This Book Belongs to:

Suzanne Beaubien

1000 CLASSIC RECIPES

1000 CLASSIC RECIPES

HH

HERMES
HOUSE

This edition published by Hermes House
27 West 20th Street, New York, NY 10011

HERMES HOUSE books are available for bulk purchase for sales promotion
and for premium use. For details, write or call the sales director,
Hermes House, 27 West 20th Street, New York, NY 10011;
(800) 354-9657

Hermes House is an imprint of
Anness Publishing Inc.

ISBN 1 901289 00 1

Publisher: Joanna Lorenz
Senior Cookery Editor: Linda Fraser
Project Manager: Anne Hildyard
Designer: Siân Keogh
Photographers: Karl Adamson, Edward Allwright, David Armstrong, Steve Baxter,
James Duncan, John Freeman, Michelle Garrett, Amanda Heywood, Tim Hill, Don Last, Patrick McLeavy, Michael Michaels
Recipes: Alex Barker, Carla Capalbo, Maxine Clark, Frances Cleary, Carole Clements,
Roz Denny, Christine France, Sarah Gates, Shirley Gill, Rosamund Grant, Patricia Lousada, Norma MacMillan, Sue Maggs,
Janice Murfitt, Annie Nichols, Louise Pickford, Katherine Richmond, Jenny Stacey, Liz Trigg, Hilaire Walden,
Laura Washburn, Steven Wheeler, Elizabeth Wolf-Cohen
Additional Photography: Sopexa UK
Food for Photography: Carla Capalbo, Joanne Craig, Carole Handslip, Wendy Lee,
Sarah Maxwell, Angela Nilsen, Jenny Shapter, Jane Stevenson, Liz Trigg and
Elizabeth Wolf-Cohen
Home Economists: Carla Capalbo, Jenny Shapter
Stylists: Madeleine Brehaut, Carla Capalbo, Michelle Garrett, Hilary Guy, Amanda Heywood, Maria Kelly, Blake Minton,
Kirsty Rawlings, Rebecca Sturrock, Fiona Tillett

Printed and bound in Germany

© Anness Publishing Limited 1997
Updated © 1999
1 3 5 7 9 10 8 6 4 2

CONTENTS

Introduction

In the modern world's quest for innovation and new taste sensations, it's often easy to forget just how delicious and fulfilling a classic recipe can be. This volume contains a definitive selection of best-ever recipes which will serve as an essential reference point for beginners and as a timely reminder to the experienced cook when planning the perfect meal.

These cosmopolitan creations have gained worldwide status through their harmonious balance of fresh ingredients, herbs and spices. Stemming from justified popularity in their homelands, they have attained universal appeal as part of the international chef's repertoire. Even more appealing is the fact that many traditional recipes are based on a natural nutritional equilibrium that was taken for granted before the days of "fast food" and a high intake of saturated fats. Many of these dishes excel when analyzed in the light of today's vogue for healthy eating. Others are unashamedly sinful (chocoholics, beware!).

The dishes presented in this book are tailored to every season and every event: you can mix and match cooking styles and influences to suit the mood and the occasion, not to mention your pocket. There is a fine selection of hearty soups such as Red Pepper Soup with Lime, which are satisfying enough for a light meal yet attractive enough to serve as an impressive dinner party appetizer. Sophisticated appetizers include Smoked Salmon and Dill Blinis or Chicken Liver Pâté with Marsala, Avocados with Tangy Topping or Pears and Stilton.

Fish and shellfish are increasingly popular in today's health-conscious society. Flavoursome dishes such as Smoked Trout with Cucumber or Grilled Fresh Sardines are classics that will

always provide a light, fresh main course to tantalize your tastebuds.

Present directions in menu planning may point away from a truly carnivorous way of life, yet there are many occasions when a sumptuous meat course will win the day. This volume will arm you with the confidence and conviction needed to present a perfect Roast Beef with Yorkshire Pudding or a melting Cottage Pie. Also included is a variety of more unusual dishes such as Duck with Chestnut Sauce, a simple yet impressive dinner party presentation, and economical yet nutritious main courses that will appeal to adults and children alike, such as Sausage and Bean Ragoût. Whether you choose western fare such as Tuna Fishcake Bites or an exotic Kashmir Coconut Fish Curry, these recipes are characterized by a distinctive depth of flavor created by a judicious blend of herbs and spices.

The vegetable dishes in this book are delicious concoctions that can be prepared at short notice as an accompaniment or a complete, well-balanced meal. Some are long-standing favorites of vegetarian fare, such as Chick-pea Stew; others are innovative versions of world-famous dishes such as a Chunky Vegetable Paella, which combines a colorful appearance with satisfying texture and harmonious flavors.

Desserts feature prominently in this collection, ranging from from light, fluffy mousses and cool, super-smooth sherbets to the richest trifles, dream puddings made from fruit, cream and chocolate, and a fabulous array of all kinds of baked treats.

Baking is one of the most satisfying of all the culinary arts. It fills the house with the most wonderful aroma, gives ample reward for minimal effort and always meets with approval, especially from younger members of the family. Bake a batch of brownies, a fresh fruit pie, a crusty loaf of bread or a luxurious cake, and watch your rating rise!

Included here is a wide range of recipes, from simple treats like drop pancakes and basic cookies to elaborate cakes for special celebrations. The step-by-step instructions are so simple and straightforward that even a novice will find them easy to follow.

In fact, novice cooks often make the best bakers, preheating the oven in plenty of time, taking care to measure ingredients accurately and following recipe methods to the letter. All these elements are important in baking, which demands more precision than many other types of cooking. With a soup or stew you can happily sling in extra ingredients or cheat a little when it comes to exact quantities, but the balance of ingredients, the temperature and the timing are all very important when you are baking a cake or pastry. It is worth reading the chosen recipe carefully before you begin, doing any advance preparation such as browning almonds or softening butter, then setting out the ingredients in the style of the TV cook.

Advice on lining pans is given in individual recipes. Wax paper is the traditional lining material, but baking parchment is even easier to use and gives excellent results. To base-line a pan, place it on the paper and draw around the outside edge, then cut out the shape. Grease the base of the pan with a dab of oil or butter to hold the paper in place, then fit it in the pan.

Grease the paper (if using greaseproof) and the sides of the tin.

Whether or not to grease tins used for pastry is a matter of choice. If the pastry is high in fat, such as shortcrust, flaky or puff, it is not usually necessary; however, spills from fillings may stick. When in doubt, grease the tins lightly.

If you are a novice baker, start with some of the simpler recipes, such as Chocolate-chip Cookies, Chive and Potato Scones or a Quick-mix Sponge. Try some of the delectable breads, from a traditional Plaited Loaf to the contemporary Saffron Focaccia.

You'll find every occasion amply catered for, from Valentine's Day through to a wedding. There are cakes for christenings, anniversaries and every possible birthday, from novelty teddies to telephones - including a mobile! For the family, the collection includes wonderful ways of keeping the cake tin and biscuit barrel brimming with healthy snacks, including a selection for those with dietary restrictions. With vegans in view, there's a special chocolate gâteau and a Dundee cake, and an entire chapter is devoted to low-fat cakes and bakes.

There's a sweet or savoury treat for every moment of the day, from breakfast Blueberry Muffins to a late-night slice of Pecan Tart.

This collection of 1000 classic recipes has been drawn together from the combined talents of some of the world's most respected cooks and food writers. With the help of this authoritative guide, your cooking will not only withstand the scrutiny of your most demanding critic – be it yourself or a fierce rival – but will win them over in style.

Carrot and Cilantro Soup

Use a good homemade stock for this soup – it adds a far greater depth of flavor than stock made from cubes.

Serves 4

4 tablespoons butter
2 leeks, sliced
1 pound carrots, sliced
1 tablespoon ground coriander
5 cups chicken stock

⅔ cup strained plain yogurt
salt and ground black pepper
2–3 tablespoons chopped fresh cilantro, to garnish

1 Melt the butter in a large saucepan. Add the leeks and carrots and stir well, coating the vegetables with the butter. Cover with a tight-fitting lid and cook for about 10 minutes, until the vegetables are beginning to soften but not color.

2 Stir in the ground coriander and cook for about 1 minute. Pour in the stock and season to taste with salt and pepper. Bring to a boil, cover and simmer for about 20 minutes, until the leeks and carrots are tender.

3 Leave to cool slightly, then purée the soup in a blender until smooth. Return the soup to the pan and add about 2 tablespoons of the yogurt, then taste the soup and adjust the seasoning again to taste. Reheat gently but do not boil.

4 Ladle the soup into bowls and put a spoonful of the remaining yogurt in the center of each. Scatter over the cilantro and serve immediately.

Leek, Potato and Arugula Soup

Arugula, with its distinctive peppery taste, is wonderful in this filling soup. Serve it hot with ciabatta croûtons.

Serves 4–6

4 tablespoons butter
1 onion, chopped
3 leeks, chopped
2 potatoes, diced
3¾ cups light chicken stock

2 large handfuls arugula, coarsely chopped
⅔ cup heavy cream
salt and ground black pepper
garlic-flavored ciabatta croûtons, to serve

1 Melt the butter in a large heavy-based saucepan, add the onion, leeks and potatoes and stir until all the vegetable pieces are coated in butter.

2 Cover with a tight-fitting lid and leave the vegetables to sweat for about 15 minutes. Pour in the stock, cover once again with the lid, then simmer for another 20 minutes, until the vegetables are tender.

3 Press the soup through a strainer and return to the rinsed-out pan. (When puréeing the soup, don't use a blender or food processor, as these will give the soup a gluey texture.) Add the chopped arugula, stir in and cook gently for about 5 minutes.

4 Stir in the cream, then season to taste with salt and pepper. Reheat gently. Ladle the soup into warmed soup bowls, then serve with a few ciabatta croûtons in each.

Cook's Tip
To make the croûtons, cut the bread into ½ inch cubes, without the crust if you wish, and either fry or bake in a roasting pan in oil until golden and crunchy.

Tomato and Basil Soup

In the summer, when tomatoes are both plentiful and cheap to buy, this is a lovely soup to make.

Serves 4

2 tablespoons olive oil
1 onion, chopped
½ teaspoon sugar
1 carrot, finely chopped
1 potato, finely chopped
1 garlic clove, crushed
1½ pounds ripe tomatoes,
*   coarsely chopped*
1 teaspoon tomato paste
1 bay leaf
1 thyme sprig

1 oregano sprig
4 fresh basil leaves,
*   coarsely torn*
1¼ cups light chicken or
*   vegetable stock*
2 – 3 pieces sun-dried
*   tomatoes in oil*
2 tablespoons shredded
*   fresh basil leaves*
salt and ground black
*   pepper*

1 Heat the oil in a large saucepan, add the onion and sprinkle with the sugar. Cook gently for 5 minutes.

2 Add the chopped carrot and potato, cover the pan and cook over a low heat for another 10 minutes, without browning the vegetables.

3 Stir in the garlic, tomatoes, tomato paste, herbs and stock, and season to taste with salt and pepper. Cover the pan with a tight-fitting lid and cook gently for about 25 – 30 minutes, or until the vegetables are tender.

4 Remove the pan from the heat and press the soup through a strainer to extract all the skins and pits. Season again with salt and pepper to taste.

5 Reheat the soup gently, then ladle into four warmed soup bowls. Finely chop the sun-dried tomatoes and mix with a little oil from the jar. Add a spoonful to each serving, then scatter the shredded basil over the top.

Corn and Shellfish Chowder

Chowder comes from the French word *chaudron*, meaning a large pot in which the soup is cooked.

Serves 4

2 tablespoons butter
1 small onion, chopped
12-ounce can corn,
*   drained*
2½ cups milk
2 scallions, finely
*   chopped*
1 cup peeled, cooked
*   shrimp*

6-ounce can white
*   crabmeat, drained and*
*   flaked*
⅔ cup light cream
pinch of cayenne pepper
salt and ground black
*   pepper*
4 whole shrimp in the
*   shell, to garnish*

1 Melt the butter in a large saucepan and gently fry the onion for 4–5 minutes, until softened.

2 Reserve 2 tablespoons of the corn for the garnish and add the rest to the pan, along with the milk. Bring the soup to a boil, then reduce the heat, cover the pan with a tight-fitting lid and simmer over a low heat for 5 minutes.

3 Pour the soup, in batches if necessary, into a blender or food processor. Process until smooth.

4 Return the soup to the pan and stir in the scallions, crabmeat, shrimp, cream and cayenne pepper. Reheat gently over a low heat.

5 Meanwhile, place the reserved corn kernels in a small frying pan without oil and dry-fry over a moderate heat until golden and toasted.

6 Season to taste with salt and pepper and serve each bowl of soup garnished with a few of the toasted corn kernels and a whole shrimp.

Spiced Parsnip Soup

Pumpkin Soup

This pale, creamy-textured soup is given a special touch with an aromatic garlic and mustard seed garnish.

The flavor of this soup will develop and improve if it is made a day in advance.

Serves 4–6
3 tablespoons butter
1 onion, chopped
1½ pounds parsnips,
   diced
1 teaspoon ground
   coriander
½ teaspoon ground cumin
½ teaspoon ground
   turmeric
¼ teaspoon chili powder

5 cups chicken stock
⅔ cup light cream
1 tablespoon sunflower oil
1 garlic clove, cut into
   julienne strips
2 teaspoons yellow
   mustard seeds
salt and ground black
   pepper

Serves 4–6
2-pound pumpkin
3 tablespoons olive oil
2 onions, chopped
2 celery stalks, chopped
1 pound tomatoes,
   chopped
6¼ cups vegetable stock
2 tablespoons tomato
   paste

1 bouquet garni
2–3 strips lean bacon,
   crisply fried and
   crumbled
2 tablespoons chopped
   fresh parsley
salt and ground black
   pepper

1   Melt the butter in a large saucepan and fry the onion and parsnips gently for about 3 minutes.

2   Stir in the spices and cook for 1 minute more. Add the stock, season to taste with salt and pepper and bring to a boil, then reduce the heat. Cover with a tight-fitting lid and simmer for about 45 minutes, until the parsnips are tender.

3   Cool slightly, then place in a blender and purée until smooth. Return the soup to the pan, add the cream and heat through gently over a low heat.

4   Heat the oil in a small pan, add the julienne strips of garlic and yellow mustard seeds and fry quickly until the garlic is beginning to brown and the mustard seeds start to pop and splutter. Remove the pan from the heat.

5   Ladle the soup into warmed soup bowls and pour a little of the hot spice mixture over each. Serve immediately.

Cook's Tip
Crushed coriander seeds may be substituted for the mustard seeds in the garnish.

1   With a sharp knife cut the pumpkin into thin slices, discarding the skin and seeds.

2   Heat the oil in a large saucepan and fry the onions and celery for about 5 minutes. Add the pumpkin and tomatoes and cook for another 5 minutes.

3   Add the vegetable stock, tomato paste and bouquet garni to the pan. Season with salt and pepper. Bring the soup to a boil, then reduce the heat, cover and simmer for 45 minutes.

4   Allow the soup to cool slightly, remove the bouquet garni, then purée (in two batches, if necessary) in a food processor or blender.

5   Press the soup through a strainer, then return it to the pan. Reheat gently and season again. Ladle the soup into warmed soup bowls. Sprinkle with the crispy bacon and parsley and serve immediately.

Jerusalem Artichoke Soup

Broccoli and Stilton Soup

Topped with saffron cream, this soup is wonderful to serve on a chilly winter's day.

A really easy, but rich, soup – choose something simple to follow, such as plainly broiled meat, poultry or fish.

Serves 4

4 tablespoons butter	⅔ cup heavy cream
1 onion, chopped	large pinch of saffron
1 pound Jerusalem	powder
artichokes, peeled and	salt and ground black
cut into chunks	pepper
3¾ cups chicken stock	chopped fresh chives, to
⅔ cup milk	garnish

1   Melt the butter in a large heavy-based saucepan and cook the onion for 5–8 minutes, until soft but not browned, stirring occasionally.

2   Add the artichokes to the pan and stir until coated in the butter. Cover with a tight-fitting lid and cook gently for 10–15 minutes; do not allow the artichokes to brown. Pour in the stock and milk, then cover again and simmer for about 15 minutes. Cool slightly, then process in a food processor or blender until smooth.

3   Strain the soup back into the pan. Add half the cream, season to taste with salt and pepper, and reheat gently. Lightly whip the remaining cream and saffron powder. Ladle the soup into warmed soup bowls and put a spoonful of saffron cream in the center of each. Scatter over the chopped chives and serve immediately.

Serves 4

3 cups broccoli florets	3 tablespoons heavy
2 tablespoons butter	cream
1 onion, chopped	4 ounces Stilton cheese,
1 leek, white part only,	rind removed,
chopped	crumbled
1 small potato, diced	salt and ground black
2½ cups hot chicken stock	pepper
1¼ cups milk	

1   Discard any tough stems from the broccoli florets. Set aside two small florets for the garnish.

2   Melt the butter in a large saucepan and cook the onion and leek until soft but not colored. Add the broccoli and potato, then pour in the stock. Cover with a tight-fitting lid and simmer for 15–20 minutes, until the vegetables are tender.

3   Cool slightly, then purée in a food processor or blender. Strain through a sieve back into the pan.

4   Add the milk, cream and seasoning to the pan and reheat gently. At the last minute add the cheese, stirring until it just melts. Do not boil.

5   Meanwhile, blanch the reserved broccoli florets and cut them vertically into thin slices. Ladle the soup into warmed bowls and garnish with the broccoli florets and a generous grinding of black pepper.

Cook's Tip
Be very careful not to boil the soup once the cheese has been added.

Minestrone with Pesto

This hearty, Italian mixed vegetable soup is a great way to use up any leftover vegetables you may have.

Serves 4

2 tablespoons olive oil
2 garlic cloves, crushed
1 onion, sliced
2 cups diced lean bacon
2 small zucchini, quartered and sliced
1½ cups green beans, chopped
2 small carrots, diced
2 celery stalks, finely chopped
bouquet garni
½ cup short cut macaroni
½ cup frozen peas
7-ounce can red kidney beans, drained and rinsed
1 cup shredded green cabbage
4 tomatoes, skinned and seeded
salt and ground black pepper

For the toasts

8 slices French bread
1 tablespoon ready-made pesto sauce
1 tablespoons grated Parmesan cheese

1 Heat the oil in a large saucepan and gently fry the garlic and onions for 5 minutes, until just softened. Add the bacon, zucchini, green beans, carrots and celery to the pan and stir-fry for another 3 minutes.

2 Pour 5 cups of cold water over the vegetables and add the bouquet garni. Cover the pan with a tight-fitting lid and simmer for 25 minutes.

3 Add the macaroni, peas and kidney beans and cook for 8 minutes more. Then add the cabbage and tomatoes and cook for an additional 5 minutes.

4 To make the toasts, spread the bread slices with the pesto, sprinkle a little Parmesan over each one and gently brown under a hot broiler. Remove the bouquet garni from the soup, season to taste and serve with the toasts.

French Onion Soup

Onion soup comes in many different guises, from smooth and creamy to this – the absolute classic from France.

Serves 4

2 tablespoons butter
1 tablespoon oil
3 large onions, thinly sliced
1 teaspoon brown sugar
1 tablespoon all-purpose flour
2 x 10-ounce cans condensed beef consommé
2 tablespoons medium sherry
2 teaspoons
Worcestershire sauce
8 slices French bread
1 tablespoon French coarse-grained mustard
1 cup grated Gruyère cheese
salt and ground black pepper
1 tablespoon chopped fresh parsley, to garnish

1 Heat the butter and oil in a large saucepan and cook the onions and brown sugar gently for about 20 minutes, stirring occasionally until the onions start to turn golden brown.

2 Stir in the flour and cook for another 2 minutes. Pour in the consommé plus two cans of water, then add the sherry and Worcestershire sauce. Season with salt and pepper, cover and simmer gently for another 25 – 30 minutes.

3 Preheat the broiler and just before serving, toast the bread lightly on both sides. Spread one side of each slice with the mustard and top with the grated cheese. Broil the toasts until bubbling and golden.

4 Ladle the soup into bowls. Pop two croutons on top of each bowl of soup and garnish with chopped fresh parsley. Serve immediately.

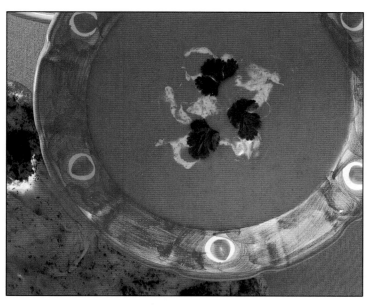

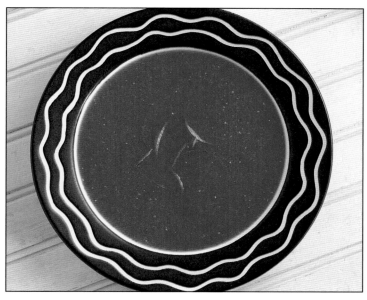

Curried Parsnip Soup

The mixture of spices in this soup impart a delicious, mild flavor to the parsnips.

Serves 4

2 tablespoons butter
1 garlic clove, crushed
1 onion, chopped
1 teaspoon ground cumin
1 teaspoon ground cilantro
1 pound (about 4) parsnips, sliced
2 teaspoons medium curry paste
scant 2 cups chicken or vegetable stock

scant 2 cups milk
4 tablespoons sour cream
good squeeze of lemon juice
salt and ground black pepper
fresh cilantro sprigs, to garnish
ready-made garlic and cilantro nan bread, to serve

1 Heat the butter in a large saucepan and fry the garlic and onion for 4–5 minutes, until lightly golden. Stir in the spices and cook for another 1–2 minutes.

2 Add the parsnips and stir until well coated with the butter, then stir in the curry paste, followed by the stock. Cover the pan with a tight-fitting lid and simmer for 15 minutes, until the parsnips are tender.

3 Ladle the soup into a blender or food processor and blend until smooth. Return to the pan and stir in the milk. Heat gently for 2–3 minutes, then add 2 tablespoons of the sour cream and the lemon juice. Season well with salt and pepper.

4 Serve in bowls topped with spoonfuls of the remaining sour cream and the fresh cilantro accompanied by the warmed, spicy nan bread.

Cook's Tip
For the best flavor, use homemade chicken or vegetable stock in this soup.

Red Pepper Soup with Lime

The beautiful rich red color of this soup makes it a very attractive appetizer or light lunch.

Serves 4–6

4 fresh red bell peppers, seeded and chopped
1 large onion, chopped
1 teaspoon olive oil
1 garlic clove, crushed
1 small red chili, sliced
3 tablespoons tomato paste

juice and finely grated rind of 1 lime
3¼ cups chicken stock
salt and ground black pepper
shreds of lime rind, to garnish

1 Cook the onion and peppers gently in the oil in a saucepan covered with a tight-fitting lid for about 5 minutes, shaking the pan occasionally, until softened.

2 Stir in the garlic, then add the chili with the tomato paste. Stir in half the stock, then bring to the boil. Cover the pan and simmer for 10 minutes.

3 Cool slightly, then purée in a food processor or blender. Return to the pan, then add the remaining stock, the lime rind and juice and seasoning.

4 Bring the soup back to a boil, then serve immediately with a few shreds of lime rind scattered into each bowl.

Thai-style Corn Soup

This is a very quick and easy soup. If you are using frozen shrimp, defrost them before adding to the soup.

Serves 4

½ teaspoon sesame or
   sunflower oil
2 scallions, thinly sliced
1 garlic clove, crushed
2½ cups chicken stock
15-ounce can cream-style
   corn
2 cups peeled, cooked
   shrimp

1 teaspoon green chili
   paste or chili sauce
   (optional)
salt and ground black
   pepper
fresh cilantro leaves, to
   garnish

Heat the oil in a large heavy-based saucepan and sauté the onions and garlic over a moderate heat for 1 minute, until softened but not browned. Stir in the chicken stock, cream-style corn, shrimp and chili paste or sauce, if using. Bring the soup to a boil, stirring occasionally. Season to taste with salt and pepper, then serve immediately, sprinkled with fresh cilantro leaves to garnish.

Haddock and Broccoli Chowder

This hearty soup makes a meal in itself when served with crusty, country-style bread.

Serves 4

4 scallions, sliced
1 pound new potatoes,
   diced
1¼ cups homemade fish
   stock, or water
1¼ cups skim milk
1 bay leaf
2 cups broccoli florets,
   sliced

1 pound smoked haddock
   fillets, skinned
7-ounce can corn,
   drained
ground black pepper
chopped scallions, to
   garnish

Place the scallions and potatoes in a pan and add the stock, milk and bay leaf. Bring to a boil, reduce the heat, cover and simmer for 10 minutes. Add the broccoli. Cut the fish into bite-size chunks; add to the pan with the corn. Season well with black pepper, then cover again and simmer until the fish is cooked through. Remove the bay leaf, scatter over the chopped scallions and serve immediately.

Cock-a-leekie Soup

This hearty main course soup is given a sweet touch by the inclusion of prunes.

Serves 4–6

Gently cook 2 chicken portions, 5 cups chicken stock and a bouquet garni for 40 minutes. Cut 4 leeks into 1 inch slices, add to the pan along with 8–12 soaked prunes and cook gently for 20 minutes. Discard the bouquet garni. Remove the chicken, discard the skin and bones and chop the flesh. Return the chicken to the pan and season to taste. Heat the soup, then serve with soft, buttered rolls.

Green Pea and Mint Soup

This soup is equally delicious lightly chilled. Stir in the swirl of cream just before serving.

Serves 4

4 tablespoons butter	2½ cups milk
4 scallions, chopped	pinch of sugar (optional)
4 cups fresh or frozen peas	salt and ground black pepper
2½ cups chicken or vegetable stock	light cream, to serve
2 large fresh mint sprigs	small fresh mint sprigs, to garnish

1 Heat the butter in a large saucepan and gently fry the scallions until just softened but not colored.

2 Stir the peas into the pan, add the stock and mint and bring to a boil. Cover and simmer very gently for about 30 minutes for fresh peas or 15 minutes if you are using frozen peas, until the peas are very tender. Remove about 3 tablespoons of the peas using a slotted spoon, and reserve for the garnish.

3 Pour the soup into a food processor or blender, add the milk and purée until smooth. Then return the soup to the pan and reheat gently. Season to taste with salt and pepper, adding a pinch of sugar if you wish.

4 Pour the soup into bowls. Swirl a little cream into each, then garnish with mint and the reserved peas.

Cook's Tip
Fresh peas are increasingly available during the summer months from grocers and supermarkets. The effort of podding them is well worthwhile, as they impart a unique flavor to this delicious, vibrant soup.

Beet and Apricot Swirl

This soup is most attractive if you swirl together the two colored purées, but mix them together if you prefer.

Serves 4

4 large cooked beets, coarsely chopped	⅞ cup ready-to-eat dried apricots
1 small onion, coarsely chopped	1 cup orange juice
2½ cups chicken stock	salt and ground black pepper

1 Place the beets and half of the onion in a saucepan with the stock. Bring to a boil, then reduce the heat, cover with a tight-fitting lid and simmer for about 10 minutes. Purée in a food processor or blender.

2 Place the rest of the onion in a pan with the apricots and orange juice, cover and simmer gently for about 15 minutes until tender. Purée in a food processor or blender.

3 Return the two mixtures to the saucepans and reheat. Season to taste with salt and pepper, then swirl the mixtures together in individual soup bowls to create a marbled effect.

Cook's Tip
Beets are available ready cooked. To cook your own, simply place in a saucepan with enough water to cover, bring to a boil, then cover and cook for 1 hour. Drain, then peel the beets with your fingers when cool enough to handle.

Thai-style Chicken Soup

New England Pumpkin Soup

Omit the red chili from the garnish if you prefer a milder flavor in this soup.

For a smooth-textured soup, process all the mixture in a food processor or blender.

Serves 4

1 tablespoon vegetable oil	peanut butter
1 garlic clove, finely chopped	1 cup thread egg noodles, broken into small pieces
2 x 6-ounce boned chicken breasts, skinned and chopped	1 tablespoon scallions, finely chopped
½ teaspoon ground turmeric	1 tablespoon chopped fresh cilantro
¼ teaspoon hot chili powder	salt and ground black pepper
3 ounces creamed coconut	2 tablespoons dried coconut and ½ red chili, seeded and finely chopped, to garnish
3¾ cups hot chicken stock	
2 tablespoons lemon or lime juice	
2 tablespoons crunchy	

1 Heat the oil in a large saucepan and fry the garlic for 1 minute until lightly golden. Add the chicken and spices and stir-fry for another 3–4 minutes. Crumble the creamed coconut into the stock and stir until dissolved. Pour onto the chicken and add the lemon juice, peanut butter and egg noodles. Cover and simmer for 15 minutes. Add the scallions and cilantro, season to taste with salt and pepper and cook for another 5 minutes.

2 Fry the coconut and chili for 2–3 minutes, stirring until the coconut is lightly browned. Use as a garnish for the soup.

Serves 4

2 tablespoons butter	1 teaspoon brown sugar
1 onion, finely chopped	
1 garlic clove, crushed	**For the croutons**
1 tablespoon all-purpose flour	1 tablespoon vegetable oil
pinch of grated nutmeg	2 slices granary bread, without the crusts
½ teaspoon ground cinnamon	2 tablespoons sunflower seeds
2¼ cups pumpkin, seeded, peeled and diced	salt and ground black pepper
2½ cups chicken stock	
⅔ cup orange juice	

1 Melt the butter in a large saucepan and gently fry the onions and garlic for 4–5 minutes, until softened.

2 Stir in the flour, spices and pumpkin, then cover and cook gently for 6 minutes, stirring occasionally.

3 Add the chicken stock, orange juice and brown sugar. Cover again, and bring to a boil, then simmer for 20 minutes until the pumpkin has softened.

4 Process half the mixture in a blender or food processor. Return the soup to the pan with the remaining chunky mixture, stirring constantly. Season to taste and heat through.

5 To make the croutons, heat the oil in a frying pan, cut the bread into cubes and gently fry until just beginning to brown. Add the sunflower seeds and fry for 1–2 minutes. Drain the croutons on paper towels. Serve the soup hot, garnished with a few of the croutons scattered over the top, and serve the remaining croutons separately.

Split Pea and Zucchini Soup

Mediterranean Tomato Soup

Rich and satisfying, this tasty and nutritious soup is ideal to serve on a chilly winter's day.

Children will love this soup – especially if you use fancy pasta such as alphabet or animal shapes.

Serves 4

1 cup yellow split peas	3¾ cups chicken stock
1 teaspoon sunflower oil	½ teaspoon ground
1 large onion, finely	turmeric
chopped	salt and ground black
2 zucchini, finely diced	pepper

1 Place the split peas in a bowl, cover with cold water and let soak for several hours or overnight. Drain, rinse in cold water and drain again.

2 Heat the oil in a saucepan. Add the onion, cover with a tight-fitting lid and cook until soft. Reserve a handful of diced zucchini and add the rest to the pan. Cook, stirring constantly, for 2–3 minutes.

3 Add the stock and turmeric to the pan and bring to a boil. Reduce the heat, then cover and simmer for about 30–40 minutes, or until the split peas are tender. Add seasoning to taste.

4 When the soup is almost ready, bring a large saucepan of water to a boil, add the reserved diced zucchini and cook for 1 minute, then drain and add to the soup before serving hot with warm crusty bread.

Cook's Tip
For a quicker alternative, use split red lentils for this soup. They do not require presoaking and cook very quickly. Adjust the amount of chicken stock used, if you need to.

Serves 4

1½ pounds ripe plum	2 tablespoons tomato
tomatoes	paste
1 onion, quartered	½ cup small pasta shapes
1 celery stalk	salt and ground black
1 garlic clove	pepper
1 tablespoon olive oil	fresh cilantro or parsley
scant 2 cups chicken	sprigs, to garnish
stock	

1 Place the tomatoes, onion, celery and garlic in a saucepan with the oil. Cover with a tight-fitting lid and cook over a gentle heat for 40–45 minutes, shaking the pan occasionally, until the vegetables become very soft.

2 Spoon the vegetables into a food processor or blender and process until smooth. Press through a sieve to remove the tomato seeds, then return to the pan.

3 Stir in the stock and tomato paste and bring to a boil. Add the pasta and simmer gently for about 8 minutes, or until the pasta is tender. Add salt and pepper to taste, then sprinkle with cilantro or parsley to garnish and serve hot.

White Bean Soup

Fish Soup

Small white lima beans or pinto beans work well in this soup, or try great northern beans for a change.

For extra flavor use some smoked fish in this soup and rub the bread with a garlic clove before toasting.

Serves 6

1½ cups dried navy or other white beans
1 bay leaf
5 tablespoons olive oil
1 onion, finely chopped
1 carrot, finely chopped
1 celery stalk, finely chopped
3 tomatoes, peeled and finely chopped

2 garlic cloves, finely chopped
1 teaspoon fresh thyme leaves or ½ teaspoon dried thyme
3⅔ cups boiling water
salt and ground black pepper
extra virgin olive oil, to serve

Serves 6

2¼ pounds mixed fish fillets such as dogfish, whiting, red mullet or cod
6 tablespoons olive oil, plus extra to serve
1 onion, finely chopped
1 celery stalk, chopped
1 carrot, chopped
4 tablespoons chopped fresh parsley

¾ cup dry white wine
3 tomatoes, peeled and chopped
2 garlic cloves, finely chopped
6¼ cups boiling water
salt and ground black pepper
French bread, to serve

1 Pick over the beans carefully, discarding any stones or other particles. Soak the beans in a large bowl of cold water overnight. Drain. Place the beans in a large saucepan of water, bring to a boil, and cook for 20 minutes. Drain. Return the beans to the pan, cover with cold water, and bring to a boil again. Add the bay leaf, and cook 1–2 hours until the beans are tender. Drain again. Remove the bay leaf.

2 Purée about three-quarters of the beans in a food processor or blender. Alternatively, pass through a strainer, adding a little water if needed.

3 Heat the oil in a large saucepan and cook the onion until softened but not browned. Add the carrot and celery, and cook for another 5 minutes.

4 Stir in the tomatoes, garlic and fresh or dried thyme. Cook for 6–8 minutes more, stirring often.

5 Pour in the boiling water. Stir in the beans and the bean purée. Season to taste with salt and pepper. Simmer for about 10–15 minutes. Serve in individual soup bowls, sprinkled with a little extra virgin olive oil.

1 Cut all the fish fillets into large pieces. Rinse well in cool water.

2 Heat the oil in a large saucepan and cook the onion over a low to moderate heat until just softened. Stir in the celery and carrot and cook for 5 minutes more. Add the parsley.

3 Pour in the wine, raise the heat and cook until it reduces by about half. Stir in the tomatoes and garlic. Cook for 3–4 minutes, stirring occasionally. Pour in the boiling water and bring back to a boil. Cook for 15 minutes.

4 Stir in the fish and simmer for 10–15 minutes, or until the fish is tender. Season to taste with salt and pepper.

5 Remove the fish from the soup with a slotted spoon. Discard any bones. Place in a food processor and purée until smooth. Taste again for seasoning. If the soup is too thick, add a little more water.

6 To serve, heat the soup to simmering. Toast the rounds of bread and sprinkle with olive oil. Place two or three in each soup plate before pouring over the soup.

Barley and Vegetable Soup

This soup comes from the Alto Adige region, in Italy's mountainous north. It is thick, nourishing and warming.

Serves 6–8

1 cup pot barley, or peas	1 bay leaf
9 cups meat stock or water, or a combination of both	3 tablespoons chopped fresh parsley
3 tablespoons olive oil	1 small fresh rosemary sprig
2 carrots, finely chopped	salt and ground black pepper
2 celery stalks, finely chopped	freshly grated Parmesan cheese, to serve
1 leek, thinly sliced	(optional)
1 large potato, finely chopped	
½ cup diced ham	

1 Pick over the barley and discard any stones or other particles. Wash the barley in cold water and soak it in cold water for at least 3 hours.

2 Drain the barley and place it in a large saucepan with the stock or water. Bring to a boil, lower the heat and simmer for 1 hour. Skim off any scum.

3 Stir in the oil, all the vegetables and the ham. Add the herbs. If necessary add more water; the ingredients should be covered by at least 1 inch. Simmer for 1–1½ hours, or until the vegetables and barley are very tender.

4 Season to taste with salt and pepper. Serve hot with grated Parmesan cheese, if desired.

Pasta and Dried Bean Soup

In Italy this soup is made with dried or fresh beans and served hot or at room temperature.

Serves 4–6

1¼ cups dried borlotti or navy beans	3½ cups water
14-ounce can plum tomatoes, chopped, with their juice	2 teaspoons salt
	scant 2 cups ditalini or other small pasta
3 garlic cloves, crushed	3 tablespoons chopped fresh parsley
2 bay leaves	freshly grated Parmesan cheese, to serve
coarsely ground black pepper	
6 tablespoons olive oil, plus extra to serve	

1 Soak the beans in water overnight. Rinse and drain well. Place them in a large saucepan and cover with water. Bring to a boil and cook for 10 minutes. Rinse and drain again.

2 Return the beans to the pan. Add enough water to cover them by 1 inch. Stir in the coarsely chopped tomatoes with their juice, the garlic, bay leaves, black pepper and the oil. Simmer for 1½–2 hours, or until the beans are tender. Add more water if necessary.

3 Remove the bay leaves. Pass about half of the bean mixture through a strainer, or purée in a food processor. Stir into the pan with the remaining bean mixture. Add the water and bring the soup to a boil.

4 Add the salt and the pasta. Stir, then cook until the pasta is just done. Stir in the parsley. Allow the dish to stand for at least 10 minutes, then serve with extra olive oil and grated Parmesan cheese.

Pasta and Lentil Soup

Small brown lentils are usually used in this wholesome soup, but green lentils may be substituted.

Serves 4–6

1 cup dried green or brown lentils	9 cups chicken stock or water
6 tablespoons olive oil	1 fresh sage leaf
¼ cup ham or salt pork, finely diced	1 fresh thyme sprig or ¼ tsp dried thyme
1 onion, finely chopped	salt and ground black pepper
1 celery stalk, finely chopped	2½ cups ditalini or other small soup pasta
1 carrot, finely chopped	

1 Carefully check the lentils for small stones. Place them in a bowl, cover with cold water and soak for 2–3 hours. Rinse and drain well through a strainer.

2 Heat the oil in a large saucepan and sauté the ham or salt pork for 2–3 minutes. Add the onion and cook gently until it softens but does not brown.

3 Stir in the celery and carrot and cook for 5 minutes more, stirring frequently. Add the lentils and stir to coat them evenly in the cooking fats.

4 Pour in the stock or water, add the herbs and bring the soup to a boil. Cook over a moderate heat for about 1 hour or until the lentils are tender. Season to taste.

5 Stir in the pasta, and cook until it is just done. Allow the soup to stand for a few minutes before serving.

Pasta and Chick-pea Soup

The addition of a fresh rosemary sprig creates a typically Mediterranean flavor in this soup.

Serves 4–6

generous 1 cup dried chick-peas	1 fresh rosemary sprig
3 garlic cloves, peeled	2½ cups water
1 bay leaf	generous 1 cup ditalini or other short hollow pasta
6 tablespoons olive oil	pinch of salt
pinch of ground black pepper	freshly grated Parmesan cheese, to serve (optional)
¼ cup diced salt pork, pancetta or bacon	

1 Soak the chick-peas in water overnight. Rinse well and drain. Place in a large saucepan with water to cover. Boil for 15 minutes. Rinse and drain.

2 Return the chick-peas to the pan. Add water to cover, one garlic clove, the bay leaf, 3 tablespoons of the oil and the pinch of pepper.

3 Simmer for about 2 hours until tender, adding more water as necessary. Remove the bay leaf. Pass about half the chick-peas through a strainer or purée in a food processor with a little cooking liquid. Return the purée to the pan with the rest of the chick-peas and the remaining cooking water.

4 Sauté the diced pork, pancetta or bacon gently in the remaining oil with the rosemary and two garlic cloves until just golden. Discard the rosemary and garlic.

5 Stir the meat with its oils into the chick-pea mixture.

6 Add 2½ cups of water to the chick-peas, and bring to a boil. Add the pinch of salt if necessary. Stir in the pasta, and cook until just *al dente*. Serve with Parmesan cheese, if you wish.

Leek and Potato Soup

Scotch Broth

If you prefer a smoother textured soup, press the mixture through a strainer.

Sustaining and warming, this traditional Scottish soup makes a delicious winter soup anywhere in the world.

Serves 4

4 tablespoons butter	3¾ cups chicken or
2 leeks, chopped	vegetable stock
1 small onion, finely	salt and ground black
chopped	pepper
12 ounces potatoes,	
chopped	

Serves 6–8

2 pounds lean shoulder of	1 turnip, chopped
lamb, cut into large	3 leeks, chopped
even-size chunks	½ small white cabbage,
7½ cups water	shredded
1 large onion, chopped	salt and ground black
¼ cup pearl barley	pepper
bouquet garni	chopped fresh parsley, to
1 large carrot, chopped	garnish

1 Heat 2 tablespoons of the butter in a large saucepan and gently cook the leeks and onions for about 7 minutes, stirring occasionally until softened but not browned.

2 Add the chopped potatoes to the pan and cook for 2–3 minutes, stirring occasionally, then add the chicken or vegetable stock and bring to a boil. Cover the pan with a tight-fitting lid and simmer gently for 30–35 minutes, until all the vegetables are very tender.

3 Season to taste with salt and pepper. Remove the pan from the heat and stir in the remaining butter in small pieces until completely melted. Serve the soup hot with warm crusty bread and butter, if you wish.

Cook's Tip
Never use a food processor or blender to purée potatoes as the starch in the vegetable will be broken down and will create an unpleasant gluey consistency.

1 Put the lamb and water into a large saucepan and bring to a boil. Skim off the scum, then stir in the onion, barley and bouquet garni.

2 Bring the soup back to a boil, then partly cover the saucepan and simmer gently for 1 hour. Add the remaining vegetables and season to taste with salt and pepper. Bring to a boil, partly cover again and simmer for about 35 minutes until the vegetables are tender.

3 Remove any extra fat from the top of the soup, then serve hot, sprinkled with chopped parsley.

Country Vegetable Soup

Vary the vegetables according to what you like and what is in season.

Serves 4

4 tablespoons butter
1 onion, chopped
2 leeks, sliced
2 celery stalks, sliced
2 carrots, sliced
2 small turnips, chopped
4 ripe tomatoes, skinned and chopped
4 cups chicken or vegetable stock
bouquet garni
1 cup green beans, chopped
salt and ground black pepper
chopped fresh herbs such as tarragon, thyme, chives and parsley, to garnish

1 Heat the butter in a large saucepan and cook the onion and leeks gently until soft but not colored.

2 Add the celery, carrots and turnips and cook them for about 3–4 minutes, stirring occasionally. Stir in the tomatoes and stock, add the bouquet garni and simmer the vegetables gently for about 20 minutes.

3 Add the beans to the soup and continue to cook until all the vegetables are tender. Season to taste with salt and pepper and serve garnished with chopped herbs.

Split Pea and Bacon Soup

This soup is also called "London Particular", because of the city's smog. The fogs in turn were named "pea-soupers".

Serves 4

1 tablespoon butter
4 ounces bacon, chopped
1 large onion, chopped
1 carrot, chopped
1 celery stalk, chopped
scant ½ cup split peas
5 cups chicken stock
2 thick slices firm bread, buttered and without crusts
2 slices lean bacon
salt and ground black pepper

1 Heat the butter in a saucepan and cook the chopped bacon until the fat runs. Stir in the onion, carrot and celery and cook for 2–3 minutes.

2 Add the split peas, followed by the stock. Bring to a boil, stirring occasionally, then cover with a tight-fitting lid and simmer for 45–60 minutes.

3 Meanwhile, preheat the oven to 350°F. Bake the bread for about 20 minutes, until crisp and brown, then dice.

4 Broil the lean bacon until very crisp, then chop finely.

5 When the soup is ready, season to taste and serve hot with the chopped bacon and croutons scattered on each portion.

Smoked Haddock and Potato Soup

This soup's traditional name is "cullen skink". A "cullen" is a town's port district and "skink" means stock or broth.

Serves 6

1 smoked haddock (about 12 ounces)
1 onion, chopped
bouquet garni
3¾ cups water
1¼ pounds (about 3 large) potatoes, quartered
2½ cups milk
3 tablespoons butter
salt and ground black pepper
chopped fresh chives, to garnish

1 Put the haddock, onion, bouquet garni and water into a large saucepan and bring to a boil. Skim the scum from the surface, then cover the pan with a tight-fitting lid. Reduce the heat and poach for about 10–15 minutes, or until the haddock flakes easily.

2 Lift the poached fish from the pan using a fish slice and remove the skin and bones. Flake the flesh and reserve. Return the skin and bones to the pan and simmer, uncovered, for 30 minutes.

3 Strain the fish stock and return to the pan, then add the potatoes and simmer for about 25 minutes or until tender. Remove the potatoes from the pan using a slotted spoon. Add the milk to the pan and bring to a boil.

4 Meanwhile, mash the potatoes with the butter, then whisk into the milk in the pan until thick and creamy. Add the flaked fish to the pan and adjust the seasoning. Sprinkle with chives and serve at once with crusty bread, if you wish.

Mulligatawny Soup

Choose red split lentils for the best color, although green or brown lentils could also be used.

Serves 4

4 tablespoons butter or 4 tablespoons oil
2 large chicken pieces, about 12 ounces each
1 onion, chopped
1 carrot, chopped
1 small turnip, chopped
about 1 tablespoon curry powder, to taste
4 cloves
6 black peppercorns, lightly crushed
¼ cup lentils
3¾ cups chicken stock
¼ cup golden raisins
salt and ground black pepper

1 Heat the butter or oil in a large saucepan and brown the chicken over a brisk heat. Transfer the chicken to a plate.

2 Add the onion, carrot and turnip to the pan and cook, stirring occasionally, until lightly colored. Stir in the curry powder, cloves and peppercorns and cook for 1–2 minutes, then add the lentils.

3 Pour the stock into the pan, bring to a boil, then add the raisins and chicken and any juices from the plate. Cover and simmer gently for about 1¼ hours.

4 Remove the chicken from the pan and discard the skin and bones. Chop the flesh into bite-size chunks, return to the soup and reheat. Season to taste with salt and pepper before serving the soup piping hot.

Smoked Haddock Pâté

Spinach, Bacon and Shrimp Salad

This easily-prepared pâté is made from small haddock which have been salted and hot-smoked.

Serve this hot salad with plenty of crusty bread to mop up the delicious juices.

Serves 6

3 large smoked haddock, about 8 ounces each
1¼ cups medium-fat cream cheese
3 eggs, beaten
2–3 tablespoons lemon juice

pinch of freshly ground black pepper
fresh chervil sprigs, to garnish
lemon wedges and lettuce leaves, to serve

Serves 4

7 tablespoons olive oil
2 tablespoons sherry vinegar
2 garlic cloves, finely chopped
1 teaspoon Dijon mustard
12 cooked jumbo shrimp, in the shell

4 ounces lean bacon, cut into strips
1 cup fresh young spinach leaves
½ head red lettuce, coarsely torn
salt and ground black

1 Preheat the oven to 325°F. Generously butter six individual ramekin dishes.

2 Lay the haddock in a baking dish and heat through in the oven for 10 minutes. Carefully remove the skin and bones from the fish, then flake the flesh into a bowl.

3 Mash the fish with a fork and work in the cheese, then the eggs. Add the lemon juice and season with pepper to taste.

4 Divide the fish mixture between the six ramekins and place in a roasting pan. Pour hot water into the roasting pan to come halfway up the dishes. Bake for 30 minutes, until just set.

5 Allow to cool for 2–3 minutes, then run a knife point around the edge of each dish and invert onto a warmed plate. Garnish with fresh chervil sprigs and serve with the lemon wedges and lettuce.

1 To make the dressing, whisk together 6 tablespoons of the olive oil with the vinegar, garlic, mustard and seasoning in a small saucepan. Heat gently until thickened slightly, then keep warm.

2 Carefully peel the jumbo shrimp, leaving their tails intact. Set aside until needed.

3 Heat the remaining oil in a frying pan and fry the bacon until golden and crisp, stirring occasionally. Add the shrimp and stir-fry for a few minutes until warmed through.

4 While the bacon and shrimp are cooking, arrange the spinach and torn lettuce leaves on four individual serving plates.

5 Spoon the bacon and shrimp onto the leaves, then pour over the hot dressing. Serve at once.

Cook's Tip
Sherry vinegar lends its pungent flavor to this delicious salad. It is readily available in large supermarkets or delicatessens. However, red or white wine vinegar could be substituted if you prefer.

Hot Tomato and Mozzarella Salad

A quick, easy appetizer with a Mediterranean flavor. It can be prepared in advance, then broiled just before serving.

Serves 4

1 pound plum tomatoes, sliced
8 ounces mozzarella cheese
1 red onion, chopped
4–6 pieces sun-dried tomatoes in oil, drained and chopped
4 tablespoons olive oil
1 teaspoon red wine vinegar
½ teaspoon Dijon mustard
4 tablespoons mixed chopped fresh herbs such as basil, parsley, oregano and chives
salt and ground black pepper
fresh herb sprigs, to garnish (optional)

1 Arrange the sliced tomatoes and mozzarella in circles in four shallow flameproof dishes. Scatter over the onion and sun-dried tomatoes. Whisk together the olive oil, vinegar, mustard, chopped herbs and seasoning. Pour over the salads.

2 Place the salads under a hot broiler for 4–5 minutes, until the mozzarella starts to melt. Grind over plenty of black pepper and serve garnished with fresh herb sprigs, if you wish.

Asparagus with Tarragon Butter

Eating fresh asparagus with your fingers is correct but messy, so serve this dish with finger bowls.

Serves 4

1¼ pounds fresh asparagus
½ cup butter
2 tablespoons chopped fresh tarragon
1 tablespoon chopped fresh parsley
grated rind of ½ lemon
1 tablespoon lemon juice
salt and black pepper

1 Trim the woody ends from the asparagus spears, then tie them into four equal bundles.

2 Place the bundles of asparagus in a large frying pan with about 1 inch of boiling water. Cover with a lid and cook for about 6–8 minutes, until the asparagus is tender but still firm. Drain well and discard the strings.

3 Arrange the asparagus spears on four warmed serving plates. Make the tarragon butter by creaming together the remaining ingredients; heat it gently and pour it over the asparagus. Serve immediately.

Deviled Kidneys

This tangy dish makes an impressive appetizer, although it is sometimes served as an English breakfast dish.

Serves 4

Mix 2 tablespoons Worcestershire sauce, 1 tablespoon each English mustard, lemon juice and tomato paste. Season with cayenne pepper and salt. Melt 3 tablespoons butter, add 1 chopped shallot; cook until softened. Stir in 8 prepared lambs' kidneys; cook for 3 minutes on each side. Coat with the sauce; serve sprinkled with chopped parsley.

Egg and Tomato Salad with Crab

You could also adjust the quantities in this tasty salad to make a quick, light and healthy weekday meal.

Serves 4

1 head of round lettuce
2 x 7-ounce cans
  crabmeat, drained
4 hard-boiled eggs, sliced
16 cherry tomatoes,
  halved
½ green bell pepper,
  seeded and thinly
  sliced
6 pitted black olives,
  sliced

For the dressing
3 tablespoons chili sauce
1 cup mayonnaise
2 teaspoons fresh lemon
  juice
½ green bell pepper,
  seeded and finely
  chopped
1 teaspoon prepared
  horseradish
1 teaspoon
  Worcestershire sauce

1 To make the dressing, place all the ingredients in a bowl and mix well. Set aside in a cool place.

2 Line four plates with the lettuce leaves. Mound the crabmeat in the center. Arrange the eggs around the outside with the tomatoes on top.

3 Spoon some of the dressing over the crabmeat. Arrange the green pepper slices on top and sprinkle with the olives. Serve immediately with the remaining dressing.

Stuffed Mushrooms

These flavorful mushrooms may also be served as an accompaniment to a main course.

Serves 4

10 ounces spinach, stalks
  removed
14-ounces medium cap
  mushrooms
2 tablespoons butter, plus
  extra for brushing
1 ounce bacon, chopped
½ small onion, chopped
5 tablespoons double
  cream

about 4 tablespoons
  grated Cheddar cheese
2 tablespoons fresh bread
  crumbs
salt and ground black
  pepper
fresh parsley sprigs, to
  garnish

1 Preheat the oven to 375°F. Butter a baking dish. Wash but do not dry the spinach. Place it in a saucepan and cook, stirring occasionally, until wilted.

2 Place the spinach in a colander and squeeze out as much liquid as possible. Chop finely. Snap the stalks from the mushrooms and chop the stalks finely.

3 Melt the butter in a pan and cook the bacon, onion and mushroom stalks for about 5 minutes. Stir in the spinach, cook for a moment or two, then remove the pan from the heat, stir in the cream and season to taste with salt and pepper.

4 Brush the mushroom caps with melted butter, then place, gills facing upwards, in a single layer in the baking dish.

5 Divide the spinach mixture among the mushrooms. Mix together the cheese and bread crumbs, sprinkle over the mushrooms, then bake for about 20 minutes until the mushrooms are tender. Serve warm, garnished with parsley.

Cook's Tip
Squeeze out all the excess water from the cooked spinach, otherwise the stuffing will be too soggy.

Pears and Stilton

Stilton is the classic British blue cheese, but you could use blue Cheshire instead, or even Gorgonzola.

Serves 4

4 ripe pears
3 ounces blue Stilton
 cheese
3 tablespoons curd cheese
pinch of ground black
 pepper
fresh watercress sprigs,
 to garnish

For the dressing
3 tablespoons light olive
 oil
1 tablespoon lemon juice
½ tablespoon toasted
 poppy seeds
salt and ground black
 pepper

1 First make the dressing. Place the olive oil, lemon juice, poppy seeds and seasoning in a screw-top jar and shake together until thoroughly blended.

2 Cut the pears in half lengthwise, then scoop out the cores and cut away the calyx from the rounded end.

3 Beat together the Stilton, curd cheese and a little pepper. Divide this mixture among the cavities in the pears.

4 Shake the dressing to mix it again, then spoon it over the pears. Serve garnished with watercress.

Cook's Tip
The pears should be lightly chilled in the fridge before they are used in this dish.

Potted Shrimp

The brown shrimp traditionally used for potting are very messy to peel. Use peeled cooked jumbo shrimp if you prefer.

Serves 4

2 cups shelled shrimps
1 cup butter
pinch of ground mace
salt and cayenne pepper

fresh dill sprigs, to
 garnish
lemon wedges and thin
 slices of brown bread
 and butter, to serve

1 Chop a quarter of the shrimp. Melt ½ cup of the butter slowly, carefully skimming off any foam that rises to the surface.

2 Stir all the shrimps, the mace, salt and cayenne pepper into the saucepan and heat gently without boiling. Pour the shrimp and butter mixture into four individual pots and set it aside to cool.

3 Heat the remaining butter in a clean small pan, then carefully spoon the clear butter over the shrimp, leaving behind the residue.

4 Let stand until the butter is almost set, then place a dill sprig in the center of each pot. Let set completely, then cover and chill in the fridge.

5 Transfer the shrimp to room temperature 30 minutes before serving with lemon wedges and thin slices of brown bread and butter.

Leek Terrine with Deli Meats

This attractive appetizer is simple yet looks spectacular. It can be made a day ahead.

Serves 6

20–24 small young leeks
about 8 ounces mixed
  sliced meats, such as
  prosciutto and salami
½ cup walnuts, toasted
  and chopped

For the dressing
4 tablespoons walnut oil
4 tablespoons olive oil
2 tablespoons wine
  vinegar
1 teaspoon whole-grain
  mustard
salt and ground black
  pepper

1 Cut off the roots and most of the green part from the leeks. Wash them thoroughly under cold running water.

2 Bring a large saucepan of salted water to a boil. Add the leeks, bring the water back to a boil, then simmer for 6–8 minutes, until the leeks are just tender. Drain well.

3 Fill a 1-pound loaf pan with the leeks, placing them top to bottom one after the other and sprinkling each layer as you go with salt and pepper.

4 Put another loaf pan inside the first and gently press down on the leeks. Carefully invert both tins and let any water drain out. Place one or two weights on top of the pans and chill the terrine for at least 4 hours, or overnight.

5 To make the dressing, whisk together the walnut and olive oils, vinegar and mustard in a small bowl. Season to taste.

6 Carefully turn out the terrine onto a board and cut into slices using a large sharp knife. Lay the slices of leek terrine on serving plates and arrange the slices of meat beside them.

7 Spoon the dressing over the slices of terrine and scatter the chopped walnuts over the top. Serve immediately.

Garlic Shrimp in Phyllo Tartlets

Tartlets made with crisp layers of phyllo pastry and filled with garlic shrimp make a tempting and unusual appetizer.

Serves 4
For the tartlets
4 tablespoons butter,
  melted
2–3 large sheets phyllo
  pastry

For the filling
½ cup butter
2–3 garlic cloves,
  crushed

1 fresh red chili, seeded
  and chopped
3 cups peeled, cooked
  shrimp
2 tablespoons chopped
  fresh parsley or fresh
  chives
salt and ground black
  pepper

1 Preheat the oven to 400°F. Brush four individual 3-inch tart pans with melted butter.

2 Cut the phyllo pastry into twelve 4-inch squares and brush with the melted butter.

3 Place three squares inside each pan, overlapping them at slight angles and carefully curling the edges and points while forming a good depression in each center. Bake the pastry for 10–15 minutes, until crisp and golden. Cool slightly and remove from the pans.

4 To make the filling, melt the butter in a large frying pan, fry the garlic, chili and shrimp for 1–2 minutes to warm through. Stir in the parsley or chives and season to taste with salt and pepper.

5 Spoon the prawn filling into the tartlets and serve immediately.

Cook's Tip
Use fresh phyllo pastry rather than frozen, then simply wrap and freeze any leftover sheets.

Smoked Salmon and Dill Blinis

Blinis, small pancakes of Russian origin, are an easy to make but sophisticated dinner party appetizer.

Serves 4

1 cup buckwheat flour	⅔ cup crème fraîche
1 cup all-purpose flour	3 tablespoons chopped
pinch of salt	fresh dill
1 tablespoon rapid-rise	8 ounces smoked salmon,
dried yeast	thinly sliced
2 eggs	fresh dill sprigs, to
1½ cups warm milk	garnish
1 tablespoon melted	
butter, plus extra for	
shallow-frying	

1 Mix together the buckwheat and all-purpose flour in a large bowl with the salt. Sprinkle in the yeast and mix well. Separate one of the eggs. Whisk together the whole egg and the yolk, the warm milk and the melted butter.

2 Pour the egg mixture onto the flour mixture. Beat well to form a smooth batter. Cover with plastic wrap and let rise in a warm place for 1–2 hours.

3 Whisk the remaining egg white in a large bowl until stiff peaks form, then gently fold into the batter.

4 Preheat a heavy-based frying pan or griddle and brush with melted butter. Drop tablespoons of the batter onto the pan, spacing them well apart. Cook for about 40 seconds, until bubbles appear on the surface.

5 Flip over the blinis and cook for 30 seconds on the other side. Wrap in foil and keep warm in a low oven. Repeat with the remaining mixture, buttering the pan each time.

6 Combine the crème fraîche and dill. Serve the blinis topped with the salmon and cream. Garnish with dill sprigs.

Celery Root Fritters with Mustard Dip

The combination of the hot, crispy fritters and the cold mustard dip is extremely tasty.

Serves 4

	For the mustard dip
1 egg	⅔ cup sour cream
1 cup ground almonds	1–2 tablespoons
3 tablespoons freshly	wholegrain mustard
grated Parmesan cheese	salt and ground black
3 tablespoons chopped	pepper
fresh parsley	sea salt flakes, for
1 celery root, about 1	sprinkling
pound	
squeeze of lemon juice	
oil, for deep-frying	

1 Beat the egg well and pour into a shallow dish. Mix together the almonds, grated Parmesan and parsley in a separate dish. Season to taste, then set aside.

2 Peel and cut the celery root into strips about ½ inch wide and 2 inches long. Drop them immediately into a bowl of water with a little lemon juice added to prevent them from becoming discolored.

3 Heat the oil in a deep-fat fryer to 350°F. Drain and then pat dry half the celery root strips. Dip them into the beaten egg, then into the ground almond mixture, making sure that the pieces are coated completely and evenly.

4 Deep-fry the fritters, a few at a time, for about 2–3 minutes until golden. Drain on paper towels and keep warm while you cook the remainder.

5 To make the mustard dip, mix together the sour cream, mustard and sea salt to taste. Spoon into a small serving bowl.

6 Heap the celery root fritters onto warmed individual serving plates. Sprinkle with sea salt flakes and serve immediately with the mustard dip.

Chicken Liver Pâté with Marsala

This is a really quick and simple pâté to make, yet it has a delicious – and quite sophisticated – flavor.

Serves 4

12 ounces chicken livers, defrosted if frozen
1 cup butter
2 garlic cloves, crushed
1 tablespoon Marsala
1 teaspoon chopped sage
salt and ground black pepper
8 fresh sage leaves, to garnish
Melba toast, to serve

1 Pick over the chicken livers, then rinse and dry with paper towels. Melt 2 tablespoons of the butter in a frying pan and fry the chicken livers with the garlic over a moderate heat for about 5 minutes, or until they are firm but still pink in their centers.

2 Transfer the livers to a food processor or blender using a slotted spoon. Add the Marsala and chopped sage.

3 Melt a generous ½ cup of the remaining butter in the frying pan, stirring to loosen any residue, then pour into the food processor or blender and process until smooth. Season well with salt and pepper.

4 Spoon the pâté into four individual pots and smooth the surface. Melt the remaining butter in a separate pan and pour over the pâtés. Garnish with sage leaves and chill in the fridge until set. Serve with triangles of Melba toast.

Cook's Tip
This delicious pâté contains Marsala, a dark, sweet, pungent dessert wine made in Sicily. If this is not available, you could substitute either brandy or a medium-dry sherry.

Salmon Rillettes

A variation on the traditional pork rillette, this appetizer is much easier to make.

Serves 6

12 ounces salmon fillets
¾ cup butter
1 celery stalk, finely chopped
1 leek, white part only, finely chopped
1 bay leaf
⅔ cup dry white wine
4 ounces smoked salmon trimmings
large pinch of ground mace
4 tablespoons ricotta cheese
salt and ground black pepper
salad greens, to serve

1 Lightly season the salmon with salt and pepper. Melt 2 tablespoons of the butter in a frying pan and cook the celery and leek for about 5 minutes. Add the salmon and bay leaf and pour over the wine. Cover with a tight-fitting lid and cook for about 15 minutes until the fish is tender.

2 Strain the cooking liquid into a saucepan and boil until reduced to 2 tablespoons. Cool. Melt 4 tablespoons of the remaining butter and gently cook the smoked salmon until it turns pale pink. Leave to cool.

3 Remove the skin and any bones from the salmon fillets. Flake the flesh into a bowl and add the cooking liquid.

4 Beat in the remaining butter, the mace and ricotta cheese. Break up the smoked salmon trimmings and fold into the mixture with the pan juices. Taste and adjust the seasoning.

5 Spoon the salmon mixture into a dish or terrine and smooth the top level. Cover and chill in the fridge.

6 To serve the salmon rillettes, shape the mixture into oval quenelles using two dessert spoons and arrange on individual plates with the salad greens. Accompany with brown bread or oatcakes, if you wish.

Mexican Dip with Chips

Omit the fresh chili and the chili powder if you prefer a dip to have a mild flavor.

Serves 4

2 medium-ripe avocados
juice of 1 lime
½ small onion, finely
    chopped
½ red chili, seeded and
    finely chopped
3 tomatoes, skinned,
    seeded and finely
    diced
2 tablespoons chopped
    fresh cilantro
2 tablespoons sour cream
salt and ground black
    pepper

1 tablespoon sour cream
    and a pinch of cayenne
    pepper, to garnish

For the chips
5-ounce bag tortilla chips
2 tablespoons finely
    grated mature
    Cheddar cheese
¼ teaspoon chili powder
2 teaspoons chopped fresh
    parsley

1 Peel, halve and pit the avocados.

2 Place the avocado in a blender or food processor with the remaining ingredients, reserving the sour cream and cayenne pepper. Process until fairly smooth. Transfer to a bowl, cover and chill in the fridge until required.

3 To make the chips, preheat the broiler, then scatter the tortilla chips over a baking sheet. Mix the grated cheese with the chili powder, sprinkle over the chips and broil for about 1–2 minutes, until the cheese has melted.

4 Remove the avocado dip from the fridge, top with the sour cream and sprinkle with cayenne pepper. Serve the bowl on a plate surrounded by the tortilla chips, garnished with the chopped fresh parsley.

French Goat Cheese Salad

The deep, tangy flavors of this salad would also make it satisfying enough for a light meal, if you wished.

Serves 4

7-ounce bag prepared
    mixed salad greens
4 strips bacon
16 thin slices French
    bread
4 ounces full-fat goat
    cheese

For the dressing
4 tablespoons olive oil
1 tablespoon tarragon
    vinegar
2 teaspoons walnut oil
1 teaspoon Dijon
    mustard
1 teaspoon wholegrain
    mustard

1 Preheat the broiler to a moderate heat. Rinse and dry the salad greens, then arrange in four individual bowls. Place the ingredients for the dressing in a screw-top jar, shake together well and reserve.

2 Lay the bacon strips on a board, then stretch with the back of a knife and cut each into four. Roll each piece up and broil for about 2–3 minutes.

3 Meanwhile, slice the goat cheese into eight and halve each slice. Top each slice of bread with a piece of goat cheese and pop under the broiler. Turn over the bacon and continue cooking with the goat cheese toasts until the cheese is golden and bubbling.

4 Arrange the bacon rolls and toasts on top of the prepared salad greens, shake the dressing well and pour a little of the dressing over each one.

Chinese Garlic Mushrooms

High in protein and low in fat, marinated tofu makes an unusual stuffing for these mushrooms.

Serves 4

8 large open mushrooms
3 scallions, sliced
1 garlic clove, crushed
2 tablespoons oyster sauce
10-ounce packet
    marinated tofu, diced

7-ounce can corn,
    drained
2 teaspoons sesame oil
salt and ground black
    pepper

1 Preheat the oven to 400°F. Finely chop the mushroom stems and mix with the next three ingredients.

2 Stir in the diced, marinated tofu and corn, season well, then spoon the filling into the mushrooms.

3 Brush the edges of the mushrooms with the sesame oil. Arrange them in a baking dish and bake for 12–15 minutes, until the mushrooms are just tender, then serve at once.

Tomato Cheese Tarts

These crisp little tartlets are easier to make than they look and are best eaten fresh from the oven.

Serves 4

2 sheets phyllo pastry
1 egg white
½ cup skimmed-milk
    cream cheese

handful of fresh basil
    leaves
3 small tomatoes, sliced
salt and ground black
    pepper

1 Preheat the oven to 400°F. Brush the sheets of phyllo pastry lightly with egg white and cut into sixteen 4-inch squares.

2 Layer the squares in twos, in eight muffin pans. Spoon the cheese into the pastry cases. Season with salt and ground black pepper and top with basil leaves.

3 Arrange the tomato slices on the tarts, add seasoning and bake for 10–12 minutes, until golden. Serve warm.

Ricotta and Pinto Bean Pâté

A lovely light yet full-flavored pâté that can be enjoyed by vegetarians.

Serves 4

Process 14 ounces pinto beans, ¾ cup ricotta cheese, 1 garlic clove, 4 tablespoons melted butter, juice of ½ lemon and seasoning. Add 2 tablespoons fresh chopped parsley and 1 tablespoon fresh thyme or dill; blend. Spoon into one serving dish or four lightly oiled and bottom-lined ramekins. Chill. Garnish with salad greens and serve with warm crusty bread or toast. If serving the pâté individually, turn each one out of its ramekin onto a plate, then remove the paper. Top the pâté with radish slices and sprigs of dill.

Avocados with Tangy Topping

Lightly broiled with a tasty topping of red onions and cheese, this dish makes a delightful appetizer.

Serves 4

1 tablespoon sunflower
    oil
1 small red onion, sliced
1 garlic clove, crushed
dash of Worcestershire
    sauce
2 ripe avocados, pitted
    and halved
2 small tomatoes, sliced

1 tablespoon chopped
    fresh basil, marjoram
    or parsley
2 ounces mozzarella
    cheese, sliced
salt and ground black
    pepper

1 Heat the oil in a frying pan and gently fry the onion and garlic for about 5 minutes until just softened. Shake in a little Worcestershire sauce.

2 Preheat a broiler. Place the avocado halves on the broiler pan and spoon the onions into the centers.

3 Divide the tomato slices and fresh herbs between the four halves and top each one with the cheese.

4 Season well with salt and pepper and broil until the cheese melts and starts to brown.

Bruschetta with Goat Cheese

Simple to prepare in advance, this Italian dish can be served as an appetizer or at a finger buffet.

Serves 4–6
For the tapenade
14-ounce can black
    olives, pitted and
    finely chopped
2 ounces sun-dried
    tomatoes in oil,
    chopped
2 tablespoons capers,
    chopped
1 tablespoon green
    peppercorns, in juice,
    crushed
2 garlic cloves, crushed
3 tablespoons chopped
    fresh basil or 1
    teaspoon dried basil

3–4 tablespoons olive oil
salt and ground black
    pepper

For the bases
12 slices ciabatta or other
    crusty bread
olive oil, for brushing
2 garlic cloves, halved
½ cup soft goat cheese or
    other whole-milk soft
    cheese
mixed fresh herb sprigs,
    to garnish

1 To make the tapenade, mix all the tapenade ingredients together and check the seasoning. It should not need too much. Allow to marinate overnight, if possible.

2 To make the bruschetta, broil both sides of the bread lightly until golden. Brush one side with oil and then rub with a cut clove of garlic. Set aside until ready to serve.

3 Spread the bruschetta with the cheese, roughing it up with a fork, and spoon the tapenade on top. Garnish with sprigs of mixed fresh herbs.

Cook's Tip
Grill the bruschetta on a barbecue for a delicious smoky flavor if you are making this appetizer in the summer.

Grilled Garlic Mussels

Use a combination of fresh herbs, such as oregano, basil and Italian parsley.

Serves 4

3–3½ pounds live
   mussels
½ cup dry white wine
4 tablespoons butter
2 shallots, finely chopped
2 garlic cloves, crushed
½ cup dried white bread
   crumbs

4 tablespoons mixed
   chopped fresh herbs
2 tablespoons freshly
   grated Parmesan
   cheese
salt and ground black
   pepper
fresh basil leaves, to
   garnish

1 Scrub the mussels well under cold running water. Remove the beards and discard any mussels that are open. Place in a large saucepan with the wine. Cover and cook over a high heat, shaking the pan occasionally, for 5–8 minutes until the mussels have opened.

2 Strain the mussels and reserve the cooking liquid. Discard any mussels that remain closed. Allow them to cool slightly, then remove and discard the top half of each shell.

3 Melt the butter in a pan and fry the shallots until softened. Add the garlic and cook for 1–2 minutes. Stir in the dried bread crumbs and cook, stirring until lightly browned. Remove the pan from the heat and stir in the herbs. Moisten with a little of the reserved mussel liquid, then season to taste with salt and pepper.

4 Spoon the breadcrumb mixture over the mussels and arrange on baking sheets. Sprinkle with the grated Parmesan.

5 Cook the mussels under a hot broiler in batches for about 2 minutes, until the topping is crisp and golden. Keep the cooked mussels warm in a low oven while broiling the rest. Garnish with fresh basil leaves and serve hot.

Nut Patties with Mango Relish

These spicy patties can be made in advance, if you wish, and reheated just before serving.

Serves 4–6

1½ cups finely chopped
   roasted and salted
   cashew nuts
1½ cups finely chopped
   walnuts
1 small onion, finely
   chopped
1 garlic clove, crushed
1 green chili, seeded and
   chopped
1 teaspoon ground cumin
2 teaspoons ground
   coriander
2 carrots, coarsely grated
1 cup fresh white bread
   crumbs
2 tablespoons chopped
   fresh cilantro

1 tablespoon lemon juice
1–2 eggs, beaten
salt and ground black
   pepper
fresh cilantro sprigs, to
   garnish

For the relish
1 large ripe mango, diced
1 small onion, cut into
   slivers
1 teaspoon grated fresh
   ginger
pinch of salt
1 tablespoon sesame oil
1 teaspoon black mustard
   seeds

1 Preheat the oven to 350°F. In a bowl, mix together the nuts, onion, garlic, chili, spices, bread crumbs, carrots, chopped cilantro and seasoning.

2 Sprinkle the lemon juice over the mixture and add enough of the beaten egg to bind the mixture together. Shape the mixture into twelve balls, then flatten slightly into round patties. Place them on a lightly greased baking sheet and bake for about 25 minutes, until golden brown.

3 To make the relish, mix together the mango, onion, fresh ginger and salt. Heat the oil in a small frying pan and fry the mustard seeds for a few seconds until they pop, then stir into the mango mixture. Serve with the nut patties, garnished with cilantro.

Dim Sum

A popular Chinese snack, these tiny dumplings are now fashionable in many specialty restaurants.

Serves 4

For the dough
1¼ cups all-purpose flour
¼ cup boiling water
⅛ cup cold water
½ tablespoon vegetable oil

For the filling
3 ounces ground pork
3 tablespoons chopped
   canned bamboo shoots

½ tablespoon light soy
   sauce
1 teaspoon dry sherry
1 teaspoon raw sugar
½ teaspoon sesame oil
1 teaspoon cornstarch
mixed fresh lettuce leaves
   such as iceberg or
   frisée

1 To make the dough, sift the flour into a bowl. Stir in the boiling water, then the cold water together with the oil. Mix to form a ball and knead until smooth. Divide the mixture into sixteen equal pieces and shape into circles.

2 For the filling, mix together the pork, bamboo shoots, soy sauce, sherry, sugar and oil. Then stir in the corn starch

3 Place a little of the filling in the center of each dim sum circle. Carefully pinch the edges of the dough together to form little "purses".

4 Line a steamer with a damp dish towel. Place the dim sum in the steamer and steam for 5–10 minutes. Serve on a bed of lettuce with soy sauce, scallion curls, sliced red chili and prawn crackers, if you wish.

Cook's Tip
As an alternative filling, substitute the pork with cooked, peeled shrimp.

Sesame Shrimp Toasts

Serve about four of these delicious toasts per person with a soy sauce for dipping.

Serves 6
6 ounces peeled, cooked
   shrimp
2 scallions, finely
   chopped
1-inch piece fresh ginger,
   peeled and grated
2 garlic cloves, crushed
2 tablespoons cornstarch
2 teaspoons soy sauce,
   plus extra for dipping

6 slices stale bread from a
   small loaf, without
   crusts
3 tablespoons sesame
   seeds
about 2½ cups vegetable
   oil, for deep-frying

1 Place the shrimp, scallions, ginger and garlic cloves into a food processor fitted with a metal blade. Add the cornstarch and soy sauce and work the mixture into a paste.

2 Spread the bread slices evenly with the paste and cut into triangles. Sprinkle with the sesame seeds, making sure they stick to the bread. Chill in the fridge for 30 minutes.

3 Heat the oil for deep-frying in a large heavy-based saucepan until it reaches a temperature of 375°F. Using a slotted spoon, lower the toasts into the oil, sesame-seed side down, and fry for 2–3 minutes, turning over for the last minute. Drain on absorbent paper towels. Keep the toasts warm while frying the rest.

4 Serve the toasts with soy sauce for dipping.

English Ploughman's Pâté

This is a roughly modern interpretation of a traditional ploughman's lunch.

Serves 4

3 tablespoons cream
  cheese
½ cup grated hard goat
  cheese
½ cup grated Cheddar
  cheese
4 pickled onions, drained
  and finely chopped
1 tablespoon apricot
  chutney

2 tablespoons butter,
  melted
2 tablespoons chopped
  fresh chives
4 slices soft-grain bread
salt and ground black
  pepper
watercress and cherry
  tomatoes, to serve

1 Mix together the cream cheese, grated cheeses, onions, chutney and butter in a bowl and season lightly with salt and ground black pepper.

2 Spoon the mixture onto a sheet of wax paper and roll up into a cylinder, smoothing the mixture into a roll with your hands. Scrunch the ends of the paper together and twist them to seal. Place in the freezer for about 30 minutes, until the parcel is just firm.

3 Spread the chives on a plate, then unwrap the chilled cheese pâté. Roll in the chives until evenly coated. Enclose in plastic wrap and chill for 10 minutes in the fridge.

4 Preheat the broiler. To make Melba toast, lightly toast the bread on both sides. Cut off the crusts and slice each piece in half horizontally. Cut each half into two triangles. Broil, untoasted side up, until golden and curled at the edges.

5 Slice the pâté into rounds with a sharp knife and serve three or four rounds per person with the Melba toast, watercress and cherry tomatoes.

Golden Cheese Puffs

Serve these deep-fried puffs – called *aigrettes* in France – with a fruity chutney and salad.

Makes 8

½ cup all-purpose flour
2 tablespoon butter
1 egg plus 1 egg yolk
½ cup finely grated
  mature Cheddar
  cheese
2 tablespoons grated
  Parmesan cheese

½ tsp mustard powder
pinch of cayenne pepper
oil, for deep-frying
salt and ground black
  pepper
mango chutney and
  green salad, to serve

1 Sift the flour onto a square of wax paper and set aside. Place the butter and ⅔ cup water in a saucepan and heat gently until the butter has melted.

2 Bring the liquid to a boil and pour in the flour all at once. Remove from the heat and stir well with a wooden spoon until the mixture begins to leave the sides of the pan and forms a ball. Let cool slightly.

3 Beat the egg and egg yolk together in a bowl with a fork and then gradually add to the mixture in the pan, beating well after each addition.

4 Stir the cheeses, mustard powder and cayenne pepper into the mixture and season to taste with salt and pepper.

5 Heat the oil in a large pan to 375°F or until a cube of bread dropped into the pan browns in 30 seconds. Drop four spoonfuls of the cheese mixture into the oil at a time and deep-fry for 2–3 minutes until golden. Drain on paper towels and keep hot in the oven while cooking the remaining mixture. Serve two puffs per person with a spoonful of mango chutney and green salad.

Kansas City Fritters

Crispy bacon and vegetable fritters are served with a spicy tomato salsa.

Makes 8

1 ¾ cups canned corn, drained well
2 eggs, separated
¾ cup all-purpose flour
5 tablespoons milk
1 small zucchini, grated
2 strips bacon, diced
2 scallions, finely chopped
large pinch of cayenne pepper
3 tablespoons sunflower oil
salt and ground black pepper

fresh cilantro sprigs, to garnish

For the salsa

3 tomatoes, skinned, seeded and diced
½ small red bell pepper, seeded and diced
½ small onion, diced
1 tablespoon lemon juice
1 tablespoon chopped fresh cilantro
dash of Tabasco sauce

1 To make the salsa, mix all the ingredients together and season to taste. Cover and chill until required.

2 Empty the corn into a bowl and mix in the egg yolks. Add the flour and blend in with a wooden spoon. When the mixture thickens, gradually blend in the milk.

3 Stir in the zucchini, bacon, scallions, cayenne pepper and seasoning and set aside. Whisk the egg whites until stiff peaks form. Gently fold into the corn batter mixture.

4 Heat the oil in a large frying pan and place four large spoonfuls of the mixture into the oil. Fry over a moderate heat for 2–3 minutes on each side until golden. Drain on paper towels and keep warm in the oven while frying the remaining four fritters.

5 Serve two fritters each, garnished with cilantro sprigs and a spoonful of the chilled tomato salsa.

Spinach and Cheese Dumplings

These tasty little dumplings are known as *gnocchi* in Italy, where they are very popular.

Serves 4

6 ounces cold mashed potato
½ cup semolina
1 cup frozen leaf spinach, defrosted, squeezed and chopped
½ cup ricotta cheese
5 tablespoons freshly grated Parmesan cheese
2 tablespoons beaten egg
½ teaspoon salt
large pinch of grated nutmeg

pinch of ground black pepper
2 tablespoons freshly grated Parmesan cheese
fresh basil sprigs, to garnish

For the butter

6 tablespoons butter
1 teaspoon grated lemon rind
1 tablespoon lemon juice
1 tablespoon chopped fresh basil

1 Place all the gnocchi ingredients except the 2 tablespoons Parmesan and the basil in a bowl and mix well. Take walnut-size pieces of the mixture and roll each one back and forth along the prongs of a fork until ridged. Make twenty-eight gnocchi in this way.

2 Bring a large pan of water to a boil, reduce to a simmer and drop in the gnocchi. They will sink at first, but as they cook they will rise to the surface; this procedure will take about 2 minutes, then simmer for 1 minute. Transfer the gnocchi to a lightly-greased and warmed casserole.

3 Sprinkle the gnocchi with the Parmesan cheese and broil under a high heat for 2 minutes, or until lightly browned. Meanwhile, heat the butter in a pan and stir in the lemon rind, lemon juice and basil. Season to taste. Pour some of this butter over each portion of gnocchi and serve hot, garnished with the basil sprigs.

Tricolor Salad

This can be a simple appetizer if served on individual salad plates, or part of a light buffet meal served on a platter.

Serves 4–6

1 small red onion, thinly sliced
6 large full-flavored tomatoes
extra-virgin olive oil, to sprinkle
2 ounces arugula or watercress, chopped

6 ounces mozzarella cheese, thinly sliced
salt and ground black pepper
2 tablespoons pine nuts (optional), to garnish

1 Soak the onion slices in a bowl of cold water for about 30 minutes, then drain and pat dry. Skin the tomatoes by slashing and dipping briefly in boiling water. Remove the cores and slice the flesh.

2 Arrange half the sliced tomatoes on a large platter or divide them among small plates.

3 Sprinkle liberally with olive oil, then layer with the chopped arugula or watercress and soaked onion slices, seasoning well with salt and pepper. Add the cheese, then sprinkle over more oil and seasoning.

4 Repeat with the remaining tomato slices, salad leaves, cheese and oil.

5 Season well to finish and complete with some oil and a good scattering of pine nuts, if using. Cover the salad and chill in the fridge for at least 2 hours before serving.

Cook's Tip
When lightly salted, tomatoes make their own dressing with their natural juices. The sharpness of the arugula or watercress offsets them wonderfully.

Minted Melon Salad

Use two different varieties of melon in this salad, such as a cantaloupe and a honeydew.

Serves 4

2 ripe melons
fresh mint sprigs, to garnish

For the dressing
2 tablespoons coarsely chopped fresh mint

1 teaspoon sugar
2 tablespoons raspberry vinegar
6 tablespoons extra-virgin olive oil
salt and ground black pepper

1 Halve the melons, then scoop out the seeds using a dessertspoon. Cut the melons into thin wedges using a large sharp knife and remove the skins.

2 Arrange the two different varieties of melon wedges alternately among four individual serving plates.

3 To make the dressing, whisk together the mint, sugar, vinegar, oil and seasoning in a small bowl, or put them in a screw-top jar and shake until blended.

4 Spoon the mint dressing over the melon wedges and garnish with mint sprigs. Serve very lightly chilled.

Garlic Mushrooms

Serve these on toast for a quick, tasty appetizer or put them into ramekins and serve with slices of warm crusty bread.

Serves 4

1 pound button
  mushrooms, sliced if
  large
3 tablespoons olive oil
3 tablespoons stock or
  water
2 tablespoons dry sherry
  (optional)

3 garlic cloves, crushed
½ cup light cream cheese
2 tablespoons chopped
  fresh parsley
1 tablespoon chopped fresh
  chives
salt and ground black
  pepper

1 Put the mushrooms into a large saucepan with the olive oil, stock or water and sherry, if using. Heat until bubbling, then cover the pan with a tight-fitting lid and simmer gently for about 5 minutes.

2 Add the crushed garlic and stir well to mix. Cook for another 2 minutes. Remove the mushrooms with a slotted spoon and set them aside. Cook the liquor until it reduces down to 2 tablespoons. Remove from the heat and stir in the cream cheese, parsley and chives.

3 Stir the mixture well until the cheese has completely melted, then return the mushrooms to the pan so that they become coated with the cheese mixture. Season to taste with salt and pepper.

4 Pile the mushrooms onto thick slabs of hot toast. Alternatively, spoon them into four ramekins and serve with slices of crusty bread.

Cook's Tip
Use a mixture of different types of mushrooms for this dish, if you prefer. Shiitake mushrooms will give this appetizer a particularly rich flavor, if you can find them.

Vegetables with Tahini

This colorful appetizer is easily prepared in advance. For an *al fresco* meal, grill the vegetables on a barbecue.

Serves 4

2 red, green or yellow bell
  peppers, quartered
2 zucchini, halved
  lengthwise
2 small eggplants
  degorged and halved
  lengthways
1 fennel bulb, quartered
dash of olive oil
4 ounces Halloumi
  cheese, sliced
salt and ground black

pepper

For the tahini cream
1 cup tahini paste
1 garlic clove, crushed
2 tablespoons olive oil
2 tablespoons fresh lemon
  juice
½ cup cold water
warm pita or nan bread,
  to serve

1 Preheat the broiler or barbecue grill until hot. Brush the vegetables with the oil and cook until just browned, turning once. (If the peppers blacken, don't worry. The skins can be peeled off when cool enough to handle.) Cook the vegetables until just softened.

2 Place all the vegetables in a shallow dish and season to taste with salt and pepper. Allow to cool. Meanwhile, brush the cheese slices with olive oil and broil these on both sides until they are just charred. Remove them from the pan with a metal spatula.

3 To make the tahini cream, place all the ingredients, except the water, in a food processor or blender. Process for a few seconds to mix, then, with the motor still running, pour in the water and blend until smooth.

4 Place the vegetables and cheese slices on a platter and trickle over the tahini cream. Serve with plenty of warm pita or nan bread.

Haddock with Parsley Sauce

The parsley sauce is enriched with cream and an egg yolk in this simple supper dish.

Serves 4

4 haddock fillets (about 6
   ounces each)
4 tablespoons butter
⅔ cup milk
⅔ cup fish stock
1 bay leaf
4 teaspoons all-purpose
   flour
4 tablespoons cream

1 egg yolk
3 tablespoons chopped
   fresh parsley
grated rind and juice of
   ½ lemon
salt and ground black
   pepper

1 Place the fish in a frying pan, add half the butter, the milk, fish stock, bay leaf and seasoning, and heat over a moderately low heat to simmering point. Lower the heat, cover the pan with a tight-fitting lid and poach the fish for 10–15 minutes, depending on the thickness of the fillets, until the fish is tender and the flesh just begins to flake.

2 Transfer the fish to a warmed serving plate with a slotted spoon, cover the fish and keep warm while you make the sauce. Return the cooking liquid to the heat and bring to a boil, stirring. Simmer for about 4 minutes, then remove and discard the bay leaf.

3 Melt the remaining butter in a saucepan and add the flour, stirring continuously for 1 minute. Remove from the heat and gradually stir in the fish cooking liquid. Return to the heat and bring to a boil, stirring. Simmer for about 4 minutes, stirring frequently.

4 Remove the pan from the heat, blend the cream into the egg yolk, then stir into the sauce with the parsley. Reheat gently, stirring for a few minutes; do not allow to boil. Remove from the heat, add the lemon juice and rind, and season to taste with salt and pepper. Pour into a warmed sauceboat and serve with the fish.

Pickled Herrings

A good basic pickled herring dish which is enhanced by the grainy mustard vinaigrette.

Serves 4

4 fresh herrings
⅔ cup white wine
   vinegar
2 teaspoons salt
12 black peppercorns
2 bay leaves
4 whole cloves
2 small onions, sliced

For the dressing
1 teaspoon coarse-grain
   mustard
3 tablespoons olive oil
1 tablespoon white wine
   vinegar
salt and ground black
   pepper

1 Preheat the oven to 325°F. Clean and bone the fish. Cut each fish into two fillets.

2 Roll up the fillets tightly and place them closely packed together in a casserole so that they can't unroll.

3 Pour the vinegar over the fish and add just enough water to cover them.

4 Add the spices and onion, cover and cook for 1 hour. Leave to cool with the liquid. To make the dressing, combine all the ingredients and shake well; serve with the fish.

Herrings with Mustard Sauce

In this delicious dish, crunchy-coated herrings are served with a piquant mayonnaise sauce.

Serves 4

1 tablespoon Dijon
   mustard
1½ teaspoons tarragon
   vinegar
¾ cup thick mayonnaise

4 herrings, about 8
   ounces each, cleaned
1 lemon, halved
1 cup medium oatmeal
salt and ground black
   pepper

1 Beat the mustard and vinegar to taste into the mayonnaise. Chill lightly in the fridge.

2 Place one fish at a time on a board, cut-side down and opened out. Press firmly along the backbone with your thumbs. Turn over the fish and carefully lift away the backbone and discard.

3 Squeeze lemon juice over both sides of the fish, then season with salt and ground black pepper. Fold the fish in half, skin-side outwards.

4 Preheat a broiler until fairly hot. Place the oatmeal on a plate, then coat each herring evenly in the oatmeal, pressing it on gently with your fingers.

5 Place the herrings on a broiler rack and broil the fish for about 3 – 4 minutes on each side, until the skin is golden brown and crisp and the flesh flakes easily. Serve hot with the mustard sauce, served separately.

Fish and Chips

The traditional British combination of battered fish and thick-cut fries is served with lemon wedges.

Serves 4

1 cup self-rising flour
⅔ cup water
1½ pound potatoes

1½ pound piece skinned
   cod fillet, cut into four

oil, for deep-frying
salt and ground black
   pepper
lemon wedges, to serve

1 Stir the flour and salt together in a bowl, then form a well in the center. Gradually pour in the water, whisking in the flour to make a smooth batter. Let stand for 30 minutes.

2 Cut the potatoes into strips about ½ inch wide and 2 inches long, using a sharp knife. Place the potatoes in a colander, rinse in cold water, then drain and dry them well.

3 Heat the oil in a deep-fat fryer or large heavy-based saucepan to 300°F. Using the wire basket, lower the potatoes in batches into the oil and cook for 5 – 6 minutes, shaking the basket occasionally until the potatoes are soft but not browned. Remove the fries from the oil and drain them thoroughly on paper towels.

4 Heat the oil in the fryer to 375°F. Season the fish. Stir the batter, then dip the pieces of fish one by one into it, allowing the excess to drain off.

5 Working in two batches if necessary, lower the fish into the oil and fry for 6 – 8 minutes, until crisp and brown. Drain the fish on paper towels and keep warm.

6 Add the fries in batches to the oil and cook them for about 2 – 3 minutes, until brown and crisp. Keep hot until ready to serve, then sprinkle with salt and serve with the fish, accompanied by lemon wedges.

Trout with Hazelnuts

The hazelnuts in this recipe make an interesting change from the almonds that are more frequently used.

Serves 4

½ cup hazelnuts, chopped
5 tablespoons butter
4 trout, about 10 ounces each
2 tablespoons lemon juice

salt and ground black pepper
lemon slices and Italian parsley sprigs, to serve

1 Preheat the broiler. Toast the nuts in a single layer, stirring frequently, until the skins split. Then tip the nuts onto a clean dish towel and rub to remove the skins. Leave the nuts to cool, then chop them coarsely.

2 Heat 4 tablespoons of the butter in a large frying pan. Season the trout inside and out, then fry two at a time for 12–15 minutes, turning once, until the trout are brown and the flesh flakes easily when tested with the point of a sharp kitchen knife.

3 Drain the cooked trout on paper towels, then transfer to a warm serving plate and keep warm while frying the remaining trout in the same way. (If your frying pan is large enough, you could, of course, cook the trout in one batch.)

4 Add the remaining butter to the frying pan and fry the hazelnuts until evenly browned. Stir the lemon juice into the pan and mix well, then quickly pour the buttery sauce over the trout and serve at once, garnished with slices of lemon and Italian parsley sprigs.

Cook's Tip
You can use a microwave to prepare the nuts instead of the broiler. Spread them out in a shallow microwave dish and leave uncovered. Cook on full power until the skins split, then remove the skins using a dish towel as described above.

Trout Wrapped in a Blanket

The "blanket" of bacon bastes the fish during cooking, keeping it moist and adding flavor at the same time.

Serves 4

juice of ½ lemon
4 trout, about 10 ounces each
4 fresh thyme sprigs
8 thin strips lean bacon

salt and ground black pepper
chopped fresh parsley and thyme sprigs, to garnish
lemon wedges, to serve

1 Preheat the oven to 400°F. Squeeze lemon juice over the skin and in the cavity of each fish, season all over with salt and ground black pepper, then put a thyme sprig in each cavity.

2 Stretch each bacon slice using the back of a knife, then wind two slices around each fish. Place the fish in a lightly greased shallow baking dish, with the loose ends of bacon tucked underneath to prevent them unwinding.

3 Bake in the oven for 15–20 minutes, until the trout flesh flakes easily when tested with the point of a sharp knife and the bacon is crisp and beginning to brown.

4 Serve garnished with chopped parsley, sprigs of thyme and accompanied by lemon wedges.

Cook's Tip
If you prefer, use fresh chopped cilantro in place of the parsley for the garnish.

Smoked Trout Salad

Horseradish goes well with smoked trout. It combines with yogurt to make a lovely dressing.

Serves 4

1 red lettuce, such as
  lollo rosso
8 ounces small ripe
  tomatoes, cut into thin
  wedges
½ cucumber, peeled and
  thinly sliced
4 smoked trout fillets,
  about 7 ounces each,
  skinned and flaked
  coarsely

For the dressing
pinch of English mustard
  powder
3 – 4 teaspoons white
  wine vinegar
2 tablespoons light olive
  oil
scant ½ cup natural
  yogurt
2 tablespoons grated
  fresh or bottled
  horseradish
pinch of caster sugar

1 To make the dressing, mix together the mustard powder and vinegar, then gradually whisk in the oil, yogurt, horseradish and sugar. Set aside for 30 minutes.

2 Place the lettuce leaves in a large bowl. Stir the dressing again, then pour half of it over the leaves and toss lightly using two spoons.

3 Arrange the lettuce on four individual plates with the tomatoes, cucumber and trout. Spoon over the remaining dressing and serve immediately.

Cook's Tip
The addition of salt to the horseradish salad dressing should not be necessary because of the saltiness of the smoked trout fillets.

Moroccan Fish Tagine

Tagine is the name of the large cooking pot used for this type of cooking in Morocco.

Serves 4

2 garlic cloves, crushed
2 tablespoons ground
  cumin
2 tablespoons paprika
1 small fresh red chili
  (optional)
2 tablespoons tomato
  paste
4 tablespoons lemon juice
4 whiting or cod cutlets,
  about 6 ounces each

12 ounces tomatoes,
  sliced
2 green bell peppers,
  seeded and thinly
  sliced
salt and ground black
  pepper
chopped fresh cilantro, to
  garnish

1 Mix together the garlic, cumin, paprika, chili, tomato paste and lemon juice. Spread this mixture over the fish, then cover and chill in the fridge for about 30 minutes to let the flavours penetrate.

2 Preheat the oven to 400°F. Arrange half of the tomatoes and peppers in a baking dish.

3 Cover with the fish, then arrange the remaining tomatoes and peppers on top. Cover the baking dish with foil and bake for about 45 minutes, until the fish is tender. Sprinkle with chopped cilantro or parsley to serve.

Cook's Tip
Try different white fish in this dish, such as hoki or pollack. If you are preparing this dish for a dinner party, it can be assembled completely and stored in the fridge until you are ready to cook it.

Shrimp and Mint Salad

Green (uncooked) shrimp make all the difference to this salad, as the flavors penetrate well into the flesh.

Serves 4

12 large green shrimp
1 tablespoon unsalted
    butter
1 tablespoon fish sauce
juice of 1 lime
3 tablespoons thin
    coconut milk
1 inch piece of fresh
    ginger, peeled and
    grated

1 teaspoon sugar
1 garlic clove, crushed
2 fresh red chilies, seeded
    and finely chopped
2 tablespoons fresh mint
    leaves
ground black pepper
8 ounces light green
    lettuce leaves, such as
    butter lettuce, to serve

1   Peel the shrimp, leaving the tails intact.

2   Melt the butter in a large frying pan and toss in the green shrimp until they turn pink.

3   Mix the fish sauce, lime juice, coconut milk, ginger, sugar, garlic, chilies and pepper together.

4   Toss the warm shrimp into the sauce with the mint leaves. Serve the shrimp mixture on a bed of green lettuce leaves.

Cook's Tip
For a really tropical touch, garnish this flavorful salad with some shavings of fresh coconut made using a potato peeler.

Mackerel with Tomatoes and Pesto

This rich and oily fish needs the sharp tomato sauce. The aromatic pesto is excellent drizzled over the fish.

Serves 4
For the pesto sauce

½ cup pine nuts
2 tablespoons fresh basil
    leaves
2 garlic cloves, crushed
2 tablespoons freshly
    grated Parmesan
    cheese
⅔ cup extra-virgin olive
    oil

salt and ground black
    pepper

For the fish

4 mackerel, gutted
2 tablespoons olive oil
4 ounces onion, coarsely
    chopped
1 pound tomatoes,
    coarsely chopped

1   To make the pesto sauce, place the pine nuts, basil and garlic cloves in a food processor fitted with a metal blade. Process until the mixture forms a rough paste. Add the Parmesan cheese and, with the machine running, gradually add the oil. Set aside until required.

2   Heat the broiler until very hot. Season the mackerel well with salt and pepper and cook for 10 minutes on either side.

3   Meanwhile, heat the oil in a large heavy-based saucepan and sauté the onions until soft.

4   Stir in the tomatoes and cook for 5 minutes. Serve the warm fish on top of the tomato mixture and top with a dollop of pesto sauce.

Cook's Tip
The pesto sauce can be made ahead and stored in the fridge until needed. Soften it again before using. For red pesto sauce, add some puréed sun-dried tomatoes after the oil.

Mackerel with Mustard and Lemon

Mackerel must be really fresh to be enjoyed. Look for bright, firm-fleshed fish.

Serves 4

4 fresh mackerel, about
    10 ounces each
1½–2 cups spinach

For the mustard and lemon butter
½ cup butter, melted
2 tablespoons wholegrain
    mustard

grated rind of 1 lemon
2 tablespoons lemon juice
3 tablespoons chopped
    fresh parsley
salt and ground black
    pepper

1 To prepare each mackerel, use a sharp knife to cut off the head just behind the gills, then cut along the belly so that the fish can be opened out flat. Remove the innards.

2 Place the fish on a board, skin-side up, and, with the heel of your hand, press along the backbone to loosen it.

3 Turn the fish the right way up and pull the bone away from the flesh. Remove the tail and cut each fish in half lengthwise. Wash and pat dry with paper towels. Score the skin three or four times, then season the fish.

4 To make the mustard and lemon butter, mix together the melted butter, mustard, lemon rind and juice and parsley. Season with salt and pepper. Place the mackerel on a broiler rack. Brush a little of the butter over the mackerel and broil for 5 minutes each side, basting occasionally, until cooked through.

5 Arrange the spinach leaves in the center of four large plates. Place the mackerel on top. Heat the remaining butter in a small saucepan until sizzling and pour over the mackerel. Serve immediately.

Smelt with Herb Sandwiches

Smelt are the tiny fry of sprats or herring and are served whole. Cayenne pepper makes them spicy hot.

Serves 4

unsalted butter, for
    spreading
6 slices whole wheat
    bread
6 tablespoons mixed
    chopped fresh herbs,
    such as parsley,
    chervil and chives
1 pound smelt,
    defrosted if frozen

scant ¾ cup all-purpose
    flour
1 tablespoon chopped
    fresh parsley
salt and cayenne pepper
peanut oil,
    for deep-frying
lemon slices, to garnish

1 Butter the bread slices. Sprinkle the herbs over three of the slices, then top with the remaining slices of bread. Remove the crusts and cut each sandwich into eight triangles. Cover with plastic wrap and set aside.

2 Rinse the smelt thoroughly. Drain and then pat dry on paper towels.

3 Put the flour, chopped parsley, salt and cayenne pepper in a large plastic bag and shake to mix. Add the smelt and toss gently in the seasoned flour until lightly coated. Heat the oil in a deep-fat fryer to 350°F.

4 Fry the fish in batches for 2–3 minutes, until golden and crisp. Lift out of the oil and drain on paper towels. Keep warm in the oven until all the fish is cooked.

5 Sprinkle the smelt with salt and more cayenne pepper, if liked, and garnish with the lemon slices. Serve immediately with the herb sandwiches.

Sole Goujons with Lime Mayonnaise

This simple dish can be rustled up quite quickly. It makes an excellent light lunch or supper.

Serves 4
1½ pound sole fillets,
    skinned
2 eggs, beaten
2 cups fresh white
    bread crumbs
oil, for deep-frying
salt and ground black
    pepper
lime wedges, to serve

1 small garlic clove,
    crushed
2 teaspoons capers,
    rinsed and chopped
2 teaspoons chopped
    small gherkins
finely grated rind
    of ½ lime
2 teaspoons lime juice
1 tablespoon chopped
    fresh cilantro

For the mayonnaise
scant 1 cup mayonnaise

1 To make the lime mayonnaise, mix together the mayonnaise, garlic, capers, gherkins, lime rind and juice and chopped cilantro. Season to taste with salt and pepper. Transfer to a serving bowl and chill until required.

2 Cut the sole fillets into finger-length strips. Dip into the beaten egg, then into the bread crumbs.

3 Heat the oil in a deep-fat fryer to 350°F. Add the fish in batches and fry until golden brown and crisp. Drain well on paper towels.

4 Pile the goujons onto warmed serving plates and serve with the lime wedges for squeezing over. Pass the lime mayonnaise around separately.

Cook's Tip
Make sure you use good-quality mayonnaise for the sauce, or – better still – make your own. But remember that some people, including pregnant women, should not eat raw egg.

Spicy Fish Rösti

Serve these delicious fish cakes crisp and hot for lunch or supper with a green salad.

Serves 4
12 ounces large, firm
    waxy potatoes
12 ounces salmon or cod
    fillet, skinned and
    boned
3–4 scallions, finely
    chopped
2 teaspoons grated fresh
    ginger

2 tablespoons chopped
    fresh cilantro
2 teaspoons lemon juice
2–3 tablespoons
    sunflower oil
salt and cayenne pepper
lemon wedges, to serve
fresh cilantro sprigs, to
    garnish

1 Bring a saucepan of water to a boil and cook the potatoes with their skins on for about 10 minutes. Drain and leave to cool for a few minutes.

2 Meanwhile, finely chop the salmon or cod fillet and place in a bowl. Stir in the chopped scallions, grated ginger, chopped cilantro and lemon juice. Season to taste with salt and cayenne pepper.

3 When the potatoes are cool enough to handle, peel off the skins and grate the potatoes coarsely. Gently stir the grated potato into the fish mixture.

4 Form the fish mixture into twelve cakes, pressing the mixture together but leaving the edges slightly rough.

5 Heat the oil in a large frying pan, and, when hot, fry the fish cakes a few at a time for 3 minutes on each side, until golden brown and crisp. Drain on paper towels. Serve hot with lemon wedges for squeezing over. Garnish with sprigs of fresh cilantro.

Mediterranean Plaice Rolls

Sun-dried tomatoes, pine nuts and anchovies make a flavorful combination for the stuffing mixture.

Serves 4

*4 plaice fillets, about 8
  ounces each, skinned
6 tablespoons butter
1 small onion, chopped
1 celery stalk, finely
  chopped
2 cups fresh white bread
  crumbs
3 tablespoons chopped
  fresh parsley*

*2 tablespoons pine nuts,
  toasted
3 – 4 pieces sun-dried
  tomatoes in oil,
  drained and chopped
2-ounce can anchovy
  fillets, drained and
  chopped
5 tablespoons fish stock
pinch of black pepper*

1 Preheat the oven to 350°F. Using a sharp knife, cut the plaice fillets in half lengthwise to make eight smaller fillets.

2 Melt the butter in a pan and add the onion and celery. Cover with a tight-fitting lid and cook over a low heat for about 15 minutes until softened. Do not allow to brown.

3 Mix together the bread crumbs, parsley, pine nuts, sun-dried tomatoes and anchovies. Stir in the softened vegetables with the buttery juices and season to taste with pepper.

4 Divide the stuffing into eight portions. Taking one portion at a time, form the stuffing into balls, then roll up each one inside a plaice fillet. Secure each roll with a toothpick.

5 Place the rolled-up fillets in a buttered casserole. Pour over the stock and cover the dish with buttered foil. Bake for about 20 minutes, or until the fish flakes easily. Remove the toothpicks, then serve with a little of the cooking juices drizzled over.

Salmon with Watercress Sauce

Adding the watercress right at the end of cooking retains much of its flavor and colour.

Serves 4

*1¼ cups crème fraîche
2 tablespoons chopped
  fresh tarragon
2 tablespoons butter
1 tablespoon sunflower
  oil
4 salmon fillets, skinned
  and boned*

*1 garlic clove, crushed
½ cup dry white wine
1 bunch watercress
salt and ground black
  pepper*

1 Gently heat the crème fraîche in a small saucepan until just beginning to boil. Remove the pan from the heat and stir in half the tarragon. Leave the herb cream to infuse while cooking the fish.

2 Heat the butter and oil in a frying pan and fry the salmon fillets for 3 – 5 minutes on each side. Remove from the pan and keep warm.

3 Add the garlic and fry for another 1 minute, then pour in the wine and let it bubble until reduced to about 1 tablespoon.

4 Meanwhile, strip the leaves off the watercress stalks and chop finely. Discard any damaged leaves. (Save the watercress stalks for soup, if you wish.)

5 Strain the herb cream into the pan and cook for a few minutes, stirring until the sauce has thickened. Stir in the remaining tarragon and watercress, then cook for a few minutes, until wilted but still bright green. Season to taste with salt and pepper and serve at once, spooned over the salmon. The dish can be accompanied by a green salad if you wish.

Warm Salmon Salad

This light salad is perfect in summer. Serve immediately, or the salad greens will lose their color.

Serves 4

1 pound salmon fillet,
   skinned
2 tablespoons sesame oil
grated rind of ½ orange
juice of 1 orange
1 teaspoon Dijon
   mustard
1 tablespoon chopped
   fresh tarragon
3 tablespoons peanut oil

4 ounces fine green
   beans, trimmed
6 ounces mixed salad
   greens, such as young
   spinach leaves,
   radicchio and frisée
1 tablespoon toasted
   sesame seeds
salt and ground black
   pepper

1 Cut the salmon into bite-size pieces, then make the dressing. Mix together the sesame oil, orange rind and juice, mustard, chopped tarragon and season to taste with salt and ground black pepper. Set aside.

2 Heat the peanut oil in a frying pan and fry the salmon pieces for 3–4 minutes, or until lightly browned but still tender on the inside.

3 While the salmon is cooking, blanch the green beans in boiling salted water for about 5–6 minutes, until tender yet still slightly crisp.

4 Add the dressing to the salmon, toss together gently and cook for 30 seconds. Remove the pan from the heat.

5 Arrange the salad on serving plates. Drain the beans and toss over the salad. Spoon over the salmon and cooking juices and serve immediately, sprinkled with the toasted sesame seeds.

Red Mullet with Fennel

Ask the fish seller to gut the mullet but not to discard the liver, as this is a delicacy and provides much of the flavor.

Serves 4

3 small fennel bulbs
4 tablespoons olive oil
2 small onions, sliced
2–4 fresh basil leaves
4 small or 2 large red
   mullet, cleaned
grated rind of ½ lemon

⅔ cup fish stock
4 tablespoons butter
juice of 1 lemon

1 Snip off the feathery leaves from the fennel bulbs, finely chop and reserve for the garnish. Cut the fennel into wedges, being careful to leave the layers attached at the root ends so the pieces stay intact.

2 Heat the oil in a frying pan large enough to take the fish in a single layer and cook the wedges of fennel and onions for about 10–15 minutes, until softened and lightly browned.

3 Tuck a basil leaf inside each mullet, then place on top of the vegetables. Sprinkle the lemon rind on top. Pour in the stock and bring just to a boil. Cover with a tight-fitting lid and cook gently for 15–20 minutes, until the fish is tender.

4 Melt the butter in a small saucepan and, when it starts to sizzle and color slightly, add the lemon juice. Pour over the mullet, sprinkle with the reserved fennel fronds and serve.

Cook's Tip
Grey mullet can also be cooked in this way. Look for fish with bright, convex eyes, firm, gleaming flesh and red gills.

Tuna with Pan-fried Tomatoes

Meaty and filling tuna steaks are served here with juicy
tomatoes and black olives.

Serves 2

2 tuna steaks, about 6
  ounces each
6 tablespoons olive oil
2 tablespoons lemon juice
2 garlic cloves, chopped
1 teaspoon chopped fresh
  thyme
4 canned anchovy fillets,
  drained and chopped

8 ounces plum tomatoes,
  halved
2 tablespoons chopped
  fresh parsley
4–6 black olives, pitted
  and chopped
pinch of ground black
  pepper
crusty bread, to serve

1   Place the tuna steaks in a shallow non-metallic dish. Mix
4 tablespoons of the oil with the lemon juice, garlic, thyme,
anchovies and pepper. Pour this mixture over the tuna and
leave to marinate for at least 1 hour.

2   Lift the tuna from the marinade and place on a broiler
rack. Broil for 4 minutes on each side, or until the tuna feels
firm to touch, basting with the marinade. Take care not to
overcook.

3   Meanwhile, heat the remaining oil in a frying pan and fry
the tomatoes for a maximum of 2 minutes on each side.

4   Divide the tomatoes equally between two serving plates
and scatter the chopped parsley and olives over them. Top
each with a tuna steak.

5   Add the remaining marinade to the pan juices and warm
through. Pour over the tomatoes and tuna steaks and serve at
once with crusty bread for mopping up the juice.

Cook's Tip
*If you are unable to find fresh tuna steaks, you could
replace them with salmon fillets, if you wish – just broil
them for one or two minutes more on each side.*

Sautéed Salmon with Cucumber

Cucumber is the classic accompaniment to salmon. Here it
is served hot, but be careful not to overcook it.

Serves 4

1 pound salmon fillet,
  skinned
3 tablespoons butter
2 scallions, chopped
½ cucumber, seeded and
  cut into strips
4 tablespoons dry white
  wine

½ cup crème fraîche
2 tablespoons chopped
  fresh chives
2 tomatoes, peeled, seeded
  and diced
salt and ground black
  pepper

1   Cut the salmon into about twelve thin slices, then cut
across into strips.

2   Melt the butter in a large frying pan and sauté the salmon
for 1–2 minutes. Remove the salmon strips using a slotted
spoon and set aside.

3   Add the scallions to the pan and cook for 2 minutes. Stir in
the cucumber and sauté for 1–2 minutes, until hot. Remove
the cucumber mixture and keep warm with the salmon.

4   Add the wine to the pan and let it bubble until well
reduced. Stir in the cucumber mixture, crème fraîche, 1
tablespoon of the chives and season to taste with salt and
pepper. Return the salmon to the pan and warm through
gently. Sprinkle the tomatoes and remaining chives over the
top. Serve at once.

Crunchy-topped Cod

It's easy to forget just how tasty and satisfying a simple, classic dish can be.

Serves 4

4 pieces cod fillet, about 4 ounces each, skinned
2 tomatoes, sliced
1 cup fresh whole wheat bread crumbs
2 tablespoons chopped fresh parsley
finely grated rind and juice of ½ lemon
1 teaspoon sunflower oil
salt and ground black pepper

1 Preheat the oven to 400°F. Arrange the cod fillets in a wide casserole.

2 Arrange the tomato slices on top. Mix together the bread crumbs, fresh parsley, lemon rind and juice and the oil with seasoning to taste.

3 Spoon the crumb mixture evenly over the fish, then bake for 15–20 minutes. Serve hot.

Fish Balls in Tomato Sauce

This quick meal is a good choice for young children, as you can guarantee there are no bones.

Serves 4

1 pound hoki or other white fish fillets, skinned
4 tablespoons fresh whole wheat bread crumbs
2 tablespoons chopped chives or scallions
14-ounce can chopped tomatoes
2 ounces button mushrooms, sliced
salt and ground black pepper

1 Cut the fish fillets into chunks; place in a food processor. Add the bread crumbs, and chives or scallions. Season and process until the fish is chopped, but still with some texture. Divide the fish mixture into about 16 even-size pieces, then mold them into balls with your hands.

2 Place the tomatoes and mushrooms in a saucepan; cook over a medium heat until boiling. Add the fish balls, cover and simmer for about 10 minutes until cooked. Serve hot.

Tuna and Corn Fish Cakes

These economical tuna fish cakes are quick to make. Use fresh mashed potatoes or instant mash.

Serves 4

Place 1½ cups mashed potato in a bowl; stir in 7 ounces tuna fish, ¼ cup canned corn and 2 tablespoons chopped parsley. Season to taste with salt and black pepper, then shape into eight patties. Press the fish cakes into 1 cup fresh bread crumbs to coat them lightly, then place on a baking sheet. Cook under a moderate broiler until crisp and golden, turning once. Serve hot with lemon wedges and fresh vegetables.

Cod Creole

Inspired by the cuisine of the Caribbean, this fish dish is both colorful and delicious.

Serves 4

1 pound cod fillets, skinned
1 tablespoon lime or lemon juice
2 teaspoons olive oil
1 onion, finely chopped
1 green bell pepper, seeded and sliced

½ teaspoon cayenne pepper
½ teaspoon garlic salt
14-ounce can chopped tomatoes
boiled rice or potatoes, to serve

1 Cut the cod fillets into bite-size chunks and sprinkle with the lime or lemon juice.

2 Heat the oil in a large, nonstick frying pan and fry the onion and pepper gently until softened. Add the cayenne pepper and garlic salt.

3 Stir in the cod and the chopped tomatoes. Bring to a boil, then cover and simmer for about 5 minutes, or until the fish flakes easily. Serve with boiled rice or potatoes.

Cook's Tip
This flavorful dish is surprisingly light in calories, so if you are worried about your waistline, this is the meal for you.

Salmon Pasta with Parsley Sauce

The parsley sauce is added at the last moment to the salmon mixture and does not have to be cooked separately.

Serves 4

1 pound salmon fillet, skinned
2 cups pasta, such as penne
6 ounces cherry tomatoes, halved
⅔ cup low-fat crème fraîche

3 tablespoons finely chopped parsley
finely grated rind of ½ orange
salt and ground black pepper

1 Cut the salmon into bite-size pieces, arrange on a heat proof plate and cover with foil.

2 Bring a large saucepan of salted water to a boil, add the pasta and return to a boil. Place the plate of salmon on top and simmer for 10–12 minutes, until the pasta and salmon are cooked.

3 Drain the pasta and toss with the tomatoes and salmon. Mix together the crème fraîche, parsley, orange rind and pepper to taste, then toss into the salmon and pasta. Serve hot or leave to cool to room temperature.

Cook's Tip
The grated orange rind in the sauce complements the salmon beautifully in this recipe. For an alternative, try trout fillets and substitute grated lemon rind.

Monkfish with Mexican Salsa

Remove the pinkish-grey membrane from the tail before cooking, or the fish will be tough.

Serves 4

1½-pound monkfish tail
3 tablespoons olive oil
2 tablespoons lime juice
1 garlic clove, crushed
1 tablespoon chopped
*   fresh cilantro*
salt and ground black
*   pepper*
fresh cilantro sprigs and
*   lime slices, to garnish*

For the salsa
4 tomatoes, seeded, peeled
*   and diced*
1 avocado, pitted, peeled
*   and diced*
½ red onion, chopped
1 green chili, seeded and
*   chopped*
2 tablespoons chopped
*   fresh cilantro*
2 tablespoons olive oil
1 tablespoon lime juice

1 To make the salsa, mix the salsa ingredients and let sit at room temperature for about 40 minutes.

2 Prepare the monkfish. Using a sharp knife, remove the pinkish-grey membrane. Cut the fillets from either side of the backbone, then cut each fillet in half to give four steaks.

3 Mix together the oil, lime juice, garlic, cilantro and seasoning in a shallow non-metallic dish. Turn the monkfish several times to coat with the marinade, then cover the dish and let marinate at cool room temperature, or in the fridge, for 30 minutes.

4 Remove the monkfish from the marinade and broil for 10–12 minutes, turning once and brushing regularly with the marinade until cooked through.

5 Serve the monkfish garnished with cilantro sprigs and lime slices and accompanied by the salsa.

Seafood Pancakes

The combination of fresh and smoked haddock imparts a wonderful flavor to the pancake filling.

Serves 4–6

12 ready-made pancakes

For the filling
8 ounces smoked haddock
*   fillet*
8 ounces fresh haddock
*   fillet*
1¼ cups milk
⅔ cup light cream
3 tablespoons butter
3 tablespoons all-purpose
*   flour*

pinch of freshly grated
*   nutmeg*
2 hard-boiled eggs,
*   shelled and chopped*
salt and ground black
*   pepper*
sprinkling of Gruyère
*   cheese*
curly salad greens, to
*   serve (optional)*

1 To make the filling, put the haddock fillets in a large pan. Add the milk and poach for 6–8 minutes, until just tender. Lift out the fish using a draining spoon and, when cool enough to handle, remove skin and bones. Reserve the milk. Measure the cream into a measuring cup, then strain enough milk into the cup to measure a scant 2 cups.

2 Melt the butter in a pan, stir in the flour and cook gently for 1 minute. Gradually mix in the milk mixture, stirring constantly to make a smooth sauce. Cook for 2–3 minutes. Season to taste with salt, pepper and nutmeg. Flake the haddock and fold into the sauce with the eggs. Let cool.

3 Preheat the oven to 350°F. Divide the filling among the pancakes. Fold the sides of each pancake into the center, then roll them up to enclose the filling completely. Butter four or six individual casseroles and arrange two or three filled pancakes in each, or butter one large dish for all the pancakes. Brush with melted butter and cook for 15 minutes. Sprinkle over the Gruyère and cook for another 5 minutes, until warmed through. Serve hot with a few curly salad greens, if you wish.

Herbed Plaice Croquettes

Deep-fry with clean oil every time as the fish will flavor the oil and spoil any other foods fried in the oil.

Serves 4

1 pound plaice fillets	*1 tablespoon unsalted*
1¼ cups milk	*butter*
1 pound cooked potatoes	*2 cups white bread*
1 fennel bulb, finely	*crumbs*
chopped	*2 tablespoons sesame*
1 garlic clove, finely	*seeds*
chopped	*oil, for deep-frying*
3 tablespoons chopped	*salt and ground black*
fresh parsley	*pepper*
2 eggs	

1 Poach the fish fillets in the milk for about 15 minutes until the fish flakes. Drain the fillets and reserve the milk.

2 Peel the skin off the fish and remove any bones. Process the fish, potatoes, fennel, garlic, parsley, eggs and butter in a food processor fitted with a metal blade.

3 Add 2 tablespoons of the reserved cooking milk and season to taste with salt and pepper.

4 Chill in the fridge for about 30 minutes, then shape into 20 croquettes with your hands.

5 Mix together the bread crumbs and sesame seeds.

6 Roll the croquettes in the mixture to form a good coating. Heat the oil in a large heavy-based saucepan and deep-fry in batches for about 4 minutes until golden brown. Drain well on paper towels and serve hot.

Mixed Smoked Fish Kedgeree

An ideal breakfast dish on a cold morning. Garnish with quartered hard-boiled eggs and season well.

Serves 6

1 pound mixed smoked	*½ tsp freshly grated*
fish such as smoked	*nutmeg*
cod, smoked haddock,	*1 tablespoon chopped*
smoked mussels or	*fresh parsley*
oysters, if available	*salt and ground black*
1¼ cups milk	*pepper*
1 cup long grain rice	*2 hard-boiled eggs, to*
1 slice lemon	*garnish*
4 tablespoons butter	
1 teaspoon medium-hot	
curry powder	

1 Poach the uncooked smoked fish in milk for 10 minutes or until it flakes. Drain off the milk and flake the fish. Mix with the other smoked fish.

2 Cook the rice in boiling water together with a slice of lemon for 10 minutes, or according to the instructions on the package, until just cooked. Drain well.

3 Melt the butter in a large saucepan and add the rice and fish. Shake the pan to mix all the ingredients together well.

4 Stir in the curry powder, nutmeg, parsley and seasoning. Serve immediately, garnished with quartered eggs.

Cook's Tip
When flaking the fish, keep the pieces fairly large to give this dish a chunky consistency.

Spanish-style Hake

Cod and haddock cutlets will work just as well as hake in this tasty fish dish.

Serves 4

2 tablespoons olive oil
2 tablespoons butter
1 onion, chopped
3 garlic cloves, crushed
1 tablespoon all-purpose
  flour
½ teaspoon paprika
4 hake cutlets, about 6
  ounces each
8 ounces fine green
  beans, cut into 1-inch
  lengths

1½ cups fish stock
generous ½ cup dry
  white wine
2 tablespoons dry sherry
15 – 20 live mussels in
  the shell, cleaned
3 tablespoons chopped
  fresh parsley
salt and ground black
  pepper
crusty bread, to serve

1 Heat the oil and butter in a sauté or frying pan and cook the onion for 5 minutes, until softened but not browned. Add the crushed garlic and cook for 1 minute more.

2 Mix together the all-purpose flour and paprika, then lightly dust over the hake cutlets. Push the sautéed onion and garlic to one side of the pan.

3 Add the hake cutlets to the pan and fry until golden on both sides. Stir in the beans, stock, wine and sherry and season to taste with salt and pepper. Bring to a boil and cook for about 2 minutes.

4 Add the mussels and parsley, cover the pan with a tight-fitting lid and cook for 5 – 8 minutes, until the mussels have opened. Discard any that do not open.

5 Serve the hake in warmed, shallow soup bowls with crusty bread to mop up the juice.

Fish Goujons

Any white fish fillets can be used for the goujons – you could try a mixture of haddock and cod for a change.

Serves 4

4 tablespoons
  mayonnaise
2 tablespoons plain
  yogurt
grated rind of ½ lemon
squeeze of lemon juice
1 tablespoon chopped
  fresh parsley
1 tablespoon capers,
  chopped
2 x 6-ounce sole fillets,
  skinned

2 x 6-ounces plaice
  fillets, skinned
1 egg, lightly beaten
2 cups fresh white bread
  crumbs
1 tablespoon sesame
  seeds
pinch of paprika
oil, for frying
salt and ground black
  pepper
4 lemon wedges, to serve

1 To make the lemon mayonnaise, mix the mayonnaise, yogurt, lemon rind and juice, parsley and capers in a bowl. Cover and chill.

2 Cut the fish fillets into thin strips. Place the beaten egg in one shallow bowl. Mix together the bread crumbs, sesame seeds, paprika and seasoning in another bowl. Dip the fish strips, one at a time, into the beaten egg, then into the bread crumb mixture and toss until coated evenly. Lay on a clean plate.

3 Heat about 1 inch of oil in a frying pan until a cube of bread browns in 30 seconds. Deep-fry the strips in batches for 2-3 minutes, until lightly golden.

4 Remove with a slotted spoon, drain on paper towels and keep warm in the oven while frying the rest. Garnish with watercress and serve hot with lemon wedges and the chilled lemon mayonnaise.

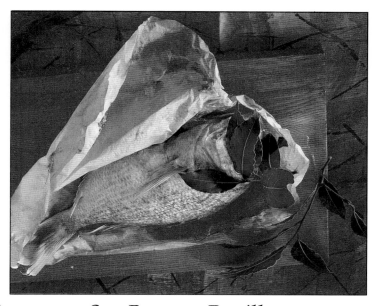

Pan-fried Garlic Sardines

Sea Bass en Papillote

Lightly fry a sliced garlic clove to garnish the fish. This dish could also be made with sprats or fresh anchovies.

Bring the unopened packages to the table and let your guests unfold their own fish to release the delicious aroma.

Serves 4

2½ pounds fresh sardines
2 tablespoons olive oil
4 garlic cloves
finely grated rind of
   2 lemons
2 tablespoons chopped
   fresh parsley

salt and ground black
   pepper

For the tomato bread
8 slices crusty bread,
   toasted
2 large ripe beefsteak
   tomatoes

1 Gut and clean the sardines thoroughly.

2 Heat the oil in a frying pan and cook the garlic cloves until they are softened.

3 Add the sardines and fry for 4–5 minutes. Sprinkle the lemon rind, parsley and seasoning over the top.

4 Cut the tomatoes in half and rub them onto the toast. Discard the skins. Serve the sardines with the tomato toast.

Cook's Tip
Make sure you use very ripe beefsteak tomatoes for this dish so they will rub onto the toast easily.

Serves 4

4 small sea bass, gutted
generous ½ cup butter
1 pound spinach
3 shallots, finely chopped
4 tablespoons white wine

4 bay leaves
salt and ground black
   pepper
new potatoes and glazed
   carrots, to serve

1 Preheat the oven to 350°F. Season both the inside and outside of the fish with salt and pepper. Melt 4 tablespoons of the butter in a large heavy-based saucepan and add the spinach. Cook gently until the spinach has broken down into a smooth purée. Set aside to cool.

2 Melt another 4 tablespoons of the butter in a clean pan and add the shallots. Gently sauté for 5 minutes until soft. Add to the spinach and let cool.

3 Stuff the insides of the fish with the spinach filling.

4 For each fish, fold a large sheet of wax paper in half and cut around the fish laid on one half, to make a heart shape when unfolded. It should be at least 2 inches larger than the fish. Melt the remaining butter and brush a little onto the paper. Set the fish on one side of the paper.

5 Add a little wine and a bay leaf to each package.

6 Fold the other side of the paper over the fish and make small pleats to seal the two edges, starting at the curve of the heart. Brush the outsides with butter. Transfer the packages to a baking sheet and bake for 20–25 minutes until the packages are brown. Serve with new potatoes and glazed carrots.

Chili Shrimp

This delightful, spicy combination makes a lovely light main course for a casual supper.

Serves 3–4

3 tablespoons olive oil
2 shallots, chopped
2 garlic cloves, chopped
1 fresh red chili, chopped
1 pound ripe tomatoes, peeled, seeded and chopped
1 tablespoon tomato paste
1 bay leaf

1 fresh thyme sprig
6 tablespoons dry white wine
4 cups peeled, cooked large shrimp
salt and ground black pepper
coarsely torn fresh basil leaves, to garnish

1 Heat the oil in a saucepan and fry the shallots, garlic and chili until the garlic starts to brown.

2 Add the tomatoes, tomato paste, bay leaf, thyme, wine and seasoning. Bring to a boil, then reduce the heat and cook gently for about 10 minutes, stirring occasionally until the sauce has thickened. Remove the herbs.

3 Stir the shrimp into the sauce and heat through for a few minutes. Taste and adjust the seasoning. Scatter the basil leaves over the top and serve immediately.

Scallops with Ginger

Scallops are at their best in winter. Rich and creamy, this dish is very simple to make and quite delicious.

Serves 4

8–12 shelled scallops
3 tablespoons butter
1-inch piece fresh ginger, finely chopped
1 bunch scallions, diagonally sliced
4 tablespoons white vermouth

1 cup crème fraîche
salt and ground black pepper
chopped fresh parsley, to garnish

1 Remove the tough muscle opposite the coral on each scallop. Separate the coral and cut the white part of the scallop in half horizontally.

2 Melt the butter in a frying pan. Add the scallops, including the corals, and sauté for about 2 minutes until lightly browned. Take care not to overcook the scallops as this will toughen them.

3 Lift out the scallops with a draining spoon and transfer to a warmed serving dish. Keep warm.

4 Add the ginger and scallions to the pan and stir-fry for 2 minutes. Pour in the vermouth and allow to bubble until it has almost evaporated. Stir in the crème fraîche and cook for a few minutes until the sauce has thickened. Season to taste with salt and pepper.

5 Pour the sauce over the scallops, sprinkle with parsley and serve immediately.

Smoked Trout Pilaf

Smoked trout might seem an unusual partner for rice, but this is a winning combination.

Serves 4

1¼ cups white basmati
   rice
3 tablespoons butter
2 onions, sliced into
   rings
1 garlic clove, crushed
2 bay leaves
2 whole cloves
2 green cardamom pods
2 cinnamon sticks
1 teaspoon cumin seeds

4 smoked trout fillets,
   skinned
½ cup slivered almonds,
   toasted
generous ½ cup seedless
   raisins
2 tablespoons chopped
   fresh parsley
mango chutney and
   poppadoms, to serve

1 Wash the rice thoroughly in water and drain well. Set aside. Melt the butter in a large frying pan and fry the onions until well browned, stirring frequently.

2 Add the garlic, bay leaves, cloves, cardamom pods, cinnamon and cumin seeds, and stir-fry for 1 minute.

3 Stir in the rice, then add 2½ cups boiling water. Bring to a boil. Cover the pan with a tight-fitting lid, reduce the heat and cook very gently for 20–25 minutes, until the water has been absorbed and the rice is tender.

4 Flake the smoked trout and add to the pan with the almonds and raisins. Fork through gently. Re-cover the pan and allow the smoked trout to warm in the rice for a few minutes. Scatter the parsley over the top and serve with mango chutney and poppadoms.

Cod with Spiced Red Lentils

This is a very tasty and filling dish, yet it is a healthy option at the same time.

Serves 4

¾ cup red lentils
¼ teaspoon ground
   turmeric
2½ cups fish stock
pinch of salt, to taste
2 tablespoons oil
1½ teaspoons cumin
   seeds
1 tablespoon grated fresh
   ginger
½ teaspoon cayenne
   pepper

1 tablespoon lemon juice
2 tablespoons chopped
   fresh cilantro
1 pound cod fillets,
   skinned and cut into
   large chunks
fresh cilantro leaves and
   lemon wedges,
   to garnish

1 Put the lentils in a saucepan with the turmeric and stock. Bring to a boil, cover with a tight-fitting lid and simmer for 20–25 minutes, until the lentils are just tender. Remove from the heat and add salt, if needed.

2 Heat the oil in a small frying pan. Add the cumin seeds and, when they begin to pop, add the ginger and cayenne pepper. Stir-fry the spices for a few seconds, then pour onto the lentils. Add the lemon juice and cilantro and stir them gently into the mixture.

3 Lay the pieces of cod on top of the lentils, cover the pan and then cook gently over a low heat for 10–15 minutes, or until the fish is tender.

4 Transfer the lentils and cod to warmed serving plates with a spatula. Sprinkle over the cilantro leaves and garnish each serving with one or two lemon wedges. Serve hot.

Mediterranean Fish Stew

Use any combination of fish you wish in this stew, which is served with an authentic rouille sauce.

Serves 4

2 cups cooked shrimp in the shell
1 pound mixed white fish, skinned and chopped (reserve skin for the stock)
3 tablespoons olive oil
1 onion, chopped
1 leek, sliced
1 carrot, diced
1 garlic clove, chopped
½ teaspoon ground turmeric
⅔ cup dry white wine or cider
14-ounce can chopped tomatoes
sprig of fresh parsley, thyme and fennel
1 bay leaf

small piece of orange peel
1 prepared squid, body cut into rings and tentacles chopped
12 mussels in the shell
salt and ground black pepper
2–3 tablespoons fresh Parmesan cheese shavings and fresh parsley, to garnish

For the rouille sauce

2 slices white bread, without crusts
2 garlic cloves, crushed
½ fresh red chili
1 tablespoon tomato paste
3–4 tablespoons olive oil

1 Peel the shrimp, leaving the tails on. Make stock with the prawn and fish skins and 1¾ cups water. Fry the onion, leek, carrot and garlic in the oil for about 6–7 minutes; stir in the turmeric. Add the wine, tomatoes, the fish stock, herbs and orange peel. Bring to a boil, cover and simmer for 20 minutes.

2 To make the rouille sauce, purée all the sauce ingredients in a food processor or blender.

3 Add the fish and seafood to the pan and simmer for about 5–6 minutes, until the mussels open. Remove the bay leaf and peel; season to taste. Serve with a spoonful of the rouille, garnished with Parmesan cheese and parsley.

Salmon with Herb Butter

Other fresh herbs could be used to flavor the butter – try mint, fennel, parsley or oregano.

Serves 4

4 tablespoons butter, softened
finely grated rind of ½ small lemon
1 tablespoon lemon juice
1 tablespoon chopped fresh dill

4 salmon steaks
2 lemon slices, halved
4 fresh dill sprigs
salt and ground black pepper

1 Place the butter, lemon rind, lemon juice, chopped dill and seasoning in a small bowl and mix together with a fork until thoroughly blended.

2 Spoon the butter onto a piece of wax paper and roll up, smoothing with your hands into a sausage shape. Twist the ends tightly, enclose in plastic wrap and place in the freezer for 20 minutes until firm.

3 Meanwhile, preheat the oven to 375°F. Cut out four squares of foil big enough to enclose the salmon steaks and grease lightly. Place a salmon steak in the center of each square.

4 Remove the butter from the freezer and slice into eight rounds. Place two rounds on top of each salmon steak with a halved lemon slice in the center and a sprig of dill on top. Lift up the edges of the foil and crinkle them together until they are well sealed.

5 Lift the parcels onto a baking sheet and bake for about 20 minutes. Remove from the oven and place the unopened parcels on warmed plates. Open the parcels and slide the contents onto the plates with the juice.

Spanish Seafood Paella

Use monkfish instead of the cod, if you wish, and add a red mullet cut into chunks.

Serves 4

4 tablespoons olive oil
8 ounces cod, skinned and cut into chunks
3 prepared baby squid, body cut into rings and tentacles chopped
1 onion, chopped
3 garlic cloves, finely chopped
1 red bell pepper, seeded and sliced
4 tomatoes, skinned and chopped
1¼ cups arborio rice
scant 2 cups fish stock

⅔ cup white wine
¼ cup frozen peas
4–5 saffron strands, soaked in 2 tablespoons hot water
1 cup peeled, cooked shrimp
8 fresh mussels in the shell, scrubbed
salt and ground black pepper
1 tablespoon chopped fresh parsley, to garnish
lemon wedges, to serve

1 Heat 2 tablespoons of the oil in a frying pan and stir-fry the cod and the squid for 2 minutes. Transfer to a bowl.

2 Heat the remaining oil in the pan and fry the onion, garlic and pepper for 6–7 minutes, stirring, until softened.

3 Stir in the tomatoes and fry for another 2 minutes, then add the rice, stirring to coat the grains with oil, and cook for 2–3 minutes more. Pour on the stock and wine and add the peas, saffron and water. Season to taste.

4 Gently stir in the reserved cooked fish with all the juice, followed by the shrimp, and then push the mussels into the rice. Cover with a tight-fitting lid and cook over a gentle heat for about 30 minutes, or until the stock has been absorbed. Remove from the heat, keep covered and let stand for 5 minutes. Sprinkle with parsley; serve with lemon wedges.

Spaghetti with Seafood Sauce

The Italian name for this tomato-based sauce is *marinara*. It is very popular in coastal regions.

Serves 4

3 tablespoons olive oil
1 onion, chopped
8 ounces spaghetti
2½ cups tomato sauce
1 tablespoon tomato paste
1 teaspoon dried oregano
1 bay leaf
1 teaspoon sugar
2 cups peeled, cooked shrimp

6 ounces cooked clam meat (rinsed well if canned or bottled)
1 tablespoon lemon juice
3 tablespoons chopped fresh parsley
2 tablespoons butter
salt and ground black pepper
4 whole cooked shrimp, to garnish

1 Heat the oil in a saucepan and fry the onion and garlic for 6–7 minutes until softened. Meanwhile, cook the spaghetti in a large pan of boiling salted water for 10–12 minutes or according to the instructions on the package, until *al dente*.

2 Stir the tomato sauce, tomato paste, oregano, bay leaf and sugar into the onions and season to taste with salt and pepper. Bring to a boil, then simmer for 2–3 minutes.

3 Add the shellfish, lemon juice and 2 tablespoons of the parsley. Stir well, then cover and cook for 6–7 minutes more.

4 Drain the spaghetti and add the butter to the pan. Return the drained spaghetti to the pan and toss in the butter. Season well.

5 Divide the spaghetti among four warmed plates and top with the seafood sauce. Sprinkle with the remaining parsley, garnish with whole shrimp and serve immediately.

Garlic Chili Shrimp

In Spain *gambas al ajillo* are traditionally cooked in small earthenware dishes, but a frying pan is just as suitable.

Serves 4

4 tablespoons olive oil
2 – 3 garlic cloves, finely
   chopped
½–1 fresh red chili,
   seeded and chopped
16 cooked whole shrimp

1 tablespoon chopped
   fresh parsley
salt and ground black
   pepper
lemon wedges and
   French bread, to serve

1 Heat the oil in a large frying pan and stir-fry the garlic and chili for 1 minute, until the garlic begins to turn brown.

2 Add the shrimp and stir-fry for about 3–4 minutes, coating them well with the flavored oil.

3 Add the parsley, remove from the heat and serve four shrimp per person in heated bowls, with the flavored oil spooned over them. Serve with lemon wedges for squeezing and French bread to mop up the juice.

Deep-fried Spicy Smelt

This is a delicious British dish – serve these tiny fish very hot and crisp.

Serves 4

1 pound smelt
3 tablespoons all-purpose
   flour
1 teaspoon paprika
pinch of cayenne pepper
12 fresh parsley sprigs

oil, for
   deep-frying
salt and ground black
   pepper
4 lemon wedges, to
   garnish

1 If using frozen smelt, defrost in the bag, then drain off any water. Spread the fish on paper towels and pat dry.

2 Place the flour, paprika, cayenne and seasoning in a large plastic bag. Add the smelt and shake gently until all the fish is lightly coated with the flour. Transfer to a plate.

3 Heat about 2 inches of oil in a saucepan or deep-fat fryer to 375°F, or until a cube of bread dropped into the oil browns in about 30 seconds.

4 Add the smelt in batches and deep-fry in the hot oil for 2–3 minutes, until the coating is lightly golden and crispy. Remove, drain on paper towels and keep warm in the oven while frying the rest.

5 When all the smelt is cooked, drop the sprigs of parsley into the hot oil (don't worry if the oil spits a bit) and fry for a few seconds until crisp. Drain on paper towels. Serve the smelt garnished with the deep-fried parsley sprigs and lemon wedges.

Baked Fish Creole-style

Fish fillets cooked in a colorful pepper and tomato sauce are topped with a cheesy crust.

Serves 4

1 tablespoon oil
2 tablespoons butter
1 onion, thinly sliced
1 garlic clove, chopped
1 red bell pepper, halved, seeded and sliced
1 green bell pepper, halved, seeded and sliced
14-ounce can chopped tomatoes with basil
1 tablespoon tomato paste
2 tablespoons chopped capers

3–4 drops Tabasco sauce
4 tail end pieces cod or haddock fillets, about 6 ounces each, skinned
6 basil leaves, shredded
3 tablespoons fresh bread crumbs
¼ cup grated Cheddar cheese
2 teaspoons chopped fresh parsley
salt and ground black pepper
fresh basil sprigs, to garnish

1 Preheat the oven to 450°F. Heat the oil and half of the butter in a saucepan, and fry the sliced onion for about 6–7 minutes until softened. Add the garlic, peppers, chopped tomatoes, tomato paste, capers and Tabasco and season to taste. Cover and cook for 15 minutes, then uncover and simmer gently for 5 minutes to reduce slightly.

2 Place the fish fillets in a buttered casserole, dot with the remaining butter and season lightly. Spoon the tomato and pepper sauce over the top and sprinkle with the shredded basil. Bake in the oven for about 10 minutes.

3 Meanwhile, mix together the bread crumbs, cheese and parsley in a bowl. Remove the fish from the oven and scatter the cheese mixture over the top. Return to the oven and bake for about another 10 minutes. Let the fish stand for about a minute, then, using a spatula, carefully transfer each topped fillet to a warmed plate. Garnish with sprigs of fresh basil and serve while still hot.

Tuna Fishcake Bites

An updated version of a traditional British tea-time dish, these little cakes would also make an elegant appetizer.

Serves 4

1½ pounds potatoes
knob of butter
2 hard-boiled eggs, chopped
3 scallions, chopped
grated rind of ½ lemon
1 teaspoon lemon juice
2 tablespoons chopped fresh parsley
7-ounce can tuna in oil, drained
2 teaspoons capers, chopped
2 eggs, lightly beaten
2 cups fresh white bread crumbs
sunflower oil, for shallow-frying

salt and ground black pepper
green salad, to serve

For the tartar sauce
4 tablespoons mayonnaise
1 tablespoon plain yogurt
1 tablespoon finely chopped small gherkins
1 tablespoon capers, chopped
1 tablespoon chopped fresh parsley

1 Boil the potatoes. Drain and mash with the butter.

2 Mix the hard-boiled eggs, scallions, lemon rind and juice, parsley, tuna, capers and 1 tablespoon of the beaten egg into the cooled potato. Season to taste, cover and chill.

3 Mix all the sauce ingredients together. Chill in the fridge.

4 Roll the fishcake mixture into about 24 balls. Dip these into the egg and then roll gently in the bread crumbs until evenly coated. Transfer to a plate.

5 Heat 6 tablespoons of the oil in a frying pan and fry the balls over a moderate heat, in batches, for about 4 minutes, turning two or three times until browned all over. Drain on paper towels and keep warm in the oven while frying the rest. Serve with the tartare sauce and a salad.

Kashmir Coconut Fish Curry

The combination of spices in this dish gives an interesting depth of flavor to the creamy curry sauce.

Serves 4

2 tablespoons vegetable
  oil
2 onions, sliced
1 green bell pepper,
  seeded and sliced
1 garlic clove, crushed
1 dried chili, seeded and
  chopped
1 teaspoon ground
  coriander
1 teaspoon ground cumin
½ teaspoon ground
  turmeric
½ teaspoon hot chili
  powder
½ teaspoon garam masala

1 tablespoon all-purpose
  flour
4 ounces creamed
  coconut, chopped
1½ pounds haddock fillet,
  skinned and chopped
4 tomatoes, skinned,
  seeded and chopped
1 tablespoon lemon juice
2 tablespoons ground
  almonds
2 tablespoons heavy
  cream
fresh cilantro sprigs, to
  garnish
naan bread and boiled
  rice, to serve

1 Heat the oil in a large saucepan and add the onions, pepper and garlic. Cook for 6–7 minutes, until the onions and pepper have softened. Stir in the chopped dried chili, all the ground spices, the chili powder, garam masala and flour, and cook for 1 minute.

2 Dissolve the coconut in 2½ cups boiling water and stir into the spicy vegetable mixture. Bring to the boil, cover and then simmer gently for 6 minutes.

3 Add the fish and tomatoes and cook for 5–6 minutes, or until the fish has turned opaque. Uncover and gently stir in the lemon juice, ground almonds and cream. Season well, garnish with cilantro and serve with nan bread and rice.

Mussels with Wine and Garlic

This famous French dish is traditionally known as *moules marinière*, and can be served as an appetizer or a main course.

Serves 4

4 pounds live mussels
1 tablespoon oil
2 tablespoons butter
1 small onion or 2
  shallots, finely
  chopped
2 garlic cloves, finely
  chopped

⅔ cup dry white wine or
  hard cider
fresh parsley sprigs
ground black pepper
2 tablespoons chopped
  fresh parsley, to
  garnish
French bread, to serve

1 Check that the mussels are closed. (Throw away any that are cracked or won't close when tapped.) Scrape the shells under cold running water and pull off the hairy beard attached to the hinge of the shell. Rinse well in two or three changes of water.

2 Heat the oil and butter in a large pan and fry the onions and garlic for 3–4 minutes.

3 Pour on the wine or cider and add the parsley sprigs, stir well, bring to a boil, then add the mussels. Cover with a tight-fitting lid and cook for about 5–7 minutes, shaking the pan once or twice until the shells open (throw away any that have not opened).

4 Serve the mussels and their juice sprinkled with the chopped parsley and some ground black pepper. Serve with hot French bread.

64

Thai Shrimp Salad

This salad has the distinctive flavor of lemon grass, the bulbous grass used widely in South-East Asian cooking.

Serves 2

2¼ cups peeled, cooked, jumbo shrimp
1 tablespoon oriental fish sauce
2 tablespoons lime juice
½ tablespoon soft light brown sugar
1 small fresh red chili, finely chopped
1 scallion, finely chopped
1 small garlic clove, crushed
1-inch piece fresh lemon grass, finely chopped
2 tablespoons chopped fresh cilantro
3 tablespoons dry white wine
8–12 Bibb lettuce leaves, to serve
fresh cilantro sprigs, to garnish

1 Place the jumbo shrimp in a bowl and add all the remaining ingredients. Stir well, cover and leave to marinate in the fridge for 2–3 hours, mixing and turning the shrimp occasionally.

2 Arrange two or three of the lettuce leaves on each of four individual serving plates.

3 Spoon the shrimp salad into the lettuce leaves. Garnish with fresh cilantro and serve immediately.

Cajun Spiced Fish

Fillets of fish are coated with an aromatic blend of herbs and spices and pan-fried in butter.

Serves 4

1 teaspoon dried thyme
1 teaspoon dried oregano
1 teaspoon ground black pepper
¼ teaspoon cayenne pepper
2 teaspoons paprika
½ teaspoon garlic salt
4 tail end pieces of cod fillet, about 6 ounces each
6 tablespoons butter
½ fresh red bell pepper, sliced
½ green bell pepper, sliced
fresh thyme sprigs, to garnish
grilled tomatoes and sweet potato purée, to serve

1 Place all the herbs and spices in a bowl and mix well. Dip the fish fillets in the spice mixture until lightly coated.

2 Heat 2 tablespoons of the butter in a large frying pan, add the peppers and fry for 4–5 minutes, until softened. Remove the peppers and keep warm.

3 Add the remaining butter to the pan and heat until sizzling. Add the cod fillets and fry over a moderate heat for about 3–4 minutes on each side, until browned and cooked.

4 Transfer the fish to a warmed serving dish, surround with the peppers and garnish with thyme. Serve the spiced fish with some grilled tomatoes and sweet potato purée.

Golden Fish Pie

This lovely light pie with a crumpled phyllo pastry topping makes a delicious lunch or supper dish.

Serves 4–6

1½ pounds white fish
  fillets
1¼ cups milk
flavoring ingredients
  such as onion slices,
  bay leaf and black
  peppercorns
1 cup peeled, cooked
  shrimp, defrosted if
  frozen
½ cup butter

½ cup all-purpose flour
1¼ cups light cream
¾ cup grated Gruyère
  cheese
1 bunch watercress,
  leaves only, chopped
1 teaspoon mustard
5 sheets phyllo pastry
salt and ground black
  pepper

1 Place the fish in a saucepan, pour over the milk and add the flavoring ingredients. Bring to a boil, cover with a lid and simmer for 10–12 minutes, until the fish is almost tender. Skin and bone the fish, then coarsely flake into a shallow ovenproof dish. Scatter the shrimp over the fish. Strain the milk and reserve.

2 Melt 4 tablespoons of the butter in a pan. Stir in the flour; cook for 1 minute. Stir in the milk and cream. Bring to the boil, stirring, then simmer for 2–3 minutes, until thickened. Remove from the heat, stir in the Gruyère, watercress and then mustard, season. Pour the mixture over the fish and leave to cool.

3 Preheat the oven to 375°F, then melt the remaining butter. Brush one sheet of phyllo pastry with a little butter, then crumple up loosely and place on top of the filling. Repeat with the remaining phyllo sheets and butter until they are all used up and the pie is completely covered.

4 Bake in the oven for 25–30 minutes, until the pastry is golden and crisp. Serve immediately.

Special Fish Pie

This fish pie is colorful, healthy and best of all, it is very simple to make.

Serves 4

12 ounces haddock fillet,
  skinned
2 tablespoons cornstarch
1 cup peeled, cooked
  shrimp
7-ounce can corn,
  drained
scant 1 cup frozen peas
¾ cup milk

¾ cup yogurt
1½ cups fresh whole
  wheat bread crumbs
generous ¼ cup grated
  Cheddar cheese
salt and ground black
  pepper

1 Preheat the oven to 375°F. Cut the haddock into bite-size pieces and toss in cornstarch to coat evenly.

2 Place the fish, shrimp, corn and peas in a baking dish. Beat together the milk, yogurt and seasoning, then pour into the dish.

3 Mix together the bread crumbs and grated cheese, then spoon evenly over the top. Bake for 25–30 minutes, or until golden brown. Serve hot with fresh vegetables.

Cook's Tip
For a more economical version of this dish, omit the shrimp and replace with more fish fillet.

Smoked Trout with Cucumber

Smoked trout provides an easy and delicious first course or light meal. Serve at room temperature for the best flavor.

Serves 4

1 large cucumber
4 tablespoons crème fraîche or strained plain yogurt
1 tablespoon chopped fresh dill

4 smoked trout fillets
salt and ground black pepper
dill sprigs, to garnish
crusty whole wheat bread, to serve

1 Peel the cucumber, cut in half lengthwise and scoop out the seeds using a teaspoon. Dice the flesh.

2 Put the cucumber in a colander, place over a plate and sprinkle with salt. Alow to drain for at least 1 hour to draw out the excess moisture.

3 Rinse the cucumber well, then pat dry on paper towels. Transfer the cucumber to a bowl and stir in the crème fraîche or yogurt, chopped dill and some freshly ground pepper. Chill the cucumber salad for about 30 minutes.

4 Arrange the trout fillets on individual plates. Spoon the cucumber and dill salad on one side and grind over a little black pepper. Garnish the dish with dill sprigs and serve with crusty bread.

Fish Cakes

Homemade fish cakes are an underrated food which bear little resemblance to the store-bought type.

Serves 4

1 pound cooked, mashed potatoes
1 pound cooked, mixed white and smoked fish such as haddock or cod, flaked
2 tablespoons butter, cubed
3 tablespoons chopped fresh parsley

1 egg, separated
1 egg, beaten
fine bread crumbs made with stale bread (about 1 cup)
pinch of pepper
oil, for shallow frying
crisp salad, to serve

1 Place the potatoes in a bowl and beat in the fish, butter, parsley and egg yolk. Season to taste with pepper.

2 Divide the fish mixture into eight equal portions, then, with floured hands, form each into a flat cake.

3 Beat the remaining egg white with the whole egg. Dip each fish cake in the beaten egg, then in bread crumbs.

4 Heat the oil in a frying pan and fry the fish cakes for about 3–5 minutes on each side, until crisp and golden. Drain on paper towels and serve hot with a crisp salad.

Cook's Tip
Make smaller fish cakes to serve as an appetizer with a salad garnish. For an extra-special version, make them with cooked fresh salmon or drained, canned red or pink salmon.

Stuffed Plaice Rolls

Plaice fillets are a good choice for families because they are economical, easy to cook and free of bones.

Serves 4
1 zucchini, grated
2 carrots, grated
4 tablespoons fresh whole
   wheat bread crumbs
1 tablespoon lime or
   lemon juice

4 plaice fillets
salt and ground black
   pepper
new potatoes, to serve

1 Preheat the oven to 400°F. Mix together the carrots and zucchini. Stir in the bread crumbs, lime or lemon juice and season with salt and pepper.

2 Lay the fish fillets skin-side up and divide the stuffing between them, spreading it evenly.

3 Roll up to enclose the stuffing and place in a baking dish. Cover and bake for about 30 minutes, or until the fish flakes easily. Serve hot with new potatoes.

Mackerel Kebabs with Parsley

Oily fish such as mackerel is ideal for broiling as it cooks quickly and needs no extra oil.

Serves 4
1 pound mackerel fillets
finely grated rind and
   juice of 1 lemon
3 tablespoons chopped
   fresh parsley
12 cherry tomatoes

8 pitted black olives
salt and ground black
   pepper
boiled rice or noodles and
   green salad, to serve

1 Cut the fish into 1½-inch chunks and place in a bowl with half the lemon rind and juice, half of the parsley and some seasoning. Cover the bowl and allow to marinate for about 30 minutes.

2 Thread the chunks of fish on to eight long wooden or metal skewers, alternating them with the cherry tomatoes and olives. Cook the kebabs under a hot broiler for 3–4 minutes, turning the kebabs occasionally, until the fish is cooked.

3 Mix the remaining lemon rind and juice with the remaining parsley in a small bowl, then season to taste with salt and pepper. Spoon the dressing over the kebabs. Serve hot with plain boiled rice or noodles and a leafy green salad.

Grilled Salmon Steaks with Fennel

Fennel grows wild all over the south of Italy. Its mild aniseed flavor goes well with fish.

Serves 4

juice of 1 lemon
3 tablespoons chopped fresh fennel, or the green feathery leaves from the top of a fennel bulb
1 teaspoon fennel seeds

3 tablespoons olive oil
4 salmon steaks of the same thickness, about 1½ pounds
salt and ground black pepper
lemon wedges, to garnish

1 Combine the lemon juice, chopped fennel and fennel seeds with the olive oil in a bowl. Add the salmon steaks, turning them to coat them with the marinade. Sprinkle with salt and ground black pepper. Cover and place in the fridge. Allow to stand for about 2 hours.

2 Preheat the broiler. Arrange the fish in one layer on a broiler pan or shallow baking pan. Broil about 4 inches from the broiler element for 3–4 minutes.

3 Turn the steaks over and spoon on the remaining marinade. Broil for 3–4 minutes, or until the edges begin to brown. Serve hot, garnished with lemon wedges.

Cook's Tip
If you wish, remove the skin from the salmon steaks before serving. Simply insert the prongs of a fork between the flesh and the skin at one end and roll the skin around the prongs in a smooth motion.

Seafood Pilaf

This one-pan dish makes a satisfying meal. For a special occasion, use dry white wine instead of orange juice.

Serves 4

2 teaspoons olive oil
1½ cups long-grain rice
1 teaspoon ground turmeric
1 red bell pepper, seeded and diced
1 small onion, finely chopped
2 zucchini, sliced
5 ounces button mushrooms, wiped and halved

1½ cups fish or chicken stock
⅔ cup orange juice
12 ounces white fish fillets
12 live mussels (or cooked shelled mussels)
salt and ground black pepper
grated rind of 1 orange, to garnish

1 Heat the oil in a large nonstick frying pan and fry the rice and turmeric over a gentle heat for about 1 minute.

2 Add the pepper, onion, zucchini and mushrooms. Stir in the stock and orange juice. Bring to a boil.

3 Reduce the heat and add the fish. Cover with a tight-fitting lid and simmer gently for about 15 minutes, until the rice is tender and the liquid absorbed. Stir in the mussels and heat thoroughly. Adjust the seasoning, sprinkle with orange rind and serve hot.

Cook's Tip
If you wish, bring the pan to the table, rather than transferring the pilaf to a serving dish, and let everyone help themselves.

Grilled Fresh Sardines

Fresh sardines are flavorful, firm-fleshed and rather different in taste and consistency from those canned in oil.

Serves 4–6

*2 pounds very heavy
    fresh sardines, gutted
    and with heads
    removed*
olive oil, for brushing

*salt and ground black
    pepper*
*3 tablespoons chopped
    fresh parsley, to serve*
lemon wedges, to garnish

1 Preheat the broiler. Rinse the sardines in water. Pat dry with kitchen paper.

2 Brush the sardines lightly with olive oil and sprinkle generously with salt and pepper. Place the sardines in one layer in a broiler pan. Broil for about 3–4 minutes.

3 Turn, and cook for 3–4 minutes more, or until the skin begins to brown. Serve immediately, sprinkled with parsley and garnished with lemon wedges.

Cook's Tip
*For a fuller flavor, you might like to leave the sardines
whole, as they do in some Mediterranean countries.*

Red Mullet with Tomatoes

**Red mullet is a popular fish in Italy, and in this recipe both
its flavor and color are accentuated.**

Serves 4

*4 red mullet, about 6–7
    ounces each*
*1 pound tomatoes, peeled,
    or 14-ounce can plum
    tomatoes*
4 tablespoons olive oil
*4 tablespoons finely
    chopped fresh parsley*

*2 cloves garlic, finely
    chopped*
½ cup dry white wine
*4 thin lemon slices, cut
    in half*
*salt and ground black
    pepper*

1 Scale and clean the fish without removing the liver. Wash and pat dry with paper towels.

2 Finely chop the tomatoes. Heat the oil in a saucepan or flameproof casserole large enough to hold the fish in one layer. Add the parsley and garlic, and sauté for 1 minute. Stir in the tomatoes and cook over a moderate heat for 15–20 minutes. Season to taste with salt and pepper.

3 Add the red mullet to the tomato sauce and cook over a moderate to high heat for 5 minutes. Add the wine and the lemon slices. Bring the sauce back to a boil, and cook for about 5 minutes more. Turn the fish over and continue to cook for 4–5 minutes more. Remove the fish to a warmed serving platter and keep warm until needed.

4 Boil the sauce for 3–4 minutes to reduce it slightly, then spoon it over the fish and serve immediately.

Cook's Tip
*To peel fresh tomatoes, use a sharp knife to make a slit
in their bases, plunge into boiling water for 30 seconds,
or until the skins split, and then plunge into cold
water. The skins should then slip off easily.*

Middle Eastern Sea Bream

Buy the smallest sea bream you can find to cook whole, allowing one for two people.

Serves 4

4-pound sea bream or 2 smaller sea bream	ground cinnamon mixed spice
2 tablespoons olive oil	3 tablespoons chopped fresh mint
¾ cup pine nuts	1¼ cups long-grain rice
1 large onion, finely chopped	3 lemon slices
1 pound ripe tomatoes, coarsely chopped	1¼ cups fish stock
½ cup raisins	salt

1 Trim, gut and scale the sea bream. Meanwhile, preheat the oven to 350°F.

2 Heat the oil in a large heavy-based saucepan and stir-fry the pine nuts for 1 minute. Add the onions and continue to stir-fry until softened but not colored.

3 Add the tomatoes and simmer for 10 minutes, then stir in the raisins, ¼ teaspoon each cinnamon and mixed spice and the mint.

4 Add the rice and lemon slices. Transfer to a large roasting pan and pour the fish stock over the top.

5 Place the fish on top and cut several slashes in the skin. Sprinkle on a little salt, mixed spice and cinnamon and bake in the preheated oven for 30–35 minutes for large fish or 20–25 minutes for smaller fish.

Cook's Tip
If you prefer, use almonds instead of pine nuts. Use the same quantity of blanched almonds and split them in half before stir-frying.

Salmon with Spicy Pesto

This pesto uses sunflower seeds and chili as its flavoring rather than the classic basil and pine nuts.

Serves 4

4 x 8-ounce salmon steaks	**For the pesto**
2 tablespoons sunflower oil	6 mild fresh red chilies
	2 garlic cloves
finely grated rind and juice of 1 lime	2 tablespoons pumpkin or sunflower seeds
pinch of salt	freshly grated rind and juice of 1 lime
	5 tablespoons olive oil
	salt and ground black pepper

1 Insert a very sharp knife close to the top of the salmon's backbone. Working closely to the bone, cut halfway through the steak all round. repeat with the other side and pull out the bone. Remove any extra visible bones with a pair of tweezers.

2 Sprinkle a little salt on the surface and take hold of the end of the salmon, skin-side down. Insert a small sharp knife under the skin and, working away from you, cut off the skin keeping as close to the skin as possible. Repeat with the three remaining pieces of fish.

3 Rub the sunflower oil into the boneless fish rounds. Add the lime juice and rind and marinate in the fridge for 2 hours.

4 To make the pesto, seed the chilies and place them together with the garlic cloves, pumpkin or sunflower seeds, lime juice, rind and seasoning in a food processor or blender. Process until well mixed. Pour the olive oil gradually over the moving blades until the sauce has thickened and emulsified. Drain the salmon from its marinade. Broil the fish steaks for about 5 minutes on either side and serve with the spicy pesto.

Roast Chicken with Celery Root

Celery root and whole wheat bread crumbs give the stuffing an unusual and delicious twist.

Serves 4

3½-pound chicken
1 tablespoon butter

For the stuffing
1 pound celery root,
  chopped
3 tablespoons butter
3 slices bacon, chopped
1 onion, finely chopped
leaves from 1 fresh thyme
  sprig, chopped

leaves from 1 fresh small
  tarragon sprig,
  chopped
2 tablespoons chopped
  fresh parsley
1½-cups fresh whole
  wheat bread crumbs
dash of Worcestershire
  sauce
1 egg
salt and ground black
  pepper

1 To make the stuffing, cook the celery root in boiling water until tender. Drain well and chop finely. Heat 2 tablespoons of the butter in a saucepan and gently cook the bacon and onion until the onion is soft. Stir in the celery root and herbs and cook, stirring occasionally, for 2–3 minutes. Meanwhile, preheat the oven to 400°F.

2 Remove the pan from the heat and stir in the fresh bread crumbs, Worcestershire sauce, enough egg to bind the mixture, and season it with salt and pepper. Use this mixture to stuff the neck cavity of the chicken. Season the bird's skin, then rub it with the remaining butter.

3 Roast the chicken, basting occasionally with the pan drippings, for 1¼–1½ hours, until the juices run clear when the thickest part of the leg is pierced. Turn off the oven, open the door slightly and allow the chicken to rest for about 10 minutes before carving.

Chicken with Lemon and Herbs

The herbs can be changed according to what is available; for example, parsley or thyme could be used.

Serves 2

4 tablespoons butter
2 scallions, white part
  only, finely chopped
1 tablespoon chopped
  fresh tarragon

1 tablespoon chopped
  fresh fennel
juice of 1 lemon
4 chicken thighs
salt and ground black
  pepper
lemon slices and herb
  sprigs, to garnish

1 Preheat the broiler to moderate. In a small saucepan, melt the butter, then add the scallions, herbs and lemon juice; season with salt and pepper.

2 Brush the chicken thighs generously with the herb mixture, then broil for 10–12 minutes, basting frequently with the herb mixture.

3 Turn the chicken over and baste again, then cook for another 10–12 minutes or until the chicken juices run clear.

4 Serve the chicken garnished with lemon slices and herb sprigs, and accompanied by any remaining herb mixture.

Chicken with Peppers

This colorful dish comes from the south of Italy, where sweet peppers are plentiful.

Serves 4

3-pound chicken, cut into serving pieces
6 tablespoons olive oil
2 red onions, finely sliced
2 garlic cloves, finely chopped
small piece of dried chili, crumbled (optional)
½ cup dry white wine

3 large bell peppers (red, yellow or green), seeded and sliced into strips
2 tomatoes, fresh or canned, peeled and chopped
3 tablespoons chopped fresh parsley
salt and ground black

1 Trim any fat off the chicken and remove all excess skin.

2 Heat half the oil in a large heavy saucepan or flameproof casserole and cook the onion over a gentle heat until soft. Reserve. Add the remaining oil to the pan, raise the heat to moderate, add the chicken pieces and brown them on all sides, 6–8 minutes. Return the onions to the pan, and add the garlic and dried chili, if using.

3 Pour in the wine and cook until it has reduced by half. Add the peppers and stir well to coat. Season to taste. After 3–4 minutes, stir in the tomatoes. Lower the heat, cover the pan with a tight-fitting lid, and cook for about 25–30 minutes, until the peppers are soft and the chicken is cooked. Stir occasionally. Stir in the parsley and serve.

Cook's Tip

For a more elegant version of this dish to serve at a dinner party, use skinless, boneless chicken breasts. Substitute the fresh parsley with different chopped fresh herbs, such as cilantro, tarragon, rosemary, chervil or marjoram.

Golden Parmesan Chicken

Served cold with the garlic mayonnaise, these morsels of chicken make good picnic food.

Serves 4

4 chicken breast fillets, skinned
1½ cups fresh white bread crumbs
½ cup finely grated Parmesan cheese
2 tablespoons chopped fresh parsley
2 eggs, beaten
4 tablespoons butter, melted

salt and ground black pepper
crisp green salad, to serve

For the garlic mayonnaise
½ cup good-quality mayonnaise
½ cup plain yogurt
1–2 garlic cloves, crushed

1 Cut each chicken fillet into four or five large chunks. Mix together the bread crumbs, Parmesan cheese, parsley and salt and pepper in a shallow dish.

2 Dip the chicken pieces in the beaten egg, then into the bread crumb mixture. Place in a single layer on a baking sheet and chill in the fridge for at least 30 minutes.

3 Meanwhile, to make the garlic mayonnaise, mix the mayonnaise, yogurt, garlic and pepper to taste. Spoon the mayonnaise into a small serving bowl. Chill in the fridge until ready to serve.

4 Preheat the oven to 350°F. Drizzle the melted butter over the chicken pieces and cook for about 20 minutes, until crisp and golden. Serve the chicken immediately with a crisp green salad and the garlic mayonnaise for dipping.

Chicken in Green Sauce

Slow, gentle cooking makes the chicken in this dish very succulent and tender.

Serves 4

2 tablespoons butter
1 tablespoon olive oil
4 chicken portions – legs, breasts or quarters
1 small onion, finely chopped
⅔ cup medium-bodied dry white wine
⅔ cup chicken stock
2 fresh thyme sprigs
2 fresh tarragon sprigs
6 ounces watercress leaves
⅔ cup heavy cream
salt and ground black pepper
watercress leaves, to garnish

1 Heat the butter and oil in a frying pan and brown the chicken evenly. Transfer the chicken to a plate using a slotted spoon and keep warm in the oven.

2 Add the onion to the pan juices and cook until softened but not colored. Stir in the wine, then boil for 2–3 minutes. Add the stock and bring to the boil. Return the chicken to the pan, cover with a tight-fitting lid and cook very gently for about 30 minutes, until the chicken juices run clear when pierced with the point of a knife. Then transfer the chicken to a warm dish, cover and keep warm.

3 Boil the pan juices hard until they are reduced to about 4 tablespoons. Remove the leaves from the herbs and add to the pan with the watercress leaves and cream. Simmer over a moderate heat until slightly thickened.

4 Return the chicken to the casserole, season to taste with salt and pepper and heat through for a few minutes. Garnish with watercress leaves to serve.

Spatchcocked Deviled Cornish Hens

"Spatchcock" refers to birds that have been split and skewered flat. This shortens the cooking time considerably.

Serves 4

1 tablespoon English mustard powder
1 tablespoon paprika
1 tablespoon ground cumin
4 teaspoons tomato ketchup
1 tablespoon lemon juice
5 tablespoons butter, melted
4 Cornish hens, about 1 pound each
pinch of salt

1 Mix together the mustard, paprika, cumin, ketchup, lemon juice and salt until smooth, then gradually stir in the butter.

2 Using game shears or strong kitchen scissors, split each Cornish hen along one side of the backbone, then cut down the other side of the backbone to remove it.

3 Open out a Cornish hen, skin-side up, then press down firmly with the heel of your hand. Pass a long skewer through one leg and out through the other to secure the bird open and flat. Repeat with the remaining birds.

4 Spread the mustard mixture evenly over the skin of the birds. Cover loosely and leave in a cool place for at least 2 hours to marinate. Preheat the broiler.

5 Place the birds, skin-side up, under the broiler and cook for about 12 minutes. Turn the birds over, baste with any pan juices, and cook for another 7 minutes, until the juices run clear when pierced with the point of a knife.

Cook's Tip
For an al fresco *meal in the summer, these spatchcocked Cornish hens may be cooked on a barbecue.*

Stoved Chicken

"Stoved" is derived from the French *étouffer*, meaning to cook in a covered pot.

Serves 4

2 pounds potatoes, cut into ¼-inch slices
2 large onions, thinly sliced
1 tablespoon chopped fresh thyme
2 tablespoons butter
1 tablespoon sunflower oil
2 large slices bacon, chopped
4 large chicken pieces, cut in half
1 bay leaf
2½ cups chicken stock
salt and ground black pepper

1 Preheat the oven to 300°F. Make a thick layer of half the potato slices in a large heavy-based casserole, then cover with half the onion. Sprinkle with half of the thyme and season.

2 Heat the butter and oil in a large frying pan and brown the bacon and chicken. Using a slotted spoon, transfer the chicken and bacon to the casserole. Reserve the fat in the pan. Sprinkle the rest of the thyme and some seasoning over the chicken and add the bayleaf. Cover with the rest of the onion, followed by a neat layer of overlapping potato slices. Sprinkle with seasoning.

3 Pour the stock into the casserole, brush the potatoes with the reserved fat, then cover with a tight-fitting lid and cook in the oven for about 2 hours, until the chicken is tender.

4 Preheat the broiler. Uncover the casserole and place under the broiler. Cook until the slices of potatoes are beginning to brown and crisp. Serve hot.

Cook's Tip
Instead of using large chicken pieces, use thighs or drumsticks, or a mixture of the two.

Chicken with Red Cabbage

Crushed juniper berries provide a distinctive flavor in this unusual casserole.

Serves 4

4 tablespoons butter
4 large chicken pieces, cut in half
1 onion, chopped
8¼ cups finely shredded red cabbage
4 juniper berries, crushed
12 cooked chestnuts
½ cup full-bodied red wine
salt and ground black pepper

1 Heat the butter in a heavy-based flameproof casserole and lightly brown the chicken pieces. Transfer to a plate.

2 Add the onion to the casserole and fry gently until soft and light golden brown. Stir the cabbage and juniper berries into the casserole, season and cook over a moderate heat for about 6–7 minutes, stirring once or twice.

3 Stir the chestnuts into the casserole, then tuck the chicken pieces under the cabbage so they are on the bottom of the casserole. Pour in the red wine.

4 Cover and cook gently for about 40 minutes until the chicken juices run clear and the cabbage is very tender. Adjust the seasoning to taste and serve immediately.

Italian Chicken

Use chicken legs, breasts or quarters in this colorful dish, and a different type of pasta if you prefer.

Serves 4

2 tablespoons all-purpose
  flour
4 chicken pieces
2 tablespoons olive oil
1 onion, chopped
2 garlic cloves, chopped
1 red bell pepper, seeded
  and chopped
14-ounce can chopped
  tomatoes
2 tablespoons red pesto
  sauce

4 sun-dried tomatoes in
  oil, chopped
⅔ cup chicken stock
1 teaspoon dried oregano
8 black olives, pitted
salt and ground black
  pepper
chopped fresh basil and
  whole basil leaves, to
  garnish
tagliatelle, to serve

1 Place the flour and seasoning in a plastic bag. Add the chicken pieces and shake well until coated. Heat the oil in a flameproof casserole and brown the chicken quickly. Remove with a slotted spoon and set aside.

2 Lower the heat and add the onion, garlic and pepper and cook for 5 minutes. Stir in the remaining ingredients, except the olives, and bring to a boil.

3 Return the sautéed chicken pieces to the casserole, season lightly, cover with a tight-fitting lid and simmer for 30–35 minutes, or until the chicken is cooked.

4 Add the black olives and simmer for another 5 minutes. Transfer to a warmed serving dish, sprinkle with the chopped basil and garnish with basil leaves. Serve with hot tagliatelle.

Cook's Tip
If you do not have red pesto sauce, use green pesto instead. Finely chop, then purée two sun-dried tomato pieces in a blender or food processor and add with the other ingredients.

Honey and Orange Glazed Chicken

This dish is popular in the United States and Australia and is ideal for an easy meal served with baked potatoes.

Serves 4

4–6 ounce boneless
  chicken breasts
1 tablespoon sunflower
  oil
4 scallions, chopped
1 garlic clove, crushed
3 tablespoons honey
4 tablespoons fresh
  orange juice

1 orange, peeled and
  segmented
2 tablespoons soy sauce
fresh lemon balm or
  Italian parsley, to
  garnish
baked potatoes and mixed
  salad, to serve

1 Preheat the oven to 375°F. Place the chicken breasts, with skins on, in a single layer in a shallow roasting pan and set aside.

2 Heat the sunflower oil in a small saucepan, and gently fry the scallions and garlic for about 2 minutes until softened but not browned. Add the honey, orange juice, orange segments and soy sauce to the pan, stirring well, and cook until the honey has completely dissolved.

3 Pour the sauce over the chicken and bake, uncovered, for about 45 minutes, basting once or twice until the chicken is cooked. Check by piercing with the point of a knife; the juices should run clear. Garnish with lemon balm or flat leaf parsley and serve with baked potatoes and a salad.

Cook's Tip
For a slightly spicier version, look out for mustard that has been flavored with honey to add to this dish instead of the honey. Use the same amount.

Cajun Chicken Jambalaya

Wonderfully spicy Cajun cooking was developed by the French-speaking immigrants in Louisiana, USA.

Serves 4

2½ pound fresh chicken
1½ onions
1 bay leaf
4 black peppercorns
2 tablespoons oil
2 garlic cloves, chopped
1 green bell pepper,
    seeded and chopped
1 celery stalk, chopped
1¼ cups long-grain rice
4 ounces chorizo sausage,
    sliced
1 cup chopped, cooked
    ham

14-ounce can chopped
    tomatoes
½ teaspoon hot chili
    powder
½ teaspoon cumin seeds
½ teaspoon ground
    cumin
1 teaspoon dried thyme
1 cup peeled, cooked
    shrimp
dash of Tabasco sauce
salt and ground black
    pepper
chopped fresh parsley, to
    garnish

1 Place the chicken in a flameproof casserole and pour over 2½ cups water. Add half an onion, the bay leaf and peppercorns and bring to a boil. Cover and simmer for 1½ hours. Then lift the chicken out of the pan. Skin, bone and chop the meat. Strain the stock and reserve.

2 Chop the remaining whole onion. Heat the oil in a large frying pan and fry the onion, garlic, green pepper and celery for 5 minutes. Stir in the rice. Add the sausage, ham and chicken and fry for 2–3 minutes, stirring frequently.

3 Pour in the tomatoes and 1¼ cups of the reserved stock, then and add the chili, cumin and thyme. Bring to a boil, cover and simmer gently for 20 minutes, or until the rice is tender and the liquid absorbed.

4 Stir in the shrimp and Tabasco. Cook for 5 minutes more, then season to taste with salt and ground black pepper. Serve hot, garnished with chopped fresh parsley.

Moroccan Chicken Couscous

The combination of sweet and spicy flavors in the sauce and couscous makes this dish irresistible.

Serves 4

1 tablespoon butter
1 tablespoon sunflower oil
4 chicken pieces
2 onions, finely chopped
2 garlic cloves, crushed
½ teaspoon ground
    cinnamon
¼ teaspoon ground
    ginger
¼ teaspoon ground
    turmeric
2 tablespoons orange
    juice
2 teaspoons honey
pinch of salt
fresh mint sprigs,
    to garnish

For the couscous

2¼ cups couscous
1 teaspoon salt
2 teaspoons caster sugar
1 tablespoon sunflower
    oil
½ teaspoon ground
    cinnamon
pinch of grated nutmeg
1 tablespoon orange
    blossom water
2 tablespoons golden
    raisins
½ cup chopped toasted
    almonds
3 tablespoons chopped
    pistachios

1 Fry the chicken pieces skin-side down in the butter and oil until golden. Turn them over. Add the onions, garlic, spices, a pinch of salt, the orange juice and 1¼ cups water. Cover and bring to a boil, then simmer for about 30 minutes.

2 Mix the couscous with the salt and 1½ cups water. Leave for 5 minutes. Add the rest of the ingredients for the couscous.

3 Line a steamer with parchment paper and spoon in the couscous. Set over the chicken and steam for 10 minutes.

4 Remove the steamer and keep covered. Stir the honey into the chicken liquid and boil rapidly for 3–4 minutes. Serve the chicken on a bed of couscous with some sauce spooned over. Garnish with fresh mint and serve with the remaining sauce.

Rabbit with Mustard

Rabbit is increasingly available in butchers and larger supermarkets, ready prepared and in serving pieces.

Serves 4

1 tablespoon all-purpose flour
1 tablespoon English mustard powder
4 large rabbit pieces
2 tablespoons butter
2 tablespoons oil
1 onion, finely chopped
⅔ cup beer
1¼ cups chicken or veal stock
1 tablespoon tarragon vinegar
2 tablespoons dark brown sugar

2 – 3 teaspoons prepared English mustard
salt and ground black pepper

To finish
4 tablespoons butter
2 tablespoons oil
1 cup fresh bread crumbs
1 tablespoon chopped fresh chives
1 tablespoon chopped fresh tarragon

1 Preheat the oven to 325°F. Mix the flour and mustard powder together, then put on a plate. Dip the rabbit pieces in the flour mixture; reserve any excess flour. Heat the butter and oil in a heavy flameproof casserole and brown the rabbit. Transfer to a plate. Stir in the onion and cook until soft.

2 Stir any reserved flour mixture into the casserole, cook for 1 minute, then stir in the beer, stock and vinegar. Bring to a boil and add the sugar and pepper. Simmer for 2 minutes. Return the rabbit and any juices that have collected on the plate to the casserole, cover with a tight-fitting lid and cook in the oven for 1 hour. Stir the mustard and salt to taste into the casserole, cover again and cook for another 15 minutes.

3 To finish, heat together the butter and oil in a frying pan and fry the bread crumbs, stirring frequently, until golden, then stir in the herbs. Transfer the rabbit to a warmed serving dish and sprinkle the bread crumb mixture over the top.

Turkey Hot-pot

Turkey and sausages combine well with kidney beans and other vegetables in this hearty stew.

Serves 4

scant ½ cup kidney beans, soaked overnight, drained and rinsed
3 tablespoons butter
2 herbed pork sausages
1 pound turkey casserole meat
3 leeks, sliced

2 carrots, finely chopped
4 tomatoes, chopped
2 – 3 teaspoons tomato paste
bouquet garni
1½ cups chicken stock
salt and ground black pepper

1 Cook the kidney beans in unsalted boiling water for 10 minutes, drain, cover with cold water, bring to the boil, and cook for about 30 minutes.

2 Meanwhile, heat the butter in a flameproof casserole, then cook the sausages until browned and the fat runs. Drain on paper towels, stir the turkey into the casserole and cook until lightly browned all over, then transfer to a bowl using a slotted spoon. Stir the leeks and carrot into the casserole and brown them lightly, stirring occasionally.

3 Add the chopped tomatoes and tomato paste and simmer gently for about 5 minutes.

4 Chop the sausages and return to the casserole with the beans, turkey, bouquet garni, stock and seasoning. Cover with a tight-fitting lid and cook gently for about 1¼ hours, until the meat is tender and there is very little liquid.

Duck with Cumberland Sauce

A sophisticated dish: the sauce contains both port and brandy, making it very rich.

Serves 4

4 duck portions	4 tablespoons port
grated rind and juice of 1 lemon	pinch of ground mace or ginger
grated rind and juice of 1 large orange	1 tablespoon brandy
4 tablespoons redcurrant jelly	salt and ground black pepper
	orange slices, to garnish

1 Preheat the oven to 375°F. Place a rack in a roasting pan. Prick the duck portions all over, sprinkle with salt and pepper. Place on the rack and cook in the oven for 45–50 minutes, until the duck skin is crisp and the juices run clear when pricked with the point of a knife.

2 Meanwhile, simmer the lemon and orange rinds and juices together in a saucepan for 5 minutes.

3 Add the redcurrant jelly and stir until melted, then stir in the port. Bring to a boil and add mace or ginger and salt and pepper, to taste.

4 Transfer the duck to a serving plate; keep warm. Pour the fat from the roasting pan, leaving the pan juices. With the pan over a gentle heat, stir in the brandy, dislodge the residue and bring to a boil. Stir in the port sauce and serve with the duck, garnished with orange slices.

Coronation Chicken

A cold chicken dish with a mild, curry-flavored sauce, ideal for summer lunch parties.

Serves 8

½ lemon	1 tablespoon curry paste
5-pound chicken	1 tablespoon tomato paste
1 onion, quartered	
1 carrot, quartered	½ cup red wine
large bouquet garni	1 bay leaf
8 black peppercorns, crushed	juice of ½ lemon, or more to taste
pinch of salt	2–3 teaspoons apricot jelly
fresh watercress sprigs, to garnish	1¼ cups mayonnaise
	½ cup whipping cream, whipped
For the sauce	salt and ground black pepper
1 small onion, chopped	
1 tablespoon butter	

1 Put the lemon half in the chicken cavity, then place the chicken in a saucepan that it just fits. Add the vegetables, bouquet garni, peppercorns and salt.

2 Add enough water to come two-thirds of the way up the chicken, bring to a boil, then cover and cook gently for about 1½ hours, until the chicken juices run clear.

3 Transfer the chicken to a large bowl, pour the cooking liquid over and allow to cool. When cool, skin and bone the chicken, then chop. (Use the liquid for making soup.)

4 To make the sauce, cook the onion in the butter until soft. Add the curry paste, tomato paste, wine, bay leaf and lemon juice, then cook for 10 minutes. Add the jelly; strain and cool.

5 Beat the sauce mixture into the mayonnaise. Fold in the cream, season to taste with salt and pepper and add the lemon juice, then stir in with the chicken.

Tandoori Chicken Kebabs

This popular dish originates from the Punjab, where it is traditionally cooked in clay ovens known as *tandoors*.

Serves 4

4 boneless chicken breasts, about 6 ounces each, skinned
1 tablespoon lemon juice
3 tablespoons tandoori paste
3 tablespoons plain yogurt
1 garlic clove, crushed
2 tablespoons chopped fresh cilantro

1 small onion, cut into wedges and separated into layers
a little oil, for brushing
salt and ground black pepper
fresh cilantro sprigs, to garnish
pilau rice and nan bread, to serve

1 Dice the chicken breasts into 1-inch pieces, place in a bowl and add the lemon juice, tandoori paste, yogurt, garlic, cilantro and seasoning. Cover and allow to marinate in the fridge for 2–3 hours.

2 Preheat the broiler. Thread alternate pieces of marinated chicken and onion onto four skewers.

3 Brush the onions with a little oil, lay the skewers on a broiler rack and cook under a high heat for 10–12 minutes, turning once. Garnish the kebabs with fresh cilantro and serve at once with pilau rice and nan bread.

Cook's Tip
If you are using wooden skewers, soak them first in cold water to prevent them catching fire under the broiler. For an economical alternative, use chicken thighs instead of breasts.

Chinese Chicken with Cashew Nuts

The cashew nuts give this oriental dish a delightful crunchy texture that contrasts well with the noodles.

Serves 4

4 boneless chicken breasts, about 6 ounces each, skinned
3 garlic cloves, crushed
4 tablespoons soy sauce
2 tablespoons cornstarch
4 cups dried egg noodles
3 tablespoons peanut or sunflower oil

1 tablespoon sesame oil
1 cup roasted cashew nuts
6 scallions, cut into 2-inch pieces and halved lengthwise
scallion curls and a little chopped fresh red chili, to garnish

1 Slice the chicken into strips, then combine with the garlic, soy sauce and cornflour. Cover and chill in the fridge for about 30 minutes.

2 Meanwhile, bring a saucepan of water to the boil and add the egg noodles. Turn off the heat and let stand for 5 minutes. Drain well and reserve.

3 Heat the oils in a large frying pan or wok and stir-fry the chilled chicken and marinade juices over a high heat for about 3–4 minutes, or until golden brown.

4 Add the cashew nuts and scallions to the pan or wok and stir-fry for another 2–3 minutes.

5 Add the drained noodles and stir-fry for 2 minutes more. Toss the noodles well and serve immediately, garnished with the scallion curls and chopped chili.

Cook's Tip
For a milder garnish, seed the red chili before chopping or finely dice some red bell pepper instead and use with the scallion curls.

Chinese-style Chicken Salad

For a variation and to add more color, add some cooked, peeled shrimp to this lovely salad.

Serves 4

4 boneless chicken breasts, about 6 ounces each
4 tablespoons dark soy sauce
pinch of Chinese five-spice powder
squeeze of lemon juice
½ cucumber, peeled and cut into matchsticks
1 teaspoon salt
3 tablespoons sunflower oil
2 tablespoons sesame oil
1 tablespoon sesame seeds

2 tablespoons dry sherry
2 carrots, cut into matchsticks
8 scallions, shredded
1 cup bean sprouts

For the sauce
4 tablespoons crunchy peanut butter
2 teaspoons lemon juice
2 teaspoons sesame oil
¼ teaspoon hot chili powder
1 scallion, finely chopped

1 Put the chicken into a saucepan and cover with water. Add 1 tablespoon of the soy sauce, the Chinese five-spice powder and lemon juice. Cover, bring to a boil, then simmer for 20 minutes. Then skin and slice into thin strips.

2 Sprinkle the cucumber matchsticks with salt, leave for 30 minutes, then rinse and pat dry.

3 Fry the sesame seeds in the oils for 30 seconds, then stir in the remaining soy sauce and the sherry. Add the carrots and stir-fry for 2 minutes, then remove from the heat.

4 Mix together the cucumber, scallions, bean sprouts, carrots, pan juices and chicken. Transfer to a shallow dish. Cover and chill for 1 hour.

5 For the sauce, cream the first four ingredients together, then stir in the scallion. Serve the chicken with the sauce.

Duck, Avocado and Berry Salad

Duck breasts are roasted until crisp with a honey and soy glaze to serve warm with fresh raspberries and avocado.

Serves 4

4 small or 2 large duck breasts, halved if large
1 tablespoon honey
1 tablespoon dark soy sauce
mixed chopped fresh salad greens such as lamb's lettuce, red chicory or frisée
2 avocados, pitted, peeled and cut into chunks
1 cup raspberries

salt and ground black pepper

For the dressing
4 tablespoons olive oil
1 tablespoon raspberry vinegar
1 tablespoon redcurrant jelly
salt and ground black pepper

1 Preheat the oven to 425°F. Prick the skin of each duck breast with a fork. Blend the honey and soy sauce together in a small bowl, then brush all over the skin.

2 Place the duck breasts on a rack set over a roasting pan and season with salt and pepper. Roast in the oven for about 15–20 minutes, until the skins are crisp and the meat cooked.

3 Meanwhile, to make the dressing, put the oil, vinegar, redcurrant jelly and seasoning in a small bowl and whisk well until evenly blended.

4 Slice the duck breasts diagonally and arrange on four individual plates with the salad greens, avocados and raspberries. Spoon the dressing over the top and serve.

Cook's Tip
Small avocados contain the most flavor and have a good texture. They should be ripe but not too soft, so avoid any with skins that are turning black.

Crumbed Turkey Steaks

The authentic Austrian dish, *Wiener schnitzel*, uses veal scallops, but turkey breasts make a tasty alternative.

Serves 4

4 turkey breast steaks, about 5 ounces each
3 tablespoons all-purpose flour, seasoned
1 egg, lightly beaten
1½ cups fresh bread crumbs

5 tablespoons finely grated Parmesan cheese
2 tablespoons butter
3 tablespoons sunflower oil
fresh parsley sprigs, to garnish
4 lemon wedges, to serve

1 Lay the turkey steaks between two sheets of pastic wrap. Hit each one with a rolling pin until flattened. Snip the edges of the steaks with scissors a few times to prevent them from curling during cooking.

2 Place the seasoned flour on one plate, the egg in a shallow bowl and the bread crumbs and Parmesan mixed together on another plate.

3 Dip each side of the steaks into the flour and shake off any extra. Next, dip them into the egg and then gently press each side into the bread crumbs and cheese until evenly coated.

4 Heat the butter and oil in a large frying pan and fry the turkey steaks over a moderate heat for 2–3 minutes on each side, until golden. Garnish with the fresh parsley sprigs and serve with lemon wedges.

Country Cider Hot-pot

Rabbit meat is regaining popularity and is a healthy, low-fat option, as is all game.

Serves 4

2 tablespoons all-purpose flour
4 boneless rabbit pieces
2 tablespoons butter
1 tablespoon oil
15 baby onions
4 slices bacon, chopped
2 teaspoons mustard
1¾ cups hard cider
3 carrots, chopped

2 parsnips, chopped
12 ready-to-eat dried prunes, pitted
1 fresh rosemary sprig
1 bay leaf
salt and ground black pepper

1 Preheat the oven to 325°F. Place the flour and seasoning in a plastic bag, add the rabbit portions and shake until coated. Set aside.

2 Heat the butter and oil in a flameproof casserole and add the onions and bacon. Fry for 4 minutes, until the onions have softened. Remove with a slotted spoon and reserve.

3 Fry the seasoned rabbit pieces in the oil left in the flameproof casserole until they are browned all over, then spread a little of the mustard over the top of each piece.

4 Return the onions and bacon to the pan. Pour on the cider and add the carrots, parsnips, prunes, rosemary and bay leaf. Season well. Bring to a boil, then cover with a tight-fitting lid and transfer to the oven. Cook for about 1½ hours until the meat and vegetables are tender.

5 Remove the rosemary sprig and bay leaf and serve the rabbit hot with creamy mashed potatoes, if you wish.

Turkey Pastitsio

A traditional Greek pastitsio is a rich, high-fat dish made with ground beef, but this lighter version is just as tasty.

Serves 4–6

1 pound lean ground turkey
1 large onion, finely chopped
4 tablespoons tomato paste
1 cup red wine or stock
1 teaspoon ground cinnamon
2½ cups macaroni
1¼ cups skimmed milk
2 tablespoons sunflower margarine

2 tablespoons all-purpose flour
1 teaspoon grated nutmeg
2 tomatoes, sliced
4 tablespoon whole wheat bread crumbs
salt and ground black pepper
green salad, to serve

1 Preheat the oven to 425°F. Fry the turkey and onion in a nonstick frying pan without fat, stirring until lightly browned.

2 Stir in the tomato paste, red wine or stock and cinnamon. Season with salt and pepper, then cover with a tight-fitting lid and simmer for 5 minutes.

3 Cook the macaroni in boiling salted water until just tender, then drain. Layer with the meat mixture in a wide casserole.

4 Place the milk, margarine and flour in a saucepan and whisk over a moderate heat until thickened and smooth. Add the nutmeg, and salt and pepper to taste.

5 Pour the sauce evenly over the pasta and meat. Arrange the tomato slices on top and sprinkle lines of bread crumbs over the surface. Bake for 30–35 minutes, or until golden brown and bubbling. Serve hot with a green salad.

Tuscan Chicken

A simple peasant casserole with all the flavors of Tuscan ingredients. The wine can be replaced by chicken stock.

Serves 4

1 teaspoon olive oil
8 chicken thighs, skinned
1 onion, thinly sliced
2 red bell peppers, seeded and sliced
1 garlic clove, crushed
1¼ cups tomato sauce
½ cup dry white wine

large fresh oregano sprig, or 1 teaspoon dried oregano
14-ounce can navy or white beans, drained
3 tablespoons fresh bread crumbs
salt and ground black pepper

1 Heat the oil in a nonstick or heavy saucepan and fry the chicken until golden brown. Remove and keep hot. Add the onion and peppers to the pan and gently sauté until softened, but not brown. Stir in the garlic.

2 Add the chicken, tomato sauce, wine and oregano. Season well with salt and pepper, bring to a boil, then cover the pan with a tight lid.

3 Lower the heat and simmer gently, stirring occasionally, for 30–35 minutes or until the chicken is tender and the juices run clear, not pink, when pierced with the point of a knife.

4 Stir in the beans and simmer for another 5 minutes until heated through. Sprinkle with the bread crumbs and cook under a hot broiler until golden brown.

Cornish Hens with Grapes in Vermouth

This sauce could also be served with roast chicken, but poussin have the stronger flavor.

Serves 4

4 oven-ready Cornish hens, about 1 pound each

4 tablespoons butter, softened

2 shallots, chopped

4 tablespoons chopped fresh parsley

2 cups white grapes, preferably Muscatel, halved and seeded

⅔ cup white vermouth

1 teaspoon cornstarch

4 tablespoons heavy cream

2 tablespoons pine nuts, toasted

salt and ground black pepper

watercress sprigs, to garnish

1 Preheat the oven to 400°F. Wash and dry the Cornish hens. Spread the softened butter all over the Cornish hens and put a hazelnut-sized piece in the cavity of each bird.

2 Mix together the shallots and parsley and place a quarter of the mixture inside each Cornish hen. Put the Cornish hens side by side in a large roasting pan and roast for 40–50 minutes, or until the juices run clear when the thickest part of the flesh is pierced with a skewer. Transfer the Cornish hens to a warmed serving plate. Cover and keep warm.

3 Skim off most of the fat from the roasting pan, then add the grapes and vermouth. Place the tin directly over a low heat for a few minutes to warm and slightly soften the grapes.

4 Lift the grapes out of the tin using a slotted spoon and scatter them around the Cornish hens. Keep covered. Stir the cornstarch into the cream, then add to the pan juices. Cook gently for a few minutes, stirring, until the sauce has thickened. Season to taste with salt and pepper. Pour the sauce around the Cornish hens. Sprinkle with the toasted pine nuts and garnish with watercress sprigs.

Chicken Parcels with Herb Butter

These delightful, individual phyllo pastry parcels contain a wonderfully moist and herby filling.

Serves 4

4 chicken breast fillets, skinned

generous ½ cup butter, softened

6 tablespoons mixed chopped fresh herbs such as thyme, parsley, oregano and rosemary

1 teaspoon lemon juice

5 large sheets phyllo pastry, defrosted if frozen

1 egg, beaten

2 tablespoons freshly grated Parmesan cheese

salt and ground black pepper

1 Season the chicken fillets. Melt 2 tablespoons of the butter in a frying pan and fry the chicken fillets to seal and brown lightly. Allow to cool.

2 Preheat the oven to 375°F. Put the remaining butter, the herbs, lemon juice and seasoning in a food processor or blender and process until smooth. Melt half of this herb butter.

3 Take one sheet of phyllo pastry and brush with melted herb butter. Keep the other sheets covered with a damp dish towel. Fold the phyllo pastry sheet in half and brush again with butter. Place a chicken fillet about 1 inch from the top end.

4 Dot the chicken with a quarter of the remaining unmelted herb butter. Fold in the sides of the pastry, then roll up to enclose it completely. Place seam-side down on a lightly greased baking sheet. Repeat with the other chicken fillets.

5 Brush the phyllo parcels with beaten egg. Cut the last sheet of filo into strips, then scrunch and arrange on top. Brush the parcels once again with the egg glaze, then sprinkle with Parmesan cheese. Bake for about 35–50 minutes, until golden brown. Serve hot.

Pot-roast of Venison

The venison is marinated for 24 hours before preparation to give this rich dish an even fuller flavor.

Serves 4–5

4–4½ pound boned leg
   of venison
5 tablespoons oil
4 cloves
8 black peppercorns,
   lightly crushed
12 juniper berries, lightly
   crushed
1 cup full-bodied red
   wine
4 ounces lean bacon,
   chopped

2 onions, finely chopped
2 carrots, chopped
5 ounces large
   mushrooms, sliced
1 tablespoon all-purpose
   flour
1 cup veal stock
2 tablespoons redcurrant
   jelly
salt and ground black
   pepper

1 Put the venison in a bowl, add half the oil, the spices and wine, cover and leave in a cool place for 24 hours, turning the meat occasionally.

2 Preheat the oven to 325°F. Remove the venison from the bowl and pat dry. Reserve the marinade. Heat the remaining oil in a shallow saucepan, then brown the venison evenly. Transfer to a plate.

3 Stir the bacon, onions, carrots and mushrooms into the pan and cook for about 5 minutes. Stir in the flour and cook for 2 minutes, then remove from the heat and stir in the marinade, stock, redcurrant jelly and seasoning. Return to the heat, bring to a boil, stirring, then simmer for 2–3 minutes.

4 Transfer the venison and sauce to a casserole and cover with a tight-fitting lid. Cook in the oven for about 3 hours, turning the meat from time to time, until tender.

Pheasant with Mushrooms

The wine and mushroom sauce in this recipe is given a lift by including anchovy fillets.

Serves 4

1 pheasant, cut in pieces
1 cup red wine
3 tablespoons oil
4 tablespoons Spanish
   sherry vinegar
1 large onion, chopped
2 strips bacon
12 ounces chestnut
   mushrooms, sliced

3 anchovy fillets,
   soaked for 10 minutes
   and drained
1½ cups game, veal or
   chicken stock
bouquet garni
salt and ground black
   pepper

1 Place the pheasant in a dish, add the wine, half the oil and half the vinegar, and scatter over half the onion. Season with salt and pepper, then cover the dish and leave in a cool place for about 8–12 hours, turning the pheasant occasionally.

2 Preheat the oven to 325°F. Lift the pheasant from the dish and pat dry with paper towels. Reserve the marinade for later.

3 Heat the remaining oil in a flameproof casserole, then brown the pheasant pieces. Transfer to a plate.

4 Add the bacon with the remaining onion to the casserole and cook until the onion is soft. Stir in the mushrooms and cook for about 3 minutes.

5 Stir in the anchovies and remaining vinegar and boil until reduced. Add the marinade, cook for 2 minutes, then add the stock and bouquet garni. Return the pheasant to the casserole, cover and bake for about 1½ hours. Transfer the pheasant to a serving dish. Boil the cooking juices to reduce. Discard the bouquet garni. Pour over the pheasant and serve at once.

Minty Yogurt Chicken

Marinated, broiled chicken thighs make a tasty light lunch or supper. Use drumsticks if you prefer.

Serves 4

8 chicken thigh portions
1 tablespoon honey
2 tablespoons lime juice
2 tablespoons plain
  yogurt
4 tablespoons chopped
  fresh mint
salt and ground black
  pepper

1 Skin the chicken thighs and slash the flesh at intervals with a sharp knife. Place in a bowl. Mix together the honey, lime juice, yogurt, seasoning and half the mint.

2 Spoon the marinade over the chicken and allow to marinate for 30 minutes. Line a broiler pan with foil and cook the chicken under a moderately hot broiler until thoroughly cooked and golden brown, turning occasionally.

3 Sprinkle with the remaining mint and serve with potatoes and tomato salad, if you wish.

Mandarin Sesame Duck

The rind, juice and flesh of sweet mandarin oranges are used in this delightful roast dish.

Serves 4

4 duck leg or boned breast
  portions
2 tablespoons light soy
  sauce
3 tablespoons clear honey
1 tablespoon sesame seeds
4 mandarin oranges
1 teaspoon cornstarch
salt and ground black
  pepper

1 Preheat the oven to 350°F. Prick the duck skin all over. Slash the breast skin diagonally at intervals. Roast the duck for 1 hour. Mix 1 tablespoon soy sauce with 2 tablespoons honey and brush over the duck. Sprinkle with sesame seeds. Roast for 15 minutes more.

2 Grate the rind from one mandarin and squeeze the juice from two. Mix in the cornstarch, remaining soy sauce and honey. Heat, stirring, until thickened and clear. Season. Peel and slice the remaining mandarins. Serve the duck with the mandarin slices and the sauce.

Sticky Ginger Chicken

For a fuller flavor, marinate the chicken drumsticks in the glaze for 30 minutes before cooking.

Serves 4

Mix 2 tablespoons lemon juice, 1 ounce light brown sugar, 1 teaspoon grated fresh ginger, 2 teaspoons, soy sauce and ground pepper to taste. Using a sharp knife, slash 8 chicken drumsticks about three times through the thickest part of the flesh, then toss the chicken in the glaze. Cook it under a hot broiler or on a barbecue, turning occasionally and brushing with the glaze, until it is golden and the juices run clear when pierced. Serve on a bed of lettuce, with crusty bread, if you wish.

Oat-crusted Chicken with Sage

Oats make a good, crunchy coating for savory foods, and offer a good way to add extra fiber.

Serves 4

3 tablespoons milk
2 teaspoons English
   mustard
½ cup rolled oats
3 tablespoons chopped
   fresh sage leaves
8 chicken thighs or
   drumsticks, skinned

½ cup plain yogurt
1 teaspoon whole-grain
   mustard
salt and ground black
   pepper
fresh sage leaves, to
   garnish

1 Preheat the oven to 400°F. Mix together the milk and English mustard.

2 Mix the oats with 2 tablespoons of the chopped sage and the seasoning on a plate. Brush the chicken with the milk and press into the oats to coat evenly.

3 Place the chicken on a baking sheet and bake for about 40 minutes, or until the juices run clear, not pink, when pierced through the thickest part.

4 Meanwhile, mix together the yogurt, whole-grain mustard, remaining sage and seasoning, transfer to a serving dish and serve with the chicken. Garnish the chicken with fresh sage leaves.

Cook's Tip
If fresh sage is not available, choose another fresh herb such as thyme or parsley rather than using a dried alternative. These chicken thighs or drumsticks may be served hot or cold.

Chicken in Creamy Orange Sauce

The brandy adds a rich flavor to the sauce, but omit it if you prefer and use orange juice alone.

Serves 4

8 chicken thighs or
   drumsticks, skinned
3 tablespoons brandy
1¼ cups orange juice
3 scallions, chopped

2 teaspoons cornstarch
6 tablespoons plain
   yogurt
salt and ground black
   pepper

1 Fry the chicken pieces without fat in a nonstick or heavy frying pan, turning until evenly browned.

2 Stir in the brandy, orange juice and scallions. Bring to the boil, then cover and simmer for 15 minutes, or until the chicken is tender and the juices run clear, not pink, when pierced with the point of a sharp knife.

3 Blend the cornstarch with a little water, then mix into the yogurt. Stir this into a small saucepan and cook over a moderate heat until boiling.

4 Adjust the seasoning to taste and serve with boiled rice or pasta and green salad, if you wish.

Normandy Roast Chicken

The chicken is turned over halfway through roasting so that it cooks evenly and stays wonderfully moist.

Serves 4

4 tablespoons butter, softened
2 tablespoons chopped fresh tarragon
1 small garlic clove, crushed
3-pound fresh chicken

1 teaspoon all-purpose flour
⅔ cup light cream
squeeze of lemon juice
salt and ground black pepper
fresh tarragon and lemon slices, to garnish

1 Preheat the oven to 400°F. Mix together the butter, a tablespoon of the chopped tarragon, the garlic and seasoning in a bowl. Spoon half the butter mixture into the cavity of the chicken.

2 Carefully lift the skin at the neck cavity of the bird from the breast flesh on each side, then gently push a little of the butter mixture into each pocket and smooth it down over the breasts with your fingers.

3 Season the bird and lay it, breast-side down, in a roasting pan. Roast in the oven for 45 minutes, then turn the chicken over and baste with the juices. Cook for another 45 minutes.

4 When the chicken is cooked, lift it to drain out any juices from the cavity into the pan, then transfer the bird to a warmed platter and keep warm.

5 Place the roasting pan on the stove top and heat until sizzling. Stir in the flour and cook for 1 minute, then stir in the cream, the remaining tarragon, ⅔ cup water, the lemon juice and seasoning. Boil and stir for 2–3 minutes, until thickened. Garnish the chicken with tarragon and lemon slices and serve with the sauce.

Duck Breasts with Orange Sauce

A simple variation on the classic French whole roast duck, which makes for a more elegant presentation.

Serves 4

4 duck breasts
1 tablespoon sunflower oil
2 oranges
⅔ cup fresh orange juice
1 tablespoon port

2 tablespoons orange marmalade
1 tablespoon butter
1 teaspoon cornstarch
salt and ground black pepper

1 Season the duck breast skin. Heat the oil in a frying pan over a moderate heat and add the duck breasts, skin-side down. Cover and cook for 3–4 minutes, until just lightly browned. Turn the breasts over, lower the heat slightly and cook uncovered for 5–6 minutes.

2 Peel the skin and pith from the oranges. Working over a bowl to catch any juice, slice either side of the membranes to release the orange segments, then set aside with the juice.

3 Remove the duck breasts from the pan with a slotted spoon, drain on paper towels and keep warm in the oven while making the sauce.

4 Drain off the fat from the frying pan. Add the segmented oranges, all but 2 tablespoons of the orange juice, the port and the orange marmalade. Bring to a boil and then reduce the heat slightly. Whisk small pats of the butter into the sauce and season with salt and pepper.

5 Blend the cornstarch with the reserved orange juice, pour into the pan and stir until slightly thickened. Add the duck breasts and cook gently for about 3 minutes. To serve, arrange the sliced breasts on plates with the sauce.

Pot-roast Cornish Hens

This dish is inspired by the French method of cooking these birds. Pot-roasting keeps them moist and succulent.

Serves 4

1 tablespoon olive oil
1 onion, sliced
1 large garlic clove, sliced
½ cup diced bacon
2 fresh Cornish hens, about 1 pound each
2 tablespoons melted butter
2 baby celery hearts, each cut into 4 pieces
8 baby carrots
2 small zucchini, cut into chunks
8 small new potatoes

2½ cups chicken stock
⅔ cup dry white wine
1 bay leaf
2 fresh thyme sprigs
2 fresh rosemary sprigs
1 tablespoon butter, softened
1 tablespoon all-purpose flour
salt and ground black pepper
fresh herbs, to garnish

1 Preheat the oven to 375°F. Heat the olive oil in a large flameproof casserole and sauté the onions, garlic and bacon for 5–6 minutes until the onions have softened. Brush the Cornish hens with half the melted butter and season. Add to the casserole with the vegetables. Pour in the stock and wine and add the herbs. Cover and bake for 20 minutes.

2 Remove the lid and brush the birds with the remaining butter. Bake for 25–30 minutes more until golden. Transfer the Cornish hens to a warmed serving platter and cut each in half with poultry shears or scissors. Remove the vegetables with a slotted spoon and arrange them around the birds. Cover with foil and keep warm.

3 Discard the herbs from the casserole. Mix the butter and flour to a paste. Bring the cooking liquid to a boil then whisk in spoonfuls of paste until thickened. Season and serve with the Cornish hens and vegetables, garnished with herbs.

Coq au Vin

Chicken is flamed in brandy, then braised in red wine with bacon, mushrooms and onions in this classic dish.

Serves 4

½ cup all-purpose flour
3-pound chicken, cut into 8 pieces
1 tablespoon olive oil
5 tablespoons butter
20 baby onions
3 ounces bacon, diced
about 20 button mushrooms
2 tablespoons brandy

1 bottle red Burgundy
bouquet garni
3 garlic cloves
1 teaspoon soft light brown sugar
salt and ground black pepper
1 tablespoon chopped fresh parsley and croûtons, to garnish

1 Place 3 tablespoons of the flour and seasoning in a large plastic bag and coat the chicken pieces. Heat the oil and 4 tablespoons of the butter in a large flameproof casserole and sauté the onions and bacon until the onions have browned lightly. Add the mushrooms and fry for 2 minutes more. Remove with a slotted spoon and reserve.

2 Add the chicken pieces to the hot oil and cook for about 5–6 minutes until browned. Add the brandy and, standing back, light it with a match, then shake the casserole gently until the flames die.

3 Add the wine, bouquet garni, garlic and sugar, and season. Bring to a boil, cover and simmer for 1 hour, stirring from time to time. Add the onions, bacon and mushrooms, cover and cook for 30 minutes. Transfer the chicken, vegetables and bacon to a warmed dish.

4 Remove the bouquet garni; boil the liquid for 2 minutes. Cream the remaining butter and flour. Whisk in spoonfuls of the mixture to thicken the liquid. Pour the sauce over the chicken and serve garnished with parsley and croûtons.

Moroccan Spiced Roast Cornish Hens

The Cornish hens are stuffed with an aromatic rice mixture and glazed with spiced yogurt in this flavorful dish.

Serves 4

1 cup cooked long-grain
    rice
1 small onion, chopped
finely grated rind and
    juice of 1 lemon
2 tablespoons chopped
    fresh mint
3 tablespoons chopped
    dried apricots
2 tablespoons plain
    yogurt

2 teaspoons ground
    turmeric
2 teaspoons ground
    cumin
2 x 1-pound Cornish
    hens
salt and ground black
    pepper
lemon slices and fresh
    mint sprigs, to
    garnish

1 Preheat the oven to 400°F. Mix together the rice, onion, lemon rind, mint and apricots. Stir in half each of the lemon juice, yogurt, turmeric, cumin, and salt and pepper.

2 Stuff the Cornish hens with the rice mixture at the neck cavity only. The spare stuffing can be served separately. Place the Cornish hens on a rack in a roasting pan.

3 Mix together the remaining lemon juice, yogurt, turmeric and cumin, then brush this over the Cornish hens. Cover loosely with foil and cook in the oven for 30 minutes.

4 Remove the foil and roast for another 15 minutes more, or until golden brown and the juices run clear, not pink, when the thickest part of the flesh is pierced with a skewer.

5 Cut both the Cornish hens in half with a sharp knife or poultry shears, and serve with warmed reserved rice. Garnish with slices of lemon and fresh mint sprigs.

Chili Chicken Couscous

Couscous is a very easy alternative to rice and makes a good base for all kinds of ingredients.

Serves 4

2 cups couscous
4 cups boiling water
1 teaspoon olive oil
14 ounces boneless,
    skinless chicken, diced
1 yellow bell pepper,
    seeded and sliced
2 large zucchini, sliced
    thickly

1 small green chili, thinly
    sliced, or 1 teaspoon
    chili sauce
1 large tomato, diced
15-ounce can
    chick-peas, drained
salt and ground black
    pepper
fresh cilantro or parsley
    sprigs, to garnish

1 Place the couscous in a large bowl and pour the boiling water over. Cover and let stand for 30 minutes.

2 Heat the oil in a large nonstick frying pan and stir-fry the chicken quickly to seal, then reduce the heat.

3 Stir in the pepper, zucchini and chili or chili sauce and cook for 10 minutes, until the vegetables are softened.

4 Stir in the tomato and chick-peas, then add the couscous. Adjust the seasoning and stir over a moderate heat until hot. Serve garnished with sprigs of fresh cilantro or parsley.

Cook's Tip
If you prefer, use 7 ounces of dried chick-peas in this recipe. Soak them overnight, then drain, place in a saucepan and add water to cover. Bring to a boil, then cook until tender, 45–60 minutes.

Mediterranean Turkey Skewers

These skewers are easy to assemble, and can be cooked under a broiler or on a charcoal barbecue.

Serves 4

6 tablespoons olive oil
3 tablespoons lemon juice
1 garlic clove, finely
   chopped
2 tablespoons chopped
   fresh basil
2 zucchini
1 long thin eggplant

11 ounces boned turkey,
   cut into 2-inch cubes
12–16 pickled onions
1 red or yellow bell
   pepper, cut into 2-inch
   squares
salt and ground black
   pepper

1 Mix the oil with the lemon juice, garlic and basil in a small bowl. Season with salt and pepper.

2 Slice the zucchini and eggplant lengthwise into strips ¼ inch thick. Cut them crosswise about two-thirds of the way along their length. Discard the shorter length. Wrap half the turkey pieces with the zucchini slices, and the other half with the eggplant slices.

3 Prepare the skewers by alternating the turkey, onions, and pepper pieces. If you are using wooden skewers, soak them in water for several minutes. This will prevent them from charring during broiling. Lay the prepared skewers on a platter and sprinkle with the flavored oil. Then let them marinate for at least 30 minutes. Preheat the broiler or light the coals to prepare a barbecue.

4 Broil or barbecue for 10 minutes, until the vegetables are tender, turning occasionally. Serve hot.

Duck with Chestnut Sauce

This autumnal dish makes use of the sweet chestnuts that are gathered in Italian woods.

Serves 4–5

1 fresh rosemary sprig
1 garlic clove, sliced
2 tablespoons olive oil
4 boned duck breasts,
   fat removed

For the sauce
4 cups chestnuts
1 teaspoon oil

1½ cups milk
1 small onion, finely
   chopped
1 carrot, finely chopped
1 small bay leaf
salt and ground black
   pepper
2-4 tablespoons light
   cream, warmed

1 Pull the leaves from the sprig of rosemary. Combine them with the garlic and oil in a shallow bowl. Pat the duck breasts dry with paper towels. Brush them with the marinade and allow to stand for at least 2 hours before cooking.

2 Preheat the oven to 350°F. Cut a cross in the flat side of each chestnut with a sharp knife. Place the chestnuts on a baking sheet with the oil and shake the sheet until they are coated with oil. Bake for 20 minutes, then peel.

3 Place the peeled chestnuts in a heavy saucepan with the milk, onion, carrot and bay leaf. Cook slowly for about 10–15 minutes until the chestnuts are tender, then season. Discard the bay leaf. Press the mixture through a strainer.

4 Return the sauce to the pan. Heat gently while the duck breasts are cooking. Just before serving, stir in the cream. If the sauce is too thick, add a little more cream. Preheat the broiler, or prepare a barbecue.

5 Broil the duck breasts until medium-rare, for about 6–8 minutes. They should be pink inside. Slice into rounds and arrange on warmed plates. Serve with the heated sauce.

Turkey Spirals

These little spirals may look difficult, but they're so easy to make, and a very good way to pep up all-purpose turkey.

Serves 4

4 thinly sliced turkey
   breast steaks, about
   3½ ounces each
4 teaspoons tomato paste
½ ounce large fresh basil
   leaves
1 garlic clove, crushed
1 tablespoon skim milk

2 tablespoons whole
   wheat flour
salt and ground black
   pepper
fresh tomato sauce and
   pasta with fresh basil,
   to serve

1 Place the turkey steaks on a board. If too thick, flatten them slightly by beating with a rolling pin.

2 Spread each turkey breast steak with tomato paste, then top with a few leaves of basil, a little crushed garlic, and salt and pepper.

3 Roll up firmly around the filling and secure with a toothpick. Brush with milk and sprinkle with flour to coat lightly.

4 Place the spirals on a foil-lined broiler pan. Cook under a moderately hot broiler for 15–20 minutes, turning them occasionally, until thoroughly cooked. Serve hot, sliced with a spoonful or two of fresh tomato sauce and pasta, sprinkled with fresh basil.

Caribbean Chicken Kebabs

These kebabs have a rich, sunshine Caribbean flavor and the marinade keeps them moist without the need for oil.

Serves 4

1¼ pounds boned chicken
   breasts, skinned
finely grated rind of
   1 lime
2 tablespoons lime juice
1 tablespoon rum or
   sherry

1 tablespoon light brown
   sugar
1 teaspoon ground
   cinnamon
2 mangoes, peeled and
   diced
rice and salad, to serve

1 Cut the chicken into bite-size chunks and place in a bowl with the lime rind and juice, rum, sugar and cinnamon. Toss well, cover and let stand for 1 hour.

2 Save the juice and thread the chicken onto four wooden skewers, alternating with the mango cubes.

3 Cook the skewers under a hot broiler or on a barbecue for about 8-10 minutes, turning occasionally and basting with the juice until the chicken is tender and golden brown. Serve at once with rice and salad.

Cook's Tip
These kebabs may be served with a colorful salad and rice. The rum or sherry adds a lovely rich flavor but it is optional, so leave it out if you prefer.

Autumn Pheasant

Pheasant is well worth buying as it is low in fat, full of flavor and never dry when cooked in this way.

Serves 4

1 oven-ready pheasant
2 small onions, quartered
3 celery stalks, thickly sliced
2 red eating apples, thickly sliced
½ cup stock
1 tablespoon honey

2 tablespoons Worcestershire sauce
pinch of freshly grated nutmeg
2 tablespoons toasted hazelnuts
salt and ground black pepper

1 Preheat the oven to 350°F. Fry the pheasant without fat in a nonstick frying pan, turning occasionally until golden. Remove and keep hot.

2 Fry the onions and celery in the pan to brown lightly. Spoon into a casserole and place the pheasant on top. Tuck the apple slices around it.

3 Spoon over the stock, honey and Worcestershire sauce. Sprinkle with nutmeg, salt and pepper, cover with a tight-fitting lid and bake for 1¼–1½ hours or until tender. Sprinkle with nuts and serve hot.

Cook's Tip
Pheasant should be hung by the neck to develop its distinctive flavor for 7–14 days, according to the degree of gaminess preferred. If you are buying the bird ready-prepared, make sure all the tendons have been removed from the legs. This recipe provides an excellent method of cooking older, cock birds which tend to be rather tough and dry if just roasted.

Chicken Stroganoff

This dish is based on the classic Russian dish, which is made with fillet of beef, and it is just as good.

Serves 4

4 boneless, skinless chicken breasts,
3 tablespoons olive oil
1 large onion, thinly sliced
8 ounces mushrooms, sliced

1¼ cups sour cream
salt and ground black pepper
1 tablespoon chopped fresh parsley, to garnish

1 Divide the chicken breasts into two natural fillets, place between two sheets of plastic wrap and flatten each to a thickness of ¼inch with a rolling pin.

2 Cut into 1-inch strips diagonally across the fillets.

3 Heat 2 tablespoons of the oil in a large frying pan and cook the sliced onion slowly until soft but not colored.

4 Add the mushrooms and cook until golden brown. Remove and keep warm.

5 Increase the heat, add the remaining oil and fry the chicken very quickly, in small batches, for 3–4 minutes until lightly colored. Remove and keep warm while frying the rest of the chicken.

6 Return all the chicken, onions and mushrooms to the pan and season with salt and pepper. Stir in the sour cream and bring to a boil. Sprinkle with fresh parsley and serve immediately.

Chicken Tikka

The red food coloring give this dish its traditional bright color. Serve with lemon wedges and a crisp mixed salad.

Serves 4

3½ pound chicken
mixed fresh salad greens
such as frisée or
radichio, to serve

For the marinade
⅔ cup plain yogurt
1 teaspoon ground
paprika

2 teaspoons grated fresh
root ginger
1 garlic clove, crushed
2 teaspoons garam masala
½ teaspoon salt
2-3 drops red food
coloring
juice of 1 lemon
salad greens, to serve

1 Cut the chicken into eight even-size pieces, using a sharp knife.

2 Mix all the marinade ingredients in a large dish, add the chicken pieces to coat and chill for 4 hours or overnight to allow the flavors to penetrate the flesh.

3 Preheat the oven to 400°F. Remove the chicken pieces from the marinade and arrange them in a single layer in a large casserole. Bake for 30–40 minutes or until tender.

4 Baste with a little of the marinade while cooking. Arrange on a bed of salad greens and serve hot or cold.

Cook's Tip
This dish would also make an excellent appetizer. Cut the chicken into smaller pieces and reduce the cooking time slightly, then serve with lemon wedges and just a simple salad garnish.

Simple Chicken Curry

Curry powder can be bought in three different strengths – mild, medium and hot. Use the type you prefer.

Serves 4

8 chicken legs, each piece
including thigh and
drumstick
2 tablespoons olive oil
1 onion, thinly sliced
1 garlic clove, crushed
1 tablespoon medium
curry powder
1 tablespoon all-purpose
flour

1¾ cups chicken stock
1 beefsteak tomato
1 tablespoon mango
chutney
1 tablespoon lemon juice
salt and ground black
pepper
2½ cups boiled rice, to
serve

1 Cut the chicken legs in half. Heat the olive oil in a large flameproof casserole and brown the chicken pieces on both sides. Remove and keep warm.

2 Add the onion and garlic clove to the casserole and cook them until tender. Add the curry powder and cook gently for another 2 minutes.

3 Add the flour and gradually blend in the chicken stock and seasoning.

4 Bring to a boil, replace the chicken pieces, cover and simmer for 20–30 minutes or until tender.

5 Skin the beefsteak tomato by blanching in boiling water for about 15 seconds, then running it under cold water to loosen the skin. Peel and dice.

6 Add to the chicken with the mango chutney and lemon juice. Heat through gently and adjust the seasoning to taste. Serve with boiled rice and Indian accompaniments.

Chicken Biryani

A *biryani* – from the Urdu – is a dish mixed with rice which resembles a risotto. It provides a one-pan meal.

Serves 4

1½ cups basmati rice, rinsed
½ teaspoon salt
5 whole cardamom pods
2 – 3 whole cloves
1 cinnamon stick
3 tablespoons oil
3 onions, sliced
1½ pounds boneless, skinless, diced chicken
¼ teaspoon ground cloves
5 cardamom pods, seeds removed and ground
¼ teaspoon hot chili powder
1 teaspoon ground cumin
1 teaspoon ground coriander

½ teaspoon freshly ground black pepper
3 garlic cloves, finely chopped
1 teaspoon finely chopped fresh ginger
juice of 1 lemon
4 tomatoes, sliced
2 tablespoons chopped fresh cilantro
⅔ cup plain yogurt
½ teaspoon saffron strands soaked in 2 teaspoons hot milk
3 tablespoons toasted flaked almonds and fresh cilantro sprigs, to garnish
plain yogurt, to serve

1 Preheat the oven to 375°F. Boil the rice mixture, salt, cardamom pods, cloves and cinnamon stick for 2 minutes. Then drain, leaving the whole spices in the rice.

2 Brown the onions in the oil. Add the chicken, ground spices, garlic, ginger and lemon juice. Stir-fry for 5 minutes.

3 Transfer to a casserole; top with the tomatoes. In layers, add the cilantro, yogurt and rice. Drizzle over the saffron and milk, then ⅔ cup water.

4 Cover and bake for 1 hour. Transfer to a warmed serving platter and remove the whole spices. Garnish with toasted almonds and cilantro and serve with yogurt.

Spatchcock of Cornish Hen

Allow one poussin per person and sharp knives to tackle them. Serve with new potatoes and salad, if wished.

Serves 4

4 Cornish hens
1 tablespoon mixed chopped fresh herbs such as rosemary and parsley, plus extra to garnish

1 tablespoon lemon juice
4 tablespoons butter, melted
salt and ground black pepper
lemon slices, to garnish

1 Remove any trussing strings from the birds, and, using a pair of kitchen scissors, cut down on either side of the backbone. Lay them flat and flatten with the help of a rolling pin or mallet, or use the heel of your hand.

2 Thread the legs and wings onto skewers to keep the poussins flat while they are cooking.

3 Brush both sides with melted butter and season with salt and pepper. Sprinkle with lemon juice and herbs.

4 Preheat the broiler to moderate heat and cook skin-side first for 6 minutes until golden brown. Turn over, brush with butter and broil for another 6 – 8 minutes or until cooked. Garnish with chopped herbs and lemon slices.

Chicken, Leek and Parsley Pie

A filling pie with a two-cheese sauce, this dish is ideal for serving on a cold winter's day.

Serves 4–6

3 boneless chicken breasts
flavorings: carrot, onion,
   peppercorns, bouquet
   garni
piecrust, made with
   2½ cups all-purpose
   flour
4 tablespoons butter
2 leeks, thinly sliced
½ cup grated Cheddar
   cheese
¼ cup grated Parmesan
   cheese

3 tablespoons chopped
   fresh parsley
2 tablespoons whole-
   grain mustard
1 teaspoon cornstarch
1¼ cups heavy cream
salt and ground black
   pepper
beaten egg, to glaze
mixed fresh green salad,
   to serve

1 Poach the chicken breasts with the flavorings in water to cover, until tender. Cool in the liquid, then cut into strips.

2 Preheat the oven to 400°F. Divide the pastry into two pieces, one slightly larger than the other. Use the larger piece to line a 7 x 11 inch baking pan. Prick the bottom, bake for 15 minutes, then let cool.

3 Fry the leeks in the butter until soft. Stir in the cheeses and parsley. Spread half the leek mixture over the pastry bottom, cover with the chicken strips, then top with the remaining leek mixture. Mix the mustard, cornstarch and cream. Season and pour into the pie.

4 Moisten the pastry bottom edges. Use the remaining pastry to cover the pie. Brush with beaten egg and bake for 30–40 minutes until golden and crisp. Serve with salad.

Hampshire Farmhouse Quiche

A traditional dish from the south of England, this quiche will satisfy the hungriest person.

Serves 4

2 cups whole wheat flour
2 ounces butter, cubed
4 tablespoons vegetable
   shortening
1 teaspoon caraway seeds
1 tablespoon oil
1 onion, chopped
1 garlic clove, crushed
2 cups cooked chicken,
   chopped
3 ounces watercress
   leaves, chopped

grated rind of ½ lemon
2 eggs, lightly beaten
¼ cup heavy cream
3 tablespoons plain
   yogurt
large pinch of grated
   nutmeg
3 tablespoons grated
   Cheddar cheese
beaten egg, to glaze
salt and ground black
   pepper

1 Rub the fats into the flour with a pinch of salt until the mixture resembles bread crumbs.

2 Stir in the caraway seeds and 3 tablespoons iced water and mix to a firm dough. Knead until smooth, then use to line a 7 x 11 inch loose-bottom tart pan. Reserve the dough scraps. Prick the bottom and chill for 20 minutes. Heat a baking sheet in the oven at 400°F.

3 Sauté the onion and garlic in the oil until softened. Remove from the heat and cool. Meanwhile, line the pastry case with wax paper and baking beans. Bake for 10 minutes, remove the paper and beans and cook for 5 minutes.

4 Mix the onion, chicken, watercress and lemon rind; spoon into the pastry shell. Beat the eggs, cream, yogurt, nutmeg, cheese and seasoning; pour over the chicken mixture. Cut the pastry scraps into ½ inch strips. Brush with egg, then twist and lay in a lattice over the quiche. Press on the ends. Bake for 35 minutes, until golden.

Chicken Charter Pie

A light pie with a fresh taste; it is versatile enough to use for light meals or informal dinners.

Serves 4

4 tablespoons butter	8 ounces ready-made puff
4 chicken legs	pastry
1 onion, finely chopped	½ cup heavy cream
⅔ cup milk	2 eggs, beaten, plus extra
⅔ cup sour cream	for glazing
4 scallions, quartered	salt and ground black
¾ ounce fresh parsley	pepper
leaves, finely chopped	

1 Melt the butter in a frying pan and brown the chicken legs. Transfer to a plate. Add the chopped onion to the pan and cook until softened but not browned. Stir the milk, sour cream, scallions, parsley and seasoning into the pan, bring to a boil, then simmer for 2 minutes.

2 Return the chicken to the pan with any juice, cover and cook gently for 30 minutes. Transfer the chicken mixture to a 5-cup pie pan. Leave to cool.

3 Preheat the oven to 425°F. Place a narrow strip of pastry on the edge of the pie pan. Moisten the strip, then cover the pan with the pastry. Press the edges together. Make a hole in the center of the pastry and insert a small funnel of foil. Brush the pastry with beaten egg, then bake for 15–20 minutes.

4 Reduce the oven temperature to 350°F. Mix the cream and eggs, then pour into the pie through the funnel. Shake the pie to distribute the cream, then return to the oven for 5–10 minutes. Leave the pie in a warm place for about 5–10 minutes before serving, or cool completely.

Chicken and Ham Pie

This is a rich pie flavored with fresh herbs and lightly spiced with mace – ideal for taking on a picnic.

Serves 8

14 ounces ready-made	2 teaspoons chopped fresh
piecrust	thyme
1¾ pounds chicken breast	grated rind and juice of
12 ounces uncooked	½ large lemon
smoked ham	1 teaspoon freshly
4 tablespoons heavy	ground mace
cream	salt and ground black
6 scallions, finely chopped	pepper
1 tablespoon chopped	beaten egg or milk, to
fresh tarragon	glaze

1 Preheat the oven to 375°F. Roll out one-third of the pastry and use it to line an 8-inch pie pan, 2 inches deep. Place on a baking sheet.

2 Grind 4 ounces of the chicken with the ham, then mix with the cream, scallions, herbs, lemon rind and 1 tablespoon of the lemon juice; season lightly. Cut the remaining chicken into ½-inch pieces and mix with the remaining lemon juice, the mace and seasoning.

3 Make a layer of one-third of the ham mixture in the pastry shell, cover with half the chopped chicken, then add another layer of one-third of the ham. Add all the remaining chicken followed by the remaining ham.

4 Moisten the edges of the pastry shell and roll out the remaining pastry to make a lid for the pie. Use the scraps to make a lattice decoration. Make a small hole in the center of the pie, brush the top with beaten egg or milk, then bake for 20 minutes. Reduce the temperature to 325°F and bake for another 1–1¼ hours. Transfer the pie to a wire rack and allow to cool.

Venison with Cranberry Sauce

Venison steaks are now readily available. Lean and low in fat, they make a healthy choice for a special occasion.

Serves 4

1 orange
1 lemon
¾ cup fresh or frozen (unthawed) cranberries
1 teaspoon grated fresh ginger
1 fresh thyme sprig
1 teaspoon Dijon mustard
4 tablespoons redcurrant jelly

⅔ cup ruby port
2 tablespoons sunflower oil
4 venison steaks
2 shallots, finely chopped
salt and ground black pepper
fresh thyme sprigs, to garnish
mashed potatoes and broccoli, to serve

1 Pare the rind from half the orange and half the lemon using a vegetable peeler, then cut into very fine strips. Blanch the strips in a small saucepan of boiling water for 5 minutes until tender. Drain the strips and refresh under cold water.

2 Squeeze the juice from the citrus fruit and pour into a small pan. Add the cranberries, ginger, thyme, mustard, redcurrant jelly and port. Cook gently until the jelly melts. Bring to a boil, stirring, cover and reduce the heat. Cook for 15 minutes, until the cranberries are just tender.

3 Fry the venison steaks in the oil over a high heat for 2–3 minutes. Turn them over and add the shallots. Cook on the other side for 2–3 minutes, to taste. Just before the end of cooking, pour in the sauce and add the strips of orange and lemon rind. Allow the sauce to bubble for a few seconds to thicken slightly, then remove the thyme sprig and adjust the seasoning to taste.

4 Transfer the venison steaks to warmed plates and spoon over the sauce. Garnish with thyme sprigs and serve accompanied by creamy mashed potatoes and broccoli.

Turkey and Snow Peas Stir-fry

Have all the ingredients prepared before you start cooking this dish, as it will be ready in minutes.

Serves 4

2 tablespoons sesame oil
6 tablespoons lemon juice
1 garlic clove, crushed
½-inch piece fresh ginger, peeled and grated
1 teaspoon honey
1 pound turkey fillets, cut into strips
1 cup snow peas, trimmed

2 tablespoons peanut oil
½ cup cashew nuts
6 scallions, cut into strips
8-ounce can water chestnuts, drained and thinly sliced
pinch of salt
saffron rice, to serve

1 Mix together the sesame oil, lemon juice, garlic, ginger and honey in a shallow non-metallic dish. Add the turkey and mix well. Cover and let marinate for 3–4 hours.

2 Blanch the snow peas in boiling salted water for about 1 minute. Drain and refresh under cold running water.

3 Drain the marinade from the turkey strips and reserve the marinade. Heat the peanut oil in a wok or large frying pan, add the cashew nuts and stir-fry for about 1–2 minutes until golden brown. Remove the cashew nuts from the wok or frying pan using a slotted spoon and set aside.

4 Add the turkey and stir-fry for 3–4 minutes, until golden brown. Add the scallions, snow peas, water chestnuts and the reserved marinade. Cook for a few minutes, until the turkey is tender and the sauce is bubbling and hot. Stir in the cashew nuts and serve with saffron rice.

Cook's Tip
This dish could be served on a bed of medium-width egg noodles for a quick meal.

Farmhouse Venison Pie

A simple and satisfying pie; the venison is cooked in a rich gravy, topped with potato and parsnip mash.

Serves 4

3 tablespoons sunflower oil
1 onion, chopped
1 garlic clove, crushed
3 slices bacon, chopped
1½ lb minced venison
4 ounces button mushrooms, chopped
2 tablespoons all-purpose flour
1¾ cups beef stock
⅔ cup ruby port
2 bay leaves
1 teaspoon chopped fresh thyme
1 teaspoon Dijon mustard
1 tablespoon redcurrant jelly
1½ pounds potatoes
1 pound parsnips
1 egg yolk
4 tablespoons butter
pinch of freshly grated nutmeg
3 tablespoons chopped fresh parsley
salt and ground black pepper

1 Heat the oil in a large frying pan and fry the onion, garlic and bacon for 5 minutes. Add the venison and mushrooms and cook for a few minutes, stirring, until browned.

2 Stir in the flour and cook for 1–2 minutes, then add the stock, port, herbs, mustard, redcurrant jelly and seasoning. Bring to a boil, cover with a tight-fitting lid and simmer for 30–40 minutes, until tender. Spoon into a large pie pan or four individual baking dishes.

3 While the venison and mushroom mixture is cooking, preheat the oven to 400°F. Cut the potatoes and parsnips into large chunks. Cook together in boiling salted water for 20 minutes or until tender. Drain and mash, then beat in the egg yolk, butter, nutmeg, parsley and seasoning.

4 Spread the potato and parsnip mixture over the meat and bake for 30–40 minutes, until piping hot and golden brown. Serve immediately with a green vegetable, if you wish.

Normandy Pheasant

Calvados, cider, apples and cream – the produce of Normandy – make this a rich and flavorful dish.

Serves 4

2 oven-ready pheasants
1 tablespoon olive oil
2 tablespoons butter
4 tablespoons Calvados
1¾ cups hard cider
bouquet garni
3 tart apples
⅔ cup heavy cream
salt and ground black pepper
fresh thyme sprigs, to garnish

1 Preheat the oven to 325°F. Cut both the pheasants into four pieces using a large sharp knife. Discard the backbones and knuckles.

2 Heat the oil and butter in a large flameproof casserole. Working in two batches, add the pheasant pieces to the casserole and brown them over a high heat. Return all the pheasant pieces to the casserole.

3 Standing far back, pour over the Calvados and set it alight with a match. Shake the casserole and when the flames have died, pour in the cider, then add the bouquet garni and season to taste with salt and pepper. Bring to a boil, cover with a tight-fitting lid and cook for about 50 minutes.

4 Peel, core and thickly slice the apples. Tuck the apple slices around the pheasant. Cover and cook for 5–10 minutes, or until the pheasant is tender. Transfer the pheasant and apples to a warmed serving plate. Keep warm.

5 Remove the bouquet garni, then boil the sauce rapidly to reduce by half to a syrupy consistency. Stir in the heavy cream and simmer for another 2–3 minutes until thickened. Taste the sauce and adjust the seasoning if necessary. Spoon the sauce over the pheasant pieces and serve immediately, garnished with fresh thyme sprigs.

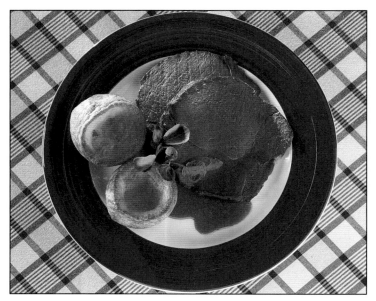

Roast Beef with Yorkshire Pudding

This classic British dish is often served at Sunday lunch, accompanied by potatoes, mustard and horseradish sauce.

Serves 6

4-pound piece of beef	**For the puddings**
2–4 tablespoons dripping or oil	½ cup all-purpose flour
1¼ cups beef stock, wine or water	1 egg, beaten
salt and ground black pepper	⅔ cup water mixed with milk
	dripping or oil, for cooking

1 Weigh the beef and calculate the cooking time. Allow 15 minutes per pound plus 15 minutes for rare meat, 20 minutes plus 20 minutes for medium, and 25–30 minutes plus 25 minutes for well-done.

2 Preheat the oven to 425°F. Heat the dripping or oil in a roasting pan in the oven. Place the meat on a rack, fat-side up, then place the rack in the roasting pan. Baste the beef with the dripping or oil, and cook for the required time, basting occasionally.

3 To make the Yorkshire puddings, stir the flour, salt and pepper together in a bowl and form a well in the centre. Pour the egg into the well, then slowly pour in the milk, stirring in the flour to give a smooth batter. Stand for 30 minutes.

4 A few minutes before the meat is ready, spoon a little dripping or oil in each of twelve patty pans and place in the oven until very hot. Remove the meat, season, then cover loosely with foil and keep warm. Quickly divide the batter among the patty tins, then bake for 15–20 minutes, until well risen and brown.

5 Spoon off the fat from the roasting pan. Add the stock, wine or water, stirring, and boil for a few minutes. Season to taste, then serve with the beef and Yorkshire puddings.

Beef Olives

So-called because of their shape, these beef rolls contain a delicious filling made with bacon and mushrooms.

Serves 4

2 tablespoons butter	1½ pounds topside of beef, cut into 8 thin slices
2 slices bacon, finely chopped	3 tablespoons all-purpose flour
4 ounces mushrooms, chopped	3 tablespoons oil
1 tablespoon chopped fresh parsley	2 onions, sliced
grated rind and juice of 1 lemon	1¾ cups beef stock
2 cups fresh bread crumbs	salt and ground black pepper

1 Preheat the oven to 325°F. Melt the butter in a saucepan and fry the bacon and mushrooms for 3 minutes. Mix them with the chopped parsley, lemon rind and juice, bread crumbs and seasoning.

2 Spread an equal amount of the bread crumb mixture evenly over the beef slices, leaving a narrow border clear around the edge. Roll up the slices and tie securely with fine string, then dip the beef rolls in the flour to coat lightly, shaking off any excess flour.

3 Heat the oil in a frying pan, then fry the beef rolls until lightly browned. Remove and keep warm. Add the onions and fry until browned. Stir in the remaining flour and cook until lightly browned. Pour in the stock, stirring constantly, bring to a boil, stirring, and simmer for 2–3 minutes.

4 Transfer the rolls to a casserole, pour the sauce over the top, then cover with a tight-fitting lid and cook in the oven for 2 hours. Lift out the "olives" using a slotted spoon and remove the string. Return them to the sauce and serve hot.

Lamb and Spring Vegetable Stew

Known as a *blanquette* in France, this stew may have blanched asparagus spears or French beans added.

Serves 4

5 tablespoons butter
2 pound lean boned
    shoulder of lamb,
    diced into 1¼-inch
    pieces
2½ cups lamb stock or
    water
⅔ cup dry white wine
1 onion, quartered
2 fresh thyme sprigs
1 bay leaf
8 ounces baby onions,
    halved
8 ounces young carrots

2 small turnips,
    quartered
¾ cup shelled lima beans
1 tablespoon all-purpose
    flour
1 egg yolk
2 tablespoons heavy
    cream
2 teaspoons lemon juice
salt and ground black
    pepper
2 tablespoons chopped
    fresh parsley, to
    garnish

1 Sauté the lamb in 2 tablespoons of the butter to seal. Add the stock or water and wine, bring to the boil and skim. Add the quartered onion, thyme and bay leaf. Cover and simmer for 1 hour.

2 Brown the baby onions in 1 tablespoon of the butter. Add to the lamb with the carrots and turnips. Cook for 20 minutes. Add the beans and cook for 10 minutes.

3 Arrange the lamb and vegetables on a serving dish. Cover and keep warm. Discard the onion quarters and herbs. Strain the stock; skim off the fat. Bring to the boil and reduce the stock to 1¾ cups. Mix the remaining butter and flour to a paste. Whisk into the stock, then simmer briefly.

4 Combine the egg yolk and cream. Add a little hot sauce then stir into the pan. Do not boil. Add the lemon juice, and season. Pour the sauce over the lamb; garnish with parsley.

Beef Paprika with Roasted Peppers

This dish is perfect for family suppers – and roasting the peppers gives an added dimension.

Serves 4

2 tablespoons olive oil
1½ pounds chuck steak,
    cut into 1½-inch pieces
2 onions, chopped
1 garlic clove, crushed
1 tablespoon all-purpose
    flour
1 tablespoon paprika,
    plus extra to garnish

14-ounce can chopped
    tomatoes
2 red bell peppers, halved
    and seeded
⅔ cup crème fraîche
salt and ground black
    pepper
buttered noodles, to serve

1 Preheat the oven to 275°F. Heat the oil in a large flameproof casserole and brown the diced chuck steak in batches. Remove the meat from the casserole using a slotted spoon and set aside.

2 Add the onions and garlic and fry gently until softened but not browned. Stir in the flour and paprika and continue cooking for 1–2 minutes more, stirring continuously to prevent sticking.

3 Return the meat and any juice that has collected on the plate to the casserole, then add the chopped tomatoes and salt and ground black pepper. Bring to a boil while stirring continuously, then cover with a tight-fitting lid and cook in the oven for 2½ hours.

4 Meanwhile, place the peppers skin-side up on a broiler rack and broil until the skins have blistered and charred. Cool, then peel off the skins. Cut the flesh into strips, then add to the casserole and cook for another 15–30 minutes, or until the meat is tender.

5 Stir in the crème fraîche and sprinkle with a little paprika. Serve hot with buttered noodles.

Beef in Guinness

Guinness gives this stew a deep, rich flavor. Use another stout if you prefer.

Serves 6

2 pounds chuck steak, cut into 1½ inch pieces
all-purpose flour, for coating
3 tablespoons oil
1 large onion, sliced
1 carrot, thinly sliced
2 celery stalks, thinly sliced
2 teaspoons granulated sugar

1 teaspoon English mustard powder
1 teaspoon tomato paste
1 x 3inch strip orange rind
2½ cups Guinness
bouquet garni
salt and ground black pepper

1 Toss the beef in flour to coat. Heat 2 tablespoons of the oil in a large shallow saucepan, then cook the beef in batches until lightly browned. Transfer to a bowl.

2 Add the remaining oil to the pan, then cook the onion until well browned, adding the thinly sliced carrot and celery towards the end.

3 Stir in the sugar, mustard, tomato paste, orange rind, Guinness and seasoning, then add the bouquet garni and bring to a boil. Return the meat, and any juice in the bowl, to the pan; add water, if necessary, so that the meat is covered. Cover the pan with a tight-fitting lid and cook gently for 2–2½ hours, until the meat is very tender.

Cottage Pie

This traditional dish is always a favorite with adults and children alike.

Serves 4

2 tablespoons oil
1 onion, finely chopped
1 carrot, finely chopped
4 ounces mushrooms, chopped
1¼ pounds ground lean chuck steak
1¼ cups ground beef stock or water
1 tablespon all-purpose flour
1 bay leaf

2–3 teaspoons Worcestershire sauce
1 tablespoon tomato paste
1½ pounds potatoes, boiled
2 tablespoons butter
3 tablespoons hot milk
1 tablespoon chopped fresh tarragon
salt and ground black pepper

1 Heat the oil in a saucepan and cook the onion, carrot and mushrooms, stirring occasionally, until browned. Stir the beef into the pan and cook, stirring to break up the lumps, until lightly browned.

2 Blend a few spoonfuls of the stock or water with the flour, then stir into the pan. Stir in the remaining stock or water and bring to a simmer, stirring. Add the bay leaf, Worcestershire sauce and tomato paste, then cover with a tight-fitting lid and cook very gently for 1 hour, stirring occasionally. Uncover towards the end of cooking to allow any excess liquid to evaporate, if necessary.

3 Preheat the oven to 375°F. Gently heat the potatoes for a couple of minutes, then mash with the butter, milk and seasoning.

4 Add the tarragon to the beef and season to taste with salt and pepper, then pour into a pie pan. Cover the beef with an even layer of potato and mark the top with the prongs of a fork. Bake for about 25 minutes, until golden brown.

Irish Stew

This wholesome and filling stew is given a slight piquancy by including a little anchovy sauce.

Serves 4

4 slices bacon
2 celery stalks, chopped
2 large onions, sliced
8 middle neck lamb
   chops, about 2¼
   pound s total weight
2¼ pounds potatoes, sliced

1¼ cups lamb stock
1½ teaspoons
   Worcestershire sauce
1 teaspoon anchovy sauce
salt and ground black
   pepper
fresh parsley, to garnish

1 Preheat the oven to 325°F. Chop and then fry the bacon for 3–5 minutes until the fat runs, then add the celery and one-third of the onions and continue to cook, stirring occasionally, until browned.

2 Layer the lamb chops, potatoes, vegetables and bacon and remaining onions in a heavy flameproof casserole, seasoning each layer with salt and pepper as you go. Finish with a layer of potatoes.

3 Pour the veal stock, Worcestershire sauce and anchovy sauce into the bacon and vegetable cooking juices in the pan, stir, and bring to a boil. Pour the mixture into the casserole, adding water if necessary so that the liquid comes halfway up the sides of the casserole.

4 Cover the casserole with a tight-fitting lid, then cook in the oven for 3 hours, until the meat and vegetables are tender. Return to the oven for longer if necessary. Serve hot, sprinkled with chopped fresh parsley.

Cook's Tip
This is a good way of cooking cheaper cuts of lamb but for a more elegant dish, use diced lamb or lamb steaks instead of the chops and cook in the oven for 2 hours.

Oatmeal and Herb Rack of Lamb

Ask the butcher to remove the chine bone that runs along the eye of the meat – this will make carving easier.

Serves 6

2 best end necks of lamb,
   about 2 pound each
finely grated rind of
   1 lemon
4 tablespoons medium
   oatmeal
1 cup fresh white bread
   crumbs
4 tablespoons chopped
   fresh parsley

2 tablespoons butter,
   melted
2 tablespoons honey
salt and ground black
   pepper
roasted baby vegetables
   and gravy, to serve
fresh herb sprigs, to
   garnish

1 Preheat the oven to 400°F. Using a small sharp knife, cut through the skin and meat of both pieces of lamb about 1 inch from the tips of the bones. Pull off the fatty meat to expose the bones, then scrape around each bone tip until completely clean.

2 Trim all the skin and most of the fat from the meat, then lightly score the remaining fat with a sharp knife. Repeat with the second rack.

3 Mix together the lemon rind, oatmeal, bread crumbs, the parsley and seasoning, then stir in the melted butter.

4 Brush the fatty side of each rack of lamb with honey, then press the oatmeal mixture evenly over the surface with your fingers until well coated.

5 Place the racks in a roasting pan with the oatmeal sides up. Roast for 40–50 minutes, depending on whether you like rare or medium lamb. Cover loosely with foil if browning too much. To serve, slice each rack into three and accompany with roasted baby vegetables and gravy made with the pan juices. Garnish with herb sprigs.

Beef Wellington

This dish is so-named because of a supposed resemblance of shape and color to the Duke of Wellington's boot.

Serves 8

3 pounds fillet of beef
1 tablespoon butter
2 tablespoons oil
½ small onion, finely
  chopped
6 ounces mushrooms,
  chopped
6 ounces liver pâté
freshly squeezed lemon
  juice
a few drops of
  Worcestershire sauce
14 ounces ready-made
  puff pastry
salt and ground black
  pepper
beaten egg, to glaze

1 Preheat the oven to 425°F. Season the beef with pepper, then tie it at intervals with string.

2 Heat the butter and oil in a roasting pan. Brown the beef over a high heat, then cook in the oven for 20 minutes. Cool and remove the string.

3 Scrape the pan juices into another pan, add the onion and mushrooms and cook until tender. Cool, then mix with the pâté. Add lemon juice and Worcestershire sauce.

4 Roll out the pastry to a large ¼-inch-thick rectangle. Spread the pâté mixture on the beef, then place it in the centre of the pastry. Moisten the edges of the pastry, then fold it over the beef to make a neat package, tucking in the ends neatly; press to seal.

5 Place the package on a baking sheet with the seam on the underneath and brush with beaten egg. Bake in the oven for 25–45 minutes, depending how well done you like the beef. Serve in generous slices.

Butterflied Cumin and Garlic Lamb

Ground cumin and garlic give the lamb a wonderful Middle-Eastern flavor in this recipe.

Serves 6

4-pound leg of lamb
4 tablespoons extra-
  virgin olive oil
2 tablespoons ground
  cumin
4–6 garlic cloves,
  crushed
salt and ground black
  pepper
toasted almond and
  raisin rice, to serve
fresh cilantro sprigs and
  lemon wedges,
  to garnish

1 To butterfly the lamb, cut away the meat from the bone using a small sharp knife. Remove any excess fat and the thin, parchment-like membrane. Bat out the meat with a rolling pin to an even thickness, then prick the fleshy side of the lamb well with the tip of the knife.

2 In a bowl, mix together the olive oil, cumin and garlic and season with pepper. Spoon the mixture all over the lamb, then rub it well into the crevices. Cover the bowl and allow the lamb to marinate overnight.

3 Preheat the oven to 400°F. Spread the lamb, skin-side down, on a rack in a roasting tin. Season with salt and roast for 45–60 minutes, until crusty brown on the outside but still pink in the center.

4 Remove the lamb from the oven and let it rest for about 10 minutes. Cut into diagonal slices and serve with the toasted almond and raisin rice. Garnish with the fresh cilantro sprigs and lemon wedges.

Cook's Tip
The lamb may be barbecued rather than roasted. Thread it on to two long skewers and barbecue for about 20-25 minutes on each side, until it is cooked to your liking.

Lamb with Mint Sauce

In this flavorful dish, the classic combination of lamb and mint is given an original twist.

Serves 4

8 lamb noisettes, ³/₄ −1 inch thick
2 tablespoons oil
3 tablespoons medium-bodied dry white wine, or light stock
salt and ground black pepper
fresh mint sprigs, to garnish

For the sauce
2 tablespoons boiling water
1 − 2 teapoons sugar
leaves from a small bunch of fresh mint, finely chopped
2-3 tablespoons white wine vinegar

1 To make the sauce, stir the water and sugar together, then add the mint, vinegar to taste and season with salt and black pepper. Leave for 30 minutes.

2 Season the lamb with pepper. Heat the oil in a large frying pan and fry the lamb, in batches if necessary so that the pan is not crowded, for about 3 minutes on each side for meat that is pink in the middle.

3 Transfer the lamb to a warmed plate and season with salt, then cover and keep warm.

4 Stir the wine or stock into the pan juices, dislodging the residue, and bring to a boil. Bubble for a couple of minutes, then pour over the lamb. Garnish the lamb noisettes with small sprigs of mint and serve hot with the mint sauce.

Somerset Pork with Apples

A creamy cider sauce accompanies tender pieces of pork and sliced apples to make a rich supper dish.

Serves 4

2 tablespoons butter
1¼-pounds pork loin, cut into bite-size pieces
12 baby onions, peeled
2 teaspoons grated lemon rind
1¼ cups hard cider
²/₃ cup ham or veal stock

2 crisp eating apples such as Granny Smith, cored and sliced
3 tablespoons chopped fresh parsley
scant ½ cup whipping cream
salt and ground black pepper

1 Heat the butter in a large sauté or frying pan and brown the pork in batches. Transfer the pork to a bowl.

2 Add the onions to the pan, brown lightly, then stir in the lemon rind, cider and stock and boil for about 3 minutes. Return all the pork to the pan and cook gently for about 25 minutes, until tender.

3 Add the apples to the pan and continue to cook for another 5 minutes. Using a slotted spoon, transfer the pork, onions and apples to a warmed serving dish, cover and keep warm. Stir the parsley and cream into the pan and allow to bubble to thicken the sauce slightly. Season, then pour over the pork and serve hot.

Pork with Plums

Plums poached in apple juice are used here to make a delightfully fruity sauce for pork chops.

Serves 4

3 tablespoons butter
1 tablespoon oil
4 pork chops, about
   7 ounces each
1 pound ripe plums,
   halved and stoned
1¼ cups apple juice

1 onion, finely chopped
pinch of freshly ground
   mace
salt and ground black
   pepper
fresh sage leaves, to
   garnish

1 Heat the butter and oil in a large frying pan and fry the chops until brown on both sides, then transfer them to a plate.

2 Meanwhile, simmer the plums in the apple juice until tender. Strain off and reserve the juice, then purée half the plums with a little of the juice.

3 Add the onion to the pan and cook gently until soft, but not colored. Return the chops to the pan. Pour over the plum purée and all the juice.

4 Simmer, uncovered, for 10–15 minutes, until the chops are cooked through. Add the remaining plums to the pan, then add the mace and seasoning. Warm the sauce through over a moderate heat and serve garnished with fresh sage leaves.

Lancashire Hot-pot

Browning the lamb and kidneys, plus the extra vegetables and herbs, adds flavor to the traditional basic ingredients.

Serves 4

3 tablespoons dripping,
   or 3 tablespoons oil
8 medium lamb chops,
   about 2 pounds total
   weight
6 ounces lambs' kidneys,
   cut into large pieces
2 pounds potatoes, thinly
   sliced
3 carrots, thickly sliced
1 pound leeks, sliced

3 celery stalks, sliced
1 tablespoon chopped
   fresh thyme
2 tablespoons chopped
   fresh parsley
small fresh rosemary
   sprig
2½ cups lamb stock
salt and ground black
   pepper

1 Preheat the oven to 325°F. Heat the dripping or oil in a frying pan and brown the chops and kidneys in batches, then reserve the fat.

2 In a large casserole, make alternate layers of lamb chops, kidneys, three-quarters of the potatoes and the carrots, leeks and celery, sprinkling the herbs and seasoning over each layer as you go. Tuck the rosemary sprig down the side.

3 Arrange the remaining potatoes on top. Pour over the stock, brush with the reserved fat, then cover the casserole with a tight-fitting lid and bake for 2½ hours. Increase the oven temperature to 425°F. Uncover and cook for another 30 minutes.

Pork Loin with Celery

Have a change from a plain Sunday roast and try this whole loin of pork in a celery and cream sauce instead.

Serves 4

1 tablespoon oil
4 tablespoons butter
2¼-pound boned, rolled
   loin of pork, rind
   removed and trimmed
1 onion, chopped
bouquet garni
3 fresh dill sprigs
⅔ cup dry white wine
⅔ cup water

stalks from 1 celery head,
   cut into 1-inch lengths
2 tablespoons all-purpose
   flour
⅔ cup heavy cream
squeeze of lemon juice
salt and ground black
   pepper
chopped fresh dill, to
   garnish

1 Heat the oil and half the butter in a heavy flameproof casserole just large enough to hold the pork and celery, then brown the pork evenly. Transfer the pork to a plate.

2 Add the onion to the casserole and cook until softened but not browned. Place the bouquet garni and the dill sprigs on the onion, then place the pork on top and add any juice from the plate. Pour the wine and water over the pork, season to taste, cover and simmer gently for 30 minutes.

3 Turn the pork, arrange the celery around it, cover again and cook for 40 minutes, until the pork and celery are tender. Transfer the pork and celery to a serving plate, cover and keep warm. Discard the bouquet garni and dill.

4 Cream the remaining butter and flour, then whisk into the cooking liquid while it is barely simmering. Cook for about 2–3 minutes, stirring occasionally. Stir the cream into the casserole, bring to a boil and add a squeeze of lemon juice.

5 Slice the pork, pour some sauce over the slices and garnish with dill. Serve the remaining sauce separately.

Spiced Lamb with Apricots

Inspired by Middle Eastern cooking, this fruity, spicy casserole is simple to make yet looks impressive.

Serves 4

4 ounces ready-to-eat
   dried apricots
scant ½ cup seedless
   raisins
½ teaspoon saffron
   strands
⅔ cup orange juice
1 tablespoon red wine
   vinegar
2–3 tablespoons olive oil
3-pound leg of lamb,
   boned and diced
1 onion, chopped
2 garlic cloves, crushed
2 teaspoons ground
   cumin

¼ teaspoon ground cloves
1 tablespoon ground
   coriander
2 tablespoons all-purpose
   flour
2½ cups lamb stock
3 tablespoons chopped
   fresh cilantro
salt and ground black
   pepper
saffron rice mixed with
   toasted almonds and
   chopped fresh cilantro,
   to serve

1 Mix together the dried apricots, raisins, saffron, orange juice and vinegar. Cover and let soak for 2–3 hours.

2 Preheat the oven to 325°F. Heat 2 tablespoons oil in a large flameproof casserole and brown the lamb in batches. Remove and set aside. Add the onion and garlic with a little more of the remaining oil and cook until softened.

3 Stir in the spices and flour and cook for 1–2 minutes more. Return the meat to the casserole. Stir in the stock, fresh cilantro and the soaked fruit with its liquid. Season to taste with salt and pepper, then bring to a boil. Cover the casserole with a tight-fitting lid and cook for 1½ hours (adding extra stock if necessary), or until the lamb is tender. Serve with saffron rice mixed with toasted almonds and fresh cilantro.

Beef and Mushroom Burgers

It's worth making your own burgers to cut down on fat – in these the meat is extended with mushrooms for extra fiber.

Serves 4

1 small onion, chopped
2 cups small cup
   mushrooms
1 pound lean ground beef
1 cup fresh bread crumbs
1 teaspoon dried mixed
   herbs

1 tablespoon tomato
   paste
flour, for shaping
salt and black pepper

1 Process the onion and mushrooms until finely chopped. Add the beef, bread crumbs, herbs, tomato paste and seasoning. Process until the mixture binds but still has some texture. Divide into 8–10 pieces and press into burger shapes.

2 Cook the burgers in a nonstick frying pan, or under a hot broiler for 12–15 minutes, turning once, until evenly cooked. Serve with relish and salad, in burger buns or pita bread.

Ruby Chops

This dish can be prepared with the minimum of effort, yet would still impress at an informal dinner party.

Serves 4

1 ruby grapefruit
4 lean pork loin chops

3 tablespoons redcurrant
   jelly
ground black pepper

1 Using a sharp knife, cut away all the peel and pith from the grapefruit. Carefully remove the segments, catching the juice in a bowl.

2 Fry the pork loin chops in a nonstick frying pan without fat, turning them once, until golden. Add the reserved grapefruit juice and redcurrant jelly to the pan and stir until melted. Add the grapefruit segments, then season with pepper and serve hot with fresh vegetables.

Beef Strips with Orange and Ginger

Stir-frying is a good way of cooking with the minimum of fat. It's also one of the quickest ways to cook.

Serves 4

Place 1 pound beef strips in a bowl; sprinkle over the rind and juice of 1 orange. Allow to marinate for at least 30 minutes. Drain the liquid and set aside, then mix the meat with 1 tablespoon soy sauce, 1 tablespoon cornstarch and 1 inch ginger. Heat 2 teaspoons sesame oil in a wok or large frying pan and add the beef. Stir-fry for 1 minute, add 1 carrot, cut into small strips and stir-fry for another 2–3 minutes. Stir in 2 sliced scallions and the reserved liquid, then boil, stirring, until thickened.

Steak, Kidney and Mushroom Pie

Lamb Pie with Mustard Thatch

If you prefer, omit the kidneys from this pie and substitute more chuck steak in their place.

Serves 4

2 tablespoons sunflower
  oil
1 onion, chopped
4 ounces bacon, finely
  chopped
1¼ pounds chuck steak,
  diced
2 tablespoons all-purpose
  flour

4 ounces lambs' kidneys
1¾ cups beef stock
large bouquet garni
4 ounces button
  mushrooms
8 ounces ready-made puff
  pastry
beaten egg, to glaze
salt and ground black
  pepper

1 Preheat the oven to 325°F. Heat the oil in a heavy-based saucepan and cook the bacon and onion until lightly browned.

2 Toss the steak in the flour. Stir the meat into the pan in batches and cook, stirring, until browned. Toss the kidneys in flour; add to the pan with the bouquet garni. Transfer to a casserole then pour in the stock, cover with a tight-fitting lid and cook in the oven for 2 hours. Stir in the mushrooms and seasoning and leave to cool.

3 Preheat the oven to 425°F. Roll out the pastry to ¾ inch larger than the top of a 5-cup pie dish. Cut off a pastry strip and then fit it around the moistened rim of the dish. Brush the pastry strip with water.

4 Turn the meat mixture into the dish. Lay the pastry over the dish, crimp the edges together to seal, cut a small vent in the pastry, brush with beaten egg and bake for 20 minutes. Lower the oven temperature to 350°F and bake for another 20 minutes, until the pastry has risen, and is golden and crisp.

This makes a pleasant change from a classic shepherd's pie – and it is a healthier option, as well.

Serves 4

1½ pounds old potatoes,
  diced
2 tablespoons skim milk
1 tablespoon wholegrain
  or French mustard
1 pound lean minced
  lamb
1 onion, chopped
2 celery stalks, sliced
2 carrots, diced
⅔ cup beef stock

4 tablespoons rolled oats
1 tablespoon
  Worcestershire sauce
2 tablespoons fresh
  rosemary, chopped, or
  2 teaspoons dried
  rosemary
salt and ground black
  pepper
fresh vegetables, to serve

1 Cook the potatoes in lightly salted boiling water until tender. Drain and mash until smooth, then stir in the milk and mustard. Meanwhile, preheat the oven to 400°F.

2 Break up the lamb with a fork and fry without any fat in a nonstick pan until lightly browned. Add the onion, celery and carrots to the saucepan and cook for 2–3 minutes, stirring constantly.

3 Stir in the stock and rolled oats. Bring to a boil, then add the Worcestershire sauce and rosemary and season to taste with salt and pepper.

4 Turn the meat mixture into a 7½-cup casserole and spread the potato topping evenly over the top, swirling with the edge of a knife. Bake for 30–35 minutes, or until golden. Serve hot with fresh vegetables.

Sausage and Bean Ragoût

An economical and nutritious main course that children
will love. Serve with garlic and herb bread, if you wish.

Serves 4

2 cups dried flageolet
 beans, soaked
 overnight
3 tablespoons olive oil
1 onion, finely chopped
2 garlic cloves, crushed
1 pound good-quality
 chunky sausages,
 skinned and thickly
 sliced
1 tablespoon tomato
 paste

2 tablespoons chopped
 fresh parsley
1 tablespoon chopped
 fresh thyme
14-ounce can chopped
 tomatoes
salt and ground black
 pepper
chopped fresh thyme and
 parsley, to garnish

1 Drain and rinse the soaked beans and place them in a
saucepan with enough water to cover. Bring to a boil, cover
the pan with a tight-fitting lid and simmer for about 1 hour, or
until tender. Drain the beans and set aside.

2 Heat the oil in a frying pan and fry the onion, garlic and
sausages until golden.

3 Stir in the tomato paste, tomatoes, chopped parsley and
thyme. Season with salt and pepper, then bring to a boil.

4 Add the beans, then cover with a lid and cook gently for
about 15 minutes, stirring occasionally, until the sausage slices
are cooked through. Garnish with chopped fresh thyme and
parsley and serve immediately.

Cook's Tip
*For a spicier version, add some skinned, thinly sliced
chorizo sausage along with the flageolet beans for the
last 15 minutes of cooking.*

Pepper Steaks with Madeira

A really easy dish for special occasions. Mixed peppercorns
have an excellent flavor, though black pepper will do.

Serves 4

1 tablespoon mixed dried
 peppercorns (green,
 pink and black)
4 fillet or sirloin steaks,
 about 6 ounces each
1 tablespoon olive oil,
 plus extra oil for
 shallow frying

1 garlic clove, crushed
4 tablespoons Madeira
 wine
6 tablespoons beef stock
⅔ cup heavy cream
pinch of salt

1 Finely crush the peppercorns using a coffee grinder or
mortar and pestle, then press them evenly onto both sides of
the steaks.

2 Place the steaks in a shallow non-metallic dish, then add
the olive oil, garlic and Madeira wine. Cover the dish and
allow to marinate in a cool place for at least 4–6 hours, or
preferably overnight for a more intense flavour.

3 Remove the steaks from the dish, reserving the marinade.
Brush a little oil over a large heavy-based frying pan and heat
until it is hot.

4 Add the steaks and cook over a high heat, according to
taste. Allow about 3 minutes' cooking time per side for a
medium steak or 2 minutes per side for rare. Remove the
steaks from the frying pan and keep them warm.

5 Add the reserved marinade and the beef stock to the pan
and bring to a boil, then let the sauce bubble until it is well
reduced.

6 Add the heavy cream to the pan, with salt to taste, and stir
until it has slightly thickened. Serve the pepper steaks on
warmed plates with the sauce.

Pork with Mozzarella and Sage

Here is a variation of the famous dish *saltimbocca alla romana* – the mozzarella adds a delicious creamy flavor.

Serves 2–3

8 ounces pork tenderloin
1 garlic clove, crushed
3 ounces mozzarella, cut into 6 slices
6 slices Parma ham
6 large sage leaves
2 tablespoons butter
salt and ground black pepper
potato wedges roasted in olive oil and green beans, to serve

1 Trim any excess fat from the pork, then cut the pork crosswise into six pieces about 1 inch thick.

2 Stand each piece of tenderloin on its end and bat down with a rolling pin to flatten. Rub with garlic and set aside for 30 minutes in a cool place.

3 Place a slice of mozzarella on top of each pork steak and season with salt and pepper. Lay a slice of Parma ham on top of each, crinkling it a little to fit.

4 Press a sage leaf onto each and secure with a toothpick. Melt the butter in a large heavy-based frying pan and cook the pork for about 2 minutes on each side until you see the mozzarella melting. Remove the toothpicks and serve immediately with roasted potatoes and green beans.

Five-spice Lamb

This aromatic lamb casserole is a perfect dish to serve at an informal supper party.

Serves 4

2–3 tablespoons oil
3–3½ pound leg of lamb, boned and cubed
1 onion, chopped
2 teaspoons grated fresh ginger
1 garlic clove, crushed
1 teaspoon five-spice powder
2 tablespoons hoisin sauce
1 tablespoon soy sauce
1¼ cups tomato paste
1 cup lamb stock
1 red bell pepper, seeded and diced
1 yellow bell pepper, seeded and diced
2 tablespoons chopped fresh cilantro
1 tablespoon sesame seeds, toasted
salt and ground black pepper

1 Preheat the oven to 325°F. In a large, flameproof casserole, heat 2 tablespoons of the oil and then brown the diced lamb in batches over a high heat. Remove to a plate and set aside.

2 Add the onion, ginger and garlic to the casserole with a little more of the oil, if necessary, and cook for 5 minutes, or until softened.

3 Return the lamb to the casserole. Stir in the five-spice powder, hoisin sauce, soy sauce, tomato purée and stock, and season to taste with salt and pepper. Bring to a boil, then cover with a tight-fitting lid and cook in the oven for about 1¼ hours.

4 Remove the casserole from the oven, stir in the peppers, then cover and return to the oven for another 15 minutes, or until the lamb is very tender.

5 Sprinkle with the chopped fresh cilantro and toasted sesame seeds. Serve hot accompanied by rice, if you wish.

Rich Beef Casserole

Use a full-bodied red wine such as a Burgundy to create the flavorful sauce in this casserole.

Serves 4–6

2 pounds chuck steak, cubed
2 onions, coarsely chopped
1 bouquet garni
6 black peppercorns
1 tablespoon red wine vinegar
1 bottle red wine
3–4 tablespoons olive oil
3 celery stalks, thickly sliced
½ cup all-purpose flour
1¼ cups beef stock
2 tablespoons tomato paste
2 garlic cloves, crushed
6 ounces chestnut mushrooms, halved
14-ounce can artichoke hearts, drained and halved
chopped fresh parsley and thyme, to garnish

1 Combine the meat, onions, bouquet garni, peppercorns, vinegar and wine. Cover and let marinate overnight.

2 The next day, preheat the oven to 325°F. Strain the meat, reserving the marinade, and pat dry. Heat the oil in a large flameproof casserole and fry the meat and onions in batches, adding a little more oil if necessary. Remove and set aside. Add the celery and fry until browned, then remove this also and set it aside with the meat.

3 Sprinkle the flour into the casserole and cook for 1 minute. Gradually add the reserved marinade and the stock, and bring to a boil, stirring continuously. Return the meat, onions and celery to the casserole, then stir in the tomato paste and crushed garlic.

4 Cover the casserole with a tight-fitting lid and cook in the oven for about 2¼ hours. Stir in the mushrooms and artichokes, cover again and cook for 15 minutes more, until the meat is tender. Garnish with parsley and thyme, and serve hot with creamy mashed potatoes, if you wish.

Pork Steaks with Gremolata

***Gremolata* is a popular Italian dressing of garlic, lemon and parsley – it adds a hint of sharpness to the pork.**

Serves 4

2 tablespoons olive oil
4 pork shoulder steaks
1 onion, chopped
2 garlic cloves, crushed
14-ounce can tomatoes
2 tablespoons tomato paste
⅔ cup dry white wine
bouquet garni
3 anchovy fillets, drained and chopped
salt and ground black pepper
salad greens, to serve

For the gremolata
3 tablespoons chopped fresh parsley
grated rind of ½ lemon
grated rind of 1 lime
1 garlic clove, chopped

1 Heat the oil in a large flameproof casserole and brown the pork steaks on both sides. Remove and set aside.

2 Add the onions to the casserole and cook until soft. Add the garlic and cook for 1–2 minutes. Chop the tomatoes and add with the tomato paste and wine. Add the bouquet garni, then boil rapidly for 3–4 minutes to reduce and thicken the sauce slightly. Return the pork to the casserole, then cover with a tight-fitting lid and cook for about 30 minutes. Stir in the chopped anchovies. Cover the casserole and cook for another 15 minutes, or until the pork is tender.

3 Meanwhile, to make the gremolata, mix together the parsley, lemon and lime rinds and garlic.

4 Remove the pork steaks and discard the bouquet garni. Reduce the sauce over a high heat, if it is not already thick. Taste and adjust the seasoning if necessary.

5 Return the pork to the casserole, then sprinkle with the gremolata. Cover and cook for another 5 minutes more, then serve hot with salad greens.

Beef Casserole and Dumplings

A traditional English recipe, this delicious casserole is topped with light herb dumplings for a filling meal.

Serves 4

1 tablespoon oil!
1 pound ground beef
16 button onions
2 carrots, thickly
    sliced
2 celery stalks, thickly
    sliced
2 tablespoons all-purpose
    flour
2½ cups beef stock

salt and ground black
    pepper

For the dumplings
4 tablespoons shredded
    beef suet
1 cup self-rising flour
1 tablespoon chopped
    fresh parsley

1 Preheat the oven to 350°F. Heat the oil in a flameproof casserole and fry the ground beef for 5 minutes until brown and sealed.

2 Add the onions; fry over a moderate heat for 5 minutes, stirring all the time.

3 Stir in the sliced carrots, the celery and the flour, then cook for another 1 minute more.

4 Add the beef stock and season to taste with salt and ground black pepper. Bring to a boil. Cover and cook in the oven for 1¼ hours.

5 For the dumplings, mix together the suet, flour and fresh parsley. Add enough cold water to form a smooth dough.

6 Roll the dumpling mixture into eight equal-size balls and place them around the top of the casserole. Return the casserole, uncovered, to the oven for another 20 minutes. Serve with broccoli florets, if liked.

Stilton Burgers

This tasty recipe contains a delicious surprise. The lightly melted Stilton cheese is enclosed in the crunchy burger.

Serves 4

1 pound ground beef
1 onion, finely chopped
1 celery stalk, chopped
1 teaspoon mixed
    dried herbs
1 teaspoon mustard

½ cup crumbled Stilton
    cheese
4 burger buns
salt and ground black
    pepper
green salad and mustard
    pickle, to serve

1 Place the ground beef in a bowl with the chopped onion and celery. Mix together, then season with salt and pepper.

2 Stir in the herbs and mustard, and bring together to form a firm mixture.

3 Divide the mixture into eight equal portions. Place four on a cutting board and flatten each one slightly.

4 Place the crumbled cheese in the center of each.

5 Flatten the remaining mixture and place on top. Mold the mixture together, enclosing the crumbled cheese, and shape into four burgers.

6 Broil under a moderate heat for turning once 10 minutes, or until cooked through. Split the burger buns and place a burger inside each. Serve with a freshly made salad and some mustard pickle.

Cook's Tip
These burgers could be made with ground lamb or pork for a variation, but make sure they are thoroughly cooked and not pink inside.

Indian Curried Lamb Samosas

Authentic samosa pastry is rather difficult to make but these samosas work equally well using puff pastry.

Serves 4

1 tablespoon oil
1 garlic clove, crushed
6 ounces ground lamb
4 scallions, finely chopped
2 teaspoons medium-hot
   curry paste
4 ready-to-eat dried
   apricots, chopped
1 small potato, diced
2 teaspoons apricot
   chutney
2 tablespoons frozen peas
 squeeze of lemon juice

1 tablespoon chopped fresh
   cilantro
8 ounces ready-made
   puff pastry
beaten egg, to glaze
1 teaspoon cumin seeds
salt and ground black
   pepper
3 tablespoons plain
   yogurt with chopped
   fresh mint, to serve
fresh mint sprigs, to
   garnish

1 Preheat the oven to 425°F and moisten a large nonstick baking sheet. Fry the garlic in the oil for 30 seconds, then add the lamb. Fry for about 5 minutes, stirring, until the meat is well browned.

2 Stir in the scallions, curry paste, apricots and potato, and cook for 2–3 minutes. Then add the chutney, peas and 4 tablespoons water. Cover and simmer for 10 minutes, stirring occasionally. Stir in the lemon juice and cilantro, season to taste, remove and let cool.

3 Roll out the pastry and cut into four 6-inch squares. Place a quarter of the curry mixture in the center of each square and brush the edges with beaten egg. Fold over to make a triangle and seal the edges. Make a small vent in the top of each.

4 Brush each samosa with beaten egg and sprinkle with cumin seeds. Place on the damp baking sheet and bake for about 20 minutes. Serve garnished with mint sprigs and with the minty yogurt passed around separately.

Breton Pork and Bean Casserole

This is a traditional French dish, called *cassoulet*. There are many variations in the different regions of France.

Serves 4

2 tablespoons olive oil
1 onion, chopped
2 garlic cloves, chopped
1 pound lean shoulder of
   pork, diced
12 ounces lean lamb
   (preferably leg), diced
8 ounces coarse pork and
   garlic sausage, cut
   into chunks
14-ounce can chopped
   tomatoes

2 tablespoons red wine
1 tablespoon tomato paste
bouquet garni
14-ounce can navy or
   white beans, drained
   and rinsed
1 cup whole wheat bread
   crumbs
salt and ground black
   pepper
green salad and French
   bread, to serve

1 Preheat the oven to 325°F. Heat the oil in a large flameproof casserole and fry the onions and garlic until softened. Remove with a slotted spoon and reserve.

2 Add the pork, lamb and sausage chunks to the casserole and fry over a high heat until browned on all sides. Add the onions and garlic to the meat.

3 Stir in the chopped tomatoes, wine and tomato paste and add 1¼ cups water. Season to taste with salt and pepper and add the bouquet garni. Cover and bring to a boil, then transfer the casserole to the preheated oven and cook for 1½ hours.

4 Remove the bouquet garni, stir in the beans and sprinkle the bread crumbs over the top. Return to the oven, uncovered, for another 30 minutes, until the top is golden brown. Serve hot with a green salad and French bread to mop up the juice.

Cook's Tip
Replace the lamb with duck breast, but be sure to drain off any fat before adding the bread crumbs.

Pan-fried Mediterranean Lamb

The warm, summery flavors of the Mediterranean are combined for a simple weekday meal.

Serves 4

8 lean lamb cutlets
1 onion, thinly sliced
2 red bell peppers, seeded and sliced
14-ounce can plum tomatoes
1 garlic clove, crushed
3 tablespoons chopped fresh basil leaves
2 tablespoons chopped black olives
salt and ground black pepper

1 Trim any excess fat from the lamb, then fry without fat in a nonstick frying pan until golden brown.

2 Add the onion and red peppers to the pan. Cook, stirring, for a few minutes to soften, then add the plum tomatoes, garlic and fresh basil leaves.

3 Cover and simmer for 20 minutes or until the lamb is tender. Stir in the olives, season to taste with salt and pepper and serve hot, with pasta if you wish.

Cook's Tip
The red peppers give this dish a slightly sweet taste. If you prefer, use green peppers for a more savory dish.

Greek Lamb Pie

Ready-made phyllo pastry is so easy to use and gives a most professional look to this lamb and spinach pie.

Serves 4

1 pound ground lamb
1 onion, sliced
1 garlic clove, crushed
14-ounce can plum tomatoes
2 tablespoons chopped fresh mint
1 teaspoon grated nutmeg
12 ounces young spinach leaves
10-ounce package ready-made phyllo pastry
sunflower oil, for brushing
1 teaspoon sesame seeds
salt and ground black pepper

1 Preheat the oven to 400°F. Lightly oil an 8½-inch round springform pan.

2 Fry the lamb and onion without fat in a nonstick pan until golden. Add the garlic, tomatoes, mint and nutmeg and season with salt and pepper. Bring to a boil, stirring from time to time. Simmer, stirring occasionally, until most of the liquid has evaporated.

3 Wash the spinach and remove any tough stalks, then cook in only the water clinging to the leaves for about 2 minutes, until just wilted.

4 Lightly brush each sheet of phyllo pastry with oil and lay in overlapping layers in the pan, leaving enough hanging over to wrap over the top.

5 Spoon in the meat and spinach, then wrap the pastry over to enclose, scrunching it slightly. Sprinkle with sesame seeds and bake for about 25–30 minutes, or until golden and crisp. Serve hot, with salad or vegetables, as you wish.

Pasta Bolognese with Cheese

If you like lasagne, you will love this dish. It is especially popular with children too.

Serves 4

2 tablespoons olive oil
1 onion, chopped
1 garlic clove, crushed
1 carrot, diced
2 celery stalks, chopped
2 slices bacon, finely
    chopped
5 button mushrooms,
    chopped
1 pound lean ground beef
½ cup red wine
1 tablespoon tomato paste
7-ounce can chopped
    tomatoes

sprig of fresh thyme
2 cups dried penne pasta
1¼ cups milk
2 tablespoons butter
2 tablespoons all-purpose
    flour
1 cup diced mozzarella
    cheese
4 tablespoons grated
    Parmesan cheese
salt and ground black
    pepper
fresh basil sprigs, to
    garnish

1 Fry the onion, garlic, carrot and celery in the olive oil until softened. Add the bacon and fry for 3–4 minutes. Add the mushrooms, fry for 2 minutes, then fry the beef until brown.

2 Add the wine, tomato paste, 3 tablespoons water, tomatoes and the sprig of fresh thyme. Bring to a boil, cover, and simmer for 30 minutes.

3 Preheat the oven to 400°F. Cook the pasta. Meanwhile, place the milk, butter and flour in a saucepan; heat gently, whisking until thickened. Stir in the mozzarella and Parmesan cheeses, and season.

4 Drain the pasta and stir into the cheese sauce. Uncover the Bolognese sauce and boil rapidly for 2 minutes. Spoon the sauce into a casserole, top with the pasta mixture and sprinkle with the remaining Parmesan. Bake for 25 minutes, or until golden. Garnish with basil and serve hot.

Corned Beef and Egg Hash

This classic American hash is a popular brunch dish and should be served with chili sauce for an authentic touch.

Serves 4

2 tablespoons oil
2 tablespoons butter
1 onion, finely chopped
1 small green bell pepper,
    seeded and diced
2 large boiled potatoes,
    diced
12-ounce can corned beef,
    diced

¼ teaspoon grated
    nutmeg
¼ teaspoon paprika
4 eggs
salt and ground black
    pepper
chopped fresh parsley, to
    garnish
chili sauce, to serve

1 Heat the oil and butter together in a large frying pan and fry the onion for 5–6 minutes until softened. In a bowl, mix together the pepper, potatoes, corned beef, nutmeg and paprika; season to taste with salt and pepper. Add to the pan and toss gently to distribute the cooked onion. Press down lightly; fry over a moderate heat for 3–4 minutes, until a golden brown crust has formed on the bottom.

2 Stir the mixture through to distribute the crust, then repeat the frying twice, until the mixture has browned.

3 Make four wells in the hash and crack an egg into each one. Cover and cook gently for about 4–5 minutes, until the egg whites are just set.

4 Sprinkle with chopped parsley and cut the hash into quarters. Serve hot with chili sauce.

Cook's Tip
Put the can of corned beef in the fridge for about 30 minutes before using. It will firm up and you will be able to cut it into cubes more easily than if it is used at room temperature.

Best-ever American Burgers

These meaty quarter-pounders are far superior in taste and texture to anything you can buy ready-made.

Makes 4 burgers

1 tablespoon oil
1 small onion, chopped
1 pound lean ground beef
1 large garlic clove, crushed
1 teaspoon ground cumin
2 teaspoons ground coriander
2 tablespoons tomato paste or ketchup
1 teaspoon wholegrain mustard
dash of Worcestershire sauce
2 tablespoons mixed chopped fresh herbs such as parsley, thyme and oregano or marjoram
1 tablespoon lightly beaten egg
salt and ground black pepper
flour, for shaping
oil, for frying (optional)
mixed salad, chips and relish, to serve

1 Heat the oil in a frying pan, add the onion and cook for 5 minutes, until softened. Remove from the pan, drain on paper towels and allow to cool.

2 Mix together the beef, garlic, spices, tomato paste or ketchup, mustard, Worcestershire sauce, herbs, beaten egg and seasoning in a bowl. Stir in the cooled onions.

3 Sprinkle a board with flour and shape the mixture into four burgers with floured hands and a palette knife. Cover and chill in the fridge for 15 minutes.

4 Heat a little oil in a pan and fry the burgers over a moderate heat for about 5 minutes each side, depending on how rare you like them. Alternatively, cook under a moderate broiler for the same time. Serve with salad, fries and relish.

Cook's Tip
If you prefer, make eight smaller burgers to serve in buns, with melted cheese and tomato slices.

Bacon and Sausage Sauerkraut

Juniper berries and crushed cilantro seeds flavour this traditional dish from Alsace.

Serves 4

2 tablespoons oil
1 large onion, thinly sliced
1 garlic clove, crushed
1 pound bottled sauerkraut, rinsed and drained
1 eating apple, cored and chopped
5 juniper berries
5 coriander seeds, crushed
1-pound piece of lightly smoked bacon loin roast
8 ounces whole smoked pork sausage, pricked
¾ cup unsweetened apple juice
⅔ cup chicken stock
1 bay leaf
8 small salad potatoes

1 Preheat the oven to 350°F. Heat the oil in a flameproof casserole and fry the onion and garlic for about 3–4 minutes, until softened. Stir in the sauerkraut, apple, juniper berries and coriander seeds.

2 Lay the piece of bacon loin and the sausage on top of the sauerkraut, pour on the apple juice and stock, and add the bay leaf. Cover and bake in the oven for about 1 hour.

3 Remove from the oven and pop the potatoes into the casserole. Add a little more stock if necessary, cover and bake for another 30 minutes, or until the potatoes are tender.

4 Just before serving, lift out the bacon and sausages onto a board and slice. Spoon the sauerkraut onto a warmed platter, top with the meat and surround with the potatoes.

Ginger Pork with Black Bean Sauce

Golden Pork and Apricot Casserole

Preserved black beans provide a unique flavor in this dish. Look for them in specialty Chinese food stores.

The rich golden color and warm spicy flavor of this simple casserole make it ideal for a chilly winter's day.

Serves 4

12-ounce pork fillet
1 garlic clove, crushed
1 tablespoon grated fresh
   ginger
6 tablespoons chicken
   stock
2 tablespoons dry sherry
1 tablespoon light soy
   sauce
1 teaspoon sugar
2 teaspoons cornstarch
3 tablespoons peanut oil

2 yellow bell peppers,
   seeded and cut into
   strips
2 red bell peppers, seeded
   and cut into strips
1 bunch scallions, sliced
   diagonally
3 tablespoons preserved
   black beans, coarsely
   chopped
fresh cilantro sprigs, to
   garnish

Serves 4

4 lean pork loin chops
1 onion, thinly sliced
2 yellow bell peppers,
   seeded and sliced
2 teaspoons medium
   curry powder
1 tablespoon all-purpose
   flour

1 cup chicken stock
4 ounces ready-to-eat
   dried apricots
2 tablespoons wholegrain
   mustard
salt and ground black
   pepper

1   Cut the pork into thin slices across the grain of the meat. Put the slices into a dish and mix them with the garlic and ginger. Let marinate at room temperature for 15 minutes.

2   Blend together the stock, sherry, soy sauce, sugar and cornstarch in a small bowl, then set the sauce mixture aside.

3   Heat the oil in a wok or large frying pan and stir-fry the marinated pork for 2–3 minutes. Add the peppers and scallions and continue to stir-fry for another 2 minutes.

4   Add the beans and sauce mixture and cook, stirring, until thick. Serve hot, garnished with the fresh cilantro sprigs.

Cook's Tip
If you cannot find preserved black beans, use the same amount of black bean sauce instead.

1   Trim the excess fat from the pork and fry without fat in a large heavy or nonstick saucepan until lightly browned.

2   Add the onion and yellow peppers to the pan and stir over a moderate heat for 5 minutes. Then stir in the curry powder and the flour.

3   Add the stock, stirring, then add the apricots and mustard. Cover with a tight-fitting lid and simmer for 25–30 minutes, until tender. Adjust the seasoning to taste and serve hot, with rice or new potatoes, if you wish.

Sukiyaki-style Beef

This dish incorporates all the traditional Japanese elements – meat, vegetables, noodles and bean curd.

Serves 4

1 pound thick round
  steak
3½ cups Japanese rice
  noodles
1 tablespoon shredded
  suet
7 ounces hard bean curd,
  cut into dice
8 shiitake mushrooms,
  trimmed
2 leeks, sliced into 1-inch
  lengths

scant 1 cup baby spinach,
  to serve

For the stock

1 tablespoon caster sugar
6 tablespoons rice wine
3 tablespoons dark soy
  sauce
½ cup water

1 Cut the beef into thin even-size slices.

2 Blanch the rice noodles in boiling water for 2 minutes, then strain well.

3 Mix together all the stock ingredients in a bowl.

4 Heat a wok, then add the suet. When the suet is melted, stir-fry the beef for 2 – 3 minutes until it is cooked, but still pink in color.

5 Pour the stock over the beef.

6 Add the remaining ingredients and cook for 4 minutes, until the leeks are tender. Serve a selection of the different ingredients, with a few baby spinach leaves, to each person.

Cook's Tip
Add a touch of authenticity and serve this complete meal with chopsticks and a porcelain spoon to collect the stock juices.

Stir-fried Pork with Mustard

Fry the apples for this dish very carefully, because they will disintegrate if they are overcooked.

Serves 4

1¼ pound pork fillet
1 tart apple, such as
  Granny Smith
3 tablespoons unsalted
  butter
1 tablespoon sugar
1 small onion, finely
  chopped
2 tablespoons Calvados
  or brandy

1 tablespoon Meaux or
  coarse grain mustard
⅔ cup heavy cream
2 tablespoons chopped
  fresh parsley
salt and ground black
  pepper
fresh Italian parsley
  sprigs, to garnish

1 Cut the pork fillet into thin even-size slices.

2 Peel and core the apple. Cut into thick slices.

3 Heat a wok, then add half the butter. When the butter is hot, add the apple slices, sprinkle on the sugar, and stir-fry for 2 – 3 minutes. Remove the apple and set aside. Wipe out the wok with paper towels.

4 Reheat the wok, then add the remaining butter and stir-fry the pork fillet and onion together for 2 – 3 minutes, until the pork is golden and the onion has begun to soften.

5 Stir in the Calvados or brandy and boil until it is reduced by half. Stir in the mustard.

6 Add the cream and simmer for about 1 minute, then stir in the parsley. Serve garnished with sprigs of Italian parsley.

Cook's Tip
If you don't have a wok, use a large frying pan, preferably with deep, sloping sides.

Hungarian Beef Goulash

Spicy beef stew served with caraway-flavored dumplings will satisfy even the largest appetites.

Serves 4
2 tablespoons oil
2 pounds beef round, cubed
2 onions, chopped
1 garlic clove, crushed
1 tablespoon all-purpose flour
2 teaspoons paprika
1 teaspoon caraway seeds
14-ounce can chopped tomatoes
1¼ cups beef stock
1 large carrot, chopped
1 red bell pepper, seeded and chopped

sour cream, to serve
paprika, to garnish

For the dumplings
1 cup self-rising flour
½ cup shredded suet
1 tablespoon chopped fresh parsley
½ teaspoon caraway seeds
salt and ground black pepper

1 Heat the oil in a flameproof casserole and fry the meat for 5 minutes over a high heat, stirring, until browned. Remove with a slotted spoon. Add the onions and garlic and fry gently for 5 minutes, until softened. Add the flour, paprika and caraway seeds, stir and cook for 2 minutes.

2 Return the meat to the casserole; stir in the tomatoes and stock. Bring to a boil, cover, simmer for 2 hours.

3 To make the dumplings, sift the flour and seasoning into a bowl, add the suet, parsley, caraway seeds and about 3–4 tablespoons water and mix to a soft dough. Divide into eight pieces and roll into balls. Cover and reserve.

4 After 2 hours, stir the carrot and red pepper into the goulash, and season. Drop the dumplings into the goulash, cover and simmer for 25 minutes. Serve in bowls topped with a spoonful of sour cream sprinkled with paprika.

Pork Satay with Peanut Sauce

These delightful little satay sticks from Thailand make a good light meal or a party snack.

Makes 8
½ small onion, chopped
2 garlic cloves, crushed
2 tablespoons lemon juice
1 tablespoon soy sauce
1 teaspoon ground coriander
½ teaspoon ground cumin
1 teaspoon ground turmeric
2 tablespoons oil
1 pound pork tenderloin
fresh cilantro sprigs, to garnish
boiled rice, to serve

For the sauce
2 ounces creamed coconut, chopped
4 tablespoons crunchy peanut butter

1 tablespoon lemon juice
½ teaspoon ground cumin
½ teaspoon ground coriander
1 teaspoon brown sugar
1 tablespoon soy sauce
1–2 dried red chilies, seeded and chopped
1 tablespoon chopped fresh cilantro

For the salad
½ small cucumber, peeled and diced
1 tablespoon white wine vinegar
1 tablespoon chopped fresh cilantro
salt and ground black pepper

1 Process the first eight ingredients until smooth. Cut the pork into strips, mix with the marinade, and chill. Preheat the broiler to hot. Thread two or three pork pieces onto each of eight soaked woodenskewers and broil for 2–3 minutes each side, basting with the marinade.

2 To make the sauce, dissolve the creamed coconut in ⅔ cup boiling water. Put the remaining ingredients into a saucepan, stir in the coconut, bring to a boil, stirring, and simmer for 5 minutes.

3 Mix together all the salad ingredients. Arrange the satay sticks on a platter, garnish with cilantro sprigs and season.

Stir-fried Pork with Lychees

No extra oil or fat is needed to cook this dish, as the pork produces enough on its own.

Serves 4

1 pound fatty pork, with
  the skin on or off
2 tablespoons hoisin
  sauce
4 scallions, sliced
  diagonally

6 ounces lychees, peeled,
  pitted and cut into
  slivers
salt and ground black
  pepper
fresh lychees and parsley
  sprigs, to garnish

1 Cut the pork into bite-size pieces.

2 Pour the hoisin sauce over the pork and leave to marinate for at least 30 minutes.

3 Heat a wok, then add the pork and stir-fry for 5 minutes until crisp and golden. Add the scallions and stir-fry for another 2 minutes.

4 Scatter the lychee slivers over the pork, and season well with salt and pepper. Garnish with fresh lychees and fresh parsley sprigs, to serve.

Cook's Tip
Lychees have a very pretty pink skin which, when peeled, reveals a soft fleshy berry with a hard shiny pit. If you cannot buy fresh lychees, this dish can be made with drained canned lychees.

Sizzling Beef with Celery Root Straw

The crisp celery root matchsticks look like fine pieces of straw when cooked and have a mild celery-like flavor.

Serves 4

1 pound celery root
⅔ cup oil
1 red bell pepper
6 scallions
1 pound rump steak
4 tablespoons beef stock
2 tablespoons sherry
  vinegar

2 teaspoons
  Worcestershire sauce
2 teaspoons tomato paste
salt and ground black
  pepper

1 Peel the celery root and then cut it into fine matchsticks, using a cleaver if you have one, or a large sharp knife.

2 Heat the wok, then add two-thirds of the oil. When the oil is hot, fry the celery root matchsticks in batches until golden brown and crispy. Drain well on paper towels.

3 Chop the red pepper and the scallions into 1-inch lengths, using diagonal cuts.

4 Chop the beef into strips, across the grain of the meat.

5 Heat the wok, then add the remaining oil. When the oil is hot, stir-fry the chopped scallions and red pepper for about 2–3 minutes.

6 Add the beef strips and stir-fry for another 3–4 minutes until well browned. Add the stock, vinegar, Worcestershire sauce and tomato paste. Season well with salt and pepper and serve with the celery root "straw".

Cook's Tip
The Chinese use a large cleaver for preparing most vegetables. With a little practice, you will discover that it is the ideal kitchen utensil for cutting fine vegetable matchsticks and chopping thin strips of meat.

Turkish Lamb and Apricot Stew

Almond and parsley–flavored couscous accompanies this rich stew of lamb, apricots and chick-peas.

Serves 4

1 large eggplant, diced
2 tablespoons sunflower
 oil
1 onion, chopped
1 garlic clove, crushed
1 teaspoon ground
 cinnamon
3 whole cloves
1 pound boned leg of
 lamb, cubed
14-ounce can chopped
 tomatoes
4 ounces ready-to-eat
 dried apricots

1 cup canned chick-peas,
 drained
1 teaspoon honey
salt and ground black
 pepper
couscous, to serve
2 tablespoons olive oil
2 tablespoons chopped
 almonds, fried in a
 little oil
chopped fresh parsley, to
 garnish

1 Place the diced eggplant in a colander, sprinkle with salt and set aside for about 30 minutes. Heat the oil in a large flameproof casserole and fry the onion and garlic for about 5 minutes, until softened but not browned.

2 Stir in the ground cinnamon and whole cloves and fry for another 1 minute. Add the lamb and cook for 5–6 minutes more, stirring occasionally to brown the pieces evenly.

3 Rinse, drain and pat dry the eggplant with paper towels, add to the casserole and cook for 3 minutes, stirring well. Add the chopped tomatoes, 1¼ cups water and the apricots, and season to taste with salt and pepper. Bring to a boil, then cover and simmer gently for about 45 minutes.

4 Stir the chick-peas and honey into the stew, then cook for a final 15–20 minutes, or until the lamb is tender. Serve the dish accompanied by couscous with the olive oil, fried almonds and chopped parsley stirred into it.

Curried Lamb and Lentils

This colorful curry is packed with protein and low in fat, and makes a flavorful yet healthy meal.

Serves 4

8 lean boned lamb leg
 steaks, about 1¼
 pounds total weight
1 onion, chopped
2 carrots, diced
1 celery stalk, chopped
1 tablespoon hot curry
 paste

2 tablespoons tomato
 paste
2 cups stock
1 cup green lentils
salt and ground black
 pepper
fresh cilantro leaves, to
 garnish
boiled rice, to serve

1 In a large nonstick saucepan, fry the lamb steaks without fat until browned, turning once.

2 Add the vegetables and cook for 2 minutes, then stir in the curry paste, tomato paste, stock and lentils.

3 Bring to a boil, cover with a tight-fitting lid and simmer gently for 30 minutes until tender. Add some extra stock, if necessary. Season to taste and serve garnished with cilantro and accompanied by rice.

Cook's Tip
Pick over the lentils carefully before adding them to the saucepan. They sometimes contain small stones which are unpleasant to find while eating a meal.

Middle-Eastern Lamb Kebabs

Skewered, broiled meats are a staple of Middle Eastern cooking. Here, marinated lamb is broiled with vegetables.

Makes 4

1 pound boned leg of
    lamb, cubed
5 tablespoons olive oil
5 tablespoon chopped
    fresh oregano or
    thyme, or 2 teaspoons
    dried oregano
1 tablespoon chopped
    fresh parsley
juice of ½ lemon

½ small eggplant, thickly
    sliced and quartered
4 baby onions, halved
2 tomatoes, quartered
4 fresh bay leaves
salt and ground black
    pepper
pita bread and plain
    yogurt, to serve

1 Place the lamb in a bowl. Mix together the olive oil, oregano or thyme, parsley, lemon juice, salt and pepper. Pour over the lamb; mix well. Cover and marinate for about 1 hour.

2 Preheat the broiler. Thread the marinated lamb, eggplant, onions, tomatoes and bay leaves alternately onto four large skewers. (If using wooden skewers, soak them first.)

3 Place the kebabs on a broiler rack and brush the vegetables liberally with the leftover marinade. Cook the kebabs under a medium heat for about 8–10 minutes on each side, basting once or twice with the juices that have collected in the bottom of the broiler pan. Serve the kebabs hot, accompanied by hot pita bread and plain yogurt.

Cook's Tip
For a more piquant marinade, add one or two cloves of garlic, peeled and crushed.

Mexican Spiced Roast Leg of Lamb

Make sure you push the garlic slices deeply into the meat or they will burn and develop a bitter flavor.

Serves 4

1 small leg or half leg of
    lamb, about 2½
    pounds
1 tablespoon dried
    oregano
1 teaspoon ground cumin
1 teaspoon hot chili
    powder

2 garlic cloves
3 tablespoons olive oil
2 tablespoons red wine
    vinegar
salt and ground black
    pepper
fresh oregano sprigs, to
    garnish

1 Preheat the oven to 425°F. Place the leg of lamb on a large cutting board.

2 Place the oregano, cumin, chili powder and one of the garlic cloves, crushed, into a bowl. Pour on half of the olive oil and mix well to form a paste. Set the paste aside.

3 Using a sharp knife, make a criss-cross pattern of fairly deep slits going through the skin and just into the meat of the leg of lamb. Press the spice paste into the meat slits with the back of a round-bladed knife. Peel and slice the remaining garlic clove thinly and cut each slice in half again. Push the pieces of garlic deeply into the slits made in the meat.

4 Mix the vinegar and remaining oil, pour over the leg and season with salt and pepper.

5 Bake for about 15 minutes at the higher temperature, then reduce the heat to 350°F and cook for another 1¼ hours (or a little longer if you like your meat well done). Serve the lamb with a delicious gravy made with the spicy pan juices and garnish with fresh oregano sprigs.

Burgundy Beef

This French classic is named after the region it comes from, Burgundy, where the local red wine is used to flavor it.

Serves 4

2 tablespoons olive oil
8 ounces piece streaky bacon, diced
12 whole baby onions
2 pounds stewing beef, cut into 2-inch squares
1 large onion, thickly sliced
1 tablespoon all-purpose flour

about 1¾ cups red Burgundy wine
bouquet garni
1 garlic clove
8 ounces button mushrooms, halved
salt and ground black pepper
chopped fresh parsley, to garnish

1 Heat the oil in a flameproof casserole and fry the bacon and baby onions for 7–8 minutes, until the onions have browned and the bacon fat is transparent. Remove with a slotted spoon and reserve.

2 Add the beef to the casserole and fry quickly on all sides until evenly browned. Add the sliced onion and continue cooking for 4–5 minutes.

3 Sprinkle on the flour and stir well. Pour on the wine and add the bouquet garni and garlic. Cover with a tightly fitting lid and simmer gently for about 2 hours. Stir in the reserved sautéed onions and bacon and add a little extra wine, if necessary.

4 Add the mushrooms. Cover again and cook for another 30 minutes more. Remove the bouquet garni and garlic and garnish with chopped fresh parsley.

Spiced Lamb Bake

A quite delicious South African shepherd's pie. The recipe was originally poached from the Afrikaners' Malay slaves.

Serves 4

1 tablespoon oil
1 onion, chopped
1½ pounds ground lamb
2 tablespoons medium curry paste
2 tablespoons mango chutney
2 tablespoons freshly squeezed lemon juice
4 tablespoons chopped, blanched almonds

2 tablespoons golden raisins
3 ounces creamed coconut, crumbled
2 eggs
2 bay leaves
salt and ground black pepper

1 Preheat the oven to 350°F. Heat the oil in a frying pan and cook the chopped onion for 5–6 minutes, until softened but not browned.

2 Add the lamb and cook over a moderate heat, turning frequently, until browned all over. Stir in the curry paste, chutney, lemon juice, almonds and raisins, season well with salt and pepper and cook for about 5 minutes.

3 Transfer the mixture to a casserole and cook in the oven, uncovered, for 10 minutes.

4 Meanwhile, dissolve the crumbled creamed coconut in a scant 1 cup of boiling water and cool slightly. Beat in the eggs and a little seasoning.

5 Remove the dish from the oven and pour the coconut custard over the meat mixture. Lay the bay leaves on the top and return the dish to the oven for 30–35 minutes, or until the top is set and golden. Serve hot.

Greek Pasta Bake

Another excellent main meal (called *pastitsio* in Greece), this recipe is both economical and filling.

Serves 4

1 tablespoon oil	2 large tomatoes
1 pound groundlamb	4-ounce cup pasta shapes
1 onion, chopped	1-pound tub strained
2 garlic cloves, crushed	plain yogurt
2 tablespoons tomato	2 eggs
paste	salt and ground black
2 tablespoons all-purpose	pepper
flour	green salad, to serve
1¼ cups lamb stock	

1 Preheat the oven to 375°F. Heat the oil in a large saucepan and fry the lamb for 5 minutes. Add the onion and garlic and continue to fry for another 5 minutes.

2 Stir in the tomato paste and flour. Cook for 1 minute.

3 Stir in the lamb stock and season to taste with salt and pepper. Bring to a boil and cook for 20 minutes.

4 Slice the tomatoes, place the meat in a baking dish and arrange the tomatoes on top.

5 Bring a pan of salted water to a boil and cook the pasta shapes for 8–10 minutes until *al dente*. Drain well.

6 Mix together the pasta, yogurt and eggs. Spoon on top of the tomatoes and cook in the preheated oven for 1 hour. Serve hot with a crisp green salad.

Cook's Tip
Choose pasta shapes for this dish rather than tubes so the sauce coats the pasta all over. Try shells, spirals or twists.

Bacon Koftas

These easy koftas are good for barbecues and summer parties, served with lots of salad.

Serves 4

8 ounces lean bacon,	ground black pepper
coarsely chopped	pinch of paprika
1½ cups fresh whole	lemon rind and fresh
wheat bread crumbs	parsley leaves, to
2 scallions, chopped	garnish
1 tablespoon chopped	lemon rice and salad, to
fresh parsley	serve
finely grated rind of	
1 lemon	
1 egg white	

1 Place the bacon in a food processor with the bread crumbs, scallions, parsley, lemon rind, egg white and pepper. Process the mixture until it is finely chopped and begins to bind together. Alternatively, use a chopper.

2 Divide the bacon mixture into eight even-size pieces and shape into long ovals around eight previously soaked wooden or bamboo skewers.

3 Sprinkle the koftas with paprika and cook under a hot broiler or on a barbecue for about 8–10 minutes, turning them occasionally, until browned and cooked through. Garnish with lemon rind and parsley leaves, then serve hot with lemon rice and salad.

Cook's Tip
This is a good way to spread a little meat a long way as each portion only requires 2 ounces of bacon. Use good quality bacon for this recipe.

Peking Beef and Pepper Stir-fry

Once the steak has marinated, this colorful dish can be prepared in just a few minutes.

Serves 4

12 ounces round or
    sirloin steak, sliced
    into strips
2 tablespoons soy sauce
2 tablespoons medium
    sherry
1 tablespoon cornstarch
1 teaspoon brown sugar
1 tablespoon sunflower
    oil
1 tablespoon sesame oil
1 garlic clove, finely
    chopped

1 tablespoon grated fresh
    ginger
1 red bell pepper, seeded
    and sliced
1 yellow bell pepper,
    seeded and sliced
1 cup snow peas
4 scallions, cut into
    2-inch pieces
2 tablespoons Chinese
    oyster sauce
hot noodles, to serve

1 In a bowl, mix together the steak strips, soy sauce, sherry, cornstarch and brown sugar. Cover and allow to marinate for 30 minutes.

2 Heat the oils in a wok or large frying pan and stir-fry the garlic and ginger for about 30 seconds. Add the peppers, peas and scallions and stir-fry over a high heat for 3 minutes.

3 Add the beef with the marinade juices to the wok or frying pan and stir-fry for another 3–4 minutes.

4 Finally, pour in the oyster sauce and 4 tablespoons water and stir until the sauce has thickened slightly. Serve immediately with hot noodles.

Texan Barbecued Ribs

This barbecue or oven-roast dish of pork spareribs cooked in a sweet and sour sauce is a favorite in the United States.

Serves 4

3 pounds (about 16) lean
    pork spareribs
1 onion, finely chopped
1 large garlic clove,
    crushed
½ cup tomato paste
2 tablespoons orange
    juice
2 tablespoons red wine
    vinegar
1 teaspoon mustard

2 teaspoons honey
2 tablespoons light
    brown sugar
dash of Worcestershire
    sauce
2 tablespoons vegetable
    oil
salt and ground black
    pepper
chopped fresh parsley, to
    garnish

1 Preheat the oven to 400°F. Place the pork spareribs in a large shallow roasting pan; bake for 20 minutes.

2 Meanwhile, in a saucepan mix together the onion, garlic, tomato paste, orange juice, wine vinegar, mustard, honey, brown sugar, Worcestershire sauce, oil and seasoning. Bring to a boil and simmer for about 5 minutes.

3 Remove the ribs from the oven and then reduce the oven temperature to 350°F. Spoon on half the sauce, covering the ribs well, and bake for 20 minutes. Turn them over, baste with the remaining sauce and cook for about another 25 minutes.

4 Sprinkle the spareribs with parsley before serving and allow three or four ribs per person. Provide finger bowls for washing sticky fingers.

Skewers of Lamb with Mint

For a more substantial meal, serve these skewers on a bed of flavored rice or couscous.

Serves 4

1¼ cups plain strained
  yogurt
½ garlic clove, crushed
generous pinch of saffron
  powder
2 tablespoons chopped
  fresh mint
2 tablespoons honey
3 tablespoons olive oil
3 lamb neck fillets (about
  1½ pounds total)

1 eggplant, in 1-inch
  pieces
2 small red onions,
  quartered
salt and ground black
  pepper
small fresh mint leaves,
  to garnish
mixed salad and hot pita
  bread, to serve

1 Mix the yogurt, garlic, saffron, mint, honey, oil and pepper together in a shallow dish.

2 Trim the lamb and cut into 1-inch cubes. Add to the marinade and stir until well coated. Cover and let marinate for at least 4 hours, or preferably overnight.

3 Blanch the diced eggplant in a saucepan of boiling salted water for about 1–2 minutes. Drain well and then pat dry on paper towels.

4 Remove the diced lamb from the marinade. Thread the lamb, eggplant and onion pieces alternately onto skewers. (If you are using wooden skewers, soak them in water first. This will prevent them from charring during broiling.) Broil for 10–12 minutes, turning and basting occasionally with the marinade, until the lamb is tender.

5 Serve the skewers garnished with mint leaves and accompanied by a mixed salad and hot pita bread.

Beef Stew with Red Wine

A slow-cooked casserole of tender beef in a red wine and tomato sauce, with black olives and red pepper.

Serves 6

5 tablespoons olive oil
2½ pounds boned beef
  chuck, in 1½-inch
  pieces
1 onion, very finely
  sliced
2 carrots, chopped
3 tablespoons finely
  chopped fresh parsley
1 garlic clove, chopped
1 bay leaf
a few fresh thyme sprigs
pinch of freshly ground
  nutmeg

1 cup red wine
14-ounce can plum
  tomatoes, chopped,
  with their juice
½ cup beef or chicken
  stock
about 15 black olives,
  pitted and halved
salt and ground black
  pepper
1 large red bell pepper,
  cut into strips

1 Preheat the oven to 350°F. Brown the meat, in batches, in 3 tablespoons of the oil in a large heavy-based flameproof casserole. Remove to a side plate as the meat is browned, and set aside until needed.

2 Add the remaining oil, the onion and carrots to the casserole. Cook over a low heat until the onion softens. Add the parsley and garlic, and cook for another 3–4 minutes.

3 Return the meat to the casserole, raise the heat, and stir well to mix the vegetables with the meat. Stir in the bay leaf, thyme and nutmeg. Add the wine, bring to a boil and cook, stirring, for 4–5 minutes. Stir in the tomatoes, stock and olives, and mix well. Season to taste with salt and pepper. Cover the casserole with a tight-fitting lid and place in the center of the preheated oven. Bake for 1½ hours.

4 Remove the casserole from the oven. Stir in the strips of pepper. Return the casserole to the oven and cook, uncovered, for 30 minutes more, or until the beef is tender.

Mixed Peppers and Salsa

Soft smoky broiled peppers make a lovely combination with the slightly tart salsa.

Serves 4

4 medium bell peppers in different colors
3 tablespoons chopped fresh Italian parsley
3 tablespoons chopped fresh dill
3 tablespoons chopped fresh mint
1 small red onion, finely chopped
1 tablespoon capers, coarsely chopped
¼ cup Greek olives, pitted and sliced
1 fresh green chili, seeded and finely chopped
4 tablespoons pistachios, chopped
5 tablespoons extra-virgin olive oil
3 tablespoons fresh lime juice
½ cup medium-fat feta cheese, crumbled
2 tablespoons finely chopped small gherkins

1 Preheat the broiler. Place the whole peppers on a tray and broil until charred and blistered.

2 Place the peppers in a plastic bag and let cool.

3 Peel, seed and cut the peppers into even strips.

4 To make the salsa, mix all the remaining ingredients together, and stir in the pepper strips.

Vegetable and Bean Curd Kebabs

A colorful mixture of vegetables and bean curd, skewered, glazed and broiled until tender.

Serves 4

1 yellow bell pepper
2 small zucchini
8 ounce piece of firm bean curd
8 cherry tomatoes
6 button mushrooms
1 tablespoon wholegrain mustard
1 tablespoon honey
2 tablespoons olive oil
salt and ground black pepper
cooked mixed rice and wild rice, to serve
lime wedges and Italian parsley, to garnish

1 Cut the pepper in half and remove the seeds. Cut each half into quarters and cut each quarter in half.

2 Cut the ends off the zucchini. Cut each zucchini into seven or eight chunks.

3 Cut the beans curd into 1½ -inch pieces.

4 Thread the pepper pieces, zucchini chunks, tofu, cherry tomatoes and mushrooms alternately on to four metal or bamboo skewers. (If you are using bamboo skewers, soak them in a bowl of cold water first. This will prevent them from charring during broiling.)

5 Whisk the mustard, honey and olive oil in a small bowl. Season to taste with salt and pepper.

6 Put the kebabs onto a baking sheet. Brush them with the mustard and honey glaze. Cook under the broiler for 8 minutes, turning once or twice during cooking. Serve with a mixture of long-grain and wild rice, and garnish with lime wedges and Italian parsley.

Soufflé Omelet

This delectable soufflé omelet is light and delicate enough to melt in the mouth.

Serves 1

2 eggs, separated
2 tablespoons cold water
1 tablespoon chopped
  fresh cilantro
½ tablespoon olive oil

2 tablespoons mango
  chutney
¼ cup grated Jarlsberg
  cheese
salt and ground black
  pepper

1 Beat the egg yolks together with the cold water, cilantro and salt and pepper.

2 Whisk the egg whites until stiff peaks form and gently fold into the egg yolk mixture.

3 Heat the oil in a frying pan, pour in the egg mixture and reduce the heat. Do not stir. Cook until the omelet becomes puffy and golden brown underneath (carefully lift one edge with a spatula to check).

4 Spoon on the chutney and sprinkle on the Jarlsberg. Fold over and slide onto a warm plate. Eat immediately. (If preferred, before adding the chutney and cheese, place the pan under a hot broiler to set the top.)

Cook's Tip
A light hand is essential to the success of this dish. Do not overmix the egg whites into the egg yolks or the mixture will be heavy.

Bubble-and-Squeak

This London breakfast dish was originally made on Mondays with leftover vegetables from the Sunday lunch.

Serves 4

3 cups mashed potato
4 cups shredded cooked
  cabbage or kale
1 egg, beaten
1 cup grated Cheddar
  cheese
pinch of freshly grated
  nutmeg

salt and ground black
  pepper
all-purpose flour, for
  coating
oil, for frying

1 Mix the potatoes with the cabbage or kale, egg, cheese, nutmeg and seasoning. Divide and shape into eight patties.

2 Chill in the fridge for an hour or so, if possible, as this allows the mixture to become firm and makes it easier to fry. Toss the patties in the flour. Heat about ½ inch oil in a frying pan until it is quite hot.

3 Carefully slide the patties into the oil and fry on each side for about 3 minutes until golden and crisp. Drain on paper towels and serve hot and crisp.

Eggplant and Red Pepper Pâté

This simple pâté of baked eggplant, pink peppercorns and red bell peppers, has more than a hint of garlic.

Serves 4
3 eggplant
2 fresh large red bell
*   peppers*
5 garlic cloves,
*   unpeeled*

1½ teaspoons pink
*   peppercorns in brine,*
*   drained and crushed*
2 tablespoons chopped
*   fresh cilantro*

1 Preheat the oven to 400°F. Arrange the whole eggplant, peppers and garlic cloves on a baking sheet and place in the oven. After 10 minutes remove the garlic cloves and turn over the eggplant and peppers.

2 Peel the garlic cloves and place in the bowl of a blender or food processor.

3 After another 20 minutes remove the blistered and charred peppers from the oven and place in a plastic bag. Leave to cool.

4 After another 10 minutes take out the eggplant. Split in half and scoop the flesh into a strainer placed over a bowl. Press the flesh with a spoon to remove the bitter juices.

5 Add the mixture to the garlic and process until smooth. Place in a large mixing bowl.

6 Peel and chop the red peppers and stir into the eggplant mixture. Mix in the pink peppercorns and chopped fresh cilantro and serve at once.

Cook's Tip
Serve the pâté with Melba toast, if you like. Simply grill some slices of crustless white bread on both sides, being careful to remove any loose crumbs, then slice the crispy golden toasts horizontally.

Red Pepper Watercress Parcels

The peppery watercress flavor combines well with sweet red pepper in these crisp little phyllo pastry parcels.

Makes 8
3 red peppers
6 ounces watercress
1 cup ricotta cheese
¼ cup toasted, chopped
*   almonds*

8 sheets phyllo pastry,
*   thawed if frozen*
2 tablespoons olive oil
salt and ground black
*   pepper*

1 Preheat the oven to 375°F. Place the peppers under a hot broiler until blistered and charred. Place in a plastic bag. When cool enough to handle, peel, seed and pat dry on paper towels.

2 Place the peppers and watercress in a food processor and pulse until coarsely chopped. Spoon into a bowl.

3 Mix in the ricotta and almonds, and season to taste with salt and pepper.

4 Working with one sheet of phyllo pastry at a time, cut out two 7-inch and two 2-inch squares from each sheet. Brush one large square with a little olive oil and place a second large square at an angle of 45 degrees to form a star shape.

5 Place one of the small squares in the center of the star shape, brush lightly with olive oil and top with a second small square.

6 Top with one-eighth of the red pepper mixture. Bring the edges together to form a purse shape and twist to seal. Place on a lightly greased baking sheet and cook for 25–30 minutes until golden. Serve immediately.

Nutty Cheese Balls

An extremely quick and simple recipe. Try making a small version to serve as canapés at a cocktail party.

Serves 4

*1 cup low-fat soft cheese
    such as Quark*
½ cup dolcelatte cheese
*1 tablespoon finely
    chopped onion*
*1 tablespoon finely
    chopped celery*
*1 tablespoon finely
    chopped fresh parsley*
*1 tablespoon finely
    chopped gherkin*

*1 teaspoon brandy or
    port (optional)*
pinch of paprika
*½ cup walnuts, coarsely
    chopped*
*6 tablespoons chopped
    fresh chives*
*salt and ground black
    pepper*

1 Beat the soft cheese and dolcelatte together using a spoon, until quite smooth.

2 Mix in all the remaining ingredients, except the chopped chives, stirring well to combine.

3 Divide the mixture into 12 pieces and roll into balls.

4 Roll each ball gently in the chopped chives. Leave to chill in the fridge for about an hour before serving.

Cook's Tip
For an alternative look, mix the chives with the rest of the ingredients but omit the walnuts. Instead, chop the walnuts finely and use to roll on to the cheese balls.

Fried Tomatoes with Polenta Crust

This recipe works well with green tomatoes freshy picked from the garden or greenhouse.

Serves 4

*4 large firm under-ripe
    tomatoes*
*1 cup polenta or coarse
    cornmeal*
*1 teaspoon dried oregano
    or marjoram*
½ teaspoon garlic powder

*all-purpose flour, for
    dredging*
*1 egg, beaten with
    seasoning*
oil, for deep-frying
green salad, to serve

1 Cut the tomatoes into thick slices. Mix the polenta or cornmeal with the oregano or marjoram and garlic powder.

2 Put the flour, egg and polenta into different bowls. Dip the tomato slices into the flour, then into the egg and finally into the polenta or cornmeal.

3 Fill a shallow frying pan one-third full of oil and heat steadily until quite hot.

4 Slip the tomato slices into the oil carefully, a few at a time, and fry on each side until crisp. Remove and drain. Repeat with the remaining tomatoes, reheating the oil in between each batch. Serve with salad.

Bean Purée with Grilled Vegetables

The slightly bitter radicchio and chicory make a wonderful marriage with the creamy citrus bean purée.

Serves 4
14-ounce can navy beans
3 tablespoons plain
   yogurt
finely grated rind and
   juice of 1 large orange
1 tablespoon finely
   chopped fresh
   rosemary

4 heads of chicory
2 radicchio
1 tablespoon walnut oil

1 Drain the beans, rinse, and drain again. Purée the beans in a food processor or blender with the yogurt, half the orange rind, orange juice and rosemary. Set aside.

2 Cut the heads of chicory in half lengthwise.

3 Cut each radicchio into eight wedges.

4 Lay out the chicory and radicchio on a baking sheet and brush with walnut oil. Broil for 2–3 minutes. Serve with the purée and scatter over the remaining orange rind.

Cook's Tip
Substitute different beans for the navy beans, if you like. Try white, mung or lima beans instead.

Broccoli and Chestnut Terrine

Served hot or cold, this versatile terrine is just as suitable for a dinner party as for a picnic.

Serves 4–6
4 cups broccoli florets
2 cups cooked chestnuts,
   coarsely chopped
1 cup fresh whole wheat
   bread crumbs
4 tablespoons low-fat
   plain yogurt

2 tablespoons finely
   grated Parmesan
   cheese
2 eggs, beaten
salt, freshly grated
   nutmeg and ground
   black pepper

1 Preheat the oven to 350°F. Bottom-line a 2-pound loaf pan with nonstick baking parchment.

2 Blanch or steam the broccoli for 3–4 minutes until just tender. Drain well. Reserve a quarter of the smallest florets and chop the rest finely.

3 Mix together the chestnuts, bread crumbs, yogurt and Parmesan, and season to taste with salt and pepper.

4 Fold in the chopped broccoli, reserved florets and the beaten eggs.

5 Spoon the broccoli mixture into the prepared pan.

6 Place in a roasting pan and pour in boiling water to come halfway up the sides of the loaf pan. Bake for 20–25 minutes. Remove from the oven and turn out onto a plate or tray. Serve cut into even slices.

Cook's Tip
If you do not have a nonstick loaf pan, grease it lightly with olive or sunflower oil after bottom-lining.

Baked Squash with Parmesan

Spaghetti squash is an unusual vegetable – when baked, the flesh separates into long strands.

Serves 2

1 spaghetti squash
½ cup butter
3 tablespoons mixed
* chopped fresh herbs*
* such as parsley, chives*
* and oregano*
1 garlic clove, crushed

1 shallot, chopped
1 teaspoons lemon juice
scant ¾ cup freshly
* grated Parmesan*
* cheese*
salt and ground black
* pepper*

1 Preheat the oven to 350°F. Cut the squash in half lengthwise. Place the halves, cut-side down, in a roasting pan. Pour a little water around them, then bake for about 40 minutes, until tender.

2 Meanwhile, put the butter, herbs, garlic, shallot and lemon juice in a food processor or blender and process until thoroughly blended and creamy in consistency. Season to taste with salt and pepper.

3 When the squash is tender, scrape out any seeds and cut a thin slice from the bottom of each half, so that they will sit level. Place the squash halves on warmed serving plates.

4 Using a fork, pull out a few of the spaghetti-like strands in the center of each. Add a dollop of herb butter, then sprinkle with a little of the grated Parmesan. Serve the remaining herb butter and Parmesan separately, adding them as you pull out more strands.

Asparagus Rolls with Herb Sauce

Tender asparagus spears wrapped in crisp phyllo pastry, served with a buttery herb sauce, tastes sensational.

Serves 2

4 tablespoons butter
5 sheets phyllo pastry
10 asparagus spears

For the sauce
2 shallots, finely chopped
1 bay leaf
⅔ cup dry white wine

¾ cup butter, softened
1 tablespoon chopped
* fresh herbs*
salt and ground black
* pepper*
chopped fresh chives, to
* garnish*

1 Preheat the oven to 400°F. Melt the butter. Cut the phyllo pastry sheets in half. Brush a half sheet with melted butter. Fold one corner of the sheet down to the bottom edge to give a wedge shape.

2 Trim the asparagus, then lay a spear on top at the longest pastry edge and roll up towards the shortest edge. Make nine more rolls in the same way.

3 Lay the rolls on a greased baking sheet. Brush with the remaining melted butter. Bake in the preheated oven for about 8 minutes until golden.

4 Meanwhile, put the shallots, bay leaf and wine into a saucepan. Cover with a tight-fitting lid and cook over a high heat until the wine is reduced to 3–4 tablespoons.

5 Strain the wine mixture into a bowl. Whisk in the butter, a little at a time, until the sauce is smooth and glossy.

6 Stir in the herbs and season to taste with salt and pepper. Return to the pan and keep the sauce warm. Serve the rolls on individual plates with a salad garnish, if liked. Serve the butter sauce separately, sprinkled with a few chopped chives.

Multi-mushroom Stroganoff

A pan-fry of sliced mushrooms swirled with sour cream makes a delicious accompaniment to pasta or rice.

Serves 3–4

3 tablespoons olive oil
1 pound fresh mixed wild and cultivated mushrooms such as ceps, shiitakes or oysters, sliced
3 scallions, sliced
2 garlic cloves, crushed
2 tablespoons dry sherry or vermouth

1¼ cups sour cream or crème fraîche
1 tablespoon chopped fresh marjoram or thyme leaves
chopped fresh parsley, to garnish
rice, pasta or boiled new potatoes, to serve

1 Heat the oil in a large frying pan and fry the mushrooms gently, stirring them from time to time until they are softened and just cooked.

2 Add the scallions, garlic and sherry or vermouth and cook for 1 minute more. Season well with salt and pepper.

3 Stir in the sour cream or crème fraîche and heat to just below boiling. Stir in the marjoram or thyme, then scatter over the parsley. Serve with rice, pasta or boiled new potatoes.

Cook's Tip
To create the most interesting flavor in this dish, use at least three different varieties of mushrooms, preferably incorporating some woodland or wild mushrooms.

Ratatouille with Cheese Croûtons

Crunchy croûtons and creamy Camembert provide a tasty topping on hot, bought or home-made ratatouille.

Serves 2

3 thick slices white bread
8 ounces firm Camembert cheese
4 tablespoons olive oil

1 garlic clove, chopped
14-ounce can ratatouille
fresh parsley sprigs, to garnish

1 Trim the crusts from the bread slices and discard. Cut the bread into 1-inch squares. Cut the Camembert cheese into 1-inch cubes.

2 Heat 3 tablespoons of the oil in a frying pan and cook the bread over a high heat for 5 minutes, stirring constantly, until golden all over. Reduce the heat, add the garlic and cook for 1 minute more. Remove the croûtons with a slotted spoon.

3 Pour the ratatouille into a saucepan and place over a moderate heat, stirring occasionally, until hot.

4 Heat the remaining oil in the frying pan. Add the cheese cubes and sear over a high heat for 1 minute. Divide the hot ratatouille between two serving bowls, spoon the croûtons and cheese on top, garnish with parsley and serve at once.

Bean Curd and Crunchy Vegetables

High protein bean curd is nicest if marinated lightly before it is cooked. If you use the smoked bean curd, it's even tastier.

Serves 4

2 – 8 ounces packages
  smoked bean curd,
  diced
3 tablespoons soy sauce
2 tablespoons dry sherry
  or vermouth
1 tablespoon sesame oil
3 tablespoons peanut or
  sunflower oil
2 leeks, thinly sliced
2 carrots, cut into sticks

1 large zucchini, thinly
  sliced
4 ounces baby corn,
  halved
4 ounces button or
  shiitake mushrooms,
  sliced
1 tablespoon sesame
  seeds
1 packet egg noodles,
  cooked

1 Marinate the bean curd in the soy sauce, sherry or vermouth and sesame oil for at least 30 minutes. Drain and reserve the marinade for later.

2 Heat the peanut or sunflower oil in a wok and stir-fry the bean curd cubes until browned all over. Remove and reserve.

3 Stir-fry the leeks, carrots, zucchini and baby corn, stirring and tossing for about 2 minutes. Add the mushrooms and cook for another 1 minute.

4 Return the bean curd to the wok and pour in the marinade. Heat until bubbling, then scatter over the sesame seeds.

5 Serve as soon as possible with the hot cooked noodles, dressed in a little sesame oil, if you wish.

Cook's Tip
The actual cooking of this dish takes just a few minutes, so have all the ingredients prepared before you start.

Sprouting Beans and Pak Choi

Supermarkets are becoming more cosmopolitan and many stock fresh ethnic vegetables.

Serves 4

3 tablespoons peranut oil
3 scallions, sliced
2 garlic cloves, cut into
  slivers
1-inch piece fresh ginger,
  cut into slivers
1 carrot, cut into thick
  sticks
scant 1 cup sprouting
  beans (lentils, mung
  beans, chick-peas)
7 ounces pak choi
  cabbage, shredded
½ cup unsalted cashew
  nuts or halved
  almonds

For the sauce
3 tablespoons light soy
  sauce
2 tablespoons dry sherry
1 tablespoon sesame oil
⅔ cup cold water
1 teaspoon cornflour
1 teaspoon honey
salt and ground black
  pepper

1 Heat the peanut oil in a large wok and stir-fry the onions, garlic, ginger and carrot for 2 minutes. Add the sprouting beans and fry for another 2 minutes, stirring and tossing all the ingredients together.

2 Add the pak choi and cashew nuts or almonds and stir-fry until the cabbage leaves are just wilting. Quickly mix all the sauce ingredients together in a bowl and pour them, stirring all the time, into the wok.

3 The vegetables will be coated in a thin glossy sauce. Season with salt and pepper and serve as soon as possible.

Cook's Tip
If you cannot find pak choi, use Chinese cabbage instead and prepare and cook in the same way.

Tomato Omelet Envelopes

These delicious chive omelets are folded and filled with tomato and melting Camembert cheese.

Serves 2

1 small onion
4 tomatoes
2 tablespoons oil
4 eggs
2 tablespoons chopped fresh chives

4 ounces Camembert cheese, rind removed and diced
salt and ground black pepper

1 Cut the onion in half. Cut each half into thin wedges. Cut the tomatoes into wedges of similar size.

2 Heat 1 tablespoon of the oil in a frying pan and cook the onion for 2 minutes over a moderate heat, then raise the heat and add the tomatoes. Cook for another 2 minutes, then remove the pan from the heat.

3 Beat the eggs with the chives in a bowl. Season to taste with salt and pepper. Heat the remaining oil in an omelet pan. Add half the egg mixture and tilt the pan to spread thinly. Cook for 1 minute.

4 Flip the omelet over and cook for 1 minute more. Remove from the pan and keep hot. Make a second omelette with the remaining egg mixture.

5 Return the tomato mixture to a high heat. Add the cheese and toss the mixture over the heat for 1 minute.

6 Divide the mixture between the omelets and fold them over. Serve immediately. Add crisp lettuce leaves and chunks of whole wheat bread, if you wish.

Cook's Tip
Add a few sliced mushrooms to the filling, if you wish, or use them in place of the tomatoes for a change.

Curried Eggs

Hard-boiled eggs are served on a mild creamy sauce base with just a hint of curry.

Serves 2

4 eggs
1 tablespoon sunflower oil
1 small onion, chopped
1-inch piece of fresh root ginger, peeled and grated
½ teaspoon ground cumin
½ teaspoon garam masala
1½ tablespoons tomato paste

2 teaspoons tandoori paste
2 teaspoons freshly squeezed lemon juice
¼ cup light cream
1 tablespoon finely chopped fresh cilantro
salt and ground black pepper
fresh cilantro sprigs, to garnish

1 Put the eggs in a saucepan of water. Bring to a boil, lower the heat and simmer for 10 minutes.

2 Meanwhile, heat the oil in a frying pan and cook the onion for 2–3 minutes. Add the fresh ginger and cook for another 1 minute.

3 Stir in the ground cumin, garam masala, tomato paste, tandoori paste, lemon juice and cream. Cook for 1–2 minutes more, then stir in the cilantro. Season with salt and pepper.

4 Drain the eggs, remove the shells and cut each egg in half. Spoon the sauce into a serving bowl, top with the eggs and garnish with fresh cilantro. Serve immediately.

Cook's Tip
If you store your eggs in the fridge, make sure you allow them to come to room temperature before you boil them. This way, they are less likely to crack.

Potatoes with Blue Cheese

We are so used to eating potatoes as a side dish, we tend to forget they can make a good main meal too, as here.

Serves 4

*1 pound small new
   potatoes
small head of celery,
   sliced
small red onion, thinly
   sliced
4 ounces blue cheese,
   mashed*

*⅔ cup light cream
salt and ground black
   pepper
scant 1 cup walnut
   pieces
2 tablespoons chopped
   fresh parsley*

1 Cover the potatoes with water and then boil for about 15 minutes, adding the sliced celery and onion to the pan for the last 5 minutes or so.

2 Drain the vegetables and put them into a shallow serving dish, making sure they are evenly distributed.

3 In a small saucepan slowly melt the cheese in the cream, stirring occasionally. Do not allow the mixture to boil.

4 Season the sauce to taste. Pour it over the vegetables and scatter the walnuts and parsley over the top. Serve hot.

Cook's Tip
*Choose any blue cheese you like, such as Stilton,
Danish blue, blue vinney or blue brie.*

Greek Spinach and Cheese Pies

These individual spinach, feta and Parmesan cheese pies are easy to make using ready-made phyllo pastry.

Makes 4

*1 tablespoon olive oil
1 small onion, finely
   chopped
2½ cups fresh spinach,
   stalks removed
4 tablespoons butter,
   melted
4 sheets phyllo pastry
1 egg*

*large pinch of freshly
   grated nutmeg
¾ cup crumbled feta
   cheese
1 tablespoon grated
   Parmesan cheese
salt and ground black
   pepper*

1 Preheat the oven to 375°F. Fry the onion in the oil for 5–6 minutes, until softened. Add the spinach leaves and cook, stirring, until the spinach has wilted and some of the liquid evaporated. Allow to cool.

2 Brush four 4-inch diameter loose-bottom tartlet pans with melted butter. Cut two sheets of phyllo into eight 4½-inch squares each. Cover the remaining sheets with a dish towel.

3 Brush four squares at a time with melted butter. Line the first tartlet pan with one square, gently easing it into the bottom and up the sides. Leave the edges overhanging. Lay the remaining squares on top of the first, turning them so the corners form a star shape. Repeat for the remaining pans.

4 Beat the egg with the nutmeg and seasoning, then stir in the cheeses and spinach. Divide the mixture between the pans and smooth level. Fold the overhanging edges over the filling.

5 Cut the third pastry sheet into eight 4-inch rounds. Brush with butter and place two on top of each tartlet. Press around the edges to seal. Brush the last pastry sheet with butter and cut into strips. Gently twist each strip and lay them on top of the tartlets. Bake for about 30–35 minutes, until golden. Serve hot or cold.

Chili Beans with Basmati Rice

Red kidney beans, chopped tomatoes and hot chili make a great combination in this colorful, flavorful dish.

Serves 4

2 cups basmati rice
2 tablespoons olive oil
1 large onion, chopped
1 garlic clove, crushed
1 tablespoon hot chili powder
1 tablespoon all-purpose flour
1 tablespoon tomato paste

14-ounce can chopped tomatoes
14-ounce can red kidney beans, drained
⅔ cup hot vegetable stock
chopped fresh parsley, to garnish
salt and ground black pepper

1 Wash the rice under cold running water. Drain well. Bring a large saucepan of water to a boil. Add the rice and cook for 10–12 minutes, until tender. Meanwhile, heat the oil in a frying pan and cook the chopped onion and garlic for about 2 minutes.

2 Stir the chili powder and flour into the onion and garlic mixture. Cook for 2 minutes more, stirring frequently.

3 Stir in the tomato paste and chopped tomatoes. Rinse and drain the kidney beans well and add to the pan with the hot vegetable stock. Cover and cook for a final 12 minutes, stirring from time to time.

4 Season the chili sauce to taste with salt and pepper. Drain the rice and serve immediately with the chili beans, garnished with a little chopped fresh parsley.

Cook's Tip
Serve the chili beans with a pasta of your choice or hot pitta bread, if you prefer.

Lentil Stir-fry

Mushrooms, artichoke hearts, sugar snap peas and green lentils make a satisfying stir-fry supper.

Serves 2–3

1 cup snow peas
2 tablespoons butter
1 small onion, chopped
4 ounces cup chestnut mushrooms, sliced
14-ounce can artichoke hearts, drained and halved

14-ounce can green lentils, drained
4 tablespoons light cream
¼ cup flaked almonds, toasted
salt and ground black pepper
French bread, to serve

1 Bring a saucepan of salted water to the boil, add the snow peas and cook for about 4 minutes until just tender. Drain, refresh under cold running water, then drain again. Pat the peas dry with paper towels and set aside.

2 Melt the butter in a frying pan and cook the chopped onion for 2–3 minutes, stirring occasionally.

3 Add the sliced mushrooms to the onions. Stir until well combined, then cook for 2–3 minutes until just tender. Add the artichoke hearts, snow peas and lentils to the pan. Stir-fry for 2 minutes.

4 Stir in the cream and almonds and cook for 1 minute. Season to taste with salt and pepper. Serve at once, with chunks of French bread.

Cook's Tip
Use dried green lentils if you prefer. Cook them according to the manufacturer's instructions first and then add them to the stir-fry with the artichokes and snow peas.

Arabian Spinach

Stir-fry spinach with onions and spices, then mix in a can of chick-peas and you have a quick, delicious main meal.

Serves 4

2 tablespoons olive or
  sunflower oil
1 onion, sliced
2 garlic cloves, crushed
3½ cups spinach, washed
  and shredded

1 teaspoon cumin seeds
15-ounce can chick-peas,
  drained
pat of butter
salt and ground black
  pepper

1 Heat the oil in a large frying pan or wok and fry the onion for about 5 minutes until softened. Add the garlic and cumin seeds, then fry for another minute.

2 Add the spinach, in stages, stirring until the leaves begin to wilt. Fresh spinach leaves condense dramatically when they are cooked and they will all fit into the pan.

3 Stir in the chick-peas and butter and season with salt and pepper. Reheat until just bubbling, then serve hot. Drain off any pan juices, if you wish, but this dish is rather good served with a little sauce.

Zucchini en Papillote

An impressive dinner party accompaniment, these puffed paper parcels should be broken open at the table.

Serves 4

2 zucchini
1 leek
8 ounces young
  asparagus, trimmed
4 tarragon sprigs

4 garlic cloves, unpeeled
1 egg, beaten
salt and ground black
  pepper

1 Preheat the oven to 400°F. Using a potato peeler, slice the zucchini lengthwise into thin strips.

2 Cut the leek into very fine julienne strips and cut the asparagus evenly into 2-inch lengths.

3 Cut out four sheets of baking parchment measuring about 12 x 15 inches and fold in half. Draw a large curve to make a heart shape when unfolded. Cut along the inside of the line and open out.

4 Divide the zucchini, asparagus and leek evenly between each paper heart, positioning the filling on one side of the fold line, and topping each with a sprig of fresh tarragon and an unpeeled garlic clove. Season to taste with salt and pepper.

5 Brush the edges lightly with the beaten egg and fold over.

6 Pleat the edges together so that each parcel is completely sealed. Lay the parcels on a baking sheet and cook for about 10 minutes. Serve immediately.

Cook's Tip
Experiment with other vegetables and herbs such as sugar snow and mint, or baby carrots and rosemary. The possibilities are endless.

Green Lentil and Cabbage Salad

This warm crunchy salad makes a satisfying meal if served with crusty French bread or whole wheat rolls.

Serves 4–6
1 cup Puy lentils
6 cups cold water
1 garlic clove
1 bay leaf
1 small onion, peeled and studded with 2 cloves
1 tablespoon olive oil
1 red onion, finely sliced
2 garlic cloves, crushed

1 tablespoon thyme leaves
6 cups finely shredded cabbage
finely grated rind and juice of 1 lemon
1 tablespoon raspberry vinegar
salt and ground black pepper

1 Rinse the lentils in cold water and place in a large saucepan with the water, garlic clove, bay leaf and clove-studded onion. Bring to a boil and cook for about 10 minutes. Reduce the heat, cover the pan with a tight-fitting lid and simmer gently for 15–20 minutes. Drain and remove the onion, garlic and bay leaf.

2 Heat the oil in a large pan and cook the red onion, crushed garlic and thyme for 5 minutes until softened.

3 Add the shredded cabbage and cook for 3–5 minutes until just cooked but still crunchy.

4 Stir in the cooked lentils, grated lemon rind and juice and the raspberry vinegar. Season with salt and pepper and serve.

Cook's Tip
Vary the type of cabbage you use in this recipe, if you like. Choose a white cabbage or a Savoy, or try fresh spring greens instead.

Tomato and Basil Tart

You could make individual tartlets instead of one large tart if you prefer, but reduce the baking time slightly.

Serves 6–8
1½ cups flour
½ teaspoon salt
½ cup butter or margarine, chilled
3–5 tablespoons water

For the filling
6 ounces mozzarella cheese, thinly sliced
12 fresh basil leaves, 6 coarsely torn

4–5 tomatoes, cut into ¼-inch slices
salt and ground black pepper
4 tablespoons freshly grated Parmesan cheese
2 tablespoons extra-virgin olive oil

1 Place the flour and salt in a bowl, then rub in the butter until the mixture resembles bread crumbs. Add 3 tablespoons water and combine with a fork until the dough holds together. Mix in more water if needed. Gather the dough into a ball, wrap in wax paper and chill for 40 minutes. Preheat the oven to 375°F.

2 Roll out the pastry to a thickness of ¼ inch and use to line an 11-inch fluted loose-bottom quiche pan. Prick the base and chill for 20 minutes in the fridge.

3 Line the pastry with a sheet of baking parchment. Fill with dried beans. Place the quiche pan on a baking sheet; bake blind for 15 minutes. Remove from the oven. Leave the oven on.

4 Remove the beans and paper. Brush the pastry with oil. Line with the mozzarella. Sprinkle the torn basil over the top.

5 Arrange the tomato slices over the cheese. Dot with the whole basil leaves. Season with salt and pepper, Parmesan and oil. Bake for 35 minutes. If the cheese oozes a lot of liquid during baking, tilt the pan and spoon it off to keep the pastry crisp. Serve hot or at room temperature.

Spinach and Potato Galette

Creamy layers of potato, spinach and fresh herbs make a warming and filling supper dish.

Serves 6

2 pounds large potatoes
4 cups fresh spinach
1¾ cups low-fat cream
   cheese
1 tablespoon grainy
   mustard
2 eggs

2 ounces mixed chopped
   fresh herbs such as
   chives, parsley, chervil
   or sorrel
salt and ground black
   pepper

1 Preheat the oven to 350°F. Base-line a deep 9-inch round cake pan with nonstick baking parchment. Place the potatoes in a large saucepan and cover with cold water. Bring to a boil and cook for 10 minutes. Drain well and allow to cool slightly before slicing thinly.

2 Wash the spinach and place in a large pan with only the water that is clinging to the leaves. Cover and cook, stirring once, until the spinach has just wilted. Drain well in a strainer and squeeze out the excess moisture with the back of a spoon. Chop the spinach finely.

3 Beat together the cream cheese, mustard and eggs, then stir in the chopped spinach and fresh herbs.

4 Place a layer of the sliced potatoes in the lined tin, arranging them in concentric circles. Top with a spoonful of the cream cheese mixture and spread out. Continue layering, seasoning with salt and pepper as you go, until all the potatoes and the cream cheese mixture are used up.

5 Cover the pan with a piece of foil, scrunched around the edge, and place in a roasting pan.

6 Half-fill the roasting pan with boiling water and cook the galette in the oven for 45–50 minutes. Turn out onto a plate and serve hot or cold.

Cowboy Hot-pot

A great dish to serve as a children's main meal, which adults will enjoy too – if they are allowed to join the posse.

Serves 4–6

3 tablespoons sunflower
   oil
1 onion, sliced
1 red bell pepper, sliced
1 sweet potato or
   2 carrots, chopped
scant ½ cup chopped
   green beans
14-ounce can baked
   beans
7-ounce can corn
1 tablespoon tomato
   paste

1 teaspoon barbecue spice
   seasoning
4 ounces cheese
   (preferably smoked),
   diced
1 pound potatoes, thinly
   sliced
2 tablespoons butter,
   melted
salt and ground black
   pepper

1 Preheat the oven to 375°F. Heat the oil in a frying pan and gently fry the onion, pepper and sweet potato or carrots until softened but not browned. Transfer to a flameproof casserole.

2 Add the green beans, baked beans, corn (and liquid), tomato paste and barbecue spice seasoning. Bring to a boil, then simmer for 5 minutes.

3 Cover the vegetable and cheese mixture with the sliced potato, brush with butter, season with salt and pepper and bake for 30–40 minutes until golden brown on top and the potato is cooked.

Cook's Tip
Use any vegetable mixture you like in this versatile hot-pot, according to what you have available.

Bean Curd with Ginger Chili

Bean curd easily absorbs different flavors and retains a good firm texture, making it ideal for stir-frying.

Serves 4

8-ounce packet bean
  curd, diced
3 tablespoons dark soy
  sauce
2 tablespoons dry sherry
  or vermouth
2 teaspoons honey
⅔ cup vegetable stock
2 teaspoons cornstarch

3 tablespoons sunflower
  or peanut oil
3 leeks, thinly sliced
1 red chili, seeded and
  sliced
1 inch piece fresh ginger,
  peeled and shredded
salt and ground black
  pepper

1 Toss the bean curd in the soy sauce and sherry or vermouth until well coated and allow to marinate for about 30 minutes.

2 Strain the bean curd from the marinade and reserve the juices in a bowl. Mix the marinade with the honey, vegetable stock and cornstarch to make a paste.

3 Heat the oil in a wok or large frying pan and when hot, stir-fry the bean curd until it is crisp on the outside. Remove the bean curd and set aside.

4 Reheat the oil and stir-fry the leeks, chili and ginger for about 2 minutes until they are just soft. Season to taste with salt and pepper.

5 Return the bean curd to the pan, together with the marinade, and stir well until the liquid is thick and glossy. Serve hot with rice or egg noodles.

Cook's Tip
Bean curd tastes bland, allowing it to absorb the flavor of marinades and ingredients with which it is cooked.

Chinese Potatoes with Chili Beans

This oriental-inspired dish gains particular appeal by way of its tasty sauce.

Serves 4

4 potatoes, cut into thick
  chunks
3 scallions, sliced
1 large fresh chili, seeded
  and sliced
2 tablespoons sunflower
  or groundnut oil
2 garlic cloves, crushed
14-ounce can red kidney
  beans

2 tablespoons dark soy
  sauce
1 tablespoon sesame oil
salt and ground black
  pepper
1 tablespoon sesame
  seeds, to sprinkle
chopped fresh cilantro or
  parsley, to garnish

1 Boil the potatoes until they are just tender. Take care not to overcook them. Drain and reserve.

2 In a large frying pan or wok, stir-fry the scallions and chili in the oil for about 1 minute, then add the garlic and fry for a few seconds longer.

3 Rinse and drain the kidney beans then add them to the pan with the potatoes, stirring well. Finally add the soy sauce and sesame oil.

4 Season to taste with salt and pepper and cook the vegetables until they are well heated through. Sprinkle with the sesame seeds and the chopped fresh cilantro or parsley.

Corn and Bean Tamale Pie

This is a hearty dish with a polenta and cheese topping which covers corn and kidney beans in a rich hot sauce.

Serves 4

2 corn on the cob
2 tablespoons oil
1 onion, chopped
2 garlic cloves, crushed
1 red bell pepper, seeded and chopped
2 green chilies, seeded and chopped
2 tablespoons ground cumin
1 pound ripe tomatoes, peeled, seeded and chopped
1 tablespoon tomato paste
15-ounce can red kidney beans, drained and rinsed

1 tablespoon chopped fresh oregano
oregano leaves, to garnish

For the topping
1 cup polenta
1 tablespoon all-purpose flour
½ teaspoon salt
2 teaspoons baking powder
1 egg, lightly beaten
½ cup milk
1 tablespoon butter, melted
½ cup grated smoked Cheddar cheese

1 Preheat the oven to 425°F. Husk the corn on the cob, then parboil for 8 minutes. Drain, let cool slightly, then remove the kernels with a sharp knife.

2 Fry the onion, garlic and pepper in the oil for 5 minutes, until softened. Add the chilies and cumin; fry for 1 minute. Stir in the tomatoes, tomato paste, beans, corn kernels and oregano. Season to taste. Simmer, uncovered, for 10 minutes.

3 To make the topping, mix the polenta, flour, salt, baking powder, egg, milk and butter to form a thick batter.

4 Transfer the bean mixture to an baking dish, spoon the polenta mixture over and spread evenly. Bake for 30 minutes. Remove from the oven, sprinkle the cheese over the top, then bake for another 5–10 minutes, until golden.

Pepper and Potato Tortilla

Traditionally a Spanish dish, tortilla is best eaten cold in chunky wedges and makes an ideal picnic food.

Serves 4

2 potatoes
3 tablespoons olive oil
1 large onion, thinly sliced
2 garlic cloves, crushed
1 green bell pepper, thinly sliced
1 red bell pepper, thinly sliced

6 eggs, beaten
1 cup grated mature Cheddar cheese
salt and ground black pepper

1 Do not peel the potatoes, but wash them well. Parboil them for about 10 minutes, then drain and, when they are cool enough to handle, slice them thickly. Switch on the broiler so that it warms up while you prepare the rest of the dish.

2 In a large nonstick or well seasoned frying pan, heat the oil and fry the onion, garlic and pepper over a moderate heat for 5 minutes until softened.

3 Add the potatoes and continue frying, stirring from time to time until the potatoes are completely cooked and the vegetables are soft. Add a little extra oil if the pan seems rather too dry.

4 Pour in half the beaten eggs, then sprinkle over half the grated Cheddar cheese, then the rest of the egg. Season with salt and pepper and finish with a layer of cheese.

5 Continue to cook over a low heat, without stirring, half covering the pan with a lid to help set the eggs.

6 When the mixture is firm, flash the pan under the hot broiler to seal the top just lightly. Leave the tortilla in the pan to cool. This helps it firm up further and makes it easier to turn out. Cut into generous wedges to serve.

Chick-pea Stew

This hearty chick-pea and vegetable stew is delicious served with garlic-flavored mashed potato.

Serves 4

2 tablespoons olive oil
1 small onion, finely chopped
8 ounces carrots, halved lengthwise and thinly sliced
½ teaspoon ground cumin
1 teaspoon ground coriander
2 tablespoons all-purpose flour

8 ounces zucchini, sliced
7-ounce can corn, drained
14-ounce can chick-peas, drained
2 tablespoons tomato paste
scant 1 cup hot vegetable stock
salt and ground black pepper
mashed potato, to serve

1 Heat the oil in a frying pan. Add the onion and carrots. Toss the vegetables to coat them in the oil, then cook over a moderate heat for 4 minutes.

2 Add the ground cumin, coriander and flour. Stir and cook for 1 minute more.

3 Cut the zucchini slices in half. Add them to the pan with the corn, chick-peas, tomato paste and vegetable stock. Stir well. Cook for 10 minutes, stirring frequently.

4 Taste the stew and season to taste with salt and pepper. Serve immediately with mashed potato.

Cook's Tip
To make garlic-flavored mashed potato, peel and crush a garlic clove, fry it lightly in butter, then stir into the mashed potato until well combined.

Potato and Broccoli Stir-fry

This wonderful stir-fry combines potato, broccoli and red pepper with just a hint of fresh ginger.

Serves 2

1 pound potatoes
3 tablespoons peanut oil
4 tablespoons butter
1 small onion, chopped
1 red pepper, seeded and chopped

8 ounces broccoli, broken into florets
1-inch piece fresh ginger, peeled and grated
salt and ground black pepper

1 Peel the potatoes and dice them into ½-inch pieces.

2 Heat the oil in a large frying pan and cook the potatoes for 8 minutes over a high heat, stirring and tossing occasionally, until browned and just tender.

3 Drain off the oil. Add the butter to the potatoes in the pan. As soon as it melts, add the chopped onion and red pepper. Stir-fry for 2 minutes.

4 Add the broccoli florets and ginger to the pan. Stir-fry for 2–3 minutes more, taking care not to break up the potatoes. Season to taste with salt and pepper and serve at once.

144

Vegetables with Lentil Bolognese

Instead of a cheese sauce, it makes a pleasant change to top lightly steamed vegetables with a delicious lentil sauce.

Serves 6

1 small cauliflower
  broken into florets
2 cups broccoli florets
2 leeks, thickly sliced
8 ounces Brussels
  sprouts, halved if large

For the lentil
Bolognese sauce

1 onion, chopped
2 garlic cloves, crushed
2 carrots, coarsely grated
2 celery stalks, chopped

3 tablespoons olive oil
½ cup red lentils
14-ounce can chopped
  tomatoes
2 tablespoons tomato
  paste
2 cups vegetable stock
1 tablespoon fresh
  marjoram, chopped,
  or 1 teaspoon dried
  marjoram
salt and ground black
  pepper

1 First make the sauce in a large saucepan, gently fry the onion, garlic, carrots and celery in the oil for about 5 minutes, until they are soft. Add the lentils, tomatoes, tomato paste, stock, marjoram and seasoning. Bring the mixture to a boil, then partially cover with a lid and simmer for 20 minutes until thick and soft.

2 Place all the vegetables in a steamer over a pan of boiling water and cook for 8–10 minutes until just tender.

3 Drain and place in a shallow serving dish. Spoon the sauce on top, stirring slightly to mix. Serve hot.

Black Bean and Vegetable Stir-fry

This colorful and very flavorful vegetable mixture is coated in a classic Chinese sauce.

Serves 4

8 scallions
8 ounces button
  mushrooms
1 red bell pepper
1 green bell pepper
2 large carrots
4 tablespoons sesame oil
2 garlic cloves, crushed

4 tablespoons black bean
  sauce
6 tablespoons warm
  water
scant 3 cups bean sprouts
salt and ground black
  pepper

1 Thinly slice the scallions and button mushrooms. Set aside in separate bowls.

2 Cut both the peppers in half, remove the seeds and slice the flesh into thin strips.

3 Cut the carrots in half. Cut each half into thin strips lengthwise. Stack the slices and cut through them to make very fine strips.

4 Heat the oil in a large wok or frying pan until very hot and stir-fry the scallions and garlic for 30 seconds.

5 Add the mushrooms, peppers and carrots. Stir-fry for another 5–6 minutes over a high heat until the vegetables are just beginning to soften.

6 Mix the black bean sauce with the water. Add to the wok or pan and cook for another 3–4 minutes. Stir in the bean sprouts and stir-fry for a final 1 minute until all the vegetables are coated in the sauce. Season to taste with salt and pepper. Serve immediately.

Tomato and Okra Stew

Okra is an unusual and delicious vegetable. It releases a sticky sap when cooked, which helps to thicken the stew.

Serves 4

1 tablespoon olive oil
1 onion, chopped
14-ounce can pimientos, drained
2 x 14-ounce cans chopped tomatoes
10 ounces okra
2 tablespoons chopped fresh parsley
salt and ground black pepper

1 Heat the oil in a saucepan and cook the chopped onion for about 2–3 minutes.

2 Coarsely chop the pimientos and add to the onion. Add the chopped tomatoes and mix well.

3 Cut the tops off the okra and cut into halves or quarters if large. Add to the tomato sauce in the pan. Season to taste with plenty of salt and pepper.

4 Bring the vegetable stew to a boil, then lower the heat, cover the pan with a tight-fitting lid and simmer for 12 minutes until the vegetables are tender and the sauce has thickened. Stir in the chopped parsley and serve immediately.

Cook's Tip
Okra is now available all year round. Do not buy them any longer than 3–4 inches and look for clean, dark green pods – a brown tinge indicates staleness. When preparing, if the ridges look tough or damaged, scrape them with a sharp knife.

Chunky Vegetable Paella

This Spanish rice dish is now enjoyed the world over. This version includes eggplant and chick-peas.

Serves 6

large pinch of saffron strands
1 eggplant, cut into thick chunks
6 tablespoons olive oil
1 large onion, thickly sliced
3 garlic cloves, crushed
1 yellow bell pepper, sliced
1 red bell pepper, sliced
2 teaspoons paprika
1¼ cups risotto rice
2½ cups stock
1 pound fresh tomatoes, skinned and chopped
4 ounces sliced mushrooms
scant ½ cup cut green beans
14-ounce can chick-peas

1 Steep the saffron in 3 tablespoons hot water. Sprinkle the eggplant with salt, let drain in a colander for 30 minutes, then rinse and dry.

2 In a large paella or frying pan, heat the oil and fry the onion, garlic, peppers and eggplant for about 5 minutes, stirring occasionally. Sprinkle in the paprika and stir again.

3 Mix in the rice, then pour in the stock, tomatoes, saffron and seasoning. Bring to a boil, then simmer the mixture for about 15 minutes, uncovered, shaking the pan frequently and stirring from time to time.

4 Stir in the mushrooms, green beans and chick-peas (with their liquid). Continue cooking for another 10 minutes, then serve hot, direct from the pan.

Onion and Gruyère Tart

The secret of this tart is to cook the onions very slowly until they almost caramelize.

Serves 4

1½ cups all-purpose flour
pinch of salt
6 tablespoons butter,
  diced
1 egg yolk

1 – 2 tablespoons
  wholegrain mustard
2 eggs, plus 1 egg yolk
1 cup heavy cream
generous ½ cup grated
  Gruyère cheese
pinch of freshly grated
  nutmeg
salt and ground black
  pepper

For the filling

4 tablespoons butter
1 pound onions, thinly
  sliced

1 To make the pastry, sift the flour and salt into a bowl. Add the butter and rub into the flour with your fingertips until the mixture resembles fine bread crumbs. Add the egg yolk and 1 tablespoon cold water and mix to a firm dough. Chill in the fridge for 30 minutes.

2 Preheat the oven to 400°F. Knead the pastry, then roll it out on a lightly floured work surface and use to line a 9-inch loose-bottomed tart pan. Prick the base all over with a fork, line the pastry case with greaseproof paper and fill with baking beans.

3 Bake the pastry case blind for 15 minutes. Remove the paper and beans and bake for another 10 – 15 minutes, until the pastry case is crisp. Meanwhile, melt the butter in a saucepan, add the onions, cover with a tight-fitting lid and cook for 20 minutes, stirring occasionally, until golden.

4 Reduce the oven temperature to 350°F. Spread the pastry case with mustard and top with the onions. Mix together the eggs, egg yolk, cream, cheese, nutmeg and seasoning. Pour over the onions. Bake for 30 – 35 minutes, until golden. Serve warm.

Potato and Spinach Gratin

Pine nuts add a satisfying crunch to this gratin of wafer-thin potato slices and spinach in a creamy cheese sauce.

Serves 2

1 pound potatoes
1 garlic clove, crushed
3 scallions, thinly sliced
⅔ cup light cream
1 cup milk
8 ounces frozen chopped
  spinach, thawed

1 cup grated mature
  Cheddar cheese
¼ cup pine nuts
salt and ground black
  pepper
lettuce and tomato salad,
  to serve

1 Peel the potatoes and cut them carefully into wafer-thin slices. Spread them out in a large, heavy-based, nonstick frying pan.

2 Scatter the crushed garlic and sliced scallions evenly over the potatoes.

3 Pour the cream and milk over the potatoes. Place the pan over a gentle heat, cover and cook for 8 minutes or until the potatoes are tender.

4 Using both hands, squeeze the spinach dry. Add the spinach to the potatoes, mixing lightly. Cover the pan with a tight-fitting lid and cook for 2 minutes more.

5 Season to taste with salt and pepper, then spoon the mixture into a gratin dish. Preheat the broiler.

6 Sprinkle the grated cheese and pine nuts over the spinach mixture. Lightly toast under the broiler for 2 – 3 minutes until the topping is golden. A simple lettuce and tomato salad makes an excellent accompaniment to this dish.

Stuffed Peppers

Sweet peppers can be stuffed and baked with a variety of fillings, from cooked vegetables to rice or pasta.

Serves 6

6 peppers, any color
generous 1 cup rice
4 tablespoons olive oil
1 large onion, chopped
3 anchovy fillets, chopped
2 garlic cloves, finely
   chopped
3 tomatoes, peeled and
   diced

4 tablespoons white wine
3 tablespoons finely
   chopped fresh parsley
scant ½ cup mozzarella
6 tablespoons freshly
   grated Parmesan
   cheese
salt and ground black
   pepper

1 Cut the tops off the peppers. Scoop out the seeds and the fibrous insides. Blanch the peppers and their tops in a large saucepan of boiling water for 3–4 minutes. Remove, and stand upside down on wire racks to drain.

2 Boil the rice according to the package instructions, but drain and rinse it in cold water 3 minutes before the recommended cooking time has elapsed. Drain again.

3 Sauté the onion in the oil until soft. Mash in the anchovies and garlic. Add the tomatoes and wine; cook for 5 minutes.

4 Preheat the oven to 375°F. Remove the tomato mixture from the heat. Stir in the rice, parsley, the mozzarella and 4 tablespoons of the Parmesan cheese. Season to taste with salt and pepper.

5 Pat the insides of the peppers dry with paper towels. Sprinkle with salt and pepper. Stuff the peppers. Sprinkle the tops with the remaining Parmesan and a little oil. Arrange the peppers in a shallow baking dish. Pour in enough water to come ½ inch up the sides of the peppers. Bake for 25 minutes. Serve immediately.

Broccoli and Ricotta Cannelloni

When piping the filling into the cannelloni tubes, hold them upright on the work surface.

Serves 4

12 dried cannelloni tubes,
   3 inches long
4 cups broccoli florets
1½ cups fresh bread
   crumbs
⅔ cup milk
4 tablespoons olive oil,
   plus extra for brushing
1 cup ricotta cheese
pinch of grated nutmeg
6 tablespoons freshly
   grated Parmesan or
   Pecorino cheese
salt and ground black
   pepper

2 tablespoons pine nuts,
   for sprinkling

For the tomato sauce
2 tablespoons olive oil
1 onion, finely chopped
1 garlic clove, crushed
2 x 14-ounce cans
   chopped tomatoes
1 tablespoon tomato paste
4 black olives, pitted and
   chopped
1 teaspoon dried thyme

1 Preheat the oven to 375°F and grease a casserole . Bring a saucepan of water to a boil, add a little olive oil and simmer the pasta, uncovered, until nearly cooked. Boil the broccoli until tender. Drain the pasta and rinse under cold water. Drain the broccoli, then process in a food processor or blender until smooth.

2 Mix together the bread crumbs, milk and oil. Add the ricotta, broccoli purée, nutmeg, 4 tablespoons Parmesan cheese and seasoning.

3 For the sauce, fry the onions and garlic in the oil for 5 minutes. Stir in the tomatoes, tomato paste, olives and thyme, and season. Boil for 2 minutes; pour in the dish.

4 Open the pasta tubes. Pipe in the filling using a ½-inch nozzle. Arrange in the dish. Brush with olive oil, then sprinkle over the remaining cheese and pine nuts. Bake for 30 minutes, or until golden on top.

Pasta with Spring Vegetables

If you are not fond of fennel, use a small onion instead. Prepare in the same way.

Serves 4

1 cup broccoli florets	*3 tablespoons mixed*
4 ounces baby leeks	*chopped fresh herbs,*
8 ounces asparagus	*such as parsley, thyme*
1 small fennel bulb	*and sage*
1 cup fresh or frozen peas	*12 ounces penne*
3 tablespoons butter	*salt and ground black*
1 shallot, chopped	*pepper*
1¼ cups heavy cream	*freshly grated Parmesan*
	cheese, to serve

1 Divide the broccoli florets into tiny sprigs. Cut the leeks and asparagus diagonally into 2-inch lengths. Trim the fennel bulb and remove any tough outer leaves. Cut into wedges, leaving the layers attached at the root ends so the pieces stay intact.

2 Cook each vegetable separately in boiling salted water until just tender – use the same water for each vegetable. Drain well and keep warm.

3 Melt the butter in a separate saucepan, and cook the chopped shallot, stirring occasionally, until softened but not browned. Stir in the herbs and cream and cook for a few minutes, until slightly thickened.

4 Meanwhile, cook the pasta in boiling salted water for 10 minutes or according to the instructions on the package. Drain well and add to the sauce with all the vegetables. Toss gently to combine and season to taste with plenty of pepper.

5 Serve the pasta hot, with plenty of freshly grated Parmesan cheese.

Pasta Carbonara

A classic Roman dish traditionally made with spaghetti, which is equally delicious with fresh egg tagliatelle.

Serves 4

12 ounces – 1 pound fresh	*5 tablespoons light cream*
tagliatelle	*salt and ground black*
1 tablespoon olive oil	*pepper*
8-ounce piece of ham,	*2 tablespoons finely*
bacon or pancetta, cut	*grated Parmesan*
into 1-inch sticks	*cheese*
4 ounces button	*fresh basil sprigs, to*
mushrooms, sliced	*garnish*
4 eggs, lightly beaten	

1 Cook the pasta in a pan of boiling salted water, with a little oil added, for 6–8 minutes or until *al dente*.

2 Meanwhile, heat the oil in a frying pan and fry the ham for 3–4 minutes, then add the mushrooms and fry for another 3–4 minutes. Turn off the heat and reserve. Lightly beat the eggs and cream together in a bowl and season well with salt and pepper.

3 When the pasta is cooked, drain it well and return to the pan. Add the ham, mushrooms and any pan juices and stir into the pasta.

4 Pour in the eggs, cream and half the Parmesan cheese. Stir well and as you do this the eggs will cook in the heat of the pasta. Pile on to warmed serving plates, sprinkle with the remaining Parmesan and garnish with basil.

Spinach and Hazelnut Lasagne

Use frozen spinach in this hearty and satisfying dish if you are short of time.

Serves 4

8 cups fresh spinach
1¼ cups vegetable stock
1 onion, finely chopped
1 garlic clove, crushed
¾ cup hazelnuts
2 tablespoons chopped
  fresh basil
6 sheets lasagne

14-ounce can chopped
  tomatoes
1 cup ricotta cheese
salt and ground black
  pepper
flaked hazelnuts and
  chopped fresh parsley

1 Preheat the oven to 400°F. Wash the spinach; cook with no extra water over a low or medium heat for 2 minutes until wilted. Drain well. Simmer the onion and garlic in 2 tablespoons of the stock until soft. Stir in the spinach, hazelnuts and basil.

2 In a large baking dish, layer the spinach, lasagne and tomatoes; season as you go. Pour in the remaining stock. Spread the ricotta over the top. Bake for 45 minutes. Serve hot, sprinkled with hazelnuts and chopped parsley.

Tagliatelle with Hazelnut Pesto

Hazelnuts are used instead of pine nuts in the pesto sauce, providing a healthier, lower-fat option.

Serves 4

2 garlic cloves, crushed
1 ounce fresh basil leaves
¼ cup chopped hazelnuts

scant 1 cup cream cheese
8 ounces tagliatelle
ground black pepper

1 Place the garlic, basil, hazelnuts and cheese in a food processor or blender and process to a thick paste.

2 Cook the tagliatelle in lightly salted boiling water until just tender, then drain well.

3 Spoon the sauce into the hot pasta, tossing until melted. Sprinkle with pepper and serve hot.

Spaghetti with Tuna Sauce

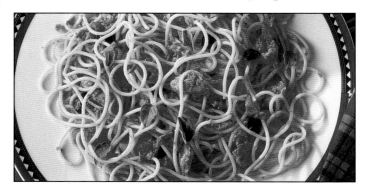

Use 1 pound fresh spaghetti in place of the dried pasta in this piquant dish, if you prefer.

Serves 4

Cook 8 ounces spaghetti, drain and keep hot. Boil 1 garlic clove and 14-ounce can chopped tomatoes and simmer for 2–3 minutes. Add 15 ounces canned tuna or 1 pound fresh tuna, cut into small chunks, and ½ teaspoon chili sauce (optional), 4 black olives and the spaghetti. Simmer until the tuna is cooked, and season to taste.

Penne with Broccoli and Chili

For a milder sauce you could omit the chili, but it does give this dish a great kick.

Serves 4

4 cups small broccoli
   florets
2 tablespoons stock
1 garlic clove, crushed
1 small red chili, finely
   sliced, or ½ teaspoon
   chili sauce

4 tablespoons plain
   low-fat yogurt
2 tablespoons toasted
   pine nuts or cashew
   nuts
12 ounces penne
salt and ground black
   pepper

1   Add the pasta to a large pan of lightly salted boiling water and return to a boil. Place the broccoli in a steamer basket over the top. Cover and cook for 8–10 minutes until both are just tender. Drain.

2   Heat the stock and add the crushed garlic and chili or chili sauce. Stir over a low heat for 2–3 minutes.

3   Stir in the broccoli, pasta and yogurt. Adjust the seasoning, sprinkle with nuts and serve hot.

Linguine with Pesto Sauce

Pesto originates in Liguria, where the sea breezes are said to give the local basil a particularly fine flavor.

Serves 5–6

2½ ounces fresh basil
   leaves
3–4 garlic cloves, peeled
3 tablespoons pine nuts
½ teaspoon salt
5 tablespoons extra-
   virgin olive oil

scant ¾ cup freshly
   grated Parmesan
   cheese
4 tablespoons freshly
   grated Pecorino cheese
salt and ground black
   pepper
1¼ pounds linguine

1   Place the basil, garlic, pine nuts, salt and olive oil in a food processor or blender and process until smooth. Place in a bowl. (If desired, the sauce may be frozen at this point, before the cheeses are added.)

2   Add the cheeses and stir to combine thoroughly. Season to taste with salt and pepper.

3   Cook the pasta in a large saucepan of rapidly boiling salted water until it is *al dente*. Just before draining it, take about 4 tablespoons of the cooking water and stir it into the pesto sauce.

4   Drain the pasta and toss with the sauce. Serve immediately, with extra cheese if desired.

Cook's Tip
Pecorino cheese is not as widely available as Parmesan. If you cannot find it, use all Parmesan instead.

Spaghetti with Herb Sauce

Fresh herbs make a wonderful aromatic sauce – the heat from the pasta releases their flavor to delicious effect.

Serves 4

*2 ounces chopped mixed
   fresh herbs such as
   parsley, basil and
   thyme
2 garlic cloves, crushed
4 tablespoons pine nuts,
   toasted
⅔ cup olive oil*

*12 ounces dried spaghetti
4 tablespoons freshly
   grated Parmesan
   cheese
salt and ground black
   pepper
fresh basil leaves, to
   garnish*

1 Put the herbs, garlic and half the pine nuts into a food processor or blender. With the machine running slowly, add the oil and process to form a thick purée.

2 Cook the spaghetti in plenty of boiling salted water for about 8 minutes, until *al dente*. Drain thoroughly.

3 Transfer the herb purée to a large warm bowl, then add the spaghetti and Parmesan. Toss well to coat the pasta with the sauce. Season with salt and peppper, sprinkle the remaining pine nuts and the basil leaves on top and serve hot.

Tagliatelle with Saffron Mussels

Tagliatelle is served with mussels in a saffron and cream sauce in this recipe, but use other pasta if you prefer.

Serves 4

*4 – 4½ pounds live
   mussels in the shell
⅔ cup dry white wine
2 shallots, finely
   chopped
12 ounces dried
   tagliatelle
2 tablespoons butter
2 garlic cloves, crushed*

*1 cup heavy cream
large pinch of saffron
   strands
1 egg yolk
salt and ground black
   pepper
2 tablespoons chopped
   fresh parsley, to
   garnish*

1 Scrub the mussels well under cold running water. Remove the beards and discard any mussels that are open. Place the mussels in a large saucepan with the wine and shallots. Cover with a tight-fitting lid and cook over a high heat, shaking the pan occasionally, for 5 – 8 minutes until the mussels have opened. Drain the mussels, reserving the liquid. Discard any that remain closed. Shell all but a few of the mussels and keep warm. Bring the reserved cooking liquid to a boil, then reduce by half. Strain into a jug.

2 Cook the pasta in a large pan of boiling salted water for 10 minutes or according to the instructions on the package.

3 Meanwhile, melt the butter in a frying pan and fry the garlic for 1 minute. Pour in the mussel liquid, cream and saffron strands. Heat gently until the sauce thickens slightly. Remove the pan from the heat and stir in the egg yolk and shelled mussels, and season to taste with salt and pepper.

4 Drain the tagliatelle and transfer to warmed serving bowls. Spoon the sauce over and sprinkle with chopped parsley. Garnish with the mussels in shells and serve immediately.

Pasta Rapido with Parsley Pesto

Here's a fresh, lively sauce that will stir the appetite and pep up any pasta supper.

Serves 4

1 pound pasta shapes	**For the sauce**
¾ cup whole almonds	1½ ounces fresh Italian
½ cup flaked almonds	parsley
toasted	2 garlic cloves, crushed
generous ¼ cup freshly	3 tablespoons olive oil
grated Parmesan	3 tablespoons lemon juice
cheese	1 teaspoon sugar
pinch of salt	1 cup boiling water

1 Bring a large saucepan of salted water to a boil and cook the pasta according to the instructions on the package. Toast the whole and flaked almonds separately under a moderate broiler until golden brown. Set the flaked almonds aside.

2 To make the sauce, chop the parsley finely in a food processor. Add the whole almonds and reduce to a fine consistency. Add the garlic, olive oil, lemon juice, sugar and water. Combine to make a sauce.

3 Drain the pasta and combine with half of the sauce. (The remainder of the sauce will keep in a screw-top jar in the fridge for up to ten days.) Top with freshly grated Parmesan cheese and the flaked almonds.

Macaroni and Cheese with Mushrooms

This macaroni and cheese is served in a light creamy sauce with mushrooms and topped with pine nuts.

Serves 4

1 pound quick-cooking	½ teaspoon celery salt
elbow macaroni	1 teaspoon Dijon
3 tablespoons olive oil	mustard
8 ounces button	1½ cups grated Cheddar
mushrooms, sliced	generous ¼ cup freshly
2 fresh thyme sprigs	grated Parmesan
4 tablespoons all-purpose	cheese
flour	¼ cup pine nuts
1 vegetable stock cube	salt and ground black
2½ cups milk	pepper

1 Bring a saucepan of salted water to a boil and cook the macaroni according to the instructions on the package.

2 Heat the oil in a heavy saucepan and cover, add mushrooms and thyme, cook over a gentle heat for 2–3 minutes. Stir in the flour and remove from the heat, add the stock cube and stir constantly until evenly blended. Return to the heat and add the milk a little at a time, stirring after each addition. Add the celery salt, mustard and Cheddar cheese and season to taste with salt and pepper. Stir and simmer for about 1–2 minutes, until the sauce has thickened.

3 Preheat a moderate broiler. Drain the macaroni well, toss into the sauce and put into four individual dishes or one large flameproof gratin dish. Scatter with grated Parmesan cheese and pine nuts, then broil until brown and bubbly.

Pasta with Roasted Pepper Sauce

Add other vegetables such as green beans or zucchini or even chick-peas to make this sauce more substantial.

Serves 4

2 red bell peppers
2 yellow bell peppers
3 tablespoons olive oil
1 onion, sliced
2 garlic cloves, crushed
14-ounce can chopped
    plum tomatoes

½ teaspoon mild chili
    powder
1 pound pasta shells or
    spirals
salt and ground black
    pepper
freshly grated Parmesan
    cheese, to serve

1 Preheat the oven to 400°F. Place the peppers on a baking sheet and bake for about 20 minutes or until they are beginning to char. Alternatively, broil the peppers, turning them from time to time.

2 Rub the skins off the peppers under cold water. Halve, remove the seeds and coarsely chop the flesh.

3 Heat the oil in a saucepan and cook the onion and garlic gently for 5 minutes until soft and golden.

4 Stir in the chili powder, cook for 2 minutes, then add the tomatoes and peppers. Bring to a boil and simmer for about 10–15 minutes until slightly thickened and reduced. Season with salt and pepper to taste.

5 Bring a pan of salted water to a boil and cook the pasta according to the instructions on the package. Drain well and toss with the sauce. Serve piping hot with lots of freshly grated Parmesan cheese.

Stir-fried Vegetables with Pasta

This is a colorful oriental-style dish, easily prepared using pasta instead of Chinese noodles.

Serves 4

1 carrot
6 ounces small zucchini
6 ounces green beans
6 ounces baby corn cobs
1 pound ribbon pasta
    such as tagliatelle
pinch of salt
2 tablespoons corn oil,
    plus extra for tossing
    the pasta
½-inch piece fresh ginger,
    peeled and finely
    chopped

2 garlic cloves, finely
    chopped
6 tablespoons yellow
    bean sauce
6 scallions, sliced into 1-
    inch pieces
2 tablespoons dry sherry
1 teaspoon sesame seeds

1 Slice the carrot and zucchini diagonally into chunks. Slice the beans diagonally, then cut the baby corn cobs diagonally in half.

2 Cook the pasta in plenty of boiling salted water according to the instructions on the package. Drain, then rinse under hot water. Toss in a little oil.

3 Heat 2 tablepoons oil until smoking in a wok or frying pan and add the ginger and garlic. Stir-fry for 30 seconds, then add the carrots, beans and zucchini.

4 Stir-fry for 3–4 minutes then stir in the yellow bean sauce. Stir-fry for 2 minutes, add the scallions, sherry and pasta and stir-fry for another minute until piping hot. Sprinkle with sesame seeds and serve immediately.

Tagliatelle with Gorgonzola Sauce

Gorgonzola is a creamy Italian blue cheese. You could use Danish Blue or Pipo Crème instead.

Serves 4

2 tablespoons butter, plus
  extra for tossing the
  pasta
8 ounces Gorgonzola
  cheese
⅔ cup heavy or whipping
  cream
2 tablepoons dry
  vermouth

1 teaspoon cornstarch
1 tablespoon chopped
  fresh sage
1 pound tagliatelle
salt and ground black
  pepper

1 Melt 2 tablepoons butter in a heavy saucepan (it needs to be thick-based to prevent the cheese from burning). Stir in 1½ cups crumbled Gorgonzola cheese and stir over very gentle heat for 2–3 minutes until the cheese is melted.

2 Pour in the cream, vermouth and cornstarch, whisking well to amalgamate. Stir in the chopped sage, then season to taste with salt and pepper. Cook, whisking all the time, until the sauce boils and thickens. Set aside.

3 Boil the pasta in plenty of salted water according to the instructions on the package. Drain well and toss with a little butter to coat evenly.

4 Reheat the sauce gently, whisking well. Divide the pasta among four serving bowls, top with the sauce and sprinkle on the remaining cheese. Serve immediately.

Cook's Tip
If you do not have vermouth, use a good-quality dry sherry in its place.

Rigatoni with Garlic Crumbs

A hot and spicy dish – halve the quantity of chili if you would prefer a milder flavor.

Serves 4–6

3 tablespoons olive oil
2 shallots, chopped
8 slices bacon, chopped
2 teaspoons crushed
  dried chilies
14-ounce can chopped
  tomatoes with herbs

6 slices white bread,
  crusts removed
½ cup butter
2 garlic cloves, chopped
1 pound rigatoni
salt and ground black
  pepper

1 Heat the oil in a saucepan and fry the shallots and bacon gently for 6–8 minutes until golden. Add the dried chilies and chopped tomatoes, half-cover with a lid and simmer for about 20 minutes.

2 Meanwhile, place the bread in a blender or food processor and process to fine crumbs.

3 Heat the butter in a frying pan and stir-fry the garlic and bread crumbs until golden and crisp. (Be careful not to let the crumbs catch and burn.)

4 Bring a pan of lightly salted water to a boil and cook the pasta according to the instructions on the package. Drain well.

5 Toss the pasta with the tomato sauce and divide among four serving bowls.

6 Sprinkle with the crumbs and serve immediately.

Cook's Tip
If you are preparing this dish for vegetarians leave out the bacon, or replace it with sliced mushrooms.

Pasta with Tomatoes and Arugula

This pretty-colored pasta dish relies for its success on the slightly peppery taste of the arugula.

Serves 4

1 pound pasta shells
1 pound ripe cherry
    tomatoes
3 tablespoons olive oil

3 ounces fresh arugula
salt and ground black
    pepper
Parmesan cheese

1 Bring a saucepan of water to a boil and cook the pasta according to the instructions on the package. Drain well.

2 Halve the tomatoes. Trim, wash and dry the arugula.

3 Heat the oil in a large saucepan and gently cook the tomatoes for barely 1 minute. The tomatoes should only just be heated through and not be allowed to disintegrate.

4 Add the pasta to the pan, then the arugula. (Coarsely tear any arugula leaves that are too large.) Carefully stir to mix and heat through. Season to taste with salt and pepper. Serve hot, with plenty of shaved Parmesan cheese.

Cook's Tip
Arugula is increasingly available in supermarkets. However, if you cannot find it, it is easy to grow in the garden.

Pasta Spirals with Pepperoni

A warming supper dish, this pepperoni and tomato sauce could be served on any type of pasta.

Serves 4

1 onion
1 red bell pepper
1 green bell pepper
2 tablepoons olive oil,
    plus extra for tossing
    the pasta
2 x 14-ounce cans
    chopped tomatoes
2 tablespoons tomato
    paste

2 teaspoons paprika
6 ounces pepperoni or
    chorizo
3 tablepoons chopped
    fresh parsley
1 pound dried green
    pasta spirals
salt and ground black
    pepper

1 Chop the onion. Halve and seed the peppers, removing the cores, then dice.

2 Heat the oil in a saucepan and cook the onion for about 2 minutes, until beginning to color. Stir in the peppers, tomatoes, tomato paste and paprika, bring to a boil and simmer uncovered for 15–20 minutes until the sauce is reduced and thickened.

3 Slice the sausage and stir into the sauce with about half the chopped parsley. Season to taste with salt and pepper.

4 While the sauce is simmering, cook the pasta in plenty of boiling salted water according to the instructions on the package. Drain well. Toss the pasta with the remaining parsley in a little extra olive oil. Divide among warmed bowls and top with the sauce.

Cook's Tip
All types of sausages are suitable to include in this dish. If using raw sausages, add them with the onion and cook thoroughly.

Pasta with Tuna and Capers

Pasta shapes are tossed in a flavorful sauce made with tuna, capers, anchovies and fresh basil.

Serves 4

14-ounce can tuna fish in oil
2 tablespoons olive oil
2 garlic cloves, crushed
2 x 14-ounce chopped tomatoes
6 canned anchovy fillets, drained

2 tablespoons capers in vinegar, drained
2 tablespoons chopped fresh basil
salt and ground black pepper
4 cups garganelle, penne or rigatoni
fresh basil sprigs, to garnish

1 Drain the oil from the tuna into a saucepan, add the olive oil and heat gently until it stops spitting.

2 Add the garlic and fry until golden. Stir in the tomatoes and simmer for 25 minutes until thickened.

3 Flake the tuna and cut the anchovies in half. Stir into the sauce with the capers and chopped basil. Season to taste with salt and pepper.

4 Cook the pasta in plenty of boiling salted water according to the instructions on the package. Drain well and toss with the sauce. Garnish with fresh basil sprigs.

Cook's Tip
This piquant sauce could be made without the addition of tomatoes – just heat the oil, add the other ingredients and heat through gently before tossing with the pasta.

Pasta Bows with Smoked Salmon

In Italy, pasta cooked with smoked salmon is becoming very fashionable. This is a quick and luxurious sauce.

Serves 4

6 scallions, sliced
4 tablepoons butter
6 tablespoons dry white wine or vermouth
1¾ cups heavy cream
pinch of freshly grated nutmeg
8 ounces smoked salmon

2 tablespoons chopped fresh dill or 1 tablespoon dried dill
freshly squeezed lemon juice
1 pound pasta bows
salt and ground black pepper

1 Slice the scallions finely. Melt the butter in a saucepan and fry the scallions for about 1 minute until they begin to soften.

2 Add the wine or vermouth and boil hard to reduce to about 2 tablespoons. Stir in the cream and add salt, pepper and nutmeg to taste. Bring to a boil and simmer for about 2–3 minutes until slightly thickened.

3 Cut the smoked salmon into 1-inch squares and stir into the sauce with the dill. Taste and add a little lemon juice. Keep the sauce warm.

4 Cook the pasta in plenty of boiling salted water according to the instructions on the package. Drain well. Toss the pasta with the sauce and serve immediately.

Cook's Tip
This dish could also be prepared with canned salmon, broken into bite-size pieces, if you prefer.

Pasta with Shrimp and Feta Cheese

This dish contains a delicious combination of fresh shrimp and sharp-tasting feta cheese.

Serves 4
4 cups medium raw
   shrimp
6 scallions
4 tablespoons butter
8 ounces feta cheese

small bunch fresh chives
1 pound garganelle or
   rigatoni
salt and ground black
   pepper

1   Remove the heads from the shrimp by twisting and pulling off. Peel the shrimp and discard the shells. Chop the scallions.

2   Melt the butter in a frying pan and cook the shrimp. When they turn pink, add the scallions and cook gently for 1 minute more.

3   Dice the feta cheese into ½-inch pieces. Stir into the shrimp mixture and season to taste with pepper.

4   Cut the chives into 1-inch pieces and stir half into the shrimp mixture.

5   Bring a saucepan of salted water to a boil and cook the pasta according to the instructions on the package. Drain well, pile into a warmed serving dish and top with the sauce. Scatter with the remaining chives and serve.

Cook's Tip
Substitute goat cheese for the feta cheese if you like; prepare the dish in the same way.

Tagliatelle with Prosciutto

This is a simple dish, prepared in minutes from the best ingredients, with a thick covering of Parmesan cheese.

Serves 4
4 ounces prosciutto
1 pound tagliatelle
6 tablepoons butter
½ cup grated Parmesan
   cheese

salt and ground black
   pepper
a few fresh sage leaves, to
   garnish

1   Cut the prosciutto into strips of the same width as the tagliatelle. Cook the pasta in plenty of boiling salted water according to the instructions on the package.

2   Meanwhile, melt the butter gently in a saucepan and heat the prosciutto strips through, but do not fry.

3   Drain the tagliatelle well and pile into a warm serving dish. Sprinkle all the Parmesan cheese over the top.

4   Pour the buttery prosciutto over the top of the tagliatelle and Parmesan. Season well with pepper and garnish with the sage leaves.

Cook's Tip
Buy Parmesan cheese in a block and grate it yourself. The flavor is far superior to that of already-grated Parmesan cheese.

Cannelloni al Forno

This recipe provides a lighter, healthier alternative to the usual beef-filled, béchamel-coated version.

Serves 4–6

*1 pound boned chicken
   breast, skinned and
   cooked
8 ounces mushrooms
2 garlic cloves, crushed
2 tablespoons chopped
   fresh parsley
1 tablespoon chopped
   fresh tarragon
1 egg, beaten*

*squeeze of lemon juice
12–18 cannelloni tubes
1 jar of tomato sauce
scant ¾ cup freshly
   grated Parmesan
   cheese
salt and ground black
   pepper
fresh parsley sprig, to
   garnish*

1 Preheat the oven to 400°F. Place the chicken in a food processor and blend until finely minced. Transfer to a bowl and set aside.

2 Place the mushrooms, garlic, parsley and tarragon in the food processor and blend until finely ground. Beat the mushroom mixture into the chicken with the egg, salt and pepper and lemon juice to taste.

3 Bring a saucepan of salted water to a boil and cook the cannelloni according to the instructions on the package. Drain well on a clean dish towel.

4 Place the filling in an icing bag fitted with a large plain nozzle. Use this to fill each tube of cannelloni.

5 Lay the filled cannelloni tightly together in a single layer in a buttered shallow dish. Spoon on the tomato sauce and sprinkle with Parmesan cheese. Bake in the oven for 30 minutes or until brown and bubbling. Serve garnished with a sprig of parsley.

Alfredo's Noodles

A classic from Rome, this dish is simply pasta tossed with heavy cream, butter and freshly grated Parmesan cheese.

Serves 4

*2 tablespoons butter
⅔ cup heavy cream, plus
   4 tablespoons extra
1 pound fettuccine
pinch of freshly grated
   nutmeg*

*salt and ground black
   pepper
scant ¾ cup freshly
   grated Parmesan
   cheese, plus extra to
   serve*

1 Place the butter and ⅔ cup cream in a heavy saucepan, bring to a boil and simmer for 1 minute until slightly thickened.

2 Bring a saucepan of salted water to a boil and cook the fettuccine according to the instructions on the package, but for about 2 minutes' less time. The pasta should still be a little firm or *al dente*.

3 Drain the pasta very thoroughly and turn into the pan with the cream sauce.

4 Place the pan on the heat and turn the pasta in the sauce to coat it evenly.

5 Add the remaining cream, the cheese, salt and pepper to taste and a little grated nutmeg. Toss until well coated and heated through. Serve immediately with some extra grated Parmesan cheese.

Cook's Tip
Popular additions to this recipe are fresh or frozen peas, and thin strips of ham if you are not catering for vegetarians.

Onion and Gorgonzola Pizzettes

Serves 4

1 quantity Basic Pizza
    Dough (see below)
2 tablespoons garlic oil
2 small red onions
5 ounces Gorgonzola

2 garlic cloves
2 teaspoons chopped fresh
    sage
pinch of black pepper

Preheat the oven to 425°F. Divide the dough into eight pieces
and roll out each one on a lightly floured surface to a small
oval about ¼-inch thick. Space well apart on two greased
baking sheets and prick with a fork. Brush the bases well with
1 tablespoon of the garlic oil. Halve, then slice the onions into
thin wedges. Scatter over the pizza bases. Remove the rind
from the Gorgonzola. Cut the cheese into small cubes, then
scatter it on the onions. Cut the garlic lengthwise into thin
strips and sprinkle on, along with the sage. Drizzle the
remaining oil on top and grind on plenty of pepper. Bake for
10–15 minutes until crisp and golden. Serve immediately.

Basic Pizza Dough

Makes one 10–12 inch round pizza base

1½ cups flour
¼ teaspoon salt
1 teaspoon rapid-rise
    dried yeast

½ –¾ cup lukewarm
    water
1 tablespoon olive oil

Sift the flour and salt into a large mixing bowl and stir in the
yeast. Make a well in the center; pour in the water and oil.
Mix to a soft dough. Knead the dough on a lightly floured
board for 10 minutes until smooth and elastic. Place in a
greased bowl, cover with plastic wrap and leave until
doubled in size – about 1 hour. Turn out on to a lightly
floured surface, knead gently for 2–3 minutes and use as
required.

Feta and Roasted Garlic Pizza

**This is a pizza for garlic lovers. Mash down the cloves as
you eat – they should be soft and sweet-tasting.**

Serves 4

1 garlic bulb, unpeeled
3 tablespoons olive oil
1 red bell pepper, seeded
    and quartered
1 yellow bell pepper,
    seeded and quartered
2 plum tomatoes

1 batch Basic Pizza
    Dough (see below left)
1½ cups feta, crumbled
pinch of black pepper
1–2 tablespoons chopped
    fresh oregano, to
    garnish

1 Preheat the oven to 425°F. Break the garlic into cloves,
discarding the outer papery layers. Toss in 1 tablespoon of the
olive oil.

2 Place the peppers skin-side up on a baking sheet and broil,
turning them until the skins are evenly charred. Place in a
covered bowl for 10 minutes, then peel off the skins. Cut the
flesh into strips.

3 Make a slash in the skin of each tomato, then put them in a
bowl and pour over boiling water. Leave for 30 seconds, then
plunge into cold water. Peel, seed and coarsely chop the flesh.
Divide the pizza dough into four pieces and roll out each one
on a lightly floured surface to an equal-sized circle of about
5 inches diameter.

4 Space the dough circles well apart on two greased baking
sheets, then push up the dough edges to form a thin rim.
Brush the dough circles with half the remaining oil and
scatter with the chopped tomatoes. Top with the peppers,
crumbled feta cheese and garlic cloves. Drizzle on the
remaining oil and season to taste with pepper. Bake in the
oven for 15–20 minutes until crisp and golden. Garnish with
chopped oregano; serve immediately.

Mussel and Leek Pizzettes

Serve these subtly flavored seafood pizzettes with a crisp green salad for a light lunch.

Serves 4

1 pound live mussels
½ cup dry white wine
1 batch Basic Pizza
  Dough
1 tablespoon olive oil

2 ounces Gruyère cheese
2 ounces mozzarella
2 small leeks
salt and ground black
  pepper

1 Preheat the oven to 425°F. Place the mussels in a bowl of cold water to soak, and scrub well. Remove the beards and discard any mussels that are open.

2 Place the mussels in a saucepan. Pour over the dry white wine, cover with a tight-fitting lid and cook over high heat, shaking the pan occasionally, for 5–10 minutes until the mussels have opened.

3 Drain off the cooking liquid. Remove the mussels from their shells, discarding any that remain closed. Let cool.

4 Divide the dough into four pieces and roll out each one on a lightly floured surface to a 5-inch circle. Space well apart on two greased baking sheets, then push up the dough edges to form a thin rim. Brush the pizza bases with the oil. Grate the cheeses and sprinkle half evenly over the bases.

5 Thinly slice the leeks, then scatter on the cheese. Bake for 10 minutes, then remove from the oven.

6 Arrange the mussels on top. Season with salt and pepper and sprinkle with the remaining cheese. Bake for another 5–10 minutes until crisp and golden. Serve immediately.

Cook's Tip
Frozen or canned mussels can also be used but will give a different flavor and texture to these pizzettes.

Wild Mushroom Pizzettes

Fresh wild mushrooms add a distinctive flavor to these pizzettes, which make an ideal starter.

Serves 4

3 tablespoons olive oil
12 ounces fresh mixed
  wild mushrooms,
  washed and sliced
2 shallots, chopped
2 garlic cloves, finely
  chopped
2 tablespoons chopped
  fresh mixed thyme and
  Italian parsley

1 batch Basic Pizza
  Dough
generous ¼ cup grated
  Gruyère cheese
2 tablespoons freshly
  grated Parmesan
salt and ground black
  pepper

1 Preheat the oven to 425°F. Heat 2 tablespoons of the oil in a frying pan and fry the mushrooms, shallots and garlic over medium heat, stirring occasionally, until all the juice has evaporated.

2 Stir in half the herbs and seasoning, then set aside to cool.

3 Divide the dough into four pieces and roll out each one on a lightly floured surface to a 5-inch circle. Place well apart on two greased baking sheets, then push up the dough edges to form a thin rim. Brush the pizza bases with the remaining oil and top with the wild mushroom mixture.

4 Mix together the Gruyère and Parmesan, then sprinkle on. Bake for 15–20 minutes until crisp and golden. Remove from the oven and scatter with the remaining herbs to serve.

Cook's Tip
If you cannot find wild mushrooms, a mixture of cultivated mushrooms, such as shiitake, oyster and chestnut, would do just as well.

Ham, Pepper and Mozzarella Pizzas

Succulent roasted peppers, salty prosciutto and creamy mozzarella make a delicious topping for these pizzas.

Serves 2

*4 thick slices ciabatta
  bread
1 red bell pepper, roasted
  and peeled
1 yellow bell pepper,
  roasted and peeled*

*4 slices prosciutto, cut
  into thick strips
3 ounces mozzarella
pinch of black pepper
tiny fresh basil leaves, to
  garnish*

1 Lightly toast the slices of ciabatta bread on both sides until they are golden.

2 Cut the roast peppers into thick strips and arrange on the toasted bread with the prosciutto ham.

3 Thinly slice the mozzarella and arrange on top. Grind on plenty of pepper. Place under a hot broiler for 2–3 minutes until the cheese is bubbling.

4 Arrange the basil leaves on top and serve immediately.

Fruity French Bread Pizza

This recipe uses French bread as a base instead of the more usual pizza dough, for a change.

Serves 4

*2 small baguettes
1 jar ready-made tomato
  sauce or pizza topping
3 ounces sliced cooked
  ham
4 rings canned pineapple,
  drained and chopped*

*½ small green bell pepper,
  seeded and cut into
  thin strips
3 ounces mature Cheddar
  cheese
salt and ground black
  pepper*

1 Preheat the oven to 400°F. Cut the baguettes in half lengthwise and toast the outsides under a broiler until crisp and golden.

2 Spread the tomato sauce or pizza topping on the toasted baguette halves.

3 Cut the ham into strips and arrange on the baguettes with the pineapple and pepper. Season with salt and pepper.

4 Grate the Cheddar and sprinkle on top. Bake for 15–20 minutes until crisp and golden. Serve immediately.

Cook's Tip
These pizzas may be broiled instead of baked in the oven. Cook them for the same length of time under a moderate heat but check that they do not burn.

162

Marinara Pizza

The combination of garlic, good-quality olive oil and oregano gives this pizza an unmistakably Italian flavor.

Serves 2–3

4 tablespoons olive oil
1½ pounds plum
    tomatoes, peeled,
    seeded and chopped
1 pizza base, 10–12
    inches diameter

4 garlic cloves, cut into
    slivers
1 tablespoon chopped
    fresh oregano
salt and ground black
    pepper

1 Preheat the oven to 425°F. In a saucepan, heat 2 tablespoons of the oil. Add the tomatoes and cook, stirring frequently, for about 5 minutes until soft.

2 Place the tomatoes in a metal strainer and allow them to drain for about 5 minutes.

3 Transfer the tomatoes to a food processor or blender and purée until smooth.

4 Brush the pizza base with half the remaining oil. Spoon on the tomatoes and sprinkle with garlic and oregano. Drizzle on the remaining oil and season to taste. Bake for 15–20 minutes until crisp and golden. Serve immediately.

Cook's Tip
Ready-made pizza bases are available from most supermarkets and come in a range of sizes. It is useful to keep a few in the freezer.

Four-Cheese Pizza

Rich and cheesy, these individual pizzas are quick to make, and the aroma of melting cheese is irresistible.

Serves 4

1 batch Basic Pizza
    Dough
1 tablespoon garlic oil
½ small red onion, very
    thinly sliced
2 ounces dolcelatte
2 ounces mozzarella

½ cup grated Gruyère
2 tablespoons freshly
    grated Parmesan
1 tablespoon chopped
    fresh thyme
pinch of black pepper

1 Preheat the oven to 425°F. Divide the dough into four pieces and roll out each one on a lightly floured surface into a 5-inch circle. Space well apart on two greased baking sheets, then push up the dough edges to make a thin rim. Brush with garlic oil and top with the red onion.

2 Dice the dolcelatte and mozzarella and scatter over the bases. Mix together the Gruyère, Parmesan and thyme and sprinkle them on.

3 Grind on plenty of pepper. Bake for 15–20 minutes until crisp and golden and the cheeses are bubbling. Serve hot.

Pizza with Fresh Vegetables

This pizza can be made with any vegetable combination. Blanch or sauté the vegetables before baking them.

Serves 4

14 ounces peeled plum
   tomatoes, weighed
   whole (or canned
   without their juice)
2 broccoli spears
8 ounces fresh asparagus
2 small zucchini
5 tablespoons olive oil
½ cup shelled peas, fresh
   or frozen
4 scallions, sliced

1 batch Basic Pizza
   Dough
generous ½ cup diced
   mozzarella cheese
10 fresh basil leaves, torn
   into pieces
2 garlic cloves, finely
   chopped
salt and ground black
   pepper

1 Preheat the oven to 475°F for at least 20 minutes before baking the pizza. Strain the tomatoes through the medium holes of a food mill placed over a bowl, scraping in all the pulp.

2 Peel the broccoli stems and asparagus, and blanch with the zucchini in a large saucepan of boiling unsalted water for 4–5 minutes. Drain and cut into bite-size pieces.

3 Heat 2 tablespoons of the olive oil in a small saucepan. Stir in the peas and scallions, and cook for 5–6 minutes, stirring frequently. Remove from the heat.

4 Roll out the pizza dough to a 10-inch circle and place on a greased baking sheet. Spread the puréed tomatoes onto the dough, leaving the rim uncovered. Add all the other vegetables, spreading them evenly over the tomatoes.

5 Sprinkle with the mozzarella, basil, garlic, salt and pepper and remaining olive oil. Immediately place the pizza in the oven. Bake for about 20 minutes, or until the crust is golden brown and the cheese has melted.

Four Seasons Pizza

The topping on this pizza is divided into four quarters, one for each "season", creating a colorful effect.

Serves 4

1 pound peeled plum
   tomatoes, weighed
   whole (or canned
   without their juice)
5 tablespoons olive oil
4 ounces mushrooms,
   thinly sliced
1 garlic clove, finely
   chopped
1 batch Basic Pizza
   Dough
scant 2½ cups diced
   mozzarella

4 thin slices of ham, cut
   into 2-inch squares
32 black olives, pitted
   and halved
8 artichoke hearts,
   preserved in oil,
   drained and cut in
   half
1 teaspoon oregano
   leaves, fresh or dried
salt and ground black
   pepper

1 Preheat the oven to 475°F for at least 20 minutes before baking the pizza. Strain the tomatoes through the medium holes of a food mill placed over a bowl, scraping in all the pulp.

2 Heat 2 tablespoons of the oil in a saucepan and lightly sauté the mushrooms. Stir in the garlic and set aside.

3 Roll out the pizza dough to a 10-inch circle and place on a greased baking sheet. Spread the puréed tomatoes on the prepared pizza dough, leaving the rim uncovered. Sprinkle evenly with the mozzarella. Spread the mushrooms on one quarter of the pizza.

4 Arrange the ham on another quarter, and the olives and artichoke hearts on the two remaining quarters. Sprinkle with oregano, salt and pepper, and the remaining olive oil. Immediately place the pizza in the oven. Bake for about 15–20 minutes, or until the crust is golden brown and the topping is bubbling.

Florentine Pizza

Spinach is the star ingredient of this pizza. A grating of nutmeg heightens its flavor.

Serves 2–3

1½ cups fresh spinach
3 tablespoons olive oil
1 small red onion, thinly sliced
1 pizza base, 10–12 inches in diameter
1 jar ready-made tomato sauce or pizza topping
pinch of freshly grated nutmeg
5 ounces mozzarella
1 egg
¼ cup grated Gruyère cheese

1 Preheat the oven to 425°F. Remove the stalks from the spinach and wash the leaves in plenty of cold water. Drain well and pat dry with paper towels.

2 Heat 1 tablespoon of the oil in a large frying pan and fry the onion until softened. Add the spinach and continue to fry until just wilted. Drain off any excess liquid.

3 Brush the pizza base with half the remaining oil. Spread on the tomato sauce or pizza topping, then top with the spinach mixture. Grate on some nutmeg.

4 Thinly slice the mozzarella and arrange over the spinach. Drizzle on the remaining oil. Bake for 10 minutes, then remove from the oven.

5 Make a small well in the center of the pizza and drop the egg into the hole.

6 Sprinkle on the Gruyère and return to the oven for another 5–10 minutes until crisp and golden.

Chili Beef Pizza

Minced beef and red kidney beans combined with oregano, cumin and chilies give this pizza a Mexican character.

Serves 4

2 tablespoons olive oil
1 red onion, finely chopped
1 garlic clove, crushed
½ red pepper, seeded and finely chopped
6 ounces lean ground beef
½ teaspoon ground cumin
2 fresh red chilies, seeded and chopped
scant ½ cup (drained weight) canned red kidney beans, rinsed
1 jar ready-made tomato sauce or pizza topping
1 tablespoon chopped fresh oregano
½ cup grated mozzarella
¾ cup grated oak-smoked Cheddar
1 pizza base, 10-12 inches in diameter
salt and ground black pepper

1 Preheat the oven to 425°F. Heat 1 tablespoon of the oil in a frying pan and gently fry the onion, garlic and pepper until soft. Increase the heat, add the beef, and brown well, stirring constantly.

2 Add the cumin and chilies and continue to cook, stirring, for about 5 minutes. Add the beans and seasoning.

3 Spread the tomato sauce on the pizza base.

4 Spoon on the beef mixture, then scatter on the oregano. Then bake.

Tuna, Anchovy and Caper Pizza

This pizza makes a substantial supper dish for two to three people when accompanied by a simple salad.

Serves 2–3

For the pizza dough
1 cup self-rising flour
1 cup self-rising whole
  wheat flour
pinch of salt
4 tablespoons butter,
  diced
⅔ cup milk

For the topping
2 tablespoons olive oil
1 jar ready-made tomato
  sauce or pizza topping

1 small red onion
7-ounce can tuna,
  drained
1 tablespoon capers
12 black olives, pitted
3 tablespoons freshly
  grated Parmesan
  cheese
2-ounce can anchovy
  fillets, drained and
  halved lengthwise
ground black pepper

1 Place the flour and salt in a bowl and rub in the butter until the mixture resembles fine bread crumbs. Add the milk and mix to a soft dough with a wooden spoon. Knead on a lightly floured surface until smooth.

2 Preheat the oven to 425°F. Roll out the dough on a lightly floured surface to a 10-inch circle. Place on a greased baking sheet and brush with 4 tablespoons of the oil. Spread the tomato sauce or pizza topping evenly over the dough, leaving the edge uncovered.

3 Cut the onion into thin wedges and arrange on top. Roughly flake the tuna with a fork and scatter on the onion. Sprinkle with the capers, black olives and Parmesan cheese. Place the anchovy fillets on the top of the pizza in a criss-cross pattern. Drizzle on the remaining oil, then grind on plenty of pepper. Bake for 15–20 minutes until crisp and golden. Serve immediately.

Salmon and Avocado Pizza

Smoked and fresh salmon make a delicious pizza topping when mixed with avocado.

Serves 3–4

5 ounces salmon fillet
½ cup dry white wine
1 pizza base, 10–12
  inches in diameter
1 tablespoon olive oil
14-ounce can chopped
  tomatoes, drained well
scant 1 cup grated
  mozzarella
1 small avocado

2 teaspoons lemon juice
2 tablespoons crème
  fraîche
3 ounces smoked salmon,
  cut into strips
1 tablespoon capers
2 tablespoons chopped
  fresh chives, to
  garnish
ground black pepper

1 Preheat the oven to 425°F. Place the salmon fillet in a frying pan, pour on the wine and season with pepper. Bring slowly to a boil over a gentle heat, remove from the heat, cover with a tight-fitting lid and cool. (The fish will cook in the cooling liquid.) Skin and flake the salmon into small pieces, removing any bones.

2 Brush the pizza base with the oil and spread the drained tomatoes on the top. Sprinkle on a scant ½ cup of mozzarella. Bake for 10 minutes, then remove from the oven.

3 Meanwhile, halve, pit and peel the avocado. Dice the flesh and toss carefully in the lemon juice.

4 Dot teaspoonfuls of the crème fraîche over the pizza base.

5 Arrange the fresh and smoked salmon, avocado, capers and remaining mozzarella on top. Season to taste with pepper. Bake for 5–10 minutes until crisp and golden.

6 Sprinkle on the chives and serve immediately.

Mushroom and Pancetta Pizzas

Use any type and combination of mushrooms you like for these simple yet tasty individual pizzas.

Serves 4

1 batch Basic Pizza
   Dough
4 tablespoons olive oil
2 garlic cloves, crushed
8 ounces fresh mixed ceps
   and chestnut
   mushrooms, coarsely
   chopped

3 ounces pancetta,
   coarsely chopped
1 tablespoon chopped
   fresh oregano
3 tablespoons freshly
   grated Parmesan
   cheese
salt and ground black
   pepper

1 Preheat the oven to 425°F. Divide the dough into four pieces and roll out each one on a lightly floured surface to a 5-inch circle. Place far apart on two greased baking sheets.

2 Heat 2 tablespoons of the olive oil in a frying pan and fry the garlic and mushrooms gently until the mushrooms are tender and the juices have evaporated. Season to taste with salt and pepper, then cool.

3 Brush the pizza bases with 1 tablespoon oil, then spoon on the mushrooms. Scatter with the pancetta and oregano. Sprinkle with Parmesan and drizzle on the remaining oil. Bake for 10–15 minutes, until crisp. Serve immediately.

Cook's Tip
Pancetta is available in larger supermarkets and Italian delicatessens. If you cannot find it, use thickly sliced fried bacon instead.

Pepperoni Pizza

Mixed peppers, mozzarella cheese and pepperoni make a delicious topping for this luxurious pizza.

Serves 4
For the sauce
2 tablespoons olive oil
1 onion, finely chopped
1 garlic clove, crushed
14-ounce can chopped
   tomatoes with herbs
1 tablespoon tomato
   paste

For the pizza base
2½ cups all-purpose flour
½ teaspoon salt
1 teaspoon rapid-rise
   dried yeast
2 tablespoons olive oil

For the topping
½ each red, yellow and
   green bell pepper,
   sliced into rings
5 ounces mozzarella
   cheese, sliced
3 ounces pepperoni
   sausage, thinly sliced
8 black olives, pitted
3 sun-dried tomatoes,
   chopped
½ teaspoon dried oregano
olive oil, for drizzling

1 For the sauce, fry the onions and garlic in the oil until softened. Add the tomatoes and tomato paste. Boil rapidly for 5 minutes until reduced slightly. Let cool.

2 To make the pizza base, sift the flour and salt into a bowl. Sprinkle on the yeast and make a well in the center. Pour in ¾ cup warm water and the olive oil. Mix to a soft dough. Knead the dough on a lightly floured surface for about 5–10 minutes, until smooth. Roll out to a 10-inch round, press up the edges slightly and place on a greased baking sheet.

3 Spread on the tomato sauce and top with the peppers, mozzarella, pepperoni, olives and tomatoes. Sprinkle with the oregano and drizzle with olive oil. Cover loosely and leave in a warm place for 30 minutes. Meanwhile, preheat the oven to 425°F. Bake for 25–30 minutes then serve.

Farmhouse Pizza

This is the ultimate party pizza. Served cut into fingers, it is ideal for a large and hungry gathering.

Serves 8

6 tablespoons olive oil
8 ounces button
   mushrooms, sliced
2 batches Basic Pizza
   Dough
1 jar ready-made tomato
   sauce or pizza topping
10 ounces mozzarella
   cheese, thinly sliced
4 ounces wafer-thin
   smoked ham slices

6 bottled artichoke hearts
   in oil, drained and
   sliced
2-ounce can anchovy
   fillets, drained and
   halved lengthwise
10 black olives, pitted
   and halved
2 tablespoons chopped
   fresh oregano
3 tablespoons grated
   Parmesan cheese
ground black pepper

1 Preheat the oven to 425°F. In a large frying pan, heat 2 tablespoons of the oil. Gently fry the mushrooms for 5 minutes until all the juices have evaporated. Remove from the heat and allow to cool.

2 Roll out the dough on a lightly floured surface to make a 12 x 10-inch rectangle. Transfer to a greased baking sheet, then push up the dough edges to form a thin rim. Brush with 2 tablespoons of the oil.

3 Spread the tomato sauce or pizza topping on the dough, then arrange the sliced mozzarella over the sauce.

4 Scrunch up the ham and arrange on top with the artichoke hearts, mushrooms and anchovies.

5 Dot with the olives, then sprinkle with the oregano and Parmesan. Drizzle with the remaining oil and season to taste with pepper. Bake for about 25 minutes until crisp and golden. Serve immediately.

Crab and Parmesan Calzonelli

These miniature calzone owe their popularity to their impressive presentation.

Makes 10–12

1 batch Basic Pizza
   Dough
4 ounces mixed prepared
   crabmeat, defrosted if
   frozen
1 tablespoon heavy cream
2 tablespoons freshly
   grated Parmesan

2 tablespoons chopped
   fresh parsley
1 garlic clove, crushed
salt and ground black
   pepper
fresh parsley sprigs, to
   garnish

1 Preheat the oven to 400°F. Roll out the pizza dough on a lightly floured surface to ⅛-inch thick. Using a 3-inch plain round pastry cutter, stamp out ten to twelve circles of dough.

2 In a bowl, mix together the crabmeat, cream, Parmesan, parsley and garlic, and season to taste with salt and pepper.

3 Spoon a little of the filling onto one half of each circle. Moisten the edges of the dough with water and fold over to enclose the filling.

4 Seal the edges by pressing with a fork. Space well apart on two greased baking sheets. Bake for 10–15 minutes until golden. Garnish with parsley sprigs.

Cook's Tip
If you prefer, use shrimp instead of crabmeat. If frozen, make sure they are fully thawed first.

Ham and Mozzarella Calzone

A calzone is a kind of "inside-out" pizza – the dough is on the outside and the filling on the inside.

Serves 2

1 batch Basic Pizza
   Dough
½ cup ricotta cheese
2 tablespoons freshly
   grated Parmesan
1 egg yolk
2 tablespoons chopped
   fresh basil

3 ounces cooked ham,
   finely chopped
3 ounces mozzarella,
   diced
olive oil, for brushing
salt and ground black
   pepper

1 Preheat the oven to 425°F. Divide the dough in half and roll out each piece on a lightly floured surface to a 7-inch circle.

2 In a bowl, mix together the ricotta and Parmesan cheeses, egg yolk, basil and seasoning.

3 Spread the mixture on half of each circle, leaving a 1-inch border, then scatter the ham and mozzarella on top. Moisten the edges with water, then fold over the other half of the dough to enclose the filling.

4 Press the edges firmly together to seal. Place on two greased baking sheets. Brush with oil and make a small hole in the top of each to allow the steam to escape. Bake for 15–20 minutes until golden. Serve immediately.

Cook's Tip
For a vegetarian version, replace the ham with fried mushrooms or chopped cooked spinach.

Eggplant and Shallot Calzone

Eggplant, shallots and sun-dried tomatoes make an unusual filling for calzone.

Serves 2

3 tablespoons olive oil
3 shallots, chopped
4 baby eggplant
1 garlic clove, chopped
2 ounces (drained
   weight) sun-dried
   tomatoes in oil,
   chopped
¼ teaspoon dried red chili
   flakes

2 teaspoons chopped fresh
   thyme
1 batch Basic Pizza
   Dough
generous ½ cup diced
   mozzarella
salt and ground black
   pepper
1–2 tablespoons freshly
   grated Parmesan
   cheese, to serve

1 Preheat the oven to 425°F. Trim the baby eggplant, then dice.

2 Fry the shallots in some oil until soft. Add the eggplant, garlic, sun-dried tomatoes, red chili flakes, thyme and season to taste. Cook for 4–5 minutes, stirring frequently, until the eggplant is beginning to soften.

3 Divide the dough in half and roll out each piece on a lightly floured surface to a 7-inch circle. Spread the eggplant mixture over half of each circle, leaving a 1-inch border, then scatter on the mozzarella.

4 Moisten the edges with water, then fold the other half of the dough over to enclose the filling. Press the edges firmly together to seal. Place on two greased baking sheets.

5 Brush with half the remaining oil and make a small hole in the top of each to allow the steam to escape. Bake for about 15–20 minutes until golden. Remove from the oven and brush with the remaining oil. Sprinkle on the Parmesan and serve the calzone immediately.

Root Vegetable Couscous

Harissa is a very fiery Tunisian chili sauce which can be bought ready-made from Middle-Eastern shops.

Serves 4

2¼ cups couscous
3 tablespoons olive oil
4 baby onions, halved
1½ pounds fresh mixed
  root vegetables such as
  carrots, rutabaga,
  turnip, celery root and
  sweet potatoes, cubed
2 garlic cloves, crushed
pinch of saffron strands
½ teaspoon each ground
  cinnamon and ginger
½ teaspoon ground
  turmeric
1 teaspoon each ground
  cumin and coriander
1 tablespoon tomato paste
1¾ cups hot vegetable
  stock

1 small fennel bulb,
  quartered
1 cup cooked or canned
  chick-peas
½ cup seedless raisins
2 tablespoons chopped
  fresh cilantro
2 tablespoons chopped
  fresh Italian parsley
salt and ground black
  pepper

For the spiced sauce
1 tablespoon olive oil
1 tablespoon lemon juice
1 tablespoon chopped
  fresh cilantro
½–1 teaspoon harissa

1 Put the couscous in a bowl, cover with hot water; drain. Gently fry the onions for 3 minutes, then add the root vegetables and fry for 5 minutes. Add the garlic and spices and cook for 1 minute, stirring. Transfer the vegetable mixture to a large deep saucepan. Stir in the tomato paste, stock, fennel, chick-peas, raisins, chopped cilantro and Italian parsley. Bring to a boil. Put the couscous into a cheesecloth-lined steamer and place this over the vegetable mixture. Cover and simmer for 20 minutes, or until the vegetables are tender.

2 To make the sauce, mix all the ingredients into 1 cup of the vegetable liquid. Spoon the couscous onto a plate and pile the vegetables on top. Serve immediately, handing around the sauce separately.

Risotto with Mushrooms

The addition of wild mushrooms gives a lovely woodland flavor to this risotto.

Serves 3–4

1 ounce dried wild
  mushrooms, preferably
  porcini
6 ounces fresh cultivated
  mushrooms
juice of ½ lemon
6 tablespoons butter
2 tablespoons finely
  chopped fresh parsley
3¾ cups meat or chicken
  stock, preferably
  homemade

2 tablespoons olive oil
1 small onion, finely
  chopped
1½ cups medium-grain
  risotto rice, such as
  arborio
½ cup dry white wine
salt and ground black
  pepper
3 tablespoons freshly
  grated Parmesan
  cheese

1 Place the dried mushrooms in a small bowl with about 1½ cups warm water. Let soak for at least 40 minutes. Rinse the mushrooms. Filter the soaking water through a strainer lined with paper towels, and reserve. Place in a pan with the stock; simmer until needed.

2 Slice the mushrooms. Toss with the lemon juice. Melt a third of the butter in a large frying pan. Stir in the mushrooms and cook until they begin to brown. Stir in the parsley, cook for 30 seconds more, and remove to another dish.

3 Heat another third of the butter with the olive oil in the mushroom pan. Cook the onion until golden. Add the rice and stir for 1–2 minutes. Add all the mushrooms. Pour in the wine, cook until it evaporates. Add the stock until it evaporates; cook the rice until *al dente*, about 20–35 minutes.

4 Remove the risotto pan from the heat. Stir in the remaining butter and the Parmesan. Grind in a little pepper, and taste again for salt; adjust if necessary. Allow the risotto to rest for 3–4 minutes before serving.

Tomato Risotto

Use plum tomatoes in this dish, if possible, for their fresh vibrant flavor and meaty texture.

Serves 4

1½ pounds firm ripe
    tomatoes
4 tablespoons butter
1 onion, finely chopped
5 cups vegetable stock
1¾ cups arborio rice
14-ounce can navy or
    white beans

½ cup finely grated
    Parmesan cheese
salt and ground black
    pepper
10 – 12 fresh basil leaves,
    shredded, and freshly
    grated Parmesan
    cheese, to serve

1 Halve the tomatoes and scoop out the seeds into a sieve placed over a bowl. Press the seeds with a spoon to extract all the juice. Set aside.

2 Broil the tomatoes skin-side up until the skins are evenly blackened and blistered. Rub off the skins and dice the flesh.

3 Melt the butter in a large frying pan and cook the onion for 5 minutes until beginning to soften. Add the tomatoes, the reserved juice and seasoning, then cook, stirring occasionally, for about 10 minutes. Meanwhile, bring the vegetable stock to a boil in another pan.

4 Add the rice to the tomatoes and stir to coat, then add a ladleful of the stock and stir gently until absorbed. Repeat, adding a ladleful of stock at a time, until all the stock is absorbed and the rice is tender and creamy.

5 Stir in the beans and grated Parmesan and heat through for a few minutes. Just before serving the risotto, sprinkle each portion with shredded basil leaves and shavings of Parmesan.

Grilled Polenta with Peppers

Grilled slices of herb-flavored polenta are topped with yellow and red pepper strips for a delicious, colorful dish.

Serves 4

scant 1 cup polenta
2 tablespoons butter
1 – 2 tablespoons mixed
    chopped herbs such as
    parsley, thyme and
    sage
melted butter, for
    brushing
4 tablespoons olive oil
1 – 2 garlic cloves, cut
    into slivers

2 roasted red bell
    peppers, peeled and
    cut into strips
2 roasted yellow bell
    peppers, peeled and
    cut into strips
1 tablespoon balsamic
    vinegar
salt and ground black
    pepper
fresh herb sprigs, to
    garnish

1 Bring 2½ cups salted water to a boil in a heavy saucepan. Trickle in the polenta, beating constantly, then cook gently for 15 – 20 minutes, stirring occasionally, until the mixture is no longer grainy and comes away from the sides of the pan.

2 Remove the pan from the heat and beat in the butter, herbs and plenty of pepper.

3 Pour the polenta into a small ovenproof bowl, smooth the surface and let stand until cold and firm.

4 Turn out the polenta onto a board and cut into thick slices. Brush the polenta slices with melted butter and broil each side for about 4 – 5 minutes, until golden brown.

5 Meanwhile, heat the olive oil in a frying pan, add the garlic and peppers and stir-fry for 1 – 2 minutes. Stir in the balsamic vinegar and seasoning.

6 Spoon the pepper mixture onto the polenta slices and garnish with fresh herb sprigs. Serve hot.

Okra Fried Rice

This spicy rich dish is given a creamy consistency by the natural juices of the sliced okra.

Serves 3–4

2 tablespoons vegetable oil
1 tablespoon butter or margarine
1 garlic clove, crushed
½ red onion, finely chopped
4 ounces okra, topped and tailed
2 tablespoons diced green and red bell peppers
½ teaspoon dried thyme

2 green chilies, finely chopped
½ teaspoon five-spice powder
1 vegetable stock cube
2 tablespoons soy sauce
1 tablespoon chopped fresh cilantro
2½ cups cooked rice
salt and ground black pepper
fresh cilantro sprigs, to garnish

1 Heat the oil and butter or margarine in a frying pan or wok and cook the garlic and onion over a moderate heat for 5 minutes until soft.

2 Thinly slice the okra, add to the pan or wok and sauté gently for 6–7 minutes.

3 Add the green and red peppers, thyme, chilies and five-spice powder and cook for 3 minutes, then crumble in the stock cube.

4 Add the soy sauce, cilantro and rice and heat through, stirring well. Season to taste with salt and pepper. Serve hot, garnished with cilantro sprigs.

Cook's Tip
Reduce the amount of chopped green chili you include in this dish, if you wish.

Asparagus and Cheese Risotto

Arborio rice is *the* risotto rice and gives this authentic Italian dish a unique creamy texture.

Serves 4

¼ teaspoon saffron strands
3⅔ cups hot chicken stock
2 tablespoons butter
2 tablespoons olive oil
1 large onion, finely chopped
2 garlic cloves, finely chopped
1¼ cups arborio rice
1¼ cups dry white wine

8 ounces asparagus tips (or asparagus cut into 2-inch pieces), cooked
1 cup finely grated Parmesan cheese
salt and ground black pepper
fresh Parmesan cheese shavings and fresh basil sprigs, to garnish
ciabatta bread rolls and green salad, to serve

1 Sprinkle the saffron over the stock and allow to infuse for 5 minutes. Heat the butter and oil in a frying pan and fry the onion and garlic for about 6 minutes until softened.

2 Add the rice and stir-fry for 1–2 minutes to coat the grains with the butter and oil. Pour on 1¼ cups of the stock and saffron. Cook gently, stirring frequently, until it is absorbed. Repeat with another 1¼ cups stock. When that is absorbed, add the wine and carry on cooking and stirring until the rice has a creamy consistency.

3 Add the asparagus and remaining stock, and stir until the liquid is absorbed and the rice is tender. Stir in the Parmesan cheese and season to taste with salt and pepper.

4 Spoon the risotto onto warmed plates and garnish with the Parmesan cheese shavings and fresh basil. Serve with hot ciabatta rolls and a crisp green salad, if you wish.

Louisiana Rice

Ground pork and chicken livers with mixed vegetables make a tasty dish that is a meal in itself.

Serves 4

4 tablespoons oil
1 small eggplant, diced
8 ounces ground pork
1 green bell pepper, seeded and chopped
2 celery stalks, chopped
1 onion, chopped
1 garlic clove, crushed
1 teaspoon cayenne pepper
1 teaspoon paprika
1 teaspoon ground black pepper

½ teaspoon salt
1 teaspoon dried thyme
½ teaspoon dried oregano
2 cups chicken stock
8 ounces chicken livers, very finely chopped
¼ cup long-grain rice
1 bay leaf
3 tablespoons chopped fresh parsley
celery leaves, to garnish

1 Heat the oil in a frying pan until really hot, then stir-fry the eggplant for about 5 minutes. Add the pork and cook for about 6–8 minutes, until browned, using a wooden spoon to break up any lumps.

2 Add the pepper, celery, onion, garlic, cayenne pepper, paprika, pepper, salt, thyme and oregano. Cover and cook over high heat for 5–6 minutes, stirring frequently from the bottom to scrape up and distribute the crispy bits of pork.

3 Pour on the chicken stock and stir to clean the bottom of the pan. Cover and cook for 6 minutes over a moderate heat. Stir in the chicken livers, cook for another 2 minutes, then stir in the rice and add the bay leaf.

4 Reduce the heat, cover and simmer for about 6–7 minutes more. Turn off the heat and let stand for 10–15 minutes more until the rice is tender. Remove the bay leaf and stir in the chopped parsley. Serve the rice hot, garnished with the celery leaves.

Indian Pilau Rice

Basmati rice is the most popular choice for Indian dishes, but you could use long-grain rice instead.

Serves 4

1¼ cups basmati rice, rinsed well
2 tablespoons oil
1 small onion, finely chopped
1 garlic clove, crushed
1 teaspoon fennel seeds
1 tablespoon sesame seeds
½ teaspoon ground turmeric
1 teaspoon ground cumin

¼ teaspoon salt
2 whole cloves
4 cardamom pods, lightly crushed
5 black peppercorns
1¾ cups chicken stock
1 tablespoon ground almonds
fresh cilantro sprigs, to garnish

1 Soak the rice in water for 30 minutes. Heat the oil in a saucepan, add the onions and garlic, then fry them gently for 5–6 minutes, until softened.

2 Stir in the fennel and sesame seeds, the turmeric, cumin, salt, cloves, cardamom pods and peppercorns and fry for about 1 minute. Drain the rice well, add to the pan and stir-fry for a further 3 minutes.

3 Pour on the chicken stock. Bring to a boil, then cover with a tight-fitting lid, reduce the heat to very low and then simmer gently for 20 minutes, without removing the lid, until all the liquid has been absorbed.

4 Remove from the heat and let stand for 2–3 minutes. Fluff up the rice with a fork and stir in the ground almonds. Garnish with cilantro sprigs.

Chinese Special Fried Rice

This staple of Chinese cuisine consists of a mixture of chicken, shrimp and vegetables with fried rice.

Serves 4

1 cup long-grain white
rice
3 tablespoons peanut oil
1 garlic clove, crushed
4 scallions, finely
chopped
1 cup diced cooked
chicken
1 cup peeled, cooked
shrimp
½ cup frozen peas

1 egg, beaten with a
pinch of salt
2 ounces lettuce, finely
shredded
2 tablespoons light soy
sauce
pinch of sugar
salt and ground black
pepper
1 tablespoon chopped,
roasted cashew nuts,
to garnish

1 Rinse the rice in warm water to wash away some of the starch. Drain well.

2 Put the rice in a saucepan and add 1 tablespoon of the oil and 1½ cups water. Cover and bring to a boil, stir once, then cover and simmer for 12–15 minutes, until nearly all the water has been absorbed. Turn off the heat and let stand, covered, for 10 minutes. Fluff up with a fork and allow to cool.

3 Heat the remaining oil in a wok or frying pan and stir-fry the garlic and scallions for 30 seconds.

4 Add the chicken, shrimp and peas and stir-fry for about 1–2 minutes, then add the cooked rice and stir-fry for another 2 minutes. Pour in the egg and stir-fry until just set. Stir in the lettuce, soy sauce, sugar and seasoning.

5 Transfer to a warmed serving bowl, sprinkle with the chopped cashew nuts and serve immediately.

Lemon Bulgur Wheat Salad

This Middle-Eastern salad, called *tabbouleh*, is delicious as an accompaniment to broiled meats or fish, or on its own.

Serves 4

1½ cups bulgur
4 scallions, finely
chopped
5 tablespoons each
chopped fresh mint
and parsley
1 tablespoon chopped
fresh cilantro

2 tomatoes, skinned and
chopped
juice of 1 lemon
5 tablespoons olive oil
salt and ground black
pepper
fresh mint sprigs, to
garnish

1 Place the bulgur in a bowl, pour on enough boiling water to cover and let soak for 20 minutes.

2 After soaking, place the bulgur in a large strainer and drain thoroughly. Transfer to a bowl.

3 Stir in the scallions, herbs, tomatoes, lemon juice, olive oil and seasoning. Mix well and chill in the fridge for about an hour. Garnish with mint.

Cook's Tip
Add some pitted, halved black olives to the salad just before serving, if you wish.

Tanzanian Vegetable Rice

Serve this tasty rice with baked chicken, or a fish dish and a delicious fresh relish – *kachumbali*.

Serves 4

2 cups basmati rice
3 tablespoons oil
1 onion, chopped
3 cups vegetable stock or
    water
2 garlic cloves, crushed

1 cup corn
½ fresh red or green bell
    pepper, chopped
1 large carrot, grated

1 Wash the rice in a strainer under cold water, then allow to drain for about 15 minutes.

2 Heat the oil in a large saucepan and fry the onion for a few minutes over moderate heat until just soft.

3 Add the rice and stir-fry for about 10 minutes, taking care to keep stirring all the time so that the rice doesn't stick to the bottom of the pan.

4 Add the stock or water and the garlic and stir well. Bring to a boil and cook over high heat for 5 minutes, then reduce the heat, cover with a tight-fitting lid and cook the rice for 20 minutes.

5 Scatter the corn over the rice, then spread the pepper on top and lastly sprinkle on the grated carrot.

6 Cover tightly and steam over low heat until the rice is cooked, then mix together with a fork and serve immediately.

Rice with Seeds and Spices

A change from plain boiled rice, this spicy dish makes a colorful accompaniment for curries or broiled meats.

Serves 4

1 teaspoon sunflower oil
½ teaspoon ground
    turmeric
6 cardamom pods, lightly
    crushed
1 teaspoon coriander
    seeds, lightly crushed
1 garlic clove, crushed
1 cup basmati rice

1⅔ cups stock
½ cup plain yogurt
1 tablespoon each toasted
    sunflower seeds and
    toasted sesame seeds
salt and ground black
    pepper
fresh cilantro leaves, to
    garnish

1 Heat the oil in a non-stick frying pan and fry the spices and garlic for about 1 minute, stirring all the time.

2 Add the rice and stock, bring to a boil, then cover and simmer for 15 minutes or until just tender.

3 Stir in the yogurt and the toasted sunflower and sesame seeds. Adjust the seasoning and serve hot, garnished with cilantro leaves.

Cook's Tip
Although basmati rice gives the best texture and flavor, you could substitute ordinary long-grain rice if you prefer.

Lemon and Herb Risotto Cake

This unusual rice dish can be served as a main course with salad, or as a satisfying side dish.

Serves 4

1 small leek, thinly sliced
2½ cups chicken stock
1¼ cups arborio rice
finely grated rind of
  1 lemon
2 tablespoons chopped
  fresh chives

2 tablespoons chopped
  fresh parsley
generous ½ cup grated
  mozzarella cheese
salt and ground black
  pepper
fresh parsley and lemon
  wedges, to garnish

1 Preheat the oven to 400°F. Lightly oil an 8½-inch round springform cake pan.

2 Cook the leek in a large saucepan with 3 tablespoons stock, stirring over moderate heat, to soften. Add the rice and the remaining stock.

3 Bring to a boil. Cover the pan with a tight-fitting lid and simmer gently, stirring occasionally, for about 20 minutes, or until all the liquid is absorbed.

4 Stir in the lemon rind, herbs, cheese and seasoning. Spoon into the pan, cover with foil and bake for 30–35 minutes or until lightly browned. Turn out and serve in slices, garnished with parsley and lemon wedges.

Cook's Tip
This risotto cake is equally delicious served cold, so makes ideal picnic food.

Bulgur and Lentil Pilaf

Bulgur is very easy to cook and can be used in almost any way you would normally use rice, hot or cold.

Serves 4

1 teaspoon olive oil
1 large onion, thinly
  sliced
2 garlic cloves, crushed
1 teaspoon ground
  coriander
1 teaspoon ground cumin
1 teaspoon ground
  turmeric

½ teaspoon ground
  allspice
1¼ cups bulgur
about 3⅔ cups stock or
  water
4 ounces button
  mushrooms, sliced
⅔ cup green lentils
salt, ground black pepper
  and cayenne pepper

1 Heat the oil in a nonstick saucepan and fry the onion, garlic and spices for 1 minute, stirring.

2 Stir in the bulgur and cook, stirring, for about 2 minutes, until lightly browned. Add the stock or water, mushrooms and lentils.

3 Simmer over very gentle heat for about 25–30 minutes, until the bulgur and lentils are tender and all the liquid is absorbed. Add more stock or water, if necessary.

4 Season well with salt, black pepper and cayenne pepper and serve hot.

Cook's Tip
Green lentils can be cooked without presoaking, as they cook quite quickly and keep their shape. However, if you have time, soaking them first will shorten the cooking time slightly.

Minted Couscous Castles

Couscous, flavored with mint and then molded, makes an unusual accompaniment to a meal.

Serves 6

1¼ cups couscous
2 cups boiling stock
1 tablespoon freshly
    squeezed lemon juice
2 tomatoes, diced
2 tablespoon chopped
    fresh mint

oil, for brushing
salt and ground black
    pepper
fresh mint sprigs, to
    garnish

1   Place the couscous in a bowl and pour on the boiling stock. Cover the bowl and let stand for 30 minutes, until all the stock is absorbed and the grains are tender.

2   Stir in the lemon juice with the tomatoes and chopped mint. Adjust the seasoning with salt and pepper.

3   Brush the insides of four cups or individual molds with oil. Spoon in the couscous mixture and pack down firmly. Chill in the fridge for several hours.

4   Turn out and serve cold, or alternatively, cover and heat gently in a low oven or microwave, then turn out and serve hot, garnished with mint.

Cook's Tip
Most couscous is sold ready-cooked so can be prepared as above. However, some types require steaming first, so check the instructions on the package.

Creole Jambalaya

This version of jambalaya is made with chicken instead of the more traditional ham.

Serves 6

4 chicken thighs, boned,
    skinned and diced
about 1¼ cups chicken
    stock
1 large green bell pepper,
    seeded and sliced
3 celery stalks, sliced
4 scallions, sliced
14-ounce can tomatoes
1 teaspoon ground cumin

1 teaspoon ground
    allspice
½ teaspoon cayenne
    pepper
1 teaspoon dried thyme
1½ cups long-grain rice
scant 2 cups peeled,
    cooked shrimp
salt and ground black
    pepper

1   Fry the chicken in a nonstick saucepan without fat, turning occasionally, until golden brown.

2   Add 1 tablespoon stock with the pepper, celery and onions. Cook for a few minutes to soften, then add the tomatoes, spices and thyme.

3   Stir in the rice and remaining stock. Cover closely and cook for about 20 minutes, stirring occasionally, until the rice is tender. Add more stock if necessary.

4   Add the peeled shrimp and heat well. Season to taste and serve with a crisp salad, if you wish.

Red Fried Rice

This vibrant rice dish owes its appeal to the bright colors of red onion, red bell pepper and cherry tomatoes.

Serves 2

¾ cup rice
2 tablespoons peanut oil
1 small red onion, chopped
1 red bell pepper, seeded and chopped
8 ounces cherry tomatoes, halved
2 eggs, beaten
salt and ground black pepper

1 Wash the rice several times under cold running water. Drain well. Bring a large saucepan of water to a boil, add the rice and cook for 10–12 minutes.

2 Meanwhile, heat the oil in a wok until very hot and stir-fry the onion and red pepper for 2–3 minutes. Add the cherry tomatoes and stir-fry for another 2 minutes.

3 Pour in the beaten eggs all at once. Cook for 30 seconds without stirring, then stir to break up the eggs as they set.

4 Drain the cooked rice thoroughly, add to the wok and toss it over the heat with the vegetable and egg mixture for 3 minutes. Season the fried rice with salt and pepper to taste.

Cook's Tip
Use basmati rice for this dish, if possible. Its slightly crunchy texture complements the softness of the egg.

Kedgeree

Popular for breakfast in Victorian England, kedgeree has its origins in *khichri*, an Indian rice and lentil dish.

Serves 4

1¼ pounds smoked haddock
scant ½ cup long-grain rice
2 tablespoons lemon juice
¾ cup single or sour cream
pinch of freshly grated nutmeg
pinch of cayenne pepper
2 hard-boiled eggs, peeled and cut into wedges
4 tablespoons butter, diced
2 tablespoons chopped fresh parsley
salt and ground black pepper
fresh parsley sprigs, to garnish

1 Poach the haddock, just covered by water, for about 10 minutes, until the flesh flakes easily. Lift the fish from the cooking liquid with a draining spoon, then remove any skin and bones. Flake the flesh.

2 Pour the fish cooking liquid into a measuring cup and add water, until it measures 1 cup.

3 Bring the fish cooking liquid to a boil, add the rice, stir, then cover with a tight-fitting lid and simmer for about 15 minutes, until the rice is tender and the liquid absorbed. While the rice is cooking, preheat the oven to 350°F, and butter a baking dish.

4 Remove the rice from the heat and stir in the lemon juice, cream, flaked fish, nutmeg and cayenne. Add the egg wedges to the rice mixture and stir in gently.

5 Turn the rice mixture into the baking dish, dot with butter and bake for about 25 minutes.

6 Stir the chopped parsley into the kedgeree, adjust the seasoning to taste and garnish with fresh parsley sprigs.

Nut Pilaf with Omelet Rolls

This pilaf combines a wonderful mixture of textures – soft fluffy rice with crunchy nuts and omelet rolls.

Serves 2

1 cup basmati rice
1 tablespoon sunflower
  oil
1 small onion, chopped
1 red bell pepper, finely
  diced
1½ cups hot vegetable
  stock

2 eggs
¼ cup salted peanuts
1 tablespoon soy sauce
salt and ground black
  pepper
fresh parsley sprigs, to
  garnish

1 Wash the rice several times under cold running water. Drain thoroughly. Heat half the oil in a large frying pan and fry the onion and red pepper for 2–3 minutes, then stir in the rice and stock. Bring to a boil and cook for 10 minutes until the rice is tender.

2 Meanwhile, beat the eggs lightly and season to taste with salt and pepper. Heat the remaining oil in a second large frying pan. Pour in the eggs and tilt the pan to cover the bottom thinly. Cook the omelet for 1 minute, then flip it over and cook the other side for 1 minute.

3 Slide the omelet onto a clean board and roll it up tightly. Cut the omelet roll into eight slices.

4 Stir the peanuts and the soy sauce into the pilaf and add pepper to taste. Turn the pilaf into a serving dish, then arrange the omelet rolls on top and garnish with the parsley. Serve immediately.

Cook's Tip
Try salted cashew nuts or toasted flaked almonds in this dish for a change.

Eggplant Pilaf

This hearty dish is made with bulgur, eggplant and pine nuts, subtly flavored with fresh mint.

Serves 2

2 eggplant
4–6 tablespoons
  sunflower oil
1 small onion, finely
  chopped
1 cup bulgur
1¾ cups vegetable stock
2 tablespoons pine nuts,
  toasted

1 tablespoon chopped
  fresh mint
salt and ground black
  pepper
lime and lemon wedges
  and fresh mint sprigs,
  to garnish

1 Remove the ends of the eggplant. Using a sharp knife, cut the eggplant into neat sticks and then dice into ½-inch pieces.

2 Heat 4 tablespoons of the oil in a large frying pan and sauté the onion for 1 minute.

3 Add the diced eggplant. Cook over high heat, stirring frequently, for about 4 minutes until just tender. Add the remaining oil if needed.

4 Stir in the bulgur, mixing well, then pour in the vegetable stock. Bring to a boil, then lower the heat and simmer for 10 minutes or until all the liquid has evaporated. Season with salt and pepper to taste.

5 Add the pine nuts, stir gently with a wooden spoon, then stir in the mint.

6 Spoon the pilaf onto individual plates and garnish each portion with lime and lemon wedges. Sprinkle with mint sprigs for extra color.

Cabbage with Bacon

In this dish, bacon enhances the flavor of cabbage, making it a delicious vegetable accompaniment.

Serves 2–4

2 tablespoons oil
1 onion, finely chopped
4 ounces bacon, finely
  chopped

1¼ pounds cabbage,
  shredded
salt and ground black
  pepper

1 Heat the oil in a large saucepan and cook the onion and bacon for about 7 minutes, stirring occasionally.

2 Add the cabbage and season with salt and pepper. Stir for a few minutes over moderately high heat until the cabbage begins to shrink in volume.

3 Continue to cook the cabbage, stirring it frequently for 8–10 minutes until tender, but still crisp. (For softer cabbage, cover the pan for part of the cooking.) Serve immediately.

Cook's Tip
This dish is equally delicious if prepared using collard greens instead of cabbage. To make a more substantial dish to serve for lunch or supper, add some chopped button mushrooms and some skinned, seeded and chopped tomatoes.

Braised Red Cabbage

Lightly spiced with a sharp, sweet flavor, this dish goes well with roast pork, duck and game dishes.

Serves 4–6

2 pounds red cabbage
2 onions, chopped
2 tart cooking apples,
  peeled, cored and
  grated
1 teaspoon freshly grated
  nutmeg
¼ teaspoon ground cloves
¼ teaspoon ground
  cinnamon

1 tablespoon dark brown
  sugar
3 tablespoons red wine
  vinegar
2 tablespoons butter or
  margarine, diced
salt and ground black
  pepper

1 Preheat the oven to 325°F. Cut off and discard the large white ribs from the outer cabbage leaves using a large sharp knife, then finely shred the cabbage.

2 Layer the shredded cabbage in a large casserole with the onions, apples, spices, sugar and seasoning. Pour on the vinegar and add the diced butter or margarine.

3 Cover the casserole and cook in the oven for about 1½ hours, stirring a couple of times, until the cabbage is very tender. Serve hot.

Cook's Tip
This recipe can be cooked in advance. Bake the cabbage for 1½ hours, then allow to cool. To complete the cooking, bake in the oven at the same temperature for about 30 minutes, stirring occasionally.

Lemon Carrots

The carrots are cooked until just tender in lemon stock which is then thickened to make a light tangy sauce.

Serves 4

2½ cups water
1 pound carrots, thinly
   sliced
bouquet garni
1 tablespoon freshly
   squeezed lemon juice
pinch of freshly grated
   nutmeg
1½ tablespoons butter
1 tablespoon all-purpose
   flour
salt and ground black
   pepper

1 Bring the water to a boil in a large saucepan, then add the carrots, bouquet garni, lemon juice, nutmeg and seasoning and simmer until the carrots are tender. Remove the carrots using a slotted spoon, then keep warm.

2 Boil the cooking liquid hard until it has reduced to about 1¼ cups. Discard the bouquet garni.

3 Mash 1 tablespoon of the butter and all of the flour together, then gradually whisk into the simmering reduced cooking liquid, whisking well after each addition, then simmer for about 3 minutes, until the sauce has thickened.

4 Return the carrots to the pan, heat through in the sauce, then remove from the heat. Stir in the remaining butter and serve immediately.

Ratatouille

Ratatouille may be served hot or cold, as an appetizer, side dish or vegetarian main course.

Serves 4

2 large eggplant, coarsely
   chopped
4 zucchini, coarsely
   chopped
⅔ cup olive oil
2 onions, sliced
2 garlic cloves, chopped
1 large red bell pepper,
   seeded and coarsely
   chopped
2 large yellow bell
   peppers, seeded and
   coarsely chopped
1 fresh rosemary sprig
1 fresh thyme sprig
1 teaspoon coriander
   seeds, crushed
3 plum tomatoes,
   skinned, seeded and
   chopped
8 basil leaves, coarsely
   torn
salt and ground black
   pepper
fresh parsley or basil
   sprigs, to garnish

1 Place the eggplant in a colander, sprinkle with salt and place a plate with a weight on top to extract the bitter juice. Leave for 30 minutes.

2 Heat the olive oil in a large saucepan and gently fry the onions for about 6–7 minutes until just softened. Add the garlic and cook for 2 minutes more.

3 Rinse, drain and pat dry the eggplant with paper towels. Add to the pan with the peppers, increase the heat and sauté until the peppers are just turning brown.

4 Add the herbs and coriander seeds, then cover the pan and cook gently for about 40 minutes.

5 Add the tomatoes and season to taste with salt and pepper. Cook gently for another 10 minutes, until the vegetables are soft but not too mushy. Remove the sprigs of herbs. Stir in the torn basil leaves and check the seasoning. Let cool slightly and serve warm or cold, garnished with sprigs of parsley or basil.

Parsnips with Almonds

Parsnips have an affinity with most nuts, so you could use walnuts or hazelnuts instead of the almonds.

Serves 4
1 pound small parsnips
scant 3 tablespoons
*   butter*
¼ cup flaked almonds
1 tablespoon light brown
*   sugar*

pinch of ground mixed
*   spice*
1 tablespoon lemon juice
salt and ground black
*   pepper*
chopped fresh chervil or
*   parsley, to garnish*

1   Cook the parsnips in boiling salted water until almost tender. Drain well. When the parsnips are cool enough to handle, cut each in half across its width, then quarter these halves lengthwise.

2   Heat the butter in a frying pan and cook the parsnips and almonds gently, stirring and turning carefully until they are lightly flecked with brown.

3   Mix together the sugar and mixed spice, sprinkle on the parsnips and stir to mix, then trickle over the lemon juice. Season to taste with salt and pepper and heat for 1 minute. Serve sprinkled with chopped fresh chervil or parsley.

Turnips with Orange

Sprinkle toasted nuts such as flaked almonds or chopped walnuts over the turnips to add contrast.

Serves 4
4 tablespoons butter
1 tablespoon oil
1 small shallot, finely
*   chopped*
1 pound small turnips,
*   quartered*

1¼ cups freshly squeezed
*   orange juice*
salt and ground black
*   pepper*

1   Heat the butter and oil in a saucepan and cook the shallot gently, stirring occasionally, until soft but not colored.

2   Add the turnips to the shallot and heat. Shake the pan frequently until the turnips start to absorb the butter and oil.

3   Pour the orange juice onto the turnips, then simmer gently for about 30 minutes, until the turnips are tender and the orange juice is reduced to a buttery sauce. Season with salt and pepper, if required, and serve hot.

Red Cabbage with Pears and Nuts

A sweet and sour, spicy red cabbage dish, with the added crunch of pears and walnuts.

Serves 6

1 tablespoon walnut oil
1 onion, sliced
2 whole star anise
1 teaspoon ground
* cinnamon*
pinch of ground cloves
1 pound red cabbage,
* finely shredded*
2 tablespoons dark brown
* sugar*

3 tablespoons red wine
* vinegar*
1¼ cup red wine
scant ¾ cup port
2 pears, cut into ½-inch
* cubes*
½ cup raisins
salt and ground black
* pepper*
½ cup walnut halves

1 Heat the oil in a large pan. Add the onion and cook gently for about 5 minutes until softened.

2 Add the star anise, cinnamon, cloves and cabbage and cook for about 3 minutes more.

3 Stir in the sugar, vinegar, red wine and port. Cover the pan and simmer gently for 10 minutes, stirring occasionally.

4 Stir in the cubed pears and raisins and cook for another 10 minutes or until the cabbage is tender. Season to taste. Mix in the walnut halves and serve.

Swiss Soufflé Potatoes

Baked potatoes are great for cold weather eating, and are both economical and satisfying.

Serves 4

4 baking potatoes
scant 1 cup grated
* Gruyère cheese*
½ cup herb-flavored
* butter*

4 tablespoons heavy
* cream*
2 eggs, separated
salt and ground black
* pepper*

1 Preheat the oven to 425°F. Scrub the potatoes, then prick them all over with a fork. Bake for about 1–1½ hours until tender. Remove them from the oven and reduce the temperature to 350°F.

2 Cut each potato in half and scoop out the insides into a bowl. Return the potato shells to the oven to crisp them while making the filling.

3 Mash the potato using a fork then add the Gruyère, herb-flavored butter, cream and egg yolks, and season to taste with salt and pepper. Beat well until smooth.

4 Whisk the egg whites in a separate bowl until stiff peaks form, then fold into the potato mixture.

5 Pile the mixture back into the potato shells and bake for 20–25 minutes, until risen and golden brown.

Cook's Tip
Choose a floury variety of potato for this dish for the best results.

Thai Vegetables with Noodles

This dish makes a delicious vegetarian supper on its own, or it could be served as an accompaniment.

Serves 4

4 cups egg noodles
1 tablespoon sesame oil
3 tablespoons peanut oil
2 garlic cloves, thinly
    sliced
1-inch piece fresh ginger,
    finely chopped
2 fresh red chilies, seeded
    and sliced
1 cup broccoli florets
4 ounces baby corn

6 ounces shiitake or
    oyster mushrooms,
    sliced
1 bunch scallions, sliced
4 ounces pak choi or
    Chinese cabbage,
    shredded
generous 1 cup bean
    sprouts
1–2 tablespoons dark
    soy sauce
salt and ground black
    pepper

1 Bring a saucepan of salted water to the boil and cook the egg noodles according to the instructions on the packet. Drain well and toss in the sesame oil. Set aside.

2 Heat the peanut oil in a wok or large frying pan and stir-fry the garlic and ginger for 1 minute. Add the chilies, broccoli, baby corn and mushrooms and stir-fry for another 2 minutes.

3 Add the scallions, shredded pak choi or Chinese cabbage and bean sprouts and stir-fry for another 2 minutes.

4 Toss in the drained noodles with the soy sauce and pepper.

5 Continue to cook over high heat, stirring, for 2–3 minutes more, until the ingredients are mixed well and warmed through. Serve immediately.

Cauliflower with Three Cheeses

The mingled flavors of three cheeses give a new twist to cauliflower cheese.

Serves 4

4 baby cauliflowers
1 cup light cream
3 ounces dolcelatte
    cheese, diced
3 ounces mozzarella
    cheese, diced

3 tablespoons freshly
    grated Parmesan
    cheese
pinch of freshly grated
    nutmeg
ground black pepper
toasted bread crumbs, to
    garnish

1 Cook the cauliflowers in a large saucepan of boiling salted water for 8–10 minutes, until just tender.

2 Meanwhile, put the cream into a small pan with the cheeses. Heat gently until the cheeses have melted, stirring occasionally. Season to taste with nutmeg and pepper.

3 When the cauliflowers are cooked, drain them thoroughly and place one on each of four warmed plates.

4 Spoon a little of the cheese sauce over each cauliflower and sprinkle each with a few of the toasted bread crumbs. Serve at once.

Cook's Tip
For a more economical dish or if baby cauliflowers are not available, use one large cauliflower instead. Cut it into quarters with a large sharp knife and remove the central core.

Potato Gnocchi with Sauce

These delicate potato dumplings are dressed with a tasty creamy hazelnut sauce.

Serves 4
1½ pounds large potatoes
1 cup all-purpose flour

For the hazelnut sauce
½ cup hazelnuts, roasted
1 garlic clove, coarsely
 chopped
½ teaspoon grated lemon
 rind

½ teaspoon lemon juice
2 tablespoons sunflower
 oil
¾ cup low-fat ricotta
 cheese
salt and ground black
 pepper

1 Place 2½ ounces of the hazelnuts in a blender with the garlic, grated lemon rind and juice. Blend until coarsely chopped. Gradually add the oil and blend until smooth. Spoon into a bowl and mix in the ricotta. Season.

2 Place the potatoes in a pan of cold water. Bring to a boil and cook for 20–25 minutes. Drain well in a colander. When cool, peel and purée the potatoes while still warm.

3 Add the flour a little at a time (you may not need all of the flour, as potatoes vary in texture). Stop adding flour when the mixture is smooth and slightly sticky. Add salt to taste.

4 Roll the mixture out onto a floured board to form a sausage ½-inch in diameter. Cut into ¾-inch pieces. Take one piece at a time and press it onto a floured fork. Roll each piece while pressing it along the prongs and off the fork. Flip onto a floured plate or tray. Continue with the rest of the mixture.

5 To cook, drop about 20–25 pieces at a time into a large pan of boiling water. They will rise to the surface quickly. Cook for about 10–15 seconds, then lift out with a slotted spoon. Heat the sauce carefully and pour over the gnocchi. Chop the remaining hazelnuts and scatter over the sauce.

Winter Vegetable Hot-pot

Use whatever vegetables you have at hand in this richly flavored and substantial one-pot meal.

Serves 4
2 onions, sliced
4 carrots, sliced
1 small rutabaga, sliced
2 parsnips, sliced
3 small turnips, sliced
½ celery root, cut into
 matchsticks
2 leeks, thinly sliced
2 tablespoons mixed
 chopped fresh herbs
 such as parsley and
 thyme

1 garlic clove, chopped
1 bay leaf, crumbled
1¼ cups vegetable stock
1 tablespoon all-purpose
 flour
1½ pounds red-skinned
 potatoes, scrubbed and
 thinly sliced
4 tablespoons butter
salt and ground black
 pepper

1 Preheat the oven to 375°F. Arrange all the vegetables, except the potatoes, in layers in a large casserole with a tight-fitting lid, seasoning them lightly with salt and pepper and sprinkling them with chopped herbs, garlic and crumbled bay leaf as you go.

2 Blend the vegetable stock into the flour and pour on the vegetables. Arrange the potatoes in overlapping layers on top. Dot with butter and cover tightly.

3 Cook in the oven for 1¼ hours, or until the vegetables are tender. Remove the lid from the casserole and cook for another 15–20 minutes until the top layer of potatoes is golden and crisp at the edges. Serve hot.

Cook's Tip
Make sure the root vegetables are cut into even slices so they cook uniformly.

Beans with Tomatoes

Young green beans are very tender and taste lovely with tomatoes and fresh tarragon.

Serves 4

2 cups young green
  beans
3 tablespoons butter
4 ripe tomatoes, peeled
  and chopped

salt and ground black
  pepper
chopped fresh tarragon,
  to garnish

1 Bring a saucepan of water to a boil, add the beans, return to a boil and cook for 3 minutes. Drain well.

2 Heat the butter in a pan, add the tomatoes and beans and season with salt and pepper. Cover the pan with a tight-fitting lid and simmer gently for about 10–15 minutes, until the beans are tender.

3 Pour the beans and tomatoes into a warm serving dish and sprinkle on the chopped tarragon to garnish. Serve hot as an accompaniment to broiled meats, poultry or fish.

Rosemary Roasties

The potatoes are roasted with their skins on, giving them far more flavor than traditional roast potatoes.

Serves 4

2 pounds small red
  potatoes
2 teaspoons walnut or
  sunflower oil

2 tablespoons fresh
  rosemary leaves
salt and paprika

1 Preheat the oven to 475°F. Leave the potatoes whole with the skins on, or if large, cut in half. Place the potatoes in a large saucepan of cold water and bring to boil, then drain immediately.

2 Return the potatoes to the saucepan and drizzle the walnut or sunflower oil over them. Shake the pan to coat the potatoes evenly in the oil.

3 Transfer the potatoes into a shallow roasting pan. Sprinkle with rosemary, salt and paprika. Roast for 30 minutes or until crisp. Served hot, these potatoes are good with roast lamb.

Vegetable Ribbons

This mixed vegetable side dish looks impressive and will delight dinner party guests.

Serves 4

Using a vegetable peeler or sharp knife, cut 3 medium carrots and 3 medium zucchini into thin ribbons. Bring ½ cup chicken stock to a boil, add the carrots. Return the stock to a boil; add the zucchini. Boil rapidly for 2–3 minutes, or until the vegetable ribbons are just tender. Stir in 2 tablespoons chopped fresh parsley, season lightly with salt and ground black pepper, and serve hot.

Zucchini and Tomato Bake

A *tian* is a heavy earthenware dish in which many French vegetable dishes are cooked. This is one example.

Serves 4

3 tablespoons olive oil
1 onion, chopped
1 garlic clove, crushed
3 slices lean bacon, chopped
4 zucchini, grated
2 tomatoes, skinned, seeded and chopped
scant ¾ cup cooked long-grain rice
2 teaspoons chopped fresh thyme
1 tablespoon chopped fresh parsley
4 tablespoons grated Parmesan cheese
2 eggs, lightly beaten
1 tablespoon sour cream
salt and ground black pepper

1 Preheat the oven to 350°F. Grease a shallow baking dish with a little olive oil.

2 Heat the oil in a frying pan and fry the onion and garlic for 5 minutes until softened.

3 Add the bacon and fry for 2 minutes, then stir in the zucchini and fry for 8 minutes more, stirring from time to time and letting some of the liquid evaporate. Remove the pan from the heat.

4 Add the tomatoes, cooked rice, herbs, 2 tablespoons of the Parmesan cheese, the eggs and sour cream, and season to taste with salt and pepper. Mix together well.

5 Spoon the zucchini mixture into the dish and sprinkle on the remaining Parmesan cheese. Bake for 45 minutes, until set and golden. Serve hot.

Cook's Tip
For a dinner party, divide the mixture among four lightly greased individual gratin dishes and bake for about 25 minutes until set and golden.

Spanish Green Beans with Ham

Judias verdes con jamón are green beans cooked with the Spanish raw-cured Serrano ham.

Serves 4

1 pound green beans
3 tablespoons olive oil
1 onion, thinly sliced
2 garlic cloves, finely chopped
3 ounces Serrano ham, chopped
salt and ground black pepper

1 Cook the beans, left whole, in boiling salted water for about 5–6 minutes, until they are just tender but still with a little bit of bite.

2 Meanwhile, heat the oil in a saucepan and fry the onions for 5 minutes, until softened and translucent. Add the garlic and ham and cook for another 1–2 minutes.

3 Drain the beans, then add them to the pan and cook, stirring occasionally, for 2–3 minutes. Season well with salt and pepper and serve hot.

Cook's Tip
Serrano ham is increasingly available in large supermarkets and has the advantage of being cheaper than prosciutto. However, if you cannot find it, use prosciutto or bacon instead.

Sweet Potatoes with Bacon

This sweet potato dish makes a good Thanksgiving offering with a tart and sweet flavor.

Serves 4

2 large sweet potatoes, 1
    pound each, washed
½ cup light brown sugar
2 tablespoons lemon juice
3 tablespoons butter
4 slices lean bacon, cut
    into thin strips

salt and ground black
    pepper
sprig of Italian parsley,
    to garnish

1 Preheat the oven to 375°F and lightly butter a shallow baking dish. Cut the unpeeled sweet potatoes crosswise into four and place the pieces in a pan of boiling water. Cover with a tight-fitting lid and cook until just tender, about 25 minutes.

2 Drain the potatoes and, when cool enough to handle, peel and slice quite thickly. Arrange in a single layer, overlapping, in the prepared dish.

3 Sprinkle on the sugar and lemon juice and dot with butter. Top with the bacon and season with salt and pepper.

4 Bake uncovered for 35–40 minutes, basting once or twice, until the potatoes are tender.

5 Preheat the broiler to high heat. Broil the potatoes for about 2–3 minutes, until they are browned and the bacon crispy. Serve hot, garnished with parsley.

Potatoes Baked with Tomatoes

This simple hearty dish from the south of Italy is best made with fresh tomatoes but canned plum tomatoes will do.

Serves 6

2 large red or yellow
    onions, thinly sliced
2¼ pounds potatoes,
    peeled and thinly
    sliced
1 pound fresh tomatoes
    (or canned, with their
    juice), sliced
6 tablespoons olive oil

1 cup freshly grated
    Parmesan or mature
    Cheddar cheese
salt and ground black
    pepper
¼ cup water
a few fresh basil leaves, to
    garnish (optional)

1 Preheat the oven to 350°F. Brush a large baking dish generously with oil.

2 Arrange a layer of onions in the dish, followed by layers of potatoes and tomatoes. Pour on a little of the oil, and sprinkle with the cheese. Season with salt and pepper.

3 Repeat until the vegetables are used up, ending with an overlapping layer of potatoes and tomatoes. Tear the basil leaves into pieces, and add them here and there among the vegetables. Sprinkle the top with cheese and a little oil.

4 Pour on the water. Bake for 1 hour, or until tender.

5 If the top begins to brown too much, place a sheet of foil or a flat baking sheet on top of the dish. Serve hot, garnished with basil leaves, if you wish.

Eggplant Baked with Cheeses

This famous dish, with its rich tomato sauce, is a specialty of Italy's southern regions.

Serves 4–6

2 pounds eggplant
flour, for coating
oil, for frying
½ cup freshly grated
  Parmesan cheese
14 ounces mozzarella
  cheese, sliced very
  thinly
salt and ground black
  pepper

For the tomato sauce
4 tablespoons olive oil
1 onion, very finely
  chopped
1 garlic clove, chopped
1 pound fresh tomatoes,
  or canned, chopped,
  with their juice
a few fresh basil leaves or
  parsley sprigs

1 Cut the eggplant into ½-inch slices, sprinkle with salt, and let drain for about 1 hour.

2 To make the tomato sauce, cook the onion in the oil until translucent. Stir in the garlic and the tomatoes (if using fresh tomatoes, add 3 tablespoons water). Season to taste; add the basil or parsley. Cook for 30 minutes. Purée in a vegetable mill.

3 Pat the aubergine slices dry, coat them lightly in flour. Heat a little oil in a large nonstick frying pan. Add one layer of eggplant, and cook over low to moderate heat with the pan covered until they soften. Turn, and cook on the other side. Remove from the pan, repeat with the remaining slices.

4 Preheat the oven to 350°F. Grease a wide shallow baking dish. Spread a little tomato sauce in the base. Cover with a layer of eggplant Sprinkle with a few teaspoons of Parmesan, season to taste with salt and pepper, and cover with a layer of mozzarella. Spoon on some tomato sauce. Repeat until all the ingredients are used up, ending with a layer of the tomato sauce and a sprinkling of Parmesan. Sprinkle with a little olive oil, and bake for about 45 minutes, until golden and bubbling.

Stuffed Onions

These savory onions make a good light lunch or supper. Small onions could be stuffed and served as a side dish.

Serves 6

6 large onions
scant ½ cup ham, cut
  into small dice
1 egg
½ cup dried bread
  crumbs
3 tablespoons finely
  chopped fresh parsley
1 garlic clove, chopped

pinch of freshly grated
  nutmeg
¾ cup freshly grated
  cheese such as
  Parmesan or mature
  Cheddar
6 tablespoons olive oil
salt and ground black
  pepper

1 Peel the onions without cutting through the bases. Cook them in a large pan of boiling water for about 20 minutes. Drain, and refresh in plenty of cold water.

2 Using a small sharp knife, cut around and scoop out each central section. Remove about half the inside (save it for soup). Lightly salt the empty cavities, and let the onions drain upside down.

3 Preheat the oven to 400°F. Beat the ham into the egg in a small bowl. Stir in the bread crumbs, parsley, garlic, nutmeg and all but 3 tablespoons of the grated cheese. Add 3 tablespoons of the oil, and season with salt and pepper.

4 Pat the insides of the onions dry with paper towels. Stuff them using a small spoon. Arrange the onions in one layer in an oiled baking dish.

5 Sprinkle the tops with the remaining cheese and then with oil. Bake for 45 minutes, or until the onions are tender and golden on top.

Baked Fennel with Parmesan Cheese

Fennel is widely eaten in Italy, both raw and cooked. It is delicious married with the sharpness of Parmesan.

Serves 4–6
2 pounds fennel bulbs, washed and cut in half
4 tablespoons butter
½ cup freshly grated Parmesan cheese

1 Cook the fennel bulbs in a large saucepan of boiling water until softened but not mushy. Drain well. Preheat the oven to 400°F.

2 Cut the fennel bulbs lengthwise into four or six pieces. Place them in a buttered baking dish.

3 Dot with butter. Sprinkle with the grated Parmesan. Bake in the hot oven until the cheese is golden brown, about 20 minutes. Serve at once.

Cook's Tip
For a more substantial version of this dish, finely chop 3 ounces ham and scatter it over the fennel before topping with the Parmesan cheese.

Zucchini with Sun-dried Tomatoes

Sun-dried tomatoes have a concentrated sweet flavor that goes well with zucchini.

Serves 6
10 sun-dried tomatoes, dry or preserved in oil and drained
¾ cup warm water
5 tablespoons olive oil
1 large onion, finely sliced
2 garlic cloves, finely chopped
2 pounds zucchini, cut into thin strips
salt and ground black pepper

1 Slice the tomatoes into thin strips. Place in a bowl with the warm water. Allow to stand for 20 minutes.

2 Heat the oil in a large frying pan or saucepan and then cook the onion over low to moderate heat until it softens but does not brown.

3 Stir in the garlic and the zucchini. Cook for about 5 minutes, continuing to stir the mixture.

4 Stir in the tomatoes and their soaking liquid. Season to taste with salt and pepper. Raise the heat slightly and cook until the zucchini is just tender. Serve hot or cold.

Broccoli Cauliflower Gratin

Broccoli and cauliflower combine well, and this dish is much lighter than a classic cauliflower cheese.

Serves 4

1 small cauliflower, about 9 ounces
1 head broccoli, about 9 ounces
½ cup plain low-fat yogurt
¼ cup grated reduced-fat Cheddar cheese
1 teaspoon whole-grain mustard
2 tablespoons whole wheat bread crumbs
salt and ground black pepper

1 Break the cauliflower and broccoli into florets and cook in lightly salted boiling water for 8–10 minutes, until just tender. Drain well and transfer to a flameproof casserole.

2 Mix together the yogurt, grated cheese and mustard, then season the mixture with pepper and spoon over the cauliflower and broccoli.

3 Sprinkle the bread crumbs over the top and place under a moderately hot broiler until golden brown. Serve hot.

Cook's Tip
When preparing the cauliflower and broccoli, discard the tougher parts of the stalks, then break the florets into even-size pieces so they will cook evenly.

Tex-Mex Baked Potatoes with Chili

A spicy chili bean sauce tops baked potatoes and is served with a dollop of sour cream.

Serves 4

2 large potatoes
1 tablespoon oil
1 garlic clove, crushed
1 small onion, chopped
½ small red bell pepper, seeded and chopped
8 ounces lean ground beef
½ small fresh red chili, seeded and chopped
1 teaspoon ground cumin
pinch of cayenne pepper
7-ounce can chopped tomatoes
2 tablespoons tomato paste
½ teaspoon dried oregano
½ teaspoon dried marjoram
7-ounce can red kidney beans, drained and rinsed
1 tablespoon chopped fresh cilantro
salt and ground black pepper
4 tablespoons sour cream
chopped fresh parsley, to garnish

1 Preheat the oven to 425°F. Rub the potatoes with a little oil. Prick with fork or thread onto skewers to speed cooking (or potato baker). Bake them on the top shelf for 30 minutes before beginning to cook the chili.

2 Heat the oil in a pan and fry the garlic, onion and pepper gently for 4–5 minutes, until softened.

3 Add the beef and fry until browned all over, then stir in the chili, cumin, cayenne pepper, tomatoes, tomato paste, 4 tablespoons water and the herbs. Cover with a tight-fitting lid and simmer for about 25 minutes, stirring occasionally.

4 Remove the lid, stir in the kidney beans and cook for 5 minutes. Turn off the heat and stir in the chopped fresh cilantro. Season to taste and set aside.

5 Cut the baked potatoes in half and place them in serving bowls. Top with the chili mixture and a dollop of sour cream,

Bombay Spiced Potatoes

Spanish Chili Potatoes

This Indian potato dish uses a delicately aromatic mixture of whole and ground spices.

Serves 4
4 large floury potatoes, diced
4 tablespoons sunflower oil
1 garlic clove, finely chopped
2 teaspoons brown mustard seeds
1 teaspoon black onion seeds (optional)
1 teaspoon ground turmeric
1 teaspoon ground cumin
1 teaspoon ground coriander
1 teaspoon fennel seeds
salt and ground black pepper
generous squeeze of lemon juice
chopped fresh cilantro and lemon wedges, to garnish

1 Bring a saucepan of salted water to a boil, add the potatoes and simmer for about 4 minutes, until just tender. Drain well.

2 Heat the oil in a large frying pan and add the garlic along with all the whole and ground spices. Stir-fry gently for 1–2 minutes, until the mustard seeds start to pop.

3 Add the potatoes and stir-fry over a moderate heat for about 5 minutes, until heated through and well coated with the spicy oil.

4 Season well and sprinkle on the lemon juice. Garnish with chopped fresh cilantro and lemon wedges. Serve as an accompaniment to curries or strongly flavored meat dishes.

Cook's Tip
Look out for black onion seeds – kalonji – in Indian or Pakistani food stores.

The Spanish name for this dish, *patatas bravas*, means fierce, hot potatoes. Reduce the amount of chili if you wish.

Serves 4
2 pounds new or salad potatoes
4 tablespoons olive oil
1 onion, finely chopped
2 garlic cloves, crushed
1 tablespoon tomato paste
7-ounce can chopped tomatoes
1 tablespoon red wine vinegar
2–3 small dried red chilies, seeded and chopped finely, or 1–2 teaspoons hot chili powder
1 teaspoon paprika
salt and ground black pepper
fresh Italian parsley sprig, to garnish

1 Boil the potatoes in their skins for 10–12 minutes until partly cooked. Drain them well and let cool, then cut in half and set aside.

2 Heat the oil in a large saucepan and fry the onions and garlic for 5–6 minutes, until just softened. Stir in the tomato paste, tomatoes, vinegar, chili and paprika and simmer for about 5 minutes.

3 Add the potatoes and mix into the sauce mixture until well coated. Cover with a tight-fitting lid and simmer gently for about 8–10 minutes, or until the potatoes are tender. Season well and transfer to a warmed serving dish. Serve garnished with a sprig of Italian parsley.

Spicy Jacket Potatoes

These lightly spiced potatoes make a glorious snack, light lunch or accompaniment to a meal.

Serves 2–4

2 large baking potatoes
1 teaspoon sunflower oil
1 small onion, chopped
1-inch piece fresh ginger, grated
1 teaspoon ground cumin
1 teaspoon ground coriander

½ teaspoon ground turmeric
generous pinch of garlic salt
plain yogurt and fresh cilantro sprigs, to serve

1 Preheat the oven to 375°F. Prick the potatoes with a fork. Bake for 40 minutes, or until soft.

2 Cut the potatoes in half and scoop out the insides. Heat the oil in a nonstick frying pan; fry the onion for a few minutes to soften. Stir in the ginger, cumin, coriander and turmeric.

3 Stir over a gentle heat for about 2 minutes, then add the potato, and garlic salt to taste.

4 Cook the potato mixture for another 2 minutes, stirring occasionally. Spoon the mixture back into the potato shells and top each with a spoonful of yogurt and a sprig or two of fresh cilantro. Serve hot.

Beans Provençal

A tasty side dish, these beans would complement a simple main course of broiled meat, poultry or fish.

Serves 4

1 teaspoon olive oil
1 small onion, finely chopped
1 garlic clove, crushed
scant 2 cups green beans

2 tomatoes, skinned and chopped
salt and ground black pepper

1 Heat the oil in a heavy-based or nonstick frying pan and sauté the chopped onion over moderate heat until softened but not browned.

2 Add the garlic, the beans and the tomatoes, then season well and cover tightly.

3 Cook over fairly gentle heat, shaking the pan from time to time, for about 30 minutes, or until the beans are tender. Serve hot.

Cook's Tip
For a dry version of this dish, omit the tomatoes. Simply fry the onion and garlic until softened, boil the beans in lightly salted water until tender, then stir into the rich mixture and combine well.

Chinese Crispy Seaweed

In northern China they use a special kind of seaweed for this dish, but collard greens make a good alternative.

Serves 4

8 ounces collard greens
peanut or sunflower oil,
    for deep-frying
¼ teaspoon salt

2 teaspoons light brown
    sugar
2–3 tablespoons toasted,
    flaked almonds

1 Cut out and discard any tough stalks from the collard greens. Place about six leaves on top of each other and roll up into a tight roll.

2 Using a sharp knife, slice across into thin shreds. Lay on a tray and leave to dry for about 2 hours.

3 Heat about 2–3 inches of oil in a wok or pan to 375°F. Carefully place a handful of the leaves into the oil – it will bubble and spit for the first 10 seconds and then die down. Deep fry for about 45 seconds, or until a slightly darker green – do not let the leaves burn.

4 Remove with a slotted spoon, drain on paper towels and transfer to a serving dish. Keep warm in the oven while frying the rest.

5 When you have fried all the shredded leaves, sprinkle with the salt and sugar and toss lightly. Garnish with the toasted almonds.

Cook's Tip
Make sure that your deep frying pan is deep enough to allow the oil to bubble up during cooking. The pan should be less than half full.

Leek and Parsnip Purée

Vegetable purées are popular in Britain and France served with meat, chicken or fish dishes.

Serves 4

2 large leeks, sliced
3 parsnips, sliced
pat of butter
3 tablespoons light cream
2 tablespoons plain
    yogurt
generous squeeze of
    lemon juice

salt and ground black
    pepper
large pinch of freshly
    grated nutmeg, to
    garnish

1 Steam or boil the leeks and parsnips together for about 15 minutes, until tender. Drain well, then place in a food processor or blender.

2 Add the remaining ingredients to the processor or blender. Combine them all until really smooth, then check the seasoning. Transfer to a warmed bowl and garnish with a sprinkling of nutmeg.

Middle-Eastern Vegetable Stew

This spiced dish of mixed vegetables can be served as a side dish or as a vegetarian main course.

Serves 4–6

3 tablespoons vegetable
  or chicken stock
1 green bell pepper,
  seeded and sliced
2 zucchini, sliced
2 carrots, sliced
2 celery stalks, sliced
2 potatoes, diced
14-ounce can chopped
  tomatoes
1 teaspoon chili powder

2 tablespoons chopped
  fresh mint
1 tablespoon ground
  cumin
14-ounce can
  chick-peas, drained
salt and ground black
  pepper
fresh mint sprigs,
  to garnish

1 Heat the vegetable or chicken stock in a large flameproof casserole until boiling, then add the sliced pepper, zucchini, carrot and celery. Stir over a high heat for 2–3 minutes, until the vegetables are just beginning to soften.

2 Add the potatoes, tomatoes, chili powder, mint and cumin. Add the chick-peas and bring to a boil.

3 Reduce the heat, cover the casserole with a tight-fitting lid and simmer for 30 minutes, or until all the vegetables are tender. Season to taste with salt and pepper and serve hot, garnished with mint leaves.

Summer Vegetable Braise

Tender young vegetables are ideal for quick cooking in a minimum of liquid. Use any vegetable mixture you like.

Serves 4

6 ounces baby carrots
1½ cups sugar snap peas
  or snow peas
4 ounces baby corn cobs
6 tablespoons vegetable
  stock

2 teaspoons lime juice
salt and ground black
  pepper
chopped fresh parsley and
  chopped fresh chives,
  to garnish

1 Place the carrots, peas and baby corn cobs in a large heavy-based saucepan with the vegetable stock and lime juice. Bring to a boil.

2 Cover the pan and reduce the heat, then simmer for about 6–8 minutes, shaking the pan occasionally, until the vegetables are just tender.

3 Season the vegetables to taste with salt and pepper, then stir in the chopped fresh parsley and chives. Cook the vegetables for a few seconds more, stirring them once or twice until the herbs are well mixed, then serve immediately with broiled lamb chops or roast chicken.

Cook's Tip
You can cook a winter version of this dish using seasonal root vegetables. Cut them into evenly sliced chunks and cook for slightly longer.

Straw Potato Cake

These potatoes are so–called in France because of their resemblance to a woven straw doormat.

Serves 4
1 pound baking potatoes
1½ tablespoons melted
   butter
1–2 tablespoons oil
salt and ground black
   pepper

1   Peel the potatoes and grate them coarsely, then immediately toss them with the melted butter and season with salt and pepper.

2   Heat the oil in a large frying pan. Add the potato mixture and press down to form an even layer that covers the pan. Cook over moderate heat for 7–10 minutes until the base is well browned.

3   Loosen the potato cake by shaking the pan or running a thin spatula under it.

4   To turn it over, invert a large baking sheet over the frying pan and, holding it tightly against the pan, turn them both over together. Lift off the frying pan, return it to the heat and add a little more oil if it looks dry. Slide the potato cake into the frying pan and continue cooking until it is crisp and browned on the second side. Serve hot.

Cook's Tip
Make several small potato cakes instead of one large one, if you prefer. Simply adjust the cooking time.

Sautéed Wild Mushrooms

This is a quick dish to prepare and makes an ideal side dish for all kinds of broiled and roast meats.

Serves 6
2 pounds fresh mixed
   wild and cultivated
   mushrooms such as
   morels, porcini,
   chanterelles, oyster or
   shiitake
2 tablespoons olive oil
2 tablespoons unsalted
   butter
2 garlic cloves, chopped
3 or 4 shallots, finely
   chopped
3 – 4 tablespoons
   chopped fresh parsley,
   or a mixture of
   different chopped fresh
   herbs
salt and ground black
   pepper

1   Wash and carefully dry the mushrooms. Trim the stems and cut the mushrooms into quarters, or slice if they are very large.

2   Heat the oil in a large frying pan over moderately high heat. Add the butter and swirl to melt, then stir in the prepared mushrooms and cook for 4–5 minutes until beginning to brown.

3   Add the garlic and shallots to the pan and cook for another 4–5 minutes until the mushrooms are tender and any liquid has evaporated. Season to taste with salt and pepper, stir in the parsley or mixed herbs and serve hot.

Cook's Tip
Use as many different varieties of cultivated and wild mushrooms as you can find to create a tasty and attractive dish.

Celery Root Purée

Many chefs add potato to celery root purée, but this recipe highlights the pure flavor of the vegetable.

Serves 4

*1 large celery root, about
    1¾ pounds, peeled
1 tablespoon butter*

*pinch of grated nutmeg
salt and ground black
    pepper*

1 Cut the celery root into large chunks, put in a saucepan with enough cold water to cover and add a little salt. Bring to a boil over moderately high heat and cook gently for about 10–15 minutes until tender.

2 Drain the celery root, reserving a little of the cooking liquid, and place in a food processor fitted with a metal blade or a blender. Process until smooth, adding a little of the cooking liquid if it needs thinning.

3 Stir in the butter and season to taste with salt, pepper and nutmeg. Reheat, if necessary, before serving.

Creamy Spinach Purée

Crème fraîche or béchamel sauce usually gives this dish its creamy richness. Here is a quick light alternative.

Serves 4

*4½ cups fresh spinach,
    stems removed
½ cup cream cheese
milk (if required)*

*pinch of freshly grated
    nutmeg
salt and ground black
    pepper*

1 Rinse the spinach, shake lightly and place in a deep frying pan or wok. Cook over moderate heat for about 3–4 minutes until wilted. Drain in a colander, pressing with the back of a spoon. The spinach does not need to be completely dry.

2 Purée the spinach and cream cheese in a food processor fitted with a metal blade or a blender until well blended, then transfer to a bowl. If the purée is too thick to fall easily from a spoon, add a little milk, spoonful by spoonful. Season to taste with salt, pepper and nutmeg. Transfer to a heavy-based saucepan and reheat gently before serving.

Navy Bean Purée

This inexpensive dip is a healthy multi-purpose option; use low-fat sour cream to lower its calorie content.

Serves 4

Drain 14-ounce can navy beans, rinse, drain again. Purée in a blender or food processor with 3 tablespoons ricotta, grated zest, rind and juice of 1 large orange and 1 tablespoon finely chopped fresh rosemary. Set aside. Cut 4 heads of Belgian endive in half lengthwise and cut 2 medium radicchio into 8 wedges. Lay them on a baking sheet and brush with 1 tablespoon walnut oil. Broil for 2–3 minutes. Serve with the purée; scatter over the orange rind.

New Potato and Chive Salad

The secret of a good potato salad is to mix the potatoes with the dressing while they are still hot so that they absorb it.

Serves 4– 6
1½ pounds new potatoes
4 scallions
3 tablespoons olive oil
1 tablespoon white wine
    vinegar
¾ teaspoon Dijon mustard
¾ cup good-quality
    mayonnaise
3 tablespoons chopped
    fresh chives
salt and ground black
    pepper

1 Cook the potatoes, unpeeled, in boiling salted water until tender. Meanwhile, finely chop the white parts of the scallions along with a little of the green parts.

2 Whisk together the oil, vinegar and mustard. Drain the potatoes well, then immediately toss lightly with the vinegar mixture and scallions and allow to cool. Stir the mayonnaise and chives into the potatoes and chill in the fridge until ready to serve with broiled pork, lamb chops or roast chicken.

Watercress Potato Salad Bowl

New potatoes are good hot or cold, and this colorful and nutritious salad makes the most of them.

Serves 4
1 pound small new
    potatoes, unpeeled
1 bunch watercress
7 ounces cherry
    tomatoes, halved
2 tablespoons pumpkin
    seeds
3 tablespoons low-fat
    ricotta
1 tablespoon cider
    vinegar
1 teaspoon light brown
    sugar
salt and paprika

1 Cook the potatoes in lightly salted boiling water until just tender, then drain and leave to cool.

2 Toss together the potatoes, watercress, tomatoes and pumpkin seeds. Place the ricotta, vinegar, sugar, salt and paprika in a screw-top jar and shake well to mix. Pour over the salad just before serving.

Frankfurter Salad

A last-minute salad you can throw together quickly using store-cupboard ingredients.

Serves 4
Boil 1½ pounds new potatoes in salted water for 20 minutes. Drain, cover and keep warm. Hard-boil 2 eggs for 12 minutes, peel and quarter. Score the skins of 12 ounces frankfurters cork-screw fashion, cover with boiling water and simmer for 5 minutes. Drain, cover and keep warm. Distribute the leaves of 1 loose-leaf lettuce and 8 ounces young spinach between 4 plates, moisten the potatoes and frankfurters with dressing and scatter on the salad. Finish with the eggs, season and serve.

Niçoise Salad

Serve this rich and filling salad as a main course, simply with crusty bread.

Serves 4

6 tablespoons olive oil
2 tablespoons tarragon
    vinegar
1 teaspoon tarragon or
    Dijon mustard
1 small garlic clove,
    crushed
1 cup green beans
12 small new potatoes
3–4 Bibb lettuces,
    coarsely chopped
7-ounce can tuna in oil,
    drained

6 anchovy fillets, halved
    lengthwise
12 black olives, pitted
4 tomatoes, chopped
4 scallions, finely
    chopped
2 teaspoons capers
2 tablespoons pine nuts
2 hard-boiled eggs,
    chopped
salt and ground black
    pepper
crusty bread, to serve

1 Mix the oil, vinegar, mustard, garlic and seasoning with a wooden spoon in the bottom of a large salad bowl.

2 Cook the green beans and potatoes in separate saucepans of boiling salted water until just tender. Drain and add to the bowl with the lettuce, tuna, anchovies, olives, tomatoes, scallions and capers.

3 Just before serving, toast the pine nuts in a small frying pan until lightly browned.

4 Sprinkle on the salad while still hot, add the eggs and toss all the ingredients together well. Serve with chunks of hot crusty bread.

Cook's Tip
Look out for salad potatoes, such as Charlotte, Belle de Fontenay or Pink Fir Apple, to use in this recipe.

Caesar Salad

Any crisp lettuce will do in this delicious salad, which was created by Caesar Cardini in the 1920s.

Serves 4

1 large Romaine lettuce
4 thick slices white or
    whole wheat bread,
    without crusts
3 tablespoons olive oil
1 garlic clove, crushed

For the dressing
1 egg
1 garlic clove, chopped

2 tablespoons lemon juice
dash of Worcestershire
    sauce
3 anchovy fillets, chopped
½ cup olive oil
5 tablespoons grated
    Parmesan cheese
salt and ground black
    pepper

1 Preheat the oven to 425°F. Separate, rinse and dry the lettuce leaves. Tear the outer leaves coarsely and chop the heart. Arrange the lettuce in a large salad bowl.

2 Dice the bread and mix with the olive oil and garlic in a separate bowl until the bread has soaked up the oil. Lay the bread chunks on a baking sheet and place in the oven for about 6–8 minutes (keeping an eye on them) until golden. Remove and allow to cool.

3 To make the dressing, break the egg into the bowl of a food processor or blender and add the garlic, lemon juice, Worcestershire sauce and one of the anchovy fillets. Process until smooth.

4 With the motor running, pour in the olive oil in a thin stream until the dressing has the consistency of light cream. Season to taste with salt and pepper, if needed.

5 Pour the dressing over the salad greens and toss well, then toss in the garlic croûtons, Parmesan cheese and finally the remaining anchovies and serve immediately.

Tuna and Bean Salad

This substantial salad makes a good light meal, and can be very quickly assembled from canned ingredients.

Serves 4–6

2 x 14-ounce cans navy
  or kidney beans
2 x 7-ounce cans tuna
  fish, drained
4 tablespoons extra
  virgin olive oil

2 tablespoons lemon juice
salt and ground black
  pepper
1 tablespoon chopped
  fresh parsley
3 scallions, thinly sliced

1 Pour the beans into a large strainer and rinse under cold water. Drain well. Place in a serving dish.

2 Break the tuna into fairly large flakes with a fork and arrange over the beans.

3 Make the dressing by combining the oil with the lemon juice in a small bowl. Season with salt and pepper, and stir in the parsley. Mix well. Pour over the beans and tuna.

4 Sprinkle the scallions over the salad and toss well before serving.

Cook's Tip
If you prefer a milder onion flavor, gently sauté the scallions in a little oil until softened, but not browned, before adding them to the salad.

Grilled Pepper Salad

This colorful salad is a southern Italian creation; all the ingredients thrive in the Mediterranean sun.

Serves 6

4 large bell peppers, red
  or yellow or a
  combination of both
2 tablespoons capers in
  salt, vinegar or brine,
  rinsed
18–20 black or green
  olives

For the dressing
6 tablespoons extra-
  virgin olive oil
2 garlic cloves, chopped
2 tablespoons balsamic or
  wine vinegar
salt and ground black
  pepper

1 Place the peppers under a hot broiler and turn occasionally until they are black and blistered on all sides. Remove from the heat and place in a paper bag. Leave for 5 minutes.

2 Peel the peppers, then cut them into quarters. Remove the stems and seeds.

3 Cut the peppers into strips, and arrange them in a serving dish. Distribute the capers and olives evenly over them.

4 To make the dressing, mix the oil and garlic together in a small bowl, crushing the garlic with a spoon to release as much flavor as possible. Mix in the vinegar, and season to taste with salt and pepper. Pour on the salad, mix well, and allow to stand for at least 30 minutes before serving.

Cook's Tip
Skinning the peppers brings out their delicious sweet flavor and is well worth the extra effort.

Chicken Liver and Tomato Salad

Warm salads are especially welcome during the autumn months when the evenings are growing shorter and cooler.

Serves 4

8 ounces young spinach, stems removed
1 frisée lettuce
7 tablespoons peanut or sunflower oil
6 ounces bacon, cut into strips

3 slices day-old bread, without crusts, cut into short slices
1 pound chicken livers
4 ounces cherry tomatoes
salt and ground black pepper

1 Wash and spin the salad greens. Put in a salad bowl. Heat 4 tablespoons of the oil in a large frying pan and cook the bacon for 3–4 minutes until crisp and brown. Remove the bacon with a slotted spoon and let drain on a piece of paper towel.

2 To make the croûtons, fry the bread in the bacon-flavored oil, tossing until crisp and golden. Drain on paper towels.

3 Heat the remaining 3 tablespoons of oil in the frying pan and fry the chicken livers briskly for 2–3 minutes. Transfer the livers to the salad greens, add the bacon, croûtons and tomatoes. Season with salt and pepper, toss, and serve.

Cook's Tip
Although fresh chicken livers are preferable, frozen ones could be used in this salad. It is important to make sure they are completely thawed before cooking.

Maryland Salad

Chicken, corn, bacon, banana and watercress are combined here in a sensational main-course salad.

Serves 4

4 free-range chicken breasts, boned
8 ounces bacon
4 baby corn
3 tablespoons soft butter, softened
4 ripe bananas, peeled and halved
4 firm tomatoes, halved
4 escarole lettuces
1 bunch watercress, about 4 ounces

salt and ground black pepper

For the dressing
5 tablespoons peanut oil
1 tablespoon white wine vinegar
1 teaspoon maple syrup
2 teaspoons mild mustard

1 Season the chicken breasts, brush with oil and barbecue or broil for 15 minutes, turning once. Barbecue or broil the bacon for 8–10 minutes or until crisp.

2 Bring a large saucepan of salted water to the boil. Trim the baby corn or leave the husks on if you prefer. Boil for 20 minutes. For extra flavor, brush with butter and brown over the barbecue or under the broiler. Barbecue or broil the bananas and tomatoes for 6–8 minutes. You can brush these with butter too if you wish.

3 To make the dressing, combine the oil, vinegar, maple syrup and mustard with 1 tablespoon water in a screw-top jar and shake well.

4 Wash, spin thoroughly and dress the escarole lettuce and the watercress.

5 Distribute the salad greens among four large plates. Slice the chicken and arrange on the leaves with the bacon, banana, corn and tomatoes.

201

Leeks with Mustard Dressing

Pour the dressing over the leeks while they are still warm so that they absorb the mustardy flavors.

Serves 4
8 slim leeks, each about
    5 inches long
1–2 teaspoons Dijon
    mustard
2 teaspoons white wine
    vinegar

1 hard-boiled egg, halved
    lengthwise
5 tablespoons light olive
    oil
2 teaspoons chopped fresh
    parsley
salt and ground black

1 Steam the leeks over a saucepan of boiling water until they are just tender.

2 Meanwhile, stir together the mustard and vinegar in a bowl. Scoop the egg yolk into the bowl and mash thoroughly into the vinegar mixture using a fork.

3 Gradually work in the oil to make a smooth sauce, then season to taste with salt and pepper.

4 Lift the leeks out of the steamer and place on several layers of paper towels, then cover the leeks with several more layers of paper towels and pat dry.

5 Transfer the leeks to a serving dish while still warm, spoon the dressing over them and let cool. Finely chop the egg white using a large sharp knife, then mix with the chopped fresh parsley and scatter on the leeks. Chill in the fridge until ready to serve.

Cook's Tip
Pencil-slim baby leeks are increasingly available nowadays, and are beautifully tender. Use three or four of these smaller leeks per serving.

Lettuce and Herb Salad

For a really quick salad, look out for prepared bags of mixed baby lettuce leaves in the supermarket.

Serves 4
½ cucumber
mixed lettuce leaves
1 bunch watercress,
    about 4 ounces
1 Belgian endive head,
    sliced
3 tablespoons mixed
    chopped fresh herbs
    such as parsley,
    thyme, tarragon,
    chives and chervil

For the dressing
1 tablespoon white wine
    vinegar
1 teaspoon prepared
    mustard
5 tablespoons olive oil
salt and ground black
    pepper

1 To make the dressing, mix the vinegar and mustard together, then whisk in the oil and seasoning.

2 Peel the cucumber, if you wish, then cut it in half lengthwise and scoop out the seeds. Thinly slice the inside. Tear the lettuce leaves into bite-size pieces.

3 Toss the cucumber, lettuce, watercress, Belgian endive and herbs together in a bowl, or arrange them in the bowl in layers, if you prefer.

4 Stir the dressing, then pour over the salad, toss lightly to coat the salad vegetables and leaves. Serve at once.

Cook's Tip
Do not dress the salad until just before serving, otherwise the lettuce leaves will wilt.

Goat Cheese Salad

The robust flavors of the cheese and buckwheat combine especially well with figs and walnuts in this salad.

Serves 4
1 cup couscous
2 tablespoons toasted buckwheat groats
1 hard-boiled egg
2 tablespoons chopped fresh parsley
4 tablespoons olive oil, preferably Sicilian
3 tablespoons walnut oil
4 ounces arugula

½ frisée lettuce
6 ounces crumbly white goat cheese
½ cup broken walnuts, toasted
4 ripe figs, trimmed and almost cut into four (leaving the pieces joined at the base)

1 Place the couscous and buckwheat groats in a bowl, cover with boiling water and let soak for 15 minutes. Place in a strainer if necessary to drain off any remaining water, then spread out on a metal tray and allow to cool.

2 Peel the hard-boiled egg and grate finely.

3 Toss the egg, parsley and couscous in a bowl. Combine the two oils and use half to moisten the couscous mixture.

4 Wash and spin the salad leaves, dress with the remaining oil and distribute among four large plates.

5 Pile the couscous in the center of the leaves, crumble on the goat cheese, scatter with toasted walnuts, and add the trimmed figs.

Cook's Tip
Serve this strongly flavored salad with a gutsy red wine from the Rhône or South of France.

Waldorf Ham Salad

Waldorf salad originally consisted of apples, celery and mayonnaise. This ham version is a meal in itself.

Serves 4
3 apples, peeled
1 tablespoon lemon juice
2 slices cooked ham, about 6 ounces each
3 celery stalks
⅔ cup mayonnaise
1 escarole or Batavia lettuce

1 small radicchio, finely shredded
½ bunch watercress
3 tablespoons walnut oil or olive oil
½ cup walnut pieces, toasted
salt and ground black pepper

1 Core, slice and shred the apples finely. Moisten with lemon juice to keep them white. Cut the cooked ham into 2-inch strips, then cut the celery into similar-size pieces, and combine in a bowl.

2 Add the mayonnaise to the apples, ham and celery and stir to combine well.

3 Wash and spin the salad greens. Shred the leaves finely, then toss with the walnut or olive oil. Distribute the greens between four plates. Pile the mayonnaise mixture in the center, scatter with toasted walnuts, season to taste with salt and pepper, and serve at once.

Baby Leaf Salad with Croutons

Crispy ciabatta croutons give a lovely crunch to this mixed leaf and avocado salad.

Serves 4

1 tablespoon olive oil
1 garlic clove, crushed
1 tablespoon freshly
    grated Parmesan
    cheese
1 tablespoon chopped
    fresh parsley
4 slices ciabatta bread,
    crusts removed, diced
1 large bunch watercress
large handful of arugula

1 bag mixed baby salad
    greens, including red
    leaf and Romaine
    lettuce
1 ripe avocado

For the dressing
3 tablespoons olive oil
1 tablespoon walnut oil
juice of ½ lemon
½ teaspoon Dijon
    mustard
salt and ground black
    pepper

1 Preheat the oven to 375°F. Put the oil, garlic, Parmesan, parsley and bread in a bowl and toss to coat well. Spread out the diced bread on a baking sheet and bake for about 8 minutes until crisp. Let cool.

2 Remove any coarse or discolored stalks or leaves from the watercress and place in a serving bowl with the arugula and baby salad greens.

3 Halve the avocado and remove the pit. Peel and cut into chunks, then add it to the salad bowl.

4 To make the dressing, mix together the oils, lemon juice, mustard and seasoning in a small bowl or screw-top jar until evenly blended. Pour over the salad and toss well. Sprinkle over the croûtons and serve immediately.

Wild Rice with Broiled Vegetables

Broiling brings out the delicious and varied flavor of these summer vegetables.

Serves 4

1¼ cups wild and long-
    grain rice mixture
1 large eggplant, thickly
    sliced
1 red, 1 yellow and 1
    green bell pepper,
    seeded and cut into
    quarters
2 red onions, sliced
8 ounces brown cap or
    shiitake mushrooms
2 small zucchini, cut in
    half lengthwise

olive oil, for brushing
2 tablespoons chopped
    fresh thyme

For the dressing
6 tablespoons extra-
    virgin olive oil
2 tablespoons balsamic
    vinegar
2 garlic cloves, crushed
salt and ground black
    pepper

1 Put the rice mixture in a saucepan of cold salted water. Bring to a boil, reduce the heat, cover with a tight-fitting lid and cook gently for 30–40 minutes or according to the package instructions, until all the grains are tender.

2 To make the dressing, mix together the olive oil, vinegar, garlic and seasoning in a small bowl or screw-topped jar until well blended. Set aside while you broil the vegetables.

3 Arrange the vegetables on a broiler rack. Brush with olive oil and broil for 8–10 minutes, until tender and well browned, turning them occasionally and brushing again with oil.

4 Drain the rice and toss in half the dressing. Turn into a serving dish and arrange the broiled vegetables on top. Pour over the remaining dressing and scatter over the chopped fresh thyme.

Russian Salad

Russian salad became fashionable in the hotel dining rooms of Europe in the 1920s and 1930s.

Serves 4

4 ounces large button mushrooms
½ cup mayonnaise
1 tablespoon freshly squeezed lemon juice
12 ounces peeled, cooked shrimp
1 large dill pickle, finely chopped, or 2 tablespoons capers
4 ounces fava beans
4 ounces small new potatoes, scrubbed or scraped

4 ounces young carrots, trimmed and peeled
4 ounces baby corn
4 ounces baby turnips, trimmed
1 tablespoon olive oil, preferably French or Italian
4 eggs, hard-boiled and shelled
pinch of salt, pepper and paprika
1 ounce canned anchovies, cut into fine strips, to garnish

1 Slice the mushrooms thinly, then cut into matchsticks. Combine the mayonnaise and lemon juice. Fold half of the mayonnaise into the mushrooms and shrimp, add the dill pickle or capers, then season to taste with salt and pepper.

2 Bring a large saucepan of salted water to a boil, add the fava beans, and cook for 3 minutes. Drain and cool under running water, then pinch the beans between thumb and forefinger to release them from their tough skins. Boil the potatoes for 20 minutes and the remaining vegetables for 6 minutes. Drain and cool under running water.

3 Toss the vegetables with the oil and divide among four shallow bowls. Spoon on the dressed shrimp and place a hard-boiled egg in the center. Garnish the egg with strips of anchovy and sprinkle with paprika.

Crunchy Coleslaw

Homemade coleslaw is quick and easy to make – and it tastes fresh, crunchy and wonderful.

Serves 4–6

¼ firm white cabbage
1 small onion, finely chopped
2 celery stalks, thinly sliced
2 carrots, coarsely grated
1–2 teaspoons caraway seeds (optional)
1 eating apple, cored and chopped (optional)

½ cup walnuts, chopped (optional)
salt and ground black pepper

For the dressing
3 tablespoons mayonnaise
2 tablespoons light cream or natural yogurt
1 teaspoon grated lemon rind

1 Cut and discard the core from the cabbage quarter, then shred the leaves finely. Place them in a large bowl.

2 Toss the onion, celery and carrot into the cabbage, plus the caraway seeds, apple and walnuts, if using. Season well with salt and pepper.

3 Mix the dressing ingredients together in a small bowl, then stir into the vegetables. Cover the salad with plastic wrap and allow to stand for 2 hours, stirring occasionally, then chill lightly in the fridge before serving.

Pear and Roquefort Salad

Choose ripe but firm Comice or Bartlett pears for this attractive and deeply flavorful salad.

Serves 4

3 ripe pears
lemon juice
about 6 ounces mixed
    fresh salad greens
6 ounces Roquefort
    cheese
½ cup hazelnuts, toasted
    and chopped

For the dressing

2 tablespoons hazelnut
    oil
3 tablespoons olive oil
1 tablespoon cider vinegar
1 teaspoon Dijon mustard
salt and ground black
    pepper

1 To make the dressing, mix together the oils, vinegar and mustard in a bowl or screw-top jar. Season to taste with salt and pepper.

2 Peel, core and slice the pears and toss them in lemon juice.

3 Divide the salad greens among four serving plates, then place the pears on top. Crumble the cheese and scatter over the salad along with the toasted hazelnuts. Spoon over the dressing and serve at once.

Mediterranean Mixed Pepper Salad

Serve this colorful salad either as a tasty appetizer or as an accompaniment to cold meats for lunch or supper.

Serves 4

2 red bell peppers, halved
    and seeded
2 yellow bell peppers,
    halved and seeded
⅔ cup olive oil
1 onion, thinly sliced

2 garlic cloves, crushed
generous squeeze of
    lemon juice
chopped fresh parsley, to
    garnish

1 Broil the pepper halves for about 5 minutes, until the skin has blistered and blackened. Pop them into a plastic bag, seal and leave for 5 minutes.

2 Meanwhile, heat 2 tablespoons of the olive oil in a frying pan and fry the onion for about 5–6 minutes, until softened and translucent. Remove from the heat and reserve.

3 Take the peppers out of the bag and peel off the skins. Discard the pepper skins and slice each pepper half into fairly thin strips.

4 Place the peppers, cooked onions and any oil from the pan in a bowl. Add the crushed garlic, pour in the remaining olive oil, add a generous squeeze of lemon juice and season to taste. Mix well, cover and marinate for 2–3 hours, stirring the mixture once or twice.

5 Just before serving, garnish the pepper salad with chopped fresh parsley.

Californian Salad

Full of vitality and vitamins, this is a lovely light and healthy salad for sunny summer days.

Serves 4

1 small crisp lettuce, torn into pieces
2 cups young spinach leaves
2 carrots, coarsely grated
4 ounces cherry tomatoes, halved
2 celery stalks, thinly sliced
½ cup raisins
½ cup blanched almonds or unsalted cashew nuts, halved

2 tablespoons sunflower seeds
2 tablespoons sesame seeds, lightly toasted

For the dressing

3 tablespoons extra-virgin olive oil
2 tablespoons cider vinegar
2 teaspoons honey
juice of 1 small orange
salt and ground black pepper

1 Put the salad vegetables, raisins, almonds or cashew nuts and seeds into a large bowl.

2 Put all the dressing ingredients into a screw-top jar, shake them up well and pour over the salad.

3 Toss the salad thoroughly and divide it among four small salad bowls. Serve chilled, sprinkled with salt and pepper.

Cucumber and Dill Salad

This Scandinavian salad is particularly complementary to hot and spicy food.

Serves 4

2 cucumbers
2 tablespoons chopped fresh chives
2 tablespoons chopped fresh dill

⅔ cup sour cream
salt and ground black pepper

1 Slice the cucumbers as thinly as possible, preferably in a food processor or with a slicer.

2 Place the slices in layers in a colander set over a plate to catch the juice. Sprinkle each layer evenly, but not too heavily, with salt.

3 Allow the cucumber to drain for up to 2 hours, then lay the slices on a clean dish towel and pat them dry.

4 Mix the cucumber with the herbs, cream and plenty of pepper. Serve as soon as possible.

Cook's Tip
The juice in this salad continues forming after salting, so only dress it when you are ready to serve.

Chicory, Fruit and Nut Salad

Mildly bitter chicory is wonderful with sweet fruit, and is delicious when complemented by a creamy curry sauce.

Serves 4

3 tablespoons
  mayonnaise
1 tablespoon strained
  plain yogurt
1 tablespoon mild curry
  paste
6 tablespoons light cream

½ iceberg lettuce
2 heads of chicory
1 cup flaked coconut
½ cup cashew nuts
2 red eating apples
½ cup currants

1 Mix together the mayonnaise, yogurt, curry paste and light cream in a small bowl. Cover and chill in the fridge until required.

2 Tear the iceberg lettuce into even-size pieces and put into a salad bowl.

3 Cut the root end off each head of chicory and discard. Slice the chicory and add it to the salad bowl. Preheat the broiler.

4 Spread out the coconut flakes on a baking sheet. Broil for 1 minute until golden. Turn into a bowl and set aside. Toast the cashew nuts for 2 minutes until golden.

5 Quarter the apples and cut out the cores. Slice the apple quarters and add to the lettuce with the toasted coconut, cashew nuts and currants.

6 Spoon the dressing over the salad, toss lightly and serve.

Cook's Tip
Choose a sweet, well-flavored variety of red apple for this salad, such as Braeburn or Royal Gala.

Tzatziki

This Greek salad is typically served with broiled lamb and chicken, but is also good with salmon and trout.

Serves 4

1 cucumber
1 teaspoon salt
3 tablespoons finely
  chopped fresh mint,
  plus a few sprigs to
  garnish

1 clove garlic, crushed
1 teaspoon sugar
scant 1 cup strained
  plain yogurt
paprika, to garnish
  (optional)

1 Peel the cucumber. Reserve a little to use as a garnish if you wish and cut the rest in half lengthwise. Remove the seeds with a teaspoon and discard. Slice the cucumber thinly and combine with salt. Let stand for about 15-20 minutes. Salt will soften the cucumber and draw out any bitter juice.

2 Combine the mint, garlic, sugar and yogurt in a bowl, reserving a few sprigs of mint as decoration.

3 Rinse the cucumber in a colander under cold running water to drain away the salt. Combine with the yogurt. Decorate with cucumber and mint. Serve cold, garnished with paprika if you wish.

Cook's Tip
If preparing tzatziki in a hurry, leave out the method for salting the cucumber at the end of step 1. The cucumber will have a more crunchy texture, and will be slightly less sweet.

Tomato and Bread Salad

This salad is a traditional peasant dish from Tuscany which was created to use up bread that was several days old.

Serves 4

14 ounces stale white or
    brown bread or rolls
4 large tomatoes
1 large red onion, or
    6 scallions
a few fresh basil leaves,
    to garnish

For the dressing

4 tablespoons extra-
    virgin olive oil
2 tablespoons white wine
    vinegar
salt and ground black
    pepper

1 Cut the bread or rolls into thick slices. Place in a shallow bowl and soak with cold water. Leave for at least 30 minutes.

2 Cut the tomatoes into chunks. Place in a serving bowl. Finely slice the onion or scallions, and add them to the tomatoes. Squeeze as much water out of the bread as possible, and add it to the vegetables.

3 Mix together the dressing ingredients. Season to taste with salt and pepper. Pour it on the salad and mix well. Decorate with the basil leaves. Allow to stand in a cool place for at least 2 hours before serving.

Fennel and Orange Salad

This salad originated in Sicily, following the seventeenth-century custom of serving fennel at a meal's end.

Serves 4

2 large fennel bulbs,
    about 1½ pounds total
2 sweet oranges
2 scallions, to garnish

For the dressing

4 tablespoons extra-
    virgin olive oil
2 tablespoons fresh lemon
    juice
salt and ground black
    pepper

1 Wash the fennel bulbs and remove any brown or stringy outer leaves. Slice the bulbs and stems into thin pieces. Place in a shallow serving bowl.

2 Peel the oranges with a sharp knife, cutting away the white pith. Slice thinly. Cut each slice into thirds. Arrange over the fennel, adding any juice from the oranges.

3 To make the dressing, mix the oil and lemon juice together. Season with salt and pepper. Pour the dressing on the salad and mix well.

4 Slice the white and green sections of the scallions thinly. Sprinkle on the salad.

Parmesan and Poached Egg Salad

Soft poached eggs, hot garlic croûtons and cool crisp salad greens make an unforgettable combination.

Serves 2
½ small loaf white bread
5 tablespoons extra-
    virgin olive oil
2 eggs
4 ounces mixed salad
    greens

2 garlic cloves, crushed
½ tablespoon white wine
    vinegar
2 tablespoons freshly
    shaved Parmesan
    cheese
black pepper

1   Remove the crust from the bread. Cut the bread into 1-inch cubes.

2   Heat 2 tablespoons of the oil in a frying pan and cook the bread for about 5 minutes, tossing the cubes occasionally, until they are golden brown.

3   Meanwhile, bring a saucepan of water to a boil. Slide in the eggs carefully, one at a time. Gently poach the eggs for 4 minutes until lightly cooked.

4   Divide the salad greens between two plates. Remove the croûtons from the pan and arrange them on the leaves. Wipe the pan clean with paper towels.

5   Heat the remaining oil in the pan and cook the garlic and vinegar over high heat for about 1 minute. Pour the warm dressing over the salad greens and croûtons.

6   Place a poached egg on each salad. Scatter with shavings of Parmesan cheese and a little freshly ground black pepper.

Cook's Tip
Add a dash of vinegar to the water before poaching the eggs. This helps to keep the whites together. To make sure that a poached egg has a good shape, swirl the water with a spoon before sliding in the egg.

Classic Greek Salad

If you have ever visited Greece you'll know that a Greek salad with a chunk of bread makes a delicious filling meal.

Serves 4
1 Romaine lettuce
½ cucumber, halved
    lengthwise
4 tomatoes
8 scallions
3 ounces Greek black
    olives

4 ounces feta cheese
6 tablespoons white wine
    vinegar
⅔ cup extra-virgin olive
    oil
salt and ground black
    pepper

1   Tear the lettuce leaves into pieces and place them in a large serving bowl. Slice the cucumber and add to the bowl.

2   Cut the tomatoes into wedges and put them into the bowl.

3   Slice the scallions. Add them to the bowl along with the olives and toss well.

4   Dice the feta cheese and add to the salad.

5   Put the vinegar and olive oil into a small bowl and season to taste with salt and pepper. Whisk well. Pour the dressing over the salad and toss to combine. Serve at once with extra olives and chunks of bread, if you wish.

Cook's Tip
This salad can be assembled in advance, but should only be dressed just before serving. Keep the dressing at room temperature as chilling deadens its flavors.

Potato Salad with Egg and Lemon

Potato salads are a popular addition to any salad spread and are enjoyed with an assortment of cold meats and fish.

Serves 4

2 pounds new potatoes, scrubbed or scraped
1 onion, finely chopped
1 hard-boiled egg
1¼ cups mayonnaise
1 garlic clove, crushed
finely grated juice and zest of 1 lemon
4 tablespoons chopped fresh parsley
salt and ground black pepper

1 Bring the potatoes to a boil in a saucepan of salted water. Simmer for 20 minutes. Drain and allow to cool. Cut the potatoes into large cubes, season with salt and pepper to taste, and combine with the onion.

2 Peel the hard-boiled egg and grate into a mixing bowl, then add the mayonnaise. Combine the garlic and lemon rind and juice in a small bowl and stir into the mayonnaise. Stir gently into the potatoes.

Cook's Tip
Use an early season variety of potato for this salad or look out for baby salad potatoes. They will not disintegrate when boiled and have a sweet flavor.

Sweet Turnip Salad

The robustly flavored turnip partners well with the taste of horseradish and caraway seeds in this delicious salad.

Serves 4

12 ounces turnips
2 scallions, white part only, chopped
1 tablespoon sugar
pinch of salt
2 tablespoons creamed horseradish
2 teaspoons caraway seeds

1 Peel, slice and shred the turnips – or you could grate them if you wish.

2 Add the scallions, sugar and salt, then rub together with your hands to soften the turnip.

3 Fold in the creamed horseradish and caraway seeds and serve the salad immediately.

Queen of Puddings

This pudding was developed from a seventeenth-century recipe by Queen Victoria's chefs at Buckingham Palace.

Serves 4

1½ cups fresh bread crumbs
4 tablespoons sugar, plus 1 teaspoon
grated rind of 1 lemon
2½ cups milk
4 eggs
3 tablespoons raspberry jam, warmed

1 Stir the bread crumbs, 2 tablespoons of the sugar and the lemon rind together in a heat proof bowl. Bring the milk to a boil in a saucepan, then stir into the bread crumbs.

2 Separate three of the eggs and beat the yolks with the whole egg. Stir into the bread crumb mixture, pour into a buttered baking dish and let stand for 30 minutes. Meanwhile, preheat the oven to 325°F. Bake the pudding for 50–60 minutes, until set.

3 Whisk the egg whites in a large clean bowl until stiff but not dry, then gradually whisk in just under 2 tablespoons sugar until the mixture is thick and glossy, taking care not to overwhip.

4 Spread the jam over the pudding, then spoon on the meringue to cover the top completely. Evenly sprinkle about 1 teaspoon sugar over the meringue, then bake for another 15 minutes, until the meringue is beginning to turn a light golden color.

Pear and Blackberry Brown Betty

All this delicious fruity pudding needs to go with it is some hot homemade custard, light cream or ice cream.

Serves 4–6

6 tablespoons butter, diced
3 cups bread crumbs
1 pound ripe pears
1 pound blackberries
grated rind and juice of 1 small orange
½ cup brown sugar
extra brown sugar, for sprinkling

1 Preheat the oven to 350°F. Heat the butter in a heavy-based frying pan over moderate heat and add the bread crumbs. Stir until golden.

2 Peel and core the pears, then cut them into thick slices and mix with the blackberries, orange rind and juice.

3 Mix the brown sugar with the bread crumbs, then layer with the fruit in a 3-cup buttered baking dish, beginning and ending with a layer of sugared bread crumbs.

4 Sprinkle the extra brown sugar over the top. Cover the baking dish, then bake the dessert for 20 minutes. Uncover the dish, then bake for a further 30–35 minutes, until the fruit is cooked and the top is brown and crisp.

Baked Stuffed Apples

When apples are plentiful, this traditional dessert is a popular and easy choice.

Serves 4

scant 1 cup ground
   almonds
2 tablespoons butter,
   softened
1 teaspoon honey

1 egg yolk
2 ounces dried apricots,
   chopped
4 cooking apples

1 Preheat the oven to 400°F. Beat together the almonds, butter, honey, egg yolk and apricots.

2 Remove the cores from the cooking apples using a large apple corer, then cut a line with the point of a sharp knife around the circumference of each apple.

3 Lightly grease a shallow baking dish, then arrange the cooking apples in the dish.

4 Divide the apricot mixture among the cavities in the apples, then bake in the oven for 45–60 minutes, until the apples are fluffy.

Kentish Cherry Batter Pudding

Kent, known as the "Garden of England", is particularly well known for cherries and the dishes made from them.

Serves 4

3 tablespoons Kirsch
   (optional)
1 pound dark cherries,
   pitted
½ cup all-purpose flour
4 tablespoons sugar

2 eggs, separated
¼ cup milk
6 tablespoons butter,
   melted
sugar, for sprinkling

1 Sprinkle the Kirsch, if using, over the cherries in a small bowl and let them to soak for about 30 minutes.

2 Mix the flour and sugar together, then slowly stir in the egg yolks and milk to make a smooth batter. Stir in half the butter and set aside for 30 minutes.

3 Preheat the oven to 425°F, then pour the remaining butter into a 2½-cup baking dish and put in the oven to heat.

4 Whisk the egg whites until stiff peaks form, then fold into the batter with the cherries. Pour into the dish and bake for 15 minutes.

5 Reduce the oven temperature to 350°F and bake for 20 minutes, or until golden and set in the center. Serve sprinkled with sugar.

Sticky Toffee Pudding

If you prefer, use pecan nuts instead of walnuts in this delightfully gooey pudding.

Serves 6

1 cup toasted walnuts, chopped
¾ cup butter
1½ cups brown sugar
4 tablespoons heavy cream
2 tablespoons lemon juice
2 eggs, beaten
1 cup self-rising flour

1 Grease a 3¾-cup ovenproof bowl and add half the nuts.

2 Heat 4 tablespoons of the butter with 4 tablespoons of the sugar, the cream and 1 tablespoon of the lemon juice in a small saucepan, stirring until smooth. Pour half into the bowl, then swirl to coat it a little way up the sides.

3 Beat the remaining butter and sugar until light and fluffy, then gradually beat in the eggs. Fold in the flour and the remaining nuts and lemon juice and spoon into the bowl.

4 Cover the bowl with baking parchment with a pleat folded in the center, then tie securely with string.

5 Steam the pudding for 1¼ hours, or until it is completely set in the center.

6 Just before serving, gently warm the remaining sauce. Unmold the pudding onto a warm plate and pour on the warm sauce.

Easy Chocolate and Orange Soufflé

The base in this soufflé is a simple semolina mixture, rather than the thick white sauce of most soufflés.

Serve 4

scant ½ cup semolina
scant ½ cup brown sugar
2½ cups milk
grated rind of 1 orange
6 tablespoons fresh orange juice
3 eggs, separated
2½ ounces plain chocolate, grated
confectioner's sugar, for sprinkling

1 Preheat the oven to 400°F. Butter a shallow 7½-cup baking dish.

2 Pour the milk into a heavy-based saucepan, sprinkle on the semolina and brown sugar, then heat, stirring the mixture all the time, until boiling and thickened.

3 Remove the pan from the heat; beat in the orange rind and juice, egg yolks and all but 1 tablespoon of the chocolate.

4 Whisk the egg whites until stiff but not dry, then lightly fold into the semolina mixture in three batches. Spoon the mixture into the dish and bake for about 30 minutes until just set in the center and risen. Sprinkle the top with the reserved chocolate and the confectioner's sugar, then serve immediately.

Plum and Walnut Crisp

Walnuts add a lovely crunch to the fruit layer in this rich dessert – almonds would be just as good.

Serves 4–6

¾ cup walnut pieces
2 pounds plums
1½ cups brown sugar

6 tablespoons butter or
  hard margarine, diced
1½ cups all-purpose flour

1 Preheat the oven to 350°F. Spread the nuts on a baking sheet and place in the oven for 8–10 minutes, until evenly colored.

2 Butter a 5-cup baking dish. Halve and pit the plums, then put them into the dish and stir in the nuts and half of the brown sugar.

3 Rub the butter or margarine into the flour until the mixture resembles coarse crumbs. (Alternatively, use a food processor.) Stir in the remaining sugar and continue to rub in until fine crumbs are formed.

4 Cover the fruit with the crumb mixture and press it down lightly. Bake the crisp for about 45 minutes, until the top is golden brown and the fruit tender.

Cook's Tip
To make an oat and cinnamon crisp, substitute rolled oats for half the flour in the crisp mixture and add ½–1 teaspoon ground cinnamon, to taste.

Baked Rice Pudding

Canned rice pudding simply cannot compare with this creamy homemade version, especially if you like the skin.

Serves 4

¼ cup short-grain rice
2 tablespoons light
  brown sugar
4 tablespoons butter
3¾ cups milk

small strip of lemon rind
pinch of freshly grated
  nutmeg
fresh mint sprigs, to
  decorate
raspberries, to serve

1 Preheat the oven to 300°F, then butter a 5-cup shallow baking dish.

2 Put the rice, sugar and butter into the dish, stir in the milk and lemon rind and sprinkle a little nutmeg over the surface.

3 Bake the rice pudding in the oven for about 2½ hours, stirring after 30 minutes and another couple of times during the next 2 hours until the rice is tender and the pudding has a thick and creamy consistency.

4 If you like skin on top, leave the rice pudding undisturbed for the last 30 minutes of cooking (otherwise, stir it again). Serve hot, decorated with fresh mint sprigs and raspberries.

Cook's Tip
Baked rice pudding is even more delicious with fruit. Add some golden raisins, raisins or chopped ready-to-eat dried apricots to the pudding, or serve it alongside sliced fresh peaches or nectarines, fresh raspberries or fresh strawberries.

Floating Islands in Plum Sauce

This unusual, low-fat dessert is simpler to make than it looks, and is quite delicious.

Serves 4
1 pound red plums
1¼ cups apple juice
2 egg whites

2 tablespoons concentrated
   apple juice syrup
pinch of freshly grated
   nutmeg

1 Halve the plums and remove the pits. Place them in a wide saucepan with the apple juice.

2 Bring to a boil, then cover with a tight-fitting lid and allow to simmer gently until the plums are tender.

3 Meanwhile, place the egg whites in a clean, dry bowl and whisk until stiff peaks form.

4 Gradually whisk in the apple juice syrup, whisking until the meringue holds fairly firm peaks.

5 Using a tablespoon, scoop the meringue mixture into the gently simmering plum sauce. (You may need to cook the "islands" in two batches.)

6 Cover again and allow to simmer gently for 2–3 minutes, until the meringues are just set. Serve immediately, sprinkled with a little freshly grated nutmeg.

Cook's Tip
For ease of preparation when you are entertaining, the plum sauce can be made in advance and reheated just before you cook the meringues.

Souffléd Rice Pudding

The inclusion of fluffy egg whites in this rice pudding makes it unusually light.

Serves 4
¼ cup short-grain rice
3 tablespoons honey
3⅔ cups low-fat milk
1 vanilla pod or ½
   teaspoon vanilla
   extract

2 egg whites
1 teaspoon finely grated
   nutmeg

1 Place the rice, honey and the milk in a heavy-based or nonstick saucepan and bring to a boil. Add the vanilla pod, if using.

2 Reduce the heat and cover with a tight-fitting lid. Leave to simmer gently for about 1–1¼ hours, stirring occasionally to prevent sticking, until most of the liquid has been absorbed.

3 Remove the vanilla pod from the saucepan, or if using vanilla extract, add this to the rice mixture now. Preheat the oven to 425°F.

4 Place the egg whites in a clean dry bowl and whisk until stiff peaks form.

5 Using a metal spoon or spatula, fold the egg whites evenly into the rice mixture and turn into a 4-cup buttered baking dish.

6 Sprinkle with grated nutmeg and bake for 15–20 minutes, until the pudding has risen well and is golden brown. Serve hot.

Cabinet Pudding

Dried and candied fruit, sponge cake and macaroons, spiked with brandy if you wish, make a rich pudding.

Serves 4

2½ teaspoons raisins, chopped

2 tablespoons brandy (optional)

1 ounce candied cherries, halved

1 ounce angelica, chopped

2 slices sponge cakes

2 ounces ratafias

2 eggs

2 egg yolks

2 tablespoons sugar

1¾ cups light cream or milk

few drops of vanilla extract

1 Soak the raisins in the brandy, if using, for several hours.

2 Butter a 3⅔ cup charlotte mold and arrange some of the cherries and angelica in the bottom.

3 Dice the sponge cake and crush the macaroons. Mix with the remaining cherries and angelica, add the raisins and spoon into the mold.

4 Lightly whisk together the eggs, egg yolks and sugar. Bring the cream or milk just to a boil, then stir into the egg mixture with the vanilla extract.

5 Strain the egg mixture into the mold, then set aside for 15–30 minutes.

6 Preheat the oven to 325°F. Place the mould in a roasting pan, cover with baking parchment and pour in enough boiling water to half-fill the pan. Bake for 1 hour, or until set. Let sit for 2–3 minutes, then turn out onto a warm plate.

Eve's Pudding

The tempting apples beneath the sponge topping are the reason for this pudding's name.

Serves 4–6

½ cup butter, softened

½ cup sugar

2 eggs, beaten

grated rind and juice of 1 lemon

scant 1 cup self-rising flour

generous ¼ cup ground almonds

½ cup brown sugar

1½ pounds cooking apples, cored and thinly sliced

¼ cup flaked almonds

1 Preheat the oven to 375°F. Beat together the butter and sugar in a large mixing bowl until the mixture is very light and fluffy.

2 Gradually beat the eggs into the butter mixture, beating well after each addition, then fold in the lemon rind, flour and ground almonds.

3 Mix the brown sugar, apples and lemon juice, turn into an ovenproof dish, add the sponge mixture, then the almonds. Bake for 40–45 minutes, until golden.

Surprise Lemon Pudding

The surprise is a delicious tangy lemon sauce that forms beneath the light topping in this pudding.

Serves 4
6 tablespoons butter, softened
1½ cups light brown sugar

4 eggs, separated
grated rind and juice of 4 lemons
½ cup self-rising flour

1 Preheat the oven to 350°F, then butter a 7-inch soufflé dish or cake pan and stand it in a roasting pan.

2 Beat the butter and sugar together in a large bowl until pale and very fluffy. Beat in one egg yolk at a time, beating well after each addition and gradually beating in the lemon rind and juice until blended; do not worry if the mixture curdles a little at this stage.

3 Sift the flour and stir into the lemon mixture until blended, then gradually stir in the milk.

4 Whisk the egg whites in a separate bowl until stiff peaks form but the whites are not dry, then lightly, but thoroughly, fold into the lemon mixture in three batches. Carefully pour the mixture into the soufflé dish or cake pan, then pour boiling water into the roasting pan to come halfway up the sides.

5 Bake the pudding in the center of the oven for about 45 minutes, or until risen, just firm to the touch and golden brown on top. Serve immediately.

Castle Puddings with Custard

These attractive puddings may be baked in ramekin dishes if you do not have dariole molds.

Serves 4
3 tablespoons blackcurrant, strawberry or raspberry jam
½ cup butter, softened
½ cup sugar
2 eggs, beaten
few drops of vanilla extract

generous 1 cup self-rising flour

For the custard
1 scant cup milk
4 eggs
1–2 tablespoons sugar
few drops of vanilla extract

1 Preheat the oven to 350°F. Butter eight dariole molds. Put about 2 teaspoons of your chosen jam in the base of each mold.

2 Beat the butter and sugar together until light and fluffy, then gradually beat in the eggs, beating well after each addition, and add the vanilla extract towards the end. Lightly fold in the flour, then divide the mixture among the molds. Bake the puddings for about 20 minutes until well risen and a light golden color.

3 To make the custard, whisk the eggs and sugar together. Bring the milk to a boil in a heavy, preferably nonstick, saucepan, then slowly pour onto the sweetened egg mixture, stirring constantly.

4 Return the milk to the pan and heat very gently, stirring, until the mixture thickens enough to coat the back of a spoon; do not allow to boil. Cover the pan and remove from the heat.

5 Remove the molds from the oven, let stand for a few minutes, then turn the puddings onto warmed plates and serve with the custard.

Bread and Butter Pudding

An unusual version of a classic recipe, this pudding is made with French bread and mixed dried fruit.

Serves 4–6

4 ready-to-eat dried
   apricots, finely
   chopped
1 tablespoon raisins
2 tablespoons golden
   raisins
1 tablespoon chopped
   mixed peel
1 French bread, about 7
   ounces, thinly sliced
4 tablespoons butter,
   melted
1¾ cups milk

⅔ cup heavy cream
½ cup caster sugar
3 eggs
½ teaspoon vanilla
   extract
2 tablespoons whiskey

For the cream
⅔ cup heavy cream
2 tablespoons plain
   strained yogurt
1–2 tablespoons whiskey
1 tablespoon sugar

1 Preheat the oven to 350°F. Butter a deep 6¼-cup baking dish. Mix together the dried fruits. Brush the bread on both sides with butter. Fill the dish with alternate layers of bread and dried fruit starting with fruit and finishing with bread. Heat the milk and cream in a saucepan until just boiling. Whisk together the sugar, eggs and vanilla extract.

2 Whisk the milk mixture into the eggs, then strain into the dish. Sprinkle the whiskey over the top. Press the bread down, cover with foil and allow to stand for 20 minutes.

3 Place the dish in a roasting pan half filled with water and bake for 1 hour, or until the custard is just set. Remove the foil and cook for 10 minutes more, until golden. Just before serving, heat all the cream ingredients in a small pan, stirring. Serve with the hot pudding.

Chocolate Amaretti Peaches

This dessert is quick and easy to prepare, yet sophisticated enough to serve at the most elegant dinner party.

Serves 4

4 ounces amaretti
   cookies, crushed
2 ounces semi-sweet
   chocolate, chopped
grated rind of ½ orange
1 tablespoon honey
¼ teaspoon ground
   cinnamon

1 egg white, lightly
   beaten
4 firm ripe peaches
⅔ cup white wine
1 tablespoon sugar
whipped cream, to serve

1 Preheat the oven to 375°F. Mix together the crushed amaretti cookies, chocolate, orange rind, honey and cinnamon in a bowl. Add the beaten egg white and mix to bind the mixture together.

2 Halve and pit the peaches and fill the cavities with the chocolate mixture, shaping it upwards slightly.

3 Arrange the stuffed peaches in a lightly buttered shallow baking dish which will just hold the fruit comfortably. Pour the wine into a measuring cup and stir in the sugar.

4 Pour the wine mixture around the peaches. Bake for 30–40 minutes, until the peaches are tender. Serve immediately with a little of the cooking juice spooned over and the whipped cream.

Cook's Tip
Prepare this dessert using fresh nectarines or apricots instead of peaches, if you wish.

Warm Autumn Compote

This is a simple yet quite sophisticated dessert featuring succulent ripe autumnal fruits.

Serves 4

generous ¼ cup sugar
1 bottle red wine
1 vanilla pod, split
1 strip pared lemon rind

4 pears
2 fresh figs, quartered
2 cups raspberries
lemon juice, to taste

1 Put the sugar and red wine in a large saucepan and heat gently until the sugar has completely dissolved. Add the vanilla pod and lemon rind and bring to a boil. Reduce the heat and simmer for 5 minutes.

2 Peel and halve the pears, then scoop out the cores, using a melon baller or teaspoon. Add the pears to the syrup and poach for about 15 minutes, turning them several times so they color evenly.

3 Add the quartered figs and poach for another 5 minutes, until the fruits are tender.

4 Transfer the poached pears and figs to a serving bowl using a slotted spoon, then scatter on the raspberries.

5 Return the syrup to the heat and boil rapidly to reduce slightly and concentrate the flavor. Add a little lemon juice to taste. Strain the syrup over the fruits and serve warm.

Apple Soufflé Omelet

Apples sautéed until they are slightly caramelized make a delicious autumn filling for this sweet omelet.

Serves 2

4 eggs, separated
2 tablespoons light cream
1 tablespoon sugar
1 tablespoon butter
sifted confectioner's
   sugar, for dredging

For the filling
1 eating apple, peeled,
   cored and sliced
2 tablespoons butter
2 tablespoons soft light
   brown sugar
3 tablespoons light cream

1 To make the filling, sauté the apple slices in the butter and sugar until just tender. Stir in the cream and keep warm, while making the omelet.

2 Place the egg yolks in a bowl with the cream and sugar and beat well. Whisk the egg whites until stiff peaks form, then fold into the yolk mixture.

3 Melt the butter in a large heavy-based frying pan, pour in the soufflé mixture and spread evenly. Cook for 1 minute until golden underneath, then place under a hot grill to brown the top.

4 Slide the omelet onto a plate, spoon the apple mixture on to one side, then fold over. Dredge the icing sugar over thickly, then quickly mark in a criss-cross pattern with a hot metal skewer. Serve the omelet immediately.

Cook's Tip
In the summer months, make the filling for the omelet using fresh raspberries or strawberries.

Warm Lemon and Syrup Cake

This simple cake is made special by the lemon syrup which is poured over it when baked.

Serves 8
3 eggs
¾ cup butter, softened
¾ cup sugar
1½ cups self-rising flour
½ cup ground almonds
¼ teaspoon freshly grated nutmeg
2 ounces candied lemon peel, finely chopped

grated rind of 1 lemon
2 tablespoons freshly squeezed lemon juice
poached pears, to serve

For the syrup
¼ cup sugar
juice of 3 lemons

1 Preheat the oven to 350°F. Lightly grease and base-line a deep round 8-inch cake pan.

2 Place all the cake ingredients in a large bowl and beat well for 2–3 minutes, until light and fluffy.

3 Turn the mixture into the prepared pan, spread evenly and bake for 1 hour, or until golden and firm to the touch.

4 To make the syrup, put the sugar, lemon juice and 5 tablespoons water in a saucepan. Heat gently, stirring until the sugar has completely dissolved, then boil, without stirring, for 1–2 minutes.

5 Turn out the cake onto a plate with a rim. Prick the surface of the cake all over with a fork, then pour on the hot syrup. Allow to soak for about 30 minutes. Serve the cake warm with thin wedges of poached pears.

Papaya and Pineapple Crisp

Crisps are always popular with children and adults, but you can make a change with this exotic variation.

Serves 4–6
For the topping
1½ cups all-purpose flour
6 tablespoons butter, diced
generous ¼ cup sugar
½ cup mixed chopped nuts

For the filling
1 medium-ripe pineapple
1 large ripe papaya
1 tablespoon sugar
1 teaspoon mixed spice
grated rind of 1 lime
plain yogurt, to serve

1 Preheat the oven to 350°F. To make the topping, sift the flour into a bowl and rub in the butter until the mixture resembles bread crumbs. Stir in the sugar and mixed chopped nuts.

2 Peel the pineapple, remove the eyes, then cut in half. Cut away the core and cut the flesh into bite-size chunks. Halve the papaya and scoop out the seeds using a spoon. Peel, then cut the fruit into similar-size pieces.

3 Put the pineapple and papaya chunks into a large pie pan. Sprinkle over the sugar, mixed spice and lime rind and toss gently to mix.

4 Spoon the crisp topping over the fruit and spread out evenly with a fork, but don't press it down. Bake in the oven for 45–50 minutes, until golden brown. Serve the crisp hot or warm with plain yogurt.

Zabaglione

A much-loved simple Italian dessert traditionally made with Marsala, an Italian fortified wine.

Serves 4
4 egg yolks
4 tablespoons sugar

4 tablespoons Marsala
amaretti cookies, to serve

1 Place the egg yolks and sugar in a large heat-proof bowl and beat with an electric hand mixer until the mixture is pale and thick.

2 Gradually add the Marsala, about 1 tablespoon at a time, beating well after each addition (at this stage the mixture will be quite runny).

3 Place the bowl over a saucepan of gently simmering water and continue to beat for at least 5–7 minutes, until the mixture becomes thick and mousse-like; when the beaters are lifted they should leave a thick trail on the surface of the mixture. (If you don't beat the mixture for long enough, the zabaglione will be too runny and will probably separate.)

4 Pour into four warmed stemmed glasses and serve immediately with the amaretti cookies for dipping.

Cook's Tip
If you don't have any Marsala, substitute Madeira, a medium-sweet sherry or a dessert wine.

Thai-fried Bananas

This is a very simple and quick Thai dessert – bananas are simply fried in butter, brown sugar and lime juice.

Serves 4
3 tablespoons unsalted
  butter
4 large slightly under-
  ripe bananas
1 tablespoon dried
  coconut

4 tablespoons ight brown
  sugar
4 tablespoons lime juice
2 lime slices, to decorate
thick and creamy plain
  yogurt, to serve

1 Heat the butter in a large frying pan or wok and fry the bananas for 1–2 minutes on each side, or until they are lightly golden in color.

2 Meanwhile, dry fry the coconut in a small frying pan until lightly browned and reserve.

3 Sprinkle the sugar into the pan with the bananas, add the lime juice and cook, stirring, until dissolved. Sprinkle the coconut over the bananas, decorate with lime slices and serve with the thick and creamy yogurt.

Crêpes Suzette

This dish is a classic of French cuisine and still enjoys worldwide popularity as a dessert or a daytime treat.

Makes 8

1 cup all-purpose flour
pinch of salt
1 egg
1 egg yolk
1¼ cups low-fat milk
1 tablespoon butter,
    melted, plus extra, for
    shallow frying

For the sauce
2 large oranges
4 tablespoons butter
½ cup soft light brown
    sugar
1 tablespoon Grand
    Marnier
1 tablespoon brandy

1 Sift the flour and salt into a bowl and make a well in the center. Crack the egg and extra yolk into the well. Stir the eggs to incorporate all the flour. When the mixture thickens, gradually pour in the milk, beating well after each addition, until a smooth batter is formed. Stir in the butter, transfer to a measuring cup, cover and chill for 30 minutes.

2 Heat a shallow frying pan, add a little butter and heat until sizzling. Pour in a little batter, tilting the pan to cover the base. Cook over moderate heat for 1–2 minutes until lightly browned underneath, then flip and cook for minute more. Make eight crêpes and stack them on a plate.

3 Pare the rind from one of the oranges and reserve about 1 teaspoon. Squeeze the juice from both oranges.

4 To make the sauce, melt the butter in a large frying pan and heat the sugar with the rind and juice until dissolved and gently bubbling. Fold each crêpe in quarters. Add to the pan one at a time, coat in the sauce and fold in half again. Move to the side of the pan to make room for the others.

5 Pour on the Grand Marnier and brandy and cook gently for 2–3 minutes, until the sauce has slightly caramelized. Sprinkle with the reserved orange rind and serve immediately.

Bananas with Rum and Raisins

Choose almost-ripe bananas with evenly colored skins, all yellow or just green at the tips for this dessert.

Serves 4

scant ¼ cup seedless
    raisins
5 tablespoons dark rum
4 tablespoons unsalted
    butter
½ cup light brown sugar
4 bananas, peeled and
    halved lengthwise
¼ teaspoon grated
    nutmeg

¼ teaspoon ground
    cinnamon
2 tablespoons slivered
    almonds, toasted
chilled cream or vanilla
    ice cream, to serve
    (optional)

1 Put the raisins in a bowl with the rum. Allow them to soak for about 30 minutes to plump up.

2 Melt the butter in a frying pan, add the sugar and stir until completely dissolved. Add the bananas and cook for a few minutes until tender.

3 Sprinkle the spices over the bananas, then pour on the rum and raisins. Carefully ignite using a long taper and stir gently to mix.

4 Scatter over the slivered almonds and serve immediately with chilled cream or vanilla ice cream, if you wish.

Cook's Tip
Stand a way back when you ignite the rum and shake the pan gently until the flames subside.

Orange Rice Pudding

In Spain, Greece, Italy and Morocco rice puddings are a favorite dish, especially when sweetened with honey.

Serves 4

¼ cup short-grain rice
2½ cups milk
2 – 3 tablespoons honey,
* to taste*
finely grated rind of
* ½ small orange*

⅔ cup heavy cream
1 tablespoon chopped
* pistachios, toasted*

1 Mix the rice with the milk, honey and orange rind in a saucepan and bring to a boil, then reduce the heat, cover with a tight-fitting lid and simmer very gently for about 1¼ hours, stirring regularly.

2 Remove the lid and continue cooking and stirring for about 15 – 20 minutes, until the rice is creamy.

3 Pour in the cream and simmer for 5 – 8 minutes longer. Serve the rice sprinkled with the chopped toasted pistachios in individual warmed bowls.

Apple and Blackberry Nut Crisp

This much-loved dish of tart apples and blackberries is topped with a golden, sweet topping.

Serves 4

2 pounds tart apples,
* peeled, cored and*
* sliced*
½ cup butter
½ cup light brown sugar
1½ cups blackberries
¾ cup whole wheat flour
¾ cup all-purpose flour

½ teaspoon ground
* cinnamon*
3 tablespoons chopped
* mixed nuts, toasted*
custard, cream or ice
* cream, to serve*

1 Preheat the oven to 350°F. Lightly butter a 5-cup baking dish.

2 Place the apples in a saucepan with 2 tablespoons of the butter, 2 tablespoons of the sugar and 1 tablespoon water. Cover with a tight-fitting lid and cook gently for about 10 minutes, until just tender but still holding their shape.

3 Remove from the heat and gently stir in the blackberries. Spoon the mixture into the baking dish and set aside while you make the topping.

4 To make the crisp topping, sift the flours and cinnamon into a bowl (add in any of the bran left in the sifter). Add the remaining 6 tablespoons butter and rub into the flour with your fingertips until the mixture resembles fine bread crumbs (or you can use a food processor).

5 Stir in the remaining generous ¼ cup sugar and the nuts and mix well. Sprinkle the crisp topping on the fruit. Bake for 35 – 40 minutes, until the top is golden brown. Serve hot with custard, cream or ice cream.

Apple Couscous Dessert

This unusual couscous mixture makes a delicious family dessert with a rich fruity flavor.

Serves 4
2½ cups apple juice
⅔ cup couscous
¼ cup golden raisins
½ teaspoon mixed spice
1 large cooking apple,
    peeled, cored and sliced

2 tablespoons light
    brown sugar
plain yogurt, to serve

1 Preheat the oven to 400°F. Place the apple juice, couscous, golden raisins and spice in a pan and bring to the boil, stirring. Cover and simmer for 10–12 minutes, until all the free liquid is absorbed.

2 Spoon half the couscous mixture into a 5-cup ovenproof dish and top with half the apple slices. Top with the remaining couscous.

3 Arrange the remaining apple slices overlapping over the top and sprinkle with the sugar. Bake for 25–30 minutes, or until golden brown. Serve hot with yogurt.

Banana, Maple and Lime Crêpes

Crêpes are a treat any day of the week, and they can be made in advance and stored in the freezer for convenience.

Serves 4
115g/4oz/1 cup plain
    flour
1 egg white
250ml/8fl oz/1 cup
    skimmed milk
50ml/2 fl oz/¼ cup cold
    water
sunflower oil, for frying

For the filling
4 bananas, sliced
45ml/3 tbsp maple or
    golden syrup
30ml/2 tbsp freshly
    squeezed lime juice
strips of lime rind, to
    decorate

1 Beat together the flour, egg white, milk and water until smooth and bubbly. Chill in the fridge until needed.

2 Heat a small amount of oil in a non-stick frying pan and pour in enough batter just to coat the base. Swirl it around the pan to coat evenly.

3 Cook until golden, then toss or turn and cook the other side. Place on a plate, cover with foil and keep hot while making the remaining pancakes.

4 To make the filling, place the bananas, syrup and lime juice in a saucepan and simmer gently for 1 minute. Spoon into the pancakes and fold into quarters. Sprinkle with shreds of lime rind to decorate. Serve hot, with yogurt or fromage frais, if you wish.

Cook's Tip
To freeze the crêpes, interleaf them with non-stick baking paper and seal in a plastic bag. They should be used within 3 months.

Spiced Pears in Cider

Any variety of pear can be used for cooking, but choose a firm variety such as Conference for this recipe.

Serves 4

4 medium-firm pears
1 cup hard cider
thinly pared strip of
    lemon rind
1 cinnamon stick

2 tablespoons light
    brown sugar
1 teaspoon arrowroot
ground cinnamon, to
    sprinkle

1 Peel the pears thinly, leaving them whole with the stalks on. Place in a saucepan with the cider, lemon rind and cinnamon. Cover and simmer gently, turning the pears occasionally, for 15–20 minutes or until tender.

2 Lift out the pears. Boil the syrup, uncovered, to reduce by about half. Remove the lemon rind and cinnamon stick, then stir in the sugar.

3 Mix the arrowroot with 1 tablespoon cold water in a small bowl until smooth, then stir into the syrup. Bring to a boil and stir over the heat until thickened and clear.

4 Pour the sauce over the pears and sprinkle with ground cinnamon. Let cool slightly, then serve warm with yogurt, if you wish.

Cook's Tip
Whole pears look impressive but if you prefer they can be halved and cored before cooking. This will shorten the cooking time slightly.

Fruity Bread Pudding

A delicious old-fashioned family favorite is given a lighter, healthier touch in this version.

Serves 4

²⁄₃ cup mixed dried fruit
²⁄₃ cup apple juice
4 ounces stale brown or
    white bread, diced
1 teaspoon mixed spice

1 large banana, sliced
²⁄₃ cup skim milk
1 tablespoon brown
    sugar
plain yogurt, to serve

1 Preheat the oven to 400°F. Place the mixed dried fruit in a small saucepan with the apple juice and bring to a boil.

2 Remove the pan from the heat and stir in the diced bread, mixed spice and banana. Spoon the mixture into a shallow 5-cup baking dish; pour over the milk.

3 Sprinkle with brown sugar and bake for about 25–30 minutes, until firm and golden brown. Serve hot or cold with plain yogurt.

Cook's Tip
Different types of bread will absorb varying amounts of liquid, so you may need to adjust the amount of milk used to allow for this.

Crunchy Gooseberry Crisp

Gooseberries are perfect for traditional family desserts such as this extra-special crisp.

Serves 4

4¼ cups gooseberries
4 tablespoons sugar
1 cup rolled oats
¼ cup whole wheat flour
4 tablespoons sunflower
  oil

4 tablespoons brown
  sugar
2 tablespoons chopped
  walnuts
plain yogurt or vanilla
  custard, to serve

1 Preheat the oven to 400°F. Place the gooseberries in a saucepan with the sugar. Cover the pan and cook over a low heat for 10 minutes, until the gooseberries are just tender. Pour into a baking dish.

2 To make the crisp, place the oats, flour and oil in a bowl and stir with a fork until evenly mixed.

3 Stir in the brown sugar and walnuts, then spread evenly over the gooseberries. Bake for 25–30 minutes, or until golden and bubbling. Serve hot with yogurt or custard.

Cook's Tip
When gooseberries are out of season substitute other fruits, such as apples, plums or rhubarb.

Gingerbread Upside-down Pudding

A proper pudding goes down well on a cold winter's day. This one is quite quick to make and looks very impressive.

Serves 4–6

sunflower oil, for
  brushing
1 tablespoon brown
  sugar
4 peaches, halved and
  pitted, or canned
  peach halves, drained
8 walnut halves

For the base
½ cup whole wheat flour
½ teaspoon baking soda
1½ teaspoons ground
  ginger
1 teaspoon ground
  cinnamon
½ cup dark brown sugar
1 egg
½ cup skim milk
¼ cup sunflower oil

1 Preheat the oven to 350°. Brush the bottom and sides of a 9-inch round springform cake pan with oil. Sprinkle the brown sugar evenly over the base.

2 Arrange the peaches, cut-side down, in the pan with a walnut half in each.

3 To make the base, sift together the flour, baking soda, ginger and cinnamon, then stir in the sugar. Beat together the egg, milk and oil, then mix into the dry ingredients until smooth.

4 Pour the mixture evenly over the peaches and bake for 35–40 minutes, until firm to the touch. Turn out onto a serving plate. Serve hot with yogurt or custard, if liked.

Cook's Tip
The brown sugar caramelizes during baking, creating a delightfully sticky topping.

Cherry Clafoutis

When fresh cherries are in season this makes a deliciously simple dessert for any occasion. Serve warm with a little light cream.

Serves 6

1½ pound fresh cherries
½ cup flour
pinch of salt
4 eggs, plus 2 egg yolks
½ cup sugar

2½ cups milk
¼ cup melted butter
sugar, for dusting
   (optional)

1 Preheat the oven to 375°F. Lightly butter the base and sides of a shallow ovenproof dish. Pit the cherries and place them in the dish.

2 Sift the flour and salt into a bowl. Add the eggs, egg yolks, sugar and a little of the milk and whisk to a smooth batter.

3 Gradually whisk in the rest of the milk and the butter, then strain the batter over the cherries. Bake for 40–50 minutes until golden and just set. Serve warm, dusted with sugar, if you like.

Cook's Tip
Use 2 x 15-ounce cans pitted black cherries, thoroughly drained, if fresh cherries are not available. For a special dessert, add 3 tablespoons kirsch to the batter.

Apple and Orange Pie

A simple but tasty two-fruit pie: make sure you choose really juicy oranges or even blood oranges.

Serves 4

400g/14oz ready-made
   shortcrust pastry
3 oranges, peeled
900g/2lb cooking apples,
   cored and thickly
   sliced

25g/1oz/2 tbsp demerara
   sugar
beaten egg, to glaze
caster sugar, for
   sprinkling

1 Roll out the pastry on a lightly floured surface to about 2cm/¾in larger than the top of a 1.2 litre/2 pint/5 cup pie dish. Cut off a narrow strip around the edge of the pastry and fit on the rim of the pie dish.

2 Preheat the oven to 190°C/375°F/Gas 5. Hold one orange at a time over a bowl to catch the juice; cut down between the membranes to remove the segments.

3 Mix the segments and juice, the apples and sugar in the pie dish. Place a pie funnel in the centre of the dish.

4 Dampen the pastry strip. Cover the dish with the rolled out pastry and press the edges to the pastry strip. Brush the top with beaten egg, then bake for 35–40 minutes, until lightly browned. Sprinkle with caster sugar before serving.

Bakewell Tart

A classic English dessert, this tart is moist with a delicious almond flavor.

Serves 4

8 ounces ready-made puff
  pastry
2 tablespoons raspberry
  or apricot jam
2 eggs
2 egg yolks
½ cup sugar

½ cup butter, melted
⅔ cup ground almonds
few drops of almond
  extract
sifted confectioner's
  sugar, for dredging

1 Preheat the oven to 400°F. Roll out the pastry on a lightly floured surface and use it to line a 7-inch pie pan or fluted loose-based tart pan. Spread the jam over the base of the pastry case.

2 Whisk the eggs, egg yolks and sugar together in a large bowl until thick and pale.

3 Gently stir the butter, ground almonds and almond extract into the mixture.

4 Pour the mixture into the pie shell and bake for about 30 minutes, until the filling is just set and browned. Dredge with confectioner's sugar before eating hot, warm or cold.

Cook's Tip

Since the pastry case isn't baked blind first, place a baking sheet in the oven while it preheats, then place the pie pan or tart pan on the hot sheet. This will make sure that the base of the pastry shell cooks through.

Yorkshire Curd Tart

The distinguishing characteristic of this tart is the allspice, or "clove pepper" as it was once known in Yorkshire, England

Serves 8

2 cups all-purpose flour
½ cup butter, cubed
1 egg yolk

For the filling
large pinch of allspice
1 scant cup light brown
  sugar

3 eggs, beaten
grated rind and juice of
  1 lemon
3 tablespoons butter,
  melted
2 cups ricotta cheese
½ cup raisins or golden
  raisins

1 Place the flour in a bowl. Add the butter and rub it into the flour with your fingertips until the mixture resembles bread crumbs. (Alternatively, you can use a food processor.) Stir the egg yolk into the flour mixture with a little water to bind the dough together.

2 Turn the dough onto a lightly floured surface, knead lightly and briefly, then form into a ball. Roll out the pastry thinly and use to line an 8-inch fluted loose-based tart pan. Chill for 15 minutes in the fridge.

3 Preheat the oven to 375°F. To make the filling, mix the allspice with the sugar, then stir in the eggs, lemon rind and juice, melted butter, ricotta cheese and the raisins or golden raisins.

4 Pour the filling into the pie shell, then bake for about 40 minutes until the pastry is cooked and the filling is lightly set and golden brown. Serve still slightly warm, cut into wedges, with cream, if you wish.

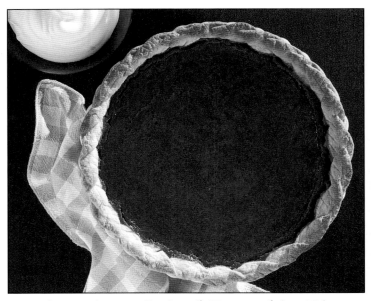

American Spiced Pumpkin Pie

This is a rich, delicately-spiced pie that deservedly goes with Thanksgiving.

Serves 4–6

1½ cups all-purpose flour
pinch of salt
6 tablespoons unsalted
*   butter*
1 tablespoon caster sugar
3 cups peeled fresh diced
*   pumpkin, or 14*
*   ounces canned*
*   pumpkin, drained*
1 cup light brown sugar

¼ teaspoon salt
¼ teaspoon ground
*   allspice*
½ teaspoon ground
*   cinnamon*
½ teaspoon ground
*   ginger*
2 eggs, lightly beaten
½ cup heavy cream
whipped cream, to serve

1 Place the flour in a bowl with a pinch of salt. Rub in the butter until the mixture resembles bread crumbs. Add the sugar and 2–3 tablespoons water. Mix to a soft dough. Knead briefly, shape into a ball, wrap and chill for 1 hour.

2 Preheat the oven to 400°F with a baking sheet inside. If using fresh pumpkin, steam for 15 minutes, then cool. Purée in a food processor or blender until smooth.

3 Line a 9½-inch x 1-inch deep pie pan with the pastry. Prick the bottom. Cut out leaf shapes from the excess pastry and mark veins with the back of a knife. Brush the edges with water and stick on the leaves. Chill.

4 Mix together the pumpkin purée, sugar, salt, spices, eggs and cream and pour into the pie shell. Place on the preheated baking sheet and bake for 15 minutes. Then reduce the temperature to 350°F and cook for another 30 minutes, or until the filling is set and the pastry golden. Serve warm with whipped cream.

Pear and Blueberry Pie

A variation on plain blueberry pie, this dessert is just as delicious served cold as it is warm.

Serves 4

2 cups all-purpose flour
pinch of salt
4 tablespoons lard, diced
4 tablespoons butter,
*   diced*
4½ cups blueberries
2 tablespoons sugar
1 tablespoon arrowroot

2 ripe but firm pears,
*   peeled, cored and*
*   sliced*
½ teaspoon ground
*   cinnamon*
grated rind of ½ lemon
beaten egg, to glaze
sugar, for sprinkling

1 Sift the flour and salt into a bowl. Rub in the fats until the mixture resembles fine bread crumbs. Mix to a dough with 3 tablespoons cold water. Chill for 30 minutes.

2 Place 2 cups of the blueberries in a saucepan with the sugar. Cover with a lid and cook gently until the blueberries have softened. Press through a nylon strainer. Blend the arrowroot with 2 tablespoons cold water and add to the blueberries. Bring to a boil, stirring until thickened. Allow to cool slightly.

3 Preheat the oven to 375°F with a baking sheet inside. Roll out just over half the pastry on a lightly floured surface and use to line an 8-inch shallow pie pan.

4 Mix together the remaining blueberries, the pears, ground cinnamon and lemon rind and spoon into the dish. Pour over the blueberry purée.

5 Use the remaining pastry to cover the pie. Make a slit in the center. Brush with egg and sprinkle with sugar. Bake on the baking sheet for 40–45 minutes, until golden. Serve warm, with crème fraîche, if you wish.

Mississippi Pecan Pie

Serve this gooey pie with a bowl of fluffy whipped cream or ice cream.

Serves 4–6
For the pastry
1 cup all-purpose flour
4 tablespoons butter
2 tablespoons caster
    sugar
1 egg yolk

For the filling
5 tablespoons maple or
    corn syrup

⅓ cup dark brown sugar
4 tablespoons butter
3 eggs, lightly beaten
½ teaspoon vanilla
    extract
1¼ cups pecan nuts
fresh cream, whipped, if
    liked or ice cream, to
    serve

1 Place the flour in a bowl. Dice the butter, then rub it into the flour with your fingertips until the mixture resembles bread crumbs. (Alternatively use a food processor.) Stir in the sugar, egg yolk and about 2 tablespoons cold water. Mix to a dough and knead on a lightly floured surface until smooth.

2 Roll out the pastry and use it to line an 8-inch fluted loose-based tart pan. Prick the bottom, then line with greaseproof paper and fill with baking beans. Chill for 30 minutes in the fridge. Preheat the oven to 400°F.

3 Bake the pie shell blind for 10 minutes. Remove the paper and beans and continue to bake for 5 more minutes. Reduce the oven temperature to 350°F.

4 To make the filling, heat the syrup, sugar and butter in a saucepan until the sugar dissolves. Remove from the heat and cool slightly. Whisk in the eggs and vanilla extract and stir in the pecan nuts.

5 Pour into the pastry case and bake for 35–40 minutes, until the filling is set. Serve with cream or ice cream.

Upside-down Apple Tart

Use tart apples in this delicious dessert with a lovely caramel layer.

Serves 4
For the pastry
4 tablespoons butter,
    softened
3 tablespoons sugar
1 egg
1 cup all-purpose flour
pinch of salt

For the apple layer
generous ¼ cup butter,
    softened
scant ½ cup light brown
    sugar
10 Granny Smith's
    apples, peeled, cored
    and thickly sliced
whipped cream, to serve

1 For the pastry, cream the butter and sugar until pale and creamy. Beat in the egg, sift in the flour and salt and mix to a soft dough. Knead, wrap and chill for 1 hour.

2 For the apple layer, grease a 9-inch cake pan, then add 4 tablespoons of the butter. Place on the stove and melt the butter. Remove from the heat and sprinkle over 4 tablespoons of the sugar. Arrange the apple slices on top, sprinkle with the remaining sugar and dot with the remaining butter.

3 Preheat the oven to 450°F. Place the cake tin on the stove again over low to moderate heat for about 15 minutes, until a light golden caramel forms on the bottom.

4 Roll out the pastry on a lightly floured surface to around the same size as the pan and lay it on top of the apples. Tuck the pastry edges down around the sides of the apples.

5 Bake for about 20–25 minutes, until the pastry is golden. Remove from the oven and let stand for 5 minutes.

6 Place an upturned plate on top of the pan and, holding the two together with a dish towel, turn the apple tart out onto the plate. Serve while still warm with whipped cream.

Mango and Coconut Stir-fry

Choose a ripe mango for this recipe. If you buy one that is a little under-ripe, leave it in a warm place for a day or two before using.

Serves 4

¼ coconut
1 large, ripe mango
juice of 2 limes
rind of 2 limes, finely
  shredded
1 tablespoon
  sunflower oil
1 tablespoon butter
1½ tablespoons honey
crème fraîche, to serve

1 Prepare the coconut flakes by draining the milk from the coconut and peeling the flesh with a vegetable peeler.

2 Peel the mango. Cut the pit out of the middle of the fruit. Cut each half of the mango into slices.

3 Place the mango slices in a bowl and pour over the lime juice and rind, to marinate them.

4 Meanwhile, heat a wok, then add 2 teaspoons of the oil. When the oil is hot, add the butter. When the butter has melted, stir in the coconut flakes and stir-fry for 1–2 minutes until the coconut is golden brown. Remove and drain on paper towels. Wipe out the wok. Strain the mango slices, reserving the juice.

5 Heat the wok and add the remaining oil. When the oil is hot, add the mango and stir-fry for 1–2 minutes, then add the juice and allow to bubble and reduce for 1 minute. Stir in the honey, sprinkle on the coconut and serve with crème fraîche.

Cook's Tip
Because of the delicate taste of desserts, always make sure your wok has been scrupulously cleaned so there is no transference of flavors.

Peach and Raspberry Crisp

A quick and easy tasty dessert, this crisp is good served hot on its own or with low fat custard.

Serves 4

⅔ cup whole wheat flour
¾ cup oatmeal
6 tablespoons butter
¼ cup soft light brown
  sugar
½ teaspoon ground
  cinnamon
14-ounce can peach slices
  in fruit juice
1⅓ cups raspberries
2 tablespoons honey

1 Preheat the oven to 350°F. Put the flour and oatmeal in a bowl and mix together.

2 Rub in the butter until the mixture resembles breadcrumbs, then stir in the sugar and cinnamon.

3 Drain the peach slices, reserving the juice.

4 Roughly chop the peaches and put them in an ovenproof dish, then scatter over the raspberries.

5 Mix together the reserved peach juice and honey, pour over the fruit and stir.

6 Spoon the topping mixture over the fruit, pressing it down lightly. Bake for about 45 minutes, until golden brown on top. Serve hot.

Cook's Tip
Use other combinations of fruit such as apples and blueberries for a tasty change.

Pineapple and Peach Dessert

A tasty combination of pineapple and peaches, serve this old favorite with custard or ice cream.

Serves 6

5 tablespoons golden
   syrup
8-ounce can pineapple
   cubes in fruit juice
⅔ cup ready-to-eat dried
   peaches, chopped
⅔ cup sugar

8 tablespoons butter
1 ½ cups self-rising whole
   wheat flour
1 teaspoon baking powder
2 eggs

1 Preheat the oven to 350°F. Lightly grease a 7-inch loose-based round cake pan and line the base with baking parchment.

2 Heat the golden syrup gently in a saucepan and pour over the bottom of the pan.

3 Strain the pineapple, reserving 3 tablespoons of the juice.

4 Mix together the pineapple and peaches and scatter them over the syrup layer.

5 Put the sugar, butter, flour, baking powder, eggs and reserved pineapple juice in a bowl and beat together until smooth.

6 Spread the cake mixture evenly over the fruit and level the surface. Bake for about 45 minutes until risen and golden brown. Turn out carefully on to a serving plate and serve hot in slices.

Cook's Tip
Other combinations of canned and dried fruit work just as well as, such as apricots and pears, or peaches and figs.

Feather-light Peach Dessert

On chilly days, try this hot fruit dessert with its tantalizing sponge topping.

Serves 4

14-ounce can peach slices
4 tablespoons butter
¼ cup soft light brown
   sugar
1 egg, beaten
½ cup flour
1 teaspoon baking
   powder

½ teaspoon ground
   cinnamon
4 tablespoons milk
½ tsp vanilla extract
2 teaspoons
   confectioners' sugar,
   for dusting
custard, to serve

1 Preheat the oven to 350°F. Drain the peaches and put into a 4-cup pie dish with 2 tablespoons of the juice.

2 Put all the remaining ingredients, except the confectioners' sugar and custard into a mixing bowl. Beat for 3–4 minutes, until thoroughly combined.

3 Spoon the sponge mixture over the peaches and level the top evenly. Cook in the oven for 35–40 minutes, or until springy to the touch.

4 Lightly dust the top with confectioners' sugar before serving hot with the custard.

Cook's Tip
For a simple sauce, blend 1 teaspoon arrowroot with 1 tablespoon peach juice in a small saucepan. Stir in the remaining peach juice from the can and bring to the boil. Simmer for 1 minute until thickened and clear.

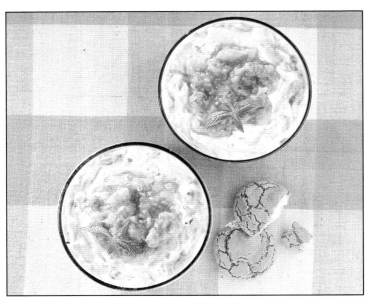

Gooseberry and Elderflower Cream

When elderflowers are in season, instead of using the cordial, cook two to three elderflower heads with the gooseberries.

Serves 4

4¼ cups gooseberries
1¼ cups heavy cream
about 1 cup sifted
  confectioner's sugar,
  to taste

2 tablespoons elderflower
  cordial or orange-
  flower water
  (optional)
fresh mint sprigs, to
  decorate
almond cookies, to serve

1 Place the gooseberries in a heavy saucepan, cover and cook over low heat, shaking the pan occasionally, until the gooseberries are tender. Transfer the gooseberries to a bowl, crush them, then leave to cool completely.

2 Beat the cream until soft peaks form, then fold in half of the crushed gooseberries. Sweeten with confectioner's sugar and add the elderflower cordial, or orange-flower water to taste, if using. Sweeten the remaining gooseberries.

3 Layer the cream mixture and the crushed gooseberries in four dessert dishes or tall glasses, then cover and chill. Decorate the dessert with the fresh mint sprigs and serve with almond cookies.

Cook's Tip
If preferred, the cooked gooseberries can be puréed and strained instead of crushed.

Eton Mess

This dish forms part of the picnic meals enjoyed by parents and pupils at Eton, a prestigious English private school.

Serves 4

4¼ cups strawberries,
  coarsely chopped
3–4 tablespoons Kirsch
1¼ cups heavy cream

6 small white meringues
fresh mint sprigs, to
  decorate

1 Put the strawberries in a bowl, sprinkle on the Kirsch, then cover and chill in the fridge for 2–3 hours.

2 Whip the cream until soft peaks form, then gently fold in the strawberries with their juice.

3 Crush the meringues into coarse chunks, then scatter on the strawberry mixture and fold in gently.

4 Spoon the strawberry mixture into a glass serving bowl, decorate with the fresh mint sprigs and serve immediately.

Cook's Tip
If you would prefer to make a less rich version of this dessert, use strained plain or thick and creamy yogurt instead of part or all of the cream. Simply beat the yogurt gently before adding the strawberries.

Atholl Brose

Crunchy toasted oatmeal and soft raspberries combine to give this dessert a lovely texture.

Serves 4

4 tablespoons honey
3 tablespoons whiskey
¾ cup medium oatmeal
1¼ cups heavy cream

3 cups raspberries
fresh mint sprigs, to
decorate

1 Gently warm the honey in the whiskey, then leave to cool.

2 Preheat the broiler. Spread the oatmeal in a very shallow layer in the broiler pan and toast, stirring occasionally, until browned. Allow to cool.

3 Whip the cream in a large bowl until soft peaks form, then gently stir in the oats, honey and whiskey until well combined.

4 Reserve a few raspberries for decoration, then layer the remainder with the oat mixture in four tall glasses. Cover and chill in the fridge for 2 hours.

5 About 30 minutes before serving, transfer the glasses to room temperature. Decorate with the reserved raspberries and mint sprigs.

Old English Trifle

If you are making this pudding for children, replace the sherry and brandy with orange juice.

Serves 6

2 cups day-old sponge
  cake, broken into
  bite-size pieces
1 cup macaroon crumbs
⅓ cup medium sherry
2 tablespoons brandy
3 cups prepared fruit
  such as raspberries,
  peaches or
  strawberries
1¼ cups heavy cream

scant ½ cup toasted
  flaked almonds, to
  decorate
strawberries, to decorate

For the custard
4 egg yolks
2 tablespoons sugar
1¾ cups light or
  whipping cream
few drops of vanilla
  extract

1 Put the sponge cake and macaroon crumbs in a glass serving dish, then sprinkle on the sherry and brandy and let sit until they have been absorbed.

2 To make the custard, whisk the egg yolks and sugar together. Bring the cream to a boil in a heavy saucepan, then pour onto the egg yolk mixture, stirring constantly.

3 Return the mixture to the pan and heat very gently, stirring all the time with a wooden spoon, until the custard thickens enough to coat the back of the spoon; do not allow to boil. Allow to cool, stirring occasionally.

4 Put the fruit in an even layer over the sponge cake and macaroon crumbs in the serving dish, then strain the custard over the fruit and allow to set. Lightly whip the cream, spread it over the custard, then chill the trifle well. Decorate with flaked almonds and strawberries just before serving.

Cherry Syllabub

This recipe follows the style of the earliest syllabubs and produces a frothy creamy layer over a liquid one.

Serves 4

2 cups ripe dark cherries, pitted and chopped
2 tablespoons Kirsch
2 egg whites
2 tablespoons lemon juice
¾ cup sweet white wine
generous ¼ cup sugar
1¼ cups heavy cream

1 Divide the chopped cherries among six tall dessert glasses and sprinkle over the Kirsch.

2 In a clean bowl, whisk the egg whites until stiff peaks form. Gently fold in the lemon juice, wine and sugar.

3 In a separate bowl (but using the same whisk), lightly beat the cream, then fold into the egg white mixture. Spoon the cream mixture over the cherries, then chill overnight in the fridge.

Damask Cream

It is important not to move this simple, light, yet elegant dessert while it is setting, otherwise it will separate.

Serves 4

2½ cups milk
3 tablespoons sugar
several drops of triple-strength rose water
2 teaspoons rennet
4 tablespoons heavy cream
sugared rose petals, to decorate (optional)

1 Gently heat the milk and 2 tablespoons of the sugar, stirring, until the sugar has melted and the temperature reaches 98.4°F, or the milk feels neither hot nor cold. Stir rose water to taste into the milk, then remove the saucepan from the heat and stir in the rennet.

2 Pour the milk into a serving dish and leave undisturbed for 2–3 hours, until set. Stir the remaining sugar into the cream, then carefully spoon on the top. Decorate with sugared rose petals, if you wish.

Mandarins in Orange-flower Syrup

Mandarins, tangerines, clementines, mineolas: any of these lovely citrus fruits are suitable to use in this recipe.

Serves 4

Pare some rind from one mandarin and cut it into fine shreds for decoration. Squeeze the juice from two mandarins and reserve it. Peel eight more mandarins, removing the white pith. Arrange the whole fruit in a wide dish. Mix the reserved juice, 1 tablespoon confectioner's sugar and 2 teaspoons orange-flower water and pour it over the fruit. Cover and chill. Blanch the rind in boiling water for 30 seconds. Drain, cool and sprinkle on the mandarins, with pistachio nuts, to serve.

Chocolate Blancmange

For a special dinner party, flavor the blancmange with peppermint extract, crème de menthe or orange liqueur.

Serves 4
4 tablespoons cornstarch
2½ cups milk
3 tablespoons sugar

2–4oz semisweet
   chocolate, chopped
vanilla extract, to taste
chocolate curls, to
   decorate

1 Rinse a 3⅔-cup fluted mold with cold water and leave it upside down to drain. Blend the cornstarch to a smooth paste with a little of the milk.

2 Bring the remaining milk to a boil, preferably in a non-stick saucepan, then pour onto the blended mixture, stirring all the time.

3 Pour all the milk back into the saucepan and bring slowly to a boil over a low heat, stirring all the time until the mixture boils and thickens. Remove the pan from the heat, then add the sugar, chopped chocolate and a few drops of vanilla extract. Stir until the chocolate has melted.

4 Pour the chocolate mixture into the mold and leave in a cool place for several hours to set.

5 To unmold the blancmange, place on a large serving plate, then holding the plate and mold firmly together, invert them. Give both plate and mold a gentle but firm shake to loosen the blancmange, then lift off the mold. Scatter white and plain chocolate curls on the top of the blancmange to decorate and serve immediately.

Cook's Tip
If you prefer, set the blancmange in four or six individual molds.

Honeycomb Mold

These honeycomb molds have a fresh lemon flavor. The layered mixture looks most attractive.

Serves 4
2 tablespoons cold water
½ ounce gelatin
2 eggs, separated
generous ¼ cup sugar

2 cups milk
grated rind of 1 small
   lemon
4 tablespoons lemon juice

1 Chill four individual molds or, if you prefer, use a 5-cup fluted mold. Mix together the water and the gelatin and let soften for 5 minutes. Place the bowl over a small saucepan of hot water and stir occasionally until dissolved.

2 Meanwhile, whisk the egg yolks and sugar together until pale, thick and fluffy.

3 Bring the milk to a boil in a heavy, preferably nonstick, saucepan, then slowly pour onto the egg yolk mixture, stirring all the time.

4 Return the milk mixture to the pan, then heat gently, stirring continuously until thickened. Do not allow to boil or it will curdle. Remove from the heat and stir in the grated lemon rind and juice.

5 Stir 2 or 3 spoonfuls of the lemon mixture into the gelatin, and then stir this back into the saucepan. In a clean dry bowl, whisk the egg whites until they are stiff but not too dry, then gently fold into the mixture in the saucepan in three batches, being careful to retain the air.

6 Rinse the molds or mold with cold water and drain well, then pour in the lemon mixture. Allow to cool, then cover and chill in the fridge until set. To serve, invert on to four individual or one serving plate.

Peach Melba

The original dish created for the opera singer Dame Nelli Melba had peaches and ice cream served upon an ice swan.

Serves 4

scant 2 cups raspberries
squeeze of lemon juice
confectioner's sugar, to
*   taste*

2 large ripe peaches or
*   15-ounce can sliced*
*   peaches*
8 scoops vanilla ice cream

1 Press the raspberries through a non-metallic strainer.

2 Add a little lemon juice to the raspberry purée and sweeten to taste with confectioner's sugar.

3 Dip fresh peaches in boiling water for 4–5 seconds, then slip off the skins, halve along the indented line, then slice; or put canned peaches into a strainer and drain them.

4 Place two scoops of ice cream in each individual glass dish, top with peach slices, then pour over the raspberry purée. Serve immediately.

Summer Pudding

You may use any seasonal berries you wish in this unique and ever-popular English dessert.

Serves 4

about 8 thin slices day-
*   old white bread, crusts*
*   removed*

4½ cups mixed summer
*   fruits*
2 tablespoons sugar

1 Cut a circle from one slice of bread to fit in the bottom of a 5-cup ovenproof bowl, then cut strips of bread about 2inches wide to line the bowl, overlapping the strips.

2 Gently heat the fruit, sugar and 2 tablespoons water in a large heavy-based saucepan, shaking the pan occasionally, until the juice begins to run.

3 Reserve about 3 tablespoons fruit juice, then spoon the fruit and remaining juice into the basin, taking care not to dislodge the bread.

4 Cut the remaining bread to fit entirely over the fruit. Stand the bowl on a plate and cover with a saucer or small plate that will just fit inside the top of the basin. Place a heavy weight on top. Chill the pudding and the reserved fruit juice overnight in the fridge.

5 Run a knife carefully around the inside of the bowl rim, then invert the pudding onto a cold serving plate. Pour over the reserved juice and serve.

Boodles' Orange Fool

This fruit fool has become the specialty of Boodles Club, a gentlemen's club in London's St James's area.

Serves 4

1¼ cup sponge cake, cubed
1¼ cups heavy cream
2–4 tablespoons sugar
grated rind and juice of 2 oranges
grated rind and juice of 1 lemon
orange and lemon slices and rind, to decorate

1 Line the bottom and halfway up the sides of a large glass serving bowl or china dish with the cubed sponge cake.

2 Whip the cream with the sugar until it starts to thicken, then gradually whip in the fruit juices, adding the fruit rinds towards the end.

3 Carefully pour the cream mixture into the bowl or dish, taking care not to dislodge the sponge. Cover and chill for about 3–4 hours. Serve the fool decorated with orange and lemon slices and rind.

Apricot and Orange Jelly

You could also make this light dessert using nectarines or peaches instead of apricots.

Serves 4

12 ounces well-flavored fresh ripe apricots, pitted
about ⅓ cup sugar
1¼ cups freshly squeezed orange juice
1 tablespoon gelatin
light cream, to serve
finely chopped candied orange peel, to decorate

1 Heat the apricots, sugar and ½ cup of the orange juice, stirring until the sugar has dissolved. Simmer gently until the apricots are tender.

2 Press the apricot mixture through a nylon strainer into a small measuring cup with a spout.

3 Pour 3 tablespoons orange juice into a small heatproof bowl, sprinkle on the gelatin and leave for about 5 minutes, until softened.

4 Place the bowl over a saucepan of hot water and heat until the gelatin has dissolved. Pour into the apricot mixture slowly, stirring all the time. Add orange juice until it measures 2½ cups.

5 Pour the apricot mixture into four individual dishes and chill in the fridge until set. Pour a thin layer of cream over the surface of the desserts before serving, decorated with candied orange peel.

Summer Berry Medley

Make the most of seasonal fruits in this refreshing dessert. The sauce is also good swirled into plain yogurt.

Serves 4–6

1½ cups red currants, stripped from their stalks
1½ cups raspberries
¼ cup sugar
2–3 tablespoons crème de framboise

4½ cups fresh mixed soft summer fruits such as strawberries, raspberries, blueberries, red currants and blackcurrants
vanilla ice cream, to serve

1 Place the red currants in a bowl with the raspberries, sugar and crème de framboise. Cover and allow to macerate for 1–2 hours.

2 Put the macerated fruit with its juices in a saucepan and cook gently for 5–6 minutes, stirring occasionally, until the fruit is just tender.

3 Pour the fruit into a blender or food processor and process until smooth. Press through a nylon strainer to remove any seeds. Let cool, then chill in the fridge.

4 Divide the mixed soft fruit among four individual glass serving dishes and pour on the sauce. Serve with scoops of vanilla ice cream.

Brown Bread Ice Cream

This delicious textured ice cream is best served with a blackcurrant sauce spiked with crème de cassis.

Serves 6

½ cup roasted and chopped hazelnuts, ground
1½ cups whole wheat bread crumbs
½ cup brown sugar
3 egg whites
½ cup sugar
1¼ cups heavy cream
few drops of vanilla extract

For the sauce

2 cups blackcurrants
generous ¼ cup sugar
1 tablespoon crème de cassis
fresh mint sprigs, to decorate

1 Combine the hazelnuts and bread crumbs on a baking sheet, then sprinkle on the brown sugar. Place under a moderate broiler and cook until crisp and browned.

2 Whisk the egg whites in a bowl until stiff, then gradually whisk in the sugar until thick and glossy. Whip the cream until soft peaks form and fold into the meringue with the bread crumb mixture and vanilla extract.

3 Spoon the mixture into a 5-cup loaf pan. Smooth the top even, then cover and freeze until firm.

4 To make the sauce, put the blackcurrants in a small bowl with the sugar. Toss gently to mix and let sit for about 30 minutes. Purée the blackcurrants in a food processor or blender, then press through a nylon strainer until smooth. Add the crème de cassis and chill in the fridge.

5 To serve, arrange a slice of ice cream on a plate, spoon on a little sauce and decorate with fresh mint sprigs.

Muscat Grape Frappé

The flavor and perfume of the Muscat grape is rarely more enticing than when captured in this icy-cool salad. Because of its alcohol content this dish is not suitable for young children.

Serves 4

½ bottle Muscat wine,
   Beaumes de Venise,
   Frontignan or
   Rivsaltes

1 pound Muscat grapes

1 Pour the wine into a stainless steel or enamel tray, add ⅔ cup water and freeze for 3 hours or until completely solid.

2 Remove the seeds from the grapes with a pair of tweezers. If you have time, peel the grapes.

3 Scrape the frozen wine with a tablespoon to make a fine ice. Combine the grapes with the ice and spoon into 4 shallow glasses and serve.

Iced Chocolate and Nut Gâteau

Autumn hazelnuts add crunchiness to this popular iced dinner-party dessert.

Serves 6–8

75g/3oz/¾ cup shelled
   hazelnuts
about 32 sponge fingers
150ml/¼ pint/⅔ cup cold
   strong black coffee
30ml/2 tbsp Cognac or
   other brandy

450ml/¾ pint/1¾ cups
   double cream
75g/3oz/scant 1 cup
   icing sugar, sifted
150g/5oz plain chocolate
icing sugar and cocoa
   powder, for dusting

1 Preheat the oven to 200°C/400°F/Gas 6. Spread out the hazelnuts on a baking sheet and toast them in the oven for 5 minutes until golden. Transfer the nuts to a clean dish towel and rub off the skins. Cool, then chop finely.

2 Line a 1.2 litre/2 pint/5 cup loaf tin with clear film and cut the sponge fingers to fit the base and sides. Reserve the remaining biscuits.

3 Mix the coffee with the Cognac or other brandy in a shallow dish. Dip the sponge fingers briefly into the coffee mixture and return to the tin, sugary-side down.

4 Whip the cream with the icing sugar until it holds soft peaks. Roughly chop 75g/3oz of the chocolate, and fold into the cream with the hazelnuts.

5 Melt the remaining chocolate in a heatproof bowl set over a saucepan of barely simmering water. Cool, then fold into the cream mixture. Spoon into the tin.

6 Moisten the remaining biscuits in the coffee mixture and lay over the filling. Wrap and freeze until firm.

7 Remove the gâteau from the freezer 30 minutes before serving. Turn out on to a serving plate and dust with icing sugar and cocoa powder.

Blackberry Brown Sugar Meringue

A rich dessert which is elegant enough in presentation to be served at an autumnal dinner party.

Serves 6

For the meringue
1½ cups light brown
    sugar
3 egg whites
1 teaspoon malt vinegar
½ teaspoon vanilla
    extract

For the filling
3–4 cups blackberries
2 tablespoons crème de
    cassis
1¼ cups heavy cream
1 tablespoon
    confectioner's sugar,
    sifted
small blackberry leaves,
    to decorate (optional)

1 Preheat the oven to 325°F. Draw an 8-inch circle on a sheet of nonstick baking parchment, turn over and place on a baking sheet. Spread the brown sugar out on a baking sheet, dry in the oven for 8–10 minutes, then sift.

2 Whisk the egg whites in a bowl until stiff. Add half the dried brown sugar, 1 tablespoon at a time, whisking well after each addition. Add the vinegar and vanilla extract, then fold in the remaining sugar.

3 Spoon the meringue onto the drawn circle on the paper, making a hollow in the center. Bake for 45 minutes, then turn off the oven and leave the meringue in the oven with the door slightly open, until cold. Meanwhile, place the blackberries in a bowl, sprinkle over the crème de cassis and leave to macerate for 30 minutes.

4 When the meringue is cold, carefully peel off the nonstick baking parchment and transfer the meringue to a serving plate. Lightly whip the cream with the confectioner's sugar and spoon into the center. Top with the blackberries and decorate with small blackberry leaves, if liked. Serve at once.

Clementines in Cinnamon Caramel

The combination of sweet, yet sharp clementines and caramel sauce with a hint of spice is divine.

Serves 4–6
8–12 clementines
1 cup sugar
1½ cups hand-hot water
2 cinnamon sticks

2 tablespoons orange-
    flavored liqueur
¼ cup shelled pistachio
    nuts

1 Pare the rind from two clementines using a vegetable peeler and cut it into fine strips. Set aside.

2 Peel the clementines, removing all the pith but keeping them intact. Put the fruits in a serving bowl.

3 Gently heat the sugar in a pan until it dissolves and turns a rich golden brown. Turn off the heat immediately.

4 Pour the water into the pan, protecting your hand with a dish towel (the mixture will bubble and splutter). Bring slowly to a boil, stirring until the caramel dissolves. Add the shredded peel and cinnamon sticks, then simmer for 5 minutes. Stir in the liqueur.

5 Allow the syrup to cool for about 10 minutes, then pour over the clementines. Cover the bowl and chill for several hours or overnight.

6 Blanch the pistachio nuts in boiling water. Drain, cool and remove the dark outer skins. Scatter over the clementines and serve at once.

Chocolate Chestnut Roulade

Don't worry if this moist sponge cracks as you roll it – this is the sign of a good roulade.

Serves 8

6 ounces semisweet
    chocolate
2 tablespoons strong
    black coffee
5 eggs, separated
1 cup sugar
1 cup heavy cream

8 ounces unsweetened
    chestnut purée
3 – 4 tablespoons
    confectioner's sugar,
    plus extra for dusting
light cream, to serve

1 Preheat the oven to 350°F, then line and oil a 13 x 9-inch jelly roll pan; use wax paper. Melt the chocolate in a bowl, then stir in the coffee. Allow to cool slightly.

2 Whisk the egg yolks and sugar together until thick and light, then stir in the cooled chocolate mixture. Whisk the egg whites in another bowl until stiff. Stir a spoonful into the chocolate mixture to lighten it, then gently fold in the rest.

3 Pour the mixture into the prepared pan, and spread evenly. Bake for 20 minutes. Remove from the oven, cover with a dish towel and let cool in the pan for several hours.

4 Whip the cream until soft peaks form. Mix together the chestnut purée and confectioner's sugar; fold into the whipped cream.

5 Dust a sheet of greaseproof paper with confectioner's sugar. Turn out the roulade onto this paper and peel off the lining paper. Trim the sides. Gently spread the chestnut cream evenly over the roulade to within 1 inch of the edges. Using the wax paper to help you, carefully roll up the roulade as tightly and evenly as possible. Chill the roulade for about 2 hours, then dust liberally with confectioner's sugar. Cut into thick slices. Serve with a little light cream on each slice.

Pasta Timbales with Apricot Sauce

If orzo cannot be found, other small soup pastas can be used for this dessert, which is made like a rice pudding.

Serves 4

1 cup orzo
⅓ cup sugar
pinch of salt
2 tablespoons butter
1 vanilla pod, split
3⅔ cups milk
1¼ cups ready-made
    custard
3 tablespoons Kirsch

1 tablespoon powdered
    gelatin
oil, for greasing
14 ounces canned
    apricots in juice
lemon juice
fresh flowers, to decorate
    (optional)

1 Place the pasta, sugar, pinch of salt, butter, vanilla pod and milk in a heavy saucepan and bring to a boil. Turn down the heat and simmer for 25 minutes until the pasta is tender and most of the liquid is absorbed. Stir frequently to prevent it from sticking.

2 Remove the vanilla pod and transfer the pasta to a bowl to cool. Stir in the custard and add 2 tablespoons of the Kirsch.

3 Sprinkle the gelatin over 2 tablespoons water in a small bowl set in a pan of barely simmering water. Allow to become spongy and heat gently to dissolve. Stir into the pasta.

4 Lightly oil 4 timbale molds and spoon in the pasta. Chill for 2 hours until set.

5 Meanwhile, blend the apricots, pass through a seive and add lemon juice and Kirsch to taste. Dilute with a little water if too thick. Loosen the timbales from their molds and turn out onto individual plates. Serve with apricot sauce, decorated with fresh flowers if you wish.

Coffee Jellies with Amaretti Cream

This impressive dessert is very easy to prepare. For the best results, use a high–roasted Arabica bean for the coffee.

Serves 4
generous ¼ cup sugar
1¾ cups hot strong coffee
2 – 3 tablespoons dark
    rum or coffee liqueur
4 teaspoons gelatin

2 – 3 teaspoons instant
    coffee granules
    dissolved in 4
    tablespoons hot water
6 large amaretti cookies,
    crushed

For the amaretti cream
⅔ cup heavy cream
1 tablespoon
    confectioner's sugar,
    sifted

1 Put the sugar in a saucepan with 5 tablespoons water and stir over a gentle heat until dissolved. Increase the heat and allow the syrup to boil steadily, without stirring, for about 3–4 minutes.

2 Stir the hot coffee and rum or coffee liqueur into the syrup, then sprinkle the gelatin over the top and stir the mixture until it is completely dissolved.

3 Carefully pour the coffee gelatin mixture into four moistened ⅔-cup molds, allow to cool and then leave in the fridge for several hours until set.

4 To make the amaretti cream, lightly whip the cream with the confectioner's sugar until the mixture holds stiff peaks. Stir in the coffee, then gently fold in all but 2 tablespoons of the crushed amaretti cookies.

5 Unmold the jellies onto four individual serving plates and spoon a little of the amaretti cream to one side. Dust over the reserved amaretti crumbs and serve immediately.

Chocolate Date Torte

A stunning cake that tastes wonderful. Rich and gooey – it's a chocoholic's delight!

Serves 8
4 egg whites
½ cup sugar
7 ounces semisweet
    chocolate
6 ounces Medjool dates,
    pitted and chopped
1½ cups walnuts or
    pecan nuts, chopped

2 teaspoons vanilla
    extract, plus a few
    extra drops

For the frosting
scant 1 cup plain yogurt
scant 1 cup mascarpone
confectioner's sugar, to
    taste

1 Preheat the oven to 350°F. Lightly grease and bottom-line an 8-inch springform cake pan.

2 To make the frosting, mix together the plain yogurt and mascarpone, add a few drops of vanilla extract and confectioner's sugar to taste, then set aside.

3 Whisk the egg whites in a bowl until stiff peaks form. Whisk in 2 tablespoons of the sugar until the meringue is thick and glossy, then fold in the remainder.

4 Chop 6 ounces of the chocolate. Carefully fold into the meringue with the dates, nuts and 1 teaspoon of the vanilla extract. Pour into the prepared pan, smooth the top evenly and bake for about 45 minutes, until risen around the edges.

5 Allow to cool in the tin for about 10 minutes, then turn out onto a wire rack. Peel off the lining paper and let stand until completely cold. When cool, swirl the frosting over the top of the torte.

6 Melt the remaining chocolate in a bowl over hot water. Spoon into a small paper icing bag, snip off the top and drizzle the chocolate over the torte. Chill in the fridge before serving, cut into wedges.

Crème Caramel

This creamy, caramel-flavored custard from France enjoys worldwide popularity.

Serves 4–6

½ cup sugar
1¼ cups milk
1¼ cups light cream
6 eggs

generous ¼ cup sugar
½ teaspoon vanilla
   extract

1 Preheat the oven to 300°F and half-fill a large roasting pan with water. Place the sugar in a saucepan with 4 tablespoons water and heat gently, swirling the pan occasionally, until the sugar has dissolved. Increase the heat and boil for a good caramel color. Immediately pour the caramel into an ovenproof soufflé dish. Place in the roasting pan and set aside.

2 To make the egg custard, heat the milk and cream together in a pan until almost boiling. Meanwhile, beat the eggs, sugar and vanilla extract together in a bowl using a large balloon whisk.

3 Whisk the hot milk into the eggs and sugar, then strain the liquid through a strainer into the soufflé dish, on top of the cooled caramel base.

4 Transfer the pan to the center of the oven and bake for about 1½–2 hours (topping up the water level after 1 hour), or until the custard has set in the center. Lift the dish carefully out of the water and let cool, then cover and chill overnight in the fridge.

5 Loosen the sides of the chilled custard with a knife and then place an inverted plate (large enough to hold the caramel sauce that will flow out as well) on top of the dish. Holding the dish and plate together, turn upside down and give the whole thing a quick shake to release the crème caramel.

Australian Hazelnut Pavlova

A hazelnut meringue base is topped with orange cream, nectarines and raspberries in this famous dessert.

Serves 4–6

3 egg whites
1 cup sugar
1 teaspoon cornstarch
1 teaspoon white wine
   vinegar
generous ¼ cup chopped
   roasted hazelnuts
1 cup heavy cream
1 tablespoon orange juice

2 tablespoons plain thick
   and creamy yogurt
2 ripe nectarines, pitted
   and sliced
2 cups raspberries,
   halved
1–2 tablespoons
   redcurrant jelly,
   warmed

1 Preheat the oven to 275°F. Lightly grease a baking sheet. Draw an 8-inch circle on a sheet of baking parchment. Place pencil-side down on the baking sheet.

2 Place the egg whites in a clean, dry, grease-free bowl and beat with an electric mixer until stiff peaks form. Beat in the sugar 1 tablespoon at a time, beating well after each addition.

3 Add the cornstarch, vinegar and hazelnuts and fold in carefully with a large metal spoon.

4 Spoon the meringue onto the marked circle and spread out to the edges, making a dip in the center.

5 Bake for about 1¼–1½ hours, until crisp. Allow to cool completely and transfer to a serving platter.

6 Whip the heavy cream and orange juice until the mixture is just thick, stir in the yogurt and spoon onto the meringue. Top with the prepared fruit and drizzle over the warmed redcurrant jelly. Serve immediately.

Chinese Fruit Salad

Apricot and Almond Jalousie

For an unusual fruit salad with an oriental flavor, try this mixture of fruits in a tangy lime and lychee syrup.

Jalousie means "shutter", and the slatted pastry topping of this pie looks exactly like French window shutters.

Serves 4

½ cup sugar
thinly pared rind and juice of 1 lime
14-ounce can lychees in syrup
1 ripe mango, pitted and sliced

1 eating apple, cored and sliced
2 bananas, chopped
1 star fruit, sliced (optional)
1 teaspoon sesame seeds, toasted

Serves 4

8 ounces ready-made puff pastry
a little beaten egg
6 tablespoons apricot conserve

2 tablespoons sugar
2 tablespoons flaked almonds
cream or plain yogurt, to serve

1 Place the sugar in a small saucepan with the lime rind and 1¼ cups water. Heat gently until the sugar dissolves completely, then increase the heat and boil gently for about 7–8 minutes. Remove the saucepan from the heat and allow the syrup to cool.

2 Drain the lychees into a pitcher and pour the juice into the cooled lime syrup with the lime juice. Place all the prepared fruit in a bowl and pour over the lime and lychee syrup. Chill in the fridge for about 1 hour. Just before serving, sprinkle with toasted sesame seeds.

Cook's Tip
Try different combinations of fruit in this salad. You might like to include pawpaw, kiwi fruit or pineapple for a change.

1 Preheat the oven to 425°F. Roll out the pastry on a lightly floured surface and cut into a square measuring 12 inches. Cut in half to make two rectangles.

2 Place one piece of pastry on a moistened baking sheet and brush all round the edges with beaten egg. Spread on the apricot conserve.

3 Fold the remaining rectangle in half lengthwise and cut about eight diagonal slits from the center fold to within about ½-inch from the edge all the way along.

4 Unfold the cut pastry and lay it on top of the pastry on the baking sheet. Press the pastry edges together well, and seal using the back of a knife.

5 Brush the slashed pastry with water and sprinkle over the sugar and flaked almonds.

6 Bake in the oven for 25–30 minutes, until well risen and golden brown. Remove the jalousie from the oven and allow to cool. Serve sliced, with cream or plain yogurt.

Cook's Tip
Make smaller individual jalousies and serve them with morning coffee, if you like. Use other flavors of fruit conserve for a change.

Baked Cheesecake

The lemon-flavored cream cheese provides a subtle filling for this classic dessert.

Makes 9 squares
For the base
1½ cups crushed graham
 crackers
3 tablespoons butter,
 melted

For the topping
2½ cups ricotta cheese or
 cream cheese
½ cup sugar
3 eggs

finely grated rind of
 1 lemon
1 tablespoon lemon juice
½ teaspoon vanilla
 extract
1 tablespoon cornstarch
2 tablespoons sour cream
⅔ cup sour cream and ¼
 teaspoon ground
 cinnamon, to decorate

1 Preheat the oven to 325°F. Lightly grease and line a 7-inch springform pan.

2 Place the crumbs and butter in a bowl and mix well. Pat into the bottom of the prepared pan and press down firmly .

3 Place the cheese in a bowl, add the sugar and beat well until smooth. Add the eggs one at a time, beating well after each addition and then stir in the lemon rind and juice, the vanilla extract, cornstarch and sour cream. Beat until the mixture is completely smooth.

4 Pour the mixture onto the base and smooth the top evenly. Bake for 1¼ hours, or until the cheesecake has set in the center. Turn off the oven but leave the cheesecake inside until completely cold.

5 Remove the cheesecake from the pan, top with the soured cream and swirl with the back of a spoon. Sprinkle with cinnamon and cut into squares.

Mango Ice Cream

Canned mangoes are used to make this deliciously rich and creamy ice cream, which has an oriental flavor.

Serves 4–6
2 x 15-ounce cans sliced
 mango, drained
¼ cup sugar
2 tablespoons lime juice
1 tablespoon gelatin

1½ cups heavy cream,
 lightly whipped
fresh mint sprigs, to
 decorate

1 Reserve four slices of mango for decoration and chop the remainder. Place the mango pieces in a bowl with the sugar and lime juice.

2 Put 3 tablespoons hot water in a small heatproof bowl and sprinkle over the gelatin. Place over a saucepan of gently simmering water and stir until dissolved. Pour onto the mango mixture and mix well.

3 Add the lightly whipped cream and fold into the mango mixture. Pour the mixture into a plastic freezer container and freeze until half frozen.

4 Place the half-frozen ice cream in a food processor or blender and process until smooth. Spoon back into the container and return to the freezer to freeze completely.

5 Remove from the freezer 10 minutes before serving and place in the fridge. Serve scoops of ice cream decorated with pieces of the reserved sliced mango and fresh mint sprigs.

Rippled Chocolate Ice Cream

Rich, smooth and packed with chocolate, this heavenly ice cream is an all-round-the-world chocoholics' favorite.

Serves 4

4 tablespoons chocolate
    and hazelnut spread
1¾ cups heavy cream
1 tablespoon
    confectioner's sugar

2 ounces semisweet
    chocolate, chopped
semisweet chocolate
    curls, to decorate

1 Mix together the chocolate and hazelnut spread and 5 tablespoons of the heavy cream in a bowl.

2 Place the remaining cream in a second bowl, sift in the confectioner's sugar and beat until softly whipped.

3 Lightly fold in the chocolate and hazelnut mixture with the chopped chocolate until the mixture is rippled. Transfer to a plastic freezer container and freeze for 3–4 hours, until firm.

4 Remove the ice cream from the freezer about 10 minutes before serving to allow it to soften slightly. Spoon or scoop into dessert dishes or glasses and top each serving with a few semisweet chocolate curls.

Fruited Rice Ring

This pudding ring looks beautiful but you could stir the fruit in and serve it in individual dishes instead.

Serves 4

¼ cup short-grain rice
3¾ cups low-fat milk
1 cinnamon stick
6 ounces dried mixed
    fruit
¾ cup orange juice

3 tablespoons sugar
finely grated rind of
    1 small orange

1 Place the rice, milk and cinnamon stick in a large saucepan and bring to a boil. Cover and simmer, stirring occasionally, for about 1½ hours, until all the liquid is absorbed.

2 Meanwhile, place the fruit and orange juice in a pan and bring to a boil. Cover and simmer very gently for about 1 hour, until the fruit is tender and all the liquid is absorbed.

3 Remove the cinnamon stick from the rice and discard. Stir in the sugar and orange rind.

4 Place the cooked fruit salad on the bottom of a lightly oiled 6-cup ring mold. Spoon the rice on, smoothing it down firmly. Chill in the fridge.

5 Run a knife around the edge of the mold and turn out the rice carefully onto a serving plate.

Apricot Mousse

This light fluffy dessert can be made with any dried fruits instead of apricots – try dried peaches, prunes or apples.

Serves 4

10 ounces ready-to-eat
   dried apricots
1¼ cups fresh orange
   juice

¾ cup plain yogurt
2 egg whites
fresh mint, to decorate

1 Place the apricots in a saucepan with the orange juice and heat gently until boiling. Cover the pan and simmer gently for 3 minutes.

2 Cool slightly, then place in a food processor or blender and process until smooth. Stir in the yogurt.

3 Whisk the egg whites until stiff enough to hold soft peaks, then fold gently into the apricot mixture.

4 Spoon the mousse into four stemmed glasses or one large serving dish. Chill in the fridge before serving. Decorate with sprigs of fresh mint.

Cook's Tip
To make a speedier, fool-type dessert, omit the egg whites and simply swirl together the apricot mixture and the yogurt.

Apple Foam with Blackberries

Any seasonal soft fruit can be used for this lovely dessert if blackberries are not available.

Serves 4

2 cups blackberries
generous ½ cup apple
   juice

1 teaspoon powdered
   gelatin
1 tablespoon honey
2 egg whites

1 Place the blackberries in a saucepan with 4 tablespoons of the apple juice and heat gently until the fruit is soft. Remove from the heat, cool then chill in the fridge.

2 Sprinkle the gelatin over the remaining apple juice in a small pan and stir over a gentle heat until dissolved. Stir in the honey.

3 Whisk the egg whites until stiff peaks form. Continue whisking hard and gradually pour in the hot gelatin mixture until well mixed.

4 Quickly spoon the foam into mounds on individual plates. Chill. To serve, spoon the blackberries and juice around the foam rounds.

Cook's Tip
Make sure you dissolve the gelatin over a very low heat. It must not boil, or it will lose its setting ability.

Raspberry Passionfruit Swirls

If passionfruit is not available, this simple dessert can be made with raspberries alone.

Serves 4

generous 2½ cups
  raspberries
2 passionfruit
1⅔ cups low-fat ricotta
  cheese

2 tablespoons sugar
raspberries and sprigs of
  fresh mint, to decorate

1 Mash the raspberries in a small bowl with a fork until the juice runs. Scoop out the passionfruit pulp into a separate bowl with the ricotta and sugar and mix well.

2 Spoon alternate spoonfuls of the raspberry pulp and the ricotta mixture into stemmed glasses or one large serving dish, stirring lightly to create a swirled effect.

3 Decorate the desserts with whole raspberries and sprigs of fresh mint. Serve chilled.

Creamy Mango Cheesecake

This low-fat cheesecake is as creamy as any other, but makes a healthier dessert option.

Serves 4

1¼ cups rolled oats
3 tablespoons sunflower
  margarine
2 tablespoons honey
1 large ripe mango
1¼ cups light cream
  cheese

⅔ cup low-fat plain
  yogurt
finely grated rind of
  1 small lime
3 tablespoons apple juice
4 teaspoons gelatin
fresh mango and lime
  slices, to decorate

1 Preheat the oven to 400°F. Mix together the oats, margarine and honey; press into the bottom of an 8-inch loose-bottomed cake pan. Bake for 12–15 minutes. Cool.

2 Peel, pit and coarsely chop the mango. Process with the cheese, yogurt and lime rind until smooth. Heat the apple juice until boiling, sprinkle the gelatin over it, stir to dissolve, then stir into the cheese mixture. Pour into the pan and chill until set. Turn out and decorate with mango and lime slices.

Frudités with Honey Dip

This dish is shared and would be ideal to serve at an informal lunch or supper party.

Serves 4

Place 1 cup plain strained yogurt in a dish, beat until smooth, then stir in 3 tablespoons honey, leaving a marbled effect. Cut a selection of fruits into wedges or bite-size pieces or leave whole, depending on your choice. Arrange on a platter with the bowl of dip in the center. Serve chilled.

Boston Banoffee Pie

This dessert's rich, creamy, toffee-style filling just can't be resisted – but who cares!

Serves 4–6

1¼ cups all-purpose flour	2 tablespoons corn syrup
1 cup butter	2 small bananas, sliced
¼ cup sugar	a little lemon juice
14-ounce can skim,	whipped cream and
sweetened condensed	grated semisweet
milk	chocolate, to decorate
⅔ cup light brown sugar	

1 Preheat the oven to 325°F. Place the flour and ½ cup of the butter in a bowl, then stir in the sugar. Squeeze the mixture together with your hands until it forms a dough. Press into the bottom of an 8-inch loose-bottom fluted tart pan. Bake blind for 25–30 minutes, until the pastry is lightly browned.

2 Place the remaining butter with the condensed milk, brown sugar and corn syrup into a nonstick saucepan and heat gently, stirring, until the butter has melted and the sugar has completely dissolved.

3 Bring to a gentle boil and cook for 7 minutes, stirring all the time (to prevent burning), until the mixture thickens and turns a light caramel color. Pour into the cooked pie shell and leave until cold.

4 Sprinkle the bananas with lemon juice and arrange in overlapping circles on top of the caramel filling, leaving a gap in the center. Pipe a swirl of whipped cream in the center and sprinkle with the grated chocolate.

Cook's Tip
Do not peel and slice the bananas until you are ready to serve or they will become slimy.

Strawberry and Blueberry Tart

This tart works equally well using either autumn or winter fruits as long as there is a riot of color.

Serves 6–8

2 cups all-purpose flour	few drops of vanilla
pinch of salt	extract
scant ¾ cup	finely grated rind of
confectioner's sugar	1 orange
generous ½ cup unsalted	4½ cups fresh mixed
butter	strawberries and
1 egg yolk	blueberries
	6 tablespoons redcurrant
For the filling	jelly
1¾ cups mascarpone	2 tablespoons orange
2 tablespoons	juice
confectioner's sugar	

1 Sift the flour, salt and sugar into a bowl. Dice the butter and rub it in until the mixture resembles coarse bread crumbs. Mix in the egg yolk and 2 teaspoons cold water. Gather the dough together, knead lightly, wrap and chill for 1 hour.

2 Preheat the oven to 375°F. Roll out the pastry and use to line a 10-inch fluted tart pan. Prick the bottom and chill for 15 minutes in the fridge.

3 Line the chilled pie shell with wax paper and baking beans, then bake blind for 15 minutes. Remove the paper and beans and bake for a further 15 minutes, until crisp and golden. Let cool in the tin.

4 Beat together the mascarpone, sugar, vanilla extract and orange rind in a mixing bowl until smooth.

5 Remove the pie shell from the pan, then spoon in the filling and pile the fruits on top. Heat the redcurrant jelly with the orange juice until runny, strain, then brush over the fruit to form a glaze.

Strawberries in Spiced Grape Jelly

This light dessert would be ideal to serve after a rich and filling main course.

Serves 4

1¾ cups red grape juice
1 cinnamon stick
1 small orange
1 tablespoon gelatin

2 cups strawberries, chopped
strawberries and shredded orange rind, to decorate

1 Place the grape juice in a saucepan with the cinnamon and thinly pared orange rind. Infuse over a gentle heat for 10 minutes, then remove the cinnamon and orange rind. Sprinkle the squeezed orange juice over the gelatin. Stir into the grape juice to dissolve. Allow to cool until just beginning to set.

2 Stir in the strawberries and then quickly turn the mixture into a 4-cup mold or serving dish. Chill in the fridge until it has set. Dip the mold quickly into hot water and invert onto a serving plate. Decorate with fresh strawberries and shreds of orange rind.

Plum and Port Sherbet

Rather a grown-up sherbet this one, but you could use fresh red grape juice in place of the port or wine.

Serves 4

2 pounds ripe red plums, pitted and halved
generous ¼ cup sugar
3 tablespoons water

3 tablespoons ruby port or red wine
crisp sweet cookies, to serve

1 Place the plums in a saucepan with the sugar and water. Stir over a gentle heat until the sugar is melted, then cover and simmer gently for about 5 minutes, until the fruit is soft.

2 Turn into a food processor or blender and purée until smooth, then stir in the port or red wine. Cool completely, then turn into a plastic freezer container and freeze until the sherbet is firm around the edges. Process until smooth. Spoon back into the freezer container and freeze until solid.

3 Allow to soften slightly at room temperature for about 15 – 20 minutes before serving in scoops, with sweet cookies.

Quick Apricot Blender Whip

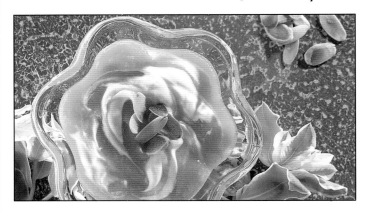

This is one of the quickest desserts you could make – and also one of the prettiest.

Serves 4

Drain the juice from 14-ounce can apricot halves in juice and place the fruit in a blender or food processor with 1 tablespoon Grand Marnier or brandy. Process until smooth. Spoon the fruit purée and ¾ cup plain strained yogurt in alternate spoonfuls into four tall glasses or glass dishes, swirling them together slightly to give a marbled effect. Lightly toast 2 tablespoons slivered almonds until they are golden. Let them cool slightly and then sprinkle them on top.

Bean Curd Berry Brulée

This is a lighter variation of a classic dessert. Use any soft fruits that are in season.

Serves 4

2 cups red berry fruits
  such as strawberries,
  raspberries and
  redcurrants
11-ounce package silken
  bean curd

3 tablespoons
  confectioner's sugar
¼ cup brown sugar

1 Halve or quarter any large strawberries, but leave the smaller ones whole. Mix with the other chosen berries.

2 Place the bean curd and confectioner's sugar in a food processor or blender and process until smooth.

3 Stir in the fruits and spoon into a flameproof dish with a 3¾-cup capacity. Sprinkle the top with enough brown sugar to cover evenly.

4 Place under a very hot broiler until the sugar melts and caramelizes. Chill in the fridge before serving.

Cook's Tip
Choose silken bean curd rather than firm bean curd as it gives a smoother texture in this type of dish. Firm bean curd is better for cooking in chunks.

Emerald Fruit Salad

This vibrant green fruit salad contains a hint of lime and is sweetened with honey.

Serves 4

2 tablespoons lime juice
2 tablespoons honey
2 green eating apples,
  cored and sliced
1 ripe honeydew melon,
  diced

2 kiwi fruit, sliced
1 star fruit, sliced
fresh mint sprigs, to
  decorate
plain yogurt, to serve

1 Mix together the lime juice and honey in a large bowl, then toss in the apple slices.

2 Stir in the melon, kiwi fruit and star fruit. Place in a glass serving dish and chill in the fridge before serving.

3 Decorate with mint sprigs and serve with yogurt, if you wish.

Cook's Tip
Color-themed fruit salads are fun to create and easy, given the wide availability of exotic fruits. You could try an orange-colored salad using cantaloupe melon, apricots, peaches or nectarines, oranges or clementines, and mango or pawpaw.

Peach and Ginger Pashka

This simpler adaptation of a Russian Easter favorite is made with lighter ingredients than the traditional version.

Serves 4–6

1½ cups low-fat cottage cheese
2 ripe peaches
½ cup low-fat plain yogurt
2 pieces preserved ginger in syrup, drained and chopped

2 tablespoons preserved ginger syrup
½ teaspoon vanilla extract
peach slices and toasted flaked almonds, to decorate

1 Drain the cottage cheese and rub through a strainer into a bowl. Pit, and coarsely chop the peaches.

2 Mix together the chopped peaches, cottage cheese, yogurt, ginger, syrup and vanilla extract.

3 Line a new clean flowerpot or a strainer with a piece of clean fine cloth such as cheesecloth.

4 Put in the cheese mixture, then wrap with the cloth and place a weight on top. Leave above a bowl in a cool place to drain overnight. To serve, unwrap the cloth and invert the pashka onto a plate. Decorate with peach slices and almonds.

Chilled Chocolate Slice

This is a very rich family dessert, but it is also designed to use up the occasional leftover.

Serves 6–8

½ cup butter, melted
8 ounces ginger cookies, finely crushed
2 ounces stale sponge cake crumbs
4–5 tablepoons orange juice
4 ounces pitted dates

¼ cup finely chopped nuts
6 ounces unsweetened chocolate
1¼ cups whipping cream
grated chocolate and confectioner's sugar, to decorate

1 Mix together the butter and ginger cookie crumbs, then pack around the sides and bottom of a 7-inch loose-bottom tart pan. Chill in the fridge while making the filling.

2 Put the cake crumbs into a large bowl with the orange juice and allow to soak. Warm the dates thoroughly, then mash and blend into the cake crumbs along with the nuts.

3 Melt the chocolate with 3–4 tablespoons of the cream. Softly whip the rest of the cream, then fold in the melted chocolate mixture.

4 Stir the cream and chocolate mixture into the crumbs and mix well. Pour into the cookie crust, mark into portions and let set. Scatter on the grated chocolate and dust with confectioner's sugar. Serve cut in wedges.

Tangerine Trifle

An unusual variation on a traditional trifle – of course, you can add a little alcohol if you wish.

Serves 4

5 ladyfingers or slices of sponge cake, halved lengthwise
2 tablespoons apricot conserve
1 cup macaroon crumbs
¾ ounce package tangerine gelatin
11-ounce can mandarin oranges, drained, reserving juice

2½ cups ready-made (or homemade) custard
whipped cream and shreds of orange rind, to decorate
sugar, for sprinkling

1 Spread the ladyfingers or sponge cake with apricot conserve and arrange in the bottom of a deep serving bowl or glass dish. Sprinkle the macaroon crumbs over the top.

2 Break up the jelly into a heat proof measuring cup, add the juice from the canned mandarins and dissolve in a saucepan of hot water or in the microwave. Stir until the liquid clears.

3 Add ice cold water until it measures 2½ cups, stir well and set aside to cool for up to 30 minutes. Scatter the mandarin orange segments on the cake and macaroon crumbs.

4 Pour the jelly over the mandarin oranges, cake and ratafias and chill in the fridge for 1 hour, or more.

5 When the jelly has set, pour the custard on the top and chill again in the fridge.

6 When ready to serve, pipe the whipped cream over the custard. Wash the orange rind shreds, sprinkle them with sugar and use to decorate the trifle.

Blackberry and Apple Romanoff

Rich yet fruity, this dessert is popular with most people and very quick and easy to make.

Serves 6–8

12 ounces tart eating apples, peeled, cored and chopped
3 tablespoons sugar
1 cup whipping cream
1 teaspoon grated lemon rind
6 tablespoons strained plain yogurt

2 ounces (about 4–6) crisp meringues, coarsely crumbled
2 cups blackberries (fresh or frozen)
whipped cream, a few blackberries and fresh mint leaves, to decorate

1 Line a 4–5 cup ovenproof bowl with plastic wrap. Toss the chopped apples into a saucepan with 2 tablespoons sugar and cook for 2–3 minutes, or until softening. Mash with a fork and allow to cool.

2 Whip the cream and fold in the lemon rind, yogurt, the remaining sugar, apples and meringues.

3 Gently stir in the blackberries, then turn the mixture into the ovenproof bowl and freeze for 1–3 hours.

4 Turn out onto a plate and remove the plastic wrap. Decorate with whirls of whipped cream, blackberries and mint leaves.

Apple and Hazelnut Shortcake

This is a variation on the classic strawberry shortcake and is equally delicious.

Serves 8–10

generous 1 cup whole
  wheat flour
½ cup ground hazelnuts
6 tablespoons
  confectioner's sugar,
  sifted
generous 1 cup unsalted
  butter
3 tart eating apples
1 teaspoon lemon juice

1–2 tablespoons sugar
1 tablespoon chopped
  fresh mint, or 1
  teaspoon dried mint
1 cup whipping cream
a few drops of vanilla
  extract
a few fresh mint leaves
  and whole hazelnuts,
  to decorate

1   Process the flour, ground hazelnuts and confectioner's sugar with the butter in a food processor in short bursts, until they come together. Bring the dough together, adding a little ice water if needed. Knead briefly, wrap and chill for 30 minutes.

2   Preheat the oven to 325°F. Cut the dough in half and roll out each half to a 7-inch round. Place on wax paper on baking sheets. Bake for 40 minutes, or until crisp. Allow to cool.

3   Peel, core and chop the apples into a saucepan with the lemon juice. Add sugar to taste; cook for 2–3 minutes, until just soft. Mash the apple gently with the mint; set aside.

4   Whip the cream with the vanilla extract. Place one shortcake round on a serving plate. Spread half the apple and half the cream on top.

5   Place the second shortcake round on top, then spread on the remaining apple and cream, swirling the top layer of cream gently. Decorate the top with mint leaves and a few whole hazelnuts, then serve immediately.

Lemon Cheesecake

A lovely light cream cheese filling is sandwiched between brandy snaps in this tasty dessert.

Serves 8

4¾-ouncs package lemon
  gelatin
2 cups light cream cheese
2 teaspoons grated lemon
  rind
about ½ cup sugar
a few drops of vanilla
  extract

½ cup strained plain
  yogurt
8 brandy snaps
a few fresh mint leaves
  and confectioner's
  sugar, to decorate

1   Dissolve the jelly in 3–4 tablespoons boiling water in a heat proof measuring cup and, when clear, add sufficient cold water to measure up to ⅔ cup. Chill in the fridge until beginning to thicken. Meanwhile, line a 1-pound loaf pan with plastic wrap.

2   Cream the cheese with the lemon rind, sugar and vanilla and beat until light and smooth. Then fold in the thickening lemon jelly and the yogurt. Spoon into the prepared pan and chill until set. Preheat the oven to 325°F.

3   Place two or three brandy snaps at a time on a baking sheet. Put in the oven for no more than 1 minute, until soft enough to unroll and flatten out completely. Leave on a cold plate or tray to harden again. Repeat with the remaining brandy snaps.

4   To serve, turn the cheesecake out onto a board with the help of the plastic wrap. Cut into eight slices and place one slice on each brandy snap base. Decorate with mint leaves and dust with confectioner's sugar.

Frozen Strawberry Mousse Cake

Children love this cake because it is pink and pretty, and it is just like an ice cream treat.

Serves 4–6

15-ounce can strawberries in syrup
1 tablespoon powdered gelatin
6 ladyfingers or slices of sponge cake

3 tablespoons strawberry conserve
scant 1 cup crème fraîche
scant 1 cup whipped cream, to decorate

1 Strain the syrup from the strawberries into a large heatproof pitcher. Sprinkle on the gelatin and stir well. Stand the pitcher in a saucepan of hot water and stir until the gelatin has dissolved.

2 Set aside to cool, then chill in the fridge for just under 1 hour, until beginning to set. Meanwhile, cut the sponge cake in half lengthwise, if using, and then spread the cut surfaces or the ladyfingers evenly with the strawberry conserve.

3 Slowly whisk the crème fraîche into the strawberry jelly, then whisk in the canned strawberries. Line a deep 8-inch loose-bottom tart pan with nonstick baking parchment.

4 Pour half the strawberry mousse mixture into the pan, arrange the sponge cake or ladyfingers over the surface and then spoon on the remaining mousse mixture, pushing down any sponge cake which rises up.

5 Freeze for 1–2 hours until firm. Unmold the cake and carefully remove the lining paper. Transfer to a serving plate. Decorate with whirls of cream, plus a few strawberry leaves and a fresh strawberry, if you have them.

Lemon and Blackberry Soufflé

This tangy dessert is complemented wonderfully by a rich blackberry sauce.

Serves 6

grated rind of 1 lemon and juice of 2 lemons
1 tablespoon powdered gelatin
5 small eggs, separated
1¼ cups sugar
a few drops of vanilla extract
1⅔ cups whipping cream

For the sauce
1½ cups blackberries (fresh or frozen)
2–3 tablespoons sugar
a few fresh blackberries and blackberry leaves, to decorate

1 Place the lemon juice in a small saucepan and heat through. Sprinkle on the gelatin and allow to dissolve, or heat further until clear. Allow to cool. Put the lemon rind, egg yolks, sugar and vanilla into a large bowl and whisk until the mixture is very thick, pale and really creamy.

2 Whisk the egg whites until almost stiff. Whip the cream until stiff. Stir the gelatin mixture into the yolks, then fold in the whipped cream and finally the egg whites. When lightly but thoroughly blended, turn into a 6-cup soufflé dish and freeze for about 2 hours.

3 To make the sauce, place the blackberries in a pan with the sugar and cook for 4–6 minutes until the juice begins to run and all the sugar has dissolved. Strain to remove the seeds, then chill until ready to serve.

4 When the soufflé is almost frozen, scoop or spoon out onto individual plates and serve with the blackberry sauce.

Apricot and Banana Compote

This compote is delicious served on its own or with custard or ice cream. Served for breakfast, it makes a tasty start to the day.

Serves 4

1 cup ready-to-eat dried
  apricots
1¼ cups orange juice
⅔ cup apple juice

1 teaspoon ground ginger
3 medium bananas, sliced
¾ cup toasted sliced
  almonds, to serve

1 Put the apricots in a saucepan with the fruit juices and ginger and stir. Cover, bring to the boil and simmer gently for 10 minutes, stirring occasionally.

2 Set aside to cool, leaving the lid on. Once cool, stir in the sliced bananas.

3 Spoon the fruit and juices into a serving dish.

4 Serve immediately, or cover and chill for several hours before serving. Sprinkle with the almonds just before serving.

Cook's Tip
Use other combinations of dried and fresh fruit such as prunes or figs and apples or peaches.

Iced Pineapple Crush

The sweet tropical flavors of pineapple and lychees combine well with richly scented strawberries to make this a most refreshing salad.

Serves 4

2 small pineapples
1 pound strawberries
14-ounce can lychees
3 tablespoons kirsch or
  white rum

2 tablespoons
  confectioners' sugar

1 Remove the crown from both pineapples by cutting around the top and twisting sharply. Reserve the leaves for decoration.

2 Cut the pineapple in half diagonally with a large serrated knife.

3 Cut around the flesh inside the skin with a small serrated knife, keeping the skin intact. Remove the core from the pineapples.

4 Chop the pineapples and combine with the strawberries and lychees, taking care not to damage the fruit.

5 Combine the kirsch or rum with the confectioners' sugar, pour over the fruit and freeze for 45 minutes.

6 Tip the fruit out into the pineapple skins and decorate with pineapple leaves.

Cook's Tip
A ripe pineapple will resist pressure when squeezed and will have a sweet, fragrant smell. In winter freezing conditions can cause the flesh to blacken.

Winter Fruit Salad

A colorful, refreshing and nutritious fruit salad that is ideal served with cream or strained plain yogurt.

Serves 6

*8-ounce can pineapple
    cubes in fruit juice*
*scant 1 cup freshly
    squeezed orange juice*
*scant 1 cup
    apple juice*
*2 tablespoons orange or
    apple liqueur*
*2 tablespoons honey
    (optional)*
2 oranges, peeled

*2 green-skinned eating
    apples, chopped*
2 pears, chopped
*4 plums, pitted and
    chopped*
*12 fresh dates, pitted and
    chopped*
*2 cups ready-to-eat dried
    apricots*
*fresh mint sprigs, to
    decorate*

1 Drain the pineapple, reserving the juice. Put the pineapple juice, orange juice, apple juice, liqueur and honey, if using, in a large serving bowl and stir.

2 Segment the oranges, catching any juice in the bowl, and put the orange segments and pineapple in the fruit juice mixture.

3 Add the apples and pears to the bowl.

4 Stir in the plums, dates and apricots, cover and chill for several hours. Decorate with fresh mint sprigs to serve.

Cook's Tip
Use other unsweetened fruit juices such as pink grapefruit and pineapple juice in place of the orange and apple juice.

Fresh Figs in Honey and Wine

Any variety of figs can be used in this recipe, their ripeness determining the cooking time. Choose ones that are plump and firm, and use quickly as they don't store well.

Serves 6

1⅞ cups dry white wine
⅓ cup honey
¼ cup sugar
1 small orange
8 whole cloves
1 pound fresh figs

1 cinnamon stick
*mint sprigs or bay leaves,
    to decorate*

For the cream
1¼ cups heavy cream

1 Put the wine, honey and sugar in a heavy-based saucepan and heat gently until the sugar dissolves.

2 Stud the orange with the cloves and add to the syrup with the figs and cinnamon. Cover and simmer very gently for 5–10 minutes until the figs are softened. Transfer to a serving dish and leave to cool.

3 Put ⅔ cup of the cream in a small saucepan with the vanilla pod. Bring almost to the boil, then leave to cool and infuse for 30 minutes. Remove the vanilla pod and mix with the remaining cream and sugar in a bowl. Whip lightly. Transfer to a serving dish. Decorate the figs with the mint sprigs or bay leaves, then serve with the cream.

Farmhouse Cookies

Delightfully wholesome, these farmhouse cookies are ideal to serve with morning coffee.

Makes 18

¹/₂ cup butter or margarine, at room temperature
7 tablespoons light brown sugar
5 tablespoons crunchy peanut butter
1 egg
¹/₂ cup all-purpose flour
¹/₂ teaspoon baking powder
¹/₂ teaspoon ground cinnamon
¹/₄ teaspoon salt
1¹/₂ cups granola
¹/₂ cup raisins
¹/₂ cup chopped walnuts

1 Preheat the oven to 350°F. Grease a baking sheet.

2 Cream the butter or margarine and sugar until light and fluffy. Beat in the peanut butter and then beat in the egg.

3 Sift the flour, baking powder, cinnamon and salt over the peanut butter mixture and stir to blend. Stir in the granola, raisins and walnuts. Taste the mixture to see if it needs more sugar, as the sugar content of granola varies.

4 Drop rounded tablespoonfuls of the mixture onto the prepared baking sheet about 1 inch apart. Press gently with the back of a spoon to spread each mound into a circle.

5 Bake until lightly colored, about 15 minutes. With a metal spatula, transfer to a wire rack to cool. Store in an airtight container.

Crunchy Oatmeal Cookies

For nutty oatmeal cookies, substitute an equal quantity of chopped walnuts or pecans for the cereal.

Makes 14

³/₄ cup butter or margarine, at room temperature
³/₄ cup superfine sugar
1 egg yolk
1¹/₂ cups all-purpose flour
1 teaspoon baking soda
¹/₂ teaspoon salt
²/₃ cup rolled oats
²/₃ cup small crunchy nugget cereal

1 Cream the butter or margarine and sugar together until light and fluffy. Mix in the egg yolk.

2 Sift over the flour, baking soda and salt, then stir into the butter mixture. Add the oats and cereal and stir to blend. Chill for at least 20 minutes.

3 Preheat the oven to 375°F. Grease a baking sheet.

4 Roll the mixture into balls. Place them on the baking sheet and flatten with the base of a floured glass.

5 Bake until golden, about 10–12 minutes. Then with a metal spatula, transfer to a wire rack to cool. Store in an airtight container.

Apricot Yogurt Cookies

These cookies do not keep well, so it is best to eat them within two days, or to freeze them.

Makes 16

1½ cups all-purpose flour
1 teaspoon baking powder
1 teaspoon ground cinnamon
scant 1 cup rolled oats
½ cup light muscovado sugar
½ cup chopped ready-to-eat dried apricots
1 tablespoon slivered hazelnuts or almonds
scant ⅔ cup plain yogurt
3 tablespoons sunflower oil
raw sugar, to sprinkle

1 Preheat the oven to 375°F. Lightly oil a large baking sheet.

2 Sift together the flour, baking powder and cinnamon. Stir in the oats, sugar, apricots and nuts.

3 Beat together the yogurt and oil, then stir evenly into the mixture to make a firm dough. If necessary, add a little more yogurt.

4 Use your hands to roll the mixture into about 16 small balls, place on the baking sheet and flatten with a fork.

5 Sprinkle with raw sugar. Bake for 15–20 minutes, or until firm and golden brown. Transfer to a wire rack to cool. Store in an airtight container.

Oat and Apricot Clusters

You can change the ingredients according to what's in your pantry – try peanuts, pecans, raisins or dates.

Makes 12

4 tablespoons butter or margarine
4 tablespoons honey
½ cup medium oatmeal
¼ cup chopped ready-to-eat dried apricots
1 tablespoon banana chips
1 tablespoon dried coconut shreds
2–3 cups cornflakes or crispy cereal

1 Place the butter or margarine and honey in a small pan and warm over low heat, stirring until well blended.

2 Add the oatmeal, apricots, banana chips, coconut and cornflakes or crispy cereal and mix well.

3 Spoon the mixture into 12 paper muffin cases, piling it up roughly. Transfer to a baking sheet and chill until set and firm.

Oaty Coconut Cookies

The coconut gives these cookies both a wonderful texture and a great taste.

Makes 48

2 cups quick-cooking oats
1¹/₂ cups dried coconut
1 cup butter
¹/₂ cup superfine sugar
¹/₄ cup dark brown sugar
2 eggs
4 tablespoons milk

1¹/₂ teaspoons vanilla
    extract
1 cup all-purpose flour,
    sifted
¹/₂ teaspoon baking soda
¹/₂ teaspoon salt
1 teaspoon ground
    cinnamon

1 Preheat the oven to 400°F. Spread the oats and coconut on a baking sheet. Bake for 8–10 minutes.

2 Cream the butter and sugars. Beat in the eggs, milk and vanilla. Fold in the dry ingredients. Add the oats and coconut. Drop spoonfuls of mixture onto two greased baking sheets. Bake for 8–10 minutes. Cool on a wire rack.

Crunchy Jumbles

For even crunchier cookies, add ½ cup walnuts, coarsely chopped, with the cereal and chocolate chips.

Makes 36

¹/₂ cup butter or
    margarine, at room
    temperature
1 cup superfine sugar
1 egg
1 teaspoon vanilla
    extract

1¹/₄ cups all-purpose
    flour, sifted
¹/₂ teaspoon baking soda
¹/₄ teaspoon salt
2¹/₄ cups crisped rice
    cereal
1 cup chocolate chips

1 Preheat the oven to 350°F. Grease two baking sheets. Cream the butter or margarine and sugar until fluffy. Add the egg and vanilla extract. Add the flour and baking soda and the salt, and fold in.

2 Add the cereal and chocolate chips and mix thoroughly. Drop spoonfuls 2 inches apart onto baking sheets and bake for 10–12 minutes. Transfer to a wire rack to cool.

Cinnamon-coated Cookies

Walnut cookies are rolled in a cinnamon and sugar mixture to give a delicate spicy flavor.

Makes 30

Preheat the oven to 375°F. Grease two baking sheets. Cream ½ cup butter, 1 cup sugar and 1 teaspoon vanilla extract. Beat in 2 eggs and ¼ cup milk. Sift over 3 cups all-purpose flour and 1 teaspoon baking soda. Stir in ½ cup chopped walnuts. Chill for 15 minutes, then roll into balls. Roll the balls in a sugar and cinnamon mixture. Bake for 10 minutes, then cool on a wire rack.

Ginger Cookies

So much tastier than store-bought varieties, these ginger cookies will disappear quickly, so make a large batch!

Makes 60

2¹/₂ cups all-purpose
  flour
1 teaspoon baking soda
1¹/₂ teaspoon ground
  ginger
¹/₄ teaspoon ground
  cinnamon
¹/₄ teaspoon ground
  cloves

¹/₂ cup butter or
  margarine, at room
  temperature
1³/₄ cups superfine sugar
1 egg, beaten
4 tablespoons molasses
1 teaspoon fresh lemon
  juice

1 Preheat the oven to 325°F. Lightly grease three to four baking sheets.

2 Sift the flour, baking soda and spices into a small bowl. Set aside.

3 Cream the butter or margarine and two-thirds of the sugar together. Stir in the egg, molasses and lemon juice. Add the flour mixture and mix in thoroughly with a wooden spoon to make a soft dough.

4 Shape the dough into ¾-inch balls. Roll the balls in the remaining sugar and place about 2 inches apart on the prepared baking sheets.

5 Bake until the cookies are just firm to the touch, about 12 minutes. With a metal spatula, transfer the cookies to a wire rack and let cool.

Cream Cheese Spirals

These cookies look so impressive and melt in the mouth, yet they are surprisingly easy to make.

Makes 32

1 cup butter, at room
  temperature
1 cup cream cheese
2 teaspoons superfine
  sugar
2 cups all-purpose flour
1 egg white, beaten with
  1 tablespoon water, for
  glazing

superfine sugar, for
  sprinkling

For the filling
1 cup finely chopped
  walnuts
³/₄ cup light brown sugar
1 teaspoon ground
  cinnamon

1 Cream the butter, cream cheese and sugar until soft. Sift over the flour and mix until combined. Gather into a ball and divide in half. Flatten each half, wrap in wax paper and chill for 30 minutes. Meanwhile, mix all the filling ingredients together and set aside.

2 Preheat the oven to 375°F. Grease two baking sheets. Working with one half of the dough at a time, roll out thinly into an 11-inch circle. Using a dinner plate as a guide, trim the edges with a knife.

3 Brush the surface with the egg white glaze, and then sprinkle evenly with half the filling.

4 Cut the circle into 16 segments. Starting from the base of the triangles, roll up to form spirals.

5 Place on the baking sheets and brush with the remaining glaze. Sprinkle with superfine sugar. Bake until golden, about 15–20 minutes. Cool on a wire rack.

Italian Almond Biscotti

Serve biscotti after a meal, for dunking in sweet white wine, such as an Italian Vin Santo or a French Muscat.

Makes 48

1¾ cups whole
    unblanched almonds
scant 2 cups all-purpose
    flour
½ cup sugar
pinch of salt

pinch of saffron powder
½ teaspoon baking soda
2 eggs
1 egg white, lightly
    beaten

1   Preheat the oven to 375°F. Grease and flour two baking sheets.

2   Spread the almonds onto an ungreased baking sheet and bake until lightly browned, about 15 minutes. When cool, grind ½ cup of the almonds in a food processor, blender, or coffee grinder until pulverized. Coarsely chop the remaining almonds in two or three pieces each. Set aside.

3   Combine the flour, sugar, salt, saffron powder, baking soda and ground almonds in a bowl and mix to blend. Make a well in the center and add the eggs. Stir to form a rough dough. Transfer to a floured surface and knead until well blended. Knead in the chopped almonds.

4   Divide the dough into three equal parts. Roll into logs about 1 inch in diameter. Place on one of the prepared sheets, brush with the egg white and bake for 20 minutes. Remove from the oven. Lower the oven temperature to 275°F.

5   With a very sharp knife, cut into each log at an angle making ½-inch slices. Return the slices on the sheets to the oven and bake for 25 minutes. Transfer to a wire rack to cool.

Orange Cookies

These classic citrus-flavored cookies are ideal for a tasty treat at any time of the day.

Makes 30

½ cup butter, at room
    temperature
1 cup sugar
2 egg yolks
1 tablespoon fresh orange
    juice
grated rind of 1 large
    orange

1¾ cups all-purpose
    flour
1 tablespoon cornstarch
½ teaspoon salt
1 teaspoon baking
    powder

1   Cream the butter and sugar until light and fluffy. Add the yolks, orange juice and rind, and continue beating to blend.

2   In another bowl, sift together the flour, cornstarch, salt and baking powder. Add to the butter mixture and stir until it forms a dough. Wrap the dough in wax paper and chill for 2 hours.

3   Preheat the oven to 375°F. Grease two baking sheets. Roll spoonfuls of the dough into balls and place 1–2 inches apart on the baking sheets.

4   Press down with a fork to flatten. Bake until golden brown, about 8–10 minutes. Using a metal spatula, transfer to a wire rack to cool.

Raspberry Sandwich Cookies

These cookies can be stored in an airtight container with sheets of wax paper between the layers.

Makes 32

1 cup blanched almonds
1½ cups all-purpose
  flour
¾ cup butter, at room
  temperature
½ cup superfine sugar
grated rind of 1 lemon
1 teaspoon vanilla
  extract

1 egg white
¼ teaspoon salt
¼ cup slivered almonds
1 cup raspberry jam
1 tablespoon fresh lemon
  juice

1 Process the blanched almonds and 3 tablespoons flour in a food processor or blender until finely ground. Cream the butter and sugar together until light and fluffy. Stir in the lemon rind and vanilla. Add the ground almonds and remaining flour and mix well. Gather into a ball, wrap in wax paper, and chill for 1 hour.

2 Preheat the oven to 325°F. Line two baking sheets with wax paper. Divide the cookie mixture into four equal parts. Working with one section at a time, roll out to a thickness of ⅛-inch on a lightly floured surface. With a 2½-inch fluted pastry cutter, stamp out circles. Using a ¾-inch icing bag nozzle or pastry cutter, stamp out the centers from half the circles. Place the rings and circles 1 inch apart on the prepared baking sheets.

3 Whisk the egg white with the salt until just frothy. Chop the slivered almonds. Brush the cookie rings with the egg white, then sprinkle over the almonds. Bake until lightly browned, about 12–15 minutes. Cool for a few minutes on the baking sheets, then transfer to a wire rack.

4 In a saucepan, melt the jam with the lemon juice until it comes to a simmer. Brush the jam over the cookie circles and sandwich together with the rings.

Christmas Cookies

Decorate these delicious cookies with festive decorations or make them at any time of year.

Makes 30

¾ cup sweet butter, at
  room temperature
1½ cups superfine
  sugar
1 egg
1 egg yolk
1 teaspoon vanilla
  extract
grated rind of 1 lemon

¼ teaspoon salt
2½ cups all-purpose
  flour

**For decorating
(optional)**
colored fondant and
  small decorations

1 Preheat the oven to 350°F. With an electric mixer, cream the butter until soft. Add the sugar gradually and continue beating until light and fluffy. Using a wooden spoon, slowly mix in the whole egg and the egg yolk. Add the vanilla extract, lemon rind and salt. Stir to mix well. Add the flour and stir until blended. Gather the mixture into a ball, wrap in wax paper, and chill for 30 minutes.

2 On a floured surface, roll out the mixture about ⅛-inch thick. Stamp out shapes or rounds with cookie cutters. Bake until lightly colored, about 8 minutes. Transfer to a wire rack and let cool completely before icing and decorating, if wished.

Apricot Specials

Try other dried fruit, such as peaches or prunes, to vary the flavor of these special bars.

Makes 12

generous ¹/₂ cup light
  brown sugar
³/₄ cup all-purpose flour
6 tablespoons cold sweet
  butter, cut in pieces

1 cup water
grated rind of 1 lemon
generous ¹/₄ cup
  superfine sugar
2 teaspoons cornstarch
¹/₂ cup chopped walnuts

For the topping

generous ¹/₂ cup dried
  apricots

1 Preheat the oven to 350°F. In a mixing bowl, combine the brown sugar and flour. With a pastry blender, cut in the butter until the mixture resembles coarse bread crumbs.

2 Transfer to an 8-inch square baking pan and press level. Bake for 15 minutes. Remove from the oven but leave the oven on.

3 Meanwhile, for the topping, combine the apricots and water in a saucepan and simmer until soft; about 10 minutes. Strain the liquid and reserve. Chop the apricots.

4 Return the apricots to the saucepan and add the lemon rind, superfine sugar, cornstarch and 4 tablespoons of the soaking liquid. Cook for 1 minute.

5 Cool slightly before spreading the topping over the base. Sprinkle over the walnuts and bake for 20 minutes more. Cool in the pan before cutting into bars.

Brandy Snaps

You could serve these brandy snaps without the cream filling and eat with rich vanilla ice cream instead.

Makes 18

4 tablespoons butter, at
  room temperature
generous ¹/₂ cup
  superfine sugar
1 rounded tablespoon
  maple syrup
¹/₃ cup all-purpose flour

¹/₂ teaspoon ground
  ginger

For the filling

1 cup whipping cream
2 tablespoons brandy

1 Cream together the butter and sugar until light and fluffy, then beat in the maple syrup. Sift over the flour and ginger and mix together. Transfer the mixture to a work surface and knead until smooth. Cover and chill for 30 minutes.

2 Preheat the oven to 375°F. Grease a baking sheet. Working in batches of four, shape the mixture into walnut-size balls. Place well apart on the baking sheet and flatten slightly. Bake until golden and bubbling, about 10 minutes.

3 Remove from the oven and let cool for a few moments. Working quickly, slide a metal spatula under each one, turn over, and wrap around the handle of a wooden spoon (have four spoons ready). If they firm up too quickly, reheat for a few seconds to soften. When firm, slide the brandy snaps off and place on a wire rack to cool.

4 When all the brandy snaps are cool, prepare the filling. Whip the cream and brandy until soft peaks form. Pipe into each end of the brandy snaps just before serving.

Chocolate Pretzels

Pretzels come in many flavors – here is a chocolate version to bake and enjoy.

Makes 28

1¼ cups all-purpose
   flour
¼ teaspoon salt
6 tablespoons cocoa
½ cup butter, at room
   temperature

scant ⅔ cup sugar
1 egg
1 egg white, lightly
   beaten, for glazing
sugar crystals, for
   sprinkling

1 Sift together the flour, salt and cocoa. Set aside. Lightly grease two baking sheets. Cream the butter until light. Add the sugar and continue beating until light and fluffy. Beat in the egg. Add the dry ingredients and stir to blend. Gather the dough into a ball, place in plastic wrap and chill for 1 hour.

2 Roll the dough into 28 small balls. Chill the balls until needed. Preheat the oven to 375°F. Roll each ball into a rope about 10 inches long. With each rope, form a loop with the two ends facing you. Twist the ends and fold back onto the circle, pressing in to make a pretzel shape. Place on the prepared baking sheets.

3 Brush the pretzels with the egg white. Sprinkle sugar crystals over the tops and bake in the oven until firm, about 10–12 minutes. Transfer to a wire rack to cool.

Ginger Shapes

If your kids enjoy cooking with you, mixing and rolling the dough, or cutting out different shapes, this is the ideal recipe to let them practise on.

Makes 16

8 tablespoons brown
   sugar
½ cup soft margarine
pinch of salt
few drops vanilla extract
1½ cups whole wheat
   flour

1 tablespoon cocoa, sifted
2 teaspoons ground
   ginger
a little milk
glacé icing and candied
   cherries, to decorate

1 Preheat the oven to 375°F. Cream the sugar, margarine, salt and vanilla extract together until very soft and light.

2 Work in the flour, cocoa and ginger, adding a little milk, if necessary, to bind the mixture. Knead lightly on a floured surface until smooth.

3 Roll out the dough on a lightly floured surface to about 1¼-inch thick. Stamp out shapes using cookie cutters and place on baking sheets.

4 Bake the cookies for 10–15 minutes, let cool on the baking sheets until firm, then transfer to a wire rack to cool completely. Decorate with the icing and cherries.

Chocolate Macaroons

Roll one side of the macaroons in chopped nuts and bake nut-side up for a crunchier variation.

Makes 24

2 ounces semisweet
  chocolate, melted
1¹/₂ cups blanched
  almonds
1 cup superfine sugar
3 egg whites

¹/₂ teaspoon vanilla
  extract
¹/₄ teaspoon almond
  extract
confectioner's sugar, for
  dusting

1 Preheat the oven to 325°F. Line two baking sheets with wax paper, then grease. Grind the almonds in a food processor or blender. Transfer to a bowl, then blend in the sugar, egg whites, vanilla and almond extract. Stir in the chocolate. The mixture should just hold its shape; if it is too soft, chill for 15 minutes.

2 Shape the mixture into walnut-size balls. Place on the baking sheets and flatten slightly. Brush with water; dust with confectioner's sugar. Bake until just firm, 10–12 minutes. With a metal spatula, transfer to a wire rack to cool.

Chocolate-orange Sponge Drops

Light and crispy, with a marmalade filling, these sponge drops are truly decadent.

Makes 14–15

2 eggs
¹/₄ cup superfine sugar
¹/₂ teaspoon grated
  orange rind
¹/₂ cup all-purpose
  flour

4 tablespoons fine
  shred orange
  marmalade
1¹/₂ ounces semisweet
  chocolate, cut into
  small pieces

1 Preheat the oven to 400°F. Line three baking sheets with parchment paper. Put the eggs and sugar in a bowl over a pan of simmering water. Whisk until thick and pale. Remove from the pan and whisk until cool. Whisk in the orange rind. Sift the flour over and fold it in gently.

2 Put 28–30 dessert spoonfuls of the mixture on the baking sheets. Bake for 8 minutes, until golden. Cool slightly, then transfer to a wire rack. Sandwich pairs together with marmalade. Melt the chocolate, and drizzle over the drops.

Coconut Macaroons

Have a change from after-dinner mints, and serve these delicious coconut macaroons with coffee instead.

Makes 24

Preheat the oven to 350°F. Grease two baking sheets. Sift ¹/₃ cup all-purpose flour and 1¹/₄ teaspoons salt into a bowl, then stir in 4 cups dried coconut. Pour in scant ³/₄ cup sweetened condensed milk. Add 1 teaspoon vanilla extract; stir from the center to a thick mixture. Drop tablespoonfuls of the mixture 1 inch apart on the baking sheets. Bake until golden brown, about 20 minutes. Cool on a wire rack.

Peanut Butter Cookies

For added crunchiness, stir in ½ cup peanuts, coarsely chopped, with the peanut butter.

Makes 24

1¼ cups all-purpose
  flour
½ teaspoon baking soda
½ teaspoon salt
½ cup butter, at room
  temperature
scant 1 cup light brown
  sugar

1 egg
1 teaspoon vanilla
  extract
scant 1¼ cups crunchy
  peanut butter

1 Sift together the flour, baking soda and salt and set aside. In another bowl, cream the butter and sugar together until light and fluffy.

2 In a third bowl, mix the egg and vanilla, then gradually beat into the butter mixture. Stir in the peanut butter and the chopped peanuts, if using, and blend thoroughly. Stir in the dry ingredients. Chill for 30 minutes, or until firm.

3 Preheat the oven to 350°. Grease two baking sheets. Spoon out rounded teaspoonfuls of the dough and roll into balls.

4 Place the balls on the baking sheets and press flat with a fork into circles about 2½ inches in diameter, making a crisscross pattern. Bake in the oven until lightly colored, about 12–15 minutes. Transfer to a wire rack to cool.

Chocolate Chip Cookies

A perennial favorite with all the family, these cookies contain walnuts as well as chocolate chips.

Makes 24

½ cup butter or
  margarine, at room
  temperature
scant ¼ cup superfine
  sugar
generous ½ cup dark
  brown sugar
1 egg

½ teaspoon vanilla
  extract
1½ cups all-purpose
  flour
½ teaspoon baking soda
¼ teaspoon salt
1 cup chocolate chips
½ cup walnuts, chopped

1 Preheat the oven to 350°F. Lightly grease two large baking sheets. With an electric mixer, cream the butter or margarine and both the sugars together until light and fluffy.

2 In another bowl, mix the egg and the vanilla extract, then gradually beat into the butter mixture. Sift over the flour, baking soda and salt, and stir. Add the chocolate chips and walnuts, and mix to combine well.

4 Place heaped teaspoonfuls of the dough 2 inches apart on the baking sheets. Bake in the oven until lightly colored, about 10–15 minutes. Transfer to a wire rack to cool.

Almond Tile Cookies

These cookies are named after the French roof tiles they so closely resemble.

Makes about 24

scant ¹/₂ cup whole
  blanched almonds,
  lightly toasted
¹/₃ cup superfine sugar
3 tablespoons sweet
  butter, softened

2 egg whites
¹/₂ teaspoon almond
  extract
¹/₃ cup all-purpose flour,
  sifted
¹/₂ cup slivered almonds

1 Preheat the oven to 400°F. Grease two baking sheets. Place the almonds and 2 tablespoons of the sugar in a blender or food processor and process until finely ground, but not pasty.

2 Beat the butter until creamy, add the remaining sugar and beat until light and fluffy. Gradually beat in the egg whites until the mixture is well blended, then beat in the almond extract. Sift the flour over the butter mixture and fold in, then fold in the almond mixture.

3 Drop tablespoonfuls of the mixture onto the baking sheets 6 inches apart. With the back of a wet spoon, spread each mound into a paper-thin 3-inch circle. Sprinkle with the slivered almonds.

4 Bake the cookies, one sheet at a time, for 5–6 minutes until the edges are golden and the centers still pale. Remove the baking sheet to a wire rack and, working quickly, use a metal spatula to loosen the edges of a cookie. Lift the cookie on the metal spatula and place over a rolling pin, then press down the sides of the cookie to curve it. Repeat with the remaining cookies, and let cool.

Brittany Butter Cookies

These little cookies are similar to shortbread, but richer in taste and texture.

Makes 18–20

6 egg yolks, lightly
  beaten
1 tablespoon milk
2 cups all-purpose flour
generous ³/₄ cup superfine
  sugar

scant 1 cup lightly salted
  butter at room
  temperature, cut into
  small pieces

1 Preheat the oven to 350°F. Lightly butter a large baking sheet. Mix 1 tablespoon of the egg yolks with the milk for a glaze. Set aside.

2 Sift the flour into a large bowl and make a central well. Add the egg yolks, sugar and butter and, using your fingertips, work the ingredients together until smooth and creamy. Gradually blend in the flour to form a smooth but slightly sticky dough.

3 Using floured hands, pat out the dough to ⅓ inch thick and cut out circles using a 3-inch cookie cutter. Transfer the circles to the baking sheet, brush with egg glaze, then score to create a lattice pattern.

4 Bake for 12–15 minutes until golden. Cool on the sheet on a wire rack for 15 minutes, then transfer to the wire rack to cool completely.

Ginger Florentines

These colorful, chewy cookies are delicious served with vanilla or other flavored ice cream.

Makes 30

4 tablespoons butter
$^1/_2$ cup superfine sugar
$^1/_4$ cup candied cherries, chopped
generous 1 tablespoon candied orange peel, chopped
$^1/_2$ cup slivered almonds
$^1/_2$ cup chopped walnuts
1 tablespoon candied ginger, chopped

2 tablespoons all-purpose flour
$^1/_2$ teaspoon ground ginger

To finish
2 ounces semisweet chocolate, melted
2 ounces white chocolate, melted

1 Preheat the oven to 350°F. Beat the butter and sugar together until light and fluffy. Thoroughly mix in all the remaining ingredients, except the melted semisweet and white chocolate.

2 Line some baking sheets with nonstick parchment paper. Put four small spoonfuls of the mixture onto each sheet, spacing them well apart to allow for spreading. Flatten the cookies and bake for 5 minutes.

3 Remove the cookies from the oven and flatten with a wet fork, shaping them into neat rounds. Return to the oven for about 3–4 minutes, until they are golden brown. Work in batches if necessary.

4 Let cool on the baking sheets for 2 minutes to firm up, and then transfer to a wire rack. When they are cold and firm, spread semisweet chocolate on the undersides of half the cookies and white chocolate on the undersides of the rest.

Christmas Shapes

These are great fun for kids to make as presents, and any shape of cookie cutter can be used.

Makes about 12

6 tablespoons butter
generous $^1/_2$ cup confectioner's sugar
finely grated rind of 1 small lemon
1 egg yolk
$1^1/_2$ cups all-purpose flour

pinch of salt

To decorate
2 egg yolks
red and green food coloring

1 Beat the butter, sugar and lemon rind together until pale and fluffy. Beat in the egg yolk, and then sift in the flour and the salt. Knead together to form a smooth dough. Wrap and chill for 30 minutes.

2 Preheat the oven to 375°F. On a lightly floured surface, roll out the dough to ⅛-inch thick. Using a 2½-inch fluted cutter, stamp out as many cookies as you can, with the cutter dipped in flour to prevent it from sticking to the dough.

3 Transfer the cookies onto lightly greased baking sheets. Mark the tops lightly with a 1-inch holly leaf cutter and use a ¼-inch plain icing bag nozzle for the berries. Chill for 10 minutes, until firm.

4 Meanwhile, put each egg yolk into a small cup. Mix red food coloring into one and green food coloring into the other. Using a small, clean paintbrush, carefully paint the colors onto the cookies. Bake for 10–12 minutes, or until they begin to color around the edges. Let them cool slightly on the baking sheets, then transfer to a wire rack.

Traditional Sugar Cookies

These lovely old-fashioned cookies would be ideal to serve at an elegant tea party.

Makes 36

3 cups all-purpose flour
1 teaspoon baking soda
2 teaspoons baking
 powder
¼ teaspoon grated
 nutmeg
½ cup butter or
 margarine, at room
 temperature

generous 1 cup superfine
 sugar
½ teaspoon vanilla
 extract
1 egg
½ cup milk
colored or raw sugar, for
 sprinkling

1 Sift the flour, baking soda, baking powder and nutmeg into a small bowl. Set aside. Cream the butter or margarine, superfine sugar and vanilla extract together until the mixture is light and fluffy. Add the egg and beat to mix well.

2 Add the flour mixture alternately with the milk, stirring with a wooden spoon to make a soft dough. Place the dough in plastic film, and chill for 30 minutes.

3 Preheat the oven to 350°F. Roll out the dough on a lightly floured surface to a ⅛-inch thickness. Cut into circles with a cookie cutter.

4 Transfer the cookies to ungreased baking sheets. Sprinkle each one with sugar. Bake until golden, 10–12 minutes. With a metal spatula, transfer the cookies to a wire rack to cool.

Spicy Pepper Cookies

Despite the warm, complex flavor added by the spices, these light cookies are simple to make.

Makes 48

¾ cup all-purpose flour
¼ cup cornstarch
2 teaspoons baking
 powder
½ teaspoon ground
 cardamom
½ teaspoon ground
 cinnamon
½ teaspoon grated
 nutmeg
½ teaspoon ground
 ginger
½ teaspoon ground
 allspice
½ teaspoon salt

½ teaspoon freshly
 ground black pepper
1 cup butter or
 margarine, at room
 temperature
½ cup light brown sugar
½ teaspoon vanilla
 extract
1 teaspoon finely grated
 lemon rind
¼ cup whipping cream
¾ cup finely ground
 almonds
2 tablespoons
 confectioner's sugar

1 Preheat the oven to 350°F . Sift the flour, cornstarch, baking powder, spices, salt and pepper into a bowl.

2 Cream the butter or margarine and brown sugar until light and fluffy. Beat in the vanilla extract and lemon rind.

3 With the mixer on low speed, add the flour mixture alternately with the cream, beginning and ending with flour. Stir in the ground almonds.

4 Shape the dough into ¾-inch balls. Place them on ungreased baking sheets about 1 inch apart. Bake until golden brown underneath, about 15–20 minutes.

5 Let cool on the baking sheets for about 1 minute before transferring to a wire rack to cool completely. Before serving, sprinkle lightly with confectioner's sugar.

Marsala Cookies

These little yellow cookies come from the Veneto region of Italy, and Marsala wine enhances their regional appeal.

Makes about 48

½ cup golden raisins	1 cup butter
½ cup finely ground yellow cornmeal	1 cup sugar
	2 eggs
1½ cups all-purpose flour	1 tablespoon Marsala or
1½ teaspoon baking powder	1 teaspoon vanilla extract
pinch of salt	

1 Soak the golden raisins in a small bowl of warm water for 15 minutes. Drain. Preheat the oven to 350°F. Sift the cornmeal and flour, the baking powder and the salt into a bowl.

2 Cream the butter and sugar together until light and fluffy. Beat in the eggs, one at a time. Beat in the Marsala or vanilla extract. Add the dry ingredients to the batter, beating until well blended. Stir in the golden raisins.

3 Drop heaped teaspoonfuls of batter onto a greased baking sheet in rows about 2 inches apart. Bake for 7–8 minutes, or until the cookies are golden brown at the edges. Transfer to a wire rack to cool.

Mexican Cinnamon Cookies

Pastelitos are traditional sweet shortbreads at weddings in Mexico, dusted in sugar to match the bride's dress.

Makes 20

½ cup butter	2 tablespoons chopped mixed nuts
2 tablespoons superfine sugar	¼ cup confectioner's sugar, sifted
1 cup all-purpose flour	
¼ cup cornstarch	
¼ teaspoon ground cinnamon	

1 Preheat the oven to 325°F. Lightly grease a baking sheet. Place the butter and sugar in a bowl and beat until pale.

2 Sift in the all-purpose flour, cornstarch and cinnamon, and gradually work in with a wooden spoon until the mixture comes together. Knead lightly until completely smooth.

3 Take tablespoonfuls of the mixture, roll into 20 small balls and arrange on the baking sheet. Press a few chopped nuts into the top of each one and then flatten slightly.

4 Bake the cookies for about 30–35 minutes, until pale golden. Remove from the oven and, while they are still warm, toss them in the sifted confectioner's sugar. Let the cookies cool on a wire rack before serving.

Toasted Oat Meringues

Meringues needn't be plain. Try these oaty ones for a lovely crunchy change.

Makes 12

generous ¹/₂ cup rolled
  oats
2 egg whites

¹/₄ teaspoon salt
1¹/₂ teaspoons cornstarch
³/₄ cup superfine sugar

1 Preheat the oven to 275°F. Spread the oats on a baking sheet and toast in the oven until golden, for about 10 minutes. Lower the heat to 250°F. Grease and flour a baking sheet.

2 Beat the egg whites and salt until they start to form soft peaks. Sift over the cornstarch and continue beating until the whites hold stiff peaks. Add half the sugar; whisk until glossy. Add the remaining sugar and fold in, then fold in the oats.

3 Place tablespoonfuls of the mixture onto the baking sheet and bake for 2 hours, then turn off the oven. Turn over the meringues, and let cool in the oven.

Meringues

Make these classic meringues as large or small as you like. Serve as a teatime treat or as an elegant dessert.

Makes about 24

4 egg whites
¹/₄ teaspoon salt
1¹/₄ cups superfine sugar

¹/₂ teaspoon vanilla or
  almond extract
  (optional)
1 cup whipping cream

1 Preheat the oven to 225°F. Grease and flour two large baking sheets. Beat the egg whites and salt in a metal bowl. When they start to form soft peaks, add half the sugar and continue beating until the mixture holds stiff peaks.

2 With a large metal spoon, fold in the remaining sugar and vanilla or almond extract, if using. Pipe or spoon the meringue mixture onto the baking sheets. Bake for 2 hours, turn off the oven. Loosen the meringues, invert, and set in another place on the sheets to prevent sticking. Let cool in the oven. Whip the cream and use to fill the meringues.

Chewy Chocolate Cookies

If you have a weakness for chocolate, add ¹/₂ cup chocolate chips to the mixture with the nuts.

Makes 18

Preheat the oven to 350°F. Line two baking sheets with wax paper and grease. Using an electric mixer, beat 4 egg whites until frothy. Sift over 2 cups confectioner's sugar and 1 teaspoon coffee. Add 1 tablespoon water, beat on low speed to blend, then on high until thick. Fold in 1 cup chopped walnuts. Place generous spoonfuls of the mixture 1 inch apart on the sheets. Bake for 12–15 minutes. Transfer to a wire rack to cool.

Lavender Cookies

Instead of lavender you can use other flavorings, such as cinnamon, lemon, orange or mint.

Makes about 30

⅔ cup butter
½ cup sugar
1 egg, beaten
1 tablespoon dried
   lavender flowers

1½ cups self-rising flour
leaves and flowers,
   to decorate

1 Preheat the oven to 350°F. Grease two baking sheets. Cream the butter and sugar together, then stir in the egg. Mix in the lavender flowers and the flour.

2 Drop spoonfuls of the mixture onto the baking sheets. Bake for about 15–20 minutes, until the cookies are golden. Serve with some fresh leaves and flowers to decorate.

Chocolate Amaretti

As an alternative decoration, lightly press a few coffee sugar crystals on top of each cookie before baking.

Makes 24

scant 1 cup blanched,
   toasted whole almonds
½ cup superfine sugar
1 tablespoon cocoa
2 tablespoons
   confectioner's sugar

2 egg whites
pinch of cream of tartar
1 teaspoon almond
   extract
slivered almonds,
   to decorate

1 Preheat the oven to 325°F. Line a large baking sheet with nonstick parchment paper or foil. In a food processor fitted with a metal blade, process the toasted almonds with half the sugar until they are finely ground but not oily. Transfer to a bowl and sift in the cocoa and confectioner's sugar; stir to blend. Set aside.

2 Beat the egg whites and cream of tartar until stiff peaks form. Sprinkle in the remaining sugar 1 tablespoon at a time, beating well after each addition, and continue beating until the whites are glossy and stiff. Beat in the almond extract.

3 Sprinkle over the almond mixture and gently fold into the egg whites until just blended. Spoon the mixture into a large icing bag fitted with a plain ½-inch nozzle. Pipe 1½-inch rounds, 1 inch apart, on the baking sheet. Press a slivered almond into the center of each.

4 Bake the cookies for 12–15 minutes or until they appear crisp. Remove the baking sheet to a wire rack to cool for 10 minutes. With a metal metal spatula, transfer the cookies to the wire rack to cool completely.

Melting Moments

These cookies are very crisp and light – and they really do melt in your mouth.

Makes 16–20

3 tablespoons butter or
    margarine
5 tablespoons vegetable
    shortening
scant ¹/₂ cup superfine
    sugar
¹/₂ egg, beaten

few drops of vanilla or
    almond extract
1¹/₄ cups self-rising flour
rolled oats, for coating
4–5 candied cherries,
    quartered, to decorate

1 Preheat the oven to 350°F. Beat together the butter or margarine, shortening and sugar, then gradually beat in the egg and vanilla or almond extract.

2 Stir the flour into the beaten mixture, with floured hands, then roll into 16–20 small balls. Spread the rolled oats on a sheet of wax paper and toss the balls in them to coat evenly.

3 Place the balls, spaced slightly apart, on two baking sheets, place a piece of cherry on top of each and bake for about 15–20 minutes, until lightly browned. Let the cookies cool on the sheets for 5 minutes before transferring to a wire rack to cool completely.

Easter Cookies

This is a seasonal recipe, but these cookies can be enjoyed at any time of the year.

Makes 16–18

¹/₂ cup butter or
    margarine
scant ¹/₂ cup superfine
    sugar, plus extra for
    sprinkling
1 egg, separated
1³/₄ cups all-purpose flour

¹/₂ teaspoon mixed spice
¹/₂ teaspoon ground
    cinnamon
4 tablespoons currants
1 tablespoon chopped
    candied peel
1–2 tablespoons milk

1 Preheat the oven to 400°F. Lightly grease two baking sheets. Cream together the butter or margarine and sugar until light and fluffy, then beat in the egg yolk.

2 Sift the flour and spices over the egg mixture, then fold in with the currants and peel, adding sufficient milk to make a fairly soft dough.

3 Turn the dough onto a floured surface, knead lightly until just smooth, then roll out using a floured rolling pin, to about a ¹/₄-inch thickness. Cut the dough into circles using a 2-inch fluted cookie cutter. Transfer the circles to the baking sheets and bake for 10 minutes.

4 Beat the egg white, then brush over the cookies. Sprinkle with superfine sugar and return to the oven for 10 minutes more, until golden. Transfer to a wire rack to cool.

Shortbread

Once you have tasted this shortbread, you'll never buy a package from a store again.

Makes 8

generous ¹/₂ cup sweet butter, at room temperature
¹/₂ cup superfine sugar
1¹/₄ cups all-purpose flour
¹/₂ cup rice flour
¹/₄ teaspoon baking powder
¹/₄ teaspoon salt

1 Preheat the oven to 325°F. Lightly grease an 8-inch shallow round cake pan. Cream the butter and sugar together until light and fluffy. Sift over the flours, baking powder and salt, and mix well.

2 Press the mixture neatly into the prepared pan, smoothing the surface with the back of a spoon. Prick all over with a fork, then score into eight equal wedges.

3 Bake until golden, about 40–45 minutes. Let sit in the pan until cool enough to handle, then unmold and recut the wedges while still hot. Store in an airtight container.

Flapjacks

For a spicier version, add 1 teaspoon ground ginger to the melted butter.

Makes 8

¹/₄ cup butter
21 rounded tablespoons maple syrup
scant ¹/₂ cup dark brown sugar
generous 1 cup quick-cooking oats
¹/₄ teaspoon salt

1 Preheat the oven to 350°F. Line and grease an 8-inch shallow round cake pan. Place the butter, maple syrup and sugar in a pan over low heat. Cook, stirring, until melted and combined.

2 Remove from heat and add the oats and salt. Stir the mixture to blend. Spoon the mixture into the prepared pan and smooth the surface. Place in the center of the oven and bake until golden brown, 20–25 minutes. Let sit in the pan until cool enough to handle, then unmold and cut into wedges while still hot. Store in an airtight container.

Chocolate Delights

This method of making cookies makes sure they are all of a uniform size.

Makes 50

1 ounce semisweet
   chocolate
1 ounce bittersweet
   chocolate
2 cups all-purpose flour
$1/2$ teaspoon salt
1 cup sweet butter, at
   room temperature

generous 1 cup superfine
   sugar
2 eggs
1 teaspoon vanilla
   extract
1 cup finely chopped
   walnuts

1 Melt the chocolate in the top of a double boiler, or in a heat proof bowl set over a pan of gently simmering water. Set aside. In a bowl, sift together the flour and salt. Set aside.

2 Cream the butter until soft. Add the sugar and continue beating until the mixture is light and fluffy. Mix the eggs and vanilla extract, then gradually stir into the butter mixture. Stir in the chocolate, then the flour. Finally, stir in the nuts.

3 Divide the mixture into four equal parts, and roll each into a 2-inch diameter log. Wrap tightly in foil and chill or freeze until firm.

4 Preheat the oven to 375°F. Grease two baking sheets. With a sharp knife, cut the logs into ¼-inch slices. Place the circles on the baking sheets and bake until lightly colored, about 10 minutes. Using a metal spatula, transfer the cookies to a wire rack to cool.

Cinnamon Treats

Place these cookies in a heart-shape basket, as here, and serve them up with love.

Makes 50

generous 2 cups all-
   purpose flour
$1/2$ teaspoon salt
2 teaspoons ground
   cinnamon
1 cup sweet butter, at
   room temperature

generous 1 cup superfine
   sugar
2 eggs
1 teaspoon vanilla
   extract

1 Sift together the flour, salt and cinnamon into a bowl. Set aside.

2 Cream the butter until soft. Add the sugar and continue beating until the mixture is light and fluffy. Beat the eggs and vanilla extract together, then gradually stir into the butter mixture. Stir in the dry ingredients.

3 Divide the mixture into four equal parts, then roll each into a 2-inch diameter log. Wrap tightly in foil and chill or freeze until firm.

4 Preheat the oven to 375°F. Grease two baking sheets. With a sharp knife, cut the logs into ¼-inch slices. Place the rounds on the baking sheets and bake until lightly colored, about 10 minutes. Using a metal spatula, transfer to a wire rack to cool.

Chunky Chocolate Drops

Do not allow these cookies to cool completely on the baking sheet or they will break when you try to lift them.

Makes 18

6 ounces semisweet chocolate
1/2 cup sweet butter
2 eggs
1/2 cup sugar
1/4 cup light brown sugar
1/3 cup all-purpose flour
1/4 cup cocoa
1 teaspoon baking powder
2 teaspoons vanilla extract
pinch of salt

1 cup pecans, toasted and coarsely chopped
1 cup semisweet chocolate chips
4 ounces fine quality white chocolate, chopped into 1/4-inch pieces
4 ounces fine quality milk chocolate, chopped into 1/4-inch pieces

1 Preheat the oven to 325°F. Grease two large baking sheets. In a medium saucepan over low heat, melt the semisweet chocolate and butter until smooth, stirring frequently. Remove from the heat to cool slightly.

2 Beat the eggs and sugars for 2–3 minutes until pale and creamy. Gradually beat in the melted chocolate mixture. Beat in the flour, cocoa, baking powder, vanilla and salt, just to blend. Add the nuts, chocolate chips and chocolate pieces.

3 Drop 4–6 heaped tablespoonfuls of the mixture onto each baking sheet 4 inches apart and flatten each to a round about 3 inches. Bake for 8–10 minutes, until the tops are shiny and cracked and the edges look crisp.

4 Transfer the baking sheets to a wire rack to cool for about 2 minutes, until the cookies are just set, then transfer them to the wire rack to cool completely. Continue to bake in batches.

Chocolate Crackle-tops

These cookies are best eaten on the day they are baked, as they dry slightly on storage.

Makes 38

7 ounces semisweet chocolate, chopped
7 tablespoons sweet butter
1/2 cup superfine sugar
3 eggs
1 teaspoon vanilla extract

scant 2 cups all-purpose flour
1/4 cup cocoa
1/2 teaspoon baking powder
pinch of salt
1 1/2 cups confectioner's sugar, for coating

1 Heat the chocolate and butter over low heat until smooth, stirring frequently. Remove from the heat. Stir in the sugar, and continue stirring until dissolved. Add the eggs, one at a time, beating well after each addition; stir in the vanilla. In a separate bowl, sift together the flour, cocoa, baking powder and salt. Gradually stir into the chocolate mixture until just blended. Cover and chill for at least 1 hour.

2 Preheat the oven to 325°F. Grease two or three large baking sheets. Place the confectioner's sugar in a small, deep bowl. Using a teaspoon, scoop the dough into small balls and roll in your hands into 1½-inch balls.

3 Drop the balls, one at a time, into the confectioner's sugar and roll until heavily coated. Remove each ball with a slotted spoon and tap against the bowl to remove any excess sugar. Place on the baking sheets 1½ inches apart.

4 Bake the cookies for 10–15 minutes or until the tops feel slightly firm when touched with your fingertip. Remove the baking sheets to a wire rack for 2–3 minutes, then, with a metal spatula, transfer the cookies to the wire rack to cool.

Chocolate Chip Oat Cookies

Oat cookies are given a delicious lift by the inclusion of chocolate chips. Try caramel chips for a change, if you like.

Makes 60

1 cup all-purpose flour
1/2 teaspoon baking soda
1/4 teaspoon baking powder
1/4 teaspoon salt
1/2 cup butter or margarine, at room temperature
generous 1/2 cup superfine sugar

generous 1/2 cup light brown sugar
1 egg
1/2 teaspoon vanilla extract
scant 1/2 cup rolled oats
1 cup semisweet chocolate chips

1 Preheat the oven to 350°F. Grease three or four baking sheets. Sift the flour, baking soda, baking powder and salt into a mixing bowl. Set aside.

2 With an electric mixer, cream the butter or margarine and the sugars together. Add the egg and vanilla, and beat until light and fluffy. Add the flour mixture and beat on low speed until thoroughly blended. Stir in the rolled oats and semisweet chocolate chips, mixing well with a wooden spoon. The dough should be crumbly.

3 Drop heaped teaspoonfuls onto the baking sheets, about 1 inch apart. Bake until just firm around the edges but still soft in the centers, about 15 minutes. With a metal spatula, transfer the cookies to a wire rack to cool.

Chocolate and Coconut Slices

These tasty family favorites are easier to slice if they are allowed to cool overnight.

Makes 24

2 cups crushed digestive cookies
1/4 cup superfine sugar
pinch of salt
1/2 cup butter or margarine, melted

1 1/2 cups dried coconut
9 ounces semisweet chocolate chips
1 cup sweetened condensed milk
1 cup chopped walnuts

1 Preheat the oven to 350°F. In a bowl, combine the crushed cookies, sugar, salt and butter or margarine. Press the mixture over the bottom of an ungreased 13 x 9-inch baking dish.

2 Sprinkle the coconut over the cookie bottom, then sprinkle the chocolate chips over the top. Pour the condensed milk evenly over the chocolate. Sprinkle the walnuts on top. Bake for 30 minutes. Unmold onto a wire rack and let cool.

Nut Lace Wafers

To create a different taste, add some finely grated orange peel to these delicate cookies.

Makes 18

scant ¹/₂ cup blanched almonds
¹/₄ cup butter
¹/₃ cup all-purpose flour
¹/₂ cup superfine sugar

2 tablespoons heavy cream
¹/₂ teaspoon vanilla extract

1 Preheat the oven to 375°F. Lightly grease two baking sheets.

2 With a sharp knife, chop the almonds as finely as possible. Alternatively, use a food processor or blender to chop the nuts very finely.

3 Melt the butter in a saucepan over low heat. Remove from the heat and stir in the remaining ingredients and the finely chopped almonds.

4 Drop teaspoonfuls 2½ inches apart on the prepared sheets. Bake until golden, about 5 minutes. Cool on the baking sheets briefly, until the wafers are just stiff enough to remove. With a metal spatula, transfer to a wire rack to cool.

Oatmeal Lace Rounds

These rich, nutty cookies are very quick and simple to make and will be enjoyed by everyone.

Makes 36

²/₃ cup butter or margarine
1¹/₄ cups quick-cooking porridge oats
³/₄ cup dark brown sugar
²/₃ cup superfine sugar
¹/₃ cup all-purpose flour

¹/₄ teaspoon salt
1 egg, lightly beaten
1 teaspoon vanilla extract
generous ¹/₂ cup pecans or walnuts, finely chopped

1 Preheat the oven to 350°F. Lightly grease two baking sheets.

2 Melt the butter or margarine in a saucepan over low heat. Set aside. In a mixing bowl, combine the oats, brown sugar, superfine sugar, flour and salt. Make a well in the center and add the butter or margarine, egg and vanilla. Mix until blended, then stir in the chopped nuts.

3 Drop rounded teaspoonfuls of the mixture about 2 inches apart on the prepared baking sheets. Bake in the oven until lightly browned on the edges and bubbling all over, about 5–8 minutes. Cool on the baking sheets for 2 minutes, then transfer to a wire rack to cool completely.

Nutty Chocolate Squares

These delicious squares are incredibly rich, so cut them smaller if you wish.

Makes 16

2 eggs
2 teaspoons vanilla
   extract
¹/₄ teaspoon salt
1¹/₂ cups pecans, coarsely
   chopped
¹/₂ cup all-purpose flour
¹/₄ cup superfine sugar

¹/₂ cup maple syrup
3 ounces semisweet
   chocolate, finely
   chopped
3 tablespoons butter
16 pecan halves, to
   decorate

1 Preheat the oven to 325°F. Line the bottom and sides of an 8-inch square baking pan with wax paper and lightly grease the paper.

2 Whisk together the eggs, vanilla and salt. In another bowl, mix together the chopped pecan and flour. Set both aside until needed.

3 In a saucepan, bring the sugar and maple syrup to a boil. Remove from the heat, stir in the chocolate and butter, and blend thoroughly with a wooden spoon. Mix in the beaten egg mixture, then fold in the pecan mixture.

4 Pour the mixture into the baking pan and bake until set, about 35 minutes. Cool in the pan for 10 minutes before unmolding. Cut into 2-inch squares and press pecan halves into the tops while warm. Cool on a wire rack.

Raisin Brownies

Cover these brownies with a light chocolate frosting for a truly decadent treat, if you wish.

Makes 16

¹/₂ cup butter or
   margarine
¹/₂ cup cocoa
2 eggs
generous 1 cup superfine
   sugar

1 teaspoon vanilla
   extract
¹/₃ cup all-purpose flour
³/₄ cup chopped walnuts
generous ¹/₂ cup raisins

1 Preheat the oven to 350°F. Line the bottom and sides of an 8-inch square baking pan with wax paper. Grease the paper.

2 Gently melt the butter or margarine in a small saucepan. Remove from the heat and stir in the cocoa. With an electric mixer, beat the eggs, sugar and vanilla together until light. Add the cocoa mixture and stir to blend.

3 Sift the flour over the cocoa mixture and gently fold in. Add the walnuts and raisins and scrape the mixture into the prepared baking tin.

4 Bake in the center of the oven for 30 minutes. Let cool in the pan before cutting into 2-inch squares and removing. The brownies should be soft and moist.

Chocolate Chip Brownies

A double dose of chocolate is incorporated into these melt-in-the-mouth brownies.

Makes 24

4 ounces semisweet
   chocolate
$^1/_2$ cup butter
3 eggs
1 cup sugar

$^1/_2$ teaspoon vanilla
   extract
pinch of salt
$1^1/_4$ cups all-purpose
   flour
1 cup chocolate chips

1 Preheat the oven to 350°F. Line a 13 x 9-inch baking pan with wax paper and grease the paper.

2 Melt the chocolate and butter together in the top of a double boiler, or in a heat proof bowl set over a pan of gently simmering water.

3 Beat together the eggs, sugar, vanilla and salt. Stir in the chocolate mixture. Sift over the flour and fold in. Add the chocolate chips.

4 Pour the mixture into the baking pan and spread evenly. Bake until just set, about 30 minutes. The brownies should be slightly moist inside. Let cool in the tin.

5 To turn out, run a knife all around the edge and invert onto a baking sheet. Remove the paper. Place another sheet on top and invert again. Cut into bars for serving.

Marbled Brownies

Flavorsome and impressive in appearance, these fancy brownies are also great fun to make.

Makes 24

8 ounces semisweet
   chocolate
$^1/_3$ cup butter
4 eggs
$1^1/_2$ cups sugar
$1^1/_4$ cups all-purpose flour
$^1/_2$ teaspoon salt
1 teaspoon baking
   powder
2 teaspoons vanilla
   extract
1 cup walnuts, chopped

For the plain mixture
4 tablespoons butter, at
   room temperature
$^3/_4$ cup cream cheese
$1^1/_2$ cups sugar
2 eggs
4 tablespoons all-purpose
   flour
1 teaspoon vanilla
   extract

1 Preheat the oven to 350°F. Line a 13 x 9-inch baking pan with wax paper and grease.

2 Melt the chocolate and butter over very low heat, stirring. Set aside to cool. Meanwhile, beat the eggs until light and fluffy. Gradually beat in the sugar. Sift over the flour, salt and baking powder and fold to combine.

3 Stir in the cooled chocolate mixture. Add the vanilla and nuts. Measure and set aside 2 cups of the chocolate mixture.

4 For the plain mixture, cream the butter and cream cheese with an electric mixer. Add the sugar and continue beating until blended. Beat in the eggs, flour and vanilla.

5 Spread the unmeasured chocolate mixture in the pan. Pour over the plain mixture. Drop spoonfuls of the reserved chocolate mixture on top.

6 With a metal spatula, swirl the mixtures to marble. Do not blend completely. Bake until just set, 35–40 minutes. Turn out when cool and cut into squares for serving.

Oatmeal and Date Brownies

These brownies are marvelous as a break-time treat. The secret of chewy, moist brownies is not to overcook them.

Makes 16

5 ounces semisweet
   chocolate
4 tablespoons butter
scant 1 cup quick-
   cooking porridge oats
3 tablespoons wheatgerm
$^1/_3$ cup milk powder
$^1/_2$ teaspoon baking
   powder

$^1/_2$ teaspoon salt
$^1/_2$ cup chopped walnuts
$^1/_3$ cup dates, chopped
$^1/_4$ cup molasses sugar
1 teaspoon vanilla
   extract
2 eggs, beaten

1 Break the chocolate into a heat proof bowl and add the butter. Place over a pan of simmering water and stir until completely melted.

2 Cool the chocolate, stirring occasionally. Preheat the oven to 350°F. Grease and line an 8-inch square cake pan.

3 Combine all the dry ingredients together in a bowl, then beat in the melted chocolate, vanilla and eggs. Pour the mixture into the cake pan, level the surface and bake in the oven for 20–25 minutes until firm around the edges yet still soft in the center.

4 Cool the brownies in the pan, then chill in the fridge. When they are more solid, turn them out of the pan and cut into 16 squares.

Banana Chocolate Brownies

Nuts traditionally give brownies their chewy texture. Here, oat bran is used instead, creating a wonderful alternative.

Makes 9

5 tablespoons cocoa
1 tablespoon superfine
   sugar
5 tablespoons milk
3 large bananas, mashed
1 cup light brown sugar

1 teaspoon vanilla
   extract
5 egg whites
$^3/_4$ cup self-rising flour
$^2/_3$ cup oat bran
confectioner's sugar, for
   dusting

1 Preheat the oven to 350°F. Line an 8-inch square cake pan with nonstick parchment paper.

2 Blend the cocoa and superfine sugar with the milk. Add the bananas, brown sugar and vanilla extract. Lightly beat the egg whites with a fork. Add the chocolate mixture and continue to beat well. Sift the flour over the mixture and fold in with the oat bran. Pour into the prepared pan.

3 Cook in the oven for 40 minutes, or until firm. Cool in the pan for 10 minutes, then turn out onto a wire rack. Cut into squares and dust with confectioner's sugar before serving.

White Chocolate Brownies

If you wish, hazelnuts can be substituted for the macadamia nuts in the topping.

Serves 12

1 cup all-purpose flour
½ teaspoon baking
    powder
pinch of salt
6 ounces fine quality
    white chocolate,
    chopped
½ cup superfine sugar
½ cup sweet butter, cut
    into pieces
2 eggs, lightly beaten

1 teaspoon vanilla
    extract
6 ounces semi-sweet
    chocolate chips

For the topping
7 ounces milk chocolate,
    chopped
1 cup unsalted
    macadamia nuts,
    chopped

1 Preheat the oven to 350°F. Grease a 9-inch springform pan. Sift together the flour, baking powder and salt, and set aside.

2 In a medium saucepan over moderate heat, melt the white chocolate, sugar and butter until smooth, stirring frequently. Cool slightly, then beat in the eggs and vanilla. Stir in the chocolate chips. Spread evenly in the prepared pan, smoothing the top.

3 Bake for 20–25 minutes until a toothpick inserted 2 inches from the side of the pan comes out clean. Remove from the oven to a heat proof surface, sprinkle chopped milk chocolate over the surface (avoid touching the side of pan) and return to the oven for 1 minute.

4 Remove from the oven and, using the back of a spoon, gently spread out the softened chocolate. Sprinkle with the macadamia nuts and gently press into the chocolate. Cool on a wire rack for 30 minutes; chill for 1 hour. Run a sharp knife around the side of the pan to loosen; then unclip and remove. Cut into thin wedges to serve.

Maple-Pecan Brownies

This recipe provides a delicious adaptation of the classic chocolate brownie.

Makes 12

½ cup butter, melted
½ cup light brown sugar
6 tablespoons maple
    syrup
2 eggs
1 cup self-rising flour

¾ cup pecans, chopped
⅔ cup semisweet
    chocolate chips
¼ cup sweet butter
12 pecan halves, to
    decorate

1 Preheat the oven to 350°F. Line and grease a 10 x 7-inch cake pan.

2 Beat together the melted butter, sugar, 4 tablespoons of the maple syrup, eggs and flour for 1 minute, or until smooth. Stir in the nuts and transfer to the cake pan. Smooth the surface and bake for 30 minutes, until risen and firm to the touch. Cool in the pan for 10 minutes, then transfer to a wire rack to cool completely.

3 Melt the chocolate chips, butter and remaining syrup over low heat. Cool slightly, then spread over the cake. Press in the pecan halves, let set for about 5 minutes, then cut into bars.

Chocolate Fudge Brownies

This is the classic recipe, but omit the frosting if you find it too rich.

Makes 12

³/₄ cup butter
6 tablespoons cocoa
2 eggs, lightly beaten
1 cup light brown sugar
¹/₂ teaspoon vanilla
  extract
1 cup chopped pecans
¹/₂ cup self-rising flour

For the frosting
4 ounces semisweet
  chocolate
2 tablespoons butter
1 tablespoon sour cream

1 Preheat the oven to 350°F. Grease, then line an 8-inch square shallow cake pan with wax paper. Melt the butter in a pan and stir in the cocoa. Set aside to cool.

2 Beat together the eggs, sugar and vanilla extract in a bowl, then stir in the cooled cocoa mixture with the nuts. Sift over the flour and fold into the mixture with a metal spoon.

3 Pour the mixture into the cake pan and bake in the oven for 30–35 minutes, until risen. Remove from the oven (the mixture will still be quite soft and wet, but it cooks further while cooling) and let cool in the pan.

4 To make the frosting, melt the chocolate and butter together in a pan and remove from the heat. Beat in the sour cream until smooth and glossy. Let cool slightly, and then spread over the top of the brownies. When set, cut into 12 pieces.

Fudge-glazed Chocolate Brownies

These brownies are just about irresistible, so hide them from friends – or make lots!

Makes 16

9 ounces bittersweet
  chocolate, chopped
1 ounce semisweet
  chocolate, chopped
¹/₂ cup sweet butter, cut
  into pieces
¹/₂ cup light brown sugar
¹/₄ cup sugar
2 eggs
1 tablespoon vanilla
  extract
¹/₂ cup all-purpose flour
1 cup pecans or walnuts,
  toasted and chopped
5 ounces white chocolate,
  chopped

pecan halves, to decorate
  (optional)

Fudgy chocolate glaze
6 ounces bittersweet
  chocolate, chopped
4 tablespoons sweet
  butter, cut into pieces
2 tablespoons maple
  syrup
2 teaspoons vanilla
  extract
1 teaspoon instant coffee

1 Preheat the oven to 350°F. Line an 8-inch square baking pan with foil, then grease the foil.

2 In a saucepan over low heat, melt the dark chocolates and butter. Remove from the heat and add the sugars. Stir for 2 minutes. Beat in the eggs and vanilla, then blend in the flour. Stir in the nuts and white chocolate. Pour into the pan. Bake for 20–25 minutes. Cool in the pan for 30 minutes then lift, using the foil, onto a wire rack to cool for 2 hours.

3 For the glaze, melt all the ingredients in a pan until smooth, stirring. Chill for 1 hour, then spread over the brownies. Chill until set, then cut into squares.

Chocolate Raspberry Macaroon Bars

Any seedless jam, such as strawberry or apricot, can be substituted for the raspberry in this recipe.

Makes 16–18

½ cup sweet butter,
softened
½ cup confectioner's
sugar
¼ cup cocoa
pinch of salt
1 teaspoon almond
extract
1¼ cups all-purpose
flour

For the topping
½ cup seedless raspberry
jam

1 tablespoon raspberry
flavor liqueur
1 cup milk chocolate
chips
1½ cups finely ground
almonds
4 egg whites
pinch of salt
1 cup superfine sugar
½ teaspoon almond
extract
½ cup slivered almonds

1 Preheat the oven to 325°F. Line a 9 x 13-inch baking pan with foil, and grease. Beat together the butter, sugar, cocoa and salt until blended. Beat in the almond extract and flour to make a crumbly dough.

2 Turn the dough into the pan and smooth the surface. Prick with a fork. Bake for 20 minutes until just set. Remove from the oven and increase the temperature to 375°F. Combine the raspberry jam and liqueur. Spread over the cooked crust, then sprinkle with the chocolate chips.

3 In a food processor fitted with a metal blade, process the almonds, egg whites, salt, sugar and almond extract. Pour over the jam layer, spreading evenly. Sprinkle with slivered almonds.

4 Bake for 20–25 minutes, until the top is golden and puffed. Cool in the pan for 20 minutes. Carefully remove from the pan and cool completely. Peel off the foil and cut into bars.

Chewy Fruit Granola Slices

The apricots give these slices a wonderful chewy texture and the apple keeps them moist.

Makes 8

scant ½ cup ready-to-eat
dried apricots,
chopped
1 eating apple, cored and
grated

1¼ cups granola
⅔ cup apple juice
1 tablespoon sunflower
margarine

1 Preheat the oven to 375°F. Place all the ingredients in a large bowl and mix well.

2 Press the mixture into an 8-inch round nonstick sandwich pan and bake for 35–40 minutes, or until lightly browned and firm. Mark the bake into wedges and let cool in the pan.

Blueberry Streusel Slice

If you are short of time, use pre-made pastry for this delightful streusel.

Makes 30
8 ounces piecrust pastry
$^1/_2$ cup all-purpose flour
$^1/_4$ teaspoon baking powder
3 tablespoons butter or margarine
2 tablespoons fresh white bread crumbs

$^1/_3$ cup light brown sugar
$^1/_4$ teaspoon salt
4 tablespoons slivered or chopped almonds
4 tablespoons blackberry or bramble jelly
1 cup blueberries, fresh or frozen

1 Preheat the oven to 350°F. Roll out the pastry on a lightly floured surface and line a 7 x 11-inch jelly roll pan. Prick the bottom evenly with a fork.

2 Rub together the flour, baking powder, butter or margarine, bread crumbs, sugar and salt until really crumbly, then mix in the almonds.

3 Spread the pastry with the jelly, sprinkle with the blueberries, then cover evenly with the streusel topping, pressing down lightly. Bake for 30–40 minutes, reducing the temperature after 20 minutes to 325°F.

4 Remove from the oven when golden on the top and the pastry is cooked through. Cut into slices while still hot, then let cool.

Sticky Date and Apple Bars

If possible, allow this mixture to mature for 1–2 days before cutting – it will get stickier and even more delicious!

Makes 16
$^1/_2$ cup margarine
$^1/_3$ cup dark brown sugar
4 tablespoons maple syrup
$^3/_4$ cup chopped dates
generous 1 cup rolled oats

1 cup whole wheat self-rising flour
2 eating apples, peeled, cored and grated
1–2 teaspoons lemon juice
20–25 walnut halves

1 Preheat the oven to 375°F. Line a 7–8-inch square or rectangular loose-based cake pan. In a large saucepan, heat the margarine, sugar, syrup and dates, stirring until the dates soften completely.

2 Gradually work in the oats, flour, apples and lemon juice until well mixed. Spoon into the pan and spread out evenly. Top with the walnut halves.

3 Bake for 30 minutes, then reduce the oven temperature to 325°F and bake for 10–20 minutes more, until firm to the touch and golden. Cut into squares or bars while still warm, or wrap in foil when nearly cold and keep for 1–2 days before eating.

Figgy Bars

Make sure you have napkins handy when you serve these deliciously sticky bars.

Makes 48

1¹/₂ cups dried figs
3 eggs
³/₄ cup superfine sugar
³/₄ cup all-purpose flour
1 teaspoon baking
    powder
¹/₂ teaspoon ground
    cinnamon
¹/₄ teaspoon ground
    cloves

¹/₄ teaspoon grated
    nutmeg
¹/₄ teaspoon salt
³/₄ cup finely chopped
    walnuts
2 tablespoons brandy or
    cognac
confectioner's sugar, for
    dusting

1 Preheat the oven to 325°F. Line a 12 x 8 x 1½-inch baking pan with wax paper and grease the paper.

2 With a sharp knife, chop the figs coarsely. Set aside. In a bowl, whisk the eggs and sugar until well blended. In another bowl, sift together the dry ingredients, then fold into the egg mixture in several batches.

3 Scrape the mixture into the baking pan and bake until the top is firm and brown, about 35–40 minutes. It should still be soft underneath.

4 Let cool in the pan for 5 minutes, then unmold and transfer to a sheet of wax paper lightly sprinkled with confectioner's sugar. Cut into bars.

Lemon Bars

A surprising amount of lemon juice goes into these bars, but you will appreciate why when you taste them.

Makes 36

¹/₂ cup confectioner's
    sugar
1¹/₂ cups all-purpose
    flour
¹/₂ teaspoon salt
³/₄ cup butter, cut in
    small pieces

For the topping
4 eggs
1¹/₂ cups superfine sugar
grated rind of 1 lemon
¹/₂ cup fresh lemon juice
³/₄ cup whipping cream
confectioner's sugar, for
    dusting

1 Preheat the oven to 325°F. Grease a 3 x 9-inch baking pan.

2 Sift the sugar, flour and salt into a bowl. With a pastry blender, cut in the butter until the mixture resembles coarse bread crumbs. Press the mixture into the bottom of the pan. Bake until golden brown, about 20 minutes.

3 Meanwhile, for the topping, whisk the eggs and sugar together until blended. Add the lemon rind and juice, and mix well.

4 Lightly whip the cream and fold into the egg mixture. Pour over the still warm bottom, return to the oven, and bake until set, about 40 minutes. Cool completely before cutting into bars. Dust with confectioner's sugar.

Spiced Raisin Bars

If you like raisins, these gloriously spicy bars are for you. Omit the walnuts, if you prefer.

Makes 30

scant 1 cup all-purpose
  flour
1¹/₂ teaspoons baking
  powder
1 teaspoon ground
  cinnamon
¹/₂ teaspoon grated
  nutmeg
¹/₄ teaspoon ground
  cloves

¹/₄ teaspoon mixed spice
1¹/₂ cups raisins
¹/₂ cup butter or
  margarine, at room
  temperature
¹/₂ cup sugar
2 eggs
scant ¹/₂ cup molasses
¹/₂ cup walnuts, chopped

1 Preheat the oven to 350°F Line a 13 x 9-inch baking pan with wax paper and grease the paper.

2 Sift together the flour, baking powder and spices. Place the raisins in another bowl and toss with a few tablespoons of the flour mixture.

3 With an electric mixer, cream the butter or margarine and sugar together until light and fluffy. Beat in the eggs, one at a time, then the molasses. Stir in the flour mixture, raisins and walnuts.

4 Spread evenly in the baking pan. Bake until just set, about 15–18 minutes. Cool in the pan before cutting into bars.

Toffee Meringue Bars

Two delicious layers complement each other beautifully in these easy-to-make bars.

Makes 12

4 tablespoons butter
scant 1¹/₄ cups dark
  brown sugar
1 egg
¹/₂ teaspoon vanilla
  extract
9 tablespoons all-purpose
  flour
¹/₂ teaspoon salt
¹/₄ teaspoon grated
  nutmeg

For the topping
1 egg white
¹/₄ teaspoon salt
1 tablespoon maple syrup
¹/₂ cup superfine sugar
¹/₂ cup walnuts, finely
  chopped

1 Combine the butter and brown sugar in a saucepan and heat until bubbling. Set aside to cool.

2 Preheat the oven to 350°F. Line the bottom and sides of an 8-inch square cake pan with wax paper and grease the paper.

3 Beat the egg and vanilla into the cooled sugar mixture. Sift over the flour, salt and nutmeg and fold in. Spread in the bottom of the cake pan.

4 For the topping, beat the egg white with the salt until it holds soft peaks. Beat in the maple syrup, then the sugar, and continue beating until the mixture holds stiff peaks. Fold in the nuts and spread on top. Bake for 30 minutes. Cut into bars when completely cool.

Chocolate Walnut Bars

These double-decker bars should be stored in the fridge in an airtight container.

Makes 24

²/₃ cup walnuts
generous ¹/₄ cup superfine sugar
scant 1 cup all-purpose flour, sifted
6 tablespoons cold sweet butter, cut into pieces

For the topping
2 tablespoons sweet butter

6 tablespoons water
¹/₄ cup cocoa
¹/₂ cup superfine sugar
1 teaspoon vanilla extract
¹/₄ teaspoon salt
2 eggs
confectioner's sugar, for dusting

1 Preheat the oven to 350°F. Grease the bottom and sides of an 8-inch square baking pan.

2 Grind the walnuts with a few tablespoons of the sugar in a food processor or blender. In a bowl, combine the ground walnuts, remaining sugar and flour. Rub in the butter until the mixture resembles coarse bread crumbs. Alternatively, use a food processor. Pat the walnut mixture evenly into the bottom of the baking pan. Bake for 25 minutes.

3 Meanwhile, for the topping, melt the butter with the water. Whisk in the cocoa and sugar. Remove from the heat, stir in the vanilla extract and salt, then cool for 5 minutes. Whisk in the eggs until blended. Pour the topping over the baked crust.

4 Return to the oven and bake until set, about 20 minutes. Set the pan on a wire rack to cool, then cut into bars and dust with confectioner's sugar.

Hazelnut Squares

These crunchy, nutty squares are made in a single bowl. What could be simpler?

Makes 9

2 ounces semisweet chocolate
5 tablespoons butter or margarine
generous 1 cup superfine sugar
¹/₂ cup all-purpose flour

¹/₂ teaspoon baking powder
2 eggs, beaten
¹/₂ teaspoon vanilla extract
1 cup skinned hazelnuts, coarsely chopped

1 Preheat the oven to 350°F. Grease an 8-inch square baking pan.

2 In a heat proof bowl set over a pan of barely simmering water, melt the chocolate and butter or margarine. Remove the bowl from the heat.

3 Add the sugar, flour, baking powder, eggs, vanilla and half of the hazelnuts to the melted mixture and stir well with a wooden spoon.

4 Pour the mixture into the prepared pan. Bake in the oven for 10 minutes, then sprinkle the reserved hazelnuts over the top. Return to the oven and continue baking until firm to the touch, about 25 minutes.

5 Cool in the tin, set on a wire rack for 10 minutes, then unmold onto the rack and cool completely. Cut into squares before serving.

Fruity Teabread

Serve this bread thinly sliced, toasted or plain, with butter or cream cheese and jam.

Makes one 9 x 5-inch loaf

2 cups all-purpose flour
generous ¹/₂ cup
  superfine sugar
1 tablespoon baking
  powder
¹/₂ teaspoon salt
grated rind of 1 large
  orange

generous ²/₃ cup fresh
  orange juice
2 eggs, lightly beaten
6 tablespoons butter or
  margarine, melted
1 cup fresh cranberries or
  bilberries
¹/₂ cup chopped walnuts

1 Preheat the oven to 350°F. Line a 9 x 5-inch loaf pan with wax paper and grease the paper.

2 Sift the flour, sugar, baking powder and salt into a mixing bowl. Then stir in the orange rind. Make a well in the center and add the fresh orange juice, eggs and melted butter or margarine. Stir from the center until the ingredients are blended; do not overmix. Add the berries and walnuts and stir until blended.

3 Transfer the mixture to the prepared pan and bake until a skewer inserted in the center of the loaf comes out clean, about 45–50 minutes. Let cool in the pan for 10 minutes before transferring to a wire rack to cool completely.

Date and Pecan Loaf

Walnuts may be used instead of pecans to make this luxurious teabread.

Makes one 9 x 5-inch loaf

1 cup chopped pitted
  dates
³/₄ cup boiling water
4 tablespoons sweet
  butter, at room
  temperature
¹/₃ cup dark brown sugar
¹/₄ cup superfine sugar
1 egg, at room
  temperature

2 tablespoons brandy
generous ¹/₄ cup all-
  purpose flour
2 teaspoons baking
  powder
¹/₂ teaspoon salt
³/₄ teaspoon freshly grated
  nutmeg
³/₄ cup coarsely chopped
  pecans

1 Place the dates in a bowl and pour over the boiling water. Set aside to cool. Preheat the oven to 350°F. Line a 9 x 5-inch loaf pan with wax paper and then grease the paper.

2 With an electric mixer, cream the butter and sugars until light and fluffy. Beat in the egg and brandy, then set aside.

3 Sift the flour, baking powder, salt and nutmeg together, at least three times. Fold the dry ingredients into the sugar mixture in three batches, alternating with the dates and water. Fold in the nuts.

4 Pour the mixture into the prepared pan and bake until a skewer inserted in the center comes out clean, 45–50 minutes. Let the loaf cool in the pan for 10 minutes before transferring to a wire rack to cool completely.

Banana Nut Loaf

A hearty and filling loaf, this would be ideal as a winter teatime treat.

Makes one 9 x 5-inch loaf

$^1/_2$ cup butter, at room
temperature
generous $^1/_2$ cup
superfine sugar
2 eggs, at room
temperature
1 cup all-purpose flour
1 teaspoon baking soda

$^1/_4$ teaspoon salt
1 teaspoon ground
cinnamon
$^1/_2$ cup whole wheat flour
3 large ripe bananas
1 teaspoon vanilla
extract
$^1/_2$ cup chopped walnuts

1 Preheat the oven to 350°F. Line the bottom and sides of a 9 x 5-inch loaf pan with wax paper and grease the paper.

2 With an electric mixer, cream the butter and sugar together until light and fluffy. Add the eggs, one at a time, beating well after each addition.

3 Sift the all-purpose flour, baking soda, salt and cinnamon over the butter mixture and stir to blend. Then stir in the whole wheat flour.

4 With a fork, mash the bananas to a purée, then stir into the mixture. Stir in the vanilla and nuts.

5 Pour the mixture into the prepared pan and spread level. Bake until a skewer inserted in the center comes out clean, about 50–60 minutes. Let stand for 10 minutes before transferring to a wire rack to cool completely.

Apricot Nut Loaf

Apricots, raisins and walnuts combine to make a lovely light teabread.

Makes one 9 x 5-inch loaf

$^1/_2$ cup ready-to-eat dried
apricots
1 large orange
generous $^1/_2$ cup raisins
$^2/_3$ cup superfine sugar
$^1/_3$ cup oil
2 eggs, lightly beaten

generous 2 cups all-
purpose flour
2 teaspoons baking
powder
$^1/_2$ teaspoon salt
1 teaspoon baking soda
$^1/_2$ cup chopped walnuts

1 Place the apricots in a bowl, cover with lukewarm water and let stand for 30 minutes. Preheat the oven to 350°F. Line a 9 x 5-inch loaf pan with wax paper and grease the paper.

2 With a vegetable peeler, remove the orange rind, leaving the pith. Chop the strips finely.

3 Drain the apricots and chop coarsely. Place in a bowl with the orange rind and raisins. Squeeze the peeled orange. Measure the juice and add enough hot water to obtain ¾ cup liquid. Add the orange juice mixture to the apricot mixture. Stir in the sugar, oil and eggs. Set aside.

4 In another bowl, sift together the flour, baking powder, salt and baking soda. Fold the flour mixture into the apricot mixture in three batches, then stir in the walnuts.

5 Spoon the mixture into the prepared pan and bake until a skewer inserted in the center of the loaf comes out clean, about 55–60 minutes. If the loaf browns too quickly, protect the top with a sheet of foil. Cool in the tin for 10 minutes, then transfer to a wire rack to cool completely.

Bilberry Teabread

A lovely crumbly topping helps to make this teabread extra special.

Makes 8 pieces

4 tablespoons butter or
   margarine, at room
   temperature
¾ cup superfine sugar
1 egg, at room
   temperature
½ cup milk
2 cups all-purpose flour
2 teaspoons baking
   powder
½ teaspoon salt

¾ cup fresh bilberries, or
   blueberries

For the topping
½ cup sugar
⅓ cup all-purpose flour
½ teaspoon ground
   cinnamon
4 tablespoons butter, cut
   into pieces

1 Preheat the oven to 375°F. Grease a 9-inch baking dish.

2 With an electric mixer, cream the butter or margarine with the sugar until light and fluffy. Add the egg, beat to combine, then mix in the milk until well blended.

3 Sift over the flour, baking powder and salt and stir just enough to blend the ingredients. Add the berries and stir. Transfer to the baking dish.

4 For the topping, place the sugar, flour, cinnamon and butter in a mixing bowl. Cut in with a pastry blender until the mixture resembles coarse bread crumbs. Sprinkle the topping over the mixture in the baking dish. Bake until a skewer inserted in the center comes out clean, about 45 minutes. Serve warm or cold.

Dried Fruit Loaf

Use any combination of dried fruit you like in this delicious teabread.

Makes one 9 x 5-inch loaf

2¾ cups mixed dried
   fruit, such as
   currants, raisins,
   chopped dried apricots
   and dried cherries
1¼ cups cold strong tea
generous 1 cup dark
   brown sugar
grated rind and juice of 1
   small orange

grated rind and juice of 1
   lemon
1 egg, lightly beaten
1¾ cups all-purpose flour
1 tablespoon baking
   powder
¼ teaspoon salt

1 In a bowl, mix the dried fruit with the cold tea and let soak overnight.

2 Preheat the oven to 350°F. Line the bottom and sides of a 9 x 5-inch loaf pan with wax paper and grease the paper.

3 Strain the fruit, reserving the liquid. In a bowl, combine the sugar, orange and lemon rind, and fruit. Pour the orange and lemon juice into a measuring cup; if the quantity is less than 1 cup, then top up with the soaking liquid. Stir the citrus juices and egg into the dried fruit mixture.

4 Sift the flour, baking powder and salt together into another bowl. Stir into the fruit mixture until blended.

5 Transfer to the pan and bake until a skewer inserted in the center comes out clean; about 1¼ hours. Let sit in the pan for 10 minutes before unmolding.

Corn Bread

Serve this bread as an accompaniment to a meal, with soup, or take it on a picnic.

Makes one 9 x 5-inch loaf

1 cup all-purpose flour
generous ¼ cup
    superfine sugar
1 teaspoon salt
1 tablespoon baking
    powder
scant 1½ cups cornmeal
    or polenta

1½ cups milk
2 eggs
6 tablespoons butter,
    melted
½ cup margarine, melted

1 Preheat the oven to 400°F. Line a 9 x 5-inch loaf pan with wax paper and grease the paper.

2 Sift the flour, sugar, salt and baking powder into a mixing bowl. Add the cornmeal or polenta and stir to blend. Make a well in the center. Whisk together the milk, eggs, melted butter and margarine. Pour the mixture into the well. Stir until just blended; do not overmix.

3 Pour into the pan and bake until a skewer inserted in the center comes out clean, about 45 minutes. Serve hot or at room temperature.

Spicy Corn Bread

An interesting variation on basic corn bread; adjust the number of chilies used according to taste.

Makes 9 squares

3–4 whole canned chilies,
    drained
2 eggs
2 cups buttermilk
4 tablespoons butter,
    melted
½ cup all-purpose flour

1 teaspoon baking soda
2 teaspoons salt
scant 1½ cups cornmeal
    or polenta
2 cups corn, canned or
    frozen and defrosted

1 Preheat the oven to 400°F. Line the bottom and sides of a 9-inch square cake pan with wax paper. Grease the paper.

2 With a sharp knife, finely chop the canned chilies and set aside until needed.

3 In a large bowl, whisk the eggs until frothy, then whisk in the buttermilk. Add the melted butter.

4 Sift the flour, baking soda and salt together into another large bowl. Fold into the buttermilk mixture in three batches, then fold in the cornmeal or polenta in three batches. Finally, fold in the chilies and corn.

5 Pour the mixture into the pan and bake until a skewer inserted in the center comes out clean, about 25–30 minutes. Leave in the pan for 2–3 minutes before unmolding. Cut into squares and serve warm.

Sweet Sesame Loaf

Lemon and sesame seeds make a great partnership in this light teabread.

Makes one 9 x 5-inch loaf

6 tablespoons sesame seeds
2½ cups all-purpose flour
2½ teaspoons baking powder
1 teaspoon salt
4 tablespoons butter or margarine, at room temperature

scant ⅔ cup sugar
2 eggs, at room temperature
grated rind of 1 lemon
1½ cups milk

1 Preheat the oven to 350°F. Line a 9 x 5-inch loaf pan with wax paper and then grease the paper.

2 Reserve 2 tablespoons of the sesame seeds. Spread the rest on a baking sheet and bake in the oven until lightly toasted, about 10 minutes.

3 Sift the flour, baking powder and salt into a bowl. Stir in the toasted sesame seeds and set aside.

4 Cream the butter or margarine and sugar together until light and fluffy. Beat in the eggs, then stir in the lemon rind and milk. Pour the milk mixture over the dry ingredients and fold in with a large metal spoon until just blended.

5 Pour into the pan and sprinkle over the reserved sesame seeds. Bake until a skewer inserted in the center comes out clean, about 1 hour. Cool in the pan for 10 minutes. Turn out onto a wire rack to cool completely.

Cardamom and Saffron Tea Loaf

An aromatic sweet bread ideal for an afternoon snack, or lightly toasted for breakfast.

Makes one 2-pound loaf

generous pinch of saffron strands
3 cups lukewarm milk
2 tablespoons butter
8 cups all-purpose bread flour
2 envelopes fast-rising dried yeast

3 tablespoons superfine sugar
6 cardamom pods, split open and seeds extracted
scant ¾ cup raisins
2 tablespoons honey
1 egg, beaten

1 Crush the saffron straight into a cup containing a little of the warm milk and leave to infuse for 5 minutes. Rub the butter into the flour, then mix in the yeast, sugar, cardamom seeds and raisins.

2 Beat the remaining milk with the honey and egg, then mix this into the flour, along with the saffron milk and strands, to form a firm dough. Turn out the dough and knead it on a lightly floured surface for 5 minutes.

3 Return the dough to the mixing bowl, cover with oiled plastic wrap and let sit in a warm place until doubled in size.

4 Preheat the oven to 400°F. Grease 2-pound loaf pan. Turn the dough out onto a floured surface, punch down, knead for 3 minutes, then shape into a fat roll and fit into the pan. Cover with a sheet of lightly oiled plastic wrap and let stand in a warm place until the dough begins to rise again.

5 Bake the loaf for 25 minutes until golden brown and firm on top. Turn out onto a wire rack, and as it cools brush the top with honey.

Zucchini Teabread

Like carrots, zucchini are a vegetable that work well in baking, adding moistness and lightness to the bread.

Makes one 9 x 5-inch loaf

4 tablespoons butter	1 teaspoon salt
3 eggs	1 teaspoon ground
1 cup vegetable oil	cinnamon
1½ cups sugar	1 teaspoon grated
2 unpeeled zucchini,	nutmeg
grated	¼ teaspoon ground
2½ cups all-purpose	cloves
flour	1 cup chopped walnuts
2 teaspoons baking soda	
1 teaspoon baking	
powder	

1 Preheat the oven to 350°F. Line the bottom and sides of a 9 x 5-inch loaf pan with wax paper and grease the paper.

2 In a saucepan, melt the butter over low heat. Set aside until needed.

3 With an electric mixer, beat the eggs and oil together until thick. Beat in the sugar, then stir in the melted butter and the zucchini. Set aside.

4 In another bowl, sift all the dry ingredients together three times. Carefully fold into the zucchini mixture. Fold in the chopped walnuts.

5 Pour into the pan and bake until a skewer inserted in the center comes out clean, about 60–70 minutes. Let stand for 10 minutes before turning out onto a wire rack to cool.

Mango Teabread

A delicious teabread with an exotic slant – baked with juicy, ripe mango.

Makes two 9 x 5-inch loaves

2½ cups all-purpose	1½ cups sugar
flour	½ cup vegetable oil
2 teaspoons baking soda	1 large ripe mango,
2 teaspoons ground	peeled and chopped
cinnamon	generous 1½ cups dried
½ teaspoon salt	coconut
½ cup margarine, at	½ cup raisins
room temperature	
3 eggs, at room	
temperature	

1 Preheat the oven to 350°F. Line the bottom and sides of two 9 x 5-inch loaf pans with wax paper and grease the paper.

2 Sift together the flour, baking soda, cinnamon and salt. Set aside until needed.

3 Cream the margarine until soft. Beat in the eggs and sugar until light and fluffy. Beat in the oil.

4 Fold the dry ingredients into the creamed ingredients in three batches, then fold in the mango, two-thirds of the coconut and the raisins.

5 Spoon the batter into the pans. Sprinkle over the remaining coconut. Bake until a skewer inserted in the center comes out clean, about 50–60 minutes. Let stand for 10 minutes before turning out onto a wire rack to cool.

Cornsticks

If you don't have a cornstick mold, use éclair pans or a muffin tray and reduce the cooking time by 10 minutes.

Makes 6

1 egg
¹/₂ cup milk
1 tablespoon vegetable oil
scant 1 cup cornmeal or polenta

¹/₂ cup all-purpose flour
2 teaspoons baking powder
3 tablespoons superfine sugar

1 Preheat the oven to 375°F. Grease a cast-iron cornstick mold.

2 Beat the egg in a small bowl. Stir in the milk and vegetable oil, and set aside.

3 In a mixing bowl, stir together the cornmeal or polenta, flour, baking powder and sugar. Pour in the egg mixture and stir with a wooden spoon to combine.

4 Spoon the mixture into the prepared mold. Bake until a skewer inserted in the center of a cornstick comes out clean, about 25 minutes. Cool in the mold on a wire rack for 10 minutes before unmolding.

Savory Corn Bread

For a spicy bread, stir ½ tablespoon chopped fresh chilies into the mixture with the cheese and corn.

Makes 9

2 eggs, lightly beaten
1 cup buttermilk
1 cup all-purpose flour
scant 1 cup cornmeal or polenta
2 teaspoons baking powder

¹/₂ teaspoon salt
1 tablespoon superfine sugar
1 cup Cheddar cheese, grated
1¹/₃ cups corn, fresh, or frozen and defrosted

1 Preheat the oven to 400°F. Grease a 9-inch square baking pan.

2 Combine the eggs and buttermilk in a small bowl and whisk until well mixed. Set aside.

3 In another bowl, stir together the flour, cornmeal or polenta, baking powder, salt and sugar. Add the egg mixture and stir with a wooden spoon to combine. Stir in the cheese and corn.

4 Pour the mixture into the baking pan. Bake until a skewer inserted in the center comes out clean, about 25 minutes. Unmold the bread onto a wire rack and let cool. Cut into squares before serving.

Herb Popovers

Popovers are delicious when flavored with herbs, and are good served as a snack or appetizer.

Makes 12

3 eggs
1 cup milk
2 tablespoons butter,
  melted
³/₄ cup all-purpose flour

¹/₄ teaspoon salt
1 small sprig each mixed
  fresh herbs, such as
  chives, tarragon, dill
  and parsley

1 Preheat the oven to 425°F. Grease 12 small ramekins or individual baking cups.

2 With an electric mixer, beat the eggs until blended. Beat in the milk and melted butter. Sift together the flour and salt, then beat into the egg mixture to combine thoroughly.

3 Strip the herb leaves from the stems and chop finely. Mix together and measure out 2 tablespoons. Stir the measured herbs into the batter.

4 Half-fill the prepared ramekins or baking cups. Bake until golden; 25–30 minutes. Do not open the oven door during baking time or the popovers may collapse. For drier popovers, pierce each one with a knife after 30 minutes baking time and then bake for 5 minutes more. Serve the herb popovers hot.

Cheese Popovers

Serve these popovers simply as an accompaniment to a meal, or make a filling and serve them as an appetizer.

Makes 12

3 eggs
1 cup milk
2 tablespoons butter,
  melted
³/₄ cup all-purpose flour

¹/₄ teaspoon salt
¹/₄ teaspoon paprika
¹/₃ cup freshly grated
  Parmesan cheese

1 Preheat the oven to 425°F. Grease 12 small ramekins or individual baking cups.

2 With an electric mixer, beat the eggs until blended. Beat in the milk and melted butter. Sift together the flour, salt and paprika, then beat into the egg mixture. Add the Parmesan cheese and stir in.

3 Half-fill the prepared cups and bake until golden, about 25–30 minutes. Do not open the oven door or the popovers may collapse. For drier popovers, pierce each one with a knife after about 30 minutes baking time and then bake for 5 minutes more. Serve hot.

Sweet Potato and Raisin Bread

Serve buttered slices of this subtly-spiced loaf at coffee or tea time.

Makes one 2-pound loaf

3 cups all-purpose flour
2 teaspoons baking powder
½ teaspoon salt
1 teaspoon ground cinnamon
½ teaspoon grated nutmeg

1 pound mashed cooked sweet potato
3½ oz light brown sugar
½ cup butter or margarine, melted and cooled
3 eggs, beaten
generous ½ cup raisins

1 Preheat the oven to 350°F. Grease a 2-pound loaf pan.

2 Sift the flour, baking powder, salt, cinnamon, and nutmeg into a small bowl. Set aside.

3 With an electric mixer, beat the mashed sweet potato with the sugar, butter or margarine, and eggs until well mixed.

4 Add the flour mixture and the raisins. Stir with a wooden spoon until the flour is just mixed in.

5 Transfer the batter to the prepared pan. Bake until a skewer inserted in the center of the loaf comes out clean, about 1–1¼ hours.

6 Let the bread cool in the pan on a wire rack for 15 minutes, then unmold onto the wire rack and let cool completely.

Lemon and Walnut Teabread

Beaten egg whites give this citrus-flavor loaf a lovely light and crumbly texture.

Makes one 9 x 5-inch loaf

½ cup butter or margarine, at room temperature
½ cup sugar
2 eggs, at room temperature, separated
grated rind of 2 lemons
2 tablespoons lemon juice

scant 2 cups all-purpose flour
2 teaspoons baking powder
½ cup milk
½ cup chopped walnuts
¼ teaspoon salt

1 Preheat the oven to 350°F. Line a 9 x 5-inch loaf pan with wax paper and grease the paper.

2 Cream the butter or margarine with the sugar until light and fluffy. Beat in the egg yolks. Add the lemon rind and juice and stir until blended. Set aside.

3 In another bowl, sift together the flour and baking powder three times. Fold into the butter mixture in three batches, alternating with the milk. Fold in the walnuts. Set aside.

4 Beat the egg whites and salt until stiff peaks form. Fold a large spoonful of the egg whites into the walnut mixture to lighten it. Fold in the remaining egg whites carefully until the mixture is just blended.

5 Pour the batter into the prepared pan and bake until a skewer inserted in the center of the loaf comes out clean, about 45–50 minutes. Cool in the pan for 5 minutes before turning out onto a wire rack to cool completely.

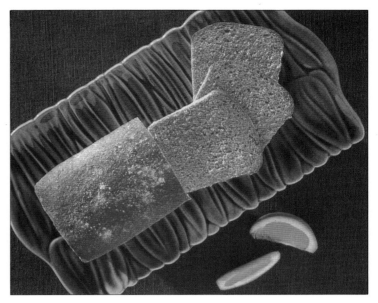

Date and Nut Maltloaf

Choose any type of nut you like to include in this very rich and fruit-packed teabread.

Makes two 1-pound loaves

2 cups all-purpose bread
  flour
2 cups plain whole wheat
  bread flour
1 teaspoon salt
6 tablespoons brown
  sugar
1 envelope fast-rising
  dried yeast
4 tablespoons butter or
  margarine

1 tablespoon molasses
4 tablespoons malt
  extract
1 cup lukewarm milk
½ cup chopped dates
½ cup chopped nuts
generous ½ cup golden
  raisins
generous ½ cup raisins
2 tablespoons honey, to
  glaze

1 Sift the flours and salt into a large bowl, then add the wheat flakes from the strainer. Stir in the sugar and yeast.

2 Put the butter or margarine in a small pan with the molasses and malt extract. Stir over low heat until melted. Let cool, then combine with the milk.

3 Stir the milk mixture into the dry ingredients and knead thoroughly for 15 minutes until the dough is elastic.

4 Knead in the fruits and nuts. Transfer the dough to an oiled bowl, cover with plastic wrap and let sit in a warm place for about 1½ hours, until the dough has doubled in size.

5 Grease two 1-pound loaf pans. Knock back the dough and knead lightly. Divide in half, form into loaves and place in the pans. Cover and let sit in a warm place for 30 minutes, until risen. Meanwhile, preheat the oven to 375°F.

6 Bake for 35–40 minutes, until well risen. Cool on a wire rack. Brush with honey while warm.

Orange Wheatloaf

Perfect just with butter as a breakfast teabread and lovely for banana sandwiches.

Makes one 1-pound loaf

2¼ cups whole wheat all-
  purpose flour
½ teaspoon salt
2 tablespoons butter
2 tablespoons light
  brown sugar

½ envelope fast-rising
  dried yeast
grated rind and juice of
  ½ orange

1 Sift the flour into a large bowl and return any wheat flakes from the strainer. Add the salt, and rub in the butter lightly with your fingertips.

2 Stir in the sugar, yeast and orange rind. Pour the orange juice into a measuring cup and use hot water to make up to scant 1 cup (the liquid should not be more than hand hot).

3 Stir the liquid into the flour and mix to a soft ball of dough. Knead gently on a lightly floured surface until quite smooth and elastic.

4 Place the dough in a greased 1-pound loaf pan and let sit in a warm place until nearly doubled in size. Preheat the oven to 425°F.

5 Bake the bread for 30–35 minutes, or until it sounds hollow when tapped underneath. Turn out of the pan and cool on a wire rack.

Orange and Honey Teabread

Honey gives a special flavor to this teabread. Serve just with a scraping of butter.

Makes one 9 x 5-inch loaf

scant 3¹/₂ cups all-purpose flour
2¹/₂ teaspoons baking powder
¹/₂ teaspoon baking soda
¹/₂ teaspoon salt
2 tablespoons margarine
1 cup honey
1 egg, at room temperature, lightly beaten
1¹/₂ tablespoons grated orange rind
³/₄ cup freshly squeezed orange juice
1 cup chopped walnuts

1 Preheat the oven to 325°F. Line the bottom and sides of a 9 x 5-inch loaf pan with wax paper and grease the paper.

2 Sift the flour, baking powder, baking soda and salt together in a bowl.

3 Cream the margarine until soft. Stir in the honey until blended, then stir in the egg. Add the orange rind and stir to combine thoroughly.

4 Fold the flour mixture into the honey and egg mixture in three batches, alternating with the orange juice. Stir in the chopped walnuts.

5 Pour into the prepared pan and bake in the oven until a skewer inserted in the center comes out clean, about 60–70 minutes. Let sit for 10 minutes before turning out onto a wire rack to cool completely.

Apple Loaf

Ring the changes with this loaf by using different nuts and dried fruit.

Makes one 9 x 5-inch loaf

1 egg
1 cup bottled or homemade apple sauce
4 tablespoons butter or margarine, melted
scant ³/₄ cup dark brown sugar
scant ¹/₄ cup superfine sugar
2¹/₂ cups all-purpose flour
2 teaspoons baking powder
¹/₂ teaspoon baking soda
¹/₂ teaspoon salt
1 teaspoon ground cinnamon
¹/₂ teaspoon grated nutmeg
¹/₂ cup currants or raisins
¹/₂ cup pecans or walnuts, chopped

1 Preheat the oven to 350°F. Line the bottom and sides of a 9 x 5-inch loaf pan with wax paper and grease the paper.

2 Break the egg into a bowl and beat lightly. Stir in the apple sauce, butter or margarine and both sugars. Set aside.

3 In another bowl, sift together the flour, baking powder, baking soda, salt, cinnamon and nutmeg. Fold the dry ingredients, including the currants or raisins and the nuts, into the apple sauce mixture in three batches.

4 Pour into the prepared pan and bake in the oven until a skewer inserted in the center of the loaf comes out clean, about 1 hour. Let stand in the pan for 10 minutes, then turn out onto a wire rack to cool completely.

Fruit and Brazil Nut Teabread

Mashed bananas are a classic ingredient in teabreads, and help to create a moist texture.

Makes one 9 x 5-inch loaf

2 cups all-purpose flour
2 teaspoons baking
  powder
1 teaspoon mixed spice
½ cup butter, diced
¾ cup light brown sugar
2 eggs, lightly beaten
2 tablespoons milk
2 tablespoons dark rum
2 bananas, peeled and
  mashed

½ cup dried figs, chopped
½ cup brazil nuts,
  chopped

To decorate
8 whole brazil nuts
4 whole dried figs, halved
2 tablespoons apricot jam
1 teaspoon dark rum

1 Preheat the oven to 350°F. Grease and line the bottom of a 9 x 5-inch loaf pan. Sift the flour, baking powder and mixed spice into a bowl. Rub in the butter until the mixture resembles fine bread crumbs. Stir in the sugar.

2 Make a well in the center and work in the eggs, milk and rum until combined. Stir in the remaining ingredients and transfer to the loaf pan.

3 Press the whole brazil nuts and halved figs gently into the mixture, to form an attractive pattern. Bake for 1¼ hours, or until a skewer inserted in the center comes out clean. Cool in the pan for 10 minutes, then transfer to a wire rack.

4 Heat the jam and rum together in a small saucepan. Increase the heat and boil for 1 minute. Remove from the heat and pass through a fine strainer. Cool the glaze slightly, brush over the warm cake, and let cool completely.

Glazed Banana Spiced Loaf

The lemony glaze perfectly sets off the flavors in this banana teabread.

Makes one 9 x 5-inch loaf

½ cup butter, at room
  temperature
generous ⅔ cup superfine
  sugar
2 eggs, at room
  temperature
scant 2 cups all-purpose
  flour
1 teaspoon salt
1 teaspoon baking soda
½ teaspoon grated
  nutmeg
¼ teaspoon mixed spice

¼ teaspoon ground
  cloves
¾ cup sour cream
1 large ripe banana,
  mashed
1 teaspoon vanilla
  extract

For the glaze
1 cup confectioner's
  sugar
1–2 tablespoons lemon
  juice

1 Preheat the oven to 350°F. Line a 9 x 5-inch loaf pan with wax paper and grease the paper.

2 Cream the butter and sugar until light and fluffy. Add the eggs, one at a time, beating well after each addition.

3 Sift together the flour, salt, baking soda, nutmeg, mixed spice and cloves. Add to the butter mixture and stir to combine well. Add the sour cream, banana and vanilla and mix to just blend. Pour into the prepared pan.

4 Bake until the top springs back when touched lightly, about 45–50 minutes. Cool in the pan for 10 minutes. Turn out onto a wire rack.

5 For the glaze, combine the confectioner's sugar and lemon juice, then stir until smooth. Place the cooled loaf on a rack set over a baking sheet. Pour the glaze over and let set.

Banana Bread

For a change, add ½–¾ cup chopped walnuts with the dry ingredients or pecans.

Makes one 8½ x 4½-inch loaf

1³/₄ cups all-purpose flour
2¹/₄ teaspoons baking powder
¹/₂ teaspoon salt
³/₄ teaspoon ground cinnamon (optional)
4 tablespoons wheatgerm
5 tablespoons butter, at room temperature
generous ¹/₂ cup superfine sugar
³/₄ teaspoon grated lemon rind
3 ripe bananas, mashed
2 eggs, beaten

1 Preheat the oven to 350°F. Grease and flour an 8½ x 4½-inch loaf pan.

2 Sift the flour, baking powder, salt and cinnamon, if using, into a bowl. Stir in the wheatgerm.

3 In another bowl, combine the butter with the superfine sugar and grated lemon rind. Beat thoroughly until the mixture is light and fluffy.

4 Add the mashed bananas and eggs, and mix well. Add the dry ingredients and blend quickly and evenly.

5 Spoon into the loaf pan. Bake for 50–60 minutes or until a wooden skewer inserted in the center comes out clean. Cool in the pan for 5 minutes, then turn out onto a wire rack to cool completely.

Banana Orange Loaf

For the best banana flavor and a really good, moist texture, make sure the bananas are ripe for this cake.

Makes one 9 x 5-inch loaf

generous ²/₃ cup whole wheat all-purpose flour
generous ³/₄ cup all-purpose flour
1 teaspoon baking powder
1 teaspoon ground mixed spice
3 tablespoons slivered hazelnuts, toasted
2 large ripe bananas
1 egg
2 tablespoons sunflower oil
2 tablespoons honey
finely grated rind and juice of 1 small orange
4 orange slices, halved
2 teaspoons confectioner's sugar

1 Preheat the oven to 350°F. Brush a 9 x 5-inch loaf pan with oil and line the bottom with nonstick parchment paper.

2 Sift the flours with the baking powder and spice into a large bowl, adding any bran that is caught in the strainer. Stir the hazelnuts into the dry ingredients.

3 Peel and mash the bananas. Beat in the egg, oil, honey and the orange rind and juice. Stir evenly into the dry ingredients.

4 Spoon into the prepared pan and smooth the top. Bake for 40–45 minutes, or until firm and golden brown. Turn out onto a wire rack to cool.

5 Sprinkle the orange slices with the confectioner's sugar and broil until golden. Use to decorate the cake.

Marmalade Teabread

If you prefer, leave the top of the loaf plain and serve sliced and lightly buttered instead.

Makes one 8½ x 4½-inch loaf

1¾ cups all-purpose flour
1 teaspoon baking
    powder
1¼ teaspoon ground
    cinnamon
7 tablespoons butter or
    margarine
⅓ cup light brown sugar

4 tablespoons chunky
    orange marmalade
1 egg, beaten
about 3 tablespoons milk
4 tablespoons glacé icing
    and shreds of orange
    and lemon rind,
    to decorate

1 Preheat the oven to 325°F. Butter an 8½ x 4½-inch loaf pan, then line the bottom with wax paper. Grease the paper.

2 Sift the flour, baking powder and cinnamon together, toss in the butter or margarine, then rub in until the mixture resembles coarse bread crumbs. Stir in the sugar.

3 In a separate bowl, mix together the marmalade, egg and most of the milk, then stir into the flour mixture to make a soft dropping consistency, adding more milk, if necessary.

4 Transfer the mixture to the pan and bake for 1¼ hours, or until firm to the touch. Let the cake cool for 5 minutes, then turn onto a wire rack, peel off the lining paper, and let cool.

5 Drizzle the icing over the top of the cake and decorate with the orange and lemon rind.

Cherry Marmalade Muffins

Purists say you should never serve a muffin cold, so enjoy these fresh from the oven.

Makes 12

2 cups self-rising flour
1 teaspoon ground mixed
    spice
scant ½ cup superfine
    sugar
½ cup candied cherries,
    quartered

2 tablespoons orange
    marmalade
⅔ cup milk
4 tablespoons sunflower
    margarine
marmalade, to glaze

1 Preheat the oven to 400°F. Lightly grease 12 deep muffin cups with oil.

2 Sift together the flour and spice, then stir in the sugar and candied cherries.

3 Mix the marmalade with the milk and beat into the dry ingredients with the margarine. Spoon into the greased cups. Bake for 20–25 minutes, until golden brown and firm. Turn out onto a wire rack and brush the tops of the muffins with warmed marmalade.

Spiced Date and Walnut Cake

Nuts and dates are a classic flavor combination. Use pecans instead of walnuts, if you wish.

Makes one 2-pound cake

2³/₄ cups whole wheat
   self-rising flour
2 teaspoons mixed spice
generous ³/₄ cup chopped
   dates
¹/₂ cup chopped walnuts
4 tablespoons sunflower
   oil

³/₄ cup dark muscovado
   sugar
1¹/₄ cups milk
walnut halves, to
   decorate

1   Preheat the oven to 350°F. Line a 2-pound loaf pan with wax paper and grease the paper.

2   Sift together the flour and spice, adding back any bran from the strainer. Stir in the dates and walnuts.

3   Mix the oil, sugar and milk, then stir evenly into the dry ingredients. Spoon into the loaf pan and arrange the walnut halves on top.

4   Bake the cake in the oven for about 45–50 minutes, or until golden brown and firm. Turn out the cake, remove the lining paper, and let cool on a wire rack.

Prune and Peel Rock Buns

The fruit content of these buns gives them plenty of flavor – and they're a low fat option, too!

Makes 12

2 cups all-purpose flour
2 teaspoons baking
   powder
¹/₂ cup raw sugar
¹/₂ cup chopped ready-to-
   eat dried prunes

¹/₃ cup chopped mixed
   candied peel
finely grated rind of
   1 lemon
¹/₄ cup sunflower oil
5 tablespoons skim milk

1   Preheat the oven to 400°F. Lightly oil a large baking sheet. Sift together the flour and baking powder, then stir in the sugar, prunes, peel and lemon rind.

2   Mix the oil and milk, then stir into the mixture, to make a dough which just binds together.

3   Spoon into rocky heaps on the baking sheet and bake for 20 minutes, until golden. Let cool on a wire rack.

Raisin Bran Buns

Serve these buns warm or at room temperature, on their own, with butter, or with cream cheese.

Makes 15

4 tablespoons butter or
   margarine
$^1/_3$ cup all-purpose flour
$^1/_2$ cup whole wheat flour
$1^1/_2$ teaspoons baking soda
$^1/_4$ teaspoon salt
1 teaspoon ground
   cinnamon

generous 1 cup bran
generous $^1/_2$ cup raisins
scant $^1/_2$ cup dark brown
   sugar
$^1/_4$ cup superfine sugar
1 egg
1 cup buttermilk
juice of $^1/_2$ lemon

1 Preheat the oven to 400°F. Lightly grease 15 muffin cups. Put the butter or margarine in a saucepan and melt over gentle heat. Set aside.

2 In a mixing bowl, sift together the flours, baking soda, salt and cinnamon. Add the bran, raisins and sugars and then stir until blended.

3 In another bowl, mix together the egg, buttermilk, lemon juice and melted butter. Add the buttermilk mixture to the dry ingredients and stir in lightly and quickly until just moistened. Do not mix until smooth.

4 Spoon the mixture into the prepared muffin cups, filling them almost to the top. Half-fill any empty cups with water. Bake until golden, about 15–20 minutes. Remove to a wire rack to cool slightly, or serve immediately.

Raspberry Crumble Buns

The crumble topping adds an unusual twist to these lovely fruit buns.

Makes 12

$1^1/_2$ cups all-purpose
   flour
$^1/_4$ cup superfine sugar
scant $^1/_3$ cup light brown
   sugar
2 teaspoons baking
   powder
$^1/_4$ teaspoon salt
1 teaspoon ground
   cinnamon
$^1/_2$ cup butter, melted
1 egg
$^1/_2$ cup milk
$^3/_4$ cup fresh raspberries
grated rind of 1 lemon

For the crumble topping

$^1/_4$ cup finely chopped
   pecans or walnuts
$^1/_3$ cup dark brown sugar
3 tablespoons all-purpose
   flour
1 teaspoon ground
   cinnamon
3 tablespoons butter,
   melted

1 Preheat the oven to 350°F. Lightly grease 12 muffin cups or use 12 paper cases. Sift the flour into a bowl. Add the sugars, baking powder, salt and cinnamon, and stir to blend.

2 Make a well in the center. Place the butter, egg and milk in the well and mix until just combined. Stir in the raspberries and lemon rind. Spoon the mixture into the prepared cups, filling them almost to the top.

3 For the crumble topping, mix the nuts, dark brown sugar, flour and cinnamon in a bowl. Add the melted butter and stir to blend.

4 Spoon some of the crumble over each bun. Bake until browned, about 25 minutes. Transfer to a wire rack to cool slightly. Serve warm.

Banana and Pecan Muffins

As a variation on this recipe, substitute an equal quantity of walnuts for the pecans.

Makes 8

1¼ cups all-purpose flour
1½ teaspoons baking
   powder
4 tablespoons butter or
   margarine, at room
   temperature
¾ cup superfine sugar

1 egg
1 teaspoon vanilla
   extract
3 bananas, mashed
½ cup pecans, chopped
5 tablespoons milk

1 Preheat the oven to 375°F. Lightly grease eight deep muffin cups. Sift the flour and baking powder into a bowl. Set aside.

2 With an electric mixer, cream the butter or margarine and sugar together. Add the egg and vanilla and beat until fluffy. Mix in the banana.

3 Add the pecans. With the mixer on low speed, beat in the flour mixture alternately with the milk.

4 Spoon the mixture into the prepared muffin cups, filling them two-thirds full. Bake until golden brown and a skewer inserted into the center of a muffin comes out clean, about 20–25 minutes.

5 Let the muffins cool in the cups on a wire rack for about 10 minutes. To loosen, run a knife gently around each muffin and unmold onto the wire rack. Let cool 10 minutes more before serving.

Blueberry and Cinnamon Muffins

These moist and "moreish" muffins appeal equally to adults and children.

Makes 8

1 cup all-purpose flour
1 tablespoon baking
   powder
pinch of salt
¼ cup light brown sugar
1 egg
¾ cup milk

3 tablespoons vegetable
   oil
2 teaspoons ground
   cinnamon
⅔ cup fresh or frozen and
   defrosted blueberries

1 Preheat the oven to 375°F. Lightly grease eight deep muffin cups.

2 With an electric mixer, beat the first eight ingredients together until smooth. Fold in the blueberries.

3 Spoon the mixture into the muffin cups, filling them two-thirds full. Bake until a skewer inserted in the center of a muffin comes out clean, about 25 minutes.

4 Let the muffins cool in the cups on a wire rack for about 10 minutes, then unmold them onto the wire rack and allow to cool completely. Serve slightly warm.

Carrot Buns

Carrots give these buns a lovely moist consistency, and a delightful taste too.

Makes 12

³/₄ cup margarine, at room temperature
generous ¹/₂ cup dark brown sugar
1 egg, at room temperature
1 tablespoon water
1¹/₂ cups grated carrots
1¹/₄ cups all-purpose flour
1 teaspoon baking powder
¹/₂ teaspoon baking soda
1 teaspoon ground cinnamon
¹/₄ teaspoon grated nutmeg
¹/₂ teaspoon salt

1 Preheat the oven to 350°F. Grease a 12-cup muffin tray or use paper cases.

2 With an electric mixer, cream the margarine and sugar until light and fluffy. Beat in the egg and water, then stir in the carrots.

3 Sift over the flour, baking powder, baking soda, cinnamon, nutmeg and salt. Stir to blend.

4 Spoon the mixture into the prepared muffin tray, filling the cups almost to the top. Bake until the tops spring back when touched lightly, about 35 minutes. Let stand for about 10 minutes in the tray before transferring to a wire rack to cool completely.

Dried Cherry Buns

Dried cherries have a wonderful tart flavor, quite unlike candied cherries.

Makes 16

1 cup plain yogurt
³/₄ cup dried cherries
¹/₂ cup butter, at room temperature
generous ³/₄ cup superfine sugar
2 eggs, at room temperature
1 teaspoon vanilla extract
generous 1³/₄ cups all-purpose flour
2 teaspoons baking powder
1 teaspoon baking soda
¹/₄ teaspoon salt

1 In a mixing bowl, combine the yogurt and cherries. Cover and let stand for 30 minutes. Preheat the oven to 350°F. Grease 16 muffin cups or use paper cases.

2 With an electric mixer, cream the butter and sugar together until light and fluffy. Add the eggs, one at a time, beating well after each addition. Add the vanilla and the cherry mixture and stir to blend. Set aside.

3 In another bowl, sift together the flour, baking powder, baking soda and salt. Fold into the cherry mixture in three batches.

4 Fill the prepared cups two-thirds full. For even baking, half-fill any empty cups with water. Bake until the tops spring back when touched lightly, about 20 minutes. Transfer to a wire rack to cool completely.

Chelsea Buns

A traditional English recipe, Chelsea buns enjoy wide popularity elsewhere in the world.

Makes 12
2 cups white bread flour
½ teaspoon salt
3 tablespoons sweet
    butter
1½ teaspoons fast-rising
    dried yeast
½ cup milk

1 egg, beaten
½ cup mixed dried fruit
2½ tablespoons chopped
    mixed candied peel
⅓ cup light brown sugar
honey, to glaze

1 Preheat the oven to 375°F. Grease a 7-inch square pan. Sift together the flour and salt; rub in 2 tablespoons of the butter.

2 Stir in the yeast and make a central well. Slowly add the milk and egg, stirring, then beat until the dough leaves the sides of the bowl clean.

3 Knead the dough until smooth. Place in an oiled bowl, cover and set aside until doubled in size. Transfer to a floured surface and roll it out to a rectangle 12 x 9 inches.

4 Mix the dried fruits, peel and sugar. Melt the remaining butter and brush over the dough. Sprinkle the fruit mixture, over the top leaving a 1-inch border. Roll up the dough from a long side. Seal the edges, then cut into 12 slices.

5 Place the slices, cut-sides up, in the greased pan. Cover and set aside until doubled in size. Bake for 30 minutes, until a rich golden brown. Brush with honey and let cool slightly in the pan before turning out.

Sticky Nut Buns

These buns will be popular, so save time by making double the recipe and freezing half for another occasion.

Makes 12
generous ⅔ cup
    lukewarm milk
1 tablespoon fast-rising
    dried yeast
2 tablespoons superfine
    sugar
4 cups white bread flour
1 teaspoon salt
½ cup cold butter, cut
    into small pieces
2 eggs, lightly beaten
finely grated rind of 1
    lemon

For the topping and filling
1¾ cups dark brown
    sugar
5 tablespoons butter
½ cup water
¾ cup chopped pecans or
    walnuts
3 tablespoons superfine
    sugar
2 teaspoons ground
    cinnamon
generous 1 cup raisins

1 Preheat the oven to 350°F. Mix the milk, yeast and sugar and leave until frothy. Combine the flour and salt, and rub in the butter. Add the yeast mixture, eggs and lemon rind. Stir to a rough dough. Knead until smooth, then return to the bowl, cover and let stand until doubled in size.

2 Cook the brown sugar, butter and water in a heavy-bottomed saucepan until syrupy, about 10 minutes. Place 1 tablespoon syrup in the bottom of 12 ½-inch muffin cups. Sprinkle a thin layer of nuts in each, reserving the remainder.

3 Punch down the dough; roll out to an 18 x 12-inch rectangle. Combine the superfine sugar, cinnamon, raisins and reserved nuts. Sprinkle over the dough. Roll up tightly from a long edge and cut into 1-inch rounds. Place in the muffin cups, cut-sides up. Let rise for 30 minutes.

4 Bake until golden, about 25 minutes. Invert the pans onto a baking sheet, let stand for 5 minutes, then remove the pans. Cool on a wire rack, sticky-sides up.

Oatmeal Buttermilk Muffins

Makes 12

1 cup rolled oats
1 cup buttermilk
¹/₂ cup butter, at room
    temperature
¹/₂ cup dark brown sugar,
    firmly packed
1 egg, at room
    temperature

1 cup all-purpose flour
1 teaspoon baking
    powder
¹/₄ teaspoon baking soda
¹/₄ cup raisins

1 In a bowl, combine the oats and buttermilk and let soak for 1 hour.

2 Grease a 12-cup muffin pan or use paper cases.

3 Preheat the oven to 400°F. With an electric mixer, cream the butter and sugar until light and fluffy. Beat in the egg.

4 In another bowl, sift together the flour, baking powder, baking soda, and salt. Stir into the butter mixture, alternating with the oat mixture. Fold in the raisins. Do not overmix.

5 Fill the prepared cups two-thirds full. Bake until a cake tester inserted in the center comes out clean, 20–25 minutes. Transfer to a rack to cool.

Pumpkin Muffins

Makes 14

²/₃ cup butter or
    margarine, at room
    temperature
³/₄ cup dark brown sugar
¹/₃ cup molasses
1 egg, at room
    temperature, beaten
1 cup cooked or canned
    pumpkin

1³/₄ cups all-purpose flour
¹/₄ teaspoon salt
1 teaspoon baking soda
1 teaspoon ground
    cinnamon
1 teaspoon grated
    nutmeg
¹/₄ cup currants or raisins

1 Preheat the oven to 400°F. Grease 14 muffin cups or use paper cases.

2 With an electric mixer, cream the butter or margarine. Add the sugar and molasses and beat until light and fluffy.

3 Add the egg and pumpkin and stir until well blended.

4 Sift over the flour, salt, baking soda, cinnamon, and nutmeg. Fold just enough to blend; do not overmix.

5 Fold in the currants or raisins.

6 Spoon the batter into the prepared muffin cups, filling them three-quarters full.

7 Bake for 12–15 minutes until the tops spring back when touched lightly. Serve warm or cold.

Blueberry Muffins

Hot blueberry muffins with a hint of vanilla are a favorite for breakfast, brunch or tea.

Makes 12

3 cups all-purpose flour
2 teaspoons baking
    powder
$^1/_4$ teaspoon salt
$^1/_2$ cup superfine sugar
2 eggs, beaten

$1^1/_4$ cups milk
$^1/_2$ cup butter, melted
1 teaspoon vanilla
    extract
$1^1/_2$ cups blueberries

1 Preheat the oven to 400°F. Grease a 12-cup muffin pan.

2 Sift the flour, baking powder and salt into a large mixing bowl and stir in the sugar.

3 Place the eggs, milk, butter and vanilla extract in a separate bowl and whisk together well.

4 Fold the egg mixture into the dry ingredients with a metal spoon, then gently stir in the blueberries.

5 Spoon the mixture into the muffin cups, filling them to just below the top. Place the muffin pan on the top shelf of the oven and bake for 20–25 minutes, until the muffins are well risen and lightly browned. Let the muffins stand in the pan for about 5 minutes, and then turn them out onto a wire rack to cool. Serve warm or cold.

Apple and Cranberry Muffins

Not too sweet, but good and spicy, these muffins will be a favorite with family and friends.

Makes 12

4 tablespoons butter
1 egg
$^1/_2$ cup superfine sugar
grated rind of 1 orange
$^1/_2$ cup fresh orange juice
$1^1/_4$ cups all-purpose flour
1 teaspoon baking powder
$^1/_2$ teaspoon baking soda
1 teaspoon ground
    cinnamon
$^1/_2$ teaspoon grated
    nutmeg

$^1/_2$ teaspoon mixed spice
$^1/_4$ teaspoon ground
    ginger
$^1/_4$ teaspoon salt
1–2 eating apples
$1^1/_2$ cups cranberries
$^1/_2$ cup chopped walnuts
confectioner's sugar, for
    dusting (optional)

1 Preheat the oven to 350°F. Grease a 12-cup muffin pan or use paper cases. Melt the butter over gentle heat. Let cool.

2 Place the egg in a mixing bowl and whisk lightly. Add the melted butter and whisk to combine, then add the sugar, orange rind and juice. Whisk to blend.

3 In a large bowl, sift together the flour, baking powder, baking soda, spices and salt. Quarter, core and peel the apples. With a sharp knife, chop coarsely.

4 Make a well in the center of the dry ingredients and pour in the egg mixture. With a spoon, stir until just blended. Add the apples, cranberries and walnuts and stir to blend.

5 Fill the cups three-quarters full and bake until the the tops spring back when touched lightly, about 25–30 minutes. Transfer to a wire rack to cool. Dust with confectioner's sugar before serving, if liked.

Yogurt and Honey Muffins

For a more substantial texture, fold in ½ cup chopped walnuts with the flour.

Makes 12

4 tablespoons butter	¼ cup lemon juice
5 tablespoons honey	¼ cup all-purpose flour
1 cup plain yogurt	½ cup whole wheat flour
1 large egg, at room	1½ teaspoon baking soda
temperature	¼ teaspoon grated
grated rind of 1 lemon	nutmeg

1 Preheat the oven to 375°F. Grease a 12-cup muffin pan or use paper cases.

2 In a saucepan, melt the butter and honey. Remove from the heat and set aside to cool slightly.

3 In a bowl, whisk together the yogurt, egg, lemon rind and juice. Add the butter and honey mixture. Set aside.

4 In another bowl, sift together the dry ingredients. Fold them into the yogurt mixture to blend.

5 Fill the prepared cups two-thirds full. Bake until the tops spring back when touched lightly, about 20–25 minutes. Cool in the pan for 5 minutes before turning out. Serve warm or at room temperature.

Prune Muffins

Prunes bring a delightful moisture to these tasty and wholesome muffins.

Makes 12

1 egg	2 teaspoons baking
1 cup milk	powder
½ cup vegetable oil	½ teaspoon salt
scant ¼ cup superfine	¼ teaspoon grated
sugar	nutmeg
2 tablespoons dark brown	½ cup cooked pitted
sugar	prunes, chopped
2½ cups all-purpose flour	

1 Preheat the oven to 400°F. Grease a 12-cup muffin pan or use paper cases.

2 Break the egg into a mixing bowl and beat with a fork. Beat in the milk and oil. Stir in the sugars and set aside.

3 Sift the flour, baking powder, salt and nutmeg into a mixing bowl. Make a well in the center, pour in the egg mixture and stir until moistened. Do not overmix; the batter should be slightly lumpy. Finally, fold in the prunes.

4 Fill the prepared cups two-thirds full. Bake until golden brown, about 20 minutes. Let stand for 10 minutes before turning out. Serve warm or at room temperature.

Crunchy Granola Muffins

The granola in these muffins gives them an unusual texture and makes them ideal to serve for breakfast.

Makes 10

1¼ cups all-purpose flour
2½ teaspoon baking
  powder
2 tablespoons superfine
  sugar
1½ cups toasted oat
  cereal with raisins

1 cup milk
4 tablespoons butter,
  melted, or corn oil
1 egg, beaten

1 Preheat the oven to 400°F. Grease 10 cups of a muffin pan or use paper cases.

2 Sift the flour, baking powder and sugar together into a large bowl. Add the oat cereal and stir to blend.

3 In a separate bowl, combine the milk, melted butter or corn oil and the beaten egg. Add to the dry ingredients. Stir until moistened, but do not overmix.

4 Spoon the mixture into the cups, leaving room for the muffins to rise. Half-fill any empty cups with water. Bake in the oven for 20 minutes, or until golden brown. Transfer to a wire rack to cool.

Raspberry Muffins

If you are using frozen raspberries, work quickly as the cold berries make the mixture solidify.

Makes 12

1 cup self-rising flour
1 cup whole wheat self-
  rising flour
3 tablespoons superfine
  sugar
½ teaspoon salt
2 eggs, beaten

scant 1 cup milk
4 tablespoons butter,
  melted
1 cup raspberries, fresh
  or frozen (defrosted for
  less than 30 minutes)

1 Preheat the oven to 375°F. Lightly grease a 12-cup muffin pan, or use paper cases. Sift the dry ingredients together, then add any wheat flakes left in the strainer.

2 Beat the eggs, milk and melted butter together and stir into the dry ingredients to make a thick batter.

3 Stir the raspberries in gently. If you mix too much, the raspberries begin to disintegrate and color the dough. Spoon into the cups or paper cases.

4 Bake for 30 minutes, until well risen and just firm. Let cool in the pan placed on a wire rack. Serve warm or cool.

Biscuits

Traditionally, biscuits should be served with butter, clotted or whipped cream and jam.

Makes 10–12
2 cups all-purpose flour
1 tablespoon baking
  powder
4 tablespoons butter,
  diced

1 egg, beaten
5 tablespoons milk
1 beaten egg, to glaze

1 Preheat the oven to 425°F. Lightly butter a baking sheet. Sift the flour and baking powder, then rub in the butter.

2 Make a well in the center of the flour mixture, add the egg and milk and mix to a soft dough using a round-bladed knife.

3 Turn out the biscuit dough onto a floured surface, and knead very lightly until smooth.

4 Roll out the dough to about a ¾-inch thickness and cut into 10 or 12 circles using a 2-inch plain or fluted cutter dipped in flour.

5 Transfer to the baking sheet, brush with egg, then bake for about 8 minutes, until risen and golden. Cool slightly on a wire rack before serving.

Drop Pancakes

If you place the cooked pancakes in a folded dish towel they will stay soft and moist.

Makes 8–10
1 cup all-purpose flour
1 teaspoon baking soda
1 teaspoon cream of
  tartar

2 tablespoons butter,
  diced
1 egg, beaten
²/₃ cup milk

1 Lightly grease a griddle or heavy-bottomed frying pan, then preheat it.

2 Sift the flour, baking soda and cream of tartar together, then rub in the butter until the mixture resembles bread crumbs. Make a well in the center, then stir in the egg and sufficient milk to give the consistency of heavy cream.

3 Drop spoonfuls of the mixture, spaced slightly apart, onto the griddle or frying pan. Cook over steady heat for 2–3 minutes, until bubbles rise to the surface and burst.

4 Turn the pancakes over and cook for 2–3 minutes more, until golden underneath. Serve warm with butter and honey.

Whole Wheat Biscuits

Split these wholesome biscuits in two with a fork while still warm and spread with butter and jam, if liked.

Makes 16

¾ cup cold butter
3 cups whole wheat flour
1¼ cups all-purpose flour
2 tablespoons sugar
½ teaspoon salt

2½ teaspoons baking soda
2 eggs
3¾ cups buttermilk
¼ cup raisins

1 Preheat the oven to 400°F. Grease and flour a large baking sheet.

2 Cut the butter into small pieces. Combine all the dry ingredients in a bowl. Add the butter and rub in until the mixture resembles coarse bread crumbs. Set aside.

3 In another bowl, whisk together the eggs and buttermilk. Set aside 2 tablespoons for glazing, then stir the remaining egg mixture into the dry ingredients until it just holds together. Stir in the raisins.

4 Roll out the dough to about ¾-inch thickness. Stamp out circles with a biscuit cutter. Place on the baking sheet and brush with the glaze.

5 Bake until golden, about 12–15 minutes. Allow to cool slightly before serving.

Orange and Raisin Biscuits

Split these biscuits when cool and toast them under a preheated broiler. Butter them while still hot.

Makes 16

2½ cups all-purpose flour
1½ teaspoons baking
    powder
generous ¼ cup sugar
½ teaspoon salt
5 tablespoons butter,
    diced

5 tablespoons margarine,
    diced
grated rind of 1 large
    orange
scant ½ cup raisins
½ cup buttermilk
milk, to glaze

1 Preheat the oven to 425°F. Grease and flour a large baking sheet.

2 Combine the dry ingredients in a large bowl. Add the butter and margarine and rub in until the mixture resembles coarse bread crumbs.

3 Add the orange rind and raisins. Gradually stir in the buttermilk to form a soft dough. Roll out the dough to about a ¾-inch thickness. Stamp out circles with a biscuit cutter. Place on the baking sheet and brush the tops with milk.

4 Bake until golden, about 12–15 minutes. Serve hot or warm, with butter, or whipped or clotted cream and jam.

Cheese and Chive Biscuits

Feta cheese makes an excellent substitute for butter in these tangy savory biscuits.

Makes 9

1 cup self-rising flour
1 cup whole wheat self-
  rising flour
½ teaspoon salt
3 ounces feta cheese
1 tablespoon chopped
  fresh chives

⅔ cup milk, plus extra to
  glaze
¼ teaspoon cayenne
  pepper

1 Preheat the oven to 400°F. Sift the flours and salt into a mixing bowl. Add any bran left in the strainer.

2 Crumble the feta cheese and rub into the dry ingredients. Stir in the chives, then add the milk and mix to a soft dough.

3 Turn out onto a floured surface and lightly knead until smooth. Roll out to a ¾-inch thickness and stamp out biscuits with a 2½-inch biscuit cutter.

4 Transfer the biscuits to a nonstick baking sheet. Brush with milk, then sprinkle over the cayenne pepper. Bake in the oven for 15 minutes, or until golden brown. Serve warm or cold.

Sunflower Golden Raisin Biscuits

Sunflower seeds give these wholesome fruit biscuits an interesting flavor and appealing texture.

Makes 10–12

2 cups self-rising flour
1 teaspoon baking
  powder
2 tablespoons soft
  sunflower margarine
2 tablespoons golden
  superfine sugar

scant ½ cup golden
  raisins
2 tablespoons sunflower
  seeds
½ cup plain yogurt
about 2–3 tablespoons
  skim milk

1 Preheat the oven to 450°F. Lightly oil a baking sheet. Sift the flour and baking powder into a bowl and rub in the margarine evenly.

2 Stir in the sugar, golden raisins and half the sunflower seeds, then mix in the yogurt, with just enough milk to make a fairly soft, but not sticky, dough.

3 Roll out on a lightly floured surface to about a ¾-inch thickness. Cut into 2½-inch flower shapes or rounds with a biscuit cutter and lift onto the baking sheet.

4 Brush with milk and sprinkle with the reserved sunflower seeds, then bake for 10–12 minutes, until well risen and golden brown. Cool the biscuits on a wire rack. Serve split and spread with jam or low fat spread.

Buttermilk Biscuits

If time is short, drop heaped tablespoonfuls of the mixture onto the baking sheet.

Makes 10

2 cups all-purpose flour
1 teaspoon baking
   powder
½ teaspoon baking soda
1 teaspoon salt
4 tablespoons butter or
   margarine, chilled
¾ cup buttermilk

1 Preheat the oven to 425°F. Sift the flour, baking powder, baking soda and salt into a mixing bowl. Cut in the butter or margarine with a fork until the mixture resembles coarse bread crumbs.

2 Add the buttermilk and mix until well combined to form a soft dough. Turn the dough onto a lightly floured surface and knead for about 30 seconds.

3 Roll out the dough to a ½-inch thickness. Use a floured 2½-inch pastry cutter to cut out rounds. Transfer the rounds to a baking sheet and bake until golden brown, about 10–12 minutes. Serve hot with butter and honey.

Date Oven Biscuits

To get light, well-risen biscuits, don't handle the dough too much or roll it out too thinly.

Makes 12

2 cups self-rising flour
pinch of salt
4 tablespoons butter
¼ cup superfine sugar
⅓ cup chopped dates
⅔ cup milk
1 beaten egg, to glaze

1 Preheat the oven to 450°F. Sift the flour and salt into a bowl and, using a pastry blender or your fingers, rub in the butter until the mixture resembles fine bread crumbs. Add the sugar and chopped dates, and stir to blend.

2 Make a well in the center of the dry ingredients and add the milk. Stir with a fork until the mixture comes together in a fairly soft dough.

3 Turn the dough out onto a lightly floured surface and knead gently for 30 seconds. Roll it out to a ¾-inch thickness. Cut out circles with a biscuit cutter. Arrange them, not touching, on an ungreased baking sheet, then glaze with the beaten egg.

4 Bake in the oven for 8–10 minutes, or until well risen and golden brown. Using a metal spatula, transfer the biscuits to a wire rack to cool completely.

Cheese and Marjoram Biscuits

A great success for a hearty tea. With savory toppings, these biscuits can make a good basis for a light lunch.

Makes 18

1 cup whole wheat flour
1 cup self-rising flour
pinch of salt
3 tablespoons butter
¼ teaspoon dry mustard
2 teaspoons dried
   marjoram

½–¾ cup finely grated
   Cheddar cheese
½ cup milk, or as
   required
½ cup pecans or walnuts,
   chopped

1 Gently sift the two flours into a bowl and add the salt. Cut the butter into small pieces, and rub into the flour until the mixture resembles fine bread crumbs.

2 Add the mustard, marjoram and grated cheese, and mix in sufficient milk to make a soft dough. Knead the dough lightly.

3 Preheat the oven to 425°F. Lightly grease two or three baking sheets. Roll out the dough on a floured surface to about a ¾-inch thickness and cut it out with a 2-inch square biscuit cutter. Place the biscuits, slightly apart, on the baking sheets.

4 Brush the biscuits with a little milk and then sprinkle the chopped pecans or walnuts over the top. Bake for about 12 minutes. Serve warm, spread with butter.

Dill and Potato Cakes

The inclusion of dill in these potato cakes makes them quite irresistible.

Makes 10

2 cups self-rising flour
3 tablespoons butter,
   softened
pinch of salt
1 tablespoon finely
   chopped fresh dill

scant 1 cup mashed
   potato, freshly made
2–3 tablespoons milk

1 Preheat the oven to 450°F. Grease a baking sheet. Sift the flour into a bowl and add the butter, salt and dill. Mix in the mashed potato and enough milk to make a soft, pliable dough.

2 Roll out the dough on a well-floured surface until fairly thin. Cut into circles with a 3-inch biscuit cutter.

3 Place the potato cakes on the baking sheet, and bake for 20–25 minutes until risen and golden.

White Bread

There is nothing quite like the smell and taste of home-baked bread, eaten while still warm.

Makes two 9 x 5-inch loaves

¼ cup lukewarm water
1 tablespoon active dried
* yeast*
2 tablespoons sugar
2 cups lukewarm milk

2 tablespoons butter or
* margarine, at room*
* temperature*
2 teaspoons salt
about 8 cups bread flour

1 Combine the water, yeast and 1 tablespoon of the sugar in a measuring cup and let stand for 15 minutes until frothy.

2 Pour the milk into a large bowl. Add the remaining sugar, butter or margarine, and salt. Stir in the yeast mixture, then stir in the flour, 1¼ cups at a time, to make a stiff dough.

3 Transfer the dough to a floured surface. Knead the dough until it is smooth and elastic, then place it in a large greased bowl, cover with a plastic bag, and let rise in a warm place until doubled in volume, about 2–3 hours.

4 Grease two 9 x 5-inch loaf pans. Punch down the dough and divide in half. Form into loaf shapes and place in the pans, seam-sides down. Cover and let rise again until almost doubled in volume, about 45 minutes. Meanwhile, preheat the oven to 375°F.

5 Bake until firm and brown, about 45–50 minutes. Turn out and tap the bottom of a loaf: if it sounds hollow, the loaf is done. If necessary, return to the oven and bake for a few minutes longer. Turn out and cool on a wire rack.

Multigrain Bread

Try different flours, such as rye, cornmeal, buckwheat or barley to replace the wheatgerm and the soy flour.

Makes two 8½ x 4½-inch loaves

1 tablespoon active dried
* yeast*
¼ cup lukewarm water
¾ cup rolled oats
2 cups milk
2 teaspoons salt
¼ cup oil
⅓ cup light brown sugar

2 tablespoons honey
2 eggs, lightly beaten
1 ounce wheatgerm
1½ cups soy flour
scant 2½ cups whole
* wheat flour*
about 4 cups bread flour

1 Combine the yeast and water, stir, and let stand for 15 minutes to dissolve. Place the oats in a large bowl. Scald the milk, then pour over the rolled oats. Stir in the salt, oil, sugar and honey. Let stand until lukewarm.

2 Stir in the yeast mixture, eggs, wheatgerm, soy and whole wheat flours. Gradually stir in enough bread flour to obtain a rough dough. Transfer the dough to a floured surface and knead, adding flour, if necessary, until smooth and elastic. Return to a clean bowl, cover and let rise in a warm place until doubled in volume, about 2½ hours.

3 Grease two 8½ x 4½-inch loaf pans. Punch down the risen dough and knead briefly. Then divide the dough into quarters. Roll each quarter into a cylinder 1½ inches thick. Twist together two cylinders and place in a pan; repeat for the remaining cylinders. Cover and let rise until doubled in volume again, about 1 hour. Preheat the oven to 375°F.

4 Bake until the bottoms sound hollow when tapped lightly, about 45–50 minutes. Turn out and cool on a wire rack.

Braided Loaf

It doesn't take much effort to turn an ordinary dough mix into this work of art.

Makes one loaf

1 tablespoon active dried
  yeast
1 teaspoon honey
1 cup lukewarm milk
4 tablespoons butter,
  melted

3¾ cups bread flour
1 teaspoon salt
1 egg, lightly beaten
1 egg yolk, beaten with
  1 teaspoon milk,
  to glaze

1 Combine the yeast, honey, milk and butter. Stir and let stand for 15 minutes to dissolve.

2 In a large bowl, mix together the flour and salt. Make a central well and add the yeast mixture and egg. With a wooden spoon, stir from the center, gradually incorporating the flour, to obtain a rough dough.

3 Transfer to a floured surface and knead until smooth and elastic. Place in a clean bowl, cover and let rise in a warm place until doubled in volume, about 1½ hours.

4 Grease a baking sheet. Punch down the dough and divide into three equal pieces. Roll each piece into a long thin strip. Begin braiding with the center strip, tucking in the ends. Cover loosely and let rise in a warm place for 30 minutes. Preheat the oven to 375°F.

5 Brush the bread with the egg and milk glaze and bake until golden, about 40–45 minutes. Turn out onto a wire rack to cool.

Oatmeal Bread

A healthy, rustic-looking bread made with rolled oats as well as flour.

Makes two loaves

2 cups milk
2 tablespoons butter
4 tablespoons dark brown
  sugar
2 teaspoons salt
1 tablespoon active dried
  yeast

¼ cup lukewarm water
4 cups rolled oats
6–8 cups strong white
  flour

1 Scald the milk. Remove from the heat and stir in the butter, brown sugar and salt. Let stand until lukewarm.

2 Combine the yeast and warm water in a large bowl and let stand until frothy. Stir in the milk mixture. Add 3 cups of the oats and enough flour to obtain a soft dough.

3 Transfer to a floured surface and knead until smooth and elastic. Place in a greased bowl, cover with a plastic bag, and let stand until doubled in volume, about 2–3 hours.

4 Grease a large baking sheet. Transfer the dough to a lightly floured surface and divide in half. Shape into rounds. Place on the baking sheet, cover with a dish towel and let rise until doubled in volume, about 1 hour. Preheat the oven to 400°F.

5 Score the tops and sprinkle with the remaining oats. Bake until the bottoms sound hollow when tapped, about 45–50 minutes. Turn out onto wire racks to cool.

Country Bread

A filling bread made with a mixture of whole wheat and white flour.

Makes two loaves

scant 2½ cups whole
   wheat flour
3 cups all-purpose flour
1¼ cups bread flour
4 teaspoons salt
4 tablespoons butter, at
   room temperature
2 cups lukewarm milk

For the starter
1 tablespoon active dried
   yeast
1 cup lukewarm water
1¼ cups all-purpose flour
¼ teaspoon superfine
   sugar

1 Combine all the starter ingredients in a bowl. Cover and let stand in a warm place for 2–3 hours.

2 Place the flours, salt and butter in a food processor or blender and process just until blended, about 1–2 minutes. Stir together the milk and starter, then slowly pour into the processor or blender, with the motor running, until the mixture forms a dough. Knead until smooth.

3 Place in an ungreased bowl, cover with a plastic bag, and let rise in a warm place until doubled in size, about 1½ hours. Knead again, then return to the bowl and let stand until tripled in size, about 1½ hours.

4 Grease a baking sheet. Divide the dough in half. Cut off one-third of the dough from each half and shape into four balls. Top each large ball with a small ball and press the center with the handle of a wooden spoon to secure. Cover with a plastic bag, slash the top, and let rise. Preheat the oven to 400°F.

5 Dust the loaves with flour and bake until browned and the bottoms sound hollow when tapped, 45–50 minutes. Cool on a wire rack.

Whole Wheat Rolls

To add interest when serving, make these individual rolls into different shapes, if you like.

Makes 12

2 tablespoons active dried
   yeast
¼ cup lukewarm water
1 teaspoon superfine
   sugar
¾ cup lukewarm
   buttermilk
¼ teaspoon baking soda

1 teaspoon salt
3 tablespoons butter, at
   room temperature
scant 1½ cups whole
   wheat flour
1¼ cups all-purpose flour
1 beaten egg, to glaze

1 In a large bowl, combine the yeast, water and sugar. Stir, and let stand for 15 minutes to dissolve.

2 Add the buttermilk, baking soda, salt and butter and stir to blend. Stir in the whole wheat flour. Add just enough of the all-purpose flour to obtain a rough dough.

3 Knead on a floured surface until smooth. Divide into three equal parts. Roll each into a cylinder, then cut in four.

4 Grease a baking sheet. Form the pieces into torpedo shapes, place on the baking sheet, cover and let stand in a warm place until doubled in size. Preheat the oven to 400°F.

5 Brush the rolls with the egg. Bake until firm, about 15–20 minutes. Let cool on a wire rack.

Whole Wheat Bread

A simple wholesome bread to be enjoyed by the whole family at any time.

Makes one 9 x 5-inch loaf

generous 4 cups whole
  wheat flour
2 teaspoons salt
4 teaspoons active dried
  yeast

1¾ cups lukewarm water
2 tablespoons honey
2 tablespoons oil
1½ ounces wheatgerm
milk, to glaze

1 Warm the flour and salt in a bowl in the oven at its lowest setting for 10 minutes. Meanwhile, combine the yeast with half of the water and let dissolve.

2 Make a central well in the flour. Pour in the yeast mixture, the remaining water, honey, oil and wheatgerm. Stir from the center until smooth.

3 Grease a 9 x 5-inch loaf pan. Knead the dough just enough to shape into a loaf. Put it in the pan and cover with a plastic bag. Let stand in a warm place until the dough is about 1 inch higher than the pan rim, about 1 hour. Preheat the oven to 400°F.

4 Brush the loaf with milk, and bake until the bottom sounds hollow when tapped, about 35–40 minutes. Cool on a wire rack.

Two-tone Bread

A tasty, malty bread that, when cut, reveals an attractive swirled interior.

Makes two 12-ounce loaves

1½ tablespoons active
  dried yeast
½ cup warm water
generous ¼ cup superfine
  sugar
6 cups white bread flour
½ tablespoon salt

2½ cups warm milk
5 tablespoons butter or
  margarine, melted and
  cooled
3 tablespoons molasses
2 cups whole wheat bread
  flour

1 Dissolve the yeast in the water with 1 teaspoon of the sugar. Sift 3 cups of the white bread flour, the salt and remaining sugar. Make a well in the center and add the yeast, milk and butter or margarine. Mix in gradually to form a smooth soft batter.

2 Divide the batter into two bowls. To one bowl, add 2½ cups of the bread flour and mix together to a soft dough. Knead until smooth. Shape into a ball, put into a greased bowl and rotate to grease all over. Cover with plastic wrap.

3 Mix the molasses and whole wheat flour into the second bowl. Add enough of the remaining white bread flour to make a soft dough. Knead until smooth. Shape into a ball, put in a greased bowl and cover. Let the doughs rise in a warm place for about 1 hour, until doubled in size. Grease two 8½ x 4½-inch loaf pans. Preheat the oven to 425°F.

4 Punch down the dough and divide each ball in half. Roll out half of the light dough to a 12 x 8-inch rectangle. Roll out half of the dark dough to the same size. Set the dark dough rectangle on the light one. Roll up tightly from a short side. Set in a loaf pan. Repeat. Cover the pans and let the dough rise until doubled in size. Bake for 30–35 minutes.

Pleated Rolls

Fancy homemade rolls show that every care has been taken to make a welcoming dinner party.

Makes 48 rolls

1 tablespoon active dried yeast	*2 teaspoons salt*
2 cups lukewarm milk	*2 eggs*
½ cup margarine	*scant 7–8 cups bread*
4 tablespoons sugar	*flour*
	4 tablespoons butter

1 Combine the yeast and ½ cup milk in a large bowl. Stir and let stand for 15 minutes to dissolve. Scald the remaining milk, let cool for 5 minutes, then beat in the margarine, sugar, salt and eggs. Let stand until lukewarm.

2 Pour the milk mixture into the yeast mixture. Stir in half the flour with a wooden spoon. Add the remaining flour, 1¼ cups at a time, to obtain a rough dough.

3 Transfer the dough to a floured surface, knead until elastic. Place in a clean bowl, cover with a plastic bag and let rise in a warm place until doubled in volume.

4 In a saucepan, melt the butter and set aside. Lightly grease two baking sheets. Punch down the dough and divide into four equal pieces. Roll each piece into a 12 x 8-inch rectangle, about ¼ inch thick.

5 Cut each of the rectangles into four long strips, then cut each strip into three 4 x 2-inch rectangles. Brush each rectangle with melted butter, then fold the rectangles in half, so that the top extends about ½ inch over the bottom.

6 Place the rectangles slightly overlapping on the baking sheet, with the longer sides facing up. Cover and chill for 30 minutes. Preheat the oven to 350°F. Bake until golden, 18–20 minutes. Cool slightly before serving.

Cheese Bread

This flavored bread is ideal to serve with hot soup for a hearty lunch snack.

Makes one 9 x 5-inch loaf

1 tablespoon active dried yeast	*3¾ cups bread flour*
1 cup lukewarm milk	*2 teaspoons salt*
2 tablespoons butter	*scant 1 cup grated aged Cheddar cheese*

1 Combine the yeast and milk. Stir and let stand for 15 minutes to dissolve. Meanwhile, melt the butter, let cool, then add to the yeast mixture.

2 Mix the flour and salt together in a large bowl. Make a central well and pour in the yeast mixture. With a wooden spoon, stir from the center to obtain a rough dough. If the dough seems too dry, add 2–3 tablespoons water.

3 Transfer to a floured surface and knead until smooth and elastic. Return to the bowl, cover and let rise in a warm place until doubled in volume, about 2–3 hours.

4 Grease a 9 x 5-inch loaf pan. Punch down the dough and knead in the cheese to distribute it evenly. Twist the dough, form into a loaf shape and place in the pan, tucking the ends under. Let stand in a warm place until the dough rises above the rim of the pan. Preheat the oven to 400°F.

5 Bake the bread for 15 minutes, then lower the oven heat to 375°F and bake until the bottom sounds hollow when tapped, about 30 minutes more.

Poppyseed Knots

The poppyseeds look attractive and add a slightly nutty flavor to these rolls.

Makes 12

1¼ cups lukewarm milk
4 tablespoons butter, at room temperature
1 teaspoon superfine sugar
2 teaspoons active dry yeast
1 egg yolk
2 teaspoons salt
4–4½ cups all-purpose flour
1 egg beaten with 2 teaspoons of water, to glaze
poppyseeds, for sprinkling

1 In a large bowl, stir together the milk, butter, sugar and yeast. Let stand for 15 minutes to dissolve. Stir in the egg yolk, salt and 2½ cups of the flour. Add half the remaining flour and stir to obtain a soft dough.

2 Transfer to a floured surface and knead, adding flour, if necessary, until smooth and elastic. Place in a bowl, cover and let stand in a warm place until the dough doubles in volume, about 1½–2 hours.

3 Grease a baking sheet. Punch down the dough with your fist and cut into 12 pieces the size of golf balls. Roll each piece into a rope, twist to form a knot and place 1 inch apart on the sheet. Cover loosely and let rise in a warm place until doubled in volume, about 1–1½ hours.

4 Preheat the oven to 350°F. Brush the knots with the egg glaze and sprinkle over the poppyseeds. Bake until the tops are lightly browned, about 30 minutes. Cool slightly on a wire rack before serving.

Clover Leaf Rolls

For a witty touch, make one "lucky four-leaf clover" in the batch.

Makes 24

1¼ cups milk
2 tablespoons superfine sugar
4 tablespoons butter, at room temperature
2 teaspoons active dried yeast
1 egg
2 teaspoons salt
4–5 cups all-purpose flour
melted butter, to glaze

1 Heat the milk to lukewarm, pour into a large bowl and stir in the sugar, butter and yeast. Let stand for 15 minutes. Stir in the egg and salt. Gradually stir in 4½ cups of the flour. Add just enough extra to obtain a rough dough. Knead until smooth. Place in a greased bowl, cover and let stand in a warm place until doubled in size, about 1½ hours.

2 Grease two 12-cup muffin trays. Punch down the dough, and make 72 equal-size balls.

3 Place three balls, in one layer, in each muffin cup. Cover loosely and let rise in a warm place until doubled in size, about 1½ hours. Preheat the oven to 400°F.

4 Brush the rolls with glaze. Bake until lightly browned, about 20 minutes. Cool slightly on a wire rack before serving.

French Bread

For a taste of France at the breakfast table, or serve with French cheeses for a supper snack.

Makes 2 loaves

1 tablespoon active dried yeast
2 cups lukewarm water
1 tablespoon salt

3½–4 cups all-purpose flour
semolina or flour, for sprinkling

1 In a large bowl, combine the yeast and water, stir, and let stand for 15 minutes. Stir in the salt.

2 Add the flour, 1¼ cups at a time, to obtain a smooth dough. Knead for 5 minutes.

3 Shape into a ball, place in a greased bowl and cover with a plastic bag. Let rise in a warm place until doubled in size, about 2–4 hours.

4 On a lightly floured surface, shape into two long loaves. Place on a baking sheet sprinkled with semolina or flour and let rise for 5 minutes.

5 Score the tops diagonally with a sharp knife. Brush with water and place in a cold oven. Place a pan of boiling water on the base of the oven and set the oven to 400°F. Bake until crusty and golden, about 40 minutes. Cool on a wire rack.

Croissants

Enjoy breakfast Continental-style with these melt-in-your-mouth croissants.

Makes 18

1 tablespoon active dried yeast
1⅓ cups lukewarm milk
2 teaspoons superfine sugar
1½ teaspoons salt

4 cups all-purpose flour
1 cup cold sweet butter
1 egg, beaten with 2 teaspoons water, to glaze

1 In an electric mixer bowl, stir together the yeast and milk. Let stand for about 15 minutes. Stir in the sugar, salt and about 1¼ cups of the flour.

2 Using a dough hook, slowly add the remaining flour. Beat on high speed until the dough pulls away from the sides of the bowl. Cover and let rise in a warm place until doubled in size, about 1½ hours. Knead until smooth, wrap in wax paper and chill for 15 minutes.

3 Roll out the butter between two sheets of wax paper to make two 6 x 4-inch rectangles. Roll out the dough to 12 x 8 inches. Interleave the butter with the dough. With a short side facing you, roll it out again to 12 x 8 inches. Fold in thirds again, wrap and chill for 30 minutes. Repeat the procedure twice, then chill for 2 hours.

4 Roll out the dough to a rectangle about ⅛ inch thick. Trim the sides. Cut into 18 equal-size triangles. Roll up from base to point. Place point-down on baking sheets and form crescents. Cover and let rise in a warm place until more than doubled in size, about 1–1½ hours. Preheat the oven to 475°F.

5 Brush with egg and bake for 2 minutes. Lower the heat to 375°F and bake until golden, about 10–12 minutes. Serve warm.

Individual Brioches

These buttery rolls with their distinctive topknots are delicious served with jam at coffee time.

Makes 8

1 tablespoon active dried
  yeast
1 tablespoon superfine
  sugar
2 tablespoons warm milk
2 eggs
1¾ cups all-purpose flour

½ teaspoon salt
6 tablespoons butter, cut
  into six pieces, at
  room temperature
1 egg yolk, beaten with
  2 teaspoons water,
  to glaze

1 Butter eight individual brioche or muffin cups. Put the yeast and sugar in a small bowl, add the milk and stir until dissolved. Let stand for 5 minutes, then beat in the eggs.

2 Put the flour and salt into a food processor or blender, then, with the machine running, slowly pour in the yeast mixture. Scrape down the sides and process until the dough forms a ball. Add the butter and pulse to blend.

3 Transfer the dough to a buttered bowl and cover with a dish towel. Let rise in a warm place for 1 hour, then punch down.

4 Shape three-quarters of the dough into eight balls and put into the pans. Shape the last quarter into eight small balls, make a depression in the top of each large ball and set a small ball into it.

5 Let rise in a warm place for 30 minutes. Preheat the oven to 400°F.

6 Brush the brioches with the egg glaze. Bake for about 15–18 minutes, until golden brown. Transfer to a wire rack and let cool completely.

Dinner Milk Rolls

Making bread especially for your dinner guests is not only a wonderful gesture, but it is also quite easy to do.

Makes 12–16

6 cups bread flour
2 teaspoons salt
2 tablespoons butter
1 envelope fast-rising
  dried yeast
1¾ cups lukewarm milk

cold milk, to glaze
poppy, sesame and
  sunflower seeds, or sea
  salt flakes, for
  sprinkling

1 Sift together the flour and salt into a large bowl. Work in the butter, then stir in the yeast. Mix to a firm dough with the milk (you may not need it all).

2 Knead the dough for 5 minutes, then return to the bowl, cover with oiled plastic wrap and let rise until doubled.

3 Grease a baking sheet. Punch down the dough and knead again, then divide into 12–16 pieces and make into shapes of your choice. Place on the baking sheet, glaze the tops with milk, and sprinkle over your chosen seeds or sea salt flakes.

4 Let rise again. Meanwhile, preheat the oven to 450°F. Bake the rolls for 12 minutes or until golden brown and cooked. Cool on a wire rack. Eat the same day – they will not keep.

Dill Bread

Tasty herb breads such as this are expensive to buy pre-made – if they can be found at all.

Makes two loaves

4 teaspoons active dried yeast	1 large bunch dill, finely chopped
2 cups lukewarm water	2 eggs, lightly beaten
2 tablespoons sugar	⅔ cup cottage cheese
scant 9½ cups bread flour	4 teaspoons salt
½ onion, chopped	milk, to glaze
4 tablespoons oil	

1 Mix together the yeast, water and sugar in a large bowl and let stand for 15 minutes to dissolve. Stir in about half of the flour. Cover and let rise in a warm place for 45 minutes.

2 In a frying pan, cook the onion in 1 tablespoon of the oil until soft. Set aside to cool, then stir into the yeast mixture. Stir the dill, eggs, cottage cheese, salt and the remaining oil into the yeast. Gradually add the remaining flour until the dough is too stiff to stir.

3 Transfer to a floured surface and knead until smooth and elastic. Place in a bowl, cover and let rise until doubled in volume, about 1–1½ hours.

4 Grease a large baking sheet. Cut the dough in half and shape into two rounds. Place on the sheet and let rise in a warm place for 30 minutes. Preheat the oven to 375°F.

5 Score the tops, brush with the milk to glaze and bake until browned, about 50 minutes. Transfer to a wire rack to cool.

Spiral Herb Bread

When you slice this unusual loaf, its herbal secret is revealed inside.

Makes two 9 x 5-inch loaves

2 tablespoons active dried yeast	1 bunch scallions, chopped
2½ cups lukewarm water	1 garlic clove, finely chopped
3¾ cups bread flour	salt and freshly ground black pepper
generous 3½ cups whole wheat flour	1 egg, lightly beaten
1 tablespoon salt	milk, for glazing
2 tablespoons butter	
1 large bunch parsley, finely chopped	

1 Combine the yeast and ¼ cup of the water, stir and let stand for 15 minutes to dissolve.

2 Combine the flours and salt in a large bowl. Make a central well and pour in the yeast mixture and the remaining water. With a wooden spoon, stir to a rough dough. Transfer to a floured surface; knead until smooth. Return to the bowl, cover with a plastic bag, and let stand until doubled in size.

3 Meanwhile, combine the butter, parsley, scallions and garlic in a large frying pan. Cook over low heat, stirring, until softened. Season and set aside.

4 Grease two 9 x 5-inch loaf pans. When the dough has risen, cut in half and roll each half into a 14 x 9-inch rectangle . Brush with the beaten egg and spread with the herb mixture. Roll up to enclose the filling, pinch the short ends to seal. Place in the pans, seam-sides down. Cover, let stand in a warm place until the dough rises above the pan rims.

5 Preheat the oven to 375°F. Brush the loaves with milk and bake until the bottoms sound hollow when tapped, about 55 minutes. Cool on a wire rack.

Sesame Seed Bread

This delicious bread breaks into individual rolls. It is ideal for entertaining.

Makes one 9-inch loaf

2 teaspoons active dried
    yeast
1¼ cups lukewarm water
1¾ cups all-purpose flour
scant 1½ cups whole
    wheat flour

2 teaspoons salt
5 tablespoons toasted
    sesame seeds
milk, to glaze
2 tablespoons sesame
    seeds, for sprinkling

1 Combine the yeast and 5 tablespoons of the water and let dissolve. Mix the flours and salt in a large bowl. Make a central well and pour in the yeast and water. Stir from the center to obtain a rough dough.

2 Transfer to a floured surface and knead until smooth and elastic. Return to the bowl and cover with a plastic bag. Let stand in a warm place until the dough has doubled in size, about 1½–2 hours.

3 Grease a 9-inch round cake pan. Punch down the dough and knead in the sesame seeds. Divide the dough into 16 balls and place in the pan. Cover with a plastic bag and let stand in a warm place until risen above the rim. Preheat the oven to 425°F.

4 Brush the loaf with milk and sprinkle with the sesame seeds. Bake for 15 minutes. Lower the heat to 375°F and bake until the bottom sounds hollow when tapped, about 30 minutes. Cool on a wire rack.

Rye Bread

To bring out the flavor of the caraway seeds, toast them lightly in the oven first.

Makes one loaf

scant 1½ cups rye flour
2 cups boiling water
½ cup molasses
5 tablespoons butter, cut
    into pieces
1 tablespoon salt
2 tablespoons caraway
    seeds

1 tablespoon active dried
    yeast
½ cup lukewarm water
about 7½ cups all-
    purpose flour
semolina or flour, for
    dusting

1 Mix the rye flour, boiling water, molasses, butter, salt and caraway seeds in a large bowl. Let cool.

2 In another bowl, mix the yeast and lukewarm water and let dissolve. Stir into the rye flour mixture. Stir in just enough all-purpose flour to obtain a stiff dough. If it becomes too stiff, stir with your hands. Transfer to a floured surface and knead thoroughly until the dough is no longer sticky and is smooth and shiny.

3 Place in a greased bowl, cover with a plastic bag, and let stand in a warm place until doubled in volume. Punch down the dough, cover, and let rise again for 30 minutes.

4 Preheat the oven to 350°F. Dust a baking sheet with semolina or flour.

5 Shape the dough into a ball. Place on the sheet and score several times across the top. Bake until the bottom sounds hollow when tapped, about 40 minutes. Cool on a wire rack.

Rosemary Focaccia

Italian flat bread is easy to make using a package mix. Additions include olives and sun-dried tomatoes.

Makes two loaves

1-pound package white
  bread mix
4 tablespoons extra
  virgin olive oil
2 teaspoons dried
  rosemary, crushed
8 sun-dried tomatoes,
  chopped

12 black olives, pitted
  and chopped
scant 1 cup lukewarm
  water
sea salt flakes, for
  sprinkling

1 Combine the bread mix with half the oil, the rosemary, tomatoes, olives and water to form a firm dough.

2 Knead the dough on a lightly floured surface for about 5 minutes. Return to the mixing bowl and cover with a piece of oiled plastic wrap. Let the dough rise in a warm place until doubled in size. Meanwhile, lightly grease two baking sheets and preheat the oven to 425°F.

3 Punch down the dough and knead again. Divide into two, and shape into flat rounds. Place on the baking sheet, and make indentations with your fingertips. Trickle over the remaining olive oil and sprinkle with sea salt flakes.

4 Bake the focaccia for 12–15 minutes until golden brown and cooked. Turn out onto wire racks to cool. This bread is best eaten slightly warm.

Saffron Focaccia

A dazzling yellow bread that is both light in texture and distinctive in flavor.

Makes one loaf

pinch of saffron strands
⅔ cup boiling water
2 cups all-purpose flour
½ teaspoon salt
1 teaspoon fast-rising
  dried yeast
1 tablespoon olive oil

For the topping
2 garlic cloves, sliced
1 red onion, cut into thin
  wedges
rosemary sprigs
12 black olives, pitted
  and coarsely chopped
1 tablespoon olive oil

1 Place the saffron in a heat proof pitcher and pour in the boiling water. Infuse until lukewarm.

2 Place the flour, salt, yeast and olive oil in a food processor or blender. Turn it on and gradually add the saffron and its liquid. Process until the dough forms a ball.

3 Turn onto a floured surface; knead for 10–15 minutes. Place in a bowl, cover and let rise until doubled in size, about 30–40 minutes.

4 Punch down the dough and roll into an oval shape about ½ inch thick. Place on a lightly greased baking sheet and let rise for 30 minutes. Preheat the oven to 400°F.

5 With your fingers, press indentations over the surface of the bread.

6 Cover with the topping ingredients, brush lightly with olive oil, and bake for 25 minutes or until the loaf sounds hollow when tapped on the bottom. Let cool on a wire rack.

Rosemary Bread

Sliced thinly, this herb bread is delicious with cheese or soup for a light meal.

Makes one 9 x 5-inch loaf

1 envelope fast-rising dried yeast	1 tablespoon sesame seeds
1¼ cups whole wheat flour	1 tablespoon dried chopped onion
1½ cups self-rising flour	1 tablespoon fresh rosemary leaves
2 tablespoons butter	1 cup cubed Cheddar cheese
¼ cup warm water	
1 cup milk, at room temperature	rosemary leaves and coarse salt, to decorate
1 tablespoon sugar	
1 teaspoon salt	

1 Mix the yeast with the flours in a large mixing bowl. Melt the butter. Then stir the warm water, milk, sugar, butter, salt, sesame seeds, onion and rosemary into the flour. Knead thoroughly until quite smooth.

2 Flatten the dough, then add the cheese cubes. Knead them in until they are well combined.

3 Place the dough into a clean bowl greased with a little melted butter. Cover with a dish towel and put in a warm place for 1½ hours, or until the dough has doubled in size.

4 Grease a 9 x 5-inch loaf pan with butter. Punch down the dough and shape into a loaf. Place in the pan, cover with the dish towel and leave for about 1 hour until doubled in size. Preheat the oven to 375°F.

5 Bake for 30 minutes. Cover the loaf with foil for the last 5–10 minutes of baking. Turn the bread out onto a wire rack to cool. Garnish with some rosemary leaves and coarse salt sprinkled on top.

Potato Bread

Don't add butter or milk to the potatoes when you mash them, or the dough will be too sticky.

Makes two 9 x 5-inch loaves

4 teaspoons active dried yeast	2 tablespoons oil
1 cup lukewarm milk	4 teaspoons salt
8oz potatoes, boiled (reserve 1 cup of the cooking liquid)	3½–4 cups all-purpose flour

1 Combine the yeast and milk in a large bowl and let dissolve, about 15 minutes. Meanwhile, mash the potatoes.

2 Add the potatoes, oil and salt to the yeast mixture and mix well. Stir in the reserved cooking water, then stir in the flour, in six separate batches, to form a stiff dough. Knead until smooth, return to the bowl, cover, and let stand in a warm place until doubled in size, about 1–1½ hours. Punch down, then let rise again for 40 minutes.

3 Grease two 9 x 5-inch loaf pans. Roll the dough into 20 small balls. Place two rows of balls in each pan. Let stand until the dough has risen above the rims of the pans.

4 Preheat the oven to 400°F. Bake the dough for 10 minutes, then lower the heat to 375°F. Bake until the bottoms of the loaves sound hollow when tapped, about 40 minutes. Cool on a wire rack.

Irish Soda Bread

Easy to make, this distinctive bread goes well with soup, cheese and traditional, rustic-style dishes.

Makes one loaf

2½ cups all-purpose flour
1 cup whole wheat flour
1 teaspoon baking soda
1 teaspoon salt
2 tablespoons butter or margarine, at room temperature

1¼ cups buttermilk
1 tablespoon all-purpose flour, for dusting

1 Preheat the oven to 400°F. Grease a baking sheet. Sift together the flours, baking soda and salt. Make a central well and add the butter or margarine and buttermilk. Working from the center, stir to combine the ingredients until a soft dough is formed.

2 With floured hands, gather the dough into a ball. Knead for 3 minutes. Shape the dough into a large round.

3 Place on the baking sheet. Cut a cross in the top with a sharp knife and dust with the flour. Bake until brown, about 40–50 minutes. Transfer to a wire rack to cool.

Sage Soda Bread

This wonderful loaf, quite unlike bread made with yeast, has a velvety texture and a powerful sage aroma.

Makes one loaf

⅔ cups whole wheat flour
1 cup bread flour
½ teaspoon salt
1 teaspoon baking soda

2 tablespoons grated fresh sage
1¼–1¾ cups buttermilk

1 Preheat the oven to 425°F. Sift the dry ingredients into a bowl. Stir in the sage and add enough buttermilk to make a soft dough.

2 Shape the dough into a round loaf and place on a lightly greased baking sheet.

3 Cut a deep cross in the top. Bake in the oven for about 40 minutes, or until the loaf is well risen and sounds hollow when tapped on the bottom. Let cool on a wire rack.

Breadsticks

If liked, use other seeds, such as poppy or caraway, in these sticks.

Makes 18–20

1 tablespoon active dried yeast
1¼ cups lukewarm water
scant 4 cups all-purpose flour
2 teaspoons salt
1 teaspoon superfine sugar

2 tablespoons olive oil
1 egg, beaten, to glaze
10 tablespoons sesame seeds, toasted
coarse salt, for sprinkling

1 Combine the yeast and water, stir and let stand for about 15 minutes. Place the flour, salt, sugar and olive oil in a food processor or blender. With the motor running, slowly pour in the yeast mixture and process until the dough forms a ball.

2 Knead until smooth. Place in a bowl, cover and let rise in a warm place for 45 minutes. Grease two baking sheets.

3 Roll the dough into 18–20 12-inch sticks. Place on the baking sheets, brush with egg then sprinkle with sesame seeds and coarse salt. Let rise, uncovered, for 20 minutes. Preheat the oven to 400°F.

4 Bake until golden, about 15 minutes. Turn off the heat but let stand in the oven for 5 minutes more. Serve warm or cool.

Tomato Breadsticks

Once you've tried this simple recipe, you'll never buy manufactured breadsticks again.

Makes 16

2 cups all-purpose flour
½ teaspoon salt
½ tablespoon fast-rising dried yeast
1 teaspoon honey
1 teaspoon olive oil

⅔ cup warm water
6 halves sun-dried tomatoes in olive oil, drained and chopped
1 tablespoon milk
2 teaspoons poppyseeds

1 Place the flour, salt and yeast in a food processor or blender. Add the honey and olive oil and, with the machine running, gradually pour in the water until the dough starts to cling together (you may not need all the water). Process for 1 minute more.

2 Turn out the dough onto a floured surface and knead for 3–4 minutes, until springy and smooth. Knead in the sun-dried tomatoes. Form into a ball and place in a lightly oiled bowl. Let rise for 5 minutes. Preheat the oven to 300°F.

3 Divide the dough into 16 pieces and roll each piece into a 11 x ½-inch stick. Place on a lightly greased baking sheet and let rise in a warm place for 15 minutes.

4 Brush the sticks with milk and sprinkle with poppy seeds. Bake for 30 minutes. Let cool on a wire rack.

Walnut Bread

This rich bread could be served at a dinner party with the cheese course, or with a country-style lunch.

Makes one loaf

3 cups whole wheat flour
1¼ cups bread flour
2½ teaspoons salt
2¼ cups lukewarm water
1 tablespoon honey

1 tablespoon active dried
    yeast
1 cup walnut pieces, plus
    more to decorate
1 beaten egg, to glaze

1 Combine the flours and salt in a large bowl. Make a well in the center and add 1 cup of the water, the honey and the yeast. Set aside until the mixture is frothy.

2 Add the remaining water. With a wooden spoon, stir from the center, incorporating flour with each turn, to obtain a smooth dough. Add more flour if the dough is too sticky and use your hands if the dough becomes too stiff to stir.

3 Transfer to a floured board and knead, adding flour, if necessary, until the dough is smooth and elastic. Place in a greased bowl and roll the dough around in the bowl to coat thoroughly on all sides. Cover with a plastic bag and let stand in a warm place until doubled in volume. Punch down the dough and knead in the walnuts evenly.

4 Grease a baking sheet. Shape the dough into a round loaf and place on the baking sheet. Press in walnut pieces to decorate the top. Cover loosely with a damp cloth and let rise in a warm place until doubled in size, 25–30 minutes. Preheat the oven to 425°F.

5 With a sharp knife, score the top. Brush with the beaten egg. Bake for 15 minutes. Lower the heat to 375°F and bake until the bottom sounds hollow when tapped, about 40 minutes. Cool on a rack.

Pecan Rye Bread

A tasty homespun loaf that recalls the old folk cooking of the United States.

Makes two 8½ x 4½-inch loaves

1½ tablespoons active
    dried yeast
2¾ cups lukewarm water
6 cups bread flour
5 cups rye flour
2 tablespoons salt

1 tablespoon honey
2 teaspoons caraway
    seeds, (optional)
8 tablespoons butter, at
    room temperature
2 cups pecans, chopped

1 Combine the yeast and ½ cup of the water. Stir and let stand for 15 minutes to dissolve. In the bowl of an electric mixer, combine the flours, salt, honey, caraway seeds and butter. With the dough hook, mix on low speed until blended.

2 Add the yeast mixture and the remaining water, and mix on medium speed until the dough forms a ball. Transfer to a floured surface and knead in the pecans.

3 Return the dough to a bowl, cover with a plastic bag and let stand in a warm place until doubled, about 2 hours. Grease two 8½ x 4½-inch loaf pans. Punch down the risen dough.

4 Divide the dough in half and form into loaves. Place in the pans, seam-sides down. Dust the tops with flour. Cover with plastic bags and let rise in a warm place until doubled in volume, about 1 hour.

5 Preheat the oven to 375°F. Bake until the bottoms sound hollow when tapped, 45–50 minutes. Transfer to wire racks to cool completely.

Prune Bread

Makes 1 loaf

1 cup dried prunes
1 tablespoon fast-rising
   dried yeast
⅔ cup whole wheat flour
3–4 cups bread flour
½ teaspoon baking soda
1 teaspoon salt

1 teaspoon pepper
2 tablespoons butter, at
   room temperature
⅔ cup buttermilk
½ cup walnuts, chopped
milk, for glazing

1 Simmer the prunes in water to cover until soft, or soak overnight. Drain, reserving 4 tablespoons of the soaking liquid. Pit and chop the prunes.

2 Combine the yeast and the reserved prune liquid, stir and let stand for 15 minutes to dissolve.

3 In a large bowl, stir together the flours, baking soda, salt and pepper. Make a well in the center.

4 Add the prunes, butter, and buttermilk. Pour in the yeast mixture. With a wooden spoon, stir from the center, folding in more flour with each turn, to obtain a rough dough.

5 Transfer to a floured surface and knead until smooth and elastic. Return to the bowl, cover with a plastic bag and let rise in a warm place until doubled in volume, for about 1½ hours. Grease a baking sheet.

6 Punch down the dough, then knead in the walnuts. Shape the dough into a long, cylindrical loaf. Place on the baking sheet, cover loosely, and let rise in a warm place for about 45 minutes. Preheat the oven to 425°F.

7 With a sharp knife, score the top. Brush with milk and bake for 15 minutes. Lower to 375°F and bake for 35 minutes more, until the bottom sounds hollow. Cool.

Zucchini Crown Bread

Adding grated zucchini and cheese to a loaf mixture will keep it tasting fresher for longer.

Serves 8

3 cups coarsely grated
   zucchini
salt, for sprinkling
5 cups all-purpose flour
2 envelopes fast-rising
   dried yeast
4 tablespoons freshly
   grated Parmesan
   cheese

freshly ground black
   pepper
2 tablespoons olive oil
lukewarm water, to mix
milk, to glaze
sesame seeds, to garnish

1 Spoon the zucchini into a colander, sprinkling them lightly with salt. Drain for 30 minutes, then dry with paper towels.

2 Mix the flour, yeast and Parmesan together and season with black pepper. Stir in the oil and zucchini, and add enough lukewarm water to make a firm dough.

3 Knead the dough on a lightly floured surface until smooth, then return to the mixing bowl, cover it with oiled plastic wrap and let rise in a warm place, until doubled in size.

4 Meanwhile, grease and line a 9-inch round sandwich pan. Preheat the oven to 400°F.

5 Punch down the dough, and knead it lightly. Break into eight balls, roll each one and arrange them, touching, in the pan. Brush the tops with milk and sprinkle the sesame seeds over the top.

6 Let rise again, then bake for 25 minutes or until golden brown. Cool in the pan, then turn out onto a wire rack.

Raisin Bread

Makes 2 loaves

1 tablespoon fast-rising
    dried yeast
1¾ cups lukewarm milk
1 cup raisins
4 tablespoons currants
1 tablespoon sherry or
    brandy
½ teaspoon grated
    nutmeg

grated rind of 1 large
    orange
7 tablespoons sugar
1 tablespoon salt
8 tablespoons butter,
    melted
about 4½ cups bread flour
1 egg beaten with
    1 tablespoon cream

1 Stir the yeast with ½ cup of the milk and let stand for
15 minutes to dissolve. Mix the raisins, currants, sherry or
brandy, nutmeg and orange rind together.

2 In another bowl, mix the remaining milk, sugar, salt and
half the butter. Add the yeast mixture. With a wooden spoon,
stir in half the flour, 1¼ cups at a time, until blended. Add the
remaining flour as needed for a stiff dough.

3 Transfer to a floured surface and knead until smooth and
elastic. Place in a greased bowl, cover and let rise in a warm
place until doubled in volume, about 2½ hours.

4 Punch down the dough, return to the bowl, cover and let
rise in a warm place for 30 minutes. Grease two 8½ x 4½-inch
bread pans. Divide the dough in half and roll each half into a
20 x 7-inch rectangle.

5 Brush the rectangles with the remaining melted butter.
Sprinkle over the raisin mixture, then roll up tightly, tucking
in the ends slightly as you roll. Place in the prepared pans,
cover, and let rise until almost doubled in volume. Preheat the
oven to 400°F.

6 Brush the loaves with the egg and milk. Bake for
20 minutes. Lower the temperature to 350°F and bake until
golden, 25–30 minutes more. Cool on racks.

Coconut Bread

**This bread is delicious served with a cup of hot chocolate
or a glass of fruit punch.**

Makes 1 loaf

¾ cup butter
⅔ cup raw sugar
2 cups self-rising flour
scant 2 cups all-purpose
    flour
4 ounces dried coconut
1 teaspoon mixed spice
2 teaspoons vanilla
    extract

1 tablespoon rum
2 eggs
about ⅔ cup milk
1 tablespoon superfine
    sugar, blended with
    2 tablespoons water,
    to glaze

1 Preheat the oven to 350°F. Grease two 1-pound loaf pans.

2 Place the butter and sugar in a large bowl and sift in the
flour. Work the ingredients together with your fingertips until
the mixture resembles fine bread crumbs.

3 Add the coconut, mixed spice, vanilla, rum, eggs and milk
and mix together well with your hands. If the mixture is too
dry, moisten with milk. Knead on a floured board until firm
and pliable.

4 Halve the mixture and place in the prepared loaf pans.
Glaze with sugared water and bake for 1 hour until the loaves
are cooked. Test with a skewer; the loaves are ready when the
skewer comes out clean.

Danish Wreath

Serves 10–12

1 teaspoon fast-rising
  dried yeast
¾ cup milk
4 tablespoons sugar
4 cups strong white flour
½ teaspoon salt
½ teaspoon vanilla
  extract
1 egg, beaten
½ cup blocks sweet butter
1 egg yolk beaten with
  2 teaspoons water

1 cup confectioner's
  sugar

For the filling
generous 1 cup dark
  brown sugar
1 teaspoon ground
  cinnamon
½ cup walnuts or pecans,
  plus extra

1 Mix the yeast, milk and ½ teaspoons of the sugar. Let stand for 15 minutes to dissolve. Mix the flour, sugar and salt. Make a well and add the yeast, vanilla and egg to make a rough dough. Knead until smooth, wrap and chill.

2 Roll the butter to form two 6 x 4-inch rectangles. Roll the dough to a 12 x 8-inch rectangle. Place one butter rectangle in the center. Fold the bottom third of dough over and seal the edge. Place the other butter rectangle on top and cover with the top third of the dough.

3 Roll the dough into a 12 x 8-inch rectangle. Fold into thirds. Wrap and chill for 30 minutes. Repeat twice more. After the third fold, chill for 1–2 hours. Grease a baking sheet.

4 Roll out the dough to a 25 x 6-inch strip. Mix the filling ingredients and spread over, leaving a ½-inch edge. Roll the dough into a cylinder, place on the sheet in a circle and seal the edges. Cover and let rise for 45 minutes. Preheat the oven to 400°F.

5 Slash the top every 2 inches, cutting ½inch deep. Brush with the egg and milk. Bake for 35–40 minutes until golden. Cool. To serve, mix the confectioner's sugar with some water, then drizzle over the wreath. Sprinkle with some nuts.

Kugelhopf

A traditional round molded bread from Germany, flavored with kirsch or brandy.

Makes one ring loaf

¾ cup raisins
1 tablespoon kirsch or
  brandy
1 tablespoon fast-rising
  dried yeast
½ cup lukewarm water
½ cup sweet butter, at
  room temperature
9½ cups sugar
3 eggs, at room
  temperature
grated rind of 1 lemon

1 teaspoon salt
½ teaspoon vanilla
  extract
3¾ cups bread flour
½ cup milk
¼ cup slivered almonds
generous ½ cup whole
  blanched almonds,
  chopped
confectioner's sugar, for
  dusting

1 Combine the raisins and kirsch or brandy in a bowl. Combine the yeast and water, stir and let stand for 15 minutes.

2 Cream the butter and sugar until thick and fluffy. Beat in the eggs, one at a time. Add the lemon rind, salt and vanilla. Stir in the yeast mixture. Add the flour, alternating with the milk, until well blended. Cover and let rise in a warm place until doubled in volume, about 2 hours.

3 Grease a 11¼-cup kugelhopf mold, then sprinkle the slivered almonds evenly over the bottom. Work the raisins and chopped almonds into the dough, then spoon into the mold. Cover with a plastic bag, and let rise in a warm place until the dough almost reaches the top of the pan, about 1 hour. Preheat the oven to 350°F.

4 Bake until golden brown, about 45 minutes. If the top browns too quickly, cover with foil. Cool in the pan for 15 minutes, then turn out onto a wire rack. Dust the top lightly with confectioner's sugar.

Open Apple Pie

If using eating apples for this pie, make sure they are firm-fleshed rather than soft.

Serves 8

3–3½ pounds tart eating or cooking apples
scant ¼ cup sugar
2 teaspoons ground cinnamon
grated rind and juice of 1 lemon
2 tablespoons butter, diced
2–3 tablespoons honey, to glaze

For the pastry
2½ cups all-purpose flour
½ teaspoon salt
½ cup butter, cut into pieces
4½ tablespoons vegetable fat or shortening, cut into pieces
5–6 tablespoons iced water

1 For the pastry, sift the flour and salt into a bowl. Add the butter and fat and rub in until the mixture resembles coarse bread crumbs. Stir in just enough water to bind the dough. Gather into a ball, wrap and chill for at least 20 minutes.

2 Preheat the oven to 400°F. Place a baking sheet in the oven.

3 Peel, core and slice the apples. Combine with the sugar, cinnamon, lemon rind and juice.

4 Roll out the pastry to a 12-inch circle. Use to line a 9-inch pie dish, leaving an overhanging edge. Fill with the apples. Fold in the edges and crimp loosely. Dot the apples with diced butter.

5 Bake on the hot baking sheet until the pastry is golden and the apples are tender, about 45 minutes.

6 Melt the honey in a saucepan and brush over the apples to glaze. Serve warm or at room temperature.

Apple and Cranberry Lattice Pie

Serves 8

grated rind of 1 orange
3 tablespoons orange juice
2 large cooking apples
1⅓ cups cranberries
½ cup raisins
4 tablespoons walnuts, chopped
generous 1 cup superfine sugar
½ cup dark brown sugar
2 tablespoons all-purpose flour

For the crust
2½ cups all-purpose flour
½ teaspoon salt
6 tablespoons cold butter, cut into pieces
½ cup cold vegetable fat or shortening, cut into pieces
4–8 tablespoons iced water

1 For the crust, sift the flour and salt, add the butter and fat and rub in well. Stir in enough water to bind the dough. Form into two equal balls, wrap and chill for at least 20 minutes.

2 Put the orange rind and juice into a bowl. Peel and core the apples and grate into the bowl. Stir in the cranberries, raisins, walnuts, all except 1 tablespoon of the superfine sugar, the brown sugar and flour. Place a baking sheet in the oven and preheat to 400°F.

3 Roll out one ball of dough about ⅛ inch thick. Transfer to a 9-inch pie plate and trim. Spoon the cranberry and apple mixture into the case.

4 Roll out the remaining dough to a circle about 11 inches in diameter. With a serrated pastry wheel, cut the dough into ten strips, ¾ inch wide. Place five strips horizontally across the top of the tart at 1-inch intervals. Weave in five vertical strips and trim. Sprinkle the top with sugar.

5 Bake for 20 minutes. Reduce the heat to 350°F and bake until the crust is golden and the filling is bubbling, about 15 minutes more.

Peach Leaf Pie

Serves 8

2½ pounds ripe peaches
juice of 1 lemon
½ cup sugar
3 tablespoons cornstarch
¼ teaspoon grated
 nutmeg
½ teaspoon ground
 cinnamon
2 tablespoons butter,
 diced

For the pastry

2½ cups all-purpose flour
¾ teaspoon salt
½ cup cold butter, cut
 into pieces
4½ tablespoons cold
 vegetable fat or
 shortening, cut into
 pieces
5–6 tablespoons iced
 water
1 egg beaten with
 1 tablespoon water

1 Make the pastry as described for Open Apple Pie on page 86. Gather into two balls, one slightly larger than the other. Wrap and chill for at least 20 minutes. Place a baking sheet in the oven and preheat to 425°F.

2 Drop the peaches into boiling water for 20 seconds, then transfer to a bowl of cold water. When cool, peel off the skins. Slice the flesh and combine with the lemon juice, sugar, cornstarch and spices. Set aside.

3 Roll out the larger dough ball to ⅛ inch thick. Use to line a 9-inch pie dish. Chill. Roll out the remaining dough to ¼ inch thick. Cut out leaves 3 inches long. Mark veins. With the scraps, roll a few balls.

4 Brush the pastry case with egg glaze. Add the peaches and dot with the butter. To assemble, start from the outside edge and cover the peaches with a ring of leaves. Place a second, staggered ring above. Continue until covered. Place the balls in the center. Brush with glaze.

5 Bake on the hot baking sheet for 10 minutes. Lower the heat to 350°F and bake for 35–40 minutes more.

Walnut and Pear Lattice Pie

For a cut-out lattice top, roll out the pastry into a circle. Use a small pastry cutter to cut out shapes in a pattern.

Serves 6–8

1 pound piecrust pastry
2 pounds pears, peeled,
 cored and thinly sliced
4 tablespoons superfine
 sugar
2 tablespoons all-purpose
 flour
½ teaspoon grated lemon
 rind
scant ¼ cup raisins or
 golden raisins

4 tablespoons chopped
 walnuts
½ teaspoon ground
 cinnamon
½ cup confectioner's
 sugar
1 tablespoon lemon juice
about 2 teaspoons cold
 water

1 Preheat the oven to 375°F. Roll out half of the pastry and use it to line a 9-inch pan that is about 2 inches deep.

2 Combine the pears, superfine sugar, flour and lemon rind. Toss to coat the fruit. Mix in the raisins, nuts and cinnamon. Put the filling into the pastry case and spread it evenly.

3 Roll out the remaining pastry and use to make a lattice top. Bake the pie for 55 minutes, or until the pastry is golden brown on top.

4 Combine the confectioner's sugar, lemon juice and water in a bowl and stir until smooth. Remove the pie from the oven. Drizzle the glaze evenly over the top, on the pastry and filling. Let the pie cool in its pan on a wire rack.

Lemon Meringue Pie

A classic dish whose popularity never seems to wane.

Serves 8

8 ounces piecrust pastry
grated rind and juice of
   1 large lemon
1 cup plus 1 tablespoon
   cold water
generous ½ cup superfine
   sugar, plus
   6 tablespoons extra

2 tablespoons butter
3 tablespoons cornstarch
3 eggs, separated
pinch of salt
pinch of cream of tartar

1 Line a 9-inch pie dish with the pastry, folding under a ½-inch overhang. Crimp the edge and chill for 20 minutes.

2 Preheat the oven to 400°F. Prick the pastry case, line with wax paper and fill with baking beans. Bake for 12 minutes. Remove the paper and beans and bake until golden, 6–8 minutes more.

3 In a saucepan, combine the lemon rind and juice with 1 cup of the water, generous ½ cup of the sugar, and the butter. Bring to a boil.

4 Meanwhile, dissolve the cornstarch in the remaining water. Add the egg yolks. Beat into the lemon mixture, return to a boil and whisk until thick, about 5 minutes. Cover the surface with wax paper and let cool.

5 For the meringue, beat the egg whites with the salt and cream of tartar until stiff peaks form. Add the remaining sugar and beat until glossy.

6 Spoon the lemon mixture into the pastry case. Spoon the meringue on top, sealing it with the pastry rim. Bake until golden, 12–15 minutes.

Blueberry Pie

Serve this tangy blueberry pie with crème fraîche or heavy cream.

Serves 6–8

1 pound piecrust pastry
5 cups blueberries
generous ⅔ cup superfine
   sugar
3 tablespoons all-purpose
   flour
1 teaspoon grated orange
   rind

¼ teaspoon grated
   nutmeg
2 tablespoons orange
   juice
1 teaspoon lemon juice

1 Preheat the oven to 375°F. On a lightly floured surface, roll out half of the pastry and use it to line a 9-inch pan that is 2 inches deep.

2 Combine the blueberries, ¾ cup of the sugar, the flour, orange rind and nutmeg. Toss the mixture gently to coat all the fruit.

3 Pour the blueberry mixture into the pastry case and spread evenly. Sprinkle over the citrus juices.

4 Roll out the remaining pastry and cover the pie. Cut out small decorative shapes from the top. Use to decorate the pastry, and finish the edge.

5 Brush the top with water and sprinkle with the remaining superfine sugar. Bake for 45 minutes, or until the pastry is golden brown. Serve warm or at room temperature.

Creamy Banana Pie

Do not prepare the topping for this pie too soon before serving, or the banana slices will discolor.

Serves 6

2¼ cups ginger cookies, finely crushed
5 tablespoons butter or margarine, melted
½ teaspoon grated nutmeg or ground cinnamon
1 ripe banana, mashed
1½ cups cream cheese, at room temperature

generous 3 tablespoons thick plain yogurt or sour cream
3 tablespoons dark rum or 1 teaspoon vanilla extract

For the topping
1 cup whipping cream
3–4 bananas

1 Preheat the oven to 375°F. For the crust, combine the crushed cookies, butter or margarine and spice. Mix thoroughly with a wooden spoon.

2 Press the biscuit mixture into a 9-inch pie dish, building up thick sides with a neat edge. Bake for 5 minutes, then let cool.

3 Beat the mashed bananas with the cream cheese. Fold in the yogurt or sour cream and rum or vanilla. Spread the filling in the biscuit case. Chill for at least 4 hours or preferably overnight.

4 For the topping, whip the cream until soft peaks form. Spread on the pie filling. Slice the bananas and arrange on top in a decorative pattern.

Red Berry Sponge Tart

When soft berry fruits are in season, serve this delicious tart warm with scoops of vanilla ice cream.

Serves 4

4 cups soft berry fruits, such as raspberries, blackberries, black currants, red currants, strawberries and blueberries
2 eggs

¼ cup superfine sugar, plus extra to taste (optional)
1 tablespoon flour
¾ cup ground almonds
vanilla ice cream, to serve

1 Preheat the oven to 375°F. Grease and line a 9-inch pie dish with wax paper. Sprinkle the fruit in the bottom of the dish with a little sugar if the fruits are tart.

2 Beat the eggs and sugar together for about 3–4 minutes, or until they leave a thick trail across the surface.

3 Mix the flour and almonds, then fold into the egg mixture with a metal spatula, retaining as much air as possible.

4 Spread the mixture on top of the fruit base and bake in the preheated oven for 15 minutes. Turn out onto a serving plate.

De Luxe Mincemeat Tart

Serves 8

2 cups all-purpose flour
2 teaspoons ground
   cinnamon
½ cup walnuts, finely
   ground
½ cup butter
4 tablespoons superfine
   sugar, plus extra for
   dusting
1 egg
2 drops vanilla extract
1 tablespoons cold water

For the mincemeat

2 eating apples, peeled,
   cored and grated
generous 1½ cups raisins
½ cup ready-to-eat dried
   apricots, chopped

½ cup ready-to-eat dried
   figs or prunes,
   chopped
8 ounces green grapes,
   halved and seeded
½ cup chopped almonds
finely grated rind of
   1 lemon
2 tablespoons lemon juice
2 tablespoons brandy or
   port
¼ teaspoon mixed spice
generous ½ cup light
   brown sugar
2 tablespoons butter,
   melted

1 Process the flour, cinnamon, nuts and butter in a food processor or blender to make fine crumbs. Turn into a bowl and stir in the sugar. Beat the egg with the vanilla and water and stir into the dry ingredients. Form a soft dough, knead until smooth, wrap and chill for 30 minutes.

2 Mix the mincemeat ingredients together. Use two-thirds of the pastry to line a 9-inch, loose-based quiche pan. Push the pastry well into the edges, then trim. Fill with the mincemeat.

3 Roll out the remaining pastry and cut into ½-inch strips. Arrange the strips in a lattice over the top of the pastry, wet the joins and press them together. Chill for 30 minutes.

4 Preheat a baking sheet in the oven at 375°F. Brush the pastry with water and dust with superfine sugar. Bake the tart on the baking sheet for 30–40 minutes. Cool in the pan on a wire rack for 15 minutes. Then remove the pan.

Crunchy Apple and Almond Flan

Don't put sugar with the apples as this produces too much liquid. The sweetness is in the pastry and topping.

Serves 8

6 tablespoons butter
1½ cups all-purpose flour
4 tablespoons ground
   almonds
2 tablespoons superfine
   sugar
1 egg yolk
1 tablespoon cold water
¼ teaspoon almond
   extract
6–7 cooking apples
2 tablespoons raisins

For the topping

1 cup all-purpose flour
¼ teaspoon ground mixed
   spice
4 tablespoons butter, cut
   in small cubes
4 tablespoons raw sugar
½ cup slivered almonds

1 To make the pastry, rub the butter into the flour until it resembles bread crumbs. Stir in the almonds and sugar. Whisk the egg yolk, water and almond extract together and mix into the dry ingredients to form a soft dough. Knead until smooth, wrap, and let rest for 20 minutes.

2 For the topping, sift the flour and spice into a bowl and work in the butter. Stir in the sugar and almonds. Roll out the pastry and use to line a 9-inch, loose-based quiche pan. Trim the top and chill for 15 minutes.

3 Preheat a baking sheet in the oven at 375°F. Peel, core and slice the apples thinly. Arrange in the flan in overlapping, concentric circles, doming the center. Sprinkle with raisins.

4 Cover with the topping mixture, pressing it on lightly. Bake on the hot baking sheet for 25–30 minutes, or until the top is golden brown and the apples are tender (test them with a fine skewer). Let the flan cool in the pan for 10 minutes before serving.

Rhubarb and Cherry Pie

The unusual partnership of rhubarb and cherries works well in this pie.

Serves 8

1 pound rhubarb, cut into 1-inch pieces
1 pound canned pitted tart red or black cherries, drained
scant 1½ cups superfine sugar
3 tablespoons quick-cooking tapioca

For the pastry
2½ cups all-purpose flour
1 teaspoon salt
6 tablespoons cold butter, cut in pieces
4 tablespoons cold vegetable fat or shortening, cut in pieces
¼–½ cup iced water
milk, for glazing

1 For the pastry, sift the flour and salt into a bowl. Add the butter and fat and rub in until the mixture resembles coarse bread crumbs. Stir in enough water to bind. Form into two balls, wrap and chill for 20 minutes.

2 Preheat a baking sheet in the oven at 400°F. Roll out one pastry ball and use to line a 9-inch pie dish, leaving a ½-inch overhang.

3 Mix together the filling ingredients and spoon into the pastry case.

4 Roll out the remaining pastry, cut out four leaf shapes, and use to cover the pie leaving a ¾-inch overhang. Fold this under the pastry base and flute. Roll small balls from the scraps, mark veins in the leaves and use to decorate the pie.

5 Glaze the top and bake on the baking sheet until golden, 40–50 minutes.

Festive Apple Pie

Serves 8

9 cooking apples
2 tablespoons all-purpose flour
generous ½ cup superfine sugar
1½ tablespoons fresh lemon juice
½ teaspoon ground cinnamon
½ teaspoon mixed spice
¼ teaspoon ground ginger
¼ teaspoon grated nutmeg

¼ teaspoon salt
4 tablespoons butter, diced

For the pastry
2½ cups all-purpose flour
1 teaspoon salt
6 tablespoons cold butter, cut in pieces
4 tablespoons cold vegetable fat or shortening, cut in pieces
¼–½ cup iced water

1 For the pastry, sift the flour and salt into a bowl. Add the butter and fat, and rub in until the mixture resembles coarse bread crumbs. Stir in just enough water to bind. Form two balls, wrap and chill for 20 minutes.

2 Roll out one ball and use to line a 9-inch pie dish. Preheat a baking sheet in the oven at 425°F.

3 Peel, core and slice the apples. Toss with the flour, sugar, lemon juice, spices and salt. Spoon into the pastry case and dot with butter.

4 Roll out the remaining pastry. Place on top of the pie and trim to leave a ¾-inch overhang. Fold this under the pastry case and press to seal. Crimp the edge. Form the scraps into leaf shapes and balls. Arrange on the pie and cut steam vents.

5 Bake on the baking sheet for 10 minutes. Reduce the heat to 350°F and bake for 40 minutes, until golden.

Black Bottom Pie

Serves 8

2 teaspoons gelatin
3 tablespoons cold water
2 eggs, separated
¾ cup superfine sugar
2 tablespoons cornstarch
½ teaspoon salt
2 cups milk
2 ounces semisweet
   chocolate, finely
   chopped
2 tablespoons rum

¼ teaspoon cream of
   tartar
chocolate curls, to
   decorate

For the crust

2 cups ginger cookies,
   crushed
5 tablespoons butter,
   melted

1 Preheat the oven to 350°F. Mix the crushed ginger cookies and melted butter. Press evenly over the base and side of a 9-inch pie plate. Bake for 6 minutes. Sprinkle the gelatin over the water and let soften.

2 Beat the egg yolks in a large mixing bowl and set aside. In a saucepan, combine half the sugar, the cornstarch and salt. Gradually stir in the milk. Boil for 1 minute, stirring constantly. Whisk the hot milk mixture into the yolks, pour back into the saucepan and return to a boil, whisking. Cook for 1 minute, still whisking. Remove from the heat.

3 Pour 8 ounces of the custard mixture into a bowl. Add the chopped chocolate and stir until melted. Stir in half the rum and pour into the pie crust. Whisk the softened gelatin into the plain custard until dissolved, then stir in the remaining rum. Set the pan in cold water to reach room temperature.

4 Beat the egg whites and cream of tartar until they peak stiffly. Add the remaining sugar gradually, beating thoroughly after each addition. Fold the custard into the egg whites, then spoon over the chocolate mixture in the pie crust. Chill until set, about 2 hours. Decorate with chocolate curls.

Pumpkin Pie

A North American classic, this pie is traditionally served at Thanksgiving.

Serves 8

scant ½ cup pecans,
   chopped
9 ounces puréed
   pumpkin
2 cups light cream
¾ cup light brown sugar
¼ teaspoon salt
1 teaspoon ground
   cinnamon
½ teaspoon ground
   ginger
¼ teaspoon ground cloves

¼ teaspoon grated
   nutmeg
2 eggs

For the pastry

1⅓ cups all-purpose flour
½ teaspoon salt
½ cup vegetable fat or
   shortening
2–3 tablespoons iced
   water

1 Preheat the oven to 425°F. For the pastry, sift the flour and salt into a mixing bowl. Rub in the fat until the mixture resembles coarse bread crumbs. Sprinkle in enough water to form the mixture into a ball.

2 Roll out the pastry to a ¼inch thickness. Use to line a 9-inch pie dish. Trim and flute the edge. Sprinkle the chopped pecans over the case.

3 Beat together the pumpkin, cream, sugar, salt, spices and eggs. Pour the pumpkin mixture into the pastry case.

4 Bake for 10 minutes, then reduce the heat to 350°F and continue baking until the filling is set, about 45 minutes. Let the pie cool in the dish, set on a wire rack.

Chocolate Nut Tart

This is a sophisticated tart – strictly for grown-ups!

Serves 6 – 8

8 ounces sweet piecrust pastry
1¾ cups dry amaretti cookies
⅔ cup blanched almonds
½ cup blanched hazelnuts
3 tablespoons sugar

7 ounces semisweet chocolate
3 tablespoons milk
4 tablespoons butter
3 tablespoons amaretto liqueur or brandy
2 tablespoons light cream

1 Grease a shallow loose-based 10-inch quiche pan. Roll out the pastry and use to line the pan. Trim the edge, prick the base with a fork and chill for 30 minutes.

2 Grind the amaretti cookies in a blender or food processor. Turn into a mixing bowl.

3 Set eight whole almonds aside and place the rest in the food processor or blender with the hazelnuts and sugar. Grind to a medium texture. Add the nuts to the amaretti, and mix well.

4 Preheat the oven to 375°F. In the top of a double boiler, melt the chocolate with the milk and butter. Stir until smooth.

5 Pour the chocolate mixture into the dry ingredients, and mix well. Add the liqueur or brandy and cream.

6 Spread the filling evenly in the pastry case. Bake for 35 minutes, or until the crust is golden brown and the filling has puffed up and is beginning to darken. Let cool to room temperature. Split the reserved almonds in half and use to decorate the tart.

Pecan Tartlets

These delightful individual tartlets make an elegant dinner party dessert.

Makes six 4-inch tartlets

1 pound piecrust pastry
1 cup pecan halves
3 eggs, beaten
2 tablespoons butter, melted
1¼ cups maple syrup

½ teaspoon vanilla extract
generous ½ cup superfine sugar
1 tablespoon all-purpose flour

1 Preheat the oven to 350°F. Roll out the pastry and use to line six 4-inch tartlet pans. Divide the pecan halves between the pastry cases.

2 Combine the eggs with the butter, and add the syrup and vanilla extract. Sift over the superfine sugar and flour, and blend. Fill the pastry cases with the mixture and let stand until the nuts rise to the surface.

3 Bake for 35–40 minutes, until a skewer inserted in the center comes out clean. Cool in the pans for 15 minutes, then turn out onto a wire rack.

Pear and Hazelnut Flan

**A delicious flan for Sunday lunch. Grind the hazelnuts
yourself, if you prefer, or use ground almonds instead.**

Serves 6–8

1 cup all-purpose flour
¾ cup whole wheat flour
½ cup sunflower
   margarine
3 tablespoons cold water

4 tablespoons superfine
   sugar
4 tablespoons butter,
   softened
2 eggs, beaten
3 tablespoons raspberry
   jam
14-ounce can pears in
   natural juice
few chopped hazelnuts, to
   decorate

For the filling

½ cup self-rising flour
1 cup ground hazelnuts
1 teaspoon vanilla
   extract

1 For the pastry, stir the flours together, then work in the
margarine until the mixture resembles fine bread crumbs. Mix
to a firm dough with the water.

2 Roll out the dough and use to line a 9–10-inch pastry dish,
pressing it up the sides after trimming, so the pastry sits a
little above the dish. Prick the base, line with wax paper and
fill with baking beans. Chill for 30 minutes.

3 Preheat the oven to 400°F. Place the dish on a baking sheet
and bake blind for 20 minutes. Remove the paper and beans
after 15 minutes.

4 Beat all the filling ingredients together except for the jam
and pears. If it is too thick, stir in some of the pear juice.
Reduce the oven temperature to 350°F. Spread the jam on the
pastry case and spoon over the filling.

5 Drain the pears and arrange them, cut-side down, in the
filling. Sprinkle the nuts over the top. Bake for 30 minutes
until risen, firm and golden brown.

Latticed Peaches

**This elegant dessert may be prepared using canned peach
halves when fresh peaches are out of season.**

Serves 6
For the pastry

1 cup all-purpose flour
3 tablespoons butter or
   sunflower margarine
3 tablespoons plain
   yogurt
2 tablespoons orange
   juice
milk, to glaze

3 tablespoons ground
   almonds
2 tablespoons plain
   yogurt
finely grated rind of
   1 small orange
¼ teaspoon almond
   extract

For the filling

3 ripe peaches

For the sauce

1 ripe peach
3 tablespoons orange
   juice

1 Lightly grease a baking sheet. Sift the flour into a bowl and
rub in the butter or margarine. Stir in the yogurt and orange
juice to make a firm dough. Roll out half the pastry thinly and
stamp out six rounds with a 3-inch cookie cutter.

2 Skin the peaches, halve and remove the pits. Mix together
the almonds, yogurt, orange rind and almond extract. Spoon
into the hollows of each peach half and place, cut-side down,
on the pastry rounds.

3 Roll out the remaining pastry thinly and cut into thin
strips. Arrange the strips over the peaches to form a lattice,
brushing with milk to secure firmly. Trim the ends. Chill for
30 minutes. Preheat the oven to 400°F. Brush with milk and
bake for 15–18 minutes, until golden brown.

4 For the sauce, skin the peach and halve it to remove the
pit. Place the flesh in a food processor or blender, with the
orange juice, and liquidize until smooth. Serve the peaches
hot, with the peach sauce spooned around.

Surprise Fruit Tarts

These delicious and simple little tarts are the perfect summer treat.

Serves 6

4 large or 8 small sheets frozen and defrosted filo pastry
5 tablespoons butter or margarine, melted
1 cup whipping cream
3 tablespoons strawberry jam
1 tablespoon Cointreau or other orange-flavor liqueur
1 cup seedless black grapes, halved

1 cup seedless white grapes, halved
5 ounces fresh pineapple, cubed, or drained canned pineapple chunks
²⁄₃ cup raspberries
2 tablespoons confectioner's sugar
6 sprigs fresh mint, to decorate

1 Preheat the oven to 350°F. Grease six cups of a muffin tray. Stack the filo sheets and cut with a sharp knife or scissors into 24 4½-inch squares.

2 Lay four squares of pastry in each of the six greased cups. Press the pastry firmly into the cups, rotating slightly to make star-shaped baskets. Brush the pastry baskets lightly with butter or margarine. Bake until the pastry is crisp and golden, 5–7 minutes. Cool on a wire rack.

3 In a bowl, lightly whip the cream until soft peaks form. Gently fold the strawberry jam and Cointreau into the cream.

4 Just before serving, spoon a little of the cream mixture into each pastry basket. Top with the fruit. Sprinkle with confectioner's sugar and decorate each basket with a small sprig of mint.

Truffle Filo Tarts

The cups can be prepared a day ahead and stored in an airtight container.

Makes 24 cups

3–6 sheets fresh or defrosted frozen filo pastry, depending on size
3 tablespoons sweet butter, melted
sugar, for sprinkling
lemon rind, to decorate

Truffle mixture
1 cup heavy cream
8 ounces bittersweet or semisweet chocolate, chopped
4 tablespoons sweet butter, cut into pieces
2 tablespoons brandy

1 Prepare the truffle mixture. In a saucepan over medium heat, bring the cream to a boil. Remove from the heat and add the chocolate, stirring until melted. Beat in the butter and add the brandy. Strain into a bowl and chill for 1 hour.

2 Preheat the oven to 400°F. Grease a muffin tray with 24 1½-inch cups. Cut each filo sheet into 2½-inch squares. Cover with a damp dish towel.

3 Keeping the filo sheets covered, place one square on a work surface. Brush lightly with melted butter, turn over and brush the other side. Sprinkle with a pinch of sugar. Butter another square and place it over the first at an angle. Sprinkle with sugar. Butter a third square and place over the first two, unevenly, so the corners form an uneven edge. Press the layered square into the tray. Continue to fill the tray.

4 Bake the filo cups for 4–6 minutes, until golden. Cool for 10 minutes on a wire rack in the tray. Remove from the tray and cool completely.

5 Stir the chocolate mixture, which should be just thick enough to pipe. Spoon the mixture into an icing bag fitted with a medium star nozzle and pipe a swirl into each cup. Decorate with lemon rind.

Apple Strudel

Premade filo pastry makes a good substitute for paper-thin strudel pastry in this classic Austrian dish.

Serves 10–12

generous ½ cup raisins
2 tablespoons brandy
5 eating apples
3 large cooking apples
generous ½ cup dark
　brown sugar
1 teaspoon ground
　cinnamon
grated rind and juice of
　1 lemon

½ cup dry bread crumbs
½ cup chopped pecans or
　walnuts
12 sheets defrosted frozen
　filo pastry
¾ cup butter, melted
confectioner's sugar, for
　dusting

1　Soak the raisins in the brandy for 15 minutes.

2　Peel, core and thinly slice the apples. Combine with the rest of the filling ingredients, reserving half the bread crumbs.

3　Preheat the oven to 375°F. Grease two baking sheets. Unfold the filo pastry and cover with a dish towel. One by one, butter and stack the sheets to make a six-sheet pile.

4　Sprinkle half the reserved bread crumbs over the last sheet and spoon half the apple mixture at the bottom edge. Roll up from this edge, jelly roll style. Place on a baking sheet, seam-side down and fold under the ends to seal. Repeat to make a second strudel. Brush both with butter.

5　Bake in the oven for 45 minutes, cool slightly, then dust with confectioner's sugar.

Cherry Strudel

A refreshing variation on traditional apple strudel. Serve with whipped cream, if you like.

Serves 8

1¼ cups fresh bread
　crumbs
¾ cup butter, melted
1 cup sugar
1 tablespoon ground
　cinnamon
1 teaspoon grated lemon
　rind

2 cups sour cherries,
　pitted
8 sheets filo pastry
confectioner's sugar, for
　dusting

1　In a frying pan, fry the bread crumbs in 5 tablespoons of the butter until golden. Set aside.

2　In a large mixing bowl, toss together the sugar, cinnamon and lemon rind. Stir in the cherries.

3　Preheat the oven to 375°F. Grease a baking sheet. Unfold the filo sheets. Keep the unused sheets covered with damp paper towels. Lift off one sheet and place on a piece of wax paper. Brush the pastry with butter. Sprinkle an eighth of the bread crumbs over the surface.

4　Lay a second sheet of filo pastry on top, brush with butter and sprinkle with bread crumbs. Continue until you have used up all the pastry.

5　Spoon the cherry mixture at the bottom edge of the strip. Starting at the cherry-filled end, roll up the dough jelly roll style. Use the paper to flip the strudel onto the baking sheet, seam-side down. Carefully fold under the ends to seal. Brush the top with melted butter.

6　Bake the strudel for 45 minutes. Cool slightly, then dust with a fine layer of confectioner's sugar.

Strawberry Tart

This tart is best assembled just before serving, but you can bake the pastry case and make the filling ahead.

Serves 6

12 ounces rough-puff or puff pastry
1 cup cream cheese
grated rind of ½ orange
2 tablespoons orange liqueur or juice

3–4 tablespoons confectioner's sugar, plus extra for dusting (optional)
4 cups ripe strawberries, hulled

1 Preheat the oven to 400°F. Roll out the pastry to about a ⅛-inch thickness and use to line an 11 x 4-inch rectangular flan pan. Trim the edges, then chill for 30 minutes.

2 Prick the bottom of the pastry all over. Line with foil, fill with baking beans and bake for 15 minutes. Remove the foil and beans and bake for 10 minutes, until the pastry is browned. Gently press down on the pastry base to deflate, then let cool on a wire rack.

3 Beat together the cheese, orange rind, orange liqueur or juice and confectioner's sugar to taste. Spread the cheese filling in the pastry case. Halve the strawberries and arrange them on top of the filling. Dust with confectioner's sugar, if you like.

Alsatian Plum Tart

Fruit and custard tarts, similar to a fruit quiche, are typical in Alsace. Sometimes they have a yeast dough base instead of pastry. You can use other seasonal fruits in this tart, or a mixture of fruit.

Serves 6–8

1 pound ripe plums, halved and pitted
2 tablespoons kirsch or plum brandy
12 ounces piecrust or sweet piecrust pastry
2 tablespoons seedless raspberry jam

For the custard filling
2 eggs
4 tablespoons confectioner's sugar
¾ cup heavy cream
grated rind of ½ lemon
¼ teaspoon vanilla extract

1 Preheat the oven to 400°F. Mix the plums with the kirsch or brandy and set aside for about 30 minutes.

2 Roll out the pastry thinly and use to line a 9-inch pie dish. Prick the pastry case all over and line with foil. Add a layer of baking beans and bake for 15 minutes until slightly dry and set. Remove the foil and the baking beans.

3 Brush the bottom of the pastry case with a thin layer of jam, then bake for 5 minutes more. Remove the pastry case from the oven and transfer to a wire rack. Reduce the oven temperature to 350°F.

4 To make the custard filling, beat the eggs and sugar until well combined, then beat in the cream, lemon rind, vanilla and any juice from the plums.

5 Arrange the plums, cut-side down, in the pastry case and pour over the custard mixture. Bake for about 30–35 minutes until a knife inserted in the center comes out clean. Serve the tart warm or at room temperature.

Almond Mincemeat Tartlets

Makes 36

2½ cups all-purpose flour
¾ cup confectioner's
  sugar
1 teaspoon ground
  cinnamon
¾ cup butter
½ cup ground almonds
1 egg yolk
3 tablespoons milk
1-pound bottle
  mincemeat
1 tablespoon brandy or
  rum

For the lemon filling

½ cup butter or
  margarine
½ cup superfine sugar
1½ cups self-rising flour
2 large eggs
finely grated rind of
  1 large lemon

For the lemon icing

1 cup confectioner's
  sugar
1 tablespoon lemon juice

1 Sift the flour, sugar and cinnamon into a bowl and work in the butter until it resembles bread crumbs. Add the ground almonds and bind with the egg yolk and milk to a soft, pliable dough. Knead until smooth, wrap and chill for 30 minutes.

2 Preheat the oven to 375°F. On a lightly floured surface, roll out the pastry and cut out 36 fluted rounds with a pastry cutter. Mix the mincemeat with the brandy or rum and put a small teaspoonful in the bottom of each pastry case. Chill.

3 For the lemon sponge filling, whisk the butter or margarine, sugar, flour, eggs and lemon rind together until smooth. Spoon on top of the mincemeat, dividing it evenly, and level the tops. Bake for 20–30 minutes, or until golden brown and springy to the touch. Remove and let cool on a wire rack.

4 For the lemon icing, sift the confectioner's sugar and mix with the lemon juice to a smooth coating consistency. Spoon into an icing bag and drizzle a zigzag pattern over each tart. If you're short of time, simply dust the tartlets with confectioner's sugar.

Mince Pies with Orange Pastry

Homemade mince pies are so much nicer than store-bought, especially with this flavorsome pastry.

Makes 18

2 cups all-purpose flour
scant ⅓ cup
  confectioner's sugar
2 teaspoons ground
  cinnamon
generous 1 cup butter

grated rind of 1 orange
4 tablespoons iced water
1½ cups mincemeat
1 egg, beaten, to glaze
confectioner's sugar, for
  dusting

1 Sift together the flour, confectioner's sugar and cinnamon. Work in the butter until it resembles fine bread crumbs. Stir in the grated orange rind.

2 Mix to a firm dough with the water. Knead lightly, then roll out to a ¼ inch thickness. Using a 2½-inch round cookie cutter, stamp out 18 circles, then stamp out 18 smaller 2-inch circles.

3 Line two muffin trays with the larger circles. Place a small spoonful of mincemeat into each pastry case and top with the smaller pastry circles, pressing the edges to seal.

4 Glaze the tops with egg and chill for 30 minutes. Preheat the oven to 400°F.

5 Bake for 15–20 minutes, or until golden brown. Remove to wire racks. Serve just warm, dusted with sugar.

Candied Fruit Pie

Use half digestive and half ginger cookies for the crust, if you prefer.

Serves 10

1 tablespoon rum
4 tablespoons mixed
    candied fruit, chopped
2 cups milk
4 teaspoons gelatin
½ cup sugar
½ teaspoon salt
3 eggs, separated
1 cup whipping cream,
    whipped

chocolate curls, to
    decorate

For the crust
2 cups digestive cookies,
    crushed
5 tablespoons butter,
    melted
1 tablespoon sugar

1 Mix the digestive cookies, butter and sugar. Press evenly over the bottom and sides of a 9-inch pie plate. Chill.

2 Stir together the rum and candied fruit. Set aside. Pour ½ cup of the milk into a small bowl. Sprinkle over the gelatin and let stand for 5 minutes to soften.

3 In the top of a double boiler, combine 4 tablespoons of the sugar, the remaining milk and salt. Stir in the gelatin mixture. Cook, stirring, until the gelatin dissolves. Whisk in the egg yolks and cook, stirring, until thick enough to coat the spoon. Pour the custard over the candied fruit mixture, set in a bowl of iced water.

4 Beat the egg whites until they peak softly. Add the remaining sugar and beat just to blend. Fold a large dollop of the egg whites into the cooled gelatin mixture. Pour into the remaining egg whites and fold together. Fold in the cream.

5 Pour into the pie crust and chill until firm. Decorate with chocolate curls.

Chocolate Chiffon Pie

As the name suggests, this is a wonderfully smooth and light-textured pie.

Serves 8

7 ounces semisweet
    chocolate, chopped
1 cup milk
1 tablespoon gelatin
1 cup sugar
2 extra-large eggs,
    separated
1 teaspoon vanilla
    extract
¼ teaspoon salt
1½ cups whipping cream,
    whipped

whipped cream and
    chocolate curls, to
    decorate

For the crust
2⅓ cups digestive
    cookies, crushed
6 tablespoons butter,
    melted

1 Place a baking sheet in the oven and preheat to 350°F. Mix the cookies and butter together and press over the bottom and sides of a 9-inch pie plate. Bake for 8 minutes.

2 Grate the chocolate in a blender or food processor. Place the milk in the top of a double boiler. Sprinkle over the gelatin and let stand for 5 minutes to soften.

3 In the top of a double boiler, put 6 tablespoons sugar, the chocolate and egg yolks. Stir until dissolved. Add the vanilla. Place the top in a bowl of ice and stir until the mixture reaches room temperature. Remove from the ice.

4 Beat the egg whites and salt until they peak softly. Add the remaining sugar and beat just to blend. Fold a dollop of egg whites into the chocolate mixture, then pour back into the whites and fold in.

5 Fold in the cream and pour into the pie crust. Freeze until just set, about 5 minutes, then chill for 3–4 hours. Decorate with whipped cream and chocolate curls.

Chocolate Pear Tart

Chocolate and pears have a natural affinity, well used in this luxurious dessert.

Serves 8

4 ounces semisweet
   chocolate, grated
3 large firm, ripe pears
1 egg
1 egg yolk
½ cup light cream
½ teaspoon vanilla
   extract
3 tablespoons superfine
   sugar

For the pastry
1¼ cups all-purpose flour
¼ teaspoon salt
2 tablespoons sugar
½ cup cold sweet butter,
   cut into pieces
1 egg yolk
1 tablespoon lemon juice

1 For the pastry, sift the flour and salt into a bowl. Add the sugar and butter. Rub in until the mixture resembles coarse bread crumbs. Stir in the egg yolk and lemon juice. Form a ball, wrap, and chill for 20 minutes.

2 Preheat the oven to 400°F. Roll out the pastry and use to line a 10-inch pie dish.

3 Sprinkle the pastry case with the grated chocolate.

4 Peel, halve and core the pears. Cut in thin slices crosswise, then fan out slightly. Transfer the pears to the tart using a metal spatula and arrange like wheel spokes.

5 Whisk together the egg and egg yolk, cream and vanilla. Ladle over the pears and sprinkle with sugar.

6 Bake on a baking sheet for 10 minutes. Reduce the heat to 350°F and cook until the custard is set and the pears begin to caramelize, about 20 minutes more. Serve while still warm.

Pear and Apple Crumble Pie

You could use just one fruit in this pie if you prefer.

Serves 8

3 firm pears
4 cooking apples
scant 1 cup superfine
   sugar
2 tablespoons cornstarch
¼ teaspoon salt
grated rind of 1 lemon
2 tablespoons fresh lemon
   juice
generous ½ cup raisins
¾ cup all-purpose flour
1 teaspoon ground
   cinnamon

6 tablespoons cold butter,
   cut in pieces

For the pastry
1¼ cups all-purpose flour
½ teaspoon salt
5 tablespoons cold
   vegetable fat or
   shortening, cut in
   pieces
2 tablespoons iced water

1 For the pastry, sift the flour and salt into a bowl. Add the fat and work in until the mixture resembles bread crumbs. Stir in enough water to bind. Form into a ball, roll out, and use to line a 9-inch pie dish, leaving a ½-inch overhang. Fold this under for double thickness. Flute the edge, then chill.

2 Preheat a baking sheet at 450°F. Peel, core and slice the fruit. Combine in a bowl with one-third of the sugar, the cornstarch, salt, lemon rind and juice, and raisins.

3 For the crumble topping, combine the remaining sugar, flour, cinnamon and butter in a bowl. Rub in until the mixture resembles coarse bread crumbs.

4 Spoon the filling into the pastry case. Sprinkle the crumbs over the top.

5 Bake on the baking sheet for 10 minutes, then reduce the heat to 350°F. Cover the pie loosely with foil and bake until browned, 35–40 minutes more.

Chocolate Lemon Tart

The unusual chocolate pastry complements the lemon filling superbly in this rich tart.

Serves 8–10

1¼ cups superfine sugar	**For the pastry**
6 eggs	generous 1½ cups all-
grated rind of 2 lemons	purpose flour
generous ⅔ cup fresh	2 tablespoons cocoa
lemon juice	4 tablespoons
generous ⅔ cup whipping	confectioner's sugar
cream	½ teaspoon salt
chocolate curls, to	½ cup butter or
decorate	margarine
	1 tablespoon water

1 Grease a 10-inch pie dish. For the pastry, sift the flour, cocoa, confectioner's sugar and salt into a bowl. Set aside.

2 Melt the butter or margarine and water over low heat. Pour over the flour mixture and stir until the dough is smooth.

3 Press the dough evenly over the base and sides of the dish. Chill while preparing the filling.

4 Preheat a baking sheet in the oven at 375°F. Whisk the sugar and eggs until the sugar is dissolved. Add the lemon rind and juice and mix well. Add the cream.

5 Pour the filling into the pastry case and bake on the hot baking sheet until the filling is set, 20–25 minutes. Cool on a wire rack, then decorate with chocolate curls.

Kiwi Ricotta Cheese Tart

A delicious filling in a rich pastry case creates an elegant dinner party dessert.

Serves 8

½ cup blanched almonds,	5 kiwi fruit
ground	
½ cup sugar	**For the pastry**
4 cups ricotta cheese	1¼ cups all-purpose flour
1 cup whipping cream	1 tablespoon sugar
1 egg and 3 egg yolks	½ teaspoon each salt and
1 tablespoon all-purpose	baking powder
flour	6 tablespoons butter, cut
pinch of salt	into pieces
2 tablespoons rum	1 egg yolk
grated rind of 1 lemon	3–4 tablespoons
2 tablespoons lemon juice	whipping cream
2 tablespoons honey	

1 For the pastry, mix the flour, sugar, salt and baking powder. Add the butter and work in. Mix in the egg yolk and cream to bind the pastry. Wrap and chill for 30 minutes.

2 Preheat the oven to 425°F. On a lightly floured surface, roll out the dough to a ⅛-inch thickness and line a 9-inch springform pan. Prick the pastry all over with a fork. Line with crumpled wax paper and fill with dried beans. Bake for 10 minutes. Remove the paper and beans and bake for another 6–8 minutes until golden. Reduce oven to 350°F.

3 Mix the almonds with 1 tablespoon of the sugar. Beat the ricotta until creamy, then add the cream, egg, yolks, remaining sugar, flour, salt, rum, lemon rind and 2 tablespoons lemon juice. Beat, add the almonds and mix.

4 Pour into pastry case and bake for 1 hour, until golden. Cool and chill. Mix the honey and remaining lemon juice. Halve the kiwis lengthwise, then slice. Arrange them over the tart and brush with the honey glaze.

Lime Tart

Use lemons instead of limes, with yellow food coloring, if you prefer.

Serves 8

3 large egg yolks
14-ounce can sweetened
   condensed milk
1 tablespoon grated lime
   rind
½ cup fresh lime juice
green food coloring
   (optional)

½ cup whipping cream

For the base
1⅓ cups crushed
   digestive cookies
5 tablespoons butter or
   margarine, melted

1 Preheat the oven to 350°F. For the base, place the crushed cookies in a bowl, add the butter or margarine and mix.

2 Press the mixture evenly over the bottom and sides of a 9-inch pie dish. Bake for 8 minutes, then cool.

3 Beat the yolks until thick. Beat in the milk, lime rind and juice and coloring, if using. Pour into the pastry case and chill until set, about 4 hours.

4 To serve, whip the cream. Pipe a lattice pattern on top, or spoon dollops around the edge.

Fruit Tartlets

You could make one large fruit tart for an elegant dessert, if you like.

Makes 8

¾ cup redcurrant jelly
1 tablespoon fresh lemon
   juice
¾ cup whipping cream
1½ pounds fresh fruit,
   such as strawberries,
   raspberries, kiwi fruit,
   peaches, grapes or
   currants, peeled and
   sliced as necessary

For the pastry
generous ½ cup cold
   butter, cut in pieces
scant ½ cup dark brown
   sugar
3 tablespoons cocoa
1¾ cups all-purpose flour
1 egg white

1 For the pastry, melt the butter, brown sugar and cocoa over low heat. Remove from the heat and sift over the flour. Stir, then add enough egg white to bind. Form into a ball, wrap, and chill for 30 minutes.

2 Grease eight 3-inch tartlet pans. Roll out the pastry between two sheets of wax paper. Stamp out eight 4-inch rounds with a fluted cookie cutter.

3 Line the tartlet pans and prick the pastry with a fork. Chill for 15 minutes. Preheat the oven to 350°F.

4 Bake the pastry cases until firm, 20–25 minutes. Cool, then turn out.

5 Melt the jelly with the lemon juice. Brush over the tartlet cases. Whip the cream and spread thinly in the tartlet cases. Arrange the fruit on top. Brush with the jelly glaze and serve.

Chocolate Cheesecake Tart

You can just use digestive cookies for the bottom of this tart, if you prefer.

Serves 8

1½ cups cream cheese
4 tablespoons whipping
   cream
generous 1 cup superfine
   sugar
½ cup cocoa
½ teaspoon ground
   cinnamon
3 eggs
whipped cream and
   chocolate curls, to
   decorate

For the base
1 cup crushed digestive
   cookies
scant 1 cup crushed
   amaretti cookies
6 tablespoons butter,
   melted

1 Preheat a baking sheet in the oven at 350°F. For the base, mix the crushed cookies and butter in a bowl. Press the mixture over the bottom and sides of a 9-inch pie dish. Bake for 8 minutes. Let cool. Keep the oven on.

2 Beat the cream cheese and cream together until smooth. Beat in the sugar, cocoa and cinnamon until blended.

3 Add the eggs, one at a time, beating just enough to blend.

4 Pour into the cookie base and bake on the baking sheet for 25–30 minutes. The filling will sink down as it cools. Decorate with whipped cream and chocolate curls.

Frozen Strawberry Tart

For a frozen raspberry tart, use raspberries in place of the strawberries.

Serves 8

1 cup cream cheese
1 cup sour cream
5 cups frozen
   strawberries, defrosted
   and sliced

For the base
1⅓ cups crushed
   digestive cookies
1 tablespoon superfine
   sugar
5 tablespoons butter,
   melted

1 For the base, mix together the cookies, sugar and butter. Press the mixture over the bottom and sides of a 9-inch pie dish. Freeze until firm.

2 Blend together the cream cheese and sour cream. Reserve 6 tablespoons of the strawberries. Add the rest to the cream cheese mixture.

3 Pour the filling into the cookie base and freeze until firm, about 6–8 hours. To serve, spoon some of the reserved strawberries on top.

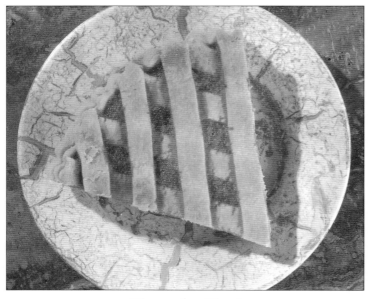

Treacle Tart

A very rich dessert, popular with all the family.

Serves 4–6

¾ cup maple syrup
1½ cups fresh white
  bread crumbs
grated rind of 1 lemon
2 tablespoons fresh lemon
  juice

For the pastry
1½ cups all-purpose flour
½ teaspoon salt
6 tablespoons cold butter,
  cut in pieces
3 tablespoons cold
  margarine, cut in
  pieces
3–4 tablespoons iced
  water

1 For the pastry, sift together the flour and salt, add the fats and work in until the mixture resembles coarse bread crumbs. Stir in enough water to bind. Form into a ball, wrap and chill for 20 minutes.

2 Roll out the pastry and use to line an 8-inch pie dish. Chill for 20 minutes. Reserve the pastry trimmings.

3 Preheat a baking sheet in the oven at 400°F. In a saucepan, warm the syrup until thin and runny. Stir in the bread crumbs and lemon rind. Let stand for 10 minutes, then stir in the lemon juice. Spread in the pastry case.

4 Roll out the pastry trimmings and cut into 12 thin strips. Lay six strips on the filling, then lay the other six at an angle over them to form a lattice.

5 Bake on the baking sheet for 10 minutes. Lower the heat to 375°F. Bake until golden, about 15 minutes more. Serve warm or cold.

Almond Syrup Tart

Serves 6

1½ cups fresh white
  bread crumbs
1 cup maple syrup
finely grated rind of
  ½ lemon
2 teaspoons lemon juice
9-inch pastry case, made
  with basic, nut or rich
  piecrust pastry

4 tablespoons slivered
  almonds
milk, to glaze (optional)
cream, custard, ice
  cream, to serve

1 Preheat the oven to 400°F. Combine the bread crumbs with the syrup and the lemon rind and juice.

2 Spoon into the pastry case and spread out evenly. Sprinkle the slivered almonds evenly over the top.

3 Brush the pastry with milk to glaze, if you like. Bake for 25–30 minutes, until the pastry and filling are golden brown.

4 Transfer to a wire rack to cool. Serve warm or cold, with cream, custard or ice cream.

Tarte Tatin

A special *tarte tatin* pan is ideal, but an oven proof frying pan can be used quite successfully.

Serves 8–10

½ pound puff or piecrust pastry
10–12 large Golden Delicious apples
½ cup butter, cut into pieces
½ cup superfine sugar
½ teaspoon ground cinnamon
crème fraîche or whipped cream, to serve

1 On a lightly floured surface, roll out the pastry to a an 11-inch round less than ¼ inch thick. Transfer to a lightly floured baking sheet and chill.

2 Peel, halve and core the apples, sprinkle with lemon juice.

3 In a 10-inch *tarte tatin* pan or ovenproof frying pan, cook the butter, sugar and cinnamon until the butter has melted and the sugar has dissolved. Cook for 6–8 minutes until the mixture is a medium caramel color. Remove from the heat and arrange the apple halves, standing on edge, in the pan.

4 Return the pan to the heat and simmer for 20–25 minutes until the apples are tender and colored. Remove from the heat and cool slightly.

5 Preheat the oven to 450°F. Place the pastry over the apples and tuck the edges inside the pan around the apples. Pierce the pastry in two or three places, then bake for 25–30 minutes until the pastry is golden and the filling is bubbling. Cool in the pan for 10–15 minutes.

6 To serve, run a sharp knife around the edge of the pan to loosen the pastry. Cover with a serving plate and carefully invert the pan and plate together. It is best to do this over a sink in case any caramel drips. Lift off the pan and loosen any apples that stick with a metal spatula. Serve the tart warm with crème fraîche or whipped cream.

Rich Chocolate Pie

A delicious pie generously decorated with chocolate curls.

Serves 8

3 ounces semisweet chocolate
4 tablespoons butter or margarine
3 tablespoons maple syrup
3 eggs, beaten
⅔ cup superfine sugar
1 teaspoon vanilla extract
4 ounces milk chocolate
2 cups whipping cream

For the pastry

1⅓ cups all-purpose flour
½ teaspoon salt
½ cup vegetable fat or shortening
2–3 tablespoons iced water

1 Preheat the oven to 425°F. For the pastry, sift the flour and salt into a bowl. Work in the fat until the mixture resembles coarse bread crumbs. Add water until the pastry forms a ball.

2 Roll out the pastry and use to line an 8–9-inch quiche pan. Flute the edge. Prick the bottom and sides of the pastry case with a fork. Bake until lightly browned, 10–15 minutes. Cool in the pan on a wire rack.

3 Reduce the oven temperature to 350°F. In the top of a double boiler, melt the semisweet chocolate, butter or margarine and syrup. Remove from the heat and stir in the eggs, sugar and vanilla. Pour the chocolate mixture into the pastry case. Bake until the filling is set, 35–40 minutes. Cool in the pan on a wire rack.

4 For the decoration, use the heat of your hands to soften the milk chocolate slightly. Use a swivel-headed vegetable peeler to shave off short, wide curls. Chill until needed.

5 Before serving, lightly whip the cream until soft peaks form. Spread the cream over the surface of the chocolate filling. Decorate with the milk chocolate curls.

Red Berry Tart with Lemon Cream

This tart is best filled just before serving so the pastry remains mouth-wateringly crisp.

Serves 6–8

1¼ cups all-purpose flour
4 tablespoons cornstarch
scant ⅓ cup
   confectioner's sugar
7 tablespoons butter
1 teaspoon vanilla
   extract
2 egg yolks, beaten

For the filling
scant 1 cup cream cheese,
   softened
3 tablespoons lemon curd
grated rind and juice of
   1 lemon
confectioner's sugar, to
   taste (optional)
2 cups mixed red berry
   fruits
3 tablespoons redcurrant
   jelly

1 Sift the flour, cornstarch and confectioner's sugar together. Rub in the butter until the mixture resembles bread crumbs.

2 Beat the vanilla into the egg yolks, then stir into the flour mixture to make a firm dough. Add cold water if necessary.

3 Roll out the pastry and use it to line a 9-inch round quiche pan. Trim the edges. Prick the pastry and let rest in the fridge for 30 minutes.

4 Preheat the oven to 400°F. Line the tart with wax paper and fill with baking beans. Place on a baking sheet and bake for 20 minutes, removing the paper and beans after 15 minutes. Let cool, then remove the pastry case from the quiche pan.

5 Cream the cheese, lemon curd and lemon rind and juice, adding confectioner's sugar, if you wish. Spread the mixture into the base of the tart. Top with the fruits.

6 Warm the redcurrant jelly and trickle over the fruits just before serving.

Peach Tart with Almond Cream

Serves 8–10

1 cup blanched almonds
2 tablespoons all-purpose
   flour
scant ¼ cup sweet butter
1 cup, plus 2 tablespoons
   superfine sugar
1 egg, plus 1 egg yolk
¼ teaspoon vanilla
   extract, or 2 teaspoons
   rum
4 large ripe peaches,
   peeled

For the pastry
generous 1½ cups all-
   purpose flour
½ teaspoon salt
scant ¼ cup cold sweet
   butter, diced
1 egg yolk
2–3 tablespoons iced
   water

1 Sift the flour and salt into a bowl. Rub in the butter until the mixture resembles coarse bread crumbs. Stir in the egg yolk and enough water to bind the pastry. Gather into a ball, wrap and chill for at least 20 minutes. Preheat a baking sheet in the center of a 400°F oven.

2 Roll out the pastry ⅛ inch thick. Transfer to a 10-inch pie dish. Trim the edge, prick with a fork and chill.

3 Grind the almonds with the flour. With an electric mixer, cream the butter and scant ¾ cup of the sugar until light and fluffy. Gradually beat in the egg and yolk. Stir in the almonds and vanilla or rum. Spread in the pastry case.

4 Halve the peaches and remove the pits. Cut crosswise in thin slices and arrange on top of the almond cream like the spokes of a wheel. Keep the slices of each peach-half together. Fan out by pressing down gently at a slight angle.

5 Bake until the pastry browns, 10–15 minutes. Lower the heat to 350°F and bake until the almond cream sets, about 15 minutes more. 10 minutes before the end of the cooking time, sprinkle with the remaining sugar.

Pear and Almond Cream Tart

This tart is equally successful made with nectarines, peaches, apricots or apples.

Serves 6

12 ounces piecrust or sweet piecrust pastry	**For the filling**
3 firm pears	generous ½ cup blanched whole almonds
lemon juice	4 tablespoons superfine sugar
1 tablespoon peach brandy or cold water	5 tablespoons butter
4 tablespoons peach jam, strained	1 egg, plus 1 egg white
	few drops almond extract

1 Roll out the pastry and use to line a 9-inch quiche pan. Chill. For the filling, put the almonds and sugar in a food processor or blender and process until finely ground but not pasty. Add the butter and process until creamy, then add the egg, egg white and almond extract and mix well.

2 Preheat a baking sheet in the oven at 375°F. Peel the pears, halve them, remove the cores and rub with lemon juice. Put the pear halves, cut-side down, on a board and slice thinly crosswise, keeping the slices together.

3 Pour the filling into the pastry case. Slide a metal spatula under one pear half and press the top to fan out the slices. Transfer to the tart, placing the fruit on the filling like spokes of a wheel.

4 Bake the tart on the baking sheet for 50–55 minutes, until the filling is set and well browned. Cool on a wire rack.

5 Heat the brandy or water with the jam. Brush over the top of the hot tart to glaze. Serve at room temperature.

Lemon Tart

This tart, a classic of France, has a refreshing tangy flavor.

Serves 8–10

12 ounces piecrust or sweet piecrust pastry	½ cup superfine sugar
grated rind of 2–3 lemons	4 tablespoons crème fraîche or heavy cream
⅔ cup freshly squeezed lemon juice	4 eggs, plus 3 egg yolks
	confectioner's sugar, for dusting

1 Preheat the oven to 375°F. Roll out the pastry and use to line a 9-inch quiche pan. Prick the pastry, line with foil and fill with baking beans. Bake for 15 minutes, or until the edges are dry. Remove the foil and beans, and bake for 5–7 minutes more, until golden.

2 Beat together the lemon rind, juice and sugar, then gradually add the crème fraîche or cream and beat until well blended. Beat in the eggs, one at a time, then beat in the yolks.

3 Pour the filling into the baked pastry case. Bake for about 15–20 minutes, until the filling is set. If the pastry begins to brown too much, cover the edges with foil. Let cool. Dust with confectioner's sugar before serving.

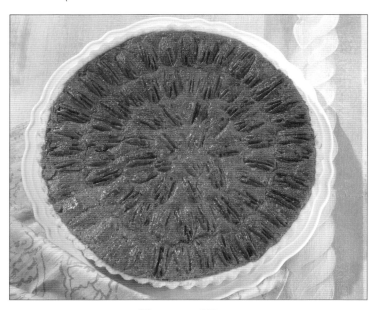

Maple Walnut Tart

Pecan Tart

Makes sure you use 100 per cent pure maple syrup in this decadent tart.

Serve this tart warm, accompanied by ice cream or whipped cream, if you wish.

Serves 8

3 eggs
¼ teaspoon salt
4 tablespoons superfine sugar
4 tablespoons butter, melted
1 cup pure maple syrup
1 cup chopped walnuts
whipped cream, to decorate

For the pastry

9 tablespoons all-purpose flour
½ cup whole wheat flour
¼ teaspoon salt
4 tablespoons cold butter, cut in pieces
3 tablespoons cold vegetable fat or shortening, cut in pieces
1 egg yolk

1 For the pastry, mix the flours and salt in a bowl. Add the fats and rub in until the mixture resembles coarse bread crumbs. Stir in the egg yolk and 2–3 tablespoons iced water to bind. Form into a ball, wrap and chill for 20 minutes.

2 Preheat the oven to 425°F. Roll out the pastry and use to line a 9-inch pie dish. Use the trimmings to stamp out heart shapes. Arrange on the pastry case rim with a little water.

3 Prick the pastry base, line with wax paper and fill with baking beans. Bake for 10 minutes. Remove the paper and beans and bake until golden, 3–6 minutes more.

4 Whisk together the eggs, salt and sugar. Stir in the butter and maple syrup. Set the pastry case on a baking sheet. Pour in the filling, then sprinkle with the nuts.

5 Bake until just set, about 35 minutes. Cool on a wire rack. Decorate with piped whipped cream.

Serves 8

3 eggs
pinch of salt
generous 1 cup dark brown sugar
½ cup maple syrup
2 tablespoons fresh lemon juice
6 tablespoons butter, melted
1¼ cups chopped pecans
½ cup pecan halves

For the pastry

1½ cups all-purpose flour
1 tablespoon superfine sugar
1 teaspoon baking powder
½ teaspoon salt
6 tablespoons cold sweet butter, cut in pieces
1 egg yolk
3–4 tablespoons whipping cream

1 For the pastry, sift together the flour, sugar, baking powder and salt. Add the butter and rub in until the mixture resembles coarse bread crumbs.

2 Blend the egg yolk and whipping cream, then stir into the flour mixture.

3 Form the pastry into a ball, then roll out and use to line a 9-inch pie dish. Flute the edge and chill for 20 minutes.

4 Preheat a baking sheet in the oven at 400°F. Lightly whisk the eggs and salt. Mix in the sugar, syrup, lemon juice and butter. Stir in the chopped nuts.

5 Pour into the pastry case and arrange the pecan halves in concentric circles on top.

6 Bake on the baking sheet for 10 minutes. Reduce the heat to 325°F and bake for 25 minutes more.

Velvety Mocha Tart

A creamy, smooth filling tops a dark, light-textured base in this wondrous dessert.

Serves 8

2 teaspoons instant
   espresso coffee
2 tablespoons hot water
6 ounces semisweet
   chocolate
1 ounce bittersweet
   chocolate
1½ cups whipping cream,
   slightly warmed
½ cup whipped cream, to
   decorate

chocolate-coated coffee
   beans, to decorate

For the base
2½ cups crushed
   chocolate wafers
2 tablespoons superfine
   sugar
5 tablespoons butter,
   melted

1 Combine the base ingredients. Press the mixture over the bottom and sides of a 9-inch pie dish. Chill.

2 Dissolve the coffee in the water. Set aside.

3 Melt the chocolates in the top of a double boiler. Set the bottom of the pan in cold water to cool.

4 Whip the cream until light and fluffy. Add the coffee and whip until the cream just holds its shape.

5 When the chocolate is at room temperature, fold it gently into the cream.

6 Pour into the cookie base and chill until firm. Decorate with piped whipped cream and chocolate-coated coffee beans just before serving.

Coconut Cream Tart

Serves 8

5 ounces dried coconut
¾ cup superfine sugar
4 tablespoons cornstarch
¼ teaspoon salt
2½ cups milk
¼ cup whipping cream
2 egg yolks
2 tablespoons unsalted
   butter
2 teaspoons vanilla
   extract

For the pastry
1¼ cups all-purpose flour
¼ teaspoon salt
3 tablespoons cold butter,
   cut in pieces
3 tablespoons cold
   vegetable fat or
   shortening
2–3 tablespoons iced
   water

1 Sift the flour and salt into a bowl, add the fats and work in until it resembles coarse bread crumbs. With a fork, stir in just enough water to bind the pastry. Gather into a ball, wrap and chill for 20 minutes. Preheat the oven to 425°F.

2 Roll out the pastry ⅛ inch thick. Line a 9-inch pie dish. Trim and flute the edges, prick the base, line with crumpled wax paper and fill with baking beans. Bake for 10–12 minutes. Remove the paper and beans, reduce heat to 350°F and bake until brown, 10–15 minutes.

3 Spread 2 ounces of the coconut on a baking sheet and toast in the oven until golden, 6–8 minutes.

4 Put the sugar, cornstarch and salt in a saucepan. In a bowl, whisk the milk, cream and yolks together. Add the egg mixture to the saucepan.

5 Cook over low heat, stirring, until the mixture comes to a boil. Boil for 1 minute, then remove from the heat. Add the butter, vanilla and remaining coconut.

6 Pour into the pre-baked pastry case. When cool, sprinkle toasted coconut in a ring in the center.

Orange Tart

If you like oranges, this is the dessert for you!

Serves 8

1 cup sugar	**For the pastry**
1 cup fresh orange juice, strained	scant 2 cups all-purpose flour
2 large navel oranges	½ teaspoon salt
scant 1 cup whole blanched almonds	4 tablespoons cold butter, cut into pieces
4 tablespoons butter	3 tablespoons cold margarine, cut into pieces
1 egg	
1 tablespoon all-purpose flour	3–4 tablespoons iced water
3 tablespoons apricot jam	

1 For the pastry, sift the flour and salt into a bowl. Add the butter and margarine and work in until the mixture resembles coarse bread crumbs. Stir in just enough water to bind the dough. Wrap and chill for 20 minutes. Roll out the pastry to a ¼-inch thickness. Use to line an 8-inch quiche pan. Trim and chill until needed.

2 In a saucepan, combine ¾ cup of the sugar and the orange juice and boil until thick and syrupy. Cut the unpeeled oranges into ¼-inch slices. Add to the syrup. Simmer gently for 10 minutes. Put on a wire rack to dry. When cool, cut in half. Reserve the syrup. Place a baking sheet in the oven and heat to 400°F.

3 Grind the almonds finely in a blender or food processor. Cream the butter and remaining sugar until light and fluffy. Beat in the egg and 2 tablespoons of the orange syrup. Stir in the almonds and flour.

4 Melt the jam over low heat, then brush over the pastry case. Pour in the almond mixture. Bake on the baking sheet until set, about 20 minutes, then cool. Arrange overlapping orange slices on top. Boil the remaining syrup until thick and brush on top to glaze.

Raspberry Tart

A luscious tart with a custard topped with juicy berries.

Serves 8

4 egg yolks	**For the pastry**
generous 4 tablespoons superfine sugar	1⅔ cups all-purpose flour
3 tablespoons all-purpose flour	½ teaspoon baking powder
1¼ cups milk	¼ teaspoon salt
¼ teaspoon salt	1 tablespoon sugar
½ teaspoon vanilla extract	grated rind of ½ orange
2⅔ cups fresh raspberries	6 tablespoons cold butter, cut in pieces
5 tablespoons redcurrant jelly	1 egg yolk
1 tablespoon orange juice	3–4 tablespoons whipping cream

1 For the pastry, sift the flour, baking powder and salt into a bowl. Stir in the sugar and orange rind. Add the butter and work in until the mixture resembles bread crumbs. Stir in the egg yolk and cream to bind. Form into a ball, wrap and chill.

2 For the filling, beat the egg yolks and sugar until thick and creamy. Gradually stir in the flour. Bring the milk and salt just to a boil, then remove from the heat. Whisk into the egg yolk mixture, return to the pan and continue whisking over moderately high heat until just bubbling. Cook for 3 minutes to thicken. Transfer to a bowl. Stir in the vanilla, then cover with wax paper.

3 Preheat the oven to 400°F. Roll out the pastry and line a 10-inch pie dish. Prick the base, line with wax paper and fill with baking beans. Bake for 15 minutes. Remove the paper and beans, and bake until golden, 6–8 minutes more. Cool.

4 Spread an even layer of the custard filling in the pastry case and arrange the raspberries on top. Melt the jelly and orange juice in a pan and brush on top to glaze.

Lattice Berry Pie

Choose any berries you like for this handsome pie.

Serves 8

about 4 cups berries,
    such as bilberries,
    blueberries and black
    currants
generous ½ cup superfine
    sugar
3 tablespoons cornstarch
2 tablespoons fresh lemon
    juice
2 tablespoons butter,
    diced

For the pastry

2½ cups all-purpose flour
¾ teaspoon salt
½ cup cold butter, diced
3 tablespoons cold
    vegetable fat or
    shortening, diced
5–6 tablespoons iced
    water
1 egg, beaten with
    1 tablespoon water,
    for glazing

1 For the pastry, sift the flour and salt into a bowl. Add the butter and fat and work in until the mixture resembles coarse bread crumbs. Stir in just enough water to bind. Form into two balls, wrap and chill for 20 minutes. Roll out one ball and use to line a 9-inch pie dish, leaving a ½-inch overhang. Brush the base with egg.

2 Mix all the filling ingredients together, except the butter (reserve a few berries for decoration). Spoon into the pastry case and dot with the butter. Brush egg around the pastry rim.

3 Preheat a baking sheet at 425°F. Roll out the remaining pastry on a baking sheet lined with wax paper. With a serrated pastry wheel, make 24 thin strips. Use the scraps to cut out leaf shapes, and mark veins. Weave the strips in a close lattice and transfer to the pie. Seal the edges and trim. Arrange the leaves around the rim. Brush with egg and bake for 10 minutes.

4 Reduce the heat to 350°F and bake for 40–45 minutes more. Decorate with berries.

Plum Pie

Treat someone special with this lightly spiced plum pie.

Serves 8

2 pounds red or purple
    plums
grated rind of 1 lemon
1 tablespoon fresh lemon
    juice
1–1¼ cups superfine
    sugar
3 tablespoons quick-
    cooking tapioca
¼ teaspoon salt
½ teaspoon ground
    cinnamon
¼ teaspoon grated
    nutmeg

For the pastry

2½ cups all-purpose flour
1 teaspoon salt
6 tablespoons cold butter,
    diced
4 tablespoons cold
    vegetable fat or
    shortening, diced
¼–½ cup iced water
milk, for glazing

1 For the pastry, sift the flour and salt into a bowl. Add the butter and fat and work in until the mixture resembles coarse bread crumbs. Stir in just enough water to bind the pastry. Form into two balls, wrap and chill for 20 minutes.

2 Preheat a baking sheet in the oven at 425°F. Roll out a pastry ball and use to line a 9-inch pie dish.

3 Halve and pit the plums, and chop coarsely. Mix all the filling ingredients together, then transfer to the pastry case.

4 Roll out the remaining pastry, place on a baking sheet lined with wax paper, and stamp out four hearts. Transfer the pastry lid to the pie using the paper.

5 Trim to leave a ¾-inch overhang. Fold this under the pastry base and pinch to seal. Arrange the hearts on top. Brush with milk and bake for 15 minutes. Reduce the heat to 350°F and bake for 30–35 minutes more.

Dorset Apple Cake

Serve this fruity apple cake warm, and spread with butter, if liked.

Makes one 7-inch round cake

2 large cooking apples, peeled, cored and chopped
juice of ½ lemon
2 cups all-purpose flour
1½ teaspoons baking powder
½ cup butter, diced

scant 1 cup light brown sugar
1 egg, beaten
about 2–3 tablespoons milk, to mix
½ teaspoon ground cinnamon

1 Preheat the oven to 350°F. Grease and line a 7-inch round cake pan.

2 Toss the apple with the lemon juice and set aside. Sift the flour and baking powder together, then work in the butter, until the mixture resembles bread crumbs.

3 Stir in ¾ cup of the brown sugar, the apple and the egg, and mix well, adding sufficient milk to make a soft dropping consistency.

4 Transfer the dough to the prepared pan. In a bowl, mix together the remaining sugar and the cinnamon. Sprinkle over the cake mixture, then bake for 45–50 minutes, until golden. Let cool in the pan for 10 minutes, then transfer to a wire rack.

Parkin

The flavor of this cake will improve if it is stored in an airtight container for several days or a week before serving.

Makes 16–20 squares

1¼ cups milk
5 tablespoons maple syrup
4 tablespoons molasses
½ cup butter or margarine, diced
scant ¼ cup dark brown sugar

4 cups all-purpose flour
½ teaspoon baking soda
1¼ teaspoons ground ginger
4 cups medium oatmeal
1 egg, beaten
confectioner's sugar, for dusting

1 Preheat the oven to 350°F. Grease and line the bottom of an 8-inch square cake pan.

2 Gently heat together the milk, syrup, molasses, butter or margarine and sugar, stirring until smooth. Do not allow the mixture to boil.

3 Stir together the flour, baking soda, ginger and oatmeal. Make a well in the center, pour in the egg, then slowly pour in the warmed mixture, stirring to make a smooth batter.

4 Pour the cake batter into the pan and bake for about 45 minutes, until firm to the touch. Cool slightly in the pan, then cool completely on a wire rack. Cut into squares and dust with confectioner's sugar.

Banana Ginger Parkin

Parkin keeps well and really improves with keeping. Store it in a covered container for up to two months.

Makes 16–20 squares

scant 2 cups all-purpose
  flour
2 teaspoons baking soda
2 teaspoons ground
  ginger
1¼ cups medium oatmeal
4 tablespoons dark
  muscovado sugar
6 tablespoons sunflower
  margarine

3 tablespoons maple
  syrup
1 egg, beaten
3 ripe bananas, mashed
¾ cup confectioner's
  sugar
preserved ginger, to
  decorate (optional)

1 Preheat the oven to 325°F. Grease and line the bottom and sides of a 7 x 11-inch cake pan.

2 Sift together the flour, baking soda and ginger, then stir in the oatmeal. Melt the sugar, margarine and syrup in a saucepan, then stir into the flour mixture. Beat in the egg and mashed bananas.

3 Spoon into the pan and bake for about 1 hour, or until firm to the touch. Allow to cool in the pan, then turn out and cut into squares.

4 Sift the confectioner's sugar into a bowl and stir in just enough water to make a smooth, runny icing. Drizzle the icing over each square and top with a piece of preserved ginger, if you like.

Gooseberry Cake

This cake is delicious served warm with whipped cream.

Makes one 7-inch square cake

½ cup butter
1⅓ cups self-rising flour
1 teaspoon baking
  powder
2 eggs, beaten
generous ½ cup superfine
  sugar
1–2 teaspoons rose water

pinch of freshly grated
  nutmeg
4-ounce bottle
  gooseberries in syrup,
  drained, juice reserved
superfine sugar, to
  decorate
whipped cream, to serve

1 Preheat the oven to 350°F. Grease a 7-inch square cake pan, line the bottom and sides with wax paper and grease the paper. Gently melt the butter, then transfer to a mixing bowl and let cool.

2 Sift together the flour and baking powder and add to the butter. Beat in the eggs, one at a time, the sugar, rose water and grated nutmeg, to make a smooth batter.

3 Mix in 1–2 tablespoons of the reserved gooseberry juice, then pour half of the batter mixture into the prepared pan. Sprinkle the gooseberries over the top and pour over the remaining batter mixture.

4 Bake for about 45 minutes, or until a skewer inserted into the center of the cake comes out clean.

5 Let rest in the pan for 5 minutes, then turn out onto a wire rack, peel off the lining paper and let cool for 5 minutes more. Dredge with sugar and serve immediately with whipped cream, or let the cake cool completely before decorating.

Crunchy-topped Sponge Loaf

This light sponge makes a perfect teatime treat.

Makes one 1-pound loaf

scant 1 cup butter,
  softened
finely grated rind of
  1 lemon
5 tablespoons superfine
  sugar
3 eggs
¾ cup all-purpose flour,
  sifted

1¼ cups self-rising flour,
  sifted

For the topping
3 tablespoons honey
¾ cup mixed candied peel
½ cup slivered almonds

1 Preheat the oven to 350°F. Grease and line a 1-pound loaf pan with wax paper. Grease the paper.

2 Beat together the butter, lemon rind and sugar until light and fluffy. Blend in the eggs, one at a time.

3 Sift together the flours, then stir into the egg mixture. Fill the loaf pan.

4 Bake for 45 minutes, or until a skewer inserted into the center comes out clean. Let stand in the pan for 5 minutes.

5 Turn the loaf out onto a wire rack, peel off the lining paper and let cool.

6 For the topping, melt the honey with the candied peel and almonds. Remove from the heat, stir briefly, then spread over the cake top. Cool before serving.

Irish Whiskey Cake

Other whiskies could be used in this cake.

Makes one 9 x 5-inch cake

1½ cups chopped walnuts
generous ½ cup raisins,
  chopped
scant ½ cup currants
1 cup all-purpose flour
1 teaspoon baking
  powder
¼ teaspoon salt
½ cup butter
scant 1½ cups superfine
  sugar

3 eggs, separated, at
  room temperature
1 teaspoon grated
  nutmeg
½ teaspoon ground
  cinnamon
5 tablespoons Irish
  whiskey
confectioner's sugar, for
  dusting

1 Preheat the oven to 325°F. Line the bottom and grease a 9 x 5-inch loaf pan. Mix the nuts and dried fruit with 2 tablespoons of the flour and set aside. Sift together the remaining flour, baking powder and salt.

2 Cream the butter and sugar until light and fluffy. Beat in the egg yolks.

3 Mix the nutmeg, cinnamon and whiskey. Fold into the butter mixture, alternating with the flour mixture.

4 Beat the egg whites until stiff. Fold into the whiskey mixture until just blended. Fold in the walnut mixture.

5 Fill the loaf pan and bake until a skewer inserted in the center comes out clean, about 1 hour. Cool in the pan. To serve, dust with confectioner's sugar over a template.

Fall Dessert Cake

Greengages, plums or semi-dried prunes are delicious in this recipe.

Serves 6–8

½ cup butter, softened
5 tablespoons superfine sugar
3 eggs, beaten
¾ cup ground hazelnuts
1¼ cups shelled pecans, chopped
½ cup all-purpose flour
1 teaspoon baking powder

½ teaspoon salt
3 cups pitted plums, greengages or semi-dried prunes
4 tablespoons lime marmalade
1 tablespoon lime juice
2 tablespoons blanched almonds, chopped, to decorate

1 Preheat the oven to 350°F. Grease a 9-inch round, fluted tart pan.

2 Beat the butter and sugar until light and fluffy. Gradually beat in the eggs, alternating with the ground hazelnuts.

3 Stir in the pecans, then sift and fold in the flour, baking powder and salt. Spoon into the tart pan.

4 Bake for 45 minutes, or until a skewer inserted into the center comes out clean.

5 Arrange the fruit on the base. Return to the oven and bake for 10–15 minutes, until the fruit has softened. Transfer to a wire rack to cool, then turn out.

6 Warm the marmalade and lime juice gently. Brush over the fruit, then sprinkle with the almonds. Let set, then chill before serving.

Apple Crumble Cake

In the fall, use windfall apples. Served warm with thick cream or custard, this cake doubles as a dessert.

Serves 8–10

For the topping
⅔ cup self-rising flour
½ teaspoon ground cinnamon
3 tablespoons butter
2 tablespoons superfine sugar

For the base
4 tablespoons butter, softened
6 tablespoons superfine sugar
1 egg, beaten

1 cup self-rising flour, sifted
2 cooking apples, peeled, cored and sliced
4 tablespoons golden raisins

To decorate
1 red dessert apple, cored, thinly sliced and tossed in lemon juice
2 tablespoons superfine sugar, sifted
pinch of ground cinnamon

1 Preheat the oven 350°F. Grease a deep 7-inch springform pan, line the bottom with wax paper and grease the paper.

2 To make the topping, sift the flour and cinnamon into a mixing bowl. Work the butter into the flour until it resembles bread crumbs, then stir in the sugar. Set aside.

3 To make the base, put the butter, sugar, egg and flour into a bowl and beat for 1–2 minutes until smooth. Spoon into the prepared pan.

4 Mix together the apple slices and golden raisins and spread them evenly over the top. Sprinkle with the topping.

5 Bake in the center of the oven for about 1 hour. Cool in the pan for 10 minutes before turning out onto a wire rack and peeling off the lining paper. Serve warm or cool, decorated with slices of red dessert apple and superfine sugar and cinnamon sprinkled over the top.

Light Fruit Cake

For the best flavor, wrap this cake in foil and store for a week before cutting.

Makes two 9 x 5-inch cakes

1 cup prunes
1⅓ cups dates
1 cup currants
generous 1½ cups golden
 raisins
1 cup dry white wine
1 cup rum
3 cups all-purpose flour
2 teaspoons baking
 powder
1 teaspoon ground
 cinnamon

½ teaspoon grated
 nutmeg
1 cup butter, at room
 temperature
scant 1¼ cups superfine
 sugar
4 eggs, lightly beaten
1 teaspoon vanilla
 extract

1 Pit the prunes and dates and chop finely. Place in a bowl with the currants and golden raisins. Stir in the wine and rum and let stand, covered, for 2 days. Stir occasionally.

2 Preheat the oven to 300°F with a tray of hot water in the bottom. Line two 9 x 5-inch loaf pans with wax paper and grease the paper.

3 Sift together the flour, baking powder, ground cinnamon and grated nutmeg.

4 Cream the butter and sugar together until light and fluffy. Gradually add the eggs and vanilla. Fold in the flour mixture in three batches. Fold in the dried fruit mixture and its liquid.

5 Divide the mixture between the pans and bake until a skewer inserted in the center comes out clean, about 1½ hours. Stand for 20 minutes, then unmold onto a wire rack.

Rich Fruit Cake

Makes one 9 x 3-inch cake

½ cup currants
generous 1 cup raisins
½ cup golden raisins
4 tablespoons candied
 cherries, halved
3 tablespoons sweet
 sherry
¾ cup butter
scant 1 cup dark brown
 sugar
2 eggs, at room
 temperature
1¾ cups all-purpose flour
2 teaspoons baking
 powder

2 teaspoons each ground
 ginger, allspice, and
 cinnamon
1 tablespoon maple syrup
1 tablespoon milk
5 tablespoons cut mixed
 candied peel
1 cup chopped walnuts

For the decoration
½ cup orange marmalade
candied citrus fruit slices
candied cherries

1 A day in advance, mix the dried fruit and cherries in a bowl. Stir in the sherry, cover and soak overnight.

2 Preheat the oven to 300°F. Line and grease the bottom and sides of a 9 x 3-inch springform pan with wax paper. Place a tray of hot water on the bottom of the oven.

3 Cream the butter and sugar. Beat in the eggs, 1 at a time. Sift the flour, baking powder and spices together three times. Fold into the butter mixture in three batches. Fold in the syrup, milk, dried fruit and liquid, candied peel and nuts.

4 Spoon into the pan, spreading out so there is a slight depression in the center. Bake for about 2½–3 hours. Cover with foil when the top is golden to prevent over-browning. Cool in the pan on a rack.

5 Melt the marmalade over low heat, then brush over the top of the cake. Decorate with the candied citrus fruit slices and cherries.

Creole Christmas Cake

Makes one 9-inch cake

3 cups raisins
1 cup currants
¾ cup golden raisins
½ cup non-soak prunes, chopped
1 cup candied orange peel, chopped
1 cup chopped walnuts
4 tablespoons dark brown sugar
1 teaspoon vanilla extract
1 teaspoon ground cinnamon
¼ teaspoon each ground nutmeg and cloves
1 teaspoon salt

4 tablespoons each rum, brandy and whisky

For the second stage
2 cups all-purpose flour
1 teaspoon baking powder
1 cup raw sugar
1 cup butter
4 eggs, beaten

For the topping
¾ cup apricot jam, strained
pecan halves and candied kumquat slices, to decorate

1 Put the first set of ingredients into a pan, mix and heat gently. Simmer over low heat for 15 minutes. Remove from the heat and cool. Transfer to a lidded jar and let stand in the fridge for 7 days, stirring at least once a day.

2 Preheat the oven to 275°F. Line a 9-inch round cake pan with a double thickness of nonstick parchment paper and grease it well. Beat the flour, baking powder, sugar and butter together until smooth, then gradually beat in the eggs until the mixture is well blended and smooth.

3 Fold in the fruit mixture and stir well to mix. Spoon the mixture into the pan, level the surface and bake in the center of the oven for 3 hours. Cover with foil and bake for 1 hour, until the cake feels springy. Cool on a wire rack, then remove from the pan. Wrap in foil. The cake will keep well for 1 year.

4 To decorate, heat the jam with 2 tablespoons water and brush half over the cake. Arrange the nuts and fruit over the cake and brush with the remaining apricot glaze.

Light Jeweled Fruit Cake

If you want to cover this cake with marzipan and icing, omit the almond decoration.

Makes one 8-inch round or 7-inch square cake

½ cup currants
¾ cup golden raisins
1 cup mixed candied cherries, quartered
½ cup mixed candied peel, finely chopped
2 tablespoons rum, brandy or sherry
1 cup butter
generous 1 cup superfine sugar
finely grated rind of 1 orange

grated rind of 1 lemon
4 eggs
½ cup chopped almonds
5 tablespoons ground almonds
2 cups all-purpose flour

To decorate
5 tablespoons whole blanched almonds (optional)
1 tablespoon apricot jam

1 A day in advance, soak the currants, golden raisins, candied cherries and peel in the rum, brandy or sherry, cover and let soak overnight.

2 Grease and line either an 8-inch round cake pan or a 7-inch square cake pan with a double thickness of wax paper. Preheat the oven to 325°F. Beat the butter, sugar and orange and lemon rinds together until light and fluffy. Beat in the eggs, one at a time. Mix in the chopped almonds, ground almonds, soaked fruits (with the liquid) and the flour. Spoon into the cake pan and level the top. Bake for 30 minutes.

3 Arrange the almonds, if using, on top of the cake (do not press them into the cake or they will sink during cooking). Return the cake to the oven and cook for 1½–2 hours, or until the center is firm to the touch.

4 Let the cake cool in the pan for 30 minutes, then turn it out in its paper onto a wire rack. When cold, wrap foil over the paper and store in a cool place. To finish, warm, then strain the jam and use to glaze the cake.

Angel Cake

This heavenly cake tastes simply divine!

Makes one 10-inch cake

generous 1 cup sifted all-
    purpose flour
2 tablespoons cornstarch
1½ cups superfine sugar
10–11 egg whites
1¼ teaspoon cream of
    tartar

¼ teaspoon salt
1 teaspoon vanilla
    extract
¼ teaspoon almond
    extract
confectioner's sugar, to
    decorate

1 Preheat the oven to 325°F. Sift the flours before measuring, then sift them four times together with ½ cup of the sugar.

2 Beat the egg whites until foamy. Sift over the cream of tartar and salt and continue to beat until the egg whites form soft peaks.

3 Add the remaining sugar in three batches, beating well after each addition. Stir in the vanilla and almond extracts. Fold in the flour mixture in two batches.

4 Transfer to an ungreased 10-inch cake pan and bake until just browned on top, about 1 hour.

5 Turn the pan upside-down onto a wire rack and cool for 1 hour. Then invert onto a serving plate. Lay a star-shaped template on top of the cake, sift over some confectioner's sugar and remove the template.

Spice Cake with Ginger Frosting

A rich three-layer cake with a creamy ginger frosting.

Makes one 8-inch round cake

1¼ cups milk
2 tablespoons maple
    syrup
2 teaspoons vanilla
    extract
¾ cup chopped walnuts
¾ cup butter, at room
    temperature
1½ cups sugar
1 whole egg, plus 3 egg
    yolks
2½ cups all-purpose flour
1 tablespoon baking
    powder
1 teaspoon grated
    nutmeg
1 teaspoon ground
    cinnamon

½ teaspoon ground cloves
¼ teaspoon ground
    ginger
¼ teaspoon mixed spice
preserved ginger pieces,
    to decorate

For the frosting
¾ cup cream cheese
2 tablespoons sweet
    butter
1⅓ cups confectioner's
    sugar
2 tablespoons finely
    chopped preserved
    ginger
2 tablespoons syrup from
    preserved ginger

1 Preheat the oven to 350°F. Line and grease the bottom and sides of three 8-inch cake pans with wax paper. In a bowl, combine the milk, maple syrup, vanilla and walnuts.

2 Cream the butter and sugar until light and fluffy. Beat in the egg and egg yolks. Add the milk mixture and stir well. Sift together the flour, baking powder and spices three times. Add to the butter mixture in four batches, folding in carefully.

3 Divide the cake mixture between the pans. Bake until the cakes spring back when touched lightly, about 25 minutes. Let stand in the pans for 5 minutes, then cool on a wire rack.

4 For the frosting, combine all the ingredients and beat until smooth. Spread the frosting between the layers and over the top. Decorate with pieces of preserved ginger.

Lemon Coconut Layer Cake

Makes one 8-inch round cake

8 eggs
scant 2 cups superfine
  sugar
1 tablespoon grated
  orange rind
grated rind of 2 lemons
juice of 1 lemon
1¼ cups sweetened,
  shredded coconut
1¼ cups all-purpose
  flour, sifted with
  ¼ teaspoon salt
2 tablespoons cornstarch

1 cup water
6 tablespoons butter

For the frosting
½ cup sweet butter
1 cup confectioner's
  sugar
grated rind of 1 lemon
6–8 tablespoons lemon
  juice
2 cups sweetened
  shredded coconut

1 Preheat the oven to 350°F. Line and grease the bottom and sides of three 8-inch cake pans with wax paper.

2 Place 6 of the eggs in a bowl set over hot water and beat until frothy. Beat in ¾ cup sugar until the mixture doubles in volume. Remove from the heat. Fold in the orange rind, half the lemon rind, 1 tablespoon of the lemon juice and the coconut. Sift over the flour mixture and fold in well.

3 Divide the mixture between the cake pans. Bake until the cakes pull away from the sides of the pans, 25–30 minutes. Let stand in the pans for 5 minutes, then cool on a wire rack.

4 Blend the cornstarch with cold water to dissolve. Whisk in the remaining eggs until blended. In a pan, mix the remaining lemon rind and juice, water, remaining sugar and butter. Bring to a boil. Whisk in the cornstarch, and return to a boil. Whisk until thick. Remove and cover with plastic wrap.

5 Cream the butter and sugar. Stir in the lemon rind and enough lemon juice to obtain a spreadable consistency. Sandwich the cake layers with the lemon custard. Spread the frosting over the top and sides. Cover with the coconut.

Lemon Yogurt Ring

The glaze gives this dessert a refreshing finishing touch.

Serves 12

1 cup butter, at room
  temperature
1½ cups superfine sugar
4 eggs, separated
2 teaspoons grated lemon
  rind
6 tablespoons lemon juice
1 cup plain yogurt
2½ cups all-purpose flour
2 teaspoons baking
  powder

1 teaspoon baking soda
½ teaspoon salt

For the glaze
1 cup confectioner's
  sugar
2 tablespoons lemon juice
3–4 tablespoons plain
  yogurt

1 Preheat the oven to 350°F. Grease a 12½-cup *bundt* or fluted tube pan and dust with flour.

2 Cream the butter and sugar until light and fluffy. Add the egg yolks, one at a time, beating well after each addition. Add the lemon rind, juice and yogurt and stir .

3 Sift together the flour, baking powder and baking soda. In another bowl, beat the egg whites and salt until they hold stiff peaks.

4 Fold the dry ingredients into the butter mixture, then fold in a dollop of egg whites. Fold in the remaining whites.

5 Pour into the pan and bake until a skewer inserted in the center comes out clean, about 50 minutes. Let stand in the pan for 15 minutes, then turn out and cool on a wire rack.

6 For the glaze, sift the confectioner's sugar into a bowl. Stir in the lemon juice and just enough of the plain yogurt to make a smooth glaze.

7 Set the cooled cake on the wire rack over a sheet of wax paper. Pour over the glaze and let set.

Carrot Cake with Geranium Cheese

Makes one 9 x 5-inch cake

1 cup self-rising flour	**For the topping**
1 teaspoon baking soda	2–3 lemon-scented
½ teaspoon ground	geranium leaves
cinnamon	2 cups confectioner's
½ teaspoon ground cloves	sugar
generous 1 cup brown	generous 4 tablespoons
sugar	cream cheese
generous 1½ cups grated	generous 2 tablespoons
carrots	softened butter
1 cup golden raisins	1 teaspoon grated lemon
½ cup finely chopped	rind
preserved ginger	
generous 1 cup pecans	
⅔ cup sunflower oil	
2 eggs, lightly beaten	

1 For the topping, put the geranium leaves, torn into small pieces, in a small bowl and mix with the confectioner's sugar. Let stand in a warm place overnight for the sugar to take up the scent.

2 For the cake, sift the flour, baking soda and spices together. Add the sugar, carrots, golden raisins, ginger and pecans. Stir well, then add the oil and beaten eggs. Mix with an electric mixer for 5 minutes.

3 Preheat the oven to 350°F. Then grease a 9 x 5-inch loaf pan, line the bottom with wax paper, and grease the paper. Pour the mixture into the pan and bake for about 1 hour. Remove the cake from the oven, let stand for a few minutes, and then cool on a wire rack.

4 Meanwhile, make the cream cheese topping. Remove the pieces of geranium leaf from the confectioner's sugar and discard. Place the cream cheese, butter and lemon rind in a bowl. Using an electric mixer, gradually add the confectioner's sugar, beating well until smooth. Spread over the top of the cooled cake.

Carrot and Zucchini Cake

If you can't resist the lure of a slice of iced cake, you'll love this spiced sponge with its delicious creamy topping.

Makes one 7-inch square cake

1 carrot	1 teaspoon confectioner's
1 zucchini	sugar, for dusting
3 eggs, separated	fondant carrots and
¾ cup light brown sugar	zucchini, to decorate
2 tablespoons ground	
almonds	**For the topping**
finely grated rind of	¾ cup low fat cream
1 orange	cheese
1¼ cups self-rising whole	1 teaspoon honey
wheat flour	
1 teaspoon ground	
cinnamon	

1 Preheat the oven to 350°F. Line a 7-inch square pan with nonstick parchment paper. Coarsely grate the carrot and zucchini.

2 Put the egg yolks, sugar, ground almonds and orange rind into a bowl and whisk until very thick and light. Sift together the flour and cinnamon and fold into the mixture together with the grated vegetables. Add any bran left in the strainer.

3 Whisk the egg whites until stiff and carefully fold them in, a half at a time. Spoon into the pan. Bake in the oven for 1 hour, covering the top with foil after 40 minutes. Let cool in the pan for 5 minutes, then turn out onto a wire rack and remove the lining paper.

4 For the topping, beat together the cheese and honey and spread over the cake. Dust with confectioner's sugar and decorate with fondant carrots and zucchini.

Banana Coconut Cake

St Clement's Cake

Slightly overripe bananas are best for this perfect morning cake.

A tangy orange-and-lemon cake makes a spectacular centerpiece when decorated with fruits and flowers.

Makes one 7-inch square cake
½ cup butter, softened
generous ½ cup superfine
   sugar
2 eggs
1 cup self-rising flour
½ cup all-purpose flour
1 teaspoon baking soda
½ cup milk
2 large bananas, peeled
   and mashed

1½ cups dried coconut,
   toasted

For the topping
2 tablespoons butter
2 tablespoons honey
2 cups shredded coconut

Makes one 9-inch ring cake
¾ cup butter
⅓ cup light brown sugar
3 eggs, separated
grated rind and juice of
   1 orange and 1 lemon
1¼ cups self-rising flour
6 tablespoons superfine
   sugar
2 tablespoons ground
   almonds

1½ cups heavy cream
1 tablespoon Grand
   Marnier
16 candied orange and
   lemon slices, silver
   dragées, sugared
   almonds and fresh
   flowers, to decorate

1 Preheat the oven to 375°F. Grease a deep 7-inch square cake pan, line with wax paper and grease the paper.

2 Beat the butter and sugar until smooth and creamy. Beat in the eggs, one at a time. Sift together the flours and baking soda, sift half into the butter mixture and stir to mix.

3 Combine the milk and mashed banana and beat half into the egg mixture. Stir in the remaining flour and banana mixtures and toasted coconut. Transfer to the cake pan and smooth the surface.

4 Bake for 1 hour, or until a skewer inserted into the center of the cake comes out clean. Let stand in the pan for about 5 minutes, then turn out onto a wire rack, peel off the paper and cool.

5 For the topping, gently melt the butter and honey. Stir in the shredded coconut and cook, stirring, for 5 minutes or until lightly browned. Remove from the heat and let cool slightly. Spoon the topping over the cake and let cool.

1 Preheat the oven to 350°F. Grease and flour a 3¾-cup ring mold.

2 Cream half the butter and all of the brown sugar until pale and light. Beat in the egg yolks, orange rind and juice and fold in ⅔ cup flour.

3 Cream the remaining butter and superfine sugar. Stir in the lemon rind and juice and fold in the remaining flour and ground almonds. Whisk the egg whites until stiff, and fold in.

4 Spoon the two mixtures alternately into the prepared pan. Using a skewer or small spoon, swirl through the mixture to create a marbled effect. Bake for 45–50 minutes until risen, and a skewer inserted in the cake comes out clean. Cool in the pan for 10 minutes then transfer to a wire rack to cool.

5 Whip the cream and Grand Marnier together until lightly thickened. Spread over the cake and swirl a pattern over the icing with a metal spatula. Decorate the ring with the candied fruits, dragées and sugared almonds to resemble a jeweled crown. Arrange a few fresh flowers in the center.

Apple Cake

Makes one ring cake

6–7 apples, peeled, cored
  and quartered
generous 2½ cups
  superfine sugar
1 tablespoon water
3 cups all-purpose flour
1¾ teaspoon baking soda
1 teaspoon ground
  cinnamon
1 teaspoon ground cloves
generous 1 cup raisins
1¼ cups chopped walnuts

1 cup butter or
  margarine, at room
  temperature
1 teaspoon vanilla
  extract

For the icing
1 cup confectioner's
  sugar
¼ teaspoon vanilla
  extract
2–3 tablespoons milk

1 Put the apples, 4 tablespoons of the sugar and the water in
a saucepan and bring to a boil. Simmer for 25 minutes,
stirring occasionally to break up any lumps. Let cool. Preheat
the oven to 325°F. Grease and flour a 7½-cup tube pan.

2 Sift the flour, baking soda and spices into a bowl. Remove
2 tablespoons of the mixture to another bowl and toss with
the raisins and 1 cup of the walnuts.

3 Cream the butter or margarine and remaining sugar
together until light and fluffy. Fold in the apple mixture
gently. Fold the flour mixture into the apple mixture. Stir in
the vanilla and the raisin and walnut mixture. Pour into the
tube pan. Bake until a skewer inserted in the center comes out
clean, about 1½ hours. Cool completely in the pan on a wire
rack, then unmold onto the rack.

4 For the icing, put the sugar in a bowl and stir in the vanilla
and 1 tablespoon milk. Add more milk until the icing is
smooth and has a thick pouring consistency. Transfer the cake
to a serving plate and drizzle the icing on top. Sprinkle with
the remaining nuts. Allow the icing to set.

Chocolate Amaretto Marquise

**This light-as-air marquise is perfect for a special occasion,
served with Amaretto cream.**

Makes one heart-shape cake

1 tablespoon sunflower
  oil
7–8 amaretti cookies,
  crushed
2 tablespoons unblanched
  almonds, toasted and
  finely chopped
1 pound semisweet
  chocolate, broken into
  pieces
5 tablespoons Amaretto
  liqueur

5 tablespoons maple
  syrup
2 cups heavy cream
cocoa, to dust

For the Amaretto cream
1½ cups whipping or
  heavy cream
2–3 tablespoons
  Amaretto liqueur

1 Lightly oil a 9-inch heart-shape or springform cake pan.
Line the base with nonstick parchment paper and oil the
paper. Mix the crushed amaretti cookies with the chopped
almonds. Sprinkle evenly over the bottom of the pan.

2 Place the chocolate, Amaretto liqueur and maple syrup in
a saucepan over very low heat. Stir frequently until the
chocolate is melted and the mixture is smooth. Let cool for
6–8 minutes, until the mixture just feels warm.

3 Beat the cream until it just begins to hold its shape. Stir a
large spoonful into the chocolate mixture, then quickly add
the remaining cream and gently fold into the chocolate
mixture. Pour into the prepared pan and tap the pan gently
on the work surface to release any large air bubbles. Cover the
pan with plastic wrap and chill overnight.

4 To unmold, run a thin-bladed sharp knife under hot water
and dry carefully. Run the knife around the edge of the pan to
loosen, place a serving plate over the pan, then invert to
unmold. Carefully peel off the paper then dust with cocoa.
Whip the cream and liqueur and serve separately.

Tangy Lemon Cake

The lemon syrup forms a crusty topping when completely cooled. Let stand in the pan until ready to serve.

Makes one 2-pound loaf

¾ cup butter
scant 1 cup superfine
    sugar
3 eggs, beaten
1½ cups self-rising flour
grated rind of 1 orange
grated rind of 1 lemon

For the syrup
generous ½ cup
    superfine sugar
juice of 2 lemons

1 Preheat the oven to 350°F. Grease a 2-pound loaf pan.

2 Beat the butter and sugar together until light and fluffy, then gradually beat in the eggs. Fold in the flour and the orange and lemon rinds.

3 Turn the cake mixture into the cake pan and bake for 1¼–1½ hours, until set in the center, risen and golden. Remove the cake from the oven, but let stand in the pan.

4 To make the syrup, gently heat the sugar in the lemon juice until melted, then boil for 15 seconds. Pour the syrup over the cake in the pan and let cool.

Pineapple and Apricot Cake

This is not a long-keeping cake, but it does freeze, well-wrapped in wax paper and then foil.

Makes one 7-inch square or 8-inch round cake

¾ cup sweet butter
generous ¾ cup superfine
    sugar
3 eggs, beaten
few drops vanilla extract
2 cups all-purpose flour
¼ teaspoon salt
1½ teaspoons baking
    powder
1¾ cups ready-to-eat
    dried apricots,
    chopped

½ cup each chopped
    candied ginger and
    candied pineapple
grated rind and juice of
    ½ orange
grated rind and juice of
    ½ lemon
a little milk

1 Preheat the oven to 350°F. Double line a 7-inch square or an 8-inch round cake pan. Cream the butter and sugar together until light and fluffy.

2 Gradually beat in the eggs with the vanilla extract, beating well after each addition. Sift together the flour, salt and baking powder, add a little with the last of the egg, then fold in the rest.

3 Gently fold in the apricots, ginger and pineapple and the fruit rinds, then add sufficient fruit juice and milk to give a fairly soft dropping consistency.

4 Spoon into the cake pan and smooth the top with a wet spoon. Bake for 20 minutes, then reduce the oven temperature to 325°F and bake for 1½–2 hours more, or until firm to the touch and a skewer comes out of the center clean. Let the cake cool completely in the pan. Wrap in fresh paper before storing in an airtight container.

Sour Cream Crumble Cake

The consistency of this cake, with its two layers of crumble, is sublime.

Makes one 9-inch square cake

½ cup butter, at room temperature
scant ¾ cup superfine sugar
3 eggs
scant 2 cups all-purpose flour
1 teaspoon baking soda
1 teaspoon baking powder
1 cup sour cream

For the topping
1 cup dark brown sugar
2 teaspoons ground cinnamon
1 cup finely chopped walnuts
4 tablespoons cold butter, cut into pieces

1 Preheat the oven to 350°F. Line the bottom of a 9-inch square cake pan with wax paper and grease the paper and sides.

2 For the topping, place the brown sugar, cinnamon and walnuts in a bowl. Mix, then add the butter and work in until the mixture resembles bread crumbs.

3 To make the cake, cream the butter until soft. Add the sugar and beat until light and fluffy. Add the eggs, one at a time, beating well after each addition.

4 In another bowl, sift the flour, baking soda and baking powder together three times. Fold the dry ingredients into the butter mixture in three batches, alternating with the sour cream. Fold until blended after each addition.

5 Pour half of the batter into the prepared pan and sprinkle over half of the topping. Pour the remaining batter on top and sprinkle over the remaining topping. Bake until browned, 60–70 minutes. Let stand in the pan for 5 minutes, then turn out and cool on a wire rack.

Plum Crumble Cake

This cake can also be made with the same quantity of apricots or cherries.

Serves 8–10

generous ½ cup butter or margarine, at room temperature
¾ cup superfine sugar
4 eggs, at room temperature
1½ teaspoons vanilla extract
1¼ cups all-purpose flour
1 teaspoon baking powder
1½ pounds red plums, halved and pitted

For the topping
1 cup all-purpose flour
generous ¾ cup light brown sugar
1½ teaspoons ground cinnamon
6 tablespoons butter, cut in pieces

1 Preheat the oven to 350°F. Using wax paper, line a 10 x 2-inch pan and grease the paper. For the topping, combine the flour, brown sugar and cinnamon in a bowl. Add the butter and work in until it resembles coarse bread crumbs.

2 Cream the butter or margarine and sugar until light and fluffy. Beat in the eggs, one at a time. Stir in the vanilla. In three batches, sift, then fold in the flour and baking powder.

3 Pour the mixture into the pan. Arrange the plums on top and sprinkle with the topping.

4 Bake until a skewer inserted in the center comes out clean, about 45 minutes. Cool in the pan.

5 To serve, run a knife around the inside edge and invert onto a plate. Invert again onto a serving plate so the topping is uppermost.

Pineapple Upside-down Cake

For an apricot cake, replace the pineapple slices with 1¾ cups dried ready-to-eat apricots.

Makes one 10-inch round cake

½ cup butter	grated rind of 1 lemon
generous 1 cup dark brown sugar	pinch of salt
1 pound canned pineapple slices, drained	generous ½ cup superfine sugar
4 eggs, separated	¾ cup all-purpose flour
	1 teaspoon baking powder

1 Preheat the oven to 350°F. Melt the butter in a 10-inch ovenproof cast-iron frying pan. Then reserve 1 tablespoon butter. Add the brown sugar to the pan and stir to blend. Place the pineapple on top in one layer. Set aside.

2 Whisk together the egg yolks, reserved butter and lemon rind until well blended. Set aside.

3 Beat the egg whites and salt until stiff. Gradually fold in the superfine sugar, then the egg yolk mixture.

4 Sift the flour and baking powder together. Carefully fold into the egg mixture in three batches.

5 Pour the mixture over the pineapple. Bake until a skewer inserted in the center comes out clean, about 30 minutes.

6 While still hot, invert onto a serving plate. Serve either hot or cold.

Upside-down Pear and Ginger Cake

This light, spicy sponge, topped with glossy baked fruit and ginger, makes an excellent dessert.

Serves 6–8

2-pound can pear halves, drained	1½ cups self-rising flour
8 tablespoons finely chopped preserved ginger	½ teaspoon baking powder
8 tablespoons ginger syrup from the jar	1 teaspoon ground ginger
	1 cup light brown sugar
	¾ cup butter, softened
	3 eggs, lightly beaten

1 Preheat the oven to 350°F. Line the bottom and grease a deep 8-inch round cake pan.

2 Fill the hollow in each pear with half the chopped preserved ginger. Arrange, flat-sides down, in the bottom of the cake pan, then spoon over half the ginger syrup.

3 Sift together the flour, baking powder and ground ginger. Stir in the sugar and butter, add the eggs and beat until creamy, 1–2 minutes.

4 Spoon the mixture into the cake pan. Bake in the oven for 50 minutes, or until a skewer inserted in the center of the cake comes out clean. Let the cake stand in the pan for 5 minutes. Turn out onto a wire rack, peel off the lining paper and let cool completely.

5 Add the reserved ginger to the pear halves and drizzle over the remaining syrup.

Cranberry and Apple Ring

Tangy cranberries add an unusual flavor to this cake which is best eaten very fresh.

Makes one ring cake
2 cups self-rising flour
1 teaspoon ground
  cinnamon
½ cup light muscovado
  sugar
1 eating apple, cored and
  diced
¾ cup fresh or frozen
  cranberries
4 tablespoons sunflower
  oil
⅔ cup apple juice
cranberry jelly and apple
  slices, to decorate

1 Preheat the oven to 350°F. Lightly grease a 4-cup ring pan with oil.

2 Sift together the flour and ground cinnamon, then stir in the muscovado sugar.

3 Toss together the diced apple and cranberries. Stir into the dry ingredients, then add the oil and apple juice and beat together well.

4 Spoon the mixture into the prepared ring pan and bake for 35–40 minutes, or until the cake is firm to the touch. Turn out and let cool completely on a wire rack.

5 To serve, drizzle warmed cranberry jelly over the cake and decorate with apple slices.

Greek Honey and Lemon Cake

A wonderfully moist and tangy cake, you could ice it once cooked, if you wished.

Makes one 7½-inch square cake
3 tablespoons sunflower
  margarine
4 tablespoons honey
finely grated rind and
  juice of 1 lemon
⅔ cup milk
1¼ cups all-purpose flour
1½ teaspoons baking
  powder
½ teaspoon grated
  nutmeg
¼ cup semolina
2 egg whites
2 teaspoons sesame seeds

1 Preheat the oven to 400°F. Lightly oil and line the bottom of a 7½-inch square deep cake pan.

2 Place the margarine and 3 tablespoons of the honey in a saucepan and heat gently until melted. Reserve 1 tablespoon lemon juice, then stir in the rest with the lemon rind and milk.

3 Sift together the flour, baking powder and nutmeg, then beat in with the semolina. Whisk the egg whites until they form soft peaks, then fold evenly into the mixture.

4 Spoon into the cake pan and sprinkle with sesame seeds. Bake for 25–30 minutes, until golden brown. Mix the reserved honey and lemon juice and drizzle over the cake while warm. Cool in the pan, then cut into fingers to serve.

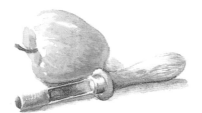

Pear and Cardamom Spice Cake

Fresh pears and cardamoms – a classic combination – are used together in this moist fruit and nut cake.

Makes one 8-inch round cake

½ cup butter
generous ½ cup superfine sugar
2 eggs, lightly beaten
2 cups all-purpose flour
1 tablespoon baking powder
2 tablespoons milk
crushed seeds from 2 cardamom pods

½ cup walnuts, chopped
1 tablespoon poppy seeds
1¼ pounds dessert pears, peeled, cored and thinly sliced
3 walnut halves, to decorate
honey, to glaze

1 Preheat the oven to 350°F. Grease and line the bottom of an 8-inch round, loose-based cake pan.

2 Cream the butter and sugar until pale and light. Gradually beat in the eggs. Sift over the flour and baking powder and fold in with the milk.

3 Stir in the cardamom seeds, chopped nuts and poppy seeds. Reserve one-third of the pear slices, and chop the rest. Fold into the creamed mixture.

4 Transfer to the cake pan. Smooth the surface, making a small dip in the center. Place the walnut halves in the center of the cake and fan the reserved pear slices around the walnuts, covering the cake mixture. Bake for 1¼–1½ hours, or until a skewer inserted in the center comes out clean.

5 Remove the cake from the oven and brush with the honey. Let stand in the pan for 20 minutes, then transfer to a wire rack to cool before serving.

Spiced Honey Nut Cake

A combination of ground pistachios and bread crumbs replaces flour in this recipe, resulting in a light, moist sponge cake.

Makes one 8-inch square cake

generous ½ cup superfine sugar
4 eggs, separated
grated rind and juice of 1 lemon
generous 1 cup ground pistachios
scant 1 cup dried bread crumbs

For the glaze
1 lemon
6 tablespoons honey
1 cinnamon stick
1 tablespoon brandy

1 Preheat the oven to 350°F. Grease and line the bottom of an 8-inch square cake pan.

2 Beat the sugar, egg yolks, lemon rind and juice together until pale and creamy. Fold in 1 cup of the ground pistachios and the bread crumbs.

3 Whisk the egg whites until stiff and fold into the creamed mixture. Transfer to the cake pan and bake for 15 minutes, until risen and springy to the touch. Cool in the pan for 10 minutes, then transfer to a wire rack.

4 For the syrup, peel the lemon and cut the rind into very thin strips. Squeeze the juice into a small pan and add the honey and cinnamon stick. Bring to a boil, add the shredded rind, and simmer fast for 1 minute. Cool slightly and stir in the brandy.

5 Place the cake on a serving plate, prick all over with a skewer, and pour over the cooled syrup, lemon shreds and cinnamon stick. Sprinkle over the reserved pistachios.

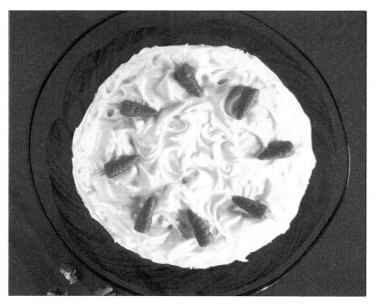

Clare's American Carrot Cake

Makes one 8-inch round cake

1 cup corn oil
1¼ cups granulated
   sugar
3 eggs
1½ cups all-purpose flour
1½ teaspoons baking
   powder
1½ teaspoons baking soda
¼ teaspoon salt
1½ teaspoons ground
   cinnamon
good pinch of grated
   nutmeg
¼ teaspoon ground
   ginger
1 cup chopped walnuts

generous 1½ cups finely
   grated carrots
1 teaspoon vanilla
   extract
2 tablespoons sour cream
8 tiny marzipan carrots,
   to decorate

For the frosting
1 cup full fat cream
   cheese
2 tablespoons butter,
   softened
2 cups confectioner's
   sugar, sifted

1 Preheat the oven to 350°F. Grease and line the bottom of two 8-inch loose-based round cake pans.

2 Put the corn oil and sugar into a bowl and beat well. Add the eggs, one at a time, and beat thoroughly. Sift the flour, baking powder, baking soda, salt, cinnamon, nutmeg and ginger into the bowl and beat well. Fold in the chopped walnuts and grated carrots and stir in the vanilla extract and sour cream.

3 Divide the mixture between the cake pans and bake in the center of the oven for about 65 minutes, or until a skewer inserted into the center of the cakes comes out clean. Let cool in the pans on a wire rack before turning out.

4 Beat all the frosting ingredients together until smooth. Sandwich the cakes together with a little frosting. Spread the remaining frosting over the top and sides of the cake. Just before serving, decorate with the marzipan carrots.

Passion Cake

This cake is associated with Passion Sunday. The carrot and banana give it a rich, moist texture.

Makes one 8-inch round cake

1¾ cups self-rising flour
2 teaspoons baking
   powder
1 teaspoon cinnamon
½ teaspoon freshly grated
   nutmeg
10 tablespoons butter,
   softened, or sunflower
   margarine
¾ cup brown sugar
grated rind of 1 lemon
2 eggs, beaten
2 carrots, coarsely grated
1 ripe banana, mashed
¾ cup raisins

½ cup chopped walnuts
   or pecans
2 tablespoons milk
6–8 walnuts, halved, to
   decorate
coffee crystal sugar, to
   decorate

For the frosting
scant 1 cup cream cheese,
   softened
scant ⅓ cup
   confectioner's sugar
juice of 1 lemon
grated rind of 1 orange

1 Preheat the oven to 350°F. Line and grease the bottom and sides of a deep 8-inch round cake pan. Sift the flour, baking powder and spices into a bowl. In another bowl, cream the butter or margarine and sugar with the lemon rind until it is light and fluffy, then beat in the eggs. Fold in the flour mixture, then the carrots, banana, raisins, chopped nuts and milk.

2 Spoon the mixture into the cake pan, level the top and bake for about 1 hour, until risen and the top is springy to touch. Turn the pan upside-down and let the cake cool in the pan for 30 minutes. Then turn out onto a wire rack. When cold, split the cake in half.

3 Cream the cheese with the confectioner's sugar, lemon juice and orange rind, then sandwich the two halves of the cake together with half of the frosting. Spread the rest of the frosting on top and decorate with walnut halves and sugar.

Caribbean Fruit and Rum Cake

Definitely a festive treat, this spicy cake contains both rum and sherry.

Makes one 10-inch round cake

2 cups currants	1¼ cups sherry, plus
2¾ cups raisins	more if needed
1 cup prunes, pitted	4 cups self-rising flour
¾ cup mixed candied peel	2 cups butter, softened
2⅔ cups dark brown	10 eggs, beaten
sugar	1 teaspoon vanilla
1 teaspoon mixed spice	extract
6 tablespoons rum, plus	
more if needed	

1 Finely chop the dried fruits and peel in a food processor or blender. Combine them in a bowl with generous ½ cup of the sugar, the mixed spice, rum and sherry. Cover and let stand for 2 weeks. Stir daily and add more alcohol if you wish.

2 Preheat the oven to 325°F. Grease and then line a 10-inch round cake pan with a double layer of wax paper.

3 Sift the flour, and set aside. Cream together the butter and remaining sugar and beat in the eggs until the mixture is smooth and creamy.

4 Add the fruit mixture, then gradually stir in the flour and vanilla extract. Mix well, adding more sherry if the mixture is too stiff; it should just fall off the back of the spoon.

5 Spoon the mixture into the prepared pan, cover loosely with foil and bake for about 2½ hours, until the cake is firm and springy. Let cool in the pan overnight.

Thai Rice Cake

A celebration gâteau made from fragrant Thai rice covered with a tangy cream icing and topped with fresh fruits.

Makes one 10-inch round cake

1¼ cups Thai fragrant	**For the topping**
rice	1¼ cups heavy cream
4½ cups milk	scant 1 cup quark
½ cup superfine sugar	1 teaspoon vanilla
6 cardamom pods,	extract
crushed open	grated rind of 1 lemon
2 bay leaves	scant ¼ cup superfine
1¼ cups whipping cream	sugar
6 eggs, separated	soft berry fruits and
	sliced star or kiwi
	fruit, to decorate

1 Grease and line a deep 10-inch round cake pan. Boil the rice in unsalted water for 3 minutes, then drain.

2 Return the rice to the pan with the milk, sugar, cardamom pods and bay leaves. Bring to a boil, then simmer for 20 minutes, stirring occasionally.

3 Let cool, then remove the bay leaves and any cardamom husks. Turn into a bowl. Beat in the cream and then the egg yolks. Preheat the oven to 350°F.

4 Whisk the egg whites until they form soft peaks and fold into the rice mixture. Spoon into the cake pan and bake for 45–50 minutes, until risen and golden brown. The center should be slightly wobbly – it will firm up as it cools.

5 Chill overnight in the pan. Turn out onto a large serving plate. Whip the cream until stiff, then mix in the quark, vanilla extract, lemon rind and sugar. Cover the top and sides of the cake with the cream, swirling it attractively. Decorate with soft berry fruits and sliced star or kiwi fruit.

Luxurious Chocolate Cake

This delicious chocolate cake contains no flour and has a light mousse-like texture.

Makes one 8-inch round cake

¾ cup butter, softened
⅔ cup superfine sugar
9 x 1-ounce squares semisweet chocolate, melted

2 cups ground almonds
4 eggs, separated
4 x 1-ounce squares white chocolate, melted, to decorate

1 Preheat the oven to 350°F. Grease and line the bottom of an 8-inch springform cake pan. Beat 8 tablespoons butter and all the sugar until light and fluffy. Add two-thirds of the semisweet chocolate, almonds and egg yolks and beat well.

2 Whisk the egg whites in another clean, dry bowl until stiff. Fold them into the chocolate mixture, then transfer to the pan and smooth the surface. Bake for 50–55 minutes or until a skewer inserted into the center comes out clean. Cool in the pan for 5 minutes, then remove from the pan and transfer to a wire rack. Remove the lining paper and cool completely.

3 Place the remaining butter and melted chocolate in a saucepan. Heat very gently, stirring constantly, until melted. Place a large sheet of wax paper under the wire rack to catch any drips. Pour the chocolate topping over the cake, allowing it to coat the top and sides. Let set for at least 1 hour.

4 To decorate, fill a paper icing bag with the melted white chocolate and snip the end. Drizzle the white chocolate around the edges. Use any remaining chocolate to make leaves. Let set, then place on top of the cake.

One-stage Chocolate Sponge

For family teas, quick-and-easy favorites like this chocolate cake are invaluable.

Makes one 7-inch round cake

¾ cup soft margarine, at room temperature
½ cup superfine sugar
4 tablespoons maple syrup
1½ cups self-rising flour, sifted
3 tablespoons cocoa, sifted

½ teaspoon salt
3 eggs, beaten
a little milk, as required
⅔ cup whipping cream
1–2 tablespoons fine shred marmalade
confectioner's sugar, for dusting

1 Preheat the oven to 350°F. Lightly grease or line two 7-inch sandwich cake pans. Place the margarine, sugar, syrup, flour, cocoa, salt and eggs in a large bowl, and cream together until well blended. If the mixture seems a little thick, stir in 1–2 tablespoons milk to get a soft dropping consistency.

2 Spoon the mixture into the prepared pans and bake for about 30 minutes, changing shelves if necessary after 15 minutes, until the tops are just firm and the cakes are springy to the touch.

3 Let the cakes cool for 5 minutes, then remove from the pans and let cool completely on a wire rack.

4 Whip the cream and fold in the marmalade, then use to sandwich the two cakes together. Sprinkle the top with sifted confectioner's sugar.

One-stage Victoria Sandwich

This versatile sponge recipe can be used for all sorts of cakes.

Makes one 7-inch round cake

1½ cups self-rising flour	**To finish**
pinch of salt	4–6 tablespoons
¾ cup butter, softened	raspberry jam
scant 1 cup superfine	superfine sugar or
sugar	confectioner's sugar
3 eggs	

1 Preheat the oven to 350°F. Grease two 7-inch sandwich cake pans, line the bottoms with wax paper and grease.

2 Whisk all the cake ingredients together until smooth and creamy. Divide the mixture between the cake pans and smooth the surfaces.

3 Bake for 25–30 minutes, or until a skewer inserted into the center of the cakes comes out clean. Turn out onto a wire rack, peel off the paper and let cool.

4 Place one of the cakes on a serving plate and spread with the raspberry jam. Place the other cake on top.

5 Cut out paper star shapes, place on the cake and dredge with sugar. Remove the paper to reveal the pattern.

Mocha Victoria Sponge

A light coffee- and cocoa-flavored sponge with a rich buttercream topping.

Makes one 7-inch round cake

¾ cup butter	**For the buttercream**
generous ¾ cup superfine	generous ½ cup butter
sugar	1 tablespoon coffee
3 eggs	extract or 2 teaspoons
1½ cups self-rising flour,	instant coffee powder
sifted	dissolved in
1 tablespoon strong black	1–2 tablespoons warm
coffee	milk
1 tablespoon cocoa mixed	2½ cups confectioner's
with 1–2 tablespoons	sugar
boiling water	

1 Preheat the oven to 350°F. Grease and line the bottoms of two 7-inch round sandwich cake pans. For the sponge, cream the butter and sugar until light and fluffy. Add the eggs, one at a time, beating well after each addition. Fold in the flour.

2 Divide the mixture into two bowls. Fold the coffee into one and the cocoa mixture into the other.

3 Place alternate spoonfuls of each mixture side by side in the cake pans. Bake for 25–30 minutes. Turn out onto a wire rack to cool.

4 For the buttercream, beat the butter until soft. Gradually beat in the remaining ingredients until smooth.

5 Sandwich the cakes, base-sides together, with a third of the buttercream. Cover the top and side with the rest.

Lemon and Apricot Cake

This cake is soaked in a tangy lemon syrup after baking to keep it really moist.

Makes one 9 x 5-inch loaf
¾ cup butter, softened
1½ cups self-rising flour
½ teaspoon baking
   powder
¾ cup superfine sugar
3 eggs, lightly beaten
finely grated rind of
   1 lemon
1½ cups ready-to-eat
   dried apricots, finely
   chopped
¾ cup ground almonds

6 tablespoons pistachios,
   chopped
½ cup slivered almonds
2 tablespoons whole
   pistachios

For the syrup
3 tablespoons superfine
   sugar
freshly squeezed juice of
   1 lemon

1 Preheat the oven to 350°F. Grease and line a 9 x 5-inch loaf pan with wax paper and grease the paper.

2 Place the butter in a mixing bowl. Sift over the flour and baking powder, then add the sugar, eggs and lemon rind. Beat for 1–2 minutes until smooth and glossy, then stir in the apricots, ground almonds and chopped pistachios.

3 Spoon the mixture into the loaf pan and smooth the surface. Sprinkle with the slivered almonds and the whole pistachios. Bake for 1¼ hours, or until a skewer inserted into the center of the cake comes out clean. Check the cake after 45 minutes and cover with a piece of foil when the top is nicely browned. Let the cake cool in the pan.

4 For the lemon syrup, gently dissolve the sugar in the lemon juice. Spoon the syrup over the cake. When the cake is completely cooled, turn it carefully out of the pan and peel off the lining paper.

Cherry Batter Cake

This colorful tray bake looks pretty cut into neat squares or fingers.

Makes one 13 x 9-inch cake
2 cups self-rising flour
1 teaspoon baking
   powder
6 tablespoons butter,
   softened
scant 1 cup light brown
   sugar
1 egg, lightly beaten
⅔ cup milk
confectioner's sugar, for
   dusting

whipped cream, to serve
   (optional)

For the topping
1½-pound bottle black
   cherries or black
   currants, drained
1 cup light brown sugar
½ cup self-rising flour
¼ cup butter, melted

1 Preheat the oven to 375°F. Grease and line a 13 x 9-inch jelly roll pan with wax paper and grease the paper.

2 To make the base, sift the flour and baking powder into a mixing bowl. Add the butter, sugar, egg and milk. Beat until the mixture becomes smooth, then turn into the prepared pan and smooth the surface.

3 Sprinkle the drained fruit evenly over the batter mixture.

4 Mix together the remaining topping ingredients and spoon evenly over the fruit. Bake for 40 minutes, or until golden brown and the center is firm to the touch.

5 Let cool, then dust with confectioner's sugar. Serve with whipped cream, if wished.

Fruit Salad Cake

You can use any combination of dried fruits in this rich, dark fruit cake.

Makes one 7-inch round cake

1 cup coarsely chopped
   mixed dried fruit,
   such as apples,
   apricots, prunes and
   peaches
1 cup hot tea
2 cups whole wheat self-
   rising flour

1 teaspoon grated
   nutmeg
⅓ cup dark muscovado
   sugar
3 tablespoons sunflower
   oil
3 tablespoons skim milk
raw sugar, for sprinkling

1   Soak the dried fruits in the tea for several hours or overnight. Drain and reserve the liquid.

2   Preheat the oven to 350°F. Grease a 7-inch round cake pan and line the bottom with nonstick parchment paper.

3   Sift the flour into a bowl with the nutmeg. Stir in the muscovado sugar, fruit and tea. Add the oil and milk, and mix well.

4   Spoon the mixture into the cake pan and sprinkle with raw sugar. Bake for 50–55 minutes, or until firm. Turn out onto a wire rack to cool.

Fairy Cakes with Blueberries

This luxurious treatment of fairy cakes means they will be as popular with adults as with kids.

Makes 8–10

½ cup soft margarine
½ cup superfine sugar
1 teaspoon grated lemon
   rind
pinch of salt
2 eggs, beaten

1 cup self-rising flour,
   sifted
½ cup whipping cream
¾–1 cup blueberries
confectioner's sugar, for
   dusting

1   Preheat the oven to 375°F. Cream the margarine, sugar, lemon rind and salt in a large bowl until pale and fluffy.

2   Gradually beat in the eggs, then fold in the flour until well mixed. Spoon the mixture into eight to ten paper muffin cases on baking sheets and bake for 15–20 minutes, until golden.

3   Let the cakes cool, then scoop out a circle of sponge from the top of each one using the point of a small, sharp knife, and set them aside.

4   Whip the cream and place a spoonful in each cake, plus a couple of blueberries. Replace the lids at an angle and sift over some confectioner's sugar.

Jewel Cake

This pretty cake is excellent served as an afternoon treat.

Makes one 9 x 5-inch cake

½ cup mixed candied
    cherries, halved,
    washed and dried
4 tablespoons preserved
    ginger in syrup,
    chopped, washed and
    dried
5 tablespoons chopped
    mixed candied peel
1 cup self-rising flour
¼ cup all-purpose flour
3 tablespoons cornstarch
¾ cup butter
scant 1 cup superfine
    sugar

3 eggs
grated rind of 1 orange

To decorate
1½ cups confectioner's
    sugar, sifted
2–3 tablespoons freshly
    squeezed orange juice
¼ cup mixed candied
    cherries, chopped
2½ tablespoons mixed
    candied peel, chopped

1 Preheat the oven to 350°F. Grease and line a 9 x 5-inch loaf pan and grease the paper.

2 Place the cherries, ginger and candied peel in a plastic bag with 4 tablespoons of the self-rising flour and shake to coat evenly. Sift together the remaining flours and cornstarch.

3 Beat together the butter and sugar until light and fluffy. Beat in the eggs, one at a time. Fold in the sifted flours with the orange rind, then stir in the dried fruit.

4 Transfer the mixture to the prepared cake pan and bake for 1¼ hours, or until a skewer inserted into the center comes out clean. Let stand in the pan for 5 minutes, then cool on a wire rack.

5 For the decoration, mix the sugar with the orange juice until smooth. Drizzle the icing over the cake. Mix together the chopped cherries and peel, then use to decorate the cake. Let the icing set before serving.

Iced Paradise Cake

Makes one 9 x 5-inch cake

3 eggs
scant ½ cup superfine
    sugar
9 tablespoons all-purpose
    flour
1 tablespoon cornstarch
6 tablespoons dark rum
1½ cups semisweet
    chocolate chips
2 tablespoons maple
    syrup

2 tablespoons water
1¾ cups heavy cream
scant 1 cup dried
    coconut, toasted
2 tablespoons sweet
    butter
2 tablespoons light cream
5 tablespoons white
    chocolate chips, melted
coconut curls, to decorate
cocoa, for dusting

1 Preheat the oven to 400°F. Grease and flour two baking sheets. Line a 9 x 5-inch pan with plastic wrap.

2 Whisk the eggs and sugar in a heat proof bowl until blended. Place over a pan of simmering water and whisk until pale and thick. Whisk off the heat until cool. Sift over the flour and cornstarch and fold in. Pipe 30 x 3-inch sponge fingers onto the baking sheets. Bake for 8 – 10 minutes. Cool slightly on the sheets, then on a wire rack.

3 Line the bottom and sides of the loaf pan with sponge fingers. Brush with rum. Melt ½ cup chocolate chips, the syrup, water and 2 tablespoons rum in a bowl over simmering water.

4 Whip the heavy cream until it holds its shape, stir in the chocolate mixture and toasted coconut. Pour into the pan and top with the remaining sponge fingers. Brush over the remaining rum. Cover with plastic wrap and freeze until firm.

5 Melt the remaining chocolate, butter and cream as before, then cool slightly. Turn the cake out onto a wire rack. Pour over the icing to coat. Chill.

6 Drizzle the white chocolate in zigzags over the cake. Chill. Sprinkle with coconut curls and dust with cocoa.

Pound Cake with Red Fruit

This orange-scented cake is good for a snack, or served as a dessert with a fruit coulis.

Makes one 8 x 4-inch cake

about 4 cups fresh
    raspberries,
    strawberries or pitted
    cherries, or a
    combination of any of
    these
¾ cup superfine sugar,
    plus 1–2 tablespoons,
    plus extra for
    sprinkling

1 tablespoon lemon juice
1½ cups all-purpose flour
2 teaspoons baking
    powder
pinch of salt
¾ cup sweet butter,
    softened
3 eggs
grated rind of 1 orange
1 tablespoon orange juice

1 Reserve a few whole fruits for decorating. In a blender or food processor, process the fruit until smooth. Add 1–2 tablespoons sugar and the lemon juice, and process again. Strain the sauce and chill.

2 Grease the bottom and sides of an 8 x 4-inch loaf pan and line the bottom with nonstick parchment paper. Grease the paper. Sprinkle with sugar and turn out any excess. Preheat the oven to 350°F.

3 Sift together the flour, baking powder and salt. Beat the butter until creamy. Add the sugar and beat until light and fluffy. Add the eggs, one at a time, beating well after each addition. Beat in the orange rind and juice. Gently fold the flour mixture into the butter mixture in three batches, then spoon the mixture into the loaf pan and tap gently to release any air bubbles.

4 Bake for 35–40 minutes, until the top is golden and springy to the touch. Let the cake stand in its pan on a wire rack for 10 minutes, then remove the cake from the pan and cool for 30 minutes. Remove the paper and serve slices of cake with the fruit sauce, decorated with the reserved fruit.

Madeleine Cakes

These little tea cakes, baked in a special pan with shell-shape cups, are best eaten on the day they are made.

Makes 12

generous 1¼ cups all-
    purpose flour
1 teaspoon baking
    powder
2 eggs
½ cup confectioner's
    sugar, plus extra for
    dusting

grated rind of 1 lemon or
    orange
1 tablespoon lemon or
    orange juice
6 tablespoons sweet
    butter, melted and
    slightly cooled

1 Preheat the oven to 375°F. Grease a 12-cup madeleine cake pan. Sift together the flour and the baking powder.

2 Beat the eggs and confectioner's sugar until the mixture is thick and creamy and leaves ribbon trails. Gently fold in the lemon or orange rind and juice.

3 Beginning with the flour mixture, alternately fold in the flour and melted butter in four batches. Let stand for 10 minutes, then spoon into the pan. Tap gently to release any air bubbles.

4 Bake for 12–15 minutes, rotating the pan halfway through cooking, until a skewer inserted in the center comes out clean. Turn out onto a wire rack to cool completely and dust with confectioner's sugar before serving.

Chocolate-orange Battenburg Cake

A tasty variation on the traditional pink-and-white Battenburg cake.

Makes one 7-inch long rectangular cake

½ cup soft margarine
½ cup superfine sugar
2 eggs, beaten
few drops vanilla extract
1 tablespoon ground almonds
1 cup self-rising flour, sifted
grated rind and juice of ½ orange
2 tablespoons cocoa, sifted
2–3 tablespoons milk
1 jar chocolate and nut spread
8 ounces white almond paste

1 Preheat the oven to 350°F. Grease and line a 7-inch square cake pan. Put a double piece of foil across the middle of the pan, to divide it into two equal oblongs.

2 Cream the margarine and sugar. Beat in the eggs, vanilla and almonds. Divide the mixture into two halves. Fold half of the flour into one half, with the orange rind and enough juice to give a soft dropping consistency. Fold the rest of the flour and the cocoa into the other half, with enough milk to give a soft dropping consistency. Fill the pan with the two mixes and level the top.

3 Bake for 15 minutes, reduce the heat to 325°F and cook for 20–30 minutes more, until the top is just firm. Let cool in the pan for a few minutes. Turn out onto a board, cut each cake into two strips and trim evenly. Let cool.

4 Using the spread, sandwich the cakes together, Battenburg-style. Roll out the almond paste on a board lightly dusted with cornstarch to a rectangle 7-inch wide and long enough to wrap around the cake. Wrap the paste around the cake, putting the joint underneath. Press to seal.

Best-ever Chocolate Sandwich

A three-layered cake that would be ideal for a birthday party or a special tea.

Makes one 8-inch round cake

1 cup all-purpose flour
½ cup cocoa
1 teaspoon baking powder
pinch of salt
6 eggs
generous 1 cup superfine sugar
2 teaspoons vanilla extract
½ cup sweet butter, melted
8 ounces semisweet chocolate, chopped
6 tablespoons sweet butter
3 eggs, separated
1 cup whipping cream
3 tablespoons superfine sugar

1 Preheat the oven to 350°F. Line three 8-inch round pans with wax paper, grease the paper and dust with flour. Sift the flour, cocoa, baking powder and salt together three times.

2 Place the eggs and sugar in a heat proof bowl set over a pan of simmering water. Beat until doubled in volume, about 10 minutes. Add the vanilla. Fold in the flour mixture in three batches, then the butter.

3 Put the mixture in the pans. Bake until the cakes pull away from the pan sides, about 25 minutes. Transfer to a wire rack.

4 For the icing, melt the chocolate in the top of a double boiler. Remove from the heat and stir in the butter and egg yolks. Return to the heat and stir until thick.

5 Whip the cream until firm. In another bowl, beat the egg whites until stiff. Add the sugar and beat until glossy. Fold the cream, then the egg whites, into the chocolate mixture. Chill for about 20 minutes, then sandwich together and cover the cake with icing.

Chocolate Layer Cake

Makes one 9-inch cake

8-ounce can cooked whole
    beetroot, drained and
    juice reserved
½ cup sweet butter,
    softened
2½ cups light brown
    sugar
3 eggs
1 tablespoon vanilla
    extract
3 ounces bittersweet
    chocolate, melted
2 cups all-purpose flour

2 teaspoons baking
    powder
½ teaspoon salt
½ cup buttermilk
chocolate curls, to
    decorate (optional)

For the frosting

2 cups heavy cream
1 pound 2 ounces
    semisweet chocolate,
    chopped
1 tablespoon vanilla
    extract

1 Preheat the oven to 350°F. Grease two 9-inch cake pans
and dust with cocoa. Grate the beetroot and add it to its juice.
Beat the butter, brown sugar, eggs and vanilla until pale and
fluffy. Beat in the chocolate.

2 Sift together the flour, baking powder and salt. With the
mixer on low speed and beginning and ending with flour
mixture, alternately beat in flour and buttermilk. Add the
beetroot and juice and beat for 1 minute. Fill the pans and
bake for 30–35 minutes, until a skewer inserted in the center
comes out clean. Cool for 10 minutes, then unmold and cool.

3 To make the frosting, heat the cream until it just begins to
boil, stirring occasionally to prevent scorching. Remove from
the heat and stir in the chocolate, until melted and smooth.
Stir in the vanilla. Strain into a bowl and chill, stirring every
10 minutes, for 1 hour.

4 Sandwich and cover the cake with frosting, and top with
chocolate curls, if using. Let set for 20–30 minutes, then chill
before serving.

Marbled Chocolate-peanut Cake

Serves 12–14

4 ounces bittersweet
    chocolate, chopped
1 cup sweet butter,
    softened
1 cup peanut butter
1 cup sugar
1 cup light brown sugar
5 eggs
2 cups all-purpose flour
2 teaspoons baking
    powder
½ teaspoon salt
½ cup milk
5 tablespoons chocolate
    chips

**For the chocolate-
peanut butter glaze**

2 tablespoons butter,
    diced
2 tablespoons smooth
    peanut butter
3 tablespoons maple
    syrup
1 teaspoon vanilla
    extract
6 ounces semisweet
    chocolate, broken into
    pieces

1 Preheat the oven to 350°F. Grease and flour a 12-cup tube
pan or ring mold. In the top of a double boiler, melt the
bittersweet chocolate.

2 Beat the butter, peanut butter and sugars until light and
creamy. Add the eggs, one at a time, beating well after each
addition. Sift together the flour, baking powder and salt. Add
to the butter mixture alternately with the milk.

3 Pour half the batter into another bowl. Stir the melted
chocolate into one half and stir the chocolate chips into the
other half. Drop alternate large spoonfuls of the two batters
into the pan or mold. Using a knife, pull through the batters
to create a swirled marbled effect; do not let the knife touch
the side or bottom of the pan. Bake for 50–60 minutes, until
the top springs back when touched. Cool in the pan on a wire
rack for 10 minutes. Then unmold onto the wire rack.

4 Combine the glaze ingredients and 1 tablespoon water in
a small saucepan. Melt over low heat, stirring. Cool slightly,
then drizzle over the cake, allowing it to run down the side.

Chocolate Fairy Cakes

Makes 24

4 ounces good-quality
    semisweet chocolate,
    cut into small pieces
1 tablespoon water
2½ cups all-purpose flour
1 teaspoon baking
    powder
½ teaspoon baking soda
pinch of salt
scant 1½ cups superfine
    sugar

¾ cup butter or
    margarine, at room
    temperature
⅔ cup milk
1 teaspoon vanilla
    extract
3 eggs
1 recipe quantity
    buttercream, flavored
    to taste

1 Preheat the oven to 350°F. Grease and flour 24 deep muffin pans, about 2¾-inch in diameter, or use paper muffin cases in the pans.

2 Put the chocolate and water in a bowl set over a pan of almost simmering water. Heat until melted and smooth, stirring. Remove from the heat and let cool.

3 Sift the flour, baking powder, baking soda, salt and sugar into a large bowl. Add the chocolate mixture, butter or margarine, milk and vanilla extract.

4 With an electric mixer on medium-low speed, beat until smoothly blended. Increase the speed to high and beat for 2 minutes. Add the eggs and beat for 2 minutes more.

5 Divide the mixture evenly among the prepared muffin pans and bake for 20–25 minutes, or until a skewer inserted into the center of a cake comes out clean. Cool in the pans for 10 minutes, then turn out to cool completely on a wire rack.

6 Ice the top of each cake with buttercream, swirling it into a peak in the center.

Chocolate Mint-filled Cupcakes

For extra mint flavor, chop eight thin mint cream-filled after-dinner mints and fold into the cake batter.

Makes 12

2 cups all-purpose flour
1 teaspoon baking soda
pinch of salt
½ cup cocoa
10 tablespoons sweet
    butter, softened
1½ cups superfine sugar
3 eggs
1 teaspoon peppermint
    extract
1 cup milk

For the filling
1¼ cups heavy or
    whipping cream
1 teaspoon peppermint
    extract

For the glaze
6 ounces semisweet
    chocolate
½ cup sweet butter
1 teaspoon peppermint
    extract

1 Preheat the oven to 350°F. Line a 12-cup muffin tray with paper cases. Sift together the flour, baking soda, salt and cocoa. In another bowl, beat the butter and sugar until light and creamy. Add the eggs, one at a time, beating well after each addition; beat in the peppermint. On low speed, beat in the flour mixture alternately with the milk, until just blended. Spoon into the paper cases.

2 Bake for 12–15 minutes, until a skewer inserted in the center of a cake comes out clean. Transfer to a wire rack to cool. When cool, remove the paper cases.

3 For the filling, whip the cream and peppermint until stiff. Spoon into an icing bag fitted with a small plain nozzle. Pipe about 1 tablespoon into each cake through the bottom.

4 For the glaze, melt the chocolate and butter, stirring until smooth. Remove from the heat and stir in the peppermint extract. Cool, then spread on top of each cake.

Rich Chocolate Nut Cake

Use walnuts or pecans for the cake sides, if you prefer.

Makes one 9-inch round cake

1 cup butter	**For the glaze**
8 ounces semisweet chocolate	4 tablespoons butter
1 cup cocoa	5 ounces bittersweet chocolate
1¾ cups superfine sugar	2 tablespoons milk
6 eggs	1 teaspoon vanilla extract
5 tablespoons brandy	
2 cups finely chopped hazelnuts	

1 Preheat the oven to 350°F. Line a 9 x 2-inch round pan with wax paper and grease the paper. Melt the butter and chocolate in the top of a double boiler. Let cool.

2 Sift the cocoa into a bowl. Add the sugar and eggs and stir until just combined. Pour in the chocolate mixture and brandy. Fold in three-quarters of the nuts, then pour the mixture into the cake pan.

3 Set the pan in a roasting pan and pour 1 inch hot water into the outer pan. Bake until the cake is firm to the touch, about 45 minutes. Let stand for 15 minutes, then unmold onto a wire rack. When cool, wrap in wax paper and chill for at least 6 hours.

4 For the glaze, melt the butter and chocolate with the milk and vanilla in the top of a double boiler.

5 Place the cake on a wire rack over a plate. Drizzle the glaze over, letting it drip down the sides. Cover the cake sides with the remaining nuts. Transfer to a serving plate when set.

Multi-layer Chocolate Cake

For a change, sandwich the cake layers with softened vanilla ice cream. Freeze before serving.

Makes one 8-inch round cake

4 ounces semisweet chocolate	1 cup chopped walnuts
¾ cup butter	**For the filling and topping**
2¼ cups superfine sugar	1½ cups whipping cream
3 eggs	8 ounces semisweet chocolate
1 teaspoon vanilla extract	1 tablespoon vegetable oil
1½ cups all-purpose flour	
1 teaspoon baking powder	

1 Preheat the oven to 350°F. Line two 8-inch round cake pans with wax paper and grease the paper.

2 Melt the chocolate and butter in the top of a double boiler. Transfer to a bowl and stir in the sugar. Add the eggs and vanilla and mix well. Sift over the flour and baking powder. Stir in the walnuts.

3 Pour the mixture into the cake pans. Bake until a skewer inserted in the center comes out clean, about 30 minutes. Let stand for 10 minutes, then unmold onto a wire rack to cool.

4 Whip the cream until firm. Slice the cakes in half horizontally. Sandwich them together and cover the cake with the cream. Chill.

5 To make the chocolate curls, melt the chocolate and oil in the top of a double boiler. Spread onto a non-porous surface. Just before it sets, hold the blade of a knife at an angle to the chocolate and scrape across the surface to make curls. Use to decorate the cake.

Chocolate Frosted Layer Cake

The contrast between the frosting and the sponge creates a
dramatic effect when the cake is cut.

Makes one 8-inch round cake

1 cup butter or
margarine, at room
temperature
1½ cups sugar
4 eggs, separated
2 teaspoons vanilla
extract
3½ cups all-purpose flour
2 teaspoons baking
powder

¼ teaspoon salt
1 cup milk

For the frosting
5 ounces semisweet
chocolate
½ cup sour cream
¼ teaspoon salt

1 Preheat the oven to 350°F. Line two 8-inch round cake
pans with wax paper and grease the paper. Dust the pans
with flour. Tap to remove any excess.

2 Cream the butter or margarine until soft. Gradually add
the sugar and beat until light and fluffy. Beat the egg yolks,
then add to the butter mixture with the vanilla.

3 Sift the flour with the baking powder three times. Set
aside. Beat the egg whites with the salt until they peak stiffly.

4 Fold the dry ingredients into the butter mixture in three
batches, alternating with the milk. Add a dollop of the egg
white and fold in to lighten the mixture. Fold in the rest until
just blended.

5 Spoon into the cake pans and bake until the cakes pull
away from the sides, about 30 minutes. Let stand in the pans
for 5 minutes, then turn out onto a wire rack.

6 For the frosting, melt the chocolate in the top of a double
boiler. When cool, stir in the sour cream and salt. Sandwich
the layers with frosting, then spread on the top and side.

Devil's Food Cake with Orange

Makes one 9-inch round cake

½ cup cocoa
¾ cup boiling water
¾ cup butter, at room
temperature
2 cups dark brown sugar
3 eggs
2½ cups all-purpose flour
1½ teaspoons baking soda
¼ teaspoon baking
powder
½ cup sour cream
blanched orange rind
shreds, to decorate

For the frosting
1½ cups superfine sugar
2 egg whites
4 tablespoons frozen
orange juice
concentrate
1 tablespoon lemon juice
grated rind of 1 orange

1 Preheat the oven to 350°F. Line two 9-inch cake pans with
wax paper and grease the paper. In a bowl, mix the cocoa and
water until smooth.

2 Cream the butter and sugar until light and fluffy. Add the
eggs, one at a time, beating well after each addition. When the
cocoa mixture is lukewarm, add to the butter mixture.

3 Sift together the flour, soda and baking powder twice. Fold
into the cocoa mixture in three batches, alternating with the
sour cream. Pour into the pans and bake until the cakes pull
away from the sides, 30–35 minutes. Let stand for 15 minutes,
then turn out onto a wire rack.

4 For the frosting, place all the ingredients in the top of a
double boiler. With an electric mixer, beat until the mixture
holds soft peaks. Continue beating off the heat until thick
enough to spread.

5 Sandwich the cake layers with frosting, then spread over
the top and side. Decorate with orange rind shreds.

French Chocolate Cake

This is typical of a French homemade cake – dense, dark and delicious. Serve with cream or a fruit coulis.

Makes one 9-inch round cake

5 tablespoons superfine sugar	5 eggs, separated
10 ounces semisweet chocolate, chopped	¼ cup all-purpose flour, sifted
¾ cup sweet butter, cut into pieces	pinch of salt
2 teaspoons vanilla extract	confectioner's sugar, for dusting

1 Preheat the oven to 325°F. Grease a 9-inch springform pan, sprinkle with sugar and tap out the excess.

2 Set aside 3 tablespoons of the sugar. Place the chocolate, butter and remaining sugar in a heavy saucepan and cook over low heat until melted. Remove from the heat, stir in the vanilla extract and let cool slightly.

3 Beat the egg yolks, one at a time, into the chocolate mixture, then stir in the flour.

4 Beat the egg whites with the salt until soft peaks form. Sprinkle over the reserved sugar and beat until stiff and glossy. Beat a third of the whites into the chocolate mixture, then fold in the rest.

5 Pour the mixture into the pan and tap it gently to release any air bubbles.

6 Bake the cake for 35–45 minutes, until well risen and the top springs back when touched lightly. Transfer to a wire rack, remove the sides of the pan and let cool. Remove the pan bottom, dust the cake with confectioner's sugar and transfer to a serving plate.

Almond Cake

Serve this wonderfully nutty cake with coffee, or, for a treat, with a glass of almond liqueur.

Makes one 9-inch round cake

1⅓ cups blanched, toasted whole almonds	4 tablespoons all-purpose flour
5 tablespoons confectioner's sugar	3 egg whites
3 eggs	1 tablespoon superfine sugar
2 tablespoons butter, melted	toasted whole almonds, to decorate
½ teaspoon almond extract	

1 Preheat the oven to 325°F. Line a 9-inch round cake pan with wax paper and grease the paper.

2 Coarsely chop the almonds and grind them with half the confectioner's sugar in a blender or food processor. Transfer to a mixing bowl.

3 Beat in the whole eggs and remaining confectioner's sugar until the mixture forms ribbon trails. Mix in the butter and almond extract. Sift over the flour and fold in.

4 Beat the egg whites until they peak softly. Add the superfine sugar and beat until stiff and glossy. Fold into the almond mixture in four batches.

5 Spoon the mixture into the cake pan and bake until golden brown, 15–20 minutes. Decorate with toasted almonds.

Caramel Layer Cake

Makes one 8-inch round cake

2½ cups all-purpose flour
1½ teaspoons baking
 powder
¾ cup butter, at room
 temperature
generous ⅔ cup superfine
 sugar
4 eggs, beaten
1 teaspoon vanilla
 extract
½ cup milk
whipped cream, to
 decorate

caramel threads, to
 decorate (optional)

For the frosting
1⅓ cups dark brown
 sugar
1 cup milk
2 tablespoons sweet
 butter
3–5 tablespoons
 whipping cream

1 Preheat the oven to 350°F. Line two 8-inch cake pans with wax paper and grease the paper. Sift the flour and baking powder together three times.

2 Cream the butter and sugar until light and fluffy. Slowly mix in the beaten eggs. Add the vanilla. Fold in the flour mixture, alternating with the milk. Divide the batter between the cake pans and spread evenly. Bake until the cakes pull away from the sides of the pan, about 30 minutes. Let stand in the pans for 5 minutes, then turn out and cool on a wire rack.

3 For the frosting, bring the brown sugar and milk to a boil, cover and cook for 2 minutes. Uncover and continue to boil, without stirring, until the mixture reaches 238°F (soft ball stage) on a sugar thermometer.

4 Remove the pan from the heat and add the butter, but do not stir it in. Let cool until lukewarm, then beat until the mixture is smooth. Stir in enough cream to obtain a spreadable consistency.

5 Sandwich the cake together with frosting and then cover the top and sides. Decorate with whipped cream, and caramel threads if liked.

Marbled Spice Cake

You could bake this cake in an 8-inch round pan if you do not have a kugelhopf.

Makes one ring cake

6 tablespoons butter,
 softened
generous ½ cup superfine
 sugar
2 eggs, lightly beaten
few drops vanilla extract
generous 1 cup all-
 purpose flour
1½ teaspoons baking
 powder

3 tablespoons milk
3 tablespoons molasses
1 teaspoon mixed spice
½ teaspoon ground
 ginger
1½ cups confectioner's
 sugar, sifted, to
 decorate

1 Preheat the oven to 350°F. Grease and flour a 2-pound kugelhopf or ring mold.

2 Cream together the butter and sugar until light and fluffy. Beat in the eggs and vanilla.

3 Sift together the flour and baking powder, then fold into the butter mixture, alternating with the milk.

4 Add the molasses and spices to a third of the mixture. Drop alternating spoonfuls of the two mixtures into the pan. Run a knife through them to give a marbled effect.

5 Bake for 50 minutes, or until a skewer inserted into the center comes out clean. Let stand in the pan for 10 minutes, then turn out onto a wire rack to cool.

6 To decorate, make a smooth icing with the confectioner's sugar and some warm water. Drizzle over the cake and let set.

Raspberry Meringue Gâteau

A rich hazelnut meringue filled with cream and raspberries makes a delicious combination of textures and tastes.

Serves 8

4 egg whites
1 cup superfine sugar
few drops vanilla extract
1 teaspoon malt vinegar
1 cup toasted chopped
  hazelnuts, ground
1¼ cups heavy cream
2 cups raspberries
confectioner's sugar, for
  dusting

raspberries and mint
  sprigs, to decorate

For the sauce
1⅓ cups raspberries
3 tablespoons
  confectioner's sugar
1 tablespoon orange
  liqueur

1 Preheat the oven to 350°F. Grease two 8-inch cake pans and line the bottoms with wax paper.

2 Whisk the egg whites in a large bowl until they hold stiff peaks, then gradually whisk in the superfine sugar a tablespoon at a time, whisking well after each addition.

3 Continue whisking the meringue mixture for a minute or two until very stiff, then fold in the vanilla, vinegar and the ground hazelnuts. Divide the meringue mixture between the prepared pans and spread level. Bake for 50–60 minutes, until crisp. Remove the meringues from the pans and let cool on a wire rack.

4 Meanwhile, make the sauce. Liquidize the raspberries with the confectioner's sugar and orange liqueur in a blender or food processor, then press it through a nylon strainer to remove any pips. Chill the sauce until ready to serve.

5 Whip the cream, then fold in the raspberries. Sandwich the meringue rounds with the raspberry cream. Dust with confectioner's sugar, decorate with fruit and mint and serve with the sauce.

Strawberry Mint Sponge

This combination of fruit, mint and ice cream will prove popular with everyone.

Makes one 8-inch round cake

6 – 10 fresh mint leaves,
  plus extra to decorate
¾ cup butter
¾ cup superfine sugar
1½ cups self-rising flour
3 eggs

5 cups strawberry ice
  cream, softened
2½ cups heavy cream
2 tablespoons mint
  liqueur
2 cups fresh strawberries

1 Tear the mint into pieces, mix with the sugar, and let stand overnight. (Remove the leaves from the sugar before use.)

2 Preheat the oven to 375°F. Grease and line an 8-inch deep springform cake pan. Cream the butter and sugar, add the flour, and then the eggs. Pour the mixture into the pan.

3 Bake for 20–25 minutes, or until a skewer inserted in the center comes out clean. Turn out onto a wire rack to cool. When cool, split into two layers.

4 Wash the cake pan and line with plastic wrap. Put the cake base back in the pan. Spread with the ice cream, then cover with the top half of the cake. Freeze for 3–4 hours.

5 Whip the cream with the liqueur. Turn the cake out onto a serving plate and quickly spread a layer of whipped cream all over it, leaving an uneven finish. Freeze until 10 minutes before serving. Decorate the cake with the strawberries and place fresh mint leaves around it.

Chestnut Cake

This rich, moist cake can be made up to 1 week in advance and kept, undecorated and wrapped, in an airtight pan.

Serves 8–10

1¼ cups all-purpose flour
pinch of salt
1 cup butter, softened
¾ cup superfine sugar
15-ounce can chestnut
   purée

9 eggs, separated
7 tablespoons dark rum
1¼ cups heavy cream
candied chestnuts and
   confectioner's sugar,
   to decorate

1 Preheat the oven to 350°F. Grease and line an 8-inch springform cake pan.

2 Sift the flour and salt and set aside. Beat the butter and sugar together until light and fluffy. Fold in two-thirds of the chestnut purée, with the egg yolks. Fold in the flour and salt.

3 Whisk the egg whites in a clean, dry bowl until stiff. Beat a little of the egg whites into the chestnut mixture, until evenly blended, then fold in the remainder. Transfer the cake mixture to the pan and smooth the surface. Bake in the center of the oven for about 1¼ hours, or until a skewer comes out clean. Let stand in the pan and place on a wire rack.

4 Using a skewer, pierce holes over the cake. Sprinkle with 4 tablespoons rum, then cool. Remove the cake from the pan, peel off the lining paper and cut horizontally into two layers. Place the bottom layer on a plate. Whisk the cream with the remaining rum, sugar and chestnut purée until smooth.

5 To assemble, spread two-thirds of the chestnut cream mixture over the bottom layer and place the other layer on top. Spread some chestnut cream over the top and sides of the cake, pipe the remainder in large swirls round the edge of the cake. Decorate with chopped candied chestnuts and confectioner's sugar.

Marbled Ring Cake

Glaze this cake with running icing if you prefer.

Makes one 10-inch ring cake

4 ounces semisweet
   chocolate
3 cups all-purpose flour
1 teaspoon baking
   powder
2 cups butter, at room
   temperature

3¾ cups superfine sugar
1 tablespoon vanilla
   extract
10 eggs, at room
   temperature
confectioner's sugar, for
   dusting

1 Preheat the oven to 350°F. Line a 10 x 4-inch ring mold with wax paper and grease the paper. Dust with flour. Melt the chocolate in the top of a double boiler, stirring occasionally. Set aside.

2 Sift together the flour and baking powder. In another bowl, cream the butter, sugar and vanilla extract until light and fluffy. Add the eggs, two at a time, then gradually blend in the flour mixture.

3 Spoon half of the mixture into the ring mold. Stir the chocolate into the remaining mixture, then spoon into the prepared ring mold. With a metal spatula, swirl the mixtures for a marbled effect.

4 Bake until a skewer inserted in the center comes out clean, about 1¾ hours. Cover with foil halfway through baking. Let stand for 15 minutes, then unmold and transfer to a wire rack. To serve, dust with confectioner's sugar.

Chocolate and Nut Gâteau

Hazelnuts give an interesting crunchy texture to this delicious iced dessert.

Serves 6–8

½ cup shelled hazelnuts
about 32 sponge fingers
¾ cup cold strong black
   coffee
2 tablespoons brandy
1¾ cups heavy cream

6 tablespoons
   confectioner's sugar,
   sifted
5 ounces semisweet
   chocolate
confectioner's sugar and
   cocoa, for dusting

1 Preheat the oven to 400°F. Spread out the hazelnuts on a baking sheet and toast them in the oven for 5 minutes until golden. Transfer the nuts to a clean dish towel and rub off the skins while still warm. Cool, then chop finely.

2 Line a 5-cup loaf pan with plastic wrap and cut enough sponge fingers to fit the bottom and sides. Reserve the remaining fingers.

3 Mix the coffee and brandy in a shallow dish. Dip the sponge fingers briefly into the coffee mixture and return to the pan, sugary-side down.

4 Whip the cream with the confectioner's sugar until it forms soft peaks. Coarsely chop 3 ounces of the chocolate, and fold into the cream with the hazelnuts. Melt the remaining chocolate in a bowl set over a pan of barely simmering water. Cool, then fold into the cream mixture. Spoon into the pan.

5 Moisten the remaining sponge fingers in the coffee mixture and lay over the filling. Wrap and freeze until firm.

6 Remove from the freezer 30 minutes before serving. Turn out onto a serving plate and dust with confectioner's sugar and cocoa.

Chocolate and Orange Angel Cake

This light-as-air sponge with its fluffy icing is the answer to a cake-lover's prayer.

Makes one 8-inch ring cake

¼ cup all-purpose flour
2 tablespoons cocoa
2 tablespoons cornstarch
pinch of salt
5 egg whites
½ teaspoon cream of
   tartar
scant ½ cup superfine
   sugar

blanched and shredded
   rind of 1 orange, to
   decorate

For the icing
1 cup superfine sugar
1 egg white

1 Preheat the oven to 350°F. Sift the flour, cocoa, cornstarch and salt together three times. Beat the egg whites in a large bowl until foamy. Add the cream of tartar, then whisk until soft peaks form.

2 Add the superfine sugar to the egg whites a spoonful at a time, whisking after each addition. Sift a third of the flour and cocoa mixture over the meringue and gently fold in. Repeat twice more.

3 Spoon the mixture into a nonstick 8-inch ring mold and level the top. Bake for 35 minutes, or until springy when lightly pressed. Turn upside-down onto a wire rack and let cool in the pan. Carefully ease out of the pan.

4 For the icing, put the sugar in a pan with 5 tablespoons cold water. Stir over low heat until dissolved. Boil until the syrup reaches soft ball stage (238°F on a sugar thermometer). Remove from the heat. Whisk the egg white until stiff. Add the syrup in a thin stream, whisking all the time, until the mixture is very thick and fluffy.

5 Spread the icing over the top and sides of the cooled cake. Sprinkle the orange rind over the top of the cake and serve.

Chocolate Date Cake

A stunning cake that tastes wonderful. Rich and gooey – it's a chocoholic's delight!

Serves 8

scant 1 cup ricotta cheese
scant 1 cup mascarpone
1 teaspoon vanilla
   extract, plus few extra
   drops
confectioner's sugar, to
   taste
4 egg whites

½ cup superfine sugar
7 ounces semisweet
   chocolate
scant 1 cup Medjool
   dates, pitted and
   chopped
1½ cups walnuts or
   pecans, chopped

1 Preheat the oven to 350°F. Grease and line the bottom of an 8-inch springform cake pan.

2 To make the frosting, mix together the ricotta cheese and mascarpone, add a few drops of vanilla extract and confectioner's sugar to taste, then set aside.

3 Whisk the egg whites until they form stiff peaks. Whisk in 2 tablespoons of the superfine sugar until the meringue is thick and glossy, then fold in the remainder.

4 Chop 6 ounces of the chocolate. Carefully fold into the meringue with the dates, nuts and 1 teaspoon of the vanilla extract. Pour into the prepared pan, spread level and bake for about 45 minutes, until risen around the edges.

5 Let cool in the pan for about 10 minutes, then unmold, peel off the lining paper and let stand until completely cold. Swirl the frosting over the top of the cake.

6 Melt the remaining chocolate in a bowl over hot water. Spoon into a small paper piping bag and drizzle the chocolate over the cake. Chill before serving.

Apple and Golden Raisin Cake

This spicy, moist and fruity cake will be a popular teatime treat for the whole family.

Serves 12

¾ cup butter
¾ cup soft light
   brown sugar
3 eggs
2 cups self-rising whole
   wheat flour
1 cup self-rising flour
1 teaspoon baking
   powder, sifted

2 teaspoons ground
   mixed spice
12 ounces cooking apples,
   peeled, cored and diced
1 cup golden raisins
5 tablespoons skim milk
2 tablespoons
   demerara sugar

1 Preheat the oven to 325°F. Lightly grease a deep 8-inch round loose-based cake pan and line with baking parchment.

2 Place the butter, sugar, eggs, flours, baking powder and spice in a large bowl and beat together until thoroughly mixed. Fold in the apples, golden raisins and enough milk to make a soft dropping consistency.

3 Spoon the mixture into the prepared pan and level the surface. Sprinkle the top with demerara sugar, then bake for about 1½ hours, until risen, golden brown and firm to the touch. Cool in the pan for a few minutes, then turn out onto a wire rack to cook completely. Serve in slices.

Strawberry Shortcake Gâteau

A light cookie-textured sponge forms the base of this summertime dessert.

Makes one 8-inch round cake

2 cups fresh strawberries, hulled
2 tablespoons ruby port
2 cups self-rising flour
2 teaspoons baking powder
6 tablespoons sweet butter, diced

3 tablespoons superfine sugar
1 egg, lightly beaten
1–2 tablespoons milk
melted butter, for brushing
1 cup heavy cream
confectioner's sugar, for dusting

1 Preheat the oven to 425°F. Grease and line the bottoms of two 8-inch round, loose-based cake pans. Reserve 5 strawberries, slice the rest and marinate in the port for 1–2 hours. Strain, reserving the port.

2 Sift the flour and baking powder into a bowl. Work in the butter until the mixture resembles fine bread crumbs and stir in the sugar. Work in the egg and 1 tablespoon of the milk to form a soft dough, adding more milk if needed.

3 Knead on a lightly floured surface and divide in two. Roll out each half, mark one half into eight wedges, and transfer to the cake pans. Brush with a little melted butter and bake for 15 minutes until risen and golden. Cool in the pans for 10 minutes, then transfer to a wire rack.

4 Cut the marked cake into wedges. Reserving a little cream for decoration, whip the rest until it holds its shape, and fold in the reserved port and strawberry slices. Spread over the cake. Place the wedges on top and dust with sugar.

5 Whip the remaining cream and use to pipe swirls on each wedge. Halve the reserved strawberries and use to decorate the cake.

Almond and Raspberry Swiss Roll

A light and airy sponge cake is rolled up with a fresh cream and raspberry filling for a decadent afternoon treat.

Makes one 9-inch long roll

3 eggs
⅓ cup superfine sugar
½ cup all-purpose flour
2 tablespoons ground almonds
superfine sugar, for dusting

1 cup heavy cream
generous 1 cup fresh raspberries
16 slivered almonds, toasted, to decorate

1 Preheat the oven to 400°F. Grease a 13 x 9-inch jelly roll pan, line with wax paper and grease the paper.

2 Whisk the eggs and sugar in a heat proof bowl until blended. Place over a pan of simmering water and whisk until thick and pale. Remove from the heat and whisk until cool. Sift over the flour and almonds and fold in gently.

3 Transfer to the prepared pan and bake for 10–12 minutes, until risen and springy to the touch. Invert the cake in its pan onto wax paper dusted with superfine sugar. Let cool, then remove the pan and lining paper.

4 Reserve a little cream, then whip the rest until it holds its shape. Fold in all but 8 raspberries and spread the mixture over the cooled cake, leaving a narrow border. Roll the cake up and sprinkle with superfine sugar.

5 Whip the reserved cream until it just holds its shape, and spoon along the cake center. Decorate with the reserved raspberries and toasted slivered almonds.

Orange and Walnut Jelly Roll

This unusual cake is tasty enough to serve alone, but you could also pour over some light cream.

Makes one 9½-inch long roll

4 eggs, separated
generous ½ cup superfine
  sugar
1 cup very finely chopped
  walnuts
pinch of cream of tartar
pinch of salt
confectioner's sugar, for
  dusting

For the filling
1¼ cups whipping cream
1 tablespoon superfine
  sugar
grated rind of 1 orange
1 tablespoon orange-
  flavor liqueur

1 Preheat the oven to 350°F. Line a 12 x 9½-inch jelly roll pan with wax paper and grease the paper.

2 Beat the egg yolks and sugar until thick. Stir in the walnuts. Beat the egg whites with the cream of tartar and salt until stiff peaks form. Fold into the walnut mixture.

3 Pour the mixture into the prepared pan and level. Bake for 15 minutes. Invert the cake onto wax paper dusted with confectioner's sugar. Peel off the lining paper. Roll up the cake with the sugared paper. Let cool.

4 For the filling, whip the cream until soft peaks form. Fold in the superfine sugar, orange rind and liqueur.

5 Unroll the cake. Spread with the filling, then re-roll. Chill. To serve, dust with confectioner's sugar.

Chocolate Jelly Roll

Makes one 13-inch long roll

8 ounces semisweet
  chocolate
3 tablespoons water
2 tablespoons rum,
  brandy or strong
  coffee
7 eggs, separated

scant 1 cup superfine
  sugar
¼ teaspoon salt
1½ cups whipping cream
confectioner's sugar, for
  dusting

1 Preheat the oven to 350°F. Line a 15 x 13-inch jelly roll pan with wax paper and grease.

2 Combine the chocolate, water and rum or other flavoring in the top of a double boiler, or in a heat proof bowl set over simmering water. Heat until melted. Set aside.

3 With an electric mixer, beat the egg yolks and sugar until thick. Stir in the melted chocolate.

4 In another bowl, beat the egg whites and salt until they hold stiff peaks. Fold a large dollop of egg whites into the yolk mixture to lighten it, then carefully fold in the rest of the egg whites.

5 Pour the mixture into the pan and smooth evenly with a metal spatula. Bake for 15 minutes. Remove from the oven, cover with wax paper and a damp cloth. Let stand for about 1–2 hours. With an electric mixer, whip the cream until stiff. Set aside.

6 Run a knife along the inside edge of the pan to loosen the cake, then invert the cake onto a sheet of wax paper that has been dusted with confectioner's sugar.

7 Peel off the lining paper. Spread with an even layer of whipped cream, then roll up the cake with the help of the sugared paper. Chill for several hours. Before serving, dust with an even layer of confectioner's sugar.

Apricot Brandy-snap Roll

A magnificent combination of soft and crisp textures, this cake looks impressive and is easy to prepare.

Makes one 13-inch long roll

4 eggs, separated
1½ teaspoons fresh
   orange juice
generous ½ cup superfine
   sugar
1½ cups ground almonds
4 brandy snaps, crushed,
   to decorate

For the filling
5 ounces canned apricots,
   drained
1¼ cups heavy cream
¼ cup confectioner's
   sugar

1 Preheat the oven to 375°F. Line a 13 x 9-inch jelly roll pan with wax paper and grease. Beat together the egg yolks, orange juice and sugar until thick and pale, about 10 minutes. Fold in the ground almonds.

2 Whisk the egg whites until they hold stiff peaks. Fold into the almond mixture, then transfer to the jelly roll pan and smooth the surface. Bake for 20 minutes, or until a skewer inserted into the center comes out clean. Let cool in the pan, covered with a just-damp dish towel.

3 For the filling, process the apricots in a blender or food processor until smooth. Whip the cream and confectioner's sugar until it holds soft peaks. Fold in the apricot purée.

4 Spread the crushed brandy snaps on a sheet of wax paper. Spread a third of the cream mixture over the cake, then invert onto the brandy snaps. Peel off the lining paper.

5 Use the remaining cream mixture to cover the whole cake, then roll up from a short end. Transfer to a serving dish.

Apricot and Orange Roll

This sophisticated dessert is very good served with a spoonful of strained yogurt or crème fraîche.

Makes one 13-inch long roll

For the roulade
4 egg whites
½ cup golden superfine
   sugar
½ cup all-purpose flour
finely grated rind of 1
   small orange
3 tablespoons orange
   juice

For the filling
½ cup ready-to-eat dried
   apricots
⅔ cup orange juice

To decorate
2 teaspoons
   confectioner's sugar
grated orange rind

1 Preheat the oven to 400°F. Line a 13 x 9-inch jelly roll pan with wax paper and grease.

2 To make the roll, place the egg whites in a large bowl and whisk until they hold soft peaks. Gradually add the sugar, whisking hard between each addition. Fold in the flour, orange rind and juice. Spoon the mixture into the pan and spread it evenly.

3 Bake for 15–18 minutes, or until the sponge is firm and light golden in color. Turn out onto a sheet of wax paper and roll it up loosely from one short side. Let cool.

4 Coarsely chop the apricots and place them in a saucepan with the orange juice. Cover and simmer until most of the liquid has been absorbed. Liquidize the apricots in a food processor or blender.

5 Unroll the cake and spread with the apricot mixture. Roll up, arrange strips of paper diagonally across the roll, sprinkle lightly with confectioner's sugar, remove the paper and sprinkle with orange rind.

Classic Cheesecake

Dust the top of the cheesecake with confectioner's sugar to decorate, if you wish.

Serves 8

⅔ cup digestive cookies, crushed
4 cups cream cheese, at room temperature
generous 1¼ cups sugar

grated rind of 1 lemon
3 tablespoons lemon juice
1 teaspoon vanilla extract
4 eggs

1 Preheat the oven to 325°F. Grease an 8-inch springform pan. Place on a 12-inch circle of foil. Press it up the sides to seal tightly. Press the cookies into the bottom of the pan.

2 Beat the cream cheese until smooth. Add the sugar, lemon rind and juice, and vanilla, and beat until blended. Beat in the eggs, one at a time.

3 Pour into the prepared pan. Set the pan in a larger baking tray and place in the oven. Pour enough hot water in the outer tray to come 1 inch up the side of the pan.

4 Bake until the top is golden brown, about 1½ hours. Cool in the pan.

5 Run a knife around the edge to loosen, then remove the rim of the pan. Chill for at least 4 hours before serving.

Chocolate Cheesecake

Substitute digestive cookies for the base to create a slightly different dessert.

Serves 10–12

10 ounces semisweet chocolate
5 cups cream cheese, at room temperature
1 cup sugar
2 teaspoons vanilla extract
4 eggs
1 tablespoon cocoa
¾ cup sour cream

For the base
2⅓ cups chocolate cookies, crushed
6 tablespoons butter, melted
½ teaspoon ground cinnamon

1 Preheat the oven to 350°F. Grease the bottom and sides of a 9 x 3-inch springform pan.

2 For the base, mix the cookies with the butter and cinnamon. Press into the bottom of the pan.

3 Melt the chocolate in the top of a double boiler. Set aside.

4 Beat the cream cheese until smooth, then beat in the sugar and vanilla. Add the eggs, one at a time.

5 Stir the cocoa into the sour cream. Add to the cream cheese mixture. Stir in the melted chocolate.

6 Pour over the crust. Bake for 1 hour. Cool in the pan, then remove the rim. Chill before serving.

Marbled Cheesecake

Serves 10

4 cups cream cheese, at
   room temperature
1 cup superfine sugar
4 eggs
1 teaspoon vanilla
   extract

½ cup cocoa, dissolved in
   5 tablespoons hot
   water
1 cup digestive cookies,
   crushed

1 Preheat the oven to 350°F. Grease and line the bottom of an 8 x 3-inch cake pan.

2 With an electric mixer, beat the cheese until smooth and creamy. Add the sugar and beat to incorporate. Beat in the eggs, one at a time. Do not overmix.

3 Divide the mixture between two bowls. Stir the vanilla into one, then add the chocolate mixture to the other. Pour a cupful of the vanilla mixture into the center of the pan to make an even layer. Slowly pour over a cupful of chocolate mixture in the center. Repeat, alternating cupfuls of the batter in a circular pattern until both are used up.

4 Set the pan in a larger baking tray and pour in hot water to come 1½ inches up the sides of the cake pan. Bake until the top of the cake is golden, about 1½ hours. It will rise during baking but will sink later. Let cool in the pan on a rack.

5 To turn out, run a knife around the inside edge. Place a flat plate, bottom-side up, over the pan and invert onto the plate.

6 Sprinkle the crushed cookies evenly over the bottom, gently place another plate over them, and invert again. Cover and chill for at least 3 hours, or overnight. To serve, cut slices with a sharp knife dipped in hot water.

Baked Cheesecake with Fresh Fruits

Vary the fruit decoration to suit the season for this rich, creamy dessert.

Serves 12

2 cups digestive cookies,
   crushed
¼ cup sweet butter,
   melted
2 cups curd cheese
⅔ cup sour cream
generous ½ cup superfine
   sugar
3 eggs, separated
grated rind of 1 lemon
2 tablespoons Marsala

½ teaspoon almond
   extract
½ cup ground almonds
scant ½ cup golden
   raisins
1 pound prepared mixed
   fruits, such as figs,
   cherries, peaches and
   strawberries, to
   decorate

1 Preheat the oven to 350°F. Grease and line the sides of a 10-inch round springform pan. Combine the cookies and butter and press into the bottom of the pan. Chill for 20 minutes.

2 For the cake mixture, beat together the cheese, cream, sugar, egg yolks, lemon rind, Marsala and almond extract until smooth and creamy.

3 Whisk the egg whites until stiff and fold into the cheese mixture with all the remaining ingredients, except the fruit, until evenly combined. Pour over the cookie base and bake for 45 minutes, until risen and just set in the center.

4 Let stand in the pan until completely cold. Carefully remove the pan and peel away the lining paper.

5 Chill the cheesecake for at least 1 hour before decorating with the prepared fruits, just before serving.

Tofu Berry "Cheesecake"

Strictly speaking, this "cheesecake" is not a cheesecake at all, since it's based on tofu (beancurd)– but who would guess?

Serves 6
For the base
4 tablespoons margarine
2 tablespoons apple juice
1 cup bran flakes

For the filling
1½ cups tofu or low fat
   soft cheese
scant 1 cup plain yogurt
1 tablespoon/1 envelope
   powdered gelatin
4 tablespoons apple juice

For the topping
1½ cups mixed summer
   soft fruit, such as
   strawberries,
   raspberries, red
   currants, blackberries
2 tablespoons red currant
   jelly
2 tablespoons hot water

1 For the base, place the margarine and apple juice in a saucepan and heat gently until melted. Crush the cereal and stir it into the pan. Turn into a 9-inch round quiche pan and press down firmly. Let set.

2 For the filling, place the tofu or cheese and yogurt in a food processor or blender and process until smooth. Dissolve the gelatin in the apple juice and stir into the tofu mixture.

3 Spread the tofu mixture over the chilled base, smoothing it evenly. Chill until set.

4 Remove the quiche pan and place the "cheesecake" on a serving plate. Arrange the fruits over the top. Melt the red currant jelly with the hot water. Let it cool, and then spoon over the fruit to serve.

Baked Blackberry Cheesecake

This light cheesecake is best made with wild blackberries; if they're not available, use cultivated ones.

Serves 6
¾ cup cottage cheese
¾ cup plain yogurt
1 tablespoon whole wheat
   flour
2 tablespoons golden
   superfine sugar
1 egg

1 egg white
finely grated rind and
   juice of ½ lemon
scant 2 cups fresh or
   frozen and defrosted
   blackberries

1 Preheat the oven to 350°F. Lightly grease and line the bottom of a 7-inch sandwich cake pan.

2 Place the cottage cheese in a food processor or blender and process until smooth. Place in a bowl, then add the yogurt, flour, sugar, egg and egg white, and mix. Add the lemon rind, juice and blackberries, reserving a few.

3 Turn the mixture into the pan and bake for 30–35 minutes, or until just set. Turn off the oven and let the cake stand in it for 30 minutes more.

4 Run a knife around the edge of the cheesecake and turn it out. Remove the lining paper and place the cheesecake on a warm serving plate.

5 Decorate the cheesecake with the reserved blackberries and serve warm.

Coffee, Peach and Almond Daquoise

Makes one 9-inch cake

5 eggs, separated
scant 2 cups superfine
　sugar
1 tablespoon cornstarch
1½ cups ground
　almonds, toasted
generous ½ cup milk
1¼ cups sweet butter,
　diced
3–4 tablespoons coffee
　extract

2 x 14-ounce cans peach
　halves in juice,
　drained
generous ½ cup slivered
　almonds, toasted
confectioner's sugar, for
　dusting
few fresh mint leaves, to
　decorate

1 Preheat the oven to 300°F. Draw three 9-inch circles onto some wax paper and place on baking sheets.

2 Whisk the egg whites until stiff. Gradually whisk in scant 1½ cups of the sugar until thick and glossy. Fold in the cornstarch and almonds. Using a ½-inch plain piping nozzle, pipe circles of the mixture onto the paper. Bake for 2 hours. Turn onto wire racks to cool.

3 For the buttercream, beat together the egg yolks and remaining sugar until thick and pale. Heat the milk to boiling point and beat into the egg mixture. Return to the pan and heat until the mixture coats the back of a spoon. Strain into a large bowl and beat until lukewarm. Gradually beat in the butter until glossy. Beat in the coffee extract.

4 Trim the meringues and crush the trimmings. Reserve 3 peach halves, chop the rest and fold into half the buttercream with the crushed meringue. Use to sandwich the meringues together and place on a serving plate.

5 Ice the cake with the plain buttercream. Cover the top with slivered almonds and dust generously with confectioner's sugar. Thinly slice the reserved peaches and use to decorate the cake edge with some mint leaves.

Mocha Brazil Layer Torte

Makes one 8-inch round cake

For the meringue

3 egg whites
generous ½ cup superfine
　sugar
1 tablespoon coffee
　extract
¾ cup Brazil nuts,
　toasted and finely
　ground
8-inch chocolate sponge
　cake

For the icing

1 cup semisweet
　chocolate chips
2 tablespoons coffee
　extract
2 tablespoons water
2½ cups heavy cream,
　whipped

To decorate

12 chocolate-coated coffee
　beans
12 chocolate triangles

1 Preheat the oven to 300°F. Draw two 8-inch circles on wax paper and place on a baking sheet. Grease, line the bottom and flour an 8-inch round springform pan.

2 For the meringue, whisk the egg whites until stiff. Whisk in the sugar until glossy. Fold in the coffee extract and nuts. Using a ½-inch plain piping nozzle, pipe circles of the mixture onto the paper. Bake for 2 hours. Cool. Increase the oven temperature to 350°F.

3 For the icing, melt the chocolate chips, coffee extract and water in a bowl over a pan of simmering water. Remove from the heat and fold in the whipped cream.

4 Cut the cake into three equal layers. Trim meringue discs to the same size and assemble the cake with a layer of sponge, a little icing and a meringue disc, ending with sponge.

5 Reserve a little of the remaining icing, use the rest to cover the cake completely, forming a swirling pattern over the top. Using the reserved icing, and an icing bag with a star nozzle, pipe 24 small rosettes on top of the cake. Top alternately with the coffee beans and the chocolate triangles.

Fresh Fruit Genoese

This Italian classic can be made with any selection of seasonal fruits.

Serves 8–10

For the sponge
1½ cups all-purpose flour
pinch of salt
4 eggs
½ cup superfine sugar
6 tablespoons orange-flavored liqueur

For the filling and topping
4 tablespoons vanilla sugar
2½ cups heavy cream
1 pound mixed fresh fruits
1¼ cups pistachios, chopped
4 tablespoons apricot jam, warmed and strained

1 Preheat the oven to 350°F. Grease and line the bottom of an 8-inch springform cake pan.

2 Sift the flour and salt together three times, then set aside. Using an electric mixer, beat the eggs and sugar together for 10 minutes until thick and pale.

3 Fold the flour mixture gently into the egg and sugar mixture. Transfer the cake mixture to the prepared pan and bake for 30–35 minutes. Let the cake stand in the pan for 5 minutes, then transfer to a wire rack, remove the lining paper and cool.

4 Cut the cake horizontally in to two layers, place the bottom layer on a plate. Sprinkle both layers with liqueur.

5 Add the vanilla sugar to the cream and whisk until the cream holds peaks. Spread two-thirds of the cream over the bottom layer and top with half of the fruit. Top with the second layer and spread the top and sides with the remaining cream. Press the nuts around the sides, arrange the remaining fruit on top and brush with the apricot jam.

Fruit Gâteau with Heartsease

This gâteau would be lovely to serve as a dessert at a summer lunch party in the garden.

Makes one ring cake
½ cup soft margarine
scant ½ cup sugar
2 teaspoons honey
1¼ cups self-rising flour
½ teaspoon baking powder
2 tablespoons milk
2 eggs
1 tablespoon rose water
1 tablespoon Cointreau

To decorate
16 heartsease pansy flowers
1 egg white, lightly beaten
superfine sugar
confectioner's sugar
4 cups strawberries
strawberry leaves

1 Preheat the oven to 375°F. Grease and lightly flour a ring mold. Put the soft margarine, sugar, honey, flour, baking powder, milk and eggs into a mixing bowl and beat well for 1 minute. Add the rose water and the Cointreau and mix well.

2 Pour the mixture into the mold and bake for 40 minutes. Let stand for a few minutes, then turn onto a serving plate.

3 Crystalize the heartsease pansies by painting them with the lightly beaten egg white and sprinkling with superfine sugar. Let dry.

4 Sift confectioner's sugar over the cake. Fill the center of the ring with strawberries – if they will not all fit, place some around the edge. Decorate with the crystalized heartsease flowers and some strawberry leaves.

Nut and Apple Gâteau

Makes one 9-inch round cake

1 cup pecans or walnuts,
  toasted
½ cup all-purpose flour
2 teaspoons baking
  powder
¼ teaspoon salt
2 large cooking apples

3 eggs
scant 1¼ cups superfine
  sugar
1 teaspoon vanilla
  extract
¾ cup whipping cream

1 Preheat the oven to 325°F. Line two 9-inch cake pans with wax paper and grease the paper.

2 Finely chop the nuts. Reserve 1½ tablespoons of them and place the rest in a mixing bowl. Sift over the flour, baking powder and salt and stir.

3 Peel and core the apples. Cut into ⅛-inch dice, then stir into the flour mixture.

4 Beat the eggs until frothy. Gradually add the sugar and vanilla and beat until ribbon trails form, about 8 minutes. Fold in the flour mixture.

5 Pour into the cake pans and bake until a skewer inserted in the center comes out clean, about 35 minutes. Let stand for 10 minutes, then turn out onto a wire rack to cool.

6 Whip the cream until firm. Use half for the filling. Pipe rosettes on the top and sprinkle over the reserved nuts.

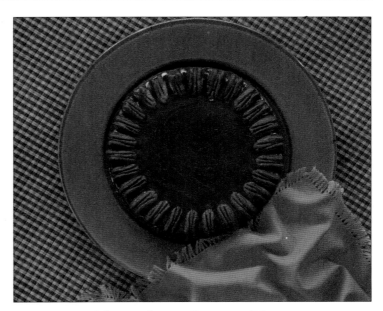

Chocolate Pecan Torte

This torte uses finely ground nuts instead of flour. Toast, then cool the nuts before grinding finely in a processor.

Makes one 8-inch round cake

7 ounces semisweet
  chocolate, chopped
10 tablespoons sweet
  butter, cut into pieces
4 eggs
½ cup superfine sugar
2 teaspoons vanilla
  extract
1 cup ground pecans
2 teaspoons ground
  cinnamon
24 toasted pecan halves,
  to decorate (optional)

**For the chocolate
honey glaze**
4 ounces semisweet
  chocolate, chopped
¼ cup sweet butter, cut
  into pieces
2 tablespoons honey
pinch of ground
  cinnamon

1 Preheat the oven to 350°F. Grease an 8-inch springform pan, line with wax paper, then grease the paper. Wrap the pan with foil.

2 Melt the chocolate and butter over low heat, stirring until smooth. Set aside. Beat the eggs, sugar and vanilla until frothy. Stir in the melted chocolate and butter, ground nuts and cinnamon. Pour into the pan. Place in a large roasting pan and pour boiling water into the roasting pan, to come ¾ inch up the side of the springform pan. Bake for 25–30 minutes, until the edge of the cake is set, but the center soft. Remove the foil and set on a wire rack.

3 For the glaze, melt the chocolate, butter, honey and cinnamon, stirring until smooth. Remove from the heat. If using, dip toasted pecan halves halfway into the glaze and place on wax paper to set. Remove the cake from its pan and invert onto a wire rack. Remove the paper. Pour the glaze over the cake, tilting the rack to spread it. Use a metal spatula to smooth the sides. Arrange the nuts on top.

Coconut Lime Gâteau

Makes one 9-inch round cake

2 cups all-purpose flour
2½ teaspoons baking
   powder
¼ teaspoon salt
1 cup butter, at room
   temperature
generous 1 cup superfine
   sugar
grated rind of 2 limes
4 eggs

4 tablespoons fresh lime
   juice
1½ cups dried coconut

For the frosting
generous 2 cups sugar
4 tablespoons water
pinch of cream of tartar
1 egg white, whisked
   stiffly

1   Preheat the oven to 350°F. Grease and line the bottom of two 9-inch sandwich cake pans. Sift together the flour, baking powder and salt.

2   Beat the butter until soft. Add the sugar and lime rind and beat until pale and fluffy. Beat in the eggs, one at a time.

3   Gradually fold in the dry ingredients, alternating with the lime juice, then stir in two-thirds of the coconut.

4   Divide the mixture between the cake pans, even the tops and bake for 30–35 minutes. Cool in the pans on a wire rack for 10 minutes, then turn out and peel off the lining paper.

5   Bake the remaining coconut until golden brown, stirring occasionally. For the frosting, heat the sugar, water and cream of tartar until dissolved, stirring. Boil to reach 250°F on a sugar thermometer. Remove from the heat and, when the bubbles subside, whisk in the egg white until thick.

6   Sandwich and cover the cake with the frosting. Sprinkle over the toasted coconut. Let set.

Exotic Celebration Gâteau

Use any tropical fruits you can find to make a spectacular display of colors and tastes.

Makes one 8-inch ring gâteau

¾ cup butter, softened
scant 1 cup superfine
   sugar
3 eggs, beaten
2¼ cups self-rising flour
2–3 tablespoons milk
6–8 tablespoons light
   rum
scant 2 cups heavy cream
¼ cup confectioner's
   sugar, sifted

To decorate
1 pound mixed fresh
   exotic and soft fruits,
   such as figs, red
   currants, star fruit
   and kiwi fruit
6 tablespoons apricot
   jam, warmed and
   strained
2 tablespoons warm
   water
confectioner's sugar

1   Preheat the oven to 375°F. Grease and flour a deep 8-inch ring mold.

2   Beat together the butter and sugar until light and fluffy. Gradually beat in the eggs, then fold in the flour and milk.

3   Spoon the mixture into the ring mold. Bake the cake for 45 minutes, or until a skewer inserted into the center comes out clean. Turn out onto a wire rack and let cool.

4   Place the cake on a serving plate. Make holes randomly over the cake with a skewer. Drizzle over the rum and allow to soak in.

5   Beat together the cream and confectioner's sugar until the mixture holds soft peaks. Spread all over the cake. Arrange the fruits in the hollow center of the cake. Mix the apricot jam and water, then brush over the fruit. Sift over some confectioner's sugar.

Chocolate and Fresh Cherry Gâteau

Makes one 8-inch round cake

½ cup butter	**For the frosting**
⅔ cup superfine sugar	⅔ cup semisweet
3 eggs, lightly beaten	chocolate chips
1 cup semisweet	¼ cup sweet butter
chocolate chips, melted	4 tablespoons heavy
4 tablespoons kirsch	cream
1¼ cups self-rising flour	
1 teaspoon ground	**To decorate**
cinnamon	½ cup white chocolate
½ teaspoon ground cloves	chips, melted
12 ounces fresh cherries,	18 fresh cherries
pitted and halved	few rose leaves, washed
3 tablespoons morello	and dried
cherry jam, warmed	
1 teaspoon lemon juice	

1 Preheat the oven to 325°F. Grease, line the bottom and flour an 8-inch round springform pan.

2 Cream the butter and ½ cup of the sugar until pale. Beat in the eggs. Stir in the chocolate and half the kirsch. Fold in the flour and spices. Put in the pan and bake for 55–60 minutes, or until a skewer inserted in the center comes out clean. Cool for 10 minutes then transfer to a wire rack.

3 For the filling, bring the cherries, remaining kirsch and sugar to a boil, cover, and simmer for 10 minutes. Uncover for 10 minutes more until syrupy. Let cool.

4 Halve the cake horizontally. Cut a ½-inch deep circle from the base, leaving a ½-inch edge. Crumble into the filling and stir to form a paste. Fill and cover the cake base.

5 Strain the jam and lemon juice. Brush all over the cake. For the frosting, melt all the ingredients. Cool, pour over the cake. Decorate with chocolate-dipped cherries and leaves.

Coffee Almond Flower Gâteau

This delicious cake can be made quite quickly. For a change, use coffee-flavored spongecakes instead of plain.

Makes one 8-inch round cake

2¼ cups coffee-flavor	3 ounces semisweet
butter icing	chocolate
2 x 8-inch round sponge	20 blanched almonds
cakes with chopped	4 chocolate-coated coffee
nuts	beans

1 Reserve 4 tablespoons of the butter icing for piping and use the rest to sandwich the sponges together and cover the top and side of the cake. Smooth the top with a metal spatula and serrate the side with a scraper.

2 Melt the chocolate in a heat proof bowl over a pan of hot water. Remove from the heat, then dip in half of each almond at a slight angle. Let dry on wax paper. Return the chocolate to the pan of hot water (off the heat) so it does not set. Remove and let cool slightly.

3 Arrange the almonds on top of the cake to represent flowers. Place a chocolate-coated coffee bean in the flower centers. Spoon the remaining melted chocolate into a wax paper icing bag. Cut a small piece off the end in a straight line. Pipe the chocolate in wavy lines over the top of the cake and in small beads around the top edge.

4 Transfer the cake to a serving plate. Place the reserved buttercream in a fresh icing bag fitted with a No 2 writing nozzle. Pipe beads of icing all around the bottom of the cake, then top with small beads of chocolate.

Vegan Chocolate Gâteau

A rare treat for vegans, this gâteau tastes really delicious.

Makes one 8-inch gâteau

2½ cups self-rising whole
   wheat flour
½ cup cocoa
1 tablespoon baking
   powder
1¼ cups superfine sugar
few drops vanilla extract
9 tablespoons sunflower
   oil
1½ cups water

sifted cocoa, to decorate
¼ cup chopped nuts, to
   decorate

For the chocolate fudge
¼ cup soy margarine
3 tablespoons water
2¼ cups confectioner's
   sugar
2 tablespoons cocoa

1 Preheat the oven to 325°F. Grease and line the bottom of a deep 8-inch round cake pan, and grease the paper.

2 Sift the flour, cocoa and baking powder into a large mixing bowl. Add the sugar and vanilla, then gradually beat in the oil and water to make a smooth batter.

3 Pour the mixture into the cake pan and smooth the surface. Bake for 45 minutes, or until a skewer inserted into the center of the cake comes out clean. Let stand in the pan for 5 minutes, then turn out onto a wire rack and let cool. Cut the cake in half.

4 For the chocolate fudge, gently melt the margarine with the water. Remove from the heat, add the confectioner's sugar and cocoa, and beat until smooth and shiny. Let cool until firm enough to spread and pipe.

5 Place a layer of cake on a serving plate and spread over two-thirds of the chocolate fudge. Top with the other layer of cake. Using a star piping nozzle, pipe chocolate fudge stars over the cake. Sprinkle with cocoa and chopped nuts.

Black Forest Gâteau

A perfect gâteau for a special tea party, or for serving as a sumptuous dinner party dessert.

Makes one 8-inch gâteau

5 eggs
scant 1 cup superfine
   sugar
½ cup all-purpose flour
½ cup cocoa
6 tablespoons butter,
   melted

For the filling
5–6 tablespoons kirsch
2½ cups heavy cream

15-ounce can black
   cherries, drained,
   pitted and chopped

To decorate
chocolate curls
15–20 fresh cherries,
   preferably with stems
confectioner's sugar

1 Preheat the oven to 350°F. Line the bottom of two deep 8-inch round cake pans with wax paper and grease.

2 Beat together the eggs and sugar for 10 minutes, or until thick and pale. Sift over the flour and cocoa, and fold in gently. Trickle in the melted butter and fold in gently.

3 Transfer the mixture to the cake pans. Bake for 30 minutes, or until springy to the touch. Let stand in the pans for 5 minutes, then turn out onto a wire rack, peel off the lining paper and let cool. Cut each cake in half horizontally and sprinkle with the kirsch.

4 Whip the cream until soft peaks form. Combine two-thirds of the cream with the chopped cherries. Place a layer of cake on a serving plate and spread with one-third of the filling. Repeat twice, and top with a layer of cake. Use the reserved cream to cover the top and sides of the gâteau.

5 Decorate the gâteau with chocolate curls, fresh cherries and dredge with confectioner's sugar.

Walnut Coffee Gâteau

Serves 8–10

1¼ cups walnuts
generous ¾ cup superfine sugar
5 eggs, separated
scant 1 cup dry bread crumbs
1 tablespoon cocoa
1 tablespoon instant coffee
2 tablespoons rum or lemon juice

¼ teaspoon salt
6 tablespoons red currant jelly, warmed
chopped walnuts, for decorating

For the frosting

8 ounces semisweet chocolate
3 cups whipping cream

1 For the frosting, combine the chocolate and cream in the top of a double boiler until the chocolate melts. Cool, then cover and chill overnight, or until the mixture is firm.

2 Preheat the oven to 350°F. Line and grease 9 x 2-inch cake pan. Grind the nuts with 3 tablespoons of the sugar in a food processor, blender or coffee grinder.

3 With an electric mixer, beat the egg yolks and remaining sugar until thick and lemon-colored. Fold in the walnuts. Stir in the bread crumbs, cocoa, coffee and rum or lemon juice.

4 In another bowl, beat the egg whites with the salt until they hold stiff peaks. Fold carefully into the walnut mixture. Pour the meringue batter into the pan and bake until the top of the cake springs back when touched, about 45 minutes. Let the cake stand for 5 minutes, then turn out and cool, before slicing in half horizontally.

5 With an electric mixer, beat the chocolate frosting mixture on low speed until it becomes lighter, about 30 seconds. Brush some of the jelly over the cut cake layer. Spread with some of the chocolate frosting, then sandwich with the remaining cake layer. Brush the top of the cake with jelly, then cover the side and top with the remaining frosting. Make a starburst pattern with a knife and sprinkle chopped walnuts around the edge.

Sachertorte

A rich cake, ideal to serve as a treat for anyone who is a self-confessed chocoholic.

Makes one 9-inch round cake

4 ounces semisweet chocolate
⅓ cup sweet butter, at room temperature
¼ cup sugar
4 eggs, separated, plus 1 egg white
¼ teaspoon salt
9 tablespoons all-purpose flour, sifted

For the topping

5 tablespoons apricot jam
1 cup water, plus 1 tablespoon
1 tablespoon sweet butter
6 ounces semisweet chocolate
⅓ cup sugar
premade chocolate decorating icing

1 Preheat the oven to 325°F. Line and grease a 9-inch cake pan. Melt the chocolate in the top of a double boiler. Set aside.

2 Cream the butter and sugar until light and fluffy. Stir in the chocolate, then beat in the egg yolks, one at a time.

3 Beat the egg whites with the salt until stiff. Fold a dollop of whites into the chocolate mixture to lighten it. Fold in the remaining whites in three batches, alternating with the sifted flour. Pour into the pan and bake until a skewer comes out clean, about 45 minutes. Turn out onto a wire rack.

4 Meanwhile, melt the jam with 1 tablespoon of the water, then strain for a smooth consistency. For the frosting, melt the butter and chocolate in the top of a double boiler. In a heavy saucepan, dissolve the sugar in the remaining water, then boil until it reaches 225°F (thread stage) on a sugar thermometer. Plunge the bottom of the pan into cold water for 1 minute. Stir into the chocolate. Cool for a few minutes.

5 Brush the warm jam over the cake. Pour over the frosting and spread over the top and sides. Let set overnight. Decorate with chocolate icing.

Dundee Cake

This is the perfect recipe for a festive occasion when a lighter fruit cake is required.

Makes one 8-inch round cake

¾ cup butter
1 cup light brown sugar
3 eggs
2 cups all-purpose flour
2 teaspoon baking powder
1 teaspoons ground cinnamon
½ teaspoon ground cloves
¼ teaspoon grated nutmeg
generous 1½ cups golden raisins

generous 1 cup raisins
¾ cup candied cherries, halved
¾ cup chopped mixed candied peel
½ cup blanched almonds, chopped
grated rind of 1 lemon
2 tablespoons brandy
1 cup whole blanched almonds, to decorate

1 Preheat the oven to 325°F. Grease and line an 8-inch round deep cake pan. Cream the butter and sugar until pale and light. Add the eggs, 1 at a time, beating after each addition.

2 Sift together the flour, baking powder and spices. Fold into the egg mixture alternately with the remaining ingredients, until evenly combined. Transfer to the cake pan. Smooth the surface, then make a small dip in the center.

3 Decorate the top of the cake by pressing the blanched almonds in decreasing circles over the entire surface. Bake for 2–2¼ hours, until a skewer inserted in the center of the cake comes out clean.

4 Let cool in the pan for 30 minutes then transfer the cake to a wire rack.

Vegan Dundee Cake

As it contains neither eggs nor dairy products, this cake is suitable for vegans.

Makes one 8-inch square cake

scant 2½ cups whole wheat flour
1 teaspoon mixed spice
¾ cup soy margarine
1 cup dark muscovado sugar, plus 2 tablespoons
generous 1 cup golden raisins
1 cup currants
generous 1 cup raisins
½ cup chopped mixed candied peel
generous ½ cup candied cherries, halved
finely grated rind of 1 orange

2 tablespoons ground almonds
¼ cup blanched almonds, chopped
1 teaspoon baking soda
½ cup soy milk
⅓ cup sunflower oil
2 tablespoons malt vinegar

To decorate
mixed nuts, such as pistachios, pecans and macadamia nuts
candied cherries
angelica
4 tablespoons honey, warmed

1 Preheat the oven to 300°F. Grease and double-line a deep 8-inch square loose-based cake pan.

2 Sift together the flour and mixed spice. Work in the margarine. Stir in the sugar, dried fruits, peel, cherries, orange rind, ground almonds and blanched almonds.

3 Dissolve the baking soda in a little of the milk. Warm the remaining milk with the oil and vinegar and add the baking soda mixture. Stir into the flour mixture.

4 Spoon into the pan and smooth. Bake for 2½ hours. Let stand in the pan for 5 minutes, then cool on a rack. Decorate with the nuts, cherries and angelica and brush with the honey.

Panforte

This rich, spicy nougat-type cake is a Christmas speciality of Siena in Italy.

Makes one 8-inch round cake

1⅔ cups mixed chopped candied exotic peel, to include lemon orange, citron, papaya and pineapple
1 cup unblanched almonds
½ cup walnut halves
½ cup all-purpose flour
1 teaspoon ground cinnamon
¼ teaspoon each grated nutmeg, ground cloves and ground coriander
1 cup superfine sugar
4 tablespoons water
confectioner's sugar, for dusting

1 Preheat the oven to 350°F. Grease and line the bottom of an 8-inch round loose-based cake pan with rice paper. Put the mixed peel and nuts in a bowl. Sift in the flour and spices and mix well.

2 Dissolve the superfine sugar and water in a small saucepan, then boil until the mixture reaches 225°F on a sugar thermometer (thread stage). Pour onto the fruit mixture, stirring to coat well. Transfer to the cake pan, pressing into the sides with a metal spoon.

3 Bake for 25–30 minutes, until the mixture is bubbling. Cool in the pan for 5 minutes.

4 Use a lightly oiled metal spatula to work around the edges of the cake to loosen it. Remove the cake from the pan, leaving the base in place. Let it go cold, then remove the base and dust generously with confectioner's sugar.

Kulich

This Russian yeast cake is traditionally made at Easter.

Makes two cakes

1 tablespoon fast-rising dried yeast
6 tablespoons lukewarm milk
scant ½ cup superfine sugar
5 cups all-purpose flour
pinch of saffron strands
2 tablespoons dark rum
½ teaspoon ground cardamom seeds
½ teaspoon ground cumin
4 tablespoons sweet butter
2 eggs, plus 2 egg yolks
½ vanilla pod, finely chopped
2 tablespoons each candied ginger, mixed peel, almonds and currants, chopped

To decorate

¾ cup confectioner's sugar, sifted
1½–2 teaspoons warm water
drop of almond extract
2 candles
blanched almonds
mixed candied peel

1 Blend together the yeast, milk, 2 tablespoons sugar and ½ cup flour. Let stand in a warm place for 15 minutes, until frothy. Soak the saffron in the rum for 15 minutes.

2 Sift together the remaining flour and spices and work in the butter. Stir in the rest of the sugar. Add the yeast mixture, saffron liquid and remaining ingredients. Knead until smooth. Put in an oiled bowl, cover and let stand until doubled in size.

3 Preheat the oven to 375°F. Grease, line and flour two 1¼-pound coffee pans or 6-inch clay flowerpots.

4 Punch down the dough and form into two rounds. Press into the pans or pots, cover and let stand for 30 minutes. Bake for 35 minutes for the pots or 50 minutes for the pans. Cool.

5 Mix together the sugar, water and almond extract. Pour over the cakes. Decorate with the candles, nuts and peel.

Yule Log

This rich seasonal treat could provide an economic alternative to a traditional iced fruit cake.

Makes one 11-inch long roll

4 eggs, separated
¾ cup superfine sugar
1 teaspoon vanilla
  extract
pinch of cream of tartar
  (optional)
1 cup all-purpose flour,
  sifted

1 cup whipping cream
11 ounces semisweet
  chocolate, chopped
2 tablespoons rum or
  Cognac
confectioner's sugar, for
  dusting

1 Preheat the oven to 375°F. Grease, line and flour a 16 x 11-inch jelly roll pan.

2 Whisk the egg yolks with all but 2 tablespoons of the sugar until pale and thick. Add the vanilla extract.

3 Whisk the egg whites (with the cream of tartar if not using a copper bowl) until they form soft peaks. Add the reserved sugar and continue whisking until stiff and glossy.

4 Fold half the flour into the yolk mixture. Add a quarter of the egg whites and fold in to lighten the mixture. Fold in the remaining flour, then the remaining egg whites.

5 Spread the mixture in the pan. Bake for 15 minutes. Turn onto paper sprinkled with sugar. Roll up and let cool.

6 Bring the cream to a boil. Put the chocolate in a bowl and add the cream. Stir until the chocolate has melted, then beat until it is fluffy and has thickened to a spreading consistency. Mix a third of the chocolate cream with the rum or Cognac.

7 Unroll the cake and spread with the rum mixture. Re-roll and cut off about a quarter, at an angle. Arrange to form a branch. Spread the chocolate cream over the cake. Mark with a fork, add Christmas decorations and dust with sugar.

Chocolate Chestnut Roll

A traditional version of Bûche de Nôel, the delicious French Christmas gâteau.

Makes one 13-inch long roll

8 ounces semisweet
  chocolate
2 ounces white chocolate
4 eggs, separated
generous ½ cup superfine
  sugar

For the chestnut filling
⅔ cup heavy cream
8-ounce can chestnut
  purée
4–5 tablespoons
  confectioner's sugar,
  plus extra for dusting
1–2 tablespoons brandy

1 Preheat the oven to 350°F. Line a 9 x 13-inch jelly roll pan and grease it.

2 For the chocolate curls, melt 2 ounces of the semisweet and all of the white chocolate in separate bowls set over saucepans of hot water. When melted, spread on a non-porous surface and let set. Hold a long sharp knife at a 45-degree angle to the chocolate and push it along the chocolate, turning the knife in a circular motion. Put the curls on wax paper.

3 Melt the remaining semisweet chocolate. Beat the yolks and superfine sugar until thick and pale. Stir in the chocolate.

4 Whisk the whites until they form stiff peaks, then fold into the mixture. Turn into the pan and bake for 15–20 minutes. Cool, covered with a just-damp dish towel, on a wire rack.

5 Sprinkle a sheet of wax paper with superfine sugar. Turn the roll out onto it. Peel off the lining paper and trim the edges of the roll. Cover with the dish towel.

6 For the filling, whip the cream until softly peaking. Beat together the chestnut purée, sugar and brandy until smooth, then fold in the cream. Spread over the cake and roll it up. Top with chocolate curls and dust with confectioner's sugar.

Chocolate Christmas Cups

To crystalize cranberries for decoration, beat an egg white until frothy. Dip each berry in egg white then in sugar.

Makes about 35 cups

*10 ounces semisweet
   chocolate, broken
   into pieces
70–80 foil or paper sweet
   cases
6 ounces cooked, cold
   Christmas pudding*

*⅓ cup brandy or whisky
chocolate leaves and a
   few candied
   cranberries, to
   decorate*

1 Place the chocolate in a bowl over a saucepan of hot water. Heat gently until the chocolate is melted, stirring until the chocolate is smooth.

2 Using a pastry brush, brush or coat the bottom and sides of about 35 sweet cases. Let set, then repeat, reheating the melted chocolate if necessary, and apply a second coat. Let cool and set completely, 4–5 hours or overnight. Reserve the remaining chocolate.

3 Crumble the Christmas pudding in a bowl, sprinkle with the brandy or whisky and let stand for 30–40 minutes, until the spirit is absorbed.

4 Spoon a little of the pudding mixture into each cup, smoothing the top. Reheat the remaining chocolate and spoon over the top of each cup to cover the surface of each cup to the edge. Let set.

5 When completely set, carefully peel off the cases and place in clean foil cases. Decorate with chocolate leaves and candied cranberries.

Eggless Christmas Cake

This simple cake contains a wealth of fruit and nuts to give it that traditional Christmas flavor.

Makes one 7-inch square cake

*½ cup golden raisins
½ cup raisins
½ cup currants
scant ½ cup candied
   cherries, halved
¼ cup mixed candied peel
1 cup apple juice
scant ¼ cup toasted
   hazelnuts
2 tablespoons pumpkin
   seeds
2 pieces preserved ginger
   in syrup, chopped*

*finely grated rind of
   1 lemon
½ cup milk
¼ cup sunflower oil
2 cups whole wheat self-
   rising flour
2 teaspoons mixed spice
3 tablespoons brandy or
   dark rum
apricot jam, for brushing
candied fruits, to
   decorate*

1 Soak the golden raisins, raisins, currants, cherries and mixed candied peel in the apple juice overnight.

2 Preheat the oven to 300°F. Grease and line a 7-inch square cake pan.

3 Add the hazelnuts, pumpkin seeds, ginger and lemon rind to the fruit. Stir in the milk and oil. Sift the flour and spice, then stir in with the brandy or rum.

4 Spoon into the cake pan and bake for about 1½ hours, or until the cake is golden brown and firm to the touch.

5 Turn out and cool on a wire rack. Brush with strained apricot jam and decorate with candied fruits.

Flourless Fruit Cake

This makes the perfect base for a birthday cake for anyone who needs to avoid eating flour.

Makes one 10-inch round cake

1⅓ cups mincemeat
2 cups dried mixed fruit
½ cup ready-to-eat dried apricots, chopped
⅔ cup ready-to-eat dried figs, chopped
½ cup candied cherries, halved
1 cup walnut pieces
8–10 cups cornflakes, crushed

4 eggs, lightly beaten
14½-ounce can evaporated milk
1 teaspoon mixed spice
1 teaspoon baking powder
mixed candied fruits, chopped, to decorate

1 Preheat the oven to 300°F. Grease a 10-inch round cake pan, line the bottom and sides with a double thickness of wax paper and grease the paper.

2 Put all the ingredients into a large mixing bowl. Beat together well.

3 Turn into the cake pan and smooth the surface.

4 Bake for about 1¾ hours or until a skewer inserted in the center of the cake comes out clean. Let the cake cool in the pan for 10 minutes, then turn out onto a wire rack, peel off the lining paper and let cool completely. Decorate with the chopped candied fruits.

Glazed Christmas Ring

Makes one 10-inch ring cake

generous 1½ cups golden raisins
generous 1 cup raisins
generous 1 cup currants
1 cup dried figs, chopped
6 tablespoons whiskey
3 tablespoons orange juice
1 cup butter
1 cup dark brown sugar
5 eggs
2¼ cups all-purpose flour
1 tablespoon baking powder
1 tablespoon mixed spice
⅔ cup candied cherries, chopped

1 cup brazil nuts, chopped
⅓ cup chopped mixed peel
½ cup ground almonds
grated rind and juice 1 orange
2 tablespoons thick-cut orange marmalade

To decorate

⅔ cup thick-cut orange marmalade
1 tablespoon orange juice
1 cup candied cherries
⅔ cup dried figs, halved
½ cup whole brazil nuts

1 Put the dried fruits in a bowl, pour over 4 tablespoons of the whiskey and all the orange juice and marinate overnight.

2 Preheat the oven to 325°F. Grease and line a 10-inch ring mold. Cream the butter and sugar. Beat in the eggs. Sift together the remaining flour, baking powder and mixed spice. Fold into the egg mixture, alternating with the rest of the ingredients, except the whiskey. Transfer to the pan and bake for 1 hour, then reduce the oven temperature to 300°F and bake for 1¾–2 hours more.

3 Prick the cake all over and pour over the reserved whiskey. Cool in the pan for 30 minutes, then transfer to a wire rack. Boil the marmalade and orange juice for 3 minutes. Stir in the fruit and nuts. Cool, then spoon over the cake and let set.

Noel Christmas Cake

If you like a traditional royal-iced cake, this is a simple design using only one icing and easy-to-pipe decorations.

Makes one 8-inch round cake

8-inch round rich fruit cake
2 tablespoons apricot jam, warmed and strained
5¼ cups marzipan
6 cups royal icing
red and green food coloring

Materials/equipment
9-inch round silver cake board
3 wax paper icing bags
No 1 writing nozzle
2 x No 0 writing nozzles
44 large gold dragées
2½ yards gold ribbon, ¾ inch wide
2½ yards red ribbon, ¼ inch wide

1 Brush the fruit cake with apricot jam, cover with the marzipan and place on the cake board.

2 Flat-ice the top of the cake with two layers of royal icing and let dry. Ice the sides of the cake and peak the royal icing, leaving a space around the center for the ribbon. Let dry. Reserve the remaining royal icing.

3 Pipe beads of icing around the top edge of the cake and place a gold dragée on alternate beads. Using a No 1 writing nozzle, write "NOEL" across the cake and pipe holly leaves, stems and berries around the top.

4 Secure the ribbons around the side of the cake. Tie a red bow and attach to the front of the cake. Use the remaining ribbon for the board. Let dry overnight.

5 Tint 2 tablespoons of the royal icing bright green and 1 tablespoon bright red. Using a No 0 writing nozzle, over-pipe "NOEL" in red, then the edging beads and berries. Over-pipe the holly in green. Let dry.

Christmas Tree Cake

No piping is involved in this bright and colorful cake, making it an easy choice.

Makes one 8-inch round cake

3 tablespoons apricot jam
8-inch round rich fruit cake
6 cups marzipan
green, red, yellow and purple food coloring

1½ cups royal icing
edible silver balls

Materials/equipment
10-inch round cake board

1 Warm, then strain the apricot jam and brush the cake with it. Color 4½ cups of the marzipan green. Use to cover the cake. Let dry overnight.

2 Secure the cake to the board with royal icing. Spread the icing halfway up the cake side. Press the flat side of a metal spatula into the icing, then pull away sharply to form peaks.

3 Make three different-size Christmas tree templates. Tint half the remaining marzipan a deeper green than the top. Using the templates, cut out three tree shapes and arrange them on the cake.

4 Divide the remaining marzipan into three and color red, yellow and purple. Use a little of each marzipan to make five 3-inch rolls. Loop them alternately around the top edge of the cake. Make small red balls and press onto the loop ends.

5 Use the remaining marzipan to make the tree decorations. Arrange on the trees, securing with water, if necessary. Finish the cake by adding silver balls to the Christmas trees.

Christmas Stocking Cake

A bright and happy cake that is sure to delight children at Christmas time.

Makes one 8-inch square cake

8-inch square rich fruit cake	**Materials/equipment**
3 tablespoons apricot jam, warmed and strained	10-inch square silver cake board
6 cups marzipan	1½ yards red ribbon, ¾ inch wide
7½ cups fondant icing	1 yard green ribbon, ¾ inch wide
1 tablespoon royal icing	
red and green food coloring	

1 Brush the cake with the apricot jam and place on the cake board. Cover with marzipan.

2 Set aside 1½ cups of the fondant icing. Cover the cake with the rest. Let dry. Secure the red ribbon around the board and the green ribbon around the cake with royal icing.

3 Divide the icing in half and roll out one half. Using a template, cut out two fondant stockings, one ¼ inch larger all around. Put the smaller one on top of the larger one.

4 Divide the other half of the fondant into two and tint one red and the other green. Roll out and cut each color into seven ½-inch strips. Alternate the strips on top of the stocking. Roll lightly to fuse and press the edges together. Let dry.

5 Shape the remaining white fondant into four packages. Trim with red and green fondant ribbons. Use the remaining red and green fondant to make thin strips to decorate the cake sides. Secure in place with royal icing. Stick small fondant balls over the joins. Arrange the stocking and packages on the cake top.

Marbled Cracker Cake

Here's a Christmas cake that's decorated in a most untraditional way!

Makes one 8-inch round cake

8-inch round rich fruit cake	**Materials /equipment**
3 tablespoons apricot jam, warmed and strained	wooden toothpicks
4½ cups marzipan	10-inch round cake board
5¼ cups fondant icing	red, green and gold thin gift-wrapping ribbon
red and green food coloring	3 red and 3 green ribbon bows
edible gold balls	

1 Brush the cake with the jam. Roll out the marzipan and use to cover the cake. Let dry overnight.

2 Form a roll with 3¾ cups of the fondant icing. With a toothpick, dab a few drops of red coloring onto the icing. Repeat with the green. Knead lightly. Roll out the icing until marbled. Brush the marzipan with water and cover with the icing. Position the cake on the cake board.

3 Color half of the remaining fondant icing red and the rest green. Use half of each color to make five crackers, about 2½ inches long. Decorate each with a gold ball. Let dry on wax paper.

4 Roll out the remaining red and green icings, and cut into ½-inch wide strips. Then cut into 12 red and 12 green diamonds. Attach them alternately around the top and bottom of the cake with water.

5 Cut the ribbons into 4-inch lengths. Arrange them with the crackers on the cake top. Attach the bows with softened fondant icing, between the diamonds at the top cake edge.

Greek New Year Cake

A "good luck," foil-wrapped gold coin is traditionally baked into this cake.

Makes one 9-inch square cake

2½ cups all-purpose flour
2 teaspoons baking
  powder
½ cup ground almonds
1 cup butter, softened
generous ¾ cup superfine
  sugar, plus extra for
  sprinkling

4 eggs
⅔ cup fresh orange juice
½ cup blanched almonds
1 tablespoon sesame
  seeds

1 Preheat the oven to 350°F. Grease a 9-inch square cake pan, line with wax paper and grease the paper.

2 Sift together the flour and baking powder and stir in the ground almonds.

3 Cream the butter and sugar until light and fluffy. Beat in the eggs, 1 at a time. Fold in the flour mixture, alternating with the orange juice.

4 Spoon the mixture into the cake pan. Arrange the blanched almonds on top, then sprinkle over the sesame seeds. Bake for 50 minutes, or until a skewer inserted in the center comes out clean.

5 Let stand in the pan for 5 minutes, then turn out onto a wire rack and peel off the lining paper. Sprinkle with superfine sugar before serving.

Starry New Year Cake

Makes one 9-inch round cake

9-inch round Madeira
  cake
3 cups butter icing
5¼ cups fondant icing
grape violet and
  mulberry food
  coloring
gold, lilac shimmer and
  primrose sparkle
  powdered food
  coloring

Materials/equipment
fine paintbrush
star-shape cutter
florist's wire, cut into
  short lengths
11-inch round cake board
purple ribbon with
  gold stars

1 Cut the cake into three layers. Sandwich together with three-quarters of the butter icing. Spread the rest thinly over the top and sides of the cake.

2 Tint 3¼ cups of the fondant icing purple with the grape violet and mulberry food coloring. Roll out and use to cover the cake. Let dry overnight.

3 Place the cake on a sheet of wax paper. Water down some gold and lilac food coloring. Use a paintbrush to flick each color in turn over the cake. Let dry.

4 For the stars, divide the remaining fondant icing into three pieces. tint one portion purple with the grape violet food coloring, one with the lilac shimmer and one with the primrose sparkle. Roll out each color to ⅛ inch thick. Cut out ten stars in each color and highlight the stars by flicking on the watered-down gold and lilac colors.

5 While the icing is soft, push the florist's wire through the middle of 15 of the stars. Let dry overnight. Put the cake on the board. Arrange the stars on top. Secure the unwired ones with water. Secure the ribbon around the bottom.

Simnel Cake

This is a traditional cake to celebrate Easter but it is delicious at any time of the year.

Makes one 8-inch round cake

1 cup butter, softened	2½ cups all-purpose flour
generous 1 cup superfine sugar	1 tablespoon mixed spice
4 eggs, beaten	1 teaspoon baking powder
3⅓ cups mixed dried fruit	4½ cups yellow marzipan
½ cup candied cherries	1 egg yolk, beaten
3 tablespoons sherry (optional)	ribbons, sugared eggs and fondant animals, to decorate

1 Preheat the oven to 325°F. Grease a deep 8-inch round cake pan, line with a double thickness of wax paper and grease.

2 Beat together the butter and sugar until light and fluffy. Gradually beat in the eggs. Stir in the dried fruit, candied cherries and sherry, if using. Sift over the flour, mixed spice and baking powder, then fold in.

3 Roll out half the marzipan to an 8-inch round. Spoon half of the cake mixture into the cake pan and place the round of marzipan on top. Add the other half of the cake mixture and smooth the surface.

4 Bake for 2½ hours, or until golden and springy to the touch. Let stand in the pan for 15 minutes, then turn out onto a wire rack, peel off the lining paper and let cool.

5 Roll out the reserved marzipan to fit the cake. Brush the cake top with egg yolk and place the marzipan on top. Flute the edges and make a pattern on top with a fork. Brush with more egg yolk. Put the cake on a baking sheet and broil for 5 minutes to brown the top lightly. Cool before decorating.

Easter Sponge Cake

This light lemon quick-mix sponge cake is decorated with lemon butter icing and cut-out marzipan flowers.

Makes one 8-inch round cake

3-egg quantity lemon-flavor quick-mix sponge cake	**To decorate**
	5⅜ cup homemade or commercial white marzipan
3 cups lemon-flavor butter icing	green, orange and yellow food coloring
½ cup flaked almonds, toasted	

1 Preheat the oven to 325°F. Bake the cakes in two lined and greased 8-inch round sandwich cake pans for 35–40 minutes until they are golden brown and spring back when lightly pressed in the center. Loosen the edges of the cakes with a metal spatula, turn out, remove the lining paper and cool on a wire rack.

2 Sandwich the cakes together with a quarter of the butter icing. Spread the side of the cake evenly with another-quarter of butter icing.

3 Press the almonds onto the sides to cover evenly. Spread the top of the cake evenly with another quarter of icing. Finish with a metal spatula dipped in hot water, spreading backward and forward to give an even lined effect.

4 Place the remaining icing into a nylon icing bag fitted with a medium-size gâteau nozzle and pipe a scroll edging.

5 Using the marzipan and food coloring, make six cut-out daffodils and ten green and eight orange cut-out marzipan flowers. Arrange them on the cake and let the icing set.

Easter Egg Nest Cake

Celebrate Easter with this colorfully adorned, fresh-tasting lemon sponge cake.

Makes one 8-inch ring cake

8-inch lemon sponge ring
  cake
1½ cups lemon-flavor
  butter icing
1½ cups marzipan
pink, green and purple
  food coloring

small foil-wrapped
  chocolate eggs

Materials/equipment
10-inch cake board

1   Cut the cake in half horizontally and sandwich together with a third of the butter icing. Place on the cake board. Use the remaining icing to cover the cake. Smooth the top and swirl the side with a metal spatula.

2   For the marzipan braids, divide the marzipan into three and tint pink, green and purple. Cut each portion in half. Using a half of each color, roll thin sausages long enough to go around the bottom. Pinch the ends together, then twist the strands into a rope. Pinch the other ends to seal.

3   Place the colored marzipan rope on the cake board around the cake.

4   For the nests, take the remaining portions of colored marzipan and divide each into five. Roll each piece into a 6½-inch rope. Take a rope of each color, pinch the ends together, twist to form a multi-colored rope and pinch the other ends. Form into a circle. Repeat to make five nests.

5   Space the nests evenly on the cake. Place small chocolate eggs in the nests.

Mother's Day Bouquet

A piped bouquet of flowers can bring as much pleasure as a fresh one for a Mother's Day treat.

Makes one 7-inch round cake

3 cups butter icing
7-inch round sponge
  cakes
green, blue, yellow and
  pink food coloring

Materials/equipment
serrated scraper
No 3 writing and petal
  nozzles
5 wax paper icing bags

1   Reserve a third of the butter icing for decorating. Sandwich together the two sponges with butter icing and place on a serving plate. Cover the top and side with the rest of the butter icing, smoothing the top with a metal spatula and serrating the side using a scraper.

2   Divide the remaining butter icing into four bowls. tint them green, blue, yellow and pink.

3   Decorate the top of the cake first. Use No 3 writing nozzles for the blue and green icing and petal nozzles for the yellow and pink. Pipe on the vase and flowers.

4   For the side decoration, spoon the remaining yellow icing into a fresh icing bag fitted with a No 3 writing nozzle. Pipe the stems, then the flowers and flower centers. Finish by piping green beads at the top and bottom edges of the cake.

Mother's Day Basket

Makes one 6-inch cake

*1½ cups self-rising flour,
    sifted*
*scant 1 cup superfine
    sugar*
¾ cup soft margarine
3 eggs
*4 cups orange-flavor
    butter icing*

Materials/equipment

*thin 6-inch round silver
    cake board*
wax paper icing bag
basketweave nozzle
foil
*1 yard mauve ribbon,
    ½ inch wide*
fresh flowers
*½ yard spotted mauve
    ribbon, ⅛ inch wide*

1 Preheat the oven to 325°F. Lightly grease and line the bottom of a 6-inch brioche mold. Place all the cake ingredients in a bowl, mix together, then beat for 1–2 minutes until smooth. Transfer to the prepared mold and bake for 1¼ hours, or until risen and golden.

2 Place the cooled cake upside-down on the board. Cover the sides with a third of the butter icing. Using a basketweave nozzle, pipe the sides with a basketweave pattern.

3 Invert the cake on the board and spread the top with butter icing. Pipe a shell edging with the basketweave nozzle. Pipe the basketweave pattern over the cake top, starting at the edge. Let set.

4 Fold a strip of foil several layers thick. Wrap the plain ribbon around the strip and bend up the ends to secure the ribbon. Form the foil into a handle and press into the icing.

5 Finish by tying a posy of fresh flowers with the spotted ribbon and making a mixed ribbon bow for the handle.

Basket Cake

This is a perfect cake for a retirement gathering or other special occasion.

Makes one basket-shaped cake

*8-inch round
    Madeira cake*
*2 cups colored butter
    icing*
*chocolates or candies and
    ribbon for decoration*

Materials/equipment

cardboard
pastillage (gum paste)
*2 wax paper icing bags,
    fitted with a plain
    tube and a
    basketweave tube*
powder food color

1 Cut a template from card to the same size as the top of the cake, fold it in half and cut along the fold. Roll out pastillage fairly thinly and cut out two pieces for the lid, using the templates as a guide. Leave to dry.

2 Coat the top of the cake with butter icing. Fill both icing bags with butter icing and on the side of the cake and about 1 inch onto the top of the cake, pipe a plain vertical line, then pipe short lengths of basketweave across the line. Pipe another plain line along the ends of the basketweave strips. Pipe the next row of basketweave strips in the spaces left between the existing strips and over the new plain line. Continue until the side of the cake and the area on the top is completely covered.

3 Brush the underside of the pastillage lid with powder food color, then pipe a basketweave on top of the lid.

4 Divide the top of the cake in half and pipe a line of basketweave along this central line. Use two or three pieces of pastillage to support each lid half in an open position on the cake. Fill the area under each lid half with chocolates or candies and decorate with ribbon.

Valentine's Heart Cake

This cake could also be used to celebrate a special birthday or anniversary.

Makes one 8-inch square cake

8-inch square light fruit cake	**Materials/equipment**
3 tablespoons apricot jam, warmed and strained	*10-inch square cake board*
6 cups marzipan	*2- and 1-inch heart-shape cutter*
9 cups royal icing	*4 wax paper icing bags*
¾ cup fondant icing	*No 1 and No 2 writing and No 42 star nozzles*
red food coloring	*heart-patterned ribbon*

1 Brush the cake with the apricot jam. Roll out the marzipan and use to cover the cake. Let dry overnight.

2 Secure the cake on the cake board with a little royal icing. Flat-ice the cake with three or four layers of smooth icing. Set aside some royal icing in an airtight container for piping.

3 Tint the fondant icing red. Roll it out and cut 12 hearts with the larger cutter. Stamp out the middles with the smaller cutter. Cut four extra small hearts. Dry on wax paper.

4 Using a No 1 writing nozzle, pipe wavy lines in royal icing around the four small hearts. Let dry. Using a fresh bag and a No 42 nozzle, pipe swirls around the top and bottom of the cake. Color 1 tablespoon of the remaining royal icing red and pipe red dots on top of each white swirl with the No 1 nozzle.

5 Secure the ribbon in place. Using a No 2 writing nozzle, pipe beads down each corner, avoiding the ribbon. Decorate the cake with the hearts, using royal icing to secure them.

Valentine's Box of Chocolates Cake

This cake would also make a wonderful surprise for Mother's Day.

Makes one 8-inch heart-shape cake

8-inch heart-shape chocolate sponge cake	**Materials/equipment**
generous 2 cups marzipan	*9-inch square piece of stiff cardboard*
8 tablespoons apricot jam, warmed and strained	*pencil and scissors*
	9-inch square cake board
6 cups fondant icing	*piece of string*
red food coloring	*small heart-shape cutter*
about 16–20 handmade chocolates	*length of ribbon and a pin*
	small paper sweet cases

1 Place the cake on the cardboard, draw around it and cut the heart shape out. It will be used to support the box lid. Cut through the cake horizontally just below the dome. Place the top section on the cardboard and the bottom on the board.

2 Use the string to measure around the outside of the bottom. Roll the marzipan into a long sausage to the measured length. Place on the cake around the outside edge. Brush both sections of the cake with jam. Tint the fondant icing red and cut off a third. Cut another 8-tablespoon portion from the larger piece. Set aside. Use the large piece to cover the bottom section of cake.

3 Stand the lid on a raised surface. Use the reserved third of fondant icing to cover the lid. Roll out the remaining piece of icing and stamp out small hearts with the cutter. Stick them around the edge of the lid with water. Tie the ribbon in a bow and secure on top of the lid with the pin.

4 Place the chocolates in the paper cases and arrange in the cake base. Position the lid slightly off-center, to reveal the chocolates. Remove the ribbon and pin before serving.

Double Heart Engagement Cake

For a celebratory engagement party, these sumptuous cakes make the perfect centerpiece.

Makes two 8-inch heart-shape cakes

12 ounces semisweet
  chocolate
2 x 8-inch heart-shape
  chocolate sponge cakes
3 cups coffee-flavor
  butter icing
confectioner's sugar, for
  dusting

fresh raspberries, to
  decorate

Materials/equipment
2 x 9-inch heart-shape
  cake boards

1 Melt the chocolate in a heat proof bowl over a saucepan of hot water. Pour the chocolate onto a smooth, non-porous surface and spread it out with a metal spatula. Let cool until just set, but not hard.

2 To make the chocolate curls, hold a large sharp knife at a 45-degree angle to the chocolate and push it along the chocolate in short sawing movements. Let set on wax paper.

3 Cut each cake in half horizontally. Use a third of the butter icing to sandwich the cakes together. Use the remaining icing to coat the tops and sides of the cakes.

4 Place the cakes on the cake boards. Generously cover the tops and sides of the cakes with the chocolate curls, pressing them gently into the butter icing.

5 Sift a little confectioner's sugar over the top of each cake and decorate with raspberries. Chill until ready to serve.

Sweetheart Cake

Makes one 8-inch heart-shape cake

8-inch heart-shape light
  fruit cake
2 tablespoons apricot
  jam, warmed and
  strained
6 cups marzipan
6 cups fondant icing
red food coloring
1½ cups royal icing

Materials/equipment
10-inch silver heart-
  shape cake board
large and medium heart-
  shape plunger cutters
1 yard red ribbon,
  1 inch wide
1 yard looped red ribbon,
  ½ inch wide
½ yard red ribbon,
  ¼ inch wide
wax paper icing bag
medium star nozzle
fresh red rosebud

1 Brush the cake with apricot jam, place on the cake board and cover with marzipan. Cover the cake and board with fondant icing. Let dry overnight.

2 Tint the fondant icing red. Cut 18 large and 21 medium-size hearts. Let dry on wax paper.

3 Secure the wide ribbon around the cake board. Secure a band of the looped ribbon around the side of the cake with a bead of icing. Tie a bow with long tails and attach to the side of the cake with a bead of icing.

4 Using the star nozzle, pipe a row of royal icing stars around the bottom of the cake and attach a medium-size heart to every third star. Pipe stars around the cake top, and arrange large red hearts on each one.

5 Tie a bow onto the rosebud stem and place on the cake top just before serving.

Cloth-of-Roses Cake

This cake simply says "congratulations." It is a very pretty cake that is bound to impress your guests.

Makes one 8-inch round cake

8-inch round light fruit
  cake
3 tablespoons apricot
  jam, warmed and
  strained
4½ cups marzipan
6 cups fondant icing
yellow, orange and green
  food coloring

¾ cup royal icing

Materials/equipment
10-inch cake board
2¼-inch plain cutter
petal cutter
thin yellow ribbon

1   Brush the cake with apricot jam. Cover with marzipan and let dry overnight.

2   Cut off 4½ cups of the fondant icing and divide in half. Color pale yellow and pale orange.

3   Make a wax paper template for the orange icing by drawing a 10-inch circle around the cake board then, using the plain cutter, draw scallops around the circle.

4   Cover the cake side with yellow fondant icing. Place the cake on the board. Using the template, cut out the orange fondant icing. Place on the cake and bend the scallops slightly. Let dry overnight.

5   For the roses and leaves, cut off three-quarters of the remaining fondant icing and divide into four. Tint pale yellow, deep yellow, orange, and marbled yellow and orange. Make 18 roses. Tint the remaining icing green, then cut out 24 leaves with a petal cutter. Dry on wax paper.

6   Secure the leaves and roses with royal icing. Decorate the cake with the ribbon.

Rose Blossom Wedding Cake

Serves 80

9-inch square rich fruit
  cake
6-inch square rich fruit
  cake
5 tablespoons apricot
  jam, warmed and
  strained
10½ cups marzipan
10½ cups royal icing, to
  coat
4½ cups royal icing, to
  pipe
pink and green food
  coloring

Materials/equipment
11-inch square cake board
8-inch square cake board
No 1 writing and No 42
  nozzles
wax paper icing bags
thin pink ribbon
8 pink bows
3–4 cake pillars
12 miniature roses
few fern sprigs

1   Brush the cakes with the jam and cover with marzipan. Let dry overnight, then secure to their boards with icing. Flat-ice the cakes with three or four layers, letting each dry overnight. Dry for several days.

2   For the sugar pieces, use the No 1 writing nozzle to pipe the double-triangle design in white icing on wax paper. You will need 40 pieces, but make extra. Tint some icing pale pink and some very pale green. Using No 1 writing nozzles, pipe pink dots on the corners of the top triangles and green on the corners of the lower triangles. Let dry.

3   Use a pin to mark out the triangles on the tops and sides of each cake. Using a No 1 writing nozzle, pipe double white lines over the pin marks, then pipe cornelli inside all the triangles. With a No 42 nozzle, pipe white shells around the top and bottom edges of each cake, between the triangles.

4   Using No 1 writing nozzles, pipe pink and green dots on the cake corners. Secure the sugar pieces to the cakes and boards with icing. Attach the ribbons and bows. Assemble the cake with the pillars and decorate with roses and fern sprigs.

Basketweave Wedding Cake

This wonderful wedding cake can be made in any flavor.

Serves 150

10-inch, 8-inch and
6-inch square Madeira
cakes
12 cups butter icing

12 small wax paper icing
bags
No 4 writing and
basketweave nozzles
1½ yards pale lilac
ribbon, 1 inch wide
2½ yards deep lilac
ribbon, ¼ inch wide
30 fresh lilac-colored
freesias

Materials/equipment
12-inch square silver
cake board
8-inch and 6-inch thin
silver cake board
smooth scraper

1 Level the cake tops, then invert the cakes onto the boards and cover with butter icing. Use a smooth scraper on the sides and a metal spatula to smooth the top. Let set for 1 hour.

2 Pipe a line of icing with the No 4 writing nozzle onto the corner of the large cake, from the bottom to the top. Using the basketweave nozzle, pipe a basketweave pattern (see above photograph). Pipe all around the side of the cake and neaten the top edge with a shell border, using the basketweave nozzle. Repeat for the second cake.

3 To decorate the top of the small cake, start at the edge with a straight plain line, then pipe across with the basketweave nozzle, spacing the lines equally apart. When the top is complete, work the design around the sides, making sure the top and side designs align. Let the cakes set overnight.

4 Fit the wide and narrow lilac ribbons around the board. Use the remaining narrow ribbon to tie eight small bows with long tails. Trim off the flower stems.

5 Assemble the cakes. Decorate with the bows and flowers.

Chocolate-iced Anniversary Cake

This attractive cake is special enough to celebrate any wedding anniversary.

Makes one 8-inch round cake
8-inch round Madeira
cake
2¼ cups chocolate-flavor
butter icing

For the chocolate icing
6 ounces semisweet
chocolate
⅔ cup light cream
½ teaspoon instant coffee
powder

To decorate
chocolate buttons,
quartered

selection of fresh fruits,
such as kiwi fruit,
nectarines, peaches,
apricots and
gooseberries, peeled
and sliced as necessary

Materials/equipment
No 22 star nozzle
wax paper icing bag
gold ribbon, about
¼ inch wide
florist's wire

1 Cut the cake horizontally into three and sandwich together with three-quarters of the butter icing. Place on a wire rack over a baking sheet.

2 To make the satin chocolate icing, put all of the ingredients in a saucepan and melt over very low heat until smooth. Immediately pour over the cake to coat completely. Use a metal spatula, if necessary. Allow to set.

3 Transfer the cake to a serving plate. Using a No 22 star nozzle, pipe butter icing scrolls around the top edge. Decorate with chocolate button pieces and fruit.

4 Make seven ribbon decorations. For each one, make two small loops from ribbon and secure the ends with a twist of florist's wire . Cut the wire to the length you want and use to position the decoration in the fruit. Remove before serving.

Silver Wedding Cake

Makes one 10-inch round cake

10-inch round rich or
light fruit cake
4 tablespoons apricot
jam, warmed and
strained
7½ cups marzipan
9 cups royal icing

For the petal paste
2 teaspoons gelatin
5 tablespoons cold water
2 teaspoons liquid glucose
2 teaspoons white
vegetable shortening
4 cups confectioner's
sugar, sifted
1 teaspoon gum
tragacanth, sifted
1 egg white

Materials/equipment
12-inch round silver cake
board
1½ yards white ribbon,
1 inch wide
2 yards silver ribbon,
1 inch wide
club cocktail cutter
tiny round cutter
wax paper icing bag
No 1 writing nozzle
50 large silver dragées
1½ yards silver ribbon,
¼ inch wide
7 silver leaves
"25" silver cake
decoration

1 Brush the cake with apricot jam and cover with marzipan. Place on the board. Flat-ice the top and side of the cake with three or four layers of royal icing. Let dry overnight, then ice the board. Reserve the remaining royal icing. Secure the wider ribbons around the board and cake with icing.

2 For the petal paste, melt the first four ingredients in a bowl set over a pan of hot water. Mix the sugar, gum tragacanth, egg white and gelatin mixture to a paste and knead until smooth. Let stand for 2 hours, then re-knead. Make 65 cut-outs using the two cutters. Let dry overnight.

3 Arrange 25 cut-outs around the top and secure with icing beads piped with a No 1 writing nozzle. Repeat at the bottom. Pipe icing beads between and press a dragée in each. Let dry. Thread the thin ribbon through. Arrange seven cut-outs and seven dragées in the center. Position the leaves and "25."

Golden Wedding Heart Cake

Makes one 9-inch round cake

4 tablespoons apricot jam
9-inch round rich fruit
cake
6 cups marzipan
6 cups fondant icing
cream food coloring
¾ cup royal icing

Materials/equipment
11-inch round cake board
crimping tool

pins
small heart-shape
plunger tool
3-inch plain cutter
dual large and small
blossom cutter
stamens
frill cutter
wooden toothpick
foil-wrapped chocolate
hearts

1 Warm, then strain the apricot jam and brush over the cake. Cover with marzipan and let dry overnight.

2 Tint 4½ cups of the fondant icing very pale cream and cover the cake. Put on the board. Crimp the top edge. With pins, mark eight equidistant points around the top edge. Crimp slanting lines to the bottom. Emboss the bottom edge with the plunger. Use the plain cutter to emboss a circle on top.

3 Divide the remaining fondant icing into two and tint cream and pale cream. Using half of each color, make flowers with the blossom cutter. Make pinholes in the large flowers. Let dry, then secure the stamens in the holes with royal icing.

4 Make eight frills with the rest of the fondant icing using the frill cutter, and a toothpick to trim and fill the edges. Attach the frills with water next to the crimped lines on the cake side. Crimp the edges of the deeper colored frills.

5 Secure the flowers on the top and sides of the cake with royal icing. Place the chocolate hearts in the center.

Marzipan Bell Cake

This cake can be easily adapted to make a christening cake if you leave out the holly decorations.

Makes one 7-inch round cake

7-inch round rich or light fruit cake	**Materials/equipment**
2 tablespoons apricot jam, warmed and strained	8-inch round silver cake board
6 cups marzipan	crimping tool
green, yellow and red food coloring	bell and holly leaf cutter
	1 yard red ribbon, ¾ inch wide
	1 yard green ribbon, ¼ inch wide
	¼ yard red ribbon, ¼ inch wide

1 Brush the cake with apricot jam and place on the cake board. Tint two-thirds of the marzipan pale green. Use to cover the cake. Crimp the top edge of the cake to make a scalloped pattern.

2 Tint a small piece of remaining marzipan bright yellow, another bright red and the rest bright green. Make two yellow bells and clappers, 11 green holly leaves (veins marked with the back of a knife), two green bell ropes, 16 red holly berries and two bell-rope ends. Let dry.

3 Secure the wide red and fine green ribbons around the side of the cake with a pin. Tie a double bow from red and green fine ribbon and attach to the side with a pin.

4 Arrange the bells, clappers, bell ropes, holly leaves and berries on top of the cake and secure with apricot jam.

Christening Sampler

Serves 30

8-inch square rich fruit cake	**Materials/equipment**
3 tablespoons apricot jam, warmed and strained	10-inch square cake board
3 cups marzipan	fine paintbrush
4½ cups fondant icing	small heart-shape cookie cutter
brown, yellow, orange, purple, cream, blue, green and pink food coloring	

1 Brush the cake with apricot jam. Roll out the marzipan, cover the cake and let dry overnight. Roll out 1 cup of the fondant icing to fit the cake top. Brush the top with water and cover with the icing.

2 Color 2 cups of the icing brown and roll out four pieces to the length and about ½ inch wider than the cake sides. Brush the sides with water and cover with icing, folding over the extra width at the top and cutting the corners at an angle to make the picture frame. Place on a cake board. With a fine paintbrush, paint over the sides with watered-down brown food coloring to represent wood grain.

3 Take the remaining icing and color small amounts yellow, orange, brown, purple and cream and two shades of blue, green and pink. Leave some white. Use the colors to shape the ducks, teddy bear, bulrushes, water, branch and leaves. Cut out a pink heart and make the baby's initial from white icing.

4 Mix the white and pink icings together for the apple blossom flowers. Make the shapes for the border. Attach the decorations to the cake with a little water.

5 Use the leftover colors to make "threads." Arrange in loops around the bottom of the cake on the board.

Teddy Bear Christening Cake

To personalize the cake, make a simple plaque for the top and pipe on the name of the new baby.

Makes one 8-inch square cake

8-inch square light fruit cake	**Materials/equipment**
3 tablespoons apricot jam, warmed and strained	10-inch square cake board
6 cups marzipan	crimping tool
5¼ cups fondant icing	cornstarch, for dipping
peach, yellow, blue and brown food coloring	fine paintbrush
¾ cup royal icing	wooden toothpick
	peach ribbon
	small blue ribbon bow

1 Brush the cake with the apricot jam. Roll out the marzipan and use to cover the cake. Let dry overnight.

2 Color 3¾ cups of the fondant icing peach, then roll it out. Brush the marzipan with water and cover the cake with the icing. Place the cake on the board. Using a crimping tool dipped in cornstarch, crimp the top and bottom edges of the cake.

3 Divide the remaining fondant into three. Leave a third white and tint a third yellow. Divide the last third in two, tint one half peach and the other blue.

4 Make flowers from the peach and blue fondant. Let dry. Reserve the blue trimmings. Make a yellow teddy bear. Paint on its face with brown food coloring. Give it a blue button. Let dry. Make a blue blanket. Frill the white edge with a toothpick. Secure the frill to the blanket with water.

5 Decorate the cake with the ribbon, place the bear on top under its blanket, securing with royal icing. Secure the flowers and the bear's bow-tie in the same way.

Daisy Christening Cake

A ring of daisies sets off this pretty pink christening cake.

Makes one 8-inch round cake

8-inch round rich fruit cake	**Materials/equipment**
3 tablespoons apricot jam, warmed and strained	10-inch round cake board
4½ cups marzipan	fine paintbrush
6 cups royal icing	2-inch fluted cutter
¾ cup fondant icing	wooden toothpick
pink and yellow food coloring	2 wax paper icing bags
	No 42 nozzle
	pink and white ribbon

1 Brush the cake with the apricot jam. Roll out the marzipan and use to cover the cake. Let dry overnight.

2 Use a little royal icing to secure the cake to the board. Tint three-quarters of the royal icing pink. Flat-ice the cake with three or four layers, using white for the top and pink for the side. Let each layer dry overnight before applying the next. Set aside a little of both icings in airtight containers.

3 Make 28 daisies. For each daisy, shape a small piece of fondant icing to look like a golf tee. Snip the edges and curl them slightly. Dry on wax paper. Trim the stems and paint the edges pink and the centers yellow.

4 To make the plaque, roll out the remaining fondant icing and cut out a circle with the fluted cutter. Roll a toothpick around the edge until it frills. Dry on wax paper, then paint the name and the edges with pink food coloring.

5 Pipe twisted ropes around the top and bottom of the cake with the reserved white royal icing. Then pipe a row of stars around the top of the cake. Stick the plaque in the center with royal icing. Stick on the daisies and decorate with the ribbons.

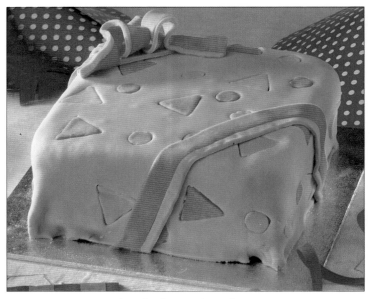

Birthday Package

Serves 10

6-inch square Madeira
   cake
1⅓ cups orange-flavor
   butter icing
3 tablespoons apricot
   jam, warmed and
   strained
3 cups fondant icing
blue, orange and green
   food coloring

confectioner's sugar, for
   dusting

Materials/equipment

7–8-inch square cake
   board
small triangular and
   round cocktail cutters

1 Cut the cake in half horizontally and sandwich together with the butter icing. Brush the cake with apricot jam. Color three-quarters of the fondant icing blue. Divide the remaining fondant icing in half and color one half orange and the other half green. Wrap the orange and green fondant separately in plastic wrap and set aside. Roll out the blue icing on a work surface lightly dusted with confectioner's sugar and use it to cover the cake. Position on the cake board.

2 While the fondant covering is still soft, use the cocktail cutters to cut out triangles and circles from the blue icing, lifting out the shapes to expose the cake.

3 Roll out the orange and green icings and cut out circles and triangles to fill the exposed holes in the blue icing. Roll out the trimmings and cut three orange strips, ¾ inch wide and long enough to go over the corner of the cake, and three very thin green strips the same length as the orange ones. Place the strips next to each other to make three striped ribbons, and secure the pieces together with a little water.

4 Place one striped ribbon over one corner of the cake, securing with a little water. Place a second strip over the opposite corner. Cut the remaining ribbon in half. Bend each half to make loops and attach both to one corner of the cake with water to form a loose bow.

Chocolate Fruit Birthday Cake

The marzipan fruits on this moist chocolate Madeira cake make an eye-catching decoration.

Makes one 7-inch square cake

7-inch square deep
   chocolate Madeira
   cake
3 tablespoons apricot
   jam, warmed and
   strained
3 cups marzipan
2 cups chocolate fudge
   icing
red, yellow, orange, green
   and purple food
   coloring

whole cloves
angelica strips

Materials/equipment

8-inch square silver cake
   board
medium gâteau nozzle
nylon icing bag
¾ yard yellow ribbon,
   ½ inch wide

1 Level the cake top and invert. Brush with apricot jam.

2 Use two-thirds of the marzipan to cover the cake. Reserve the trimmings.

3 Place the cake on a wire rack over a tray and pour three-quarters of the chocolate fudge icing over, spreading with a metal spatula. Let stand for 10 minutes, then place on the cake board.

4 Using the reserved icing and a medium-size gâteau nozzle, pipe stars around the top edge and bottom of the cake. Let set.

5 Using the reserved marzipan, food coloring, cloves and angelica strips, model a selection of fruits.

6 Secure the ribbon around the sides of the cake. Decorate the top with the marzipan fruits.

Eighteenth Birthday Cake

A really striking cake for an eighteenth birthday. Change the shape if you cannot hire the pan.

Serves 80

13½ x 8-inch diamond-shape deep rich or light fruit cake
3 tablespoons apricot jam, warmed and strained
7½ cups marzipan
10½ cups fondant
black food coloring
2 tablespoons royal icing

Materials/equipment
15 x 9-inch diamond-shape cake board
"18" template
small wax paper icing bag
No 1 writing nozzle
2 yards white ribbon, 1 inch wide
2 yards black ribbon, ⅛ inch wide

1 Make the cake using quantities for a 9-inch round cake. Brush with apricot jam. Cover in marzipan. Place on the cake board. Cover the cake using 7½ cups fondant icing. Knead the trimmings into the remaining fondant and tint black.

2 Use two-thirds of the black fondant to cover the board.

3 Use a quarter of the remaining fondant to cut out a number "18" using a template. Use the rest to cut out a variety of bow ties, wine glasses and music notes. Let dry on wax paper.

4 Tint the royal icing black. Using a No 1 writing nozzle, attach the cut-outs to the cake top and sides.

5 Tie four small bows with the black ribbon. Secure with icing to the top corners. Position and secure black ribbon around the cake bottom and white ribbon around the board.

Flickering Birthday Candle Cake

Flickering, stripy candles are ready to blow out on this birthday cake for all ages.

Makes one 8-inch square cake

8-inch square Madeira cake
1½ cups butter icing
3 tablespoons apricot jam, warmed and strained
5¼ cups fondant icing
pink, yellow, purple and jade food coloring
edible silver balls

Materials/equipment
9-inch square cake board
small round cutter
pink and purple food coloring pens
¼-inch wide jade-colored ribbon

1 Cut the cake into three layers. Sandwich together with the butter icing and brush the cake with the apricot jam. Roll out 3¾ cups of the fondant icing and use to cover the cake. Position on the cake board.

2 Divide the remaining fondant into four pieces and tint them pink, yellow, pale purple and jade.

3 Make the candles from jade and the flames from yellow icing. Press a silver ball into their bases. Position the candles and flames on the cake with a little water. Mold strips in yellow and purple icing to go around the candles. Secure with water. Cut small, wavy pieces from the pink and purple icing for smoke, and arrange them, using water, above the candles.

4 Cut out yellow circles with the cutter for the side decorations. Mold small pink balls and press a silver ball into their centers. Attach using water.

5 Using food coloring pens, draw wavy lines and dots coming from the purple and pink wavy icings. Decorate the sides of the cake board with the ribbon, securing at the back with a little softened fondant.

Flower Birthday Cake

A simple birthday cake decorated with piped yellow and white flowers and ribbons.

Makes one 7-inch round cake

7-inch round light fruit cake	**Materials/equipment**
2 tablespoons apricot jam, warmed and strained	9-inch round silver cake board
4½ cups marzipan	petal nozzle, Nos 1 and 2 writing nozzles, and medium star nozzle
7½ cups royal icing	wax paper icing bags
yellow and orange food coloring	1 yard white ribbon, ¾ inch wide
	2 yards coral ribbon, ½ inch wide
	10-inch coral ribbon, ¼ inch wide

1 Brush the cake with apricot jam and cover with marzipan. Place on the board.

2 Flat-ice the top and side of the cake with three layers of royal icing. Let dry, then ice the board. Reserve the remaining royal icing.

3 Tint one-third of the reserved royal icing yellow and 1 tablespoon of it orange. Using the petal nozzle for the petals and No 1 writing nozzle for the centers, make four white narcissi with yellow centers and nine yellow narcissi with orange centers. Make nine plain white flowers with a snipped icing bag with yellow centers. When dry, secure to the top.

4 Use the star nozzle to pipe shell edgings to the cake top and bottom. Pipe "Happy Birthday" using the No 2 writing nozzle. Overlay in orange using the No 1 writing nozzle.

5 Secure the ribbons around the board and cake side. Finish with a coral bow.

Jazzy Chocolate Gâteau

This cake is made with Father's Day in mind, though you can make it for anyone who loves chocolate.

Serves 12–15

2 x quantity chocolate-flavor quick-mix sponge cake mix	8 tablespoons chocolate hazelnut spread
3 squares semisweet chocolate	**Materials/equipment**
3 squares white chocolate	2 x 8-inch round cake pans
6 ounces fudge frosting	wax paper icing bag
1 cup glacé icing	No 1 writing nozzle
1 teaspoon weak coffee	

1 Preheat the oven to 325°F. Grease the cake pans, line the bottoms with wax paper and grease the paper. Divide the cake mixture evenly between the pans and smooth the surfaces. Bake in the center of the oven for 20–30 minutes, or until firm to the touch. Turn out onto a wire rack, peel off the lining paper and let cool.

2 Melt the chocolates in two separate bowls, pour onto parchment paper and spread evenly. As it begins to set, place another sheet of parchment paper on top and turn the chocolate "sandwich" over. When set, peel off the paper and turn the chocolate sheets over. Cut out haphazard shapes of chocolate and set aside.

3 Sandwich the two cakes together with fudge frosting. Place the cake on a plate. Color the glacé icing using the weak coffee and add enough water to form a spreading consistency. Spread the icing on top of the cake almost to the edges. Cover the side of the cake with chocolate hazelnut spread.

4 Press the chocolate pieces around the side of the cake and, using an icing bag fitted with a No 1 nozzle, decorate the top of the cake with "jazzy" lines over the glacé icing.

Petal Retirement Cake

Makes one 8-inch petal-shape cake

8-inch petal-shape deep
  light fruit cake
3 tablespoons apricot
  jam, warmed and
  strained
6 cups marzipan
mulberry and pink food
  coloring
6 cups fondant icing
10 ounces petal paste
1 tablespoon royal icing

foam sponge
large and small blossom
  plunger cutters
2 yards white ribbon,
  ¾ inch wide
2 yards fuchsia ribbon,
  ½ inch wide
2 yards fuchsia ribbon,
  ⅛ inch wide
wax paper icing bag
No 1 writing nozzle
pink food coloring pen
fresh flowers

Materials/equipment
9-inch petal-shape silver
  cake board

1 Brush the cake with jam and put on the board. Cover with marzipan. Knead mulberry coloring into the fondant icing. Use to cover the cake and board. Dry overnight.

2 Tint the petal paste with pink coloring. Roll and cut out a 2 x 1-inch rectangle. Fold in half and dry over a foam sponge to make the card. Make holes in the top edges of the fold for the ribbon. Cut out 30 large and four small plunger blossom flowers. Let dry.

3 Using the royal icing and a No 1 writing nozzle, secure the white and narrow fuchsia ribbons around the board and the medium ribbon around the cake bottom. Tie six small bows from the narrow ribbon for the base.

4 Attach the large flowers to the side of the cake with icing. Secure the small flowers to the board. Draw a design and write a message inside the card with the pen. Thread ribbon through the holes and tie a bow. Place on the cake top with the fresh flowers.

Pansy Retirement Cake

You can use other edible flowers such as nasturtiums, roses or tiny daffodils for this cake, if you prefer.

Makes one 8-inch round cake

8-inch round light fruit
  cake
3 tablespoons apricot
  jam, warmed and
  strained
4½ cups marzipan
7½ cups royal icing
orange food coloring
about 7 sugar-frosted
  pansies (orange and
  purple)

Materials/equipment
10-inch round cake board
2 wax paper icing bags
No 19 star and No 1
  writing nozzles
¾-inch wide purple
  ribbon
⅛-inch wide dark purple
  ribbon

1 Brush the cake with the apricot jam. Roll out the marzipan and use to cover the cake. Let dry overnight.

2 Secure the cake to the cake board with a little royal icing. Tint a quarter of the royal icing pale orange. Flat-ice the cake with three layers of smooth icing. Use the orange icing for the top and the white for the sides. Set aside a little of both icings in airtight containers for decoration.

3 Spoon the reserved white royal icing into a wax paper icing bag fitted with a No 19 star nozzle. Pipe a row of scrolls around the cake top. Pipe a second row directly underneath the first row in the reverse direction. Pipe another row of scrolls around the bottom of the cake.

4 Spoon the reserved orange icing into a fresh icing bag fitted with a No 1 writing nozzle. Pipe around the outline of the top of each scroll. Pipe a row of single orange dots below the lower row of reverse scrolls at the top and a double row of dots above the bottom row of scrolls. Arrange the pansies on top of the cake. Decorate the side with the ribbons.

Halloween Pumpkin Patch Cake

Celebrate Halloween with this fall-colored cake, colorfully decorated with fondant pumpkins.

Makes one 8-inch round cake

generous 1 cup fondant
   icing
brown and orange food
   coloring
2 x 8-inch round
   chocolate sponge cakes
3 cups orange-flavor
   butter icing
chocolate chips
angelica

Materials/equipment
wooden toothpick
fine paintbrush
9-inch round cake board
serrated scraper
No 7 writing nozzle
wax paper icing bag

1 For the pumpkins, tint a very small piece of the fondant icing brown, and the rest orange. Shape some balls of the orange icing the size of walnuts and some a bit smaller. Make ridges with a toothpick. Make stems from the brown icing and secure with water. Paint highlights on the pumpkins in orange. Let dry on wax paper.

2 Cut both cakes in half horizontally. Use a quarter of the butter icing to sandwich the cakes together. Place the cake on the board. Use two-thirds of the remaining icing to cover the cake. Texture the icing with a serrated scraper.

3 Using a No 7 writing nozzle, pipe a twisted rope pattern around the top and bottom edges of the cake with the remaining butter icing. Decorate with chocolate chips.

4 Cut the angelica into diamond shapes and arrange on the cake with the pumpkins.

Fudge-frosted Starry Roll

Whether it's for a birthday or another occasion, this sumptuous-looking cake is sure to please.

Makes one 13-inch long roll

9 x 13-inch jelly roll
   sponge
¾ cup chocolate butter
   icing
2 ounces white chocolate
2 ounces semisweet
   chocolate

3 cups confectioner's
   sugar, sifted
6 tablespoons butter or
   margarine
4½ tablespoons milk or
   light cream
1½ teaspoons vanilla
   extract

For the fudge frosting

3 ounces semisweet
   chocolate, broken into
   pieces

Materials/equipment
small star cutter
wax paper icing bags
No 19 star nozzle

1 Unroll the sponge and spread with the butter icing. Re-roll and set aside.

2 For the decorations, melt the white chocolate in a bowl set over a pan of hot water and spread onto a non-porous surface. Let firm, then cut out stars with the cutter. Let set on wax paper. To make lace curls, melt the semisweet chocolate and then cool slightly. Cover a rolling pin with wax paper. Pipe zigzags on the paper and let cool on the rolling pin.

3 For the frosting, stir all the ingredients over low heat until melted. Remove from the heat and beat frequently until cool and thick. Cover the cake with two-thirds of the frosting, swirling with a metal spatula.

4 With a No 19 star nozzle, use the remaining frosting to pipe diagonal lines on the cake.

5 Position the lace curls and stars. Transfer the cake to a serving plate and decorate with more stars.

Lucky Horseshoe Cake

This horseshoe-shape cake, made to wish "good luck", is made from a round cake and the shape is then cut out.

Makes one 10-inch horseshoe cake

10-inch rich fruit cake	**Materials/equipment**
4 tablespoons apricot	12-inch round cake board
jam, warmed and	crimping tool
strained	pale blue ribbon, ⅛ inch
5¼ cups marzipan	wide
6¾ cups fondant icing	scalpel
peach and blue food	large and small blossom
coloring	cutters
edible silver balis	
¾ cup royal icing	

1 Make a horseshoe template and use to shape the cake. Brush the cake with the apricot jam. Roll out 2¼ cups of the marzipan to a 10-inch circle. Using the template, cut out the shape and place on the cake. Measure the inside and outside of the cake. Cover with the remaining marzipan. Place the cake on the board and let stand overnight.

2 Tint 5¼ cups of the fondant icing peach. Cover the cake in the same way. Crimp the top edge.

3 Draw and measure the ribbon insertion on the template. Cut 13 pieces of ribbon fractionally longer than each slit. Make the slits through the template with a scalpel. Insert the ribbon with a painted tool. Let dry overnight.

4 Make a small horseshoe template. Tint half the remaining fondant icing pale blue. Using the template, cut out nine blue shapes. Mark each horseshoe with a sharp knife. Cut out 12 large and 15 small blossoms. Press a silver ball into the centers of the larger blossoms. Let dry. Repeat with the white icing. Decorate the cake and board with the ribbon, horseshoes and blossoms, securing with royal icing.

Bluebird Bon-voyage Cake

This cake is sure to see someone off on an exciting journey in a very special way.

Makes one 8-inch round cake

3 cups royal icing	**Materials/equipment**
blue food coloring	No 1 writing nozzle
5¼ cups fondant icing	wax paper icing bags
8-inch round Madeira	10-inch round cake board
cake	thin pale blue ribbon
1½ cups butter icing	
3 tablespoons apricot	
jam, warmed and	
strained	
edible silver balls	

1 Make two-thirds of the royal icing softer to use for the run-outs. Make the rest stiffer for the outlines and piping. Tint the softer icing bright blue. Cover and let stand overnight.

2 Make two bird templates in different sizes, and use to pipe the run-outs on wax paper. Using a No 1 writing nozzle, pipe the outlines, and then fill in. You need four large and five small birds. Let dry for at least 2 days.

3 Tint two-thirds of the fondant icing blue. Form all the icing into small rolls and place them alternately together on a work surface. Form into a round and lightly knead to marble.

4 Cut the cake horizontally into three and sandwich together with the butter icing. Place the cake on the board, flush with an edge, and brush with apricot jam. Roll out the marbled icing and use to cover the cake and board.

5 Using the No 1 writing nozzle and the stiffer royal icing, pipe a wavy line around the edge of the board. Position the balls evenly in the icing. Secure the birds to the cake with royal icing. Pipe beads of white icing for eyes and stick on a ball. Drape the ribbon between the beaks, securing with icing.

Ghost Cake

This children's cake is really simple to make yet very effective. It is ideal for a Halloween party.

Serves 15–20
6 cups fondant icing
black food coloring
2 Madeira cakes, baked in
a 7-inch square cake
pan and a 1¼-cup
ovenproof bowl

1½ cups butter icing

Materials/equipment
9-inch round cake board
fine paintbrush

1 Tint ¾ cup of the fondant icing dark gray and use to cover the cake board.

2 Cut two small corners off the large cake. Cut two larger wedges off the other two corners, then stand the cake on the board. Divide the larger trimmings in half and wedge around the bottom of the cake.

3 Secure the small cake to the top of the larger cake with butter icing. Completely cover both of the cakes with the remaining butter icing.

4 Roll out the remaining fondant icing to a 20 x 12-inch oval shape. Lay it over the cake, letting the icing fall into folds around the sides. Gently smooth the icing over the top half of the cake and trim off any excess.

5 Using black food coloring and a fine paintbrush, paint two oval eyes onto the head.

Cat-in-a-Basket Cake

Makes one 6-inch round cake
5¼ cups marzipan
red, green, yellow and
brown food coloring
6-inch round deep sponge
cake
2 tablespoons apricot
jam, warmed and
strained

4 tablespoons butter
icing
4 tablespoons white
fondant icing

Materials/equipment
8-inch round cake board
fine paintbrush

1 Tint 2 cups of the marzipan pink. Divide the rest in half and tint one half green and the other yellow. Brush the cake with the apricot jam and place it on the board.

2 Roll out the pink marzipan to a 6 x 10-inch rectangle. Cut five ½-inch wide strips, about 9½ inches long, keeping them attached to the rectangle at one end. Roll out the green marzipan and cut it into 3-inch lengths of the same width. Fold back alternate pink strips and lay a green strip across widthwise. Bring the pink strips over the green strip to form the weave. Keep repeating the process until the entire length is woven. Press lightly to join. Repeat with the rest of the rectangle and more strips of green marzipan.

3 Press the two pieces of basketweave onto the side of cake, joining them neatly. Model a yellow marzipan cat about 3 inches across. Let dry overnight.

4 Roll out the fondant icing and place on the center of the cake. Put the cat on top and arrange the icing in folds around it. Trim the edges neatly.

5 Make long ropes from any leftover pink and green marzipan. Twist together and press onto the top edge of the cake. Paint the cat's features in brown food coloring.

Fish-shaped Cake

A very easy, but colorful cake, perfect for a small child's birthday party.

Makes one fish-shape cake

3 cups fondant icing
blue, orange, red, mauve
    and green food
    coloring
sponge cake, baked in a
    15-cup ovenproof bowl
1½ cups butter icing
1 blue Smartie

Materials/equipment
large oval cake board
1-inch plain cookie cutter
wax paper icing bag

1 Tint two-thirds of the fondant icing blue, roll out very thinly and use to cover the dampened cake board.

2 Invert the cake and trim into the fish shape. Slope the sides. Place on the cake board.

3 Tint all but 1 tablespoon of the butter icing orange. Use to cover the cake, smoothing with a metal spatula. Score curved lines for scales, starting from the tail end.

4 Tint half the remaining fondant icing red. Shape and position two lips. Cut out the tail and fins. Mark with lines using a knife and position on the fish. Make the eye from white fondant and the blue Smartie.

5 Tint a little fondant mauve, cut out crescent-shape scales using a cookie cutter and place on the fish. Tint the remaining fondant green and cut into long thin strips. Twist each strip and arrange around the board.

6 To make the bubbles around the fish, place the reserved butter icing in an icing bag, snip off the end and pipe small circles onto the board.

Pink Monkey Cake

This cheeky little monkey could be made in any color icing you wish.

Makes one 8-inch cake

8-inch round sponge cake
½ cup butter icing
3 tablespoons apricot
    jam, warmed and
    strained
3 cups marzipan
scant 3¾ cups fondant
    icing

red, blue and black food
    coloring

Materials/equipment
10-inch round cake board
2 candles and holders

1 Trace the outline and paws of the monkey from the photograph. Enlarge to fit the cake and cut a template.

2 Split and fill the cake with butter icing. Place on the cake board and use the template to cut out the basic shape of the monkey. Use the trimmings to shape the nose and tummy. Brush with apricot jam and cover with a layer of marzipan.

3 Tint 3 cups of the fondant icing pale pink and use to cover the cake. Let dry overnight.

4 Mark the position of the face and paws. Tint a little of the fondant icing blue and use for the eyes. Tint a little icing black and cut out the pupils and tie.

5 Tint the remaining fondant icing dark pink and cut out the nose, mouth, ears and paws. Stick all the features in place with water. Roll the trimmings into balls and place on the board to hold the candles.

Porcupine Cake

Melt-in-the-mouth strips of chocolate flake give this porcupine its spiky coating.

Serves 15–20

2 chocolate sponge cakes,
  baked in a 5-cup and a
  2½-cup ovenproof
  bowl
2½ cups chocolate-flavor
  butter icing
cream, black, green,
  brown and red food
  coloring

5–6 chocolate flakes
⅓ cup white marzipan

Materials/equipment
14-inch long rectangular
  cake board
wooden toothpick
fine paintbrush

1 Use the smaller cake for the head and shape a pointed nose at one end. Reserve the trimmed wedges.

2 Place the cakes side-by-side on the board, inverted, and use the trimmings to fill in the sides and top where they meet. Secure with butter icing.

3 Cover the cake with the remaining butter icing and mark the nose with a toothpick.

4 Make the spikes by breaking the chocolate flakes into thin strips and sticking them into the butter icing all over the body part of the porcupine.

5 Reserve a small portion of marzipan. Divide the remainder into three, and tint cream, black and green. Tint a tiny portion of the reserved marzipan brown. Shape cream ears and feet, black-and-white eyes, and black claws and nose. Arrange all the features on the cake. Make green apples and highlight in red with a fine paintbrush. Make the stalks from the brown marzipan and push them into the apples.

Mouse-in-Bed Cake

This cake is suitable for almost any age. Make the mouse well in advance to give it time to dry.

Makes one 8 x 6-inch cake

8-inch square sponge
  cake
½ cup butter icing
3 tablespoons apricot
  jam, warmed and
  strained
3 cups marzipan
4½ cups fondant icing
blue and red food
  coloring

Materials/equipment
10-inch square cake
  board
flower cutter
blue and red food
  coloring pens

1 Cut 2 inches off one side of the cake. Split and fill the main cake with butter icing. Place on the cake board, brush with apricot jam and cover with a layer of marzipan. With the cake off-cut, shape a hollowed pillow, the torso and the legs of the mouse. Cover with marzipan and let dry overnight.

2 Cover the cake and pillow with white fondant icing. Lightly frill the edge of the pillow with a fork. To make the valance, roll out 2¼ cups of fondant icing and cut into four 3-inch wide strips. Attach to the bed with water. Arrange the pillow and mouse body on the cake.

3 For the quilt, tint ½ cup of fondant icing blue and roll out to a 7-inch square. Mark with a diamond pattern and the flower cutter. Cover the mouse with the quilt.

4 Cut a 1 x 7½-inch white fondant icing strip for the sheet, mark the edge and place over the quilt, tucking it under at the top edge.

5 Tint 2 tablespoons of marzipan pink and make the head and paws of the mouse. Put the head on the pillow, tucked under the sheet, and the paws over the edge of the sheet. Use food coloring pens to draw on the face of the mouse.

Teddy's Birthday

After all the pieces have been assembled and stuck into the cake with a little water, an icing smoother is very useful to flatten the design.

Makes one 8-inch round cake

8-inch round cake	**Materials/equipment**
½ cup butter icing	10-inch round cake board
3 tablespoons apricot jam, warmed and strained	small wax paper icing bags
	No 7 shell and No 7 star nozzles
2 cups marzipan	
3 cups fondant icing	1½ yards red ribbon
brown, red, blue and black food coloring	2 candles and holders
¾ cup royal icing	
edible silver bails	

1 Split and fill the cake with butter icing. Place on the cake board and brush with apricot jam. Cover with a layer of marzipan then a layer of fondant icing. Using a template, mark the design on top of the cake.

2 Color a third of the remaining fondant icing pale brown. Color a piece pink, a piece red, some blue and a tiny piece black. Using the template, cut out the pieces and place in position on the cake. Stick down by lifting the edges carefully and brushing the undersides with a little water. Roll small ovals for the eyes and stick in place with the nose and eyebrows. Cut out a mouth and press flat.

3 Tie the ribbon around the cake. Color the royal icing blue and pipe the border around the bottom of the cake with the shell nozzle and tiny stars around the small cake with the star nozzle, inserting silver balls. Put the candles on the cake.

Party Teddy Bear Cake

The teddy on this cake is built up with royal icing and colored coconut.

Makes one 8-inch square cake

8-inch square sponge cake	**Materials/equipment**
½ cup butter icing	10-inch square cake board
3 tablespoons apricot jam, warmed and strained	2 small wax paper icing bags
3 cups marzipan	small red bow
2 cups white fondant icing	No 7 shell nozzle
½ cup dried coconut	1½ yards red ribbon
blue and black food coloring	6 candles and holders
¾ cup royal icing	

1 Cut the cake in half and sandwich together with butter icing. Place on the cake board and brush with apricot jam. Cover with a thin layer of marzipan and then white fondant icing. Let dry overnight. Using a template, carefully mark the position of the teddy onto the cake.

2 Put the coconut into a bowl and mix in a drop of blue coloring to color it pale blue. Spread a thin layer of royal icing within the outline of the teddy. Before the icing dries, sprinkle on some pale blue coconut and press it down lightly.

3 Roll out the fondant trimmings and cut out a nose, ears and paws. Stick in place with a little royal icing. Tint some royal icing black and pipe on the eyes, nose and mouth. Use the bow as a tie and stick it in place. Pipe a white royal icing border around the bottom of the cake, tie the ribbon around the cake and position the candles on top.

Iced Fancies

These cakes are ideal for a children's tea party. Premade cake decorating products may be used instead, if preferred.

Makes 16

½ cup butter, at room temperature
generous 1 cup superfine sugar
2 eggs, at room temperature
1½ cups all-purpose flour
¼ teaspoon salt
1½ teaspoons baking powder
½ cup milk
1 teaspoon vanilla extract

For the icing
2 large egg whites
3½ cups sifted confectioner's sugar
1–2 drops glycerine
juice of 1 lemon
food colorings
colored vermicelli, to decorate
candied lemon and orange slices, to decorate

1 Preheat the oven to 375°F. Line a 16-cup muffin tray with paper cases.

2 Cream the butter and sugar until light and fluffy. Add the eggs, 1 at a time, beating well after each addition. Sift over and stir in the flour, salt and baking powder, alternating with the milk. Add the vanilla extract.

3 Half-fill the cups and bake for about 20 minutes, or until the tops spring back when touched. Stand in the tray to cool for 5 minutes, then unmold onto a wire rack.

4 For the icing, beat the egg whites until stiff. Gradually add the sugar, glycerine and lemon juice, and beat for 1 minute.

5 Tint the icing with different food colorings. Ice the cakes.

6 Decorate the cakes with colored vermicelli and candied lemon and orange slices. Make freehand decorations using a paper icing bag.

Fairy Castle Cake

If the icing on this cake dries too quickly, dip a metal spatula into hot water to help smooth the surface.

Makes one castle-shape cake

8-inch round sponge cake
½ cup butter icing
3 tablespoons apricot jam, warmed and strained
4½ cups marzipan
8 mini jelly rolls
4½ cups royal icing
red, blue and green food coloring

jelly diamonds
4 ice cream cones
2 ice cream wafers
1 cup dried coconut
8 marshmallows

Materials/equipment
12-inch square cake board
wooden toothpick

1 Split and fill the cake with butter icing, place in the center of the board and brush with apricot jam. Cover with a layer of marzipan. Cover each of the jelly rolls with marzipan. Stick four of them around the cake and cut the other four in half.

2 Tint two-thirds of the royal icing pale pink and cover the cake. Ice the extra pieces of jelly roll and stick them around the top of the cake. Use a toothpick to score the walls with a brick pattern. Make windows on the corner towers from jelly diamonds. Cut the ice cream cones to make the tower spires and stick them in place. Let dry overnight.

3 Tint half the remaining royal icing pale blue and cover the cones. Use a fork to pattern the icing. Shape the wafers for the gates, stick to the cake and cover with blue icing. Use the back of a knife to mark planks.

4 Tint the coconut with a few drops of green coloring. Spread the board with the remaining royal icing and sprinkle over the coconut. Stick on the marshmallows with a little royal icing to make the small turrets.

Sailing Boat

For chocoholics, make this cake using chocolate sponge.

Makes one boat-shape cake

8-inch square sponge
   cake
1 cup butter icing
1 tablespoon cocoa
4 large chocolate flakes
¾ cup royal icing
blue food coloring

Materials/equipment
10-inch square cake
   board
rice paper
blue and red powder tints
paintbrush
plastic drinking straw
wooden toothpick
2 small cake ornaments

1 Split and fill the cake with half of the butter icing. Cut 2¾ inches from one side of the cake. Shape the larger piece to resemble the hull of a boat. Place diagonally across the cake board. Mix the cocoa into the remaining butter icing and spread evenly over the top and sides of the boat.

2 Make the rudder and tiller from short lengths of flake and place them at the stern of the boat. Split the rest of the flakes lengthwise and press onto the sides of the boat, horizontally, to resemble planks of wood. Sprinkle the crumbs over the top.

3 Cut two rice paper rectangles, one 5¾ x 6½ inches and the other 6 x 3 inches. Cut the bigger one in a gentle curve to make the large sail and the smaller one into a triangle. Brush a circle of blue powder tint onto the large sail. Wet the edges of the sails and stick onto the straw. Make a hole for the straw 3 inches from the bow of the boat and push into the cake.

4 Cut a rice paper flag and brush with red powder tint. Stick the flag onto a toothpick and insert into the top of the straw. Tint the royal icing blue and spread on the board in waves. Place the small ornaments on the boat.

Spiders' Cake

A spooky cake for any occasion, fancy dress or otherwise.

Makes one 2-pound cake

2-pound dome-shape
   lemon sponge cake
¾ cup lemon-flavor glacé
   icing
black and yellow food
   coloring

cocoa, for dusting
chocolate vermicelli
2–3 liquorice wheels,
   candy centers removed
2 tablespoons fondant
   icing

For the spiders

4 ounces semisweet
   chocolate, broken into
   pieces
⅔ cup heavy cream
3 tablespoons ground
   almonds

Materials/equipment
wax paper
small wax paper icing
   bag
wooden skewer
8-inch cake board

1 Place the cake on wax paper. Tint 3 tablespoons of the glacé icing black. Tint the rest yellow and pour it over the cake, letting it run down the sides.

2 Fill an icing bag with the black icing and, starting at the center top, drizzle it around the cake in an evenly-spaced spiral. Finish the web by drawing downward through the icing with a skewer. When set, place on the cake board.

3 For the spiders, gently melt the chocolate with the cream, stirring frequently. Transfer to a bowl, let cool, then beat the mixture for 10 minutes, or until thick and pale. Stir in the ground almonds, then chill until firm enough to handle. Dust your hands with a little cocoa, then make walnut-size balls with the mixture. Roll the balls in chocolate vermicelli.

4 For the legs, cut the liquorice into 1½-inch lengths. Make holes in the sides of the spiders and insert the legs. For the spiders' eyes, tint a piece of fondant icing black and form into tiny balls. Make larger balls with white icing. Stick on using water. Arrange the spiders on and around the cake.

Toy Telephone Cake

The child's name could be piped in a contrasting color of icing, if you wish.

Makes one telephone-shaped cake

6-inch square sponge
  cake
¼ cup butter icing
2 tablespoons apricot
  jam, warmed and
  strained
2 cups marzipan
2 cups fondant icing
yellow, blue, red and
  black food coloring

liquorice strips
¾ cup royal icing

Materials/equipment
8-inch square cake board
piping nozzle
small wax paper icing
  bag
No 1 writing nozzle

1 Split and fill the cake with butter icing. Trim to the shape of a telephone. Round off the edges and cut a shallow groove where the receiver rests on the telephone. Place the cake on the board and brush with apricot jam.

2 Cover the cake with marzipan then fondant icing. Tint half the remaining fondant icing yellow, a small piece blue and the rest of the icing red. To make the dial, cut out a 3½-inch diameter circle in yellow and a 1½-inch diameter circle in blue. Stamp out 12 red discs for the numbers with the end of a piping nozzle and cut out a red receiver. Position on the cake with water.

3 Twist the liquorice around to form a curly cord and use royal icing to stick one end to the telephone and the other end to the receiver. Tint the royal icing black and pipe the numbers on the discs and the child's name on the telephone.

Bumble Bee Cake

The edible sugar flowers that are used to decorate this cake were bought premade.

Makes one bee-shape cake

8-inch round sponge cake
½ cup butter icing
3 tablespoons apricot
  jam, warmed and
  strained
2¼ cups marzipan
3¾ cups fondant icing
yellow, black, blue and
  red food coloring

¾ cup royal icing
1 cup dried coconut

Materials/equipment
10-inch square cake
  board
6 fondant daisies
1 paper doily
sticky tape
1 pipe cleaner

1 Split and fill the cake with butter icing. Cut in half to make semicircles, sandwich the halves together and stand upright on the cake board. Trim the ends to shape the head and tail. Brush with apricot jam and cover with a layer of marzipan. Tint 2¼ cups of the fondant icing yellow and cover the cake.

2 Tint ¾ cup of the fondant icing black. Roll out and cut three stripes, each 1 x 10 inches. Space evenly on the cake and stick on with water. Use the remaining icing to make the eyes and mouth, tinting the icing blue for the pupils and pink for the mouth. Stick on with water.

3 Tint the coconut with a drop of yellow coloring. Cover the cake board with royal icing then sprinkle with coconut. Place the daisies on the board.

4 To make the wings, cut the doily in half, wrap each half into a cone shape and stick together with sticky tape. Cut the pipe cleaner in half and stick the pieces into the cake, just behind the head. Place the wings over the pipe cleaners.

Toy Car Cake

You can add a personalized number plate with the child's name and age to the back of this car.

Makes one car-shape cake

8-inch round sponge cake
½ cup butter icing
3 tablespoons apricot jam, warmed and strained
3 cups marzipan
3¾ cups fondant icing
yellow, red and black food coloring
2 tablespoons royal icing
red and green candies

Materials/equipment
10-inch round cake board
wooden toothpick
cutters, 1½ inches and 1 inch
small wax paper icing bag
No 1 writing nozzle
2 candles and holders

1 Split and fill the cake with the butter icing. Cut in half and sandwich the halves together. Stand upright and slice off pieces to create the windscreen and bonnet. Place on the cake board and brush with apricot jam.

2 Cut a strip of marzipan to cover the top of the cake to level the joins. Then cover the cake all over with marzipan. Tint 3 cups of the fondant icing yellow and use to cover the cake. Let dry overnight.

3 Mark the outlines of the doors and windows onto the car with a toothpick.

4 Tint the remaining fondant icing red. Cut out four wheels with the larger cutter. Stick in place with water. Mark the hubs in the center of each wheel with the smaller cutter.

5 Tint the royal icing black and pipe over the outline marks of the doors and windows. Stick on candies for headlights with royal icing. Press the candles into candies and stick to the board with royal icing.

Fire Engine Cake

This jolly fire engine is simplicity itself as the decorations are mainly bought candies and novelties.

Makes one 8 x 4-inch cake

8-inch square sponge cake
½ cup butter icing
3 tablespoons apricot jam, warmed and strained
2¼ cups marzipan
3 cups fondant icing
red, black and green food coloring
liquorice strips

4 tablespoons royal icing
candies
1 cup dried coconut

Materials/equipment
10-inch round cake board
small wax paper icing bag
No 2 plain nozzle
2 silver bells
3 candles and holders

1 Split and fill the cake with the butter icing. Cut in half and sandwich one half on top of the other. Place on the cake board and brush with apricot jam.

2 Trim a thin wedge off the front edge to make a sloping windscreen. Cover with marzipan. Tint 2¼ cups of the fondant icing red and use to cover the cake.

3 For the ladder, cut the liquorice into two strips and some short pieces for the rungs. Tint half the royal icing black and use some to stick the ladder to the top of the cake. Roll out the remaining fondant icing, cut out windows and stick them on with a little water.

4 Pipe around the windows in black royal icing. Stick candies in place for headlights, lamps and wheels and stick the silver bells on the roof. Tint the coconut green, spread a little royal icing over the cake board and sprinkle with the coconut. Stick candies to the board with royal icing and press the candles into the candies.

Sandcastle Cake

Crushed digestive cookies make convincing-looking sand when used to cover this fun cake.

Makes one 6-inch round cake

2 x 6-inch round sponge
  cakes
½ cup butter icing
3 tablespoons apricot
  jam, warmed and
  strained
¾ cup digestive cookies
¾ cup royal icing
blue food coloring

shrimp-shape candies

Materials/equipment
10-inch square cake
  board
rice paper
plastic drinking straw
4 candles and holders

1 Split both of the cakes, then sandwich all the layers together with the butter icing. Place in the center of the cake board. Cut 1¼ inches off the top just above the filling and set aside. Shape the rest of the cake with slightly sloping sides.

2 Cut four 1¼-inch cubes from the reserved piece of cake. Stick on the cubes for the turrets and brush with apricot jam.

3 Crush the cookies and press through a sifter to make the "sand." Press some crushed cookies onto the cake, using a metal spatula to get a smooth finish.

4 Color some royal icing blue and spread on the board around the sandcastle to make a moat. Spread a little royal icing on the board around the outside edge of the moat and sprinkle on some crushed cookie.

5 To make the flag, cut a small rectangle of rice paper and stick onto half a straw with water. Push the end of the straw into the cake. Stick candles into each turret and arrange the shrimp-shape candies on the board.

Clown Face Cake

Kids love this happy clown whose frilly collar is surprisingly simple to make.

Makes one 8-inch cake

8-inch round sponge cake
½ cup butter icing
3 tablespoons apricot
  jam, warmed and
  strained
3 cups marzipan
3 cups fondant icing
¾ cup royal icing
edible silver balls
red, green, blue and black
  food coloring

Materials/equipment
10-inch round cake board
small wax paper icing
  bag
No 8 star nozzle
wooden toothpick
cotton wool
two candles and holders

1 Split and fill the cake with butter icing. Place on the cake board and brush with apricot jam. Cover with a thin layer of marzipan then with white fondant icing. Mark the position of the features. Pipe stars around the bottom of the cake with some royal icing, placing silver balls as you work, and let dry overnight.

2 Make a template for the face and features. Tint half the remaining fondant icing pink and cut out the face base. Tint and cut out all the features, rolling a sausage to make the mouth. Cut thin strands for the hair. Stick all the features and hair in place with a little water.

3 Tint the remaining fondant icing green. Cut three strips 1½ inches wide. Give each a scalloped edge and stretch by rolling a toothpick along it to make the frill. Stick on with water and arrange the frills, holding them in place with cotton wool until dry. Place the candles at the top of the head.

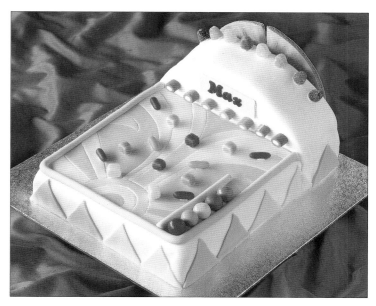

Pinball Machine

Serves 8–10

10-inch square sponge cake
1½ cups butter icing
3 tablespoons apricot jam, warmed and strained
3 cups marzipan
¾ cup royal icing
3 cups fondant icing
yellow, blue, green and red food coloring
candies
2 ice cream fan wafers

Materials/equipment
8-inch round cake tin
12-inch square cake board
small wax paper icing bag
No 1 writing nozzle

1 Split and fill the sponge cake with butter icing. Cut off a 2-inch strip from one side and reserve. Cut a thin wedge off the top of the cake, diagonally along its length, to end just above the halfway mark. This will give a sloping table.

2 Using the cake pan as a guide, cut the reserved strip of cake to make a rounded back for the pinball table. Brush the back and table with apricot jam, then cover separately with marzipan and place on the board. Stick them together with royal icing. Let dry overnight.

3 Cover with a layer of fondant icing and let dry. Use a template to mark out the pinball design on the top of the cake. Color the remaining fondant icing yellow, blue, green and pink. Roll out the colors and cut to fit the design. Stick on the pieces with water and smooth the joins carefully.

4 Using royal icing, stick candies on the cake as buffers, flippers, lights and knobs. Roll some blue fondant icing into a long sausage and edge the pinball table and divider. Cut zigzags for the sides and a screen for the back. Stick on with water. Stick the ice cream fans at the back of the screen. Load the pinball candies. Add the child's name on the screen with run-out letters or piping.

Pirate's Hat

If you prefer, buy premade black fondant icing rather than tinting it yourself.

Serves 8–10

10-inch round sponge cake
1 cup butter icing
3 tablespoons apricot jam, warmed and strained
3 cups marzipan
3¾ cups fondant icing
black and gold food coloring
chocolate money
jewel candies

Materials/equipment
12-inch square cake board
fine paint brush

1 Split and fill the cake with butter icing. Cut in half and sandwich the halves together. Stand upright diagonally across the cake board and cut shallow dips from each end to create the brim of the hat. Brush with apricot jam.

2 Cut a strip of marzipan to lay over the top of the cake. Then cover the whole of the cake with a layer of marzipan. Tint 3 cups of the fondant icing black. Use to cover the cake.

3 Roll out the remaining fondant icing and cut some ½-inch strips. Stick the strips in place with a little water around the brim of the pirate's hat and mark with the prongs of a fork to make a braid.

4 Make a skull and crossbones template and mark onto the hat. Cut the shapes out of the white fondant icing and stick in place with water. Paint the braid strip gold and arrange the chocolate money and jewel candies on the board.

Noah's Ark Cake

This charming cake is decorated with small animals, about 1½ inches high, available from cake decorating stores.

Makes one 8 x 5-inch cake

8-inch square sponge
 cake
½ cup butter icing
3 tablespoons apricot
 jam, warmed and
 strained
3 cups marzipan
3 cups fondant icing
brown, yellow and blue
 food coloring

¾ cup royal icing
chocolate mint stick

Materials/equipment
10-inch square cake
 board
skewer
rice paper flag
small animal cake
 ornaments

1 Split and fill the cake with butter icing. Cut off and set aside a 3-inch strip. Shape the remaining piece of cake to form the hull of the boat. Place diagonally on the cake board.

2 Cut a 4 x 2½-inch rectangle for the cabin from the set aside piece of cake and a triangular piece for the roof. Sandwich together with butter icing or apricot jam.

3 Cover the three pieces with a layer of marzipan. Tint the fondant icing brown and use most of it to cover the hull and cabin. Use the remaining brown icing to make a long sausage. Stick around the edge of the hull with water. Mark planks with the back of a knife. Let dry overnight.

4 Tint a third of the royal icing yellow and spread it over the cabin roof with a metal spatula. Roughen it with a skewer to create a thatch effect.

5 Tint the remaining royal icing blue and spread over the cake board, making rough waves. Stick a rice paper flag onto the chocolate mint stick and press on the back of the boat. Stick the small animals onto the boat with a dab of icing.

Balloons Cake

This is a simple yet effective cake design that can be adapted to suit any age.

Makes one 8-inch round cake

8-inch round cake
½ cup butter icing
3 tablespoons apricot
 jam, warmed and
 strained
3 cups marzipan
3 cups fondant icing
red, blue, green and
 yellow food coloring
¾ cup royal icing

Materials/equipment
10-inch round cake board
2 small wax paper icing
 bags
No 2 plain and No 7 star
 nozzles
1½ yards blue ribbon
3 candles and holders

1 Split and fill the cake with butter icing. Place on the cake board and brush with apricot jam. Cover with a layer of marzipan then fondant icing.

2 Divide the remaining fondant icing into three pieces and tint pink, blue and green. Make a balloon template, roll out the colored fondant and cut out one balloon from each color. Stick onto the cake with water and rub the edges gently to round them off.

3 Tint the royal icing yellow. With a plain nozzle, pipe on the balloon strings and a number on each balloon. Using the star nozzle, pipe a border around the bottom of the cake.

4 Tie the ribbon around the cake and place the candles on the top.

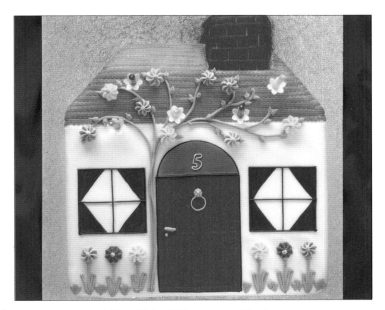

Horse Stencil Cake

Use a fairly dry brush when painting the design on this cake and allow each color to dry before adding the next.

Makes one 8-inch round cake

8-inch round sponge cake
½ cup butter icing
3 tablespoons apricot jam, warmed and strained
3 cups marzipan
3 cups fondant icing
yellow, brown, black, red, orange and blue food coloring

Materials/equipment
10-inch round cake board
spoon with decorative handle
fine paintbrush
horse and letter stencils
1½ yards blue ribbon
7 candles and holders

1 Split and fill the cake with butter icing. Place on the cake board and brush with apricot jam. Cover with a layer of marzipan. Tint the fondant icing yellow, roll out and use to cover the cake. Roll the trimmings into two thin ropes, long enough to go halfway around the cake. Brush water in a thin band around the bottom of the cake, lay on the ropes and press together. Pattern the border with the decorative spoon handle. Let dry overnight.

2 If you do not have a stencil, make one by tracing a simple design onto a thin piece of cardboard and cutting out the shape with a craft knife. Place the horse stencil in the center of the cake. With a fairly dry brush, gently paint over the parts you want to color first. Let these dry completely before adding another color, otherwise the colors will run into each other. Clean the stencil between colors.

3 When the horse picture is finished, carefully paint on the lettering. Tie the ribbon around the side of the cake and place the candles on top.

Doll's House Cake

Serves 8–10

10-inch square sponge cake
1 cup butter icing
3 tablespoons apricot jam, warmed and strained
3 cups marzipan
3 cups fondant icing red, yellow, blue, black, green and gold food coloring
¾ cup royal icing

Materials/equipment
12-inch square cake board
pastry wheel
large and fine paintbrushes
wooden toothpick
small wax paper icing bags
No 2 writing nozzle
flower decorations

1 Split and fill the cake with butter icing. Cut triangles off two corners and use the pieces to make a chimney. Place on the cake board and brush with apricot jam. Cover with a layer of marzipan then fondant icing.

2 Mark the roof with a pastry wheel and the chimney with the back of a knife. Paint the chimney red and the roof yellow.

3 Tint 2 tablespoons of fondant icing red and cut out a 3 x 4½-inch door. Tint enough fondant icing blue to make a fanlight. Stick to the cake with water. Mark 2½-inch square windows with a toothpick. Paint on curtains with blue food coloring. Tint half the royal icing black and pipe around the windows and the door.

4 Tint the remaining royal icing green. Pipe the flower stems and leaves under the windows and the climber up onto the roof. Stick the flowers in place with a little icing and pipe green flower centers. Pipe the house number or child's age, the knocker and handle on the door. Let dry for 1 hour, then paint with gold food coloring.

Treasure Chest Cake

Allow yourself a few days before the party to make this cake as the lock and handles need to dry for 48 hours.

Makes one 8 x 4-inch cake

8-inch square sponge
  cake
½ cup butter icing
3 tablespoons apricot
  jam, warmed and
  strained
2 cups marzipan
2½ cups fondant icing
brown and green food
  coloring

1 cup dried coconut
¾ cup royal icing
edible gold dusting
  powder
edible silver balls
chocolate money

Materials/equipment
12-inch round cake board
fine paintbrush

1 Split and fill the cake with butter icing. Cut the cake in half and sandwich the halves on top of each other with butter icing. Place on the cake board.

2 Shape the top into a rounded lid and brush with apricot jam. Cover with a layer of marzipan. Tint 2¼ cups of the fondant icing brown and use to cover the cake.

3 Use the brown fondant trimmings to make strips. Stick onto the chest with water. Mark the lid with a sharp knife.

4 Tint the coconut with a few drops of green coloring. Spread a little royal icing over the cake board and press the green coconut lightly into it to make the grass.

5 From the remaining fondant icing, cut out the padlock and handles. Cut a keyhole shape from the padlock and shape the handles over a small box. Let dry. Stick the padlock and handles in place with royal icing and paint them gold. Stick silver balls on to look like nails. Arrange the chocolate money on the board.

Lion Cake

For an animal lover or a celebration cake for a Leo horoscope sign, this cake is ideal.

Makes one 11 x 9-inch oval cake

10 x 12-inch sponge cake
1½ cups orange-flavor
  butter icing
orange and red food
  coloring
4½ cups yellow marzipan
generous 4 tablespoons
  fondant icing
red and orange liquorice
  bootlaces

long and round
  marshmallows

Materials/equipment
12-inch square cake
  board
cheese grater
small heart-shape cutter

1 With the flat side of the cake uppermost, cut it to make an oval shape with an uneven scallop design around the edge. Turn the cake over and trim the top level.

2 Place the cake on the cake board. Tint the butter icing orange and use it to cover the cake.

3 Roll ¾ cup of marzipan to a 6-inch square. Place in the center of the cake for the lion's face.

4 Grate the remaining marzipan and use to cover the sides and the top of the cake up to the face panel.

5 Tint the fondant icing red. Use the heart-shape cutter to stamp out the lion's nose and position on the cake with water. Roll the remaining red icing into two thin, short strands to make the lion's mouth, and stick on with water.

6 Cut the liquorice into graduated lengths, and place on the cake for the whiskers. Use two flattened round marshmallows for the eyes and two snipped long ones for the eyebrows.

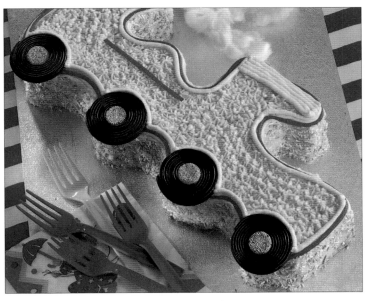

Train Cake

This cake is made in a train-shape pan, so all you need to do is decorate it.

Makes one train-shape cake

train-shape sponge cake, about 14 inches long
3 cups butter icing
yellow food coloring
red liquorice bootlaces
6–8 tablespoons colored vermicelli
4 liquorice wheels

Materials/equipment
10 x 15-inch cake board
2 fabric icing bags
small round and small star nozzles
pink and white cotton wool balls

1 Slice off the top surface of the cake to make it flat. Place it diagonally on the cake board.

2 Tint the butter icing yellow. Use half of it to cover the cake.

3 Using a round nozzle and a quarter of the remaining butter icing, pipe a straight double border around the top edge of the cake.

4 Place the red liquorice bootlaces on the piped border. Cut the bootlaces around the curves on the train.

5 Using a small star nozzle and the remaining butter icing, pipe small stars over the top of the cake. Add extra liquorice and piping, if you like. Use a metal spatula to press on the colored vermicelli all around the sides of the cake.

6 Pull a couple of balls of cotton wool apart for the steam and stick them onto the cake board with butter icing. Press the liquorice wheels in place for the wheels.

Number 7 Cake

Any combination of colors will work well for this cake with its marble effect.

Makes one 12-inch long cake

9 x 12-inch sponge cake
1½ cups orange-flavor butter icing
4 tablespoons apricot jam, warmed and strained
4½ cups fondant icing

blue and green food coloring
rice paper candies

Materials /equipment
10 x 13-inch cake board
small "7" cutter

1 Place the cake flat-side up and cut out the number seven. Slice the cake horizontally, sandwich together with the butter icing and place on the board.

2 Brush the cake evenly with apricot jam. Divide the fondant icing into three and tint one of the pieces blue and another green. Set aside scant ½ cup from each of the colored icings. Knead together the large pieces of blue and green icing with the third piece of white icing to marble. Cover the cake.

3 Immediately after covering, use the cutter to remove fondant shapes in a random pattern from the covered cake.

4 Roll out the reserved blue and green fondant icing and stamp out shapes with the same cutter. Use these to fill the stamped-out shapes from the cake. Decorate the board with some rice paper candies.

Musical Cake

Creating a sheet of music on a cake requires very delicate piping work, so it is best to practice first.

Makes one 8 x 10-inch cake

10-inch square sponge cake
1 cup butter icing
3 tablespoons apricot jam, warmed and strained
3 cups marzipan
3 cups fondant icing
¾ cup royal icing
black food coloring

Materials/equipment
10 x 12-inch cake board
wooden toothpick
2 small wax paper icing bags
No 0 writing and No 7 shell nozzles
1½ yards red ribbon

1 Split and fill the cake with a little butter icing. Cut a 2-inch strip off one side of the cake. Place the cake on the cake board and brush with apricot jam. Cover with a layer of marzipan then fondant icing. Let dry overnight.

2 Make a template and mark out the sheet of music and child's name with a toothpick.

3 Using white royal icing and a No 0 nozzle, begin by piping the lines and bars. Let dry.

4 Tint the remaining icing black and pipe the clefs, name and notes. With the shell nozzle, pipe a royal icing border around the bottom of the cake. Tie a ribbon around the side.

Magic Rabbit Cake

Makes one 6-inch tall round cake

2 x 6-inch round cakes
1 cup butter icing
¾ cup royal icing
3 tablespoons apricot jam, warmed and strained
4½ cups marzipan
4½ cups fondant icing
black and pink food coloring

edible silver balls

Materials/equipment
10-inch square cake board
2 small wax paper icing bags
star nozzle
1½ yards pink ribbon

1 Split and fill the cakes with butter icing, then sandwich them one on top of the other. Stick on the center of the cake board with a little royal icing. Brush with apricot jam. Use 3 cups of the marzipan to cover the cake.

2 Tint the fondant icing gray. Use about two-thirds of it to cover the cake. Roll out the rest to an 8-inch round. Cut a 6-inch circle from its center. Lower the brim over the cake. Shape the brim sides over wooden spoon handles until dry.

3 Cut a cross in the 6-inch gray circle and place on the hat. Curl the triangles over a wooden spoon handle to shape. Smooth the join at the top and sides of the hat.

4 Tint the remaining marzipan pink and make the rabbit's head, about 2 inches wide with a pointed face. Mark the position of the eyes, nose and mouth. Let dry overnight.

5 Stick the rabbit in the center of the hat with a little royal icing. Pipe a border of royal icing around the top and bottom of the hat and decorate with silver balls while still wet. Tint the remaining royal icing black and pipe the rabbit's eyes and mouth. Tie the ribbon around the hat.

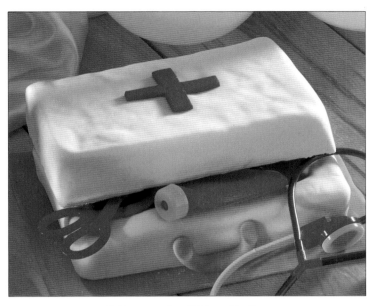

Nurse's Kit Cake

The box is easy to make and is simply filled with toy kit.

Makes one 8 x 6½-inch cake

*14 x 8-inch chocolate
  sponge cake
½ cup apricot jam,
  warmed and strained
4½ cups fondant icing
red food coloring*

Materials/equipment
*10-inch square cake
  board
selection of toy medical
  equipment*

1 Place the cake dome-side down and cut in half widthwise.

2 To make the bottom of the nurse's box, turn one cake half dome-side up and hollow out the center to a depth of ½ inch, leaving a ½-inch border on the three uncut edges. Brush the tops and sides of both halves with jam.

3 Tint generous ½ cup fondant icing deep pink. Use a little to make a small handle for the box. Wrap in plastic wrap and set aside. Cover the cake board with the rest of the pink icing. Tint 2 tablespoons of the fondant icing red. Cover with plastic wrap and set aside.

4 Tint the remaining icing light pink and divide into two portions, one slightly bigger than the other. Roll out the bigger portion and use to cover the bottom of the box, easing it into the hollow and along the edges. Trim, then position the bottom on the cake board.

5 Roll out the other portion and use to cover the lid of the box. Trim, then place on top of the bottom at a slight angle.

6 Stick the handle to the bottom of the box using water. Cut a small cross out of red icing and stick it on the lid. Place a few toy items under the lid, protruding slightly. Arrange some more items around the board and cake.

Ballerina Cake

Use flower cutters with ejectors to make the tiny flowers.

Makes one 8-inch round cake

*8-inch round sponge cake
½ cup butter icing
3 tablespoons apricot
  jam, warmed and
  strained
3 cups marzipan
3 cups fondant icing
pink, yellow, blue and
  green food coloring
¾ cup royal icing*

Materials/equipment
*10-inch round cake board
small flower cutter
small circle cutter
wooden toothpick
cotton wool
fine paintbrush
3 small wax paper icing
  bags
No 7 shell nozzle
1½ yards pink ribbon*

1 Split and fill the cake with butter icing. Place on the board and brush with apricot jam. Cover with marzipan then fondant icing. Let dry overnight. Divide the rest of the fondant into three. Tint flesh tone, light pink and dark pink. Stamp out 15 pale pink flowers. Let dry.

2 Make a template of the ballerina. Mark her position on the cake. Cut out a flesh-tone body and dark pink bodice. Stick on with water, rounding off the edges.

3 Cut two dark pink underskirts, a pale pink top skirt and a dark pink bodice extension to make the tutu. Stamp out hollow, fluted circles, divide the circles into four and frill the fluted edges with a toothpick. Stick the tutu in place, supported with cotton wool. Cut out and stick on pale pink shoes. Let dry overnight.

4 Paint the ballerina's face and hair. Position 12 hoop and three headdress flowers. Tint some royal icing green and dark pink to complete the flowers and ballet shoes. Pipe a border around the bottom with the shell nozzle. Tie the ribbon on.

Monsters on the Moon

A great cake for little monsters! This cake is best eaten on the day of making.

Serves 12–15

1 quantity quick-mix
    sponge cake
3¾ cups fondant icing
1½ cups marzipan
black food coloring
edible silver glitter
    powder (optional)
¾ cups superfine sugar
2 egg whites
4 tablespoons water

Materials/equipment
ovenproof wok
various sizes of plain
    round and star cutters
12-inch round cake board
small monster toys

1   Preheat the oven to 350°F. Grease and line the wok. Spoon in the cake mixture and smooth the surface. Bake in the center of the oven for 35–40 minutes. Let stand for 5 minutes, then turn out onto a wire rack and peel off the paper.

2   With the cake dome-side up, use the round cutters to cut out craters. Press in the cutters to about 1 inch deep, then remove and cut the craters out of the cake with a knife.

3   Use ¾ cup of the fondant icing to cover the cake, pulling off small pieces and pressing them in uneven strips around the edges of the craters. Tint the remaining fondant icing black. Roll out and cover the board. Stamp out stars and replace with marzipan stars of the same size. Dust with glitter powder, if using, and place on the board.

4   Put the sugar, egg whites and water in a heat proof bowl over a pan of simmering water. Beat until thick and peaks form. Spoon the icing over the cake, swirling it into the craters and peaking it unevenly. Sprinkle over the silver glitter powder, if using, then position the monsters on the cake.

Circus Cake

This colorful design is easy to achieve and is sure to delight young children.

Makes one 8-inch cake

8-inch round sponge cake
½ cup butter icing
3 tablespoons apricot
    jam, warmed and
    strained
3 cups marzipan
3 cups fondant icing
red and blue food
    coloring
¾ cup royal icing

edible silver balls
3 digestive cookies

Materials/equipment
10-inch round cake board
small wax paper icing
    bag
No 5 star nozzle
2-inch plastic circus
    ornaments

1   Split and fill the cake with butter icing. Place on the cake board and brush with apricot jam. Cover with a layer of marzipan then fondant icing.

2   Tint ¾ cup fondant icing pink, then roll into a rope and stick around the top edge of the cake with a little water.

3   Tint half the remaining fondant icing red and half blue. Roll out each color and cut into twelve 1-inch squares. Stick the squares alternately at an angle around the side of the cake with a little water. Pipe stars around the bottom of the cake with royal icing and stick in the edible silver balls.

4   Crush the cookies by pressing through a sifter to make the "sand" for the circus ring. Sprinkle over the top of the cake and place small circus ornaments on top.

Frog Prince Cake

Serves 8–10

8-inch round sponge cake	green, red, black and gold
½ cup butter icing	food coloring
3 tablespoons apricot	
jam, warmed and	**Materials/equipment**
strained	10-inch square cake
3 cups marzipan	board
cornstarch, for dusting	glass
3¾ cups fondant icing	fine paintbrush
¾ cup royal icing	

1 Split and fill the cake with butter icing. Cut in half and sandwich the halves together with apricot jam. Stand upright diagonally across the cake board. Brush the cake with apricot jam and cover with marzipan.

2 Tint 3 cups of the fondant icing green and cover the cake. Roll the remaining green fondant icing into ½-inch diameter sausages. You will need two folded 8-inch lengths for the back legs and 14 x 4-inch lengths for the front legs and feet. Stick in place with a little royal icing. Roll balls for the eyes and stick in place.

3 Roll out the reserved icing and cut a 2 x 7½-inch strip. Cut out triangles along one edge to make the crown shape. Wrap around a glass dusted with cornstarch and moisten the edges to join. Let dry.

4 Cut a 4-inch circle for the white shirt. Stick in place and trim the bottom edge. Cut white circles and stick to the eyes. Tint a little fondant pink, roll into a sausage and stick on for the mouth. Tint the rest black and use for the pupils and the bow tie. Stick in place.

5 Paint the crown with gold food coloring. Let dry, then stick into position with royal icing.

Ladybird Cake

Children will love this colorful and appealing ladybird, and it is very simple to make.

Serves 10–12

3-egg quantity quick-mix	food colorings
sponge cake	5 marshmallows
¾ cup butter icing	4 tablespoons marzipan
4 tablespoons lemon	
curd, warmed	**Materials/equipment**
confectioner's sugar, for	wooden skewer
dusting	garlic crusher
7 cups fondant icing	2 pipe cleaners

1 Cut the cake in half crosswise and sandwich together with the butter icing. Cut vertically through the cake, about a third of the way in. Brush both pieces with the lemon curd.

2 Color 1 pound of the fondant icing red. Dust a work surface with confectioner's sugar and roll out the icing to about ¼ inch thick. Use to cover the larger piece of cake for the body. Using a wooden skewer, make an indentation down the center for the wings.

3 Color 1½ cups of fondant icing black, roll out three-quarters and use to cover the smaller piece of cake for the head. Place both cakes on a cakeboard, press together.

4 Roll out 2 ounces fondant icing and cut out two 2-inch circles for the eyes, and stick to the head with water. Roll out the remaining black icing and cut out eight 1½-inch circles. Use two of these for the eyes and stick the others onto the body.

5 Color some icing green and squeeze through a garlic crusher to make grass. Flatten the marshmallows and stick a marzipan in the center of each. Color pipe cleaners black and press a ball of black icing onto the end of each. Arrange the grass around the cake with the ladybird and decorations.

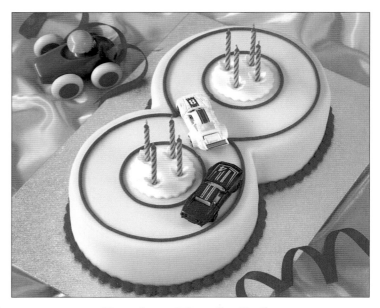

Spaceship Cake

Serves 10–12

*10-inch square sponge
cake
1 cup butter icing
4 tablespoons apricot
jam, warmed and
strained
2¼ cups marzipan
3 cups fondant icing
blue, red and black food
coloring*

Materials/equipment
*12-inch square cake
board
4 silver candles and
holders
gold paper stars*

1 Split and fill the sponge cake with butter icing. Cut a 4-inch wide piece diagonally across the middle of the cake, about 10 inches long. Shape the nose end and straighten the other end.

2 From the off-cuts make three 3-inch triangles for the wings and top of the ship. Cut two smaller triangles for the booster jets. Position the main body, wings and top of the cake diagonally across the board. Add extra pieces of cake in front of the top triangle. Brush the cake and booster jets with apricot jam, then cover with a layer of marzipan and fondant icing.

3 Divide the remaining fondant icing into three. Tint blue, pink and black. Roll out the blue icing and cut it into ½-inch strips. Stick around the bottom of the cake with water and outline the boosters. Cut a 1-inch strip and stick down the center of the spaceship.

4 Roll out the pink and black fondant icing separately and cut shapes, numbers and the child's name to finish the design. When complete, position the boosters.

5 Make small cubes with the off-cuts of fondant icing and use to stick the candles to the cake board. Decorate the board with gold stars.

Racing Track Cake

This cake will delight eight-year-old racing car enthusiasts.

Serves 10–12

*2 x 6-inch round sponge
cakes
½ cup butter icing
4 tablespoons apricot
jam, warmed and
strained
3 cups marzipan
3¾ cups fondant icing
blue and red food
coloring
¾ cup royal icing*

Materials/equipment
*10 x 14-inch cake board
2-inch fluted cutter
2 small wax paper icing
bags
No 8 star and No 2 plain
nozzles
8 candles and holders
2 small racing cars*

1 Split and fill the cakes with a little butter icing. Cut off a ½-inch piece from the side of each cake and place the cakes on the cake board, cut edges together.

2 Brush the cake with apricot jam and cover with a layer of marzipan. Tint 3 cups of the fondant icing pale blue and use to cover the cake.

3 Mark a 2-inch circle in the center of each cake. Roll out the remaining white fondant icing and cut out two fluted 2-inch circles and stick them in the marked spaces.

4 Tint the royal icing red. Pipe a shell border around the bottom of the cake using the star nozzle. Pipe a track for the cars on the cake using the plain nozzle and stick the candles into the two white circles. Place the cars on the track.

Floating Balloons Cake

Makes one 8-inch round cake

8-inch round sponge or
   fruit cake, covered
   with 5½ cups
   marzipan, if liked
6 cups fondant icing
red, green and yellow
   food coloring
3 eggs
2 egg whites
4 cups confectioner's
   sugar

Materials/equipment

10-inch round cake board
3 bamboo skewers, 10,
   9½ and 9 inches long
small star cutter
wax paper icing bags
fine writing nozzle
1 yard fine colored ribbon
8 candles

1 Place the cake on the board. Tint scant ½ cup of the fondant icing red, scant ½ cup green and 1 cup yellow. Cover the cake with the remaining icing. Use just under half the yellow icing to cover the board.

2 Using a skewer, pierce the eggs and carefully empty the contents. Wash and dry the shells. Cover them carefully with the tinted fondant and insert a bamboo skewer in each. Use the trimmings to stamp out a star shape of each color. Thread onto the skewers for the balloon knots.

3 Trace 16 balloon shapes onto parchment paper. Beat the egg whites with the confectioner's sugar until smooth and divide among four bowls. Leave one white and tint the others red, green and yellow. With the fine writing nozzle and white icing, trace around the balloon shapes. Thin the tinted icings with water. Fill the run-outs using cut icing bags. Let dry overnight.

4 Stick the run-outs around the side of the cake with icing. Pipe white balloon strings. Push the large balloons into the center and decorate with the ribbon. Push the candles into the icing around the edge.

Number 6 Cake

Use the round cake pan as a guide to cut the square cake to fit neatly around the round cake.

Serves 10–12

6-inch round and 6-inch
   square sponge cakes
½ cup butter icing
4 tablespoons apricot
   jam, warmed and
   strained
3 cups marzipan
3¾ cups fondant icing
yellow and green food
   coloring
¾ cup royal icing

Materials/equipment

10 x 14-inch cake board
2 small wax paper icing
   bags
3-inch fluted cutter
No 1 plain and No 8 star
   nozzles
plastic train set with 6
   candles

1 Split and fill the cakes with butter icing. Cut the square cake in half and cut, using the round cake pan as a guide, a rounded end from one rectangle to fit around the round cake. Trim the cakes to the same depth and assemble the number on the cake board. Brush with apricot jam and cover with a thin layer of marzipan.

2 Tint 3 cups of the fondant icing yellow and the rest green. Cover the cake with the yellow icing. With the cutter, mark a circle in the center of the round cake. Cut out a green fondant icing circle. Stick in place with water and let dry overnight.

3 Mark a track the width of the train on the top of the cake. Tint the royal icing yellow and pipe the track with the plain nozzle. Use the star nozzle to pipe a border around the bottom and top of the cake. Pipe the name on the green circle and attach the train and candles with royal icing.

Spider's Web Cake

Make the marzipan spider several days before you need the cake to give it time to dry.

Makes one 8-inch round cake

8-inch round deep sponge cake

1 cup butter icing

3 tablespoons apricot jam, warmed and strained

2 tablespoons cocoa

chocolate vermicelli

4 tablespoons marzipan

yellow, red, black and brown food coloring

1½ cups confectioner's sugar

1–2 tablespoons water

Materials/equipment

10-inch round cake board

2 small wax paper icing bags

wooden toothpick

star nozzle

8 candles and holders

1 Split and fill the cake with half the butter icing. Brush the sides with apricot jam, add the cocoa to the remaining butter icing then smooth a little over the sides of the cake. Roll the sides of the cake in chocolate vermicelli. Place on the board.

2 For the spider, tint the marzipan yellow. Roll half of it into two balls for the head and body. Tint a small piece red and make three balls and a mouth. Tint a tiny piece black for the eyes. Roll the rest of the marzipan into eight legs and two smaller feelers. Stick together.

3 Gently heat the confectioner's sugar and water over a saucepan of hot water. Use two-thirds of the glacé icing to cover the cake top.

4 Tint the remaining glacé icing brown and use it to pipe concentric circles onto the cake. Divide the web into eighths by drawing lines across with a toothpick. Let set.

5 Put the rest of the chocolate butter icing into an icing bag fitted with a star nozzle and pipe a border around the web. Put candles around the border and the spider in the center.

Dart Board

Makes one 10-inch round cake

10-inch round sponge cake

¾ cup butter icing

3 tablespoons apricot jam, warmed and strained

3 cups marzipan

3 cups fondant icing

¾ cup royal icing

black, red, yellow and silver food coloring

Materials/equipment

12-inch round cake board

icing smoother

½-inch plain circle cutter

small wax paper icing bag

No 1 writing nozzle

3 candles and holders

1 Split and fill the cake with butter icing and put onto the board. Brush with jam and cover with marzipan. Color some of the fondant icing black, a small piece red and the remaining yellow. Cover the cake with black fondant icing. Cut an 8-inch circular template out of wax paper. Fold it in quarters, then divide each quarter into fifths.

2 Using the template, mark the center and wedges on the top of the cake with a sharp knife. Cut out ten wedges from the yellow fondant, using the template as a guide. Place on alternate sections but do not stick in place yet. Repeat with the black fondant. Cut ⅛ inch off each wedge and swop the colors. Mark a 5-inch circle in the center of the board and cut out ⅛-inch pieces to swop with adjoining colors. Stick in place and use an icing smoother to flatten.

3 Use the cutter to remove the center for the bull's eye. Replace with a circle of red fondant, cut with the same cutter. Surround it with a strip of black fondant. Roll the remaining black fondant into a long sausage to fit around the bottom of the cake and stick in place with a little water. Mark numbers on the board and pipe on with royal icing. Let dry, then paint with silver food coloring. Stick candles in at an angle to resemble darts.

Camping Tent Cake

Makes one 8 x 4-inch cake

8-inch square sponge
  cake
½ cup butter icing
3 tablespoons apricot
  jam, warmed and
  strained
3 cups marzipan
3¾ cups fondant icing
brown, orange, green, red
  and blue food coloring
¾ cup royal icing
1 cup dried coconut
chocolate mint sticks

Materials/equipment
10-inch square cake
  board
wooden toothpicks
fine paintbrush
4 small wax paper icing
  bags
No 1 basketweave and
  plain nozzles

1 Split and fill the cake with butter icing. Cut the cake in half. Cut one half in two diagonally from the top right edge to the bottom left edge to form the roof of the tent. Stick the two wedges, back-to-back, on top of the rectangle with jam. Trim to 4 inches high and use the trimmings on the bottom. Place the cake diagonally on the board and brush with jam.

2 Cover with marzipan, reserving some for modeling. Tint scant ½ cup of the fondant icing brown and cover one end of the tent. Tint the rest orange and cover the rest of the cake. Cut a semicircle for the tent opening and a central 3-inch slit. Lay over the brown end. Secure the flaps with royal icing. Put halved toothpicks in the corners and ridge.

3 Tint the coconut green. Spread the board with a thin layer of royal icing and sprinkle with the coconut.

4 Tint the reserved marzipan flesh-color and use to make a model of a child. Paint on a blue T-shirt and let dry. Tint some royal icing brown and pipe on the hair with a basketweave nozzle. Tint the icing and pipe on the mouth and eyes. Make a bonfire with broken chocolate mint sticks.

Army Tank Cake

Create an authentic camouflaged tank by combining green and brown fondant icing.

Makes one 10 x 6-inch cake

10-inch square sponge
  cake
1 cup butter icing
3 tablespoons apricot
  jam, warmed and
  strained
3 cups marzipan
3 cups fondant icing
brown, green and black
  food coloring

chocolate flake
liquorice strips
4 tablespoons royal icing
round cookies
candies

Materials/equipment
10 x 14 -inch cake board

1 Split and fill the sponge cake with butter icing. Cut off a 4-inch strip from one side of the cake. Use the off-cut to make a 6 x 3-inch rectangle, and stick on the top.

2 Shape the sloping top and cut a 1-inch piece from both ends between the tracks. Shape the rounded ends for the wheels and tracks. Place on the cake board and brush with apricot jam. Cover with a layer of marzipan.

3 Tint a quarter of the fondant icing brown and the rest green. Roll out the green to a 10-inch square. Break small pieces of brown icing and place all over the green. Flatten and roll out together to give a camouflage effect. Turn the icing over and repeat.

4 Continue to roll out until the icing is ⅛ inch thick. Lay it over the cake and gently press to fit. Cut away the excess. Cut a piece into a 2½-inch disc and stick on the top with a little water. Cut a small hole in it for the gun and insert the chocolate flake. Stick liquorice on for the tracks, using a little black royal icing. Stick on cookies for the wheels and candies for the lights and portholes.

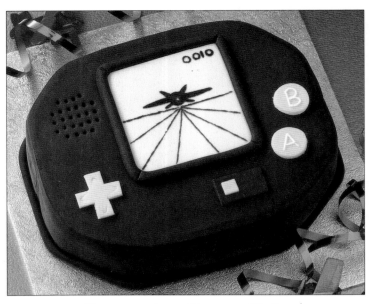

Computer Game Cake

Making a cake look like a computer is easier than you think. This cake is ideal for a computer game fan.

Makes one 5½ x 5-inch cake

6-inch square sponge
   cake
½ cup butter icing
3 tablespoons apricot
   jam, warmed and
   strained
1½ cups marzipan
scant 2 cups fondant
   icing
black, blue, red and
   yellow food coloring

royal icing, to decorate

Materials/equipment
8-inch square cake board
wooden toothpick
fine paintbrush
small wax paper icing
   bag

1 Split and fill the cake with a little butter icing. Cut 1 inch off one side of the cake and ½ inch off the other side. Round the corners slightly. Place on the cake board and brush with apricot jam. Cover with a layer of marzipan.

2 Tint 1½ cups of the fondant black. Use to cover the cake. Reserve the trimmings. With a toothpick, mark the speaker holes and position of the screen and knobs.

3 Tint half the remaining fondant pale blue, roll and cut out a 2½-inch square for the screen. Stick in the center of the game with a little water. Tint a small piece of fondant red and the remainder yellow. Use to cut out the switch and controls. Stick them in position with water. Roll the reserved black fondant icing into a long, thin sausage and edge the screen and bottom of the cake.

4 With a fine paintbrush, draw the game onto the screen with a little blue coloring. Pipe letters onto the buttons with royal icing.

Chessboard Cake

To make this cake look most effective, make sure that the squares have very sharp edges.

Makes one 10-inch square cake

10-inch square sponge
   cake
1 cup butter icing
4 tablespoons apricot
   jam, warmed and
   strained
5¼ cups marzipan
3¾ cups fondant icing
black and red food
   coloring

edible silver balls
¾ cup royal icing

Materials/equipment
12-inch square cake
   board
small wax paper icing
   bag
No 8 star nozzle

1 Split and fill the cake with butter icing. Place on the board and brush with jam. Roll out 3 cups of marzipan and use to cover the cake. Then cover with 3 cups of the fondant icing. Let dry overnight.

2 Divide the remaining marzipan into two, and tint black and red. To shape the chess pieces, roll 4 tablespoons of each color into a sausage and cut into eight equal pieces. Shape into pawns.

3 Divide generous 4 tablespoons of each color into six equal pieces and use to shape into two castles, two knights and two bishops.

4 Divide 2 tablespoons of each color marzipan in half and shape a queen and a king. Decorate with silver balls. Let dry overnight.

5 Cut ½-inch black strips of marzipan to edge the board, and stick in place with water. Pipe a border around the bottom of the cake with royal icing. Place the chess pieces in position.

Kite Cake

The happy face on this cheerful kite is a great favorite with kids of all ages.

Serves 10–12

10-inch square sponge cake
1 cup butter icing
3 tablespoons apricot jam, warmed and strained
4½ cups fondant icing yellow, red, green, blue and black food coloring
3 cups marzipan
¾ cup royal icing

Materials/equipment
12-inch square cake board
wooden toothpick
small wax paper icing bag
No 8 star nozzle
6 candles and holders

1 Trim the cake into a kite shape, then split and fill with butter icing. Place diagonally on the cake board and brush with apricot jam. Cover with a layer of marzipan

2 Tint 1½ cups of the fondant icing pale yellow and cover the cake. Make a template of the face, tie and buttons and mark onto the cake with a toothpick. Divide the rest of the fondant icing into four and tint red, green, blue and black. Cut out the features and stick on with water.

3 Pipe a royal icing border around the bottom of the cake.

4 For the kite's tail, roll out each color separately and cut two 1½ x ½-inch lengths in blue, red and green. Pinch each length to shape into a bow.

5 Roll the yellow into a long rope and lay it on the board in a wavy line from the narrow end of the kite. Stick the bows in place with water. Roll balls of yellow fondant, stick onto the board with a little royal icing and press in the candles.

Hotdog Cake

Makes one 9-inch long cake

9 x 13-inch jelly roll sponge
¾ cup coffee-flavor butter icing
6 tablespoons apricot jam, warmed and strained
3 cups fondant icing brown and red food coloring
1–2 tablespoons toasted sesame seeds
¾ cup glacé icing

Filling
6 ounces sponge cake pieces
¼ cup dark brown sugar
3 tablespoons orange juice
5 tablespoons honey

Materials/equipment
fine paintbrush
2 small wax paper icing bags
napkin, plate, knife and fork

1 Unroll the jelly roll, spread with butter icing, then roll up again. Slice the jelly roll along the center lengthwise, almost to the bottom and ease the two halves apart.

2 Mix all the filling ingredients in a food processor or blender until smooth. Shape the mixture with your hands to a 9-inch sausage shape.

3 Tint all the fondant icing brown. Set aside scant ½ cup and use the remainder to cover the cake.

4 Paint the top of the "bun" with diluted brown food coloring to give a toasted effect. Position the "sausage."

5 Divide the glacé icing in half. Tint one half brown and the other red. Pipe red icing along the sausage, then overlay with brown icing. Sprinkle the sesame seeds over the bun.

6 Cut the reserved brown fondant icing into thin strips. Place on the cake with the joins under the sausage. Place the cake on a napkin on a serving plate, with a knife and fork.

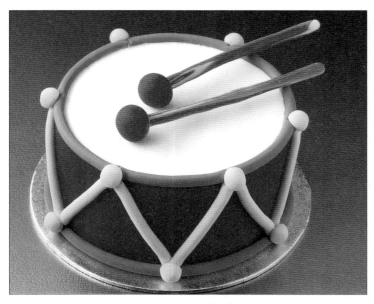

Drum Cake

This is a colorful cake for very young children. It even come complete with drumsticks.

Makes one 6-inch round cake

6-inch round sponge cake
4 tablespoons butter icing
3 tablespoons apricot jam, warmed and strained
2 cups marzipan

3 cups fondant icing
red, blue and yellow food coloring
royal icing, for sticking

Materials/equipment
8-inch round cake board

1 Split and fill the cake with a little butter icing. Place on the cake board and brush with apricot jam. Cover with a layer of marzipan and let dry overnight.

2 Tint half of the fondant icing red and roll it out to a rectangle 10 x 12 inches. Cut in half and stick to the side of the cake with water.

3 Roll out a circle of white fondant icing to fit the top of the cake and divide the rest in half. Tint one half blue and the other yellow. Divide the blue into four pieces and roll into sausages long enough to go halfway around the cake. Stick around the bottom and top of the cake with a little water.

4 Mark the cake into six around the top and bottom. Roll the yellow fondant icing into 12 strands long enough to cross diagonally from top to bottom to form the drum strings. Roll the rest of the yellow icing into 12 small balls and stick where the strings join the drum.

5 Knead together the red and white fondant icing until streaky, then roll two balls and sticks 6 inches long. Let dry overnight. Stick together with royal icing to make the drumsticks and place on top of the cake.

Ice Cream Cones

Individual cakes make a change for a party. Put a candle in the special person's one.

Makes 9

¾ cup marzipan
9 ice cream cones
9 sponge fairy cakes
1½ cups butter icing
red, green and brown food coloring
colored and chocolate vermicelli, wafers and chocolate sticks

candies

Materials/equipment
3 x 12-egg egg boxes
foil

1 Make the stands for the cakes by turning the egg boxes upside down and pressing three balls of marzipan into evenly spaced holes in each box. Wrap the boxes in foil. Pierce the foil above the marzipan balls and insert the cones, pressing them in gently.

2 Gently push a fairy cake into each cone. If the bottoms of the cakes are too large, trim them down with a small, sharp knife. The cakes should be quite secure in the cones.

3 Divide the butter icing into three bowls and tint them pale red, green and brown.

4 Using a small metal spatula, spread each cake with some of one of the icings, making sure that the finish on the icing is a little textured so it looks like ice cream.

5 To insert a wafer or chocolate stick into an ice cream, use a small, sharp knife to make a hole through the icing and into the cake, then insert the wafer or stick. Add the finishing touches to the cakes by sprinkling over some colored and chocolate vermicelli. Arrange candies around the cones.

Treasure Map

Makes one 8 x 10-inch cake

*10-inch square sponge
cake*
1½ cups butter icing
*3 tablespoons apricot
jam, warmed and
strained*
3 cups marzipan
4½ cups fondant icing
*yellow, brown, paprika,
green, black and red
food coloring*
¾ cup royal icing

Materials/equipment
10 x 14-inch cake board
fine paintbrush
paper towels
*4 small wax paper icing
bags*
*No 7 shell and No 1
writing nozzles*
6 candles and holders

1 Split and fill the cake with butter icing, cut it into a
8 x 10-inch rectangle and place on the cake board. Brush with
apricot jam. Cover with a layer of marzipan then with 3 cups
fondant icing.

2 Color the remaining fondant icing yellow and cut out with
an uneven outline. Stick onto the cake with water and let dry
overnight. Mark the island, river, lake, mountains and trees
on the map.

3 With brown and paprika colors and a fine paintbrush,
paint the edges of the map to look old, smudging the colors
together with paper towels. Paint the island pale green and
the water around the island, the river and the lake pale blue.
Dry overnight before painting on the other details, otherwise
the colors will run.

4 Pipe a border of royal icing around the bottom of the cake
with a shell nozzle. Color a little royal icing red and pipe the
path to the treasure, marked with an "X." Color some icing
green and pipe on grass and trees. Finally color some icing
black and pipe on a North sign with the writing nozzle.

Royal Crown Cake

This regal cake is sure to delight any prince or princess.

Serves 16–20

*8-inch and 6-inch round
sponge cake*
¾ cup butter icing
*3 tablespoons apricot
jam, warmed and
strained*
3 cups marzipan
3¾ cups fondant icing
red food coloring
3 cups royal icing

small black jelly candies
4 ice cream fan wafers
edible silver balls
jewel candies

Materials/equipment
*12-inch square cake
board*
wooden toothpicks

1 Split and fill the cakes with butter icing. Sandwich one on
top of the other and place on the board. Shape the top cake
into a dome.

2 Brush the cake with apricot jam and cover with marzipan.
Set aside ¾ cup of the fondant icing and use the remainder to
cover the cake.

3 Tint the reserved fondant icing red, and use to cover the
dome of the cake. Trim away the excess.

4 Spoon uneven mounds of royal icing around the bottom of
the cake and stick a black jelly candy on each mound.

5 Cut the ice cream wafers in half. Spread both sides of the
wafers with royal icing and stick to the cake, smoothing the
icing level with the sides of the cake.

6 Use toothpicks to support the wafers until they are dry.
Put silver balls on top of each point and stick jewel candies
around the side of the crown with a little royal icing.

Box of Chocolates Cake

This sophisticated cake is perfect for an adult's birthday and will delight chocolate lovers.

Makes one 6-inch square cake

6-inch square sponge
  cake
4 tablespoons butter
  icing
2 tablespoons apricot
  jam, warmed and
  strained
2¼ cups marzipan
2¼ cups fondant icing

red food coloring
wrapped chocolates

Materials/equipment
8-inch square cake board
small paper sweet cases
1½ yards x 1½-inch wide
  gold and red ribbon

1 Split and fill the cake with butter icing. Cut a shallow square from the top of the cake, leaving a ¼-inch border around the edge. Place on the cake board and brush with apricot jam. Cover with a layer of marzipan.

2 Roll out the fondant icing and cut a 7-inch square. Ease it into the hollow dip and trim. Tint the remaining fondant icing red and use to cover the sides.

3 Put the chocolates into paper cases and arrange in the box. Tie the ribbon around the sides and tie a big bow.

Strawberry Cake

Makes one 2-pound cake

scant 4½ cups marzipan
green, red and yellow
  food coloring
2 tablespoons apricot
  jam, warmed and
  strained
2-pound heart-shape
  sponge cake

superfine sugar, for
  dusting

Materials/equipment
12-inch round cake board
icing smoother
teaspoon

1 Tint generous 1 cup of the marzipan green. Brush the cake board with apricot jam, roll out the green marzipan and use to cover the board. Trim the edges. Use an icing smoother to flatten and smooth the marzipan.

2 Brush the remaining apricot jam over the top and sides of the cake. Position the cake on the cake board. Tint scant 2 cups of the remaining marzipan red. Roll it out to ¼ inch thick and use to cover the cake, smoothing down the sides. Trim the edges. Use the handle of a teaspoon to indent the "strawberry" evenly and lightly all over.

3 For the stalk, tint generous 1 cup of the marzipan bright green. Cut it in half and roll out one portion into a 4 x 6-inch rectangle. Cut "V" shapes out of the rectangle, leaving a 1-inch border across the top, to form the calyx. Position on the cake, curling the "V" shapes to make them look realistic.

4 Roll the rest of the green marzipan into a sausage shape 5 inches long. Bend it slightly, then position it on the board to form the stalk.

5 For the strawberry pips, tint the remaining marzipan yellow. Pull off tiny pieces and roll them into tear-shape pips. Place them in the indentations all over the strawberry. Dust the cake and board with sifted sugar.

Gift-wrapped Package

If you don't have a tiny flower cutter for the "wrapping paper" design, then press a small decorative button into the icing while still soft to create a pattern.

Makes one 6-inch square cake

6-inch square cake
4 tablespoons butter icing
3 tablespoons apricot jam, warmed and strained
3 cups marzipan
2¼ cups pale lemon yellow fondant icing

red and green food coloring
2 tablespoons royal icing

Materials/equipment
8-inch square cake board
small flower cutter (optional)

1 Split and fill the cake with butter icing. Place on the cake board and brush with jam. Cover with half the marzipan, then yellow fondant and mark with a small flower cutter.

2 Divide the remaining marzipan in half, color one half pink and the other pale green. Roll out the pink marzipan and cut into four 1 x 7-inch strips. Roll out the green marzipan and cut into four ½-inch strips the same length. Center the green strips on top of the pink strips and stick onto the cake with a little water. Cut two 2-inch strips from each color and cut a "V" from the ends to form the ends of the ribbon. Stick in place and let dry overnight.

3 Cut the rest of the green into four 1 x 3-inch lengths and the pink into four ½ x 3-inch lengths. Center the pink on top of the green, fold in half, stick the ends together and slip over the handle of a wooden spoon, dusted with cornstarch. Let dry overnight.

4 Cut the ends in "V" shapes to fit neatly together on the cake. Cut two pieces for the join in the center. Remove the bows from the spoon and stick in position with royal icing.

Sweetheart Cake

The heart-shape run-outs can be made a week before the cake is made to make sure that they are completely dry.

Makes one 8-inch round cake

8-inch round sponge cake
½ cup butter icing
3 tablespoons apricot jam, warmed and strained
3 cups marzipan
4½ cups fondant icing
red food coloring
¾ cup royal icing

Materials/equipment
10-inch round cake board
spoon with decorative handle
small wax paper icing bag
No 1 writing nozzle
8 candles and holders
1½ yards x 1-inch wide ribbon

1 Split and fill the cake with butter icing. Place on the cake board and brush with apricot jam. Cover with a layer of marzipan. Tint the fondant icing pale pink and cover the cake and board. Mark the edge with the decorative handle of a spoon.

2 Tint the royal icing dark pink. Make a heart-shape template and use to pipe the run-outs on wax paper. Using a No 1 writing nozzle, pipe the outlines in a continuous line. Then fill in until the hearts are rounded. You will need eight for the cake top. Let dry for at least 2 days.

3 Arrange the hearts on top of the cake and place the candles in the center. Tie the ribbon around the cake.

Rosette Cake

This cake is quick to decorate and looks truly professional.

Makes one 8-inch square cake

8-inch square sponge cake	**Materials/equipment**
2 cups butter icing	10-inch square cake board
4 tablespoons apricot jam, warmed and strained	serrated scraper
	icing bag
mulberry red food coloring	No 8 star nozzle
candied violets	4 candles and holders

1 Split and fill the cake with a little butter icing. Place in the center of the cake board and brush with apricot jam. Tint the remaining butter icing dark pink. Spread the top and sides with butter icing.

2 Using the serrated scraper, hold it against the cake and move it from side to side across the top to make waves. Hold the scraper against the side of the cake, resting the flat edge on the board and draw it along to give straight ridges along each side.

3 Put the rest of the butter icing into an icing bag fitted with a No 8 star nozzle. Mark a 6-inch circle on the top of the cake and pipe stars around it and around the bottom of the cake. Place the candles and violets in the corners.

Number 10 Cake

This is a very simple cake to decorate. If you can't master the shell edge, pipe stars instead.

Makes one 8-inch tall round cake

8-inch and 6-inch round sponge cakes	**Materials/equipment**
2 cups butter icing	10-inch round cake board
5 tablespoons apricot jam, warmed and strained	wooden toothpick
	plastic "10" cake decoration
colored vermicelli	small wax paper icing bag
cream food coloring	No 7 shell and No 7 star nozzles
	10 candles and holders

1 Split and fill both cakes with a little butter icing. Brush the sides with apricot jam. When cold, spread a layer of butter icing on the sides then roll in colored vermicelli to cover.

2 Tint the rest of the icing cream, spread over the top of each cake. Place the small cake on top of the large cake. Using a toothpick, make a pattern in the icing on top of the cake.

3 Using the remaining icing, pipe around the bottom of the cakes and around the edge. Stick the "10" decoration in the center of the top tier and two candles on either side. Arrange the other candles evenly around the bottom cake.

Shirt and Tie Cake

Makes one 7½ x 10½-inch cake

coffee sponge cake, baked
   in a 7½ x 5-inch loaf
   pan
1½ cups coffee-flavor
   butter icing
6 tablespoons apricot
   jam, warmed and
   strained
generous 7 cups fondant
   icing
blue food coloring
1 cup confectioner's
   sugar, sifted

3–4 tablespoons water

Materials/equipment
15½ x 12-inch cake board
steel ruler
small wax paper icing
   bag
small round nozzle
cardboard collar template
"Happy Birthday"
   decoration
tissue paper (optional)

1 Cut the cake in half horizontally and sandwich together
with the butter icing. Brush the cake with apricot jam. Color
4½ cups fondant icing light blue and roll out to about ¼ inch
thick. Use to cover the whole cake. Trim away any excess
icing. Place the cake on the cake board.

2 Using a steel ruler, make grooves down the length and
sides of the cake, about 1 inch apart. Mix the confectioner's
sugar and water to make an icing to pipe into the grooves.

3 To make the collar, roll out 1½ cups fondant icing to a
16½ x 4-inch rectangle. Lay the piece of cardboard for the
collar on top. Brush water around the edges, then carefully lift
one edge over the cardboard to encase it completely. Trim the
two short ends to match the angles of the cardboard. Lift the
collar and gently bend it around and position on the cake.

4 Color 1 cup fondant icing dark blue. Cut off one-third and
shape into a tie knot. Position the knot. Roll out the rest to
about ½ inch thick. Cut out a tie piece to fit under the knot
and long enough to hang over the edge of the cake. Position
the tie piece, tucking it under the knot and securing in place
with a little water. Finish the cake with the "Happy Birthday"
decoration and tissue paper, if using.

Mobile Phone Cake

Makes one 9 x 5-inch cake

sponge cake, baked in a
   9 x 5-inch loaf pan
2 tablespoons apricot
   jam, warmed and
   strained
2¼ cups fondant icing
black food coloring
10 small square candies
2 striped liquorice sweets
2–3 tablespoons
   confectioner's sugar

½–1 teaspoon water

Materials/equipment
10 x 7-inch cake board
diamond-shaped cookie
   cutter
small piece of foil
small wax paper icing
   bag .
small, round nozzle

1 Turn the cake upside-down. Make a 1-inch diagonal cut
1 inch from one end. Cut down vertically to remove the
wedge. Remove the middle of the cake to the wedge depth up
to 1½ inches from the other end.

2 Place the cake on the board and brush with apricot jam.
Tint 1¼ cups of the fondant icing black. Use to cover the cake,
smoothing it over the carved shape. Reserve the trimmings.

3 Tint ½ cup of the fondant icing gray. Cut a piece to fit the
hollowed center, leaving a ½-inch border, and another piece
1-inch square. Stamp out the center of the square with the
cutter. Secure all the pieces on the cake with water.

4 Position the candies and the foil for the display pad. For
the glacé icing, mix the confectioner's sugar with the water
and tint black. With the small, round nozzle, pipe border lines
around the edges of the phone, including the gray pieces of
fondant. Pipe the numbers on the keys.

5 Roll a sausage shape from the reserved black fondant for
the aerial. Indent one side of the top with a knife and secure
the aerial with water.

Heart Cake

Makes one 8-inch heart-shape cake

3 egg whites
1¾ cups superfine sugar
2 tablespoons cold water
2 tablespoons fresh
    lemon juice
¼ teaspoon cream of
    tartar
red food coloring
8-inch heart-shape
    sponge cake

¾–1 cup confectioner's
    sugar

Materials/equipment
12-inch square cake
    board
small wax paper icing
    bag
small nozzle

1 Make the icing by combining 2 of the egg whites, the superfine sugar, water, lemon juice and cream of tartar in the top of a double boiler or in a bowl set over simmering water. With an electric mixer, beat until thick and holding soft peaks, about 7 minutes. Remove from the heat and continue beating until the mixture is thick enough to spread. Color the icing pale pink.

2 Put the cake on the cake board and spread the icing evenly on the cake. Smooth the top and sides. Let set for 3–4 hours, or overnight.

3 Place 1 tablespoon of the remaining egg white in a bowl and whisk until frothy. Gradually beat in enough confectioner's sugar to make a stiff mixture suitable for piping.

4 Spoon the white icing into an icing bag and pipe the decorations on the top and sides of the cake as shown in the photograph above.

Bowl-of-Strawberries Cake

The strawberry theme of the painting is carried on into the molded decorations on this summery birthday cake.

Makes one 8-inch petal-shape cake

1½ cups butter icing
red, yellow, green and
    claret food coloring
8-inch petal-shape
    Madeira cake
3 tablespoons apricot
    jam, warmed and
    strained
4½ cups fondant icing
yellow powder tint

Materials/equipment
10-inch petal-shape cake
    board
paint palette or small
    saucers
fine paintbrushes
thin red and green
    ribbons

1 Tint the butter icing pink. Cut the cake horizontally into three. Sandwich together with the butter icing. Brush the cake with apricot jam. Use 3¾ cups of the fondant icing to cover the cake. Place on the cake board and let dry overnight.

2 For the strawberries, tint three-quarters of the remaining fondant icing red, and equal portions of the rest yellow and green. Make the strawberries, securing with water, if necessary. Let dry on wax paper.

3 Put the red, green, yellow and claret food coloring in a palette and water them down slightly. Paint the bowl and strawberries, using yellow powder tint to highlight the bowl.

4 Decorate the cake with the ribbons. Secure two strawberries to the top of the cake, and arrange the others around the bottom.

Barley Twist Cake

Makes one 8-inch round cake

8-inch round sponge cake	**Materials/equipment**
½ cup butter icing	10-inch round cake board
3 tablespoons apricot	wooden toothpick
jam, warmed and	fine paintbrush
strained	No 1 plain nozzle
3 cups marzipan	small wax paper icing
3 cups pale yellow	bags
fondant icing	6 small blue bows
¾ cup white fondant	
icing	
¾ cup royal icing	
blue food coloring	
pink dusting powder	

1 Split and fill the cake with butter icing. Place on the board and brush with jam. Cover with marzipan, then yellow fondant icing, extending it over the board. Mark six equidistant points around the cake with a toothpick.

2 Color 1 tablespoon of white fondant icing pale blue and roll out thinly. Moisten a paintbrush with water and brush lightly over it. Roll out the same quantity of white icing, lay on top and press together. Roll out to an 8-inch square.

3 Cut ¼-inch strips, carefully twist each one, moisten the six marked points around the cake with water and drape each barley twist into place, pressing lightly to stick to the cake.

4 Cut out a sweater shape from white icing and stick on with water. Roll some icing into a ball and color a small amount dark blue. Roll into two tapering 3-inch needles with a small ball at the end. Let dry overnight. Stick the needles and ball in position. Using royal icing and a No 1 nozzle, pipe the stitches and wool in position. Pipe a white border around the bottom of the cake. Stick small bows around the edge of the cake with a little royal icing and carefully brush the knitting with red powder tint.

Tablecloth Cake

Makes one 8-inch round cake

8-inch round sponge cake	**Materials/equipment**
½ cup butter icing	10-inch round cake board
3 tablespoons apricot	spoon with decorative
jam, warmed and	handle
strained	8 wooden toothpicks
3 cups marzipan	sharp needle
4½ cups fondant icing	skewer
¾ cup royal icing	8 red ribbon bows
red food coloring	small wax paper icing
	bags
	No 2 and No 0 plain
	nozzles

1 Split and fill the cake with butter icing. Place on the board and brush with apricot jam. Cover with a layer of marzipan. Tint 3 cups of the fondant icing red and cover the cake and board. Roll the rest of the red fondant into a thin rope long enough to go around the cake. Stick around the bottom of the cake with water. Mark with the decorative handle of a spoon. Let dry overnight.

2 Roll out the remaining icing to a 10-inch circle and trim. Lay this icing over the cake and drape the "cloth" over the wooden toothpicks set at equidistant points.

3 Mark a 4-inch circle in the center of the cake. Make a template of the flower design and transfer to the cake with a needle. Use a skewer to make the flowers; the red color should show through.

4 Remove the toothpicks and stick on the bows with royal icing. With a No 2 plain nozzle and white royal icing, pipe around the circle in the center. With a No 0 plain nozzle, pipe small dots around the edge of the cloth. Color some royal icing red and pipe a name in the center.

Pizza Cake

Quick-and-easy, this really is a definite winner for pizza fans everywhere.

Makes one 9-inch round cake

9-inch shallow sponge
  cake
1½ cups butter icing
red and green food
  coloring
generous 1 cup yellow
  marzipan
4 tablespoons fondant
  icing

1 tablespoon dried
  coconut

Materials/equipment
10-inch pizza plate
cheese grater
leaf cutter

1 Place the cake on the pizza plate. Tint the butter icing red and spread evenly over the cake, leaving a ½-inch border.

2 Knead the marzipan for a few minutes, to soften slightly, then grate it like cheese, and sprinkle all over the top of the red butter icing.

3 Tint the fondant icing green. Use the leaf cutter to cut out two leaf shapes. Mark the veins with the back of a knife and place on the pizza cake.

4 For the chopped herbs, tint the dried coconut dark green. Then sprinkle over the pizza cake.

Flowerpot Cake

Makes one round cake

Madeira cake, baked in a
  5-cup ovenproof bowl
½ cup jam
¾ cup butter icing
2 tablespoons apricot
  jam, warmed and
  strained
4¼ cups fondant icing
¾ cup royal icing
dark orange-red, red,
  silver, green, purple
  and yellow food
  coloring

2 chocolate flakes,
  coarsely crushed

Materials/equipment
fine paintbrush
wooden spoon

1 Slice the cake into three layers and stick together again with jam and butter icing. Cut out a shallow circle from the cake top, leaving a ½-inch rim. Brush the outside of the cake and rim with apricot jam. Tint 2¼ cups of the fondant orange-red and cover the cake, molding it over the rim. Reserve the trimmings. Let dry.

2 Use the trimmings to make decorations and handles for the flowerpot. Let dry on wax paper. Sprinkle the chocolate flakes into the pot for soil.

3 Tint a small piece of fondant very pale orange-red. Use to make a seed bag. When dry, paint on a pattern in food coloring. Tint two small pieces of icing red and silver. Make a trowel and dry over a wooden spoon handle.

4 Tint the remaining icing green, purple and a small piece yellow. Use to make the flowers and leaves, attaching together with royal icing. Score leaf veins with the back of a knife. Let dry on wax paper.

5 Attach all the decorations to the flowerpot and arrange the plant, seed bag and trowel with soil, seeds and grass made from leftover tinted fondant.

Glittering Star Cake

With a quick flick of a paintbrush you can give a sparkling effect to this glittering cake.

Makes one 8-inch round cake

8-inch round rich fruit cake
2½ tablespoons apricot jam, warmed and strained
4½ cups marzipan
4 cups fondant icing
¾ cup royal icing

silver, gold, lilac-shimmer, red-sparkle, glitter-green and primrose-sparkle food coloring and powder tints

Materials/equipment
paintbrush
10-inch round cake board

1 Brush the cake with the apricot jam. Use two-thirds of the marzipan to cover the cake. Let dry overnight.

2 Cover the cake with the fondant icing. Let dry.

3 Place the cake on a large sheet of wax paper. Dilute a little powdered silver food coloring and, using a loaded paintbrush, flick it all over the cake to give a spattered effect. Let dry.

4 Make templates of two different-size moon shapes and three irregular star shapes. Divide the remaining marzipan into six pieces and tint silver, gold, lilac, pink, green and yellow. Cut into stars and moons using the templates as a guide, cutting some of the stars in half.

5 Place the cut-outs on wax paper and brush each with its own color powder tint. Let dry.

6 Secure the cake on the board with royal icing. Arrange the stars and moons at different angles all over the cake, attaching with royal icing, and position the halved stars upright as though coming out of the cake. Let set.

Racing Ring Cake

Serves 12

ring mold sponge cake
1½ cups butter icing
4⅛ cups fondant icing
¾ cup royal icing, for fixing
black, blue, yellow, green, orange, red, purple food coloring
selection of liquorice candies, dolly mixtures and teddy bears

4½-ounce package liquorice Catherine wheels

Materials/equipment
10-inch round cake board
wooden kebab skewer
fine paintbrush

1 Cut the cake in half horizontally and fill with some butter icing. Cover the outside with the remaining butter icing.

2 Use 2¼ cups of fondant icing to coat the top and inside of the cake. Use the trimmings to roll an oblong for the flag. Cut the skewer to 15 inches and fold one end of the flag around it, securing with water. Paint on the pattern with black food coloring. Color a ball of icing black, and stick on top of the skewer. Make a few folds and let dry.

3 Color the remaining fondant icing blue, yellow, green, orange, red and a very small amount purple. Shape each car in two pieces, attaching in the center with royal icing where the seat joins the body of the car. Add decorations and headlights and attach dolly mixture wheels with royal icing. Place a teddy bear in each car and Let set.

4 Unwind the Catherine wheels and remove the center sweets. Fix them to the top of the cake with royal icing. Secure one strip round the bottom. Cut some of the liquorice into small strips and attach round the middle of the outside of the cake with royal icing. Arrange small liquorice sweets around the bottom of the cake. Position the cars on top of the cake on the tracks and attach the flag to the outside with royal icing.

Artist's Cake

Making cakes is an art in itself, and this cake proves it!

Makes one 8-inch square cake

8-inch square rich fruit
   cake
3 tablespoons apricot
   jam, warmed and
   strained
3 cups marzipan
5¼ cups fondant icing
¾ cup royal icing
chestnut, yellow, blue,
   black, silver, paprika,
   green and mulberry
   food coloring

Materials/equipment
10-inch square cake
   board
fine paintbrush

1 Brush the cake with the apricot jam. Cover in marzipan and let dry overnight.

2 Make a template of a painter's palette that will fit the cake top. Tint generous 1 cup of the fondant very pale chestnut. Cut out the palette shape, place on wax paper and let dry overnight.

3 Tint 3 cups of the fondant icing dark chestnut, cover the cake and secure it to the board with royal icing. Let dry.

4 Divide half the remaining fondant icing into seven equal parts and tint yellow, blue, black, silver, paprika, green and mulberry. Make all the decorative pieces for the box and palette, using the remaining white fondant for the paint tubes. Let dry on wax paper.

5 Paint black markings on the paint tubes and chestnut wood markings on the box.

6 Position all the fondant pieces on the cake and board using royal icing. Let dry.

Liquorice Candy Cake

Makes one 8-inch square cake

8-inch and 6-inch square
   Madeira cakes
3 cups butter icing
3 tablespoons apricot
   jam, warmed and
   strained
2¼ cups marzipan
5¼ cups fondant icing

egg-yellow, black, blue
   and mulberry food
   coloring

Materials/equipment
10-inch square cake
   board
1¾-inch round cutter

1 Cut both cakes horizontally into three. Fill with butter icing, reserving a little to coat the smaller cake. Wrap and set aside the smaller cake. Brush the larger cake with apricot jam. Cover with marzipan and secure on the cake board with butter icing. Let dry overnight.

2 Tint 2¼ cups of the fondant icing yellow. Take ¾ cup of the fondant icing and tint half black and leave the other half white. Cover the top and a third of the sides of the cake with yellow fondant icing.

3 Use the white icing to cover the lower third of the sides of the cake. Use the black icing to fill the central third.

4 Cut the smaller cake into three equal strips. Divide two of the strips into three squares each. Cut out two circles from the third strip, using a cutter as a guide.

5 Tint ¾ cup of the remaining fondant black. Divide the rest into four equal portions, leave one white and tint the others blue, pink and yellow.

6 Coat the outsides of the cake cut-outs with the reserved butter icing. Use the tinted and white fondant to cover the pieces to resemble candies. Make small rolls from the trimmings. Arrange on and around the cake.

Sun Cake

Makes one 8-inch star-shaped cake

2 8 x 2-inch sponge cakes
2 tablespoons sweet
   butter
4 cups sifted
   confectioner's sugar
½ cup apricot jam
2 tablespoons water
2 large egg whites
1–2 drops glycerine

juice of 1 lemon
yellow and orange food
   coloring

Materials/equipment
16-inch square cake
   board
fabric icing bag
small star nozzle

1   Cut one of the cakes into eight wedges. Trim the outsides to fit around the other cake. Make butter icing with the butter and 2 tablespoons of the confectioner's sugar. Place the whole cake on the board and attach the sunbeams with butter icing.

2   Melt the jam with the water and brush over the cake.

3   For the icing, beat the egg whites until stiff. Gradually add the confectioner's sugar, glycerine and lemon juice, and beat for 1 minute. Tint yellow and spread over the cake. Tint the remaining icing bright yellow and orange. Pipe the details onto the cake.

Strawberry Basket Cake

Makes one small rectangular cake

sponge cake baked in a
   3-cup loaf pan
3 tablespoons apricot
   jam, warmed and
   strained
4½ cups marzipan
1½ cups chocolate-flavor
   butter icing
red food coloring
4 tablespoons superfine
   sugar

Materials/equipment
small star nozzle
small wax paper icing
   bag
10 plastic strawberry
   stalks
12 x 3-inch strip foil
12 inches thin red ribbon

1   Level the top of the cake and make it perfectly flat. Score a ¼-inch border around the edge and scoop out the inside to make a shallow hollow.

2   Brush the sides and border edges of the cake with apricot jam. Roll out scant 2 cups of the marzipan, cut into rectangles and use to cover the sides of the cake, overlapping the borders. Press the edges together to seal.

3   Using the star nozzle, pipe vertical lines 1 inch apart all around the sides of the cake. Pipe short horizontal lines of butter icing alternately crossing over and then stopping at the vertical lines to give a basketweave effect. Pipe a decorative line of icing around the top edge of the basket to finish.

4   Tint the remaining marzipan red and mold it into ten strawberry shapes. Roll in the superfine sugar and press a plastic stalk into each top. Arrange in the "basket."

5   For the basket handle, fold the foil into a thin strip and wind the ribbon around it to cover. Bend up the ends and then bend into a curve. Push the ends into the sides of the cake. Decorate with bows made from the ribbon.

Banana Gingerbread Slices

Bananas make this spicy bake delightfully moist. The flavor develops on keeping, so store the gingerbread for a few days before cutting, if possible.

Makes 20 slices

2¹/₂ cups all-purpose
   flour
4 teaspoons ground
   ginger
2 teaspoons mixed spice
1 teaspoon baking soda
¹/₂ cup light brown sugar
4 tablespoons corn oil
2 tablespoons molasses

2 tablespoons malt
   extract
2 eggs, beaten
4 tablespoons orange
   juice
3 ripe bananas
scant 1 cup raisins or
   golden raisins

1 Preheat the oven to 350°F. Line and grease a 11 x 7-inch baking pan.

2 Sift the flour, spices and baking soda into a mixing bowl. Spoon some of the mixture back into the sifter, add the brown sugar and sift the mixture back into the bowl.

3 Make a well in the center of the dry ingredients and add the oil, molasses, malt extract, eggs, and orange juice. Mix together thoroughly.

4 Mash the bananas in a bowl. Add to the gingerbread mixture with the raisins or golden raisins. Mix well.

5 Scrape the mixture into the prepared pan. Bake for 35–40 minutes or until the center springs back when the surface of the cake is lightly pressed.

6 Let the gingerbread stand in the pan to cool for 5 minutes, then turn onto a wire rack, remove the lining paper and let cool completely. Cut into 20 slices to serve.

Banana and Apricot Chelsea Buns

Old favorites get a new twist with a delectable filling.

Serves 9

2 cups bread flour
2 teaspoons mixed spice
¹/₂ teaspoon salt
2 tablespoons soft
   margarine
1¹/₂ teaspoons fast-rising
   dried yeast
¹/₄ cup superfine sugar
6 tablespoons hand-hot
   milk
1 egg, beaten

For the filling
1 large, ripe banana
1 cup ready-to-eat dried
   apricots
2 tablespoons light
   brown sugar

For the glaze
2 tablespoons superfine
   sugar
2 tablespoons water

1 Grease a 7-inch square cake pan. Prepare the filling. Mash the banana in a bowl. Using kitchen scissors, cut in the apricots, then stir in the brown sugar. Mix well.

2 Sift the flour, spice and salt into a mixing bowl. Work in the margarine, then stir in the yeast and sugar. Make a well in the center and pour in the milk and the egg. Mix to a soft dough, adding a little extra milk, if necessary.

3 Turn the dough onto a floured surface and knead for 5 minutes until smooth and elastic. Roll out to a 12 x 9-inch rectangle. Spread the filling over the dough and roll up lengthwise like a jelly roll, with the join underneath. Cut into nine pieces and place cut-side downward in the pan. Cover and let stand in a warm place until doubled in size.

4 Preheat the oven to 400°F. Bake the Chelsea buns for 20–25 minutes until golden brown. Meanwhile make the glaze: mix the superfine sugar and water in a small saucepan. Heat, stirring, until dissolved, then boil for 2 minutes. Brush the glaze over the buns while still hot, then remove from the tin and cool on a wire rack.

Lemon Sponge Fingers

These sponge fingers are perfect for serving with fruit salads or light, creamy desserts.

Makes about 20
2 eggs
6 tablespoons superfine
    sugar
grated rind of 1 lemon

$^{1}/_{2}$ cup all-purpose flour,
    sifted
superfine sugar, for
    sprinkling

1 Preheat the oven to 375°F. Line two baking sheets with nonstick parchment paper. Whisk the eggs, sugar and lemon rind together with a hand-held electric whisk until thick and mousse-like: when the whisk is lifted, a trail should remain on the surface of the mixture for at least 30 seconds.

2 Carefully fold in the flour with a large, metal spoon using a figure-of-eight action.

3 Place the mixture in an icing bag fitted with a ½-inch plain nozzle. Pipe into finger lengths on the prepared baking sheets, leaving room for spreading.

4 Sprinkle the fingers with superfine sugar. Bake for about 6–8 minutes until golden brown, then remove to a wire rack to cool completely.

Variation
To make Hazelnut Fingers, omit the lemon rind and fold in $^{1}/_{4}$ cup toasted ground hazelnuts and 1 teaspoon mixed spice with the flour.

Apricot and Almond Fingers

These delicious almond fingers will stay moist for several days, thanks to the addition of apricots.

Makes 18
2 cups self-rising flour
½ cup light brown sugar
⅓ cup semolina
1 cup ready-to-eat dried
    apricots, chopped
2 tablespoons honey
2 tablespoons malt
    extract

2 eggs, beaten
4 tablespoons skim milk
4 tablespoons sunflower
    oil
few drops of almond
    extract
2 tablespoons slivered
    almonds

1 Preheat the oven to 325°F. Grease and line an 11 x 7-inch baking pan. Sift the flour into a bowl and stir in the sugar, semolina and apricots. Make a well in the center and add the honey, malt extract, eggs, milk, oil and almond extract. Mix well until combined.

2 Turn the mixture into the prepared pan, spread to the edges and sprinkle with the slivered almonds.

3 Bake for 30–35 minutes, or until the center springs back when lightly pressed. Invert the cake on a wire rack to cool. Remove the lining paper, if necessary, and cut into 18 slices with a sharp knife.

Cook's Tip
If you cannot find ready-to-eat dried apricots, soak chopped, dried apricots in boiling water for 1 hour, then drain them and add to the mixture. This works well with other dried fruit too. Try ready-to-eat dried pears or peaches for a change.

Raspberry Muffins

These muffins are beautifully light and spongy.

Makes 10 – 12

2¹/₂ cups all-purpose
    flour
1 tablespoon baking
    powder
¹/₂ cup superfine sugar

1 egg
1 cup buttermilk
4 tablespoons sunflower
    oil
1 cup raspberries

1   Preheat the oven to 400°F. Arrange 12 paper cases in a deep muffin pan. Sift the flour and baking powder into a mixing bowl, stir in the sugar, then make a well in the center.

2   Mix the egg, buttermilk and oil together in a pitcher, pour into the bowl and mix quickly until just combined.

3   Add the raspberries and lightly fold in with a metal spoon. Spoon into the paper cases to within a third of the top.

4   Bake the muffins for 20–25 minutes until golden brown and firm in the middle. Remove to a wire rack and serve while still warm.

Cook's Tip
This is a fairly moist mixture which should only be lightly mixed. Over-mixing toughens the muffins and breaks up the fruit. Use blackberries, blueberries or black currants instead of raspberries, if you prefer.

Date and Apple Muffins

These tasty muffins are delicious with morning coffee or breakfast. You'll only need one or two per person as they are very filling.

Makes 12

1¹/₄ cups self-rising whole
    wheat flour
1¹/₄ cups self-rising white
    flour
1 teaspoon ground
    cinnamon
1 teaspoon baking
    powder
2 tablespoons soft
    margarine

6 tablespoons light
    brown sugar
1 cup apple juice
2 tablespoons pear and
    apple spread
1 egg, lightly beaten
1 eating apple
¹/₂ cup chopped dates
1 tablespoon chopped
    pecans

1   Preheat the oven to 400°F. Arrange 12 paper cases in a deep muffin pan. Put the whole wheat flour in a mixing bowl. Sift in the white flour with the cinnamon and baking powder. Work in the margarine until the mixture resembles bread crumbs, then stir in the brown sugar.

2   In a bowl, stir a little of the apple juice with the pear and apple spread until smooth. Add the remaining juice, mix well, then add to the flour mixture with the egg. Peel and core the apple, chop the flesh finely and add it to the bowl with the dates. Mix quickly until just combined.

3   Divide the mixture among the muffin cases. Sprinkle with the chopped pecans.

4   Bake the muffins for 20–25 minutes until golden brown and firm in the middle. Turn onto a wire rack and serve while still warm.

Filo and Apricot Purses

Filo pastry is very easy to use and is low in fat. Always keep a package in the freezer ready for rustling up a speedy afternoon treat.

Makes 12
1 cup ready-to-eat dried
  apricots
3 tablespoons apricot
  compote
3 amaretti cookies,
  crushed

3 sheets filo pastry
4 teaspoons soft
  margarine, melted
confectioner's sugar, for
  dusting

1 Preheat the oven to 350°F. Grease two baking sheets. Chop the apricots, put them in a bowl and stir in the apricot compote. Mix in the amaretti cookies.

2 Cut the filo pastry into 24 x 5-inch squares, pile the squares on top of each other and cover with a clean dish towel to prevent the pastry from drying out.

3 Lay one pastry square on a flat surface, brush lightly with melted margarine and lay another square diagonally on top. Brush the top square with melted margarine. Spoon a small mound of apricot mixture in the center of the pastry, bring up the edges and pinch together in a money-bag shape. The margarine will help to make the pastry stick.

4 Repeat with the remaining filo squares and filling to make 12 purses in all. Arrange on the prepared baking sheets and bake for 5–8 minutes until golden brown. Dust with confectioner's sugar and serve warm.

Cook's Tip
The easiest way to crush the amaretti cookies is to put them in a plastic bag and roll with a rolling pin.

Filo Scrunchies

Quick-and-easy to make, these are an ideal afternoon snack. Eat them warm or they will lose their crispness.

Makes 6
5 apricots or plums
4 sheets filo pastry
4 teaspoons soft
  margarine, melted
¼ cup raw sugar

2 tablespoons slivered
  almonds
confectioner's sugar, for
  dusting

1 Preheat the oven to 375°F. Cut the apricots or plums in half, remove the pits and slice the fruit thinly.

2 Cut the filo pastry into 12 x 7-inch squares. Pile the squares on top of each other and cover with a clean dish towel to prevent the pastry from drying out. Remove one square and brush it with melted margarine. Lay a second filo square on top, then, using your fingers, mold the pastry into neat folds.

3 Lay the scrunched filo square on a baking sheet. Make five more scrunchies in the same way, working quickly so that the pastry does not dry out. Arrange a few slices of fruit in the folds of each scrunchie, then sprinkle generously with raw sugar and almonds.

4 Bake the scrunchies for 8–10 minutes until golden brown, then loosen from the baking sheet with a metal spatula. Place on a plate, dust with confectioner's sugar and serve immediately.

Cook's Tip
Filo pastry dries out very quickly. Keep it covered as much as possible with plastic wrap or a dry cloth to limit exposure to the air, or it will become too brittle to use.

Coffee Sponge Drops

These light cookies are delicious on their own, but taste even better with a filling made by mixing low-fat cream cheese with chopped preserved ginger.

Makes about 24

¹/₂ cup all-purpose flour
1 tablespoon instant
   coffee powder
2 eggs
6 tablespoons superfine
   sugar

For the filling (optional)
¹/₂ cup low fat cream
   cheese
¹/₄ cup chopped preserved
   ginger

1 Preheat the oven to 375°F. Line two baking sheets with nonstick parchment paper. Sift the flour and instant coffee powder together.

2 Combine the eggs and superfine sugar in a heat proof bowl. Place over a saucepan of simmering water. Beat with a hand-held electric whisk until thick and mousse-like: when the whisk is lifted a trail should remain on the surface of the mixture for at least 30 seconds.

3 Carefully fold in the sifted flour mixture with a large metal spoon, being careful not to knock out any air.

4 Spoon the mixture into an icing bag fitted with a ¹/₂-inch plain nozzle and pipe 1¹/₂-inch rounds on the prepared baking sheets. Bake for 12 minutes. Cool on a wire rack. Sandwich together in pairs with a ginger-cheese filling (above) or a coffee icing, if you like.

Variation
To make Chocolate Sponge Drops, replace the coffee with 2 tablespoons reduced-fat cocoa.

Oaty Crisps

These cookies are very crisp and crunchy – ideal to serve with morning coffee.

Makes 18

1¹/₂ cups rolled oats
6 tablespoons light
   brown sugar
1 egg

4 tablespoons sunflower
   oil
2 tablespoons malt
   extract

1 Preheat the oven to 375°F. Grease two baking sheets. Mix the oats and brown sugar in a bowl, breaking up any lumps in the sugar.

2 Add the egg, oil and malt extract, mix well, then let soak for 15 minutes.

3 Using a teaspoon, place small heaps of the mixture on the prepared baking sheets, leaving room for spreading. Press into 3-inch rounds with a dampened fork.

4 Bake the cookies for 10–15 minutes until golden brown. Let cool for 1 minute, then remove with a metal spatula and cool on a wire rack.

Variation
Add ¹/₂ cup chopped almonds or hazelnuts to the mixture. You can also add some jumbo oats to give a coarser texture.

Snowballs

These light and airy morsels make a good accompaniment to yogurt ice cream.

Makes about 20
2 egg whites
$^1/_2$ cup superfine sugar
1 tablespoon cornstarch,
   sifted
1 teaspoon white wine
   vinegar
$^1/_4$ teaspoon vanilla
   extract

1 Preheat the oven to 300°F and line two baking sheets with nonstick parchment paper. Whisk the egg whites in a clean bowl, using a hand-held electric whisk, until very stiff.

2 Add the superfine sugar, a little at a time, whisking until the meringue is very stiff. Whisk in the cornstarch, vinegar and vanilla extract.

3 Using a teaspoon, mound the mixture into snowballs on the prepared baking sheets. Bake for 30 minutes.

4 Cool on the baking sheets, then remove the snowballs from the paper with a metal spatula.

Variation
Make Pineapple Snowballs by lightly folding about $^1/_3$ cup finely chopped semi-dried pineapple into the meringue.

Caramel Meringues

Muscovado sugar gives these meringues a marvelous caramel flavor. Take care not to overcook them, so that they stay chewy in the middle.

Makes about 20
$^1/_2$ cup muscovado sugar
2 egg whites
1 teaspoon finely chopped
   walnuts

1 Preheat the oven to 325°F. Line two baking sheets with nonstick parchment paper. Press the sugar through a metal sifter into a bowl. Whisk the egg whites in a clean bowl until very stiff and dry, then add the sifted brown sugar, about 1 tablespoon at a time, whisking it into the meringue until it is thick and glossy.

2 Spoon small mounds of the mixture onto the prepared baking sheets. Sprinkle with the walnuts.

3 Bake for 30 minutes, then let cool for 5 minutes on the baking sheets. Transfer the meringues to a wire rack to cool completely.

Cook's Tip
For an easy, sophisticated filling, mix $^1/_2$ cup low-fat cream cheese with 1 tablespoon confectioner's sugar. Chop 2 slices of fresh pineapple and add to the mixture. Sandwich the meringues together in pairs.

Chocolate Banana Cake

A delicious sticky chocolate cake, moist enough to eat without the icing if you want to cut down on the calories.

Serves 8

2 cups self-rising flour
3 tablespoons fat-reduced cocoa
½ cup light brown sugar
2 tablespoons malt extract
2 tablespoons maple syrup
2 eggs, beaten
4 tablespoons skim milk

4 tablespoons sunflower oil
2 large ripe bananas

For the icing
1½ cups confectioner's sugar, sifted
2 tablespoons fat-reduced cocoa, sifted
1–2 tablespoons warm water

1 Preheat the oven to 325°F. Line and grease a deep 8-inch round cake pan. Sift the flour into a mixing bowl with the cocoa. Stir in the sugar.

2 Make a well in the center and add the malt extract, syrup, eggs, milk and oil. Mix well. Mash the bananas thoroughly and stir them into the mixture until thoroughly combined.

3 Spoon the mixture into the prepared pan and bake for 1–1¼ hours or until the center of the cake springs back when lightly pressed. Remove the cake from the pan and turn onto a wire rack to cool.

4 Make the icing: put the confectioner's sugar and cocoa in a mixing bowl and gradually add enough water to make a mixture thick enough to coat the back of a wooden spoon. Pour over the top of the cake and ease to the edges, allowing the icing to dribble down the sides.

Spiced Apple Cake

Grated apple and dates give this cake a natural sweetness. It may not be necessary to add all the sugar.

Serves 8

2 cups self-rising whole wheat flour
1 teaspoon baking powder
2 teaspoons ground cinnamon
1 cup chopped dates
scant ½ cup light brown sugar

1 tablespoon pear and apple spread
½ cup apple juice
2 eggs, beaten
6 tablespoons sunflower oil
2 eating apples, cored and grated
1 tablespoon chopped walnuts

1 Preheat the oven to 350°F. Line and grease an 8-inch deep round cake pan. Sift the flour, baking powder and cinnamon into a mixing bowl, then mix in the dates and make a well in the center.

2 Mix the sugar with the pear and apple spread in a small bowl. Gradually stir in the apple juice. Add to the dry ingredients with the eggs, oil and apples. Mix thoroughly.

3 Spoon into the prepared cake pan, sprinkle with the walnuts and bake for 60–65 minutes or until a skewer inserted into the center of the cake comes out clean. Invert onto a wire rack, remove the lining paper and let cool.

Cook's Tip
It is not necessary to peel the apples – the skin adds extra fiber and softens on cooking.

Irish Whiskey Cake

This moist, rich fruit cake is drizzled with whiskey as soon as it comes out of the oven.

Serves 10

*scant 1 cup golden
  raisins
scant 1 cup raisins
½ cup currants
½ cup candied cherries
1 cup light brown sugar*

*1¼ cups cold tea
1 egg, beaten
2½ cups self-rising flour,
  sifted
3 tablespoons Irish
  whiskey*

1   Mix the dried fruit, cherries, sugar and tea in a large bowl. Let soak overnight until the tea has been absorbed.

2   Preheat the oven to 350°F. Line and grease a 2¼-pound loaf pan. Add the egg and flour to the fruit mixture and beat thoroughly until well mixed.

3   Pour into the prepared pan and bake for 1½ hours or until a skewer inserted into the center comes out clean.

4   Prick the top of the cake with a skewer and drizzle over the whiskey while still hot. Let stand for 5 minutes, then remove from the pan and cool on a wire rack.

Cook's Tip
If time is short, use hot tea and soak the fruit for 2 hours instead of overnight.

Fruit and Nut Cake

A rich fruit cake that matures with keeping.

Serves 12–14

*1½ cups self-rising whole
  wheat flour
1½ cups self-rising white
  flour
2 teaspoons mixed spice
1 tablespoon apple and
  apricot spread
3 tablespoons honey
1 tablespoon molasses*

*6 tablespoons sunflower
  oil
¾ cup orange juice
2 eggs, beaten
4 cups luxury mixed
  fruit
½ cup candied cherries,
  halved
3 tablespoons split
  almonds*

1   Preheat the oven to 325°F. Line and grease a deep 8-inch cake pan. Tie a band of newspaper around the outside of the pan and stand it on a pad of newspaper on a baking sheet.

2   Combine the flours in a mixing bowl. Stir in the mixed spice and make a well in the center.

3   Put the apple and apricot spread in a small bowl. Gradually stir in the honey and molasses. Add to the bowl with the oil, orange juice, eggs and mixed fruit. Stir with a wooden spoon to mix thoroughly.

4   Scrape the mixture into the prepared pan and smooth the surface. Arrange the cherries and almonds in a decorative pattern over the top. Bake for 2 hours or until a skewer inserted into the center of the cake comes out clean. Turn onto a wire rack to cool, then remove the lining paper.

Cook's Tip
For a less elaborate cake, omit the cherries, chop the almonds coarsely and sprinkle them over the top.

Angel Cake

Served with ricotta cheese and fresh raspberries, this makes a light dessert.

Serves 10

scant ½ cup cornstarch
scant ½ cup all-purpose
   flour
8 egg whites
1 cup superfine sugar,
   plus extra for
   sprinkling

1 teaspoon vanilla
   extract
confectioner's sugar, for
   dusting

1   Preheat the oven to 350°F. Sift both flours into a bowl.

2   Whisk the egg whites in a large, clean bowl until very stiff, then gradually add the sugar and vanilla extract, whisking until the mixture is thick and glossy.

3   Fold in the flour mixture with a large, metal spoon. Spoon into an ungreased 10-inch angel cake pan, smooth the surface and bake for 40–45 minutes.

4   Sprinkle a piece of wax paper with superfine sugar and set an egg cup in the center. Invert the cake pan over the paper, balancing it carefully on the egg cup. When cold, the cake will drop out of the pan. Transfer it to a plate, dust generously with confectioner's sugar and serve.

Variation
Make a lemon icing by mixing 1½ cups confectioner's sugar with 1–2 tablespoons lemon juice. Drizzle the icing over the cake and decorate with lemon slices and mint sprigs or physalis.

Peach Jelly Roll

This is the perfect cake for a summer afternoon snack in the garden.

Serves 6–8

3 eggs
½ cup superfine sugar
¾ cup all-purpose flour,
   sifted
1 tablespoon boiling
   water

6 tablespoons peach jam
confectioner's sugar, for
   dusting (optional)

1   Preheat the oven to 400°F. Line and grease a 12 x 8-inch jelly roll pan. Combine the eggs and sugar in a bowl. Beat with a hand-held electric whisk until thick and mousse-like: when the whisk is lifted a trail should remain on the surface of the mixture for at least 30 seconds.

2   Carefully fold in the flour with a large, metal spoon, then add the boiling water in the same way.

3   Spoon into the prepared pan, spread evenly to the edges and bake for 10–12 minutes until the cake springs back when lightly pressed.

4   Spread a sheet of wax paper on a flat surface, sprinkle it with superfine sugar, then invert the cake on top. Peel off the lining paper.

5   Make a neat cut two-thirds of the way through the cake, about ½ inch from the short edge nearest you – this will make it easier to roll. Trim the remaining edges.

6   Spread the cake with the peach jam and roll up quickly from the partially-cut end. Hold in position for a minute, making sure the join is underneath. Cool on a wire rack. Dust with confectioner's sugar before serving, if you like.

Pear and Golden Raisin Teabread

This is an ideal teabread to make when pears are plentiful. There's no better use for windfalls.

Serves 6–8

3 cups rolled oats
¼ cup light brown sugar
2 tablespoons pear or
    apple juice
2 tablespoons sunflower
    oil
1 large or 2 small pears

1 cup self-rising flour
scant 1 cup golden
    raisins
½ teaspoon baking
    powder
2 teaspoons mixed spice
1 egg

1 Preheat the oven to 350°F. Line a 1-pound loaf pan with nonstick parchment paper. Put the oats in a bowl with the sugar, pour over the pear or apple juice and oil, mix well and let stand for 15 minutes.

2 Quarter, core and grate the pear(s). Add to the bowl with the flour, golden raisins, baking powder, spice and egg. Using a wooden spoon, mix thoroughly.

3 Spoon the teabread mixture into the prepared loaf pan. Bake for 55–60 minutes or until a skewer inserted into the center comes out clean.

4 Invert the teabread onto a wire rack and remove the lining paper. Let cool.

Cook's Tip
Health-food stores sell concentrated pear juice, ready for diluting as required.

Banana and Ginger Teabread

The bland creaminess of banana is given a delightful lift with chunks of preserved ginger in this tasty teabread. If you like a strong ginger flavor add 1 teaspoon ground ginger with the flour.

Serves 6–8

1½ cups self-rising flour
1 teaspoon baking
    powder
3 tablespoons soft
    margarine

¼ cup light brown sugar
⅓ cup drained preserved
    ginger, chopped
4 tablespoons skim milk
2 ripe bananas, mashed

1 Preheat the oven to 350°F. Line and grease a 1-pound loaf pan. Sift the flour and baking powder into a mixing bowl.

2 Work in the margarine until the mixture resembles bread crumbs, then stir in the sugar.

3 Add the ginger, milk and mashed bananas and mix to a soft dough.

4 Spoon into the prepared pan and bake for 40–45 minutes. Run a metal spatula around the edges to loosen them, turn the teabread onto a wire rack and let cool.

Variation
To make Banana and Walnut Teabread, add 1 teaspoon mixed spice and omit the chopped preserved ginger. Stir in ½ cup chopped walnuts and add scant ½ cup golden raisins.

Olive and Oregano Bread

This is an excellent accompaniment to all salads and is very good with broiled goat cheese.

Serves 8–10

1 tablespoon olive oil
1 onion, chopped
4 cups bread flour
2 teaspoons fast-rising
    dried yeast
1 teaspoon salt
¹/₄ teaspoon black pepper
¹/₃ cup pitted black olives,
    coarsely chopped

1 tablespoon black olive
    paste
1 tablespoon chopped
    fresh oregano
1 tablespoon chopped
    fresh parsley
1¹/₄ cups hand-hot water

1 Lightly oil a baking sheet. Heat the olive oil in a frying pan and fry the onion until golden brown.

2 Sift the flour into a mixing bowl. Add the yeast, salt and pepper. Make a well in the center. Add the fried onion (with the oil), the olives, olive paste, herbs and water. Gradually incorporate the flour and mix to a soft dough, adding a little extra water, if necessary.

3 Turn the dough onto a floured surface and knead for 5 minutes until it is smooth and elastic. Shape into an 8-inch round and place on the prepared baking sheet. Using a sharp knife, make crisscross cuts over the top, cover and let stand in a warm place until doubled in size. Preheat the oven to 425°F.

4 Bake the loaf for 10 minutes, then lower the oven temperature to 400°F. Bake for 20 minutes more, or until the loaf sounds hollow when tapped underneath. Let cool on a wire rack.

Sun-dried Tomato Braid

This makes a marvelous centerpiece for a summer buffet.

Serves 8–10

2 cups whole wheat flour
2 cups bread flour
1 teaspoon salt
¹/₄ teaspoon black pepper
2 teaspoons fast-rising
    dried yeast
pinch of sugar
1¹/₄ cups hand-hot water

³/₄ cup drained sun-dried
    tomatoes in oil,
    chopped, plus
    1 tablespoon oil from
    the jar
¹/₄ cup freshly grated
    Parmesan cheese
2 tablespoons red pesto
¹/₂ teaspoon coarse
    sea salt

1 Lightly oil a baking sheet. Put the whole wheat flour in a mixing bowl. Sift in the bread flour, salt and pepper. Add the yeast and sugar. Make a well in the center and add the water, sun-dried tomatoes, oil, Parmesan and pesto. Gradually incorporate the flour and mix to a soft dough, adding a little extra water, if necessary.

2 Turn the dough onto a floured surface and knead for 5 minutes until it is smooth and elastic. Shape into three 13-inch long sausages.

3 Dampen the ends of the three sausages. Press them together at one end, braid them loosely, then press them together at the other end. Place on the baking sheet, cover and let stand in a warm place until doubled in size. Preheat the oven to 425°F.

4 Sprinkle the braid with coarse sea salt. Bake in the oven for 10 minutes, then lower the temperature to 400°F and bake for 15–20 minutes more, or until the loaf sounds hollow when tapped underneath. Let cool on a wire rack.

Cheese and Onion Herb Stick

An extremely tasty bread that is very good with soup or salads. Use a strong cheese to give plenty of flavor.

Makes 2 sticks, each serving 4–6

1 tablespoon sunflower
  oil
1 red onion, chopped
4 cups bread flour
1 teaspoon salt
1 teaspoon mustard
  powder
2 teaspoons fast-rising
  dried yeast

3 tablespoons chopped
  fresh herbs, such as
  thyme, parsley,
  marjoram or sage
¾ cup grated reduced-fat
  Cheddar cheese
1¼ cups hand-hot water

1 Lightly oil two baking sheets. Heat the oil in a frying pan and fry the onion until well browned.

2 Sift the flour, salt and mustard powder into a mixing bowl. Stir in the yeast and herbs. Set aside 2 tablespoons of the cheese. Add the rest to the flour mixture and make a well in the center. Add the water with the fried onions and oil; gradually incorporate the flour and mix to a soft dough, adding a little extra water, if necessary.

3 Turn the dough onto a floured surface and knead for 5 minutes until it is smooth and elastic. Divide the mixture in half and roll each piece into a stick 12 inches in length.

4 Place each stick on a baking sheet, make diagonal cuts along the top and sprinkle with the reserved cheese. Cover and let stand until doubled in size. Preheat the oven to 425°F.

5 Bake the loaves for 25 minutes or until the bread sounds hollow when tapped underneath.

Focaccia

This Italian flatbread is best served warm. It makes a delicious snack with olives and feta cheese.

Serves 8

3 cups bread flour
1 teaspoon salt
¼ teaspoon freshly
  ground black pepper
2 teaspoons fast-rising
  dried yeast
1¼ cups hand-hot water
pinch of sugar
1 tablespoon pesto

⅔ cup pitted black olives,
  chopped
3 tablespoons drained
  sun-dried tomatoes in
  oil, chopped, plus
  1 tablespoon oil from
  the jar
1 teaspoon coarse sea salt
1 teaspoon chopped fresh
  rosemary

1 Lightly oil a 12 x 8-inch jelly roll pan. Sift the flour, salt and pepper into a bowl. Add the yeast and sugar and make a well in the center.

2 Add the water with the pesto, olives and sun-dried tomatoes (reserve the oil). Mix to a soft dough, adding a little extra water, if necessary.

3 Turn the dough onto a floured surface and knead for 5 minutes until it is smooth and elastic. Roll into a rectangle measuring 13 x 9 inches. Place over the rolling pin and place in the prepared pan. Let rise until doubled in size. Preheat the oven to 425°F.

4 Using your fingertips, make indentations all over the dough. Brush with the oil from the sun-dried tomatoes, then sprinkle with salt and rosemary. Bake for 20–25 minutes until golden. Transfer to a wire rack and serve warm.

Spinach and Bacon Bread

This bread is so good that it is a good idea to make double the quantity and freeze one of the loaves.

Makes 2 loaves, each serving 8

1 tablespoon olive oil
1 onion, chopped
4 ounces rindless smoked bacon rashers, chopped
6 cups all-purpose flour
1¹/₂ teaspoon salt
¹/₂ teaspoon grated nutmeg

1 envelope fast-rising dried yeast
2 cups hand-hot water
8 ounces chopped spinach, defrosted if frozen
¹/₄ cup grated reduced-fat Cheddar cheese

1 Lightly oil two 9-inch cake pans. Heat the oil and fry the onion and bacon for 10 minutes until golden brown.

2 Sift the flour, salt and nutmeg into a mixing bowl, add the yeast and make a well in the center. Add the water, the fried bacon and onion, with the oil, then add the drained spinach. Gradually incorporate the flour and mix to a soft dough.

3 Turn the dough onto a floured surface and knead for 5 minutes until it is smooth and elastic. Divide the mixture in half. Shape each half into a ball, flatten slightly and place in a pan, pressing the dough so that it extends to the edges.

4 Mark each loaf into six wedges and sprinkle with the cheese. Cover loosely with a plastic bag and let stand in a warm place until each loaf has doubled in size. Preheat the oven to 400°F.

5 Bake the loaves for 25–30 minutes, or until they sound hollow when tapped underneath. Let cool on a wire rack.

Parma Ham and Parmesan Bread

This nourishing bread can be made very quickly, and is a meal in itself when served with a tomato and feta salad.

Serves 8

2 cups self-rising whole wheat flour
2 cups self-rising all-purpose flour
1 teaspoon salt
1 teaspoon freshly ground black pepper
3 ounces Parma ham, chopped

2 tablespoons chopped fresh parsley
2 tablespoons freshly grated Parmesan cheese
3 tablespoons Meaux mustard
1¹/₂ cups buttermilk
skim milk, to glaze

1 Preheat the oven to 400°F. Flour a baking sheet. Put the whole wheat flour in a bowl and sift in the all-purpose flour, salt and pepper. Stir in the ham and parsley. Set aside about half of the grated Parmesan and add the rest to the flour mixture. Make a well in the center.

2 Mix the mustard and buttermilk in a pitcher, pour into the bowl and quickly mix to a soft dough.

3 Turn onto a well-floured surface and knead very briefly. Shape into an oval loaf and place on the baking sheet.

4 Brush the loaf with milk, sprinkle with the reserved Parmesan and bake for 25–30 minutes until golden brown. Cool on a wire rack.

Cook's Tip
When chopping the ham, sprinkle it with flour so that it does not stick together. Do not knead the mixture as for a yeast dough, or it will become tough. It should be mixed quickly and kneaded very briefly before shaping.

Austrian Three-Grain Bread

A mixture of grains gives this close-textured bread a delightful nutty flavor.

Makes 1 large loaf
2 cups bread flour
1¹/₂ teaspoons salt
2 cups malted brown
    flour
2 cups rye flour
¹/₂ cup medium oatmeal
1 envelope fast-rising
    dried yeast

3 tablespoons sunflower
    seeds
2 tablespoons linseeds
2 cups hand-hot water
2 tablespoons malt
    extract

1 Sift the all-purpose flour and salt into a mixing bowl and add the remaining flours, oatmeal, yeast and sunflower seeds. Set aside 1 teaspoon of the linseeds and add the rest to the flour mixture. Make a well in the center.

2 Add the water to the bowl with the malt extract. Gradually incorporate the flour and mix to a soft dough, adding extra water, if necessary.

3 Flour a baking sheet. Turn the dough onto a floured surface and knead for 5 minutes until it is smooth and elastic. Divide it in half. Roll each half into a sausage, about 12 inches in length. Twist the two pieces together, dampen each end and press together firmly.

4 Lift the loaf onto the prepared baking sheet. Brush with water, sprinkle with the remaining linseeds and cover loosely with a large plastic bag (balloon it to trap the air inside). Let stand in a warm place until doubled in size. Preheat the oven to 425°F.

5 Bake the bread for 10 minutes, then lower the oven temperature to 400°F and cook for 20 minutes more, or until the loaf sounds hollow when tapped underneath. Let cool on a wire rack.

Rye Bread

Rye bread is popular in Northern Europe and makes an excellent base for open sandwiches.

Makes 2 loaves, each serving 10
3 cups whole wheat flour
2 cups rye flour
1 cup bread flour
1¹/₂ teaspoons salt
1 envelope fast-rising
    dried yeast

2 tablespoons caraway
    seeds
2 cups hand-hot water
2 tablespoons molasses
2 tablespoons sunflower
    oil

1 Grease a baking sheet. Put the flours in a bowl with the salt and yeast. Set aside 1 teaspoon of the caraway seeds and add the rest to the bowl. Mix, then make a well in the center.

2 Add the water to the bowl with the molasses and oil. Gradually incorporate the flour and mix to a soft dough, adding a little extra water, if necessary.

3 Turn the dough onto a floured surface and knead for 5 minutes until it is smooth and elastic. Divide the dough in half and shape into two 9-inch long oval loaves.

4 Flatten the loaves slightly and place them on the baking sheet. Brush them with water and sprinkle with the remaining caraway seeds. Cover and let stand in a warm place until doubled in size. Preheat the oven to 425°F.

5 Bake the loaves for 30 minutes until they sound hollow when tapped underneath. Let cool on a wire rack.

Soda Bread

Finding the bread bin empty need never be a problem when your repertoire includes a recipe for soda bread. It takes only a few minutes to make and needs no rising or proving. If possible, eat soda bread warm from the oven as it does not keep well.

Serves 8

4 cups all-purpose flour
1 teaspoon salt
1 teaspoon baking soda

1 teaspoon cream of
   tartar
1½ cups buttermilk

1 Preheat the oven to 425°F. Flour a baking sheet. Sift the dry ingredients into a mixing bowl and make a well in the center.

2 Add the buttermilk and mix quickly to a soft dough. Turn onto a floured surface and knead lightly. Shape into a round about 7 inches in diameter; place on the baking sheet.

3 Cut a deep cross on top of the loaf and sprinkle with a little flour. Bake for 25–30 minutes, then transfer to a wire rack to cool.

Cook's Tip
Soda bread needs a light hand. The ingredients should be bound together quickly in the bowl and kneaded very briefly. The aim is just to get rid of the largest cracks, as the dough becomes tough if handled for too long.

Malt Loaf

This is a rich and sticky loaf. If it lasts long enough to go stale, try toasting it for a delicious afternoon treat.

Serves 8

3 cups all-purpose flour
¼ teaspoon salt
1 teaspoon fast-rising
   dried yeast
pinch of superfine sugar
2 tablespoons light
   brown sugar
generous 1 cup golden
   raisins
⅔ cup hand-hot skim
   milk

1 tablespoon sunflower
   oil
3 tablespoons malt
   extract

To glaze
2 tablespoons superfine
   sugar
2 tablespoons water

1 Sift the flour and salt into a mixing bowl, stir in the yeast, pinch of sugar, brown sugar and golden raisins, and make a well in the center. Add the hot milk with the oil and malt extract. Gradually incorporate the flour and mix to a soft dough, adding a little extra milk, if necessary.

2 Turn onto a floured surface and knead for about 5 minutes until it is smooth and elastic. Lightly oil a 1-pound loaf pan.

3 Shape the dough and place it in the prepared pan. Cover with a damp dish cloth and let stand in a warm place until doubled in size. Preheat the oven to 375°F.

4 Bake the loaf for 30–35 minutes, or until it sounds hollow when tapped underneath.

5 Meanwhile make the glaze by dissolving the sugar in the water in a small saucepan. Bring to a boil, stirring, then lower the heat and simmer for 1 minute. Brush the loaf while hot, then transfer it to a wire rack to cool.

Banana and Cardamom Bread

The combination of banana and cardamom is delicious in this soft-textured moist loaf.

Serves 6

10 cardamom pods	⅔ cup hand-hot water
3½ cups bread flour	2 tablespoons malt
1 teaspoon salt	extract
1 teaspoon fast-rising	2 ripe bananas, mashed
dried yeast	1 teaspoon sesame seeds

1 Grease a 1-pound loaf pan. Split the cardamom pods. Remove the seeds and chop the pods finely.

2 Sift the flour and salt into a mixing bowl, add the yeast and make a well in the center. Add the water with the malt extract, chopped cardamom pods and bananas. Gradually incorporate the flour and mix to a soft dough, adding a little extra water, if necessary.

3 Turn the dough onto a floured surface and knead for 5 minutes until it is smooth and elastic. Shape into a braid and place in the prepared pan. Cover loosely with a plastic bag (ballooning it to trap the air) and let stand in a warm place until well risen. Preheat the oven to 425°F.

4 Brush the braid lightly with water and sprinkle with the sesame seeds. Bake for 10 minutes, then lower the oven temperature to 400°F. Cook for 15 minutes more, or until the loaf sounds hollow when tapped underneath. Transfer to a wire rack to cool.

Swedish Golden Raisin Bread

A lightly sweetened bread that goes very well with the cheeseboard and is also excellent toasted as a teabread.

Serves 10

2 cups whole wheat flour	½ cup walnuts, chopped
2 cups bread flour	1 tablespoon honey
1 teaspoon fast-rising	⅔ cup hand-hot water
dried yeast	¾ cup hand-hot skim
1 teaspoon salt	milk, plus extra for
scant 1 cup golden	glazing
raisins	

1 Grease a baking sheet. Put the flours in a bowl with the yeast, salt and golden raisins. Set aside 1 tablespoon of the walnuts and add the rest to the bowl. Mix lightly and make a well in the center.

2 Dissolve the honey in the water and add it to the bowl with the milk. Gradually incorporate the flour, mixing to a soft dough and adding a little extra water, if necessary.

3 Turn the dough onto a floured surface and knead for 5 minutes until smooth and elastic. Shape into an 11-inch long sausage shape. Place on the prepared baking sheet.

4 Make diagonal cuts down the length of the loaf, brush with milk, sprinkle with the remaining walnuts and let stand in a warm place until doubled in size. Preheat the oven to 425°F.

5 Bake the loaf for 10 minutes, then lower the temperature to 400°F and bake for 20 minutes more, or until the loaf sounds hollow when tapped underneath. Transfer to a wire rack and let cool.

Poppy Seed Rolls

Pile these soft rolls in a basket and serve them for breakfast or with dinner.

Makes 12

4 cups bread flour
1 teaspoon salt
1 teaspoon fast-rising
   dried yeast
1¹/₄ cups hand-hot skim
   milk

1 egg, beaten

For the topping
1 egg, beaten
poppy seeds

1 Lightly grease two baking sheets. Sift the flour and salt into a mixing bowl. Add the yeast. Make a well in the center and pour in the milk and the egg. Gradually incorporate the flour and mix to a soft dough.

2 Turn the dough onto a floured surface and knead for 5 minutes until it is smooth and elastic. Cut into 12 pieces and shape into rolls.

3 Place the rolls on the prepared baking sheets, cover loosely with a large plastic bag (ballooning it to trap the air inside) and let stand in a warm place until the rolls have doubled in size. Preheat the oven to 425°F.

4 Glaze the rolls with beaten egg, sprinkle with poppy seeds and bake for 12–15 minutes until golden brown.

Variations
Vary the toppings. Linseed, sesame and caraway seeds all look good; try adding caraway seeds to the dough, too, for extra flavor.

Granary Baps

These make excellent picnic fare and are also good buns for hamburgers.

Makes 8

4 cups malted brown
   flour
1 teaspoon salt
2 teaspoons fast-rising
   dried yeast

1 tablespoon malt extract
1¹/₄ cups hand-hot water
1 tablespoon rolled oats

1 Lightly oil a large baking sheet. Put the malted flour, salt and yeast in a mixing bowl and make a well in the center. Dissolve the malt extract in the water and add it to the well. Gradually incorporate the flour and mix to a soft dough.

2 Turn the dough onto a floured surface and knead for 5 minutes until it is smooth and elastic. Divide it into eight pieces. Shape into balls and flatten with the palm of your hand to make 4-inch rounds.

3 Place the rounds on the prepared baking sheet, cover loosely with a large plastic bag (ballooning it to trap the air inside), and let stand in a warm place until the baps have doubled in size. Preheat the oven to 425°F.

4 Brush the baps with water, sprinkle with the oats and bake for 20–25 minutes or until they sound hollow when tapped underneath. Cool on a wire rack.

Variation
To make a large loaf, shape the dough into a round, flatten it slightly and bake for 30–40 minutes. Test by tapping the bottom of the loaf – if it sounds hollow, it is cooked.

Whole Wheat Herb Triangles

These make a good lunchtime snack when stuffed with ham and salad and also taste good when served with soup.

Makes 8

2 cups whole wheat flour
1 cup bread flour
1 teaspoon salt
¹/₂ teaspoon baking soda
1 teaspoon cream of
   tartar
¹/₂ teaspoon chili powder

¹/₄ cup soft margarine
1 cup skim milk
4 tablespoons chopped
   mixed fresh herbs
1 tablespoon sesame
   seeds

1 Preheat the oven to 425°F. Flour a baking sheet. Put the whole wheat flour in a bowl. Sift in the other dry ingredients, including the chili powder. Work in the margarine.

2 Add the milk and herbs and mix quickly to a soft dough. Turn onto a lightly floured surface. Knead very briefly or the dough will become tough.

3 Roll out to a 9-inch circle and place on the baking sheet. Brush lightly with water and sprinkle with the sesame seeds.

4 Cut the dough round into eight wedges, separate slightly and bake for 15–20 minutes. Transfer the triangles to a wire rack to cool. Serve warm or cold.

Variation
Sun-dried Tomato Triangles: replace the mixed herbs with 2 tablespoons chopped, drained sun-dried tomatoes in oil, and add 1 tablespoon mild paprika, 1 tablespoon chopped fresh parsley and 1 tablespoon chopped fresh marjoram.

Caraway Breadsticks

Ideal to eat with drinks, these can be made in many flavors, including cumin seed, poppy seed and celery seed, as well as the coriander and sesame variation given below.

Makes about 20

2 cups all-purpose flour
¹/₂ teaspoon salt
¹/₂ teaspoon fast-rising
   dried yeast

2 teaspoons caraway
   seeds
²/₃ cup hand-hot water
   pinch of sugar

1 Grease two baking sheets. Sift the flour, salt, yeast and sugar into a mixing bowl, stir in the caraway seeds and make a well in the center. Add the water and gradually mix the flour to make a soft dough, adding a little extra water, if necessary.

2 Turn the dough onto a lightly floured surface and knead for 5 minutes until it is smooth and elastic. Divide the mixture into 20 pieces and roll each one into a 12-inch stick.

3 Arrange the breadsticks on the baking sheets, leaving room to allow for rising. Let stand for 30 minutes until well risen. Meanwhile, preheat the oven to 425°F.

4 Bake the breadsticks for 10–12 minutes until golden brown. Cool on the baking sheets.

Variation
Coriander and Sesame Sticks: replace the caraway seeds with 1 tablespoon crushed coriander seeds. Dampen the breadsticks lightly and sprinkle them with sesame seeds before baking.

Curry Crackers

These spicy, crisp little crackers are ideal for serving with drinks or cheese.

Makes 12
$^1/_2$ cup all-purpose flour
1 teaspoon curry powder
$^1/_4$ teaspoon chili powder
$^1/_4$ teaspoon salt

1 tablespoon chopped
   fresh cilantro
2 tablespoons water

1 Preheat the oven to 350°F. Sift the flour, curry powder, chili powder and salt into a mixing bowl and make a well in the center. Add the chopped cilantro and water. Gradually incorporate the flour and mix to a fine dough.

2 Turn the dough onto a lightly floured surface, knead until it is smooth, then let rest for 5 minutes.

3 Cut the dough into 12 pieces and knead into small balls. Roll each ball out very thinly to a 4-inch round.

4 Arrange the rounds on two ungreased baking sheets. Bake for 15 minutes, turning over once during cooking.

Variations
These can be flavored in many different ways. Omit the curry and chili powders and add 1 tablespoon caraway, fennel or mustard seeds. Any of the stronger spices such as nutmeg, cloves or ginger will give a good flavor but you will only need to add 1 teaspoon.

Oatcakes

These are traditionally served with cheese, but are also delicious topped with thick honey for breakfast.

Makes 8
1 cup medium oatmeal,
   plus extra for
   sprinkling
pinch of baking soda

$^1/_2$ teaspoon salt
1 tablespoon butter
5 tablespoons water

1 Preheat the oven to 300°F. Grease a baking sheet. Put the oatmeal, baking soda and salt in a mixing bowl.

2 Melt the butter with the water in a small saucepan. Bring to a boil, then add to the oatmeal and mix to a moist dough.

3 Turn onto a surface sprinkled with oatmeal and knead to a smooth ball. Turn a large baking sheet upside down, sprinkle it lightly with oatmeal and place the ball of dough on top. Dust with oatmeal; roll out thinly to a 10-inch round.

4 Cut the round into eight sections, ease apart slightly and bake for 50–60 minutes until crisp. Let cool on the baking sheet, then remove the oatcakes with a metal spatula.

Cook's Tip
To get a neat circle, place a 10-inch cake board or plate on top of the oatcake. Cut away any excess dough with a metal spatula, then remove the board or plate.

Chive and Potato Biscuits

These little biscuits should be fairly thin, soft and crisp. They are delicious served for breakfast.

Makes 20

1 pound potatoes
1 cup all-purpose flour, sifted
2 tablespoons olive oil
2 tablespoons chopped chives
salt and freshly ground black pepper
low-fat spread, for topping

1 Cook the potatoes in a saucepan of boiling salted water for 20 minutes, then drain thoroughly. Return the potatoes to the clean pan and mash them. Preheat a griddle or heavy-bottomed frying pan over low heat.

2 Tip the hot mashed potato into a bowl. Add the flour, oil and chives, with a little salt and pepper. Mix to a soft dough.

3 Roll out the dough on a well-floured surface to a thickness of ¼ inch and stamp out rounds with a 2-inch biscuit cutter, re-rolling and cutting the trimmings.

4 Cook the biscuits, in batches, on the hot griddle or frying pan for about 10 minutes until they are golden brown. Keep the heat low and turn the biscuits once. Spread with a little low-fat spread and serve immediately.

Cook's Tip
Use floury potatoes such as King Edwards. The potatoes must be freshly cooked and mashed and should not be allowed to cool before mixing. Cook the biscuits over low heat so that the outside does not burn before the inside is cooked.

Ham and Tomato Biscuits

These make an ideal accompaniment for soup. If you have any left over the next day, halve them, sprinkle with cheese, and toast under the broiler.

Makes 12

2 cups self-rising flour
1 teaspoon mustard powder
1 teaspoon paprika, plus extra for topping
¹/₂ teaspoon salt
2 tablespoons soft margarine
2 ounces Black Forest ham, chopped
1 tablespoon chopped fresh basil
¹/₃ cup drained sun-dried tomatoes in oil, chopped
¹/₃–¹/₂ cup skim milk, plus extra for brushing

1 Preheat the oven to 400°F. Flour a large baking sheet. Sift the flour, mustard, paprika and salt into a bowl. Work in the margarine until the mixture resembles bread crumbs.

2 Stir in the ham, basil and sun-dried tomatoes and mix lightly. Pour in enough milk to mix to a soft dough.

3 Turn the dough onto a lightly floured surface, knead lightly and roll out to a 8 x 6-inch rectangle. Cut into 2-inch squares and arrange on the baking sheet.

4 Brush sparingly with milk, sprinkle with paprika and bake for 12–15 minutes. Transfer to a wire rack to cool.

Cook's Tip
Biscuit dough should be soft and moist and mixed for just long enough to bind the ingredients together. Too much kneading makes the biscuits tough.

Drop Pancakes

Children love making – and eating – these little pancakes.

Makes 18
2 cups self-rising flour
½ teaspoon salt
1 tablespoon superfine
sugar

1 egg, beaten
1¼ cups skim milk
oil, for brushing

1 Preheat a griddle, heavy-bottomed frying pan or an electric frying pan. Sift the flour and salt into a mixing bowl. Stir in the sugar and make a well in the center.

2 Add the egg and half the milk and gradually incorporate the surrounding flour to make a smooth batter. Beat in the remaining milk.

3 Lightly grease the griddle or pan. Drop tablespoons of the batter onto the surface, letting them bubble and the bubbles begin to burst.

4 Turn the drop pancakes with a metal spatula and cook until the underside is golden brown. Keep the cooked pancakes warm and moist by wrapping them in a clean napkin while cooking successive batches. Serve with jam.

Variation
For a savory version of these tasty pancakes, add 2 chopped scallions and 1 tablespoon freshly grated Parmesan cheese to the batter. Serve with cottage cheese.

Pineapple and Spice Drop Pancakes

Making the batter with pineapple or orange juice instead of milk cuts down on fat and adds to the taste. Semi-dried pineapple has an intense flavor that makes it ideal to use in baking.

Makes 24
1 cup self-rising whole
wheat flour
1 cup self-rising white
flour
1 teaspoon ground
cinnamon
1 tablespoon superfine
sugar

1 egg, beaten
1¼ cups pineapple juice
½ cup semi-dried
pineapple, chopped
oil, for greasing

1 Preheat a griddle, heavy-bottomed frying pan or an electric frying pan. Put the whole wheat flour in a mixing bowl. Sift in the white flour, ground cinnamon and sugar and make a well in the center.

2 Add the egg with half the pineapple juice and gradually incorporate the surrounding flour to make a smooth batter. Beat in the remaining juice with the chopped pineapple.

3 Lightly grease the griddle or pan. Drop tablespoons of the batter onto the surface, letting them bubble and the bubbles begin to burst.

4 Turn the drop pancakes with a metal spatula and cook until the underside is golden brown. Keep the cooked pancakes warm and moist by wrapping them in a clean napkin while cooking successive batches.

Cook's Tip
Drop pancakes do not keep well and are best eaten freshly cooked. These taste good with cottage cheese.

Peach and Amaretto Cake

Try this delicious cake for dessert, with reduced-fat ricotta cheese, or serve it solo as an afternoon snack.

Serves 8

3 eggs, separated
¾ cup superfine sugar
grated rind and juice of
*   1 lemon*
⅓ cup semolina
scant ½ cup ground
*   almonds*
¼ cup all-purpose flour

For the syrup
6 tablespoons superfine
*   sugar*
6 tablespoons water
2 tablespoons Amaretto
*   liqueur*
2 peaches or nectarines,
*   halved and pitted*
4 tablespoons apricot
*   jam, strained, to glaze*

1 Preheat the oven to 350°F. Grease an 8-inch round loose-bottomed cake pan. Whisk the egg yolks, sugar, lemon rind and juice in a bowl until thick, pale and creamy, then fold in the semolina, almonds and flour until smooth.

2 Whisk the egg whites in a clean bowl until fairly stiff. Using a metal spoon, stir a generous spoonful of the whites into the semolina mixture to lighten it, then fold in the remaining egg whites. Spoon into the prepared cake pan.

3 Bake for 30–35 minutes, then remove the cake from the oven and carefully loosen the edges. Prick the top with a skewer and let cool slightly in the pan.

4 Meanwhile, make the syrup. Heat the sugar and water in a small saucepan, stirring until dissolved, then boil without stirring for 2 minutes. Add the Amaretto liqueur and drizzle slowly over the cake.

5 Remove the cake from the pan and transfer it to a serving plate. Slice the peaches or nectarines, arrange them in concentric circles over the top and brush with the glaze.

Chestnut and Orange Roll

A very moist roll – ideal to serve as a dessert.

Serves 8

3 eggs, separated
½ cup superfine sugar
15½-ounce can
*   unsweetened chestnut*
*   purée*
grated rind and juice of
*   1 orange*
confectioner's sugar, for
*   dusting*

For the filling
1 cup low-fat cream
*   cheese*
1 tablespoon honey
1 orange

1 Preheat the oven to 350°F. Line and grease a 12 x 8-inch jelly roll pan. Whisk the egg yolks and sugar in a mixing bowl until thick and creamy. Put the chestnut purée in a separate bowl. Whisk the orange rind and juice into the purée, then whisk into the egg mixture.

2 Whisk the egg whites until fairly stiff. Stir a generous spoonful of the whites into the chestnut mixture to lighten it, then fold in the remaining egg whites. Spoon the mixture into the prepared pan and bake for 30 minutes until firm. Cool for 5 minutes, then cover with a clean damp dish cloth and let stand until cold.

3 Meanwhile, make the filling. Put the cream cheese in a bowl with the honey. Finely grate the orange rind and add to the bowl. Peel away all the pith from the orange, cut the fruit into segments, chop coarsely and set aside. Add any juice to the bowl, then beat until smooth. Mix in the orange segments.

4 Sprinkle a sheet of wax paper with confectioner's sugar. Turn the cake out onto the paper and peel off the lining paper. Spread the filling over the cake and roll up like a jelly roll. Transfer to a plate and dust with confectioner's sugar.

Cinnamon and Apple Gâteau

Make this lovely gâteau for a fall teatime treat.

Serves 8
3 eggs
¹/₂ cup superfine sugar
¾ cup all-purpose flour
1 teaspoon ground
* cinnamon*

4 tablespoons honey
¹/₂ cup golden raisins
¹/₂ teaspoon ground
* cinnamon*
1¹/₂ cups low-fat cream
* cheese*
4 tablespoons reduced-fat
* ricotta cheese*
2 teaspoons lemon juice

For the filling and topping
4 large eating apples
1 tablespoon water

1 Preheat the oven to 375°F. Line and grease a 9-inch sandwich cake pan. Whisk the eggs and sugar until thick, then sift the flour and cinnamon over the surface and carefully fold in with a large, metal spoon.

2 Pour into the prepared pan and bake for 25–30 minutes, or until the cake springs back when lightly pressed. Let cool on a wire rack.

3 To make the filling, peel, core and slice three of the apples and cook them in a covered pan with the water and half the honey until softened. Add the golden raisins and cinnamon, stir well, replace the lid and let cool.

4 Put the cream cheese in a bowl with the ricotta cheese, the remaining honey and half the lemon juice and beat until smooth. Split the sponge cake in half, place the bottom half on a plate and drizzle over any liquid from the apples. Spread with two-thirds of the cheese mixture, then top with the apple filling. Fit the top of the cake in place.

5 Swirl the remaining filling over the top of the sponge. Quarter, core and slice the remaining apple, dip the slices in the remaining lemon juice and use to decorate the edges.

Lemon Chiffon Cake

Lemon mousse makes a tangy and delicious sponge filling.

Serves 8
1 lemon sponge cake mix
lemon glacé icing
shreds of blanched
* lemon rind*

grated rind and juice of
* 1 small lemon*
4 teaspoons water
2 teaspoons gelatin
¹/₂ cup reduced-fat ricotta
* cheese*

For the filling
2 eggs, separated
6 tablespoons superfine
* sugar*

1 Preheat the oven to 350°F. Line and grease an 8-inch loose-bottomed cake pan, add the sponge mixture and bake for 20–25 minutes until firm and golden. Cool on a wire rack, then split in half. Return the lower half of the cake to the clean cake pan and set aside.

2 Make the filling. Whisk the egg yolks, sugar, lemon rind and juice in a bowl until thick, pale and creamy. In a clean bowl, whisk the egg whites to soft peaks.

3 Sprinkle the gelatin over the water in a bowl. When spongy, dissolve over simmering water. Cool slightly, then whisk into the yolk mixture. Fold in the ricotta cheese. When the mixture begins to set, fold in a generous spoonful of the egg whites to lighten it, then fold in the remaining whites.

4 Spoon the lemon mousse over the sponge in the cake pan. Set the second layer of sponge on top and chill until set.

5 Carefully transfer the cake to a serving plate. Pour the glacé icing over the cake and spread it evenly to the edges. Decorate with the lemon shreds.

Strawberry Gâteau

It is difficult to believe that a cake that tastes so delicious can be low fat.

Serves 6

2 eggs
6 tablespoons superfine
  sugar
grated rind of ¹/₂ orange
¹/₂ cup all-purpose flour

For the filling
1¹/₄ cups low-fat cream
  cheese
grated rind of ¹/₂ orange

2 tablespoons superfine
  sugar
4 tablespoons reduced-fat
  ricotta cheese
8 ounces strawberries,
  halved and chopped
¹/₄ cup chopped almonds,
  toasted

1 Preheat the oven to 375°F. Line an 8-inch jelly roll pan with nonstick parchment paper.

2 In a bowl, whisk the eggs, sugar and orange rind until thick and mousse-like, then fold in the flour lightly. Turn the mixture into the prepared pan. Bake for 15–20 minutes, or until firm and golden. Let cool on a wire rack, removing the lining paper.

3 Meanwhile make the filling. In a bowl, mix the cream cheese with the orange rind, sugar and ricotta cheese until smooth. Divide between two bowls. Add half the strawberries to one bowl. Cut the sponge widthwise into three equal pieces and sandwich together with the strawberry filling. Place on a serving plate.

4 Spread the plain filling over the top and sides of the cake. Press the toasted almonds over the sides and decorate the top with the remaining strawberry halves.

Tia Maria Gâteau

A feather-light coffee sponge with a creamy liqueur-flavored filling spiked with preserved ginger.

Serves 8

¾ cup all-purpose flour
2 tablespoons instant
  coffee powder
3 eggs
¹/₂ cup superfine sugar

For the filling
¾ cup low-fat cream
  cheese
1 tablespoon honey
1 tablespoon Tia Maria

¹/₃ cup preserved ginger,
  chopped

For the icing
2 cups confectioner's
  sugar, sifted
2 teaspoons coffee extract
1 teaspoon fat-reduced
  cocoa
coffee beans (optional)

1 Preheat the oven to 375°F. Line and grease an 8-inch round cake pan. Sift the flour and coffee powder together.

2 Whisk the eggs and sugar in a bowl until thick and mousse-like, then fold in the flour mixture lightly. Turn the mixture into the prepared pan. Bake for 30–35 minutes or until firm and golden. Let cool on a wire rack.

3 Make the filling. Mix the cream cheese with the honey in a bowl. Beat until smooth, then stir in the Tia Maria and ginger. Split the cake in half horizontally and sandwich together with the Tia Maria filling.

4 Make the icing. In a bowl, mix the confectioner's sugar and coffee extract with enough water to make an icing which will coat the back of a wooden spoon. Pour three-quarters of the icing over the cake. Stir the cocoa into the remaining icing, spoon it into an icing bag fitted with a writing nozzle and drizzle the mocha icing over the coffee icing. Decorate with coffee beans, if desired.

Quick-mix Sponge Cake

Choose either chocolate or lemon flavoring for this light and versatile sponge cake, or leave it plain.

Makes 1 x 8-inch round cake

1 cup self-rising flour	**For the flavorings**
1 teaspoon baking powder	*Chocolate: 1 tablespoon cocoa blended with*
½ cup soft margarine	*1 tablespoon boiling*
½ cup superfine sugar	*water*
2 eggs	*Lemon: 2 teaspoons grated lemon rind*

1 Preheat the oven to 325°F. Grease an 8-inch round cake pan, line the bottom with wax paper and grease the paper.

2 Sift the flour and baking powder into a bowl. Add the margarine, sugar and eggs with the chosen flavorings, if using.

3 Beat with a wooden spoon for 2–3 minutes. The mixture should be pale in color and slightly glossy.

4 Spoon the mixture into the cake pan and smooth the surface. Bake in the center of the oven for 30–40 minutes, or until a skewer inserted into the center of the cake comes out clean. Turn out onto a wire rack, remove the lining paper and let cool completely.

Genoese Sponge Cake

This sponge cake has a firm texture due to the addition of butter and is suitable for cutting into layers for gâteaux.

Makes 1 x 8-inch round cake

4 eggs	**For the flavorings**
½ cup superfine sugar	*Citrus: 2 teaspoons grated orange, lemon*
6 tablespoons sweet butter, melted and cooled slightly	*or lime rind*
¾ cup all-purpose flour	*Chocolate: 2 ounces bittersweet chocolate, melted*
	Coffee: 2 teaspoons coffee granules, dissolved 1 teaspoon boiling water

1 Preheat the oven to 350°F. Grease an 8-inch round cake pan, line the bottom with wax paper and grease the paper.

2 Whisk the eggs and sugar together in a heat proof bowl until thoroughly blended. Place the bowl over a saucepan of simmering water and continue to whisk the mixture until thick and pale.

3 Remove the bowl from the saucepan and continue to whisk until the mixture is cool and leaves a thick trail on the surface when beaters are lifted.

4 Pour the butter carefully into the mixture, leaving any sediment behind.

5 Sift the flour over the surface. Using a plastic spatula, carefully fold the flour, butter and any flavorings into the mixture until smooth and evenly blended. Scrape the mixture into the prepared pan, tilt to level and bake for 30–40 minutes, until firm to the touch and golden. Cool on a wire rack.

Madeira Cake

Enjoy this cake in the traditional way with a large glass of Madeira or a schooner of sherry.

Serves 6–8

2 cups all-purpose flour
1 teaspoon baking
   powder
1 cup butter or
   margarine, at room
   temperature

1 cup superfine sugar
grated rind of 1 lemon
1 teaspoon vanilla
   extract
4 eggs

1 Preheat the oven to 325°F. Grease a 9 x 5-inch loaf pan, line the bottom with wax paper and grease the paper.

2 Sift the flour and baking powder into a bowl. Set the mixture aside.

3 Cream the butter or margarine, adding the superfine sugar about 2 tablespoons at a time, until light and fluffy. Stir in the lemon rind and vanilla. Add the eggs one at a time, beating for 1 minute after each addition. Add the flour mixture and stir until just combined.

4 Pour the cake mixture into the prepared pan and tap lightly to level. Bake for about 1¼ hours, or until a metal skewer inserted in the center comes out clean.

5 Cool in the pan on a wire rack for 10 minutes, then turn the cake out onto a wire rack and let cool completely.

Jelly Roll

Vary the flavor of the jelly roll by adding a little grated orange, lime or lemon rind to the mixture.

Serves 6–8

4 eggs, separated
½ cup superfine sugar
1 cup all-purpose flour
1 teaspoon baking
   powder

For a chocolate flavoring
Replace 1½ tablespoons
   of the flour with
   1½ tablespoons cocoa

1 Preheat the oven to 350°F. Grease a 13 x 9-inch jelly roll pan, line the bottom with wax paper and grease the paper. Whisk the egg whites until stiff. Beat in 2 tablespoons of the superfine sugar.

2 Beat the egg yolks with the remaining superfine sugar and 1 tablespoon water for about 2 minutes until the mixture is pale and leaves a thick ribbon trail.

3 Sift together the flour and baking powder. Carefully fold the beaten egg yolks into the egg whites, then fold in the flour mixture.

4 Pour the mixture into the prepared pan and gently smooth the surface. Bake in the center of the oven for 12–15 minutes, or until the cake starts to come away from the edges of the pan.

5 Turn out onto a piece of wax paper lightly sprinkled with superfine sugar. Peel off the lining paper and cut off any crisp edges. Spread with jam, if wished, and roll up, using the wax paper as a guide. Let cool completely on a wire rack.

Rich Fruit Cake

Make this cake a few weeks before icing, wrap well and store in an airtight container to mature.

Makes 1 x 8-inch round or 7-inch square cake

1¾ cups currants	1¼ teaspoons mixed spice
scant 2 cups golden raisins	½ teaspoon grated nutmeg
1 cup raisins	generous ½ cup ground almonds
scant ½ cup candied cherries, halved	scant 1 cup soft margarine or butter
scant 1 cup almonds, chopped	1¼ cups brown sugar
scant ½ cup mixed candied peel	1 tablespoon molasses
grated rind of 1 lemon	5 eggs, beaten
2½ tablespoons brandy	
2¼ cups all-purpose flour, sifted	

1 Preheat the oven to 275°F. Grease a deep 8-inch round or 7-inch square cake pan, line the bottom and sides with a double thickness of wax paper and grease the paper.

2 Combine the ingredients in a large mixing bowl. Beat with a wooden spoon for 5 minutes until well mixed.

3 Spoon the mixture into the prepared cake pan. Make a slight depression in the center.

4 Bake in the center of the oven for 3–3½ hours. Test the cake after 3 hours. If it is ready it will feel firm and a skewer inserted in the center will come out clean. Cover the top loosely with foil if it starts to brown too quickly.

5 Let the cake cool completely in the pan. Then turn out. The lining paper can be left on to help keep the cake moist.

Light Fruit Cake

For those who prefer a slightly less dense fruit cake, here is one that is still ideal for marzipanning and icing.

Makes 1 x 8-inch round or 7-inch square cake

1 cup soft margarine or butter	¾ cup currants
1 cup superfine sugar	generous 1 cup raisins
grated rind of 1 orange	generous 1 cup golden raisins
5 eggs, beaten	⅓ cup dried, ready-to-eat apricots
2¾ cups all-purpose flour	⅔ cup mixed candied peel
½ teaspoon baking powder	
2 teaspoons mixed spice	

1 Preheat the oven to 300°F. Grease a deep 8-inch round or 7-inch square cake pan, line the bottom and sides with a double thickness of wax paper and grease the paper.

2 Combine all the ingredients in a large mixing bowl, cutting the apricots in strips, using kitchen scissors. Beat thoroughly with a wooden spoon for 3–4 minutes until thoroughly mixed.

3 Spoon the mixture into the cake pan. Make a slight depression in the center. Bake in the center of the oven for 2½–3¼ hours. Test the cake after 2½ hours. If it is ready it will feel firm and a skewer inserted in the center will come out clean. Test at intervals if necessary. Cover the top loosely with foil if it starts to brown too quickly.

4 Let the cake cool completely in the pan. Then turn out. The lining paper can be left on to help keep the cake moist.

Marzipan

Marzipan can be used on its own, under an icing or for modeling.

Makes 3 cups

2 cups ground almonds
½ cup superfine sugar
1 cup confectioner's
  sugar, sifted
1 teaspoon lemon juice

a few drops of almond
  extract
1 small egg, or 1 large
  egg white

1 Stir the ground almonds and sugars together in a bowl until evenly mixed. Make a well in the center and add the lemon juice, almond extract and enough egg or egg white to mix to a soft but firm dough, using a wooden spoon.

2 Form the marzipan into a ball. Lightly dust a surface with confectioner's sugar and knead the marzipan until smooth. Wrap in plastic wrap or store in a polythene bag until needed. Tint with food coloring if required.

Fondant Icing

Fondant icing is wonderfully pliable and can be colored, molded and shaped in imaginative ways.

Makes 2¼ cups

1 egg white
1 tablespoon liquid
  glucose, warmed

3 cups confectioner's
  sugar, sifted

1 Put the egg white and glucose in a mixing bowl. Stir them together to break up the egg white.

2 Add the confectioner's sugar and mix together with a metal spatula, using a chopping action, until well blended and the icing begins to bind together. Knead the mixture with your fingertips until it forms a ball.

3 Knead the fondant on a work surface lightly dusted with confectioner's sugar for several minutes until smooth, soft and pliable. If the icing is too soft, knead in some more sifted sugar until it reaches the right consistency.

Marzipan Roses

To decorate a cake, shape the roses in a variety of colors and sizes, then arrange on top.

Form a small ball of colored marzipan into a cone shape. This forms the central core which supports the petals. To make the petals, take a piece of marzipan about the size of a large pea, and make a petal shape which is thicker at the base. Wrap the petal around the cone, pressing the petal to the cone to secure. Bend back the ends of the petal to curl. Repeat with more petals, each overlapping. Make some petals bigger until the required size is achieved.

Royal Icing

Royal icing gives a professional finish. This recipe makes enough icing to cover the top and sides of a 7-inch cake.

Makes 4½ cups
3 egg whites
about 6 cups
  confectioner's sugar,
  sifted
1½ teaspoons glycerine
few drops of lemon juice
food coloring (optional)

1 Put the egg whites in a bowl and stir lightly with a fork to break them up.

2 Add the confectioner's sugar gradually, beating well with a wooden spoon after each addition. Add enough sugar to make a smooth, shiny icing that has the consistency of very stiff meringue.

3 Beat in the glycerine, lemon juice and food coloring, if using. Let stand for 1 hour before using, covered with damp plastic warp, then stir to burst any air bubbles.

Storing
The icing will keep for up to three days, stored in a plastic container with a tight-fitting lid in a fridge.

Icing consistencies
This recipe is for an icing consistency suitable for flat icing a marzipan-covered rich fruit cake. When the spoon is lifted, the icing should form a sharp point, with a slight curve at the end, known as "soft peak." For piping, the icing needs to be slightly stiffer. It should form a fine sharp peak when the spoon is lifted.

Butter Icing

The creamy, rich flavor and silky smoothness of butter icing is popular with both children and adults.

Makes 1½ cups
6 tablespoons soft
  margarine or butter,
  softened
2 cups confectioner's
  sugar, sifted
1 teaspoon vanilla
  extract
2–3 teaspoons milk

For the flavorings
*Chocolate: blend
  1 tablespoon cocoa
  with 1 tablespoon hot
  water and let cool
  before beating into the
  icing.*

*Coffee: blend 2 teaspoons
  coffee powder with
  1 tablespoon boiling
  water, omit the milk
  and let cool before
  beating into the icing.*

*Lemon, orange or lime:
  substitute the vanilla
  extract and milk for
  lemon, orange or lime
  juice and 2 teaspoons
  of finely grated citrus
  rind. Omit the rind if
  using the icing for
  piping. Lightly tint
  the icing with food
  coloring, if wished.*

1 Put the margarine or butter, confectioner's sugar, vanilla extract and 1 teaspoon of the milk in a bowl.

2 Beat with a wooden spoon or an electric mixer, adding sufficient extra milk to give a light, smooth and fluffy consistency. For flavored butter icing, follow the instructions above for the flavor of your choice.

Storing
The icing will keep for up to three days in an airtight container stored in a fridge.

Fudge Frosting

A darkly delicious frosting, this can transform a simple sponge cake into one worthy of a very special occasion. Spread fudge frosting smoothly over the cake or swirl it. Or be even more elaborate with a little piping – it really is very versatile. This recipe makes enough to fill and coat the top and sides of a 8-inch or 9-inch round sponge cake.

Makes 1½ cups
2 ounces semisweet chocolate
2 cups confectioner's sugar, sifted
4 tablespoons butter
3 tablespoons milk or light cream
1 teaspoon vanilla extract

1 Break or chop the chocolate into small pieces. Put the chocolate, confectioner's sugar, butter, milk or cream and vanilla extract in a heavy-bottomed saucepan.

2 Stir over very low heat until both the chocolate and the butter have melted. Remove the mixture from the heat and stir until evenly blended.

3 Beat the icing frequently as it cools until it thickens sufficiently to use for spreading or piping. Use the icing immediately and work quickly once it has reached the right consistency.

Storing
This icing should be used straightaway.

Crème au Beurre

The rich, smooth, light texture of this icing makes it ideal for spreading, filling or piping onto cakes and gâteaux for all occasions.

Makes 1½ cups
4 tablespoons water
6 tablespoons superfine sugar
2 egg yolks
generous ½ cup sweet butter, softened

Chocolate: add 2 ounces semisweet chocolate, melted
Coffee: add 2 teaspoons instant coffee granules, dissolved in 1 teaspoon boiling water, cooled

For the flavorings
Citrus: replace water with orange, lemon or lime juice and 2 teaspoons grated rind

1 Bring the water to a boil, remove from the heat and stir in the sugar. Heat gently, stirring, until the sugar has dissolved. Then boil rapidly until the mixture becomes syrupy, or reaches the "thread" stage. To test, place a little syrup on the back of a dry teaspoon. Press a second teaspoon onto the syrup and gently pull apart. The syrup should form a fine thread. If not, return to the heat, boil rapidly and re-test a minute later.

2 Whisk the egg yolks together in a bowl. Continue to whisk while slowly adding the sugar syrup. Whisk until thick, pale and cool.

3 Beat the butter until light and fluffy. Add the egg mixture gradually, beating well after each addition, until thick and fluffy. For Chocolate or Coffee Crème au Beurre, fold in the flavoring at the end. If you prefer a citrus flavor, follow the instructions above.

American Frosting

A light marshmallow icing which crisps on the outside when left to dry – swirl or peak it into a soft coating.

Makes 1½ cups

1 egg white
2 tablespoons water
1 tablespoon maple syrup
*1 teaspoon cream of
    tartar*

*1½ cups confectioner's
    sugar, sifted*

1 Place the egg white with the water, syrup and cream of tartar in a heat proof bowl. Whisk together until blended.

2 Stir the confectioner's sugar into the mixture and place the bowl over a saucepan of simmering water. Whisk until the mixture becomes thick and white.

3 Remove the bowl from the saucepan and continue to whisk the frosting until cool and thick, and the mixture stands up in soft peaks. Use immediately to fill or cover cakes.

Glacé Icing

An instant icing for finishing large or small cakes.

Makes 1½ cups

*2 cups confectioner's
    sugar*
*2–3 tablespoons hot
    water*
food coloring (optional)

For the flavorings

*Citrus: replace the water
    with orange, lemon or
    lime juice*
*Chocolate: sift
    2 teaspoons cocoa with
    the confectioner's*
*Coffee: replace water
    with strong coffee*

1 Sift the confectioner's sugar into a bowl. Using a wooden spoon, gradually stir in enough water to obtain the consistency of thick cream.

2 Beat until white and smooth, and the icing thickly coats the back of the spoon. Tint with a few drops of food coloring, if desired, or flavor the icing as suggested above. Use immediately to cover the top of the cake.

Simple Piped Flowers

Bouquets of iced blossoms, such as roses, pansies and bright summer flowers make colorful cake decorations.

For a rose, make a fairly firm icing. Color the icing. Fit a petal nozzle into a paper icing bag, half-fill with icing and fold over top to seal. Hold the icing bag so the wider end is pointing at what will be the bottom of the rose and hold a toothpick in the other hand. Pipe a small cone shape around the tip of the toothpick, pipe a petal half way around the cone, lifting it so it is at an angle and curling outward, turning the toothpick at the same time. Repeat with more petals so they overlap. Remove from the toothpick and let dry.

Butterscotch Frosting

Makes 3 cups

6 tablespoons sweet
    butter
3 tablespoons milk
2 tablespoons light
    brown sugar
1 tablespoon molasses
3 cups confectioner's
    sugar, sifted

Citrus: replace the
    molasses with maple
    syrup and add
    2 teaspoons finely
    grated orange, lemon
    or lime rind
Coffee: replace the
    molasses with
    1 tablespoon coffee
    granules

For the flavorings
Chocolate: sift
    1 tablespoon cocoa
    with the confectioner's
    sugar

1 Place the butter, milk, sugar and molasses in a bowl over a pan of simmering water. Stir until the butter and sugar melt.

2 Remove the bowl and stir in the confectioner's sugar. Beat until smooth and glossy. For flavoring, follow instructions above. Pour over the cake, or cool for a thicker consistency.

Chocolate Fudge Icing

A rich, glossy icing which sets like chocolate fudge, this is versatile enough to smoothly coat, swirl or pipe, depending on the temperature of the icing when it is used.

Makes 2 cups

4 ounces semisweet
    chocolate, in squares
¼ cup sweet butter

1 egg, beaten
1½ cups confectioner's
    sugar, sifted

1 Place the chocolate and butter in a heat proof bowl over a saucepan of hot water.

2 Stir occasionally with a wooden spoon until both the chocolate and butter are melted. Add the egg and beat well.

3 Remove the bowl from the saucepan and stir in the confectioner's sugar, then beat until smooth and glossy.

4 Pour immediately over the cake for a smooth finish, or let cool for a thicker spreading or piping consistency.

Making Caramel

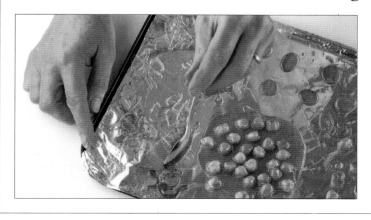

Caramel has endless uses – for dipping fruits and nuts, crushing for cake coating, or drizzling into shapes.

Place ⅔ cup water in a saucepan. Bring to a boil, remove from the heat and stir in ¾ cup superfine sugar. Heat gently until the sugar has dissolved. Bring the syrup to a boil, boil rapidly until the bubbles begin to subside and the syrup begins to turn a pale golden brown. For praline, add ¾ cup toasted almonds to the caramel, shake to mix, then pour onto a sheet of oiled foil on a baking sheet. Cool, then crush with a rolling pin, or process in a food processor or blender until finely ground.

Apricot Glaze

It is a good idea to make a large quantity of apricot glaze, especially when making celebration cakes.

Makes 1½ cups
1½ cups apricot jam
3 tablespoons water

1 Place the jam and water in a saucepan. Heat gently, stirring occasionally until melted. Boil rapidly for 1 minute, then rub through a strainer, pressing the fruit against the sides of the strainer with the back of a wooden spoon. Discard the skins left in the strainer. Use the warmed glaze to brush cakes before applying marzipan, or use for glazing fruits on gâteaux and cakes.

Glossy Chocolate Icing

A rich, smooth glossy icing, this can be made with semi-sweet or milk chocolate.

Makes 1¼ cups
6 ounces semisweet
chocolate
⅔ cup light cream

1 Break up the chocolate into small pieces and place it in a saucepan with the cream.

2 Heat gently, stirring occasionally, until the chocolate has melted and the mixture is smooth.

3 Let the icing cool until it is thick enough to coat the back of a wooden spoon. Use it at this stage for a smooth glossy icing, or allow it to thicken to obtain an icing which can be swirled or patterned with a cake decorating scraper.

Sugar-frosting Flowers

Choose edible flowers such as pansies, primroses, violets, roses, freesias, tiny daffodils or nasturtiums.

Lightly beat an egg white in a small bowl and sprinkle some superfine sugar on a plate. Wash the flowers then dry on paper towels. If possible, leave some stem attached. Evenly brush both sides of the petals with the egg white. Hold the flower by its stem over a plate lined with paper towels, sprinkle it evenly with the sugar, then shake off any excess. Place on a flat board or wire rack covered with paper towels and let dry in a warm place. Use to decorate a cake.

Petal Paste

Makes 1¼ pound

2 teaspoons gelatin
1½ teaspoons cold water
2 teaspoons liquid
  glucose
2 teaspoons white
  vegetable fat

4 cups confectioner's
  sugar, sifted
1 teaspoon gum
  tragacanth
1 egg white

1 Place the gelatin, water, liquid glucose and white fat in a heat proof bowl over a saucepan of hot water until melted, stirring occasionally. Remove the bowl from the heat.

2 Sift the sugar and gum tragacanth into a bowl. Make a well in the center and add the egg white and the gelatin mixture. Mix together to form a soft, malleable white paste.

3 Knead on a surface dusted with confectioner's sugar until smooth, white and free from cracks. Place in a plastic bag or plastic wrap, sealing well to exclude all the air. Let stand for two hours before use, then knead again and use small pieces at a time, leaving the remaining petal paste well sealed.

Meringue Frosting

Makes 1½ cups

2 egg whites
1 cup confectioner's
  sugar, sifted
⅔ cup butter, softened

For the flavorings
Chocolate: 2 ounces
  semisweet chocolate

Citrus: 2 teaspoons finely
  grated orange, lemon
  or lime rind.
Coffee: 2 teaspoons coffee
  granules, blended with
  1 teaspoon boiling
  water, cooled

1 Whisk the egg whites in a clean, heat proof bowl, add the sugar and gently whisk to mix well. Place the bowl over a saucepan of simmering water and whisk until thick and white. Remove the bowl from the saucepan and continue to whisk until cool and the meringue stands up in soft peaks.

2 Beat the butter in a separate bowl until light and fluffy. Add the meringue gradually, beating well after each addition, until thick and fluffy. Fold in the chosen flavoring, using a metal spatula, until evenly blended. Use immediately for coating, filling and piping onto cakes.

Marbling

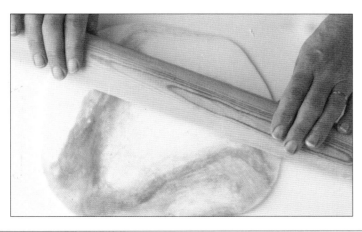

Fondant, lends itself to tinting in all shades and marbling is a good way to color the paste.

Using a toothpick, add a few drops of the chosen edible food color to some fondant icing. Do not knead the food coloring fully into the icing.
When the fondant is rolled out, the color disperses in such a way that it gives a marbled appearance.
Marbled fondant icing can be used to cover novelty cakes. Several colors can be used in the same icing to give an interesting multi-colored effect.